Standard C++ Library Header Files

Algorithms

\<algorithm\>	Defines numerous general algorithms as template functions.
\<numeric\>	Defines several function templates useful for computing numeric va

Containers

\<bitset\>	Describes an object that stores a set of Boolean values as a sequence of N bits. A bit is set if its value is 1, and reset if its value is 0.
\<deque\>	Describes an object controlling a varying-length sequence of elements of type T, permitting insertion and removal of an element at either end—a double-ended queue of T.
\<list\>	Defines the container class template list along with three supporting templates—a doubly linked list of T.
\<map\>	Defines the container class templates map and multimap, along with their supporting templates, providing an associative array of T.
\<queue\>	Defines the class templates priority_queue and queue, along with two supporting templates.
\<set\>	Defines the container class templates set and multiset, along with their supporting templates, providing a set of T.
\<stack\>	Defines the template class stack and two supporting templates, providing a stack of T.
\<vector\>	Defines the container class template vector, along with three supporting templates, providing a one-dimensional array of T.

Diagnostics

\<cassert\>	Includes the Standard C header \<assert.h\> within the std namespace, providing Standard C assertions.
\<cerrno\>	Includes the Standard C header \<errno.h\> within the std namespace, providing C-style error handling.
\<stdexcept\>	Defines several classes used for reporting Standard C++ exceptions.

General Utilities

\<ctime\>	Includes the Standard C header \<time.h\> within the std namespace, providing C-style data and time.
\<functional\>	Define several templates that help construct function objects.
\<memory\>	Defines a class, an operator, and several templates used to allocate and free objects—allocators for containers.
\<utility\>	Defines several general-use templates useful throughout the Standard Template Library, including operators and pairs.

Input/Output

\<cstdio\>	Includes the Standard C header \<stdio.h\> within the std namespace.
\<fstream\>	Defines several class templates that support iostream operations on sequences stored in external files.
\<iomanip\>	Defines several *manipulators* that each take a single argument. A manipulator performs actions on streams.
\<ios\>	Defines several types and functions essential to the operation of iostreams—iostream base classes.
\<iosfwd\>	Declares forward references to several class templates used throughout the iostreams library.
\<iostream\>	Declares objects that control reading from, and writing to, the standard streams.
\<istream\>	Defines the class template basic_istream, which handles extractions for the iostreams, and the class template basic_iostream, which handles insertions **and** extractions—handles input streams.
\<ostream\>	Defines class template basic_ostream, which handles extractions for the iostream classes, and also defines several related manipulators—handles output streams.
\<sstream\>	Defines several class templates supporting iostreams operations on sequences stored in an array object.

Input/Output

<streambuf>	Defines class template `basic_streambuf`, which is essential to the operation of the iostream classes—stream buffers.
<strstream>	Defines several classes that support iostreams operations on sequences stored in an array of `char` objects.

Iterator

<iterator>	Defines a number of classes, class templates, and function templates used for the declaration and manipulation of iterators—iterators and iterator support.

Language Support

<cfloat>	Includes the Standard C header `<float.h>` within the `std` namespace, providing C-style floating-point limit macros.
<ciso646>	Includes the Standard C header `<iso646.h>` within the `std` namespace.
<climits>	Includes the Standard C header `<limits.h>` within the `std` namespace, providing C-style numeric scalar-limit macros.
<csetjmp>	Includes the Standard C header `<setjmp.h>` within the `std` namespace, providing C-style stack unwinding.
<csignal>	Includes the Standard C header `<signal.h>` within the `std` namespace, providing C-style signal handling.
<cstdarg>	Includes the Standard C header `<stdarg.h>` within the `std` namespace, providing variable-length function argument lists.
<cstddef>	Includes the Standard C header `<stddef.h>` within the `std` namespace, providing C library language support.
<exception>	Defines several types and functions related to exception handling.
<limits>	Defines the class template `numeric_limits`, whose specializations describe arithmetic properties of scalar data types.

Localization

<clocale>	Includes the Standard C header `<locale.h>` within the `std` namespace, representing cultural differences C-style.
<locale>	Defines many class templates and function templates that encapsulate and manipulate locales, which represent cultural differences.

Numerics

<cmath>	Includes the Standard C header `<math.h>` within the `std` namespace, providing standard math functions.
<complex>	Provides a class template describing an object that stores both the real part and the imaginary part of a complex number.
<cstdlib>	Includes the Standard C header `<stdlib.h>` within the `std` namespace, providing pseudo-random numbers.
<numeric>	Defines several function templates useful for computing numeric values—generalized numeric operations.
<valarray>	Defines the class template `valarray` along with many supporting template classes and functions, providing numeric vectors and operations.

Strings

<cctype>	Includes the Standard C header `<ctype.h>` within the `std` namespace—character classsification.
<cstdlib>	Includes the Standard C header `<stdlib.h>` within the `std` namespace, providing C-style string and character functions.
<cstring>	Includes the Standard C header `<string.h>` within the `std` namespace, providing C-style string and character functions.
<cwchar>	Includes the Standard C header `<wchar.h>` within the `std` namespace, providing C-style wide character support.
<cwctype>	Includes the Standard C header `<wctype.h>` within the `std` namespace, providing C-style wide character string functions.
<string>	Defines the container template class `basic_string` and various supporting templates—a string of T.

Using C++

Rob McGregor

que

A Division of Macmillan Computer Publishing, USA
201 W. 103rd Street
Indianapolis, Indiana 46290

Contents at a Glance

Using C++

Copyright©1999 by Que Corporation

International Standard Book Number: 0-7897-1667-4

Library of Congress Catalog Card Number: 98-84812

Printed in the United States of America

First Printing: October 1998

00   99   98   4   3   2   1

Trademarks

Warning and Disclaimer

Executive Editor
Tracy Dunkelberger

Aquisitions Editor
David Mayhew
Tracy Dunkelberger

Development Editor
Sean Dixon

Managing Editor
Jodi Jensen

Senior Editor
Susan Ross Moore

Copy Editor
Alice Martina-Smith

Indexer
Kevin Fulcher

Proofreader
Mona Brown

Technical Editor
Poney Carpenter

Team Coordinator
Michelle Newcomb

Cover Designers
Dan Armstrong
Ruth Harvey

Interior Designers
Nathan Clement
Ruth Harvey

Layout Technicians
Marcia Deboy
Susan Geiselman

Contents

vi

Using C++

About the Author

Fascinated by computers since the early days of *Star Trek*, **Rob McGregor** began exploring computer programming with BASIC as a teenager in the late 1970s. Over the years he has worked professionally as a programmer, rock musician, software consultant, 3D computer artist, and network administrator (among other things). Rob has authored or co-authored numerous books about computer programming, including *Peter Norton's Guide to Windows 95/NT 4 Programming with MFC*, also by Macmillan Computer Publishing. In 1992 he founded Screaming Tiki Interactive, a software development company that specializes in business and 3D graphics applications for Microsoft Windows. Rob lives in Rockledge, Florida, and in his free time enjoys ray tracing, reading, writing, programming, composing music, and playing classical and electric guitar. You can contact Rob via email at:

rob_mcgregor@compuserve.com

Dedication

For Frank and Olive—I couldn't have done it without you!!

Acknowledgments

I'd like to thank Grace Buechlein for getting the ball rolling, and David Barnhart for everything he's done to help make my life easier during the writing of this book (including introducing me to some cool new music!).

Special thanks to Development Editor Sean Dixon for his valuable guidance and direction for this book, and to Dr. Don Argo for his insight into the inner workings of how computers think—even if he's not aware that he provided such insight. Thanks, Don!

Most importantly, uncounted thanks to my lovely Carleen for her diligent proofreading and critique sessions, and for making sure that I remembered to eat and sleep occasionally while writing the manuscript and source code for this book. (You're the best, Imzadi!)

Tell Us What You Think!

As the reader of this book, *you* are our most important critic and commentator. We value your opinion and want to know what we're doing right, what we could do better, what areas you'd like to see us publish in, and any other words of wisdom you're willing to pass our way.

As the Executive Editor for the Advanced Programming and Distributed Architecture team at Macmillan Computer Publishing, I welcome your comments. You can fax, email, or write me directly to let me know what you did or didn't like about this book—as well as what we can do to make our books stronger.

Please note that I cannot help you with technical problems related to the topic of this book, and that due to the high volume of mail I receive, I might not be able to reply to every message.

When you write, please be sure to include this book's title and author as well as your name and phone or fax number. I will carefully review your comments and share them with the author and editors who worked on the book.

Fax: 317-817-7070

Email: programming@mcp.com

Mail: Tracy Dunkelberger
          Executive Editor
          Advanced Programming and Distributed Architecture Team
          Macmillan Computer Publishing
          201 West 103rd Street
          Indianapolis, IN 46290 USA

Who Should Read This Book

This book was written for anyone who wants to understand how C++ programming works. *Using C++* will get you up to speed fast on the essential elements of C++ that you will use every day in your programs. It provides you with a thorough grounding in using the power of the C++ language to create object-oriented programs. Whether you already know how to program in some other language or have never programmed before, this book will help you learn C++ quickly and will help to simplify the often complex application development process.

What Experience Do You Need?

The concepts and sample code presented in this book should work under any standard C++ compiler, with few exceptions. If you're familiar and comfortable with fundamental programming and object-oriented concepts, then you'll have a head start—but the book assumes no previous programming experience in C, C++, or any other language.

The History and Evolution of C++

The C++ language was conceived and developed in the early 1980s by Dr. Bjarne Stroustrup at AT&T's Bell Labs in New Jersey. Dr. Stroustrup developed C++ as an object-oriented C, or "C with Classes" as it was originally called. The C programming language was developed at Bell Labs a decade earlier, and by the early 1980s, C had become the *lingua franca* of computer programming.

Dr. Stroustrup wanted an elegant, object-oriented programming language that would be compatible with existing C code; C++ was the result. Even today, after several developmental and conceptual changes, C++ retains full compatibility with C. The C programming language was finally standardized in 1989 by a joint committee made up of representatives from the American National Standards Institute (ANSI) and the International Standards Organization (ISO).

Just after C was standardized, another joint committee was formed to look into standardizing C++. After seven years of modification and purposeful evolution of C++ into the industrial strength, robust programming language it is today, the standards committee approved a final draft of the C++ standard, and Standard C++ became a reality at long last in February 1998.

Today, C++ is quickly replacing C as the predominant programming language on the planet. In terms of flexibility, speed, portability, and power, C++ has no equal.

How This Book Is Organized

The book is divided into six parts, each part covering a specific set of related concepts or issues. Before you dive in and start reading about how to write programs with C++, please take the time to peruse this brief overview.

Part I: C++ Basics

In this first part of the book, you learn the basic syntax and idiosyncrasies of the C++ language. Topics covered in Part I include data types, expressions and statements, programmatic decision making, loops, arrays, and functions.

Part II: Beyond the Basics

In the second part of this book, you'll learn about some more advanced features of the C++ language. Topics covered in Part II include function and operator overloading, user-defined data types (structures and unions), pointers and references, dynamic memory allocation, preprocessing, function pointers, error trapping, namespaces, bit manipulation, and the program build process.

Part III: Object-Oriented Programming

In the third part of this book, you are introduced to object-oriented programming and the C++ language features that support this programming model. Topics covered in Part III include C++ classes, class inheritance and polymorphism, dynamic storage, object-oriented design and development, class templates, dynamic casting, and runtime type identification.

Part IV: Using the Standard C++ Library

In the fourth part of this book, you'll discover the advantages and details of using the Standard C++ Library, an international C++ standard set of functions, classes, and algorithms. Topics covered in Part IV include iterators and containers, standard strings, numerics, files and streams, and standard algorithms.

Formatting Conventions

This book and its text have been formatted to be easily read and used. Most of the text is formatted exactly as you see here in this paragraph, although some words, phrases, or lines may have additional formatting. This additional formatting provides the following types of emphasis:

- *Italic type* is used to highlight words or terms being introduced and defined. It is also used occasionally for emphasis.

- `Monospace type` is used for all terms and text that are part of programming code. For example, function names are formatted with this special typeface: the `Allocate()` function. In addition, all structure names (`Point2d`), class names (`CVertex`), C++ keywords (`bool` and `return`), and all parameter names are formatted in this way.

Source Code on the Web: The *Using* C++ Web Site

Because this book has no accompanying CD-ROM, all the published source code from the book, along with additional code and sample programs, are available on the World Wide Web. To access this information, type the ten digits of this book's ISBN (0789716674) on the following page:

`http://www.mcp.com/info`

This page can take you to a little corner of cyberspace in which I've created a small Web site as a resource for those of you who spend your hard-earned money to buy this book. Thanks!

How to Contact the Author

I think this book is a good one, and that the sample code does a good job of demonstrating the concepts presented. Please realize that, for clarity, the sample code uses very little error checking in most cases, and is written merely to demonstrate the concepts presented. The samples are not meant to be production-quality code; they are teaching tools.

If you have any questions, suggestions, or bug reports that will help improve future editions of this book, please feel free to contact me directly, with email, at this address:

rob_mcgregor@compuserve.com

I check my email at least once a day, so I'll get back to you (maybe sooner, maybe later).

C++ Basics

Getting Started
with C++

See how to write source code

Find out about compiling and linking source files

Get a peek at functions

Learn to use C-style and C++-style comments

Tour the basic input, output, and error streams

Creating a C++ Program

Procedural Programming

A programming paradigm that uses sub-programs or sub-routines that allow replacement of a group of statements with a single statement.

Object-Oriented Programming

A programming paradigm that is an evolution of procedural programming where the procedures and the data they act upon are encapsulated into objects.

Paradigm

A type of programming model, such as procedural programming or object-oriented programming. It is a school of thought, a way of thinking about your programs.

The C++ Superset

The C++ programming language is a superset of the C programming language. That means that everything C can do, C++ can do too—and much more. C++ extends the capabilities of C, adding support for truly object-oriented programming techniques.

Why would anyone choose C++ as a favorite programming language? Maybe you've heard the nasty rumors that C++ is obtuse, difficult to understand, and downright unintuitive and unfriendly—that it's mainly used by rocket scientists and egghead geeks. That couldn't be further from the truth! C++ is a rich, robust programming language with features that make it stand head and shoulders above most other languages.

Imagine yourself as an aspiring artist. When you start learning to draw, you create rough sketches with a pencil; eventually, you can produce fantastic pencil drawings. As your talent develops, you may want to expand the expressiveness of your work by adding color and working with different artistic mediums such as watercolors and oil paints. After a few years of hard work, diligent study, and lots of practice, you may find yourself creating paintings that rival those of the masters.

The C++ language is to a C++ programmer what various artistic mediums are to an artist. The best thing about C++ is that it works at the same level you do, whether you're a beginning or an advanced programmer. C++ is the medium you use to create computer programs. As a beginner, you can use a small subset of C++ functionality to write simple programs, much as the beginning artist creates rough sketches with a pencil. As you get better at C++, more advanced language features become available to you, allowing you to create complex, highly useful programs. This process can be likened to the experienced artist using the expanded range of color and expressiveness offered by oil paints, which allows the artist to create great works of art.

C++ supports the two most popular programming *paradigms* (or models): *procedural programming* and *object-oriented programming*. The differences between these two paradigms will become readily apparent as you progress through this book. Because the procedural model is easier for most people to grasp in the beginning, I'll start off using the procedural approach. In later chapters, I'll introduce the object-oriented features of the language and show you how object-oriented programming is really just a natural evolutionary step beyond procedural programming, which makes it a far superior methodology.

Writing Source Code

A C++ program consists of human-readable source code composed of one or more files. These program files are just ordinary text files that contain the instructions a computer will follow when the program executes. A C++ program can contain as little as one line of code, or as many as a million (or more) lines of code—it just depends on what the program is supposed to do.

Creating a Program

1. Decide what the program is supposed to do.

2. Figure out how you want the program to do it.

3. Write the source code for the program.

4. Debug and test the program.

When you create the source code for a C++ program, you simply type it into any text editor and save the file as plain text. There are two basic types of source code files used in C++ programming: *interface files* (also called header files) and *implementation files* (also called source files). The standard file extension for a C++ header file is .h, although you may sometimes see the extension .hpp used instead. The standard file extension for a C++ source file is .cpp. You'll see more about writing header (.h) files in later chapters—for now, we're only concerned with source (.cpp) files.

Compiling and Linking Source Files

Before you can run a program you've written, you must *build* an executable file. When creating C++ programs—especially large ones that use multiple source and header files—it's important to understand what's going on under the hood at compile time. Generally speaking, *compiling* is the process of converting text files (your source code) into binary object code files (the machine code).

A program called a *compiler* does the compiling. Another program, called a *linker*, links together all the compiled object files needed by your program, resulting in an executable file. Most programs use more than one source file and typically use several

---

Implementation File

An implementation file is another name for a source file.

Interface File

An interface file is another name for a header file.

What's an Include File?

You may hear the term *include file* from time to time, but what does it mean? It really means a header file, one that's included in some other file using the C++ #include directive.

Linker

A program that links object modules into an executable file.

header files as well. After you have written the source code for a program, you must compile and link your source files.

Building Executable Programs

Almost all C++ compilers ship with a utility program called a *make utility*. A special script file, called a *make file* (usually having a .mak file extension), contains information about your source files, object files, and any library files that have to be linked with them to create your resulting executable program. The make utility automates much or, with many compilers, all of the compiling and linking process. Compiling and linking is called the *build process*.

SEE ALSO

➤ *To learn more about make files, see page 453*

Compiling

A C++ compiler makes several passes over your source code, converting a plain-text source file into a binary object code file that usually has either a .obj or a .o file extension. An object code file contains *machine code*, the native language of the computer. This object code is the main part of what's required for your source code to become an executable program. Compilers target specific operating systems and hardware platforms, so be aware that code compiled on one system may not run on another. Assuming your code is Standard C++, and doesn't use implementation dependent extensions to the language, the same source code can be recompiled to run on as many platforms as you like.

SEE ALSO

➤ *To learn more about compiling, see page 448*

Linking

The linker takes any object code files compiled from your source code and links them with special execution code and with any C++ library code required by your program. The code in a library consists of several object modules grouped together logically and combined by a special *librarian* program into a single

Make Utility

A program that runs the compiler, linker, and other tools to build a C++ program according to specifications given in a script.

Make File

A script, defining the build options for a program, that's used by a make utility.

Machine Code

The fundamental binary language of the computer that tells the CPU (Central Processing Unit) what to do first and what to do last. It is written as binary strings.

library file (usually having a .lib extension). The end result is an executable file, having an .exe file extension, that your target computer platform's operating system can load and run.

SEE ALSO

➤ *To learn more about linking, see page 451*

Again, the process of compiling and linking your code is called the *build process*; Figure 1.1 shows the steps involved.

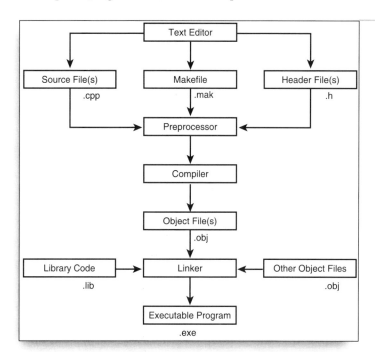

FIGURE 1.1

The steps involved in building an executable file.

Testing Your Code

It's rare, if not impossible, to find a programmer who can write flawless code the first time through. Most programmers go through several iterations of coding, compiling, linking, and testing their programs for bugs and then starting the process over again until the program works properly. The entire program development process of coding, compiling, linking, and testing is shown in Figure 1.2.

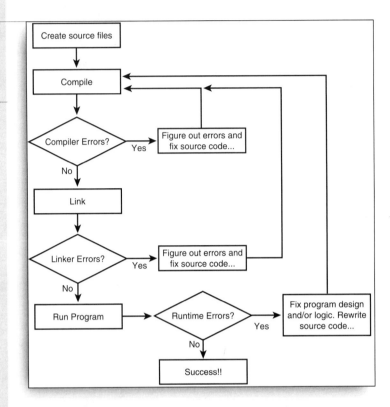

FIGURE 1.2

The program development process of coding, compiling, linking, and testing.

Case Sensitivity

C++ is an extremely *case sensitive* programming language. If you mistakenly capitalize a keyword or identifier, the compiler won't understand what the word represents and will usually generate an error message. For example, the following variable names are all considered completely different identifiers:

```
MyVariable
myVariable
myvariable
```

Be careful to follow some sort of convention when creating new names for data items in your programs. Inadvertently using the wrong case can create program bugs that are hard to track down.

Introducing Functions

C++ programs make extensive use of programming constructs called *functions*, which you use to break complex programming problems down into bite-size pieces. Functions are covered thoroughly in Chapter 7, "Creating and Using Functions," but because they are so important and so common in C++ programs, I'll go over the basics a bit right now.

You call a function, as needed, to perform some task for you. A function can either return a value of some specified type to its caller, or it can return no value at all (a void value). A function can call another function, which can call still another function, and so on. Eventually, all called functions return to their caller. Confused? Don't worry—it'll all become clear to you in no time.

SEE ALSO

➤ *For a more in-depth look at functions, see page 170*

Declaring Functions

You must *declare* a function before you can use it in a program, which simply means you must tell the compiler that the function exists and a few things about it. The basic syntax of a function declaration is as follows:

```
return-type  FunctionName(parameter-list);
```

This syntax contains several elements, as shown in Table 1.1.

TABLE 1.1   The Basic Components of a Function Declaration

Item	Description
return-type	Describes the type of value a function returns to the caller. This return value might be a number, a word, a letter, some other type of data, or void (nothing at all).
FunctionName	A descriptive name for the function, which can be almost anything you want it to be.
parameter-list	A list of data elements, separated by commas, that the function uses internally to perform its work.

Function

A subprogram called from within an expression that has a single value that is computed and returned to the main program.

Declare

To make an identifier visible within the scope of your program.

Choose Descriptive Names

When you choose names for the data in your program—including names for constants, variables, and functions—you should choose descriptive names that reflect their intent. For example, instead of giving a function the name Function1(), give the function a name that describes its purpose: GoToTheStoreAndBack(). When you (or your co-workers) go back to review and test your code, you'll be glad your data is self-documented.

Variable

A location in memory where a data value that can be changed is stored and referenced by an identifier.

Semicolons and Function Declarations

Each C++ statement in a C++ program must be terminated by a trailing semicolon. The term "C++ statement" includes function declarations.

If no parameters are needed for a function, the function declaration must still contain an empty parameter list—a set of empty parentheses, like this: (). The function declaration must be terminated by a trailing semicolon.

SEE ALSO

➤ *For a better understanding of function parameters, see page 171*

Making a Sandwich: A Study in Problem Solving

To make the concept of functions and function calls a little clearer, let's think of the basic steps needed to make a sandwich. Here is a set of steps in the sandwich-making process; you can use these steps regardless of the type of sandwich you are making:

1. Gather all the items needed for the sandwich.

2. Apply any desired condiments (mayonnaise, mustard, and so on) to two slices of bread.

3. Apply the main sandwich ingredients (meat, cheese, lettuce, and so on) to one of the bread slices.

4. Finish by placing the second slice of bread on top of the sandwich ingredients, effectively "sandwiching" the ingredients between the two slices of bread.

5. Clean up the mess.

Of course, you might make sandwiches differently than I do, but that's okay—various programmers solve various problems differently, too. If this series of steps was to be broken out into a set of functions, the functions might use these descriptive names:

1. GatherSandwichItems()

2. ApplyCondiments()

3. ApplySandwichIngredients()

4. ApplySecondSliceOfBread()

5. CleanUp()

Of course, you would probably want to eat the sandwich, too, but that's up to you. The function declarations (also called *function prototypes*) for these functions might look like this:

```
void GatherSandwichItems();
void ApplyCondiments();
void ApplySandwichIngredients();
void ApplySecondSliceOfBread();
void CleanUp();
```

Creating and Using Code Blocks

A C++ program is simply a sequence of instructions that we want the computer to follow. The instructions are often broken into functions. You've seen function declarations, but what about the actual functions themselves? The instruction code within a function is grouped into a *code block*, which makes up the *function body*. A code block starts with an opening brace ({) and ends with a closing brace (}). The code that lies between the braces comprises the code block. The code within a block can consist of any number of lines, with each statement terminated by a semicolon (;).

SEE ALSO

➤ *For more information about C++ statements, see page 70*

For example, the hypothetical GatherSandwichItems() function described earlier would use a code block to define the body of the function:

```
void GatherSandwichItems() { }
```

Earlier, I mentioned that functions can call other functions. Now is a good time to explain this a little more. Why? Because calling the five functions in the order listed earlier is a bit tedious, and it would be easy to mix up the proper calling order, resulting in a messy sandwich. Let's introduce a new function called MakeSandwich(). This new function will call the other five functions for us. Once it's created, we only need to remember one function call—MakeSandwich()—and it'll handle the details for us.

Function Prototype

The function interface describing return type, function name, and parameter list of a function.

Code Block

A set of statements that fall between opening ({) and closing (}) braces.

Compiler

A program that translates high-level code such as C++ into machine code.

I'll put everything you've seen so far to use in this MakeSandwich() function. First, let's declare the function so that the compiler will know about it. The function just performs the tedious work of assembling the sandwich, so it doesn't need to return a value—that's why it uses the void return type:

```
void MakeSandwich();
```

That was easy. Next comes the function body, complete with a code block to mark the beginning and end of the function and calls to the five functions within the block:

```
void MakeSandwich()
{
    GatherSandwichItems();
    ApplyCondiments();
    ApplySandwichIngredients();
    ApplySecondSliceOfBread();
    CleanUp();
}
```

Now, by simply by calling MakeSandwich(), you effectively call GatherSandwichItems(), ApplyCondiments(), ApplySandwichIngredients(), ApplySecondSliceOfBread(), and CleanUp().

Of course, this is all hypothetical. Computer programs don't typically make sandwiches, so let's move on to something a little more concrete—a real program you can type and compile yourself!

Introducing the *main()* Function

At its heart, a C++ program contains a special function called main(). The main() function is the entry point of program execution, and it must be present in every C++ program. The main() function contains the code that tells the computer what to do as a program executes. Because main() is a function, you can write other functions within your source files and main() can call them, in effect acting as a host for all the other code.

To better understand the concept of the role of main() as the program entry point and host, take a look at Figure 1.3.

This figure shows the operating system calling main(). The program begins execution when the main() function begins—which makes main() the program entry point. Each of the three functions in this figure lives in its own box. The main() function calls the other two, and execution returns from them back to main().

Think of a talk-show host calling guests to the stage. The host calls a guest, and attention switches to the guest while he or she is speaking. Attention returns to the host when the guest leaves. The main() function calls the other functions, each does its thing and returns execution back to main(), which finally ends execution and returns control to the operating system.

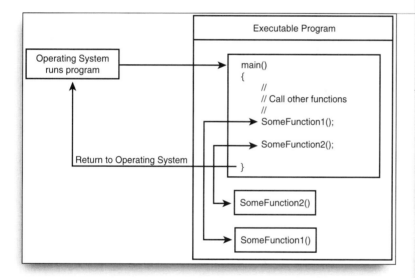

FIGURE 1.3

The main() function acts as the entry point of program execution; it hosts all the program code.

As you progress through the chapters in this book, you'll learn more about the syntax and capabilities of the C++ language. The main() function will become a familiar sight, although it will likely contain different code for every program, reflecting the differing needs of each program.

The main() function must follow the same function syntax described earlier. If main() were to return a value, the value would be returned to the operating system that executed the program—the operating system would act as the function's caller.

Receiving and Sending Values

Sometimes the main() function returns a value to the operating system when it terminates, and sometimes it doesn't. This is up to the programmer to decide and implement. The main() function can also receive values *from* the operating system when the program executes (you'll learn more about this in Chapter 7).

For now, we don't want `main()` to return a value, so we must declare it using the `void` return type. Also, there are no parameters that we want to pass to the function, so the parameter list will consist of an empty set of opening and closing parentheses.

Like all other functions, the `main()` function uses a block to define the code within its function body, for example:

```
void main() { }
```

This is the shortest possible C++ program, and as you might expect, it doesn't do anything at all—the function's *body* (code block) consists of a pair of braces containing no source code. This is the empty shell of the `main()` function.

Whitespace

Space between characters and lines within an input or output string. Also refers to tabs, spaces, and hard returns in your source code that is ignored by the compiler.

In general, the C++ compiler doesn't care about *whitespace*, such as tab characters, line breaks, hard returns, and spaces. This means that the code just shown can just as easily be written like this:

```
void main()
    { }
```

It can also be written like this:

```
void
main()
{
}
```

All these examples define the empty code block making up the `main()` function, and the compiler sees all these variations as being the same code. There is no actual instruction code to tell the computer to do anything, though. To actually make the program do something, you have to expand your C++ knowledge and add some more code. I'll show you how a little later in this chapter.

Using C-Style and C++-Style Comments

When writing a program, it's very important to document what the source code does. The best place to do this is within the program itself, by writing comments in the code. This makes it easy to know, at a glance, what the program does each step of the way. The compiler ignores all comments completely—anything you type as a comment is for humans only. The computer never even knows the comments exist.

The first simple programs you create may not need many comments, if any. As programs grow in complexity, however, the number of comments the program contains should grow proportionally. Even if you understand the code today, six months from now you might not, and the comments will make your life much easier!

C++ supports two styles of comments. The first style was inherited from the C programming language, which is fully contained as a subset within C++. The second style was introduced specifically for C++.

C-Style Comments

The C-style comment uses a matched pair of slashes and stars, with the slashes on the outside and the stars on the inside, like this:

```
/* This is a C-style comment */
```

This comment style is very useful because it can span multiple lines of code. The same comment can also look like this:

```
/*
This is a C-style comment
*/
```

The comment can also look like this:

```
/************************
This is a C-style comment
************************/
```

In fact, you will often see comments like these in professional production code. Because anything between /* and */ is considered a comment, you can use such comments to temporarily remove entire sections of source code from a program file. For example, if I place these comment symbols around the main()

function, the entire program becomes "commented out," and the compiler won't see the main() function at all:

```
/* Commenting out the entire main() function
void main()
{
}
End of comment */
```

C++-Style Comments

The C++-style comment can exist on only a single line in a source file. It uses a double-slash to mark the beginning of the comment, like this:

```
// This is a C++-style comment
```

This comment style includes everything from the double-slash to the end of the line. You can string several of these comments together, one per line, as you see fit, for example:

```
//
// This is also a C++-style comment
//
```

The compiler ignores all these lines. Comments not only tell the reader of the code what's going on, they are also useful for letting the reader know some things about the code they are reading, such as who wrote the code, when, and why. Both types of comments can occur anywhere in the source code. Take a look at a few examples of comment style and use. First, comments can be at the end of code lines, like these:

```
void main()      // this is the program entry point
{                // start of function body
}                /* end of function body */
```

C-style comments can be within a line of code, like this:

```
short /*int*/ x = 45;
```

In this case, the author of the code is trying to tell us either that a short is a type of int, or that he is "commenting out" one data type or the other, compiling each to see which is the better choice. He could rewrite this code like this:

```
/*short*/ int x = 45;
```

Consider the code in Listing 1.1, which is simply a well-commented version of the do-nothing program shown above (it still does nothing).

Beware of Line Numbers

Note that the code listings in this book use line number/colon combinations (such as 1:, 2:, 3:, and so on) at the beginning of each line of code. These line numbers are for illustrative purposes only, to aid your understanding of the code. Don't type these line numbers into your source files—doing so will cause compiler errors galore!

LISTING 1.1 A Well-Commented Program That Does Absolutely Nothing

```
1: /////////////////////////////////////////////////////////////
2: //  Module  : first.cpp
3: //
4: //  Purpose : Demonstrates comments and the main() function
5: /////////////////////////////////////////////////////////////
6:
7: void main()
8: {
9:    /*
10:      Useful executable statements would go here...in the
11:      main() code block...this program does absolutely
12:      nothing...
13:    */
14: }
```

In this program, lines 1 through 5 are comments making up a simple program description. Line 7 begins the main() function, and line 8 begins the code block that makes up the body of main(). Lines 9 through 13 use a multiple-line comment to describe that the program does nothing, and line 14 ends the program by closing the main() block.

Important C++ Keywords

There are many keywords built in to the C++ language that you commonly use in your programs, and many more obscure keywords that you use less often. Keywords are divided into categories, such as data type keywords or flow control keywords. Table 1.2 lists some commonly used, important C++ keywords.

TABLE 1.2   Some Commonly Used C++ Keywords, Presented Alphabetically

Keyword	Category
break	Flow control statement
case	Flow control statement
class	Abstract data type
const	Type modifier
continue	Flow control statement
delete	Memory management keyword
do	Loop statement
double	Data type
else	Decision statement
float	Data type
for	Loop statement
goto	Flow control statement
if	Decision statement
int	Data type
long	Data type
namespace	Access specifier
new	Memory management keyword
operator	Function declarator
private	Access specifier
protected	Access specifier
public	Access specifier
struct	Abstract data type
switch	Flow control statement
union	Abstract data type
void	Data type
while	Loop statement

You'll learn about all these keywords later in this book.

Using Basic Input/Output Streams

To make your programs actually do something, you've got to put some code in the body of the `main()` function. To do this, you need to know more about C++ language syntax and commands. Writing data to the screen is traditionally where C++ programmers begin, and I'll continue that tradition by doing the same thing here. I'll also show you how to read user input from the keyboard.

Realizing That Input/Output Streams Are C++ Objects

As I mentioned earlier, C++ supports object-oriented programming (OOP) and was designed with OOP as its main goal. For this reason, many of the native programming concepts in C++ involve the use of C++ *objects*, which are data constructs that are "smart enough" to know how to do certain things.

SEE ALSO

➤ *For more information about object-oriented programming and C++ objects, see page 473*

Reading user input from the keyboard and writing text to the screen are actually somewhat complex tasks, but C++ makes it easy by providing the input/output stream library (`iostream`). This library gives us access to C++ objects called *streams*. For now, just accept the fact that you can use streams to write text to the screen and to read user input from the keyboard.

Three Standard C++ stream objects are used for input, output, and error output. By default, the standard input object (`cin`) reads from the keyboard; the standard output object (`cout`) and the standard error object (`cerr`) print to the screen.

Writing data to the screen is accomplished through the `cout` object and its *insertion operator* (`<<`). Reading user input from the keyboard is accomplished through the `cin` object and its *extraction operator* (`>>`).

SEE ALSO

➤ *For an in-depth look at input and output streams, see page 788*

Objects

Variables or constants used in programming.

Stream

A linear, ordered sequence of bytes.

Extraction Operator

An operator that extracts bytes from an input stream object.

Insertion Operator

An overloaded < operator that inserts data into an output stream.

Using the *#include* Directive

The first portion of the C++ compile process involves something called *preprocessing*, which is one of the things that makes C++ so flexible. The *preprocessor* portion of the compiler looks for certain commands, called *preprocessor directives*, that perform special tasks during the compilation of source code. One of these preprocessor directives is #include.

SEE ALSO

> *For more information about the preprocessor, see page 297*

The #include directive tells the preprocessor that what follows is the name of a file from the Standard C++ Library, and that the file should be opened and read into the source code as if you typed the entire thing there yourself, effectively including its text in your program.

The iostream library we'll use for basic input and output in the following sections is defined in the header file <iostream.h>. To give your program access to the library, you must include this header file in your source code, like this:

```
#include <iostream.h>
```

The angle brackets (< and >) around the header filename tell the preprocessor to look in all directories that should contain header files. These directories are typically specified in configuration files your compiler uses when it runs. Check your specific compiler's documentation for details about how to specify include directories. All header files that should be found in your compiler's include directory will be shown with angle brackets.

The Standard Output Stream

The standard output stream object cout uses its insertion operator (<<) to redirect text output to the screen. By simply using a literal string of characters (a character string, or string) enclosed in quotation marks, you can write some text to the screen. For example, to write the title of this book to the screen, we'd use cout in a statement that looks like this:

```
cout << "Using C++\n";
```

Preprocessor

A program that prepares source code for compiling. May arrange data into groups or different internal formats.

Preprocessing

The process of arranging data into groups and internal formats that the computer can interpret when compiling.

Preprocessor Directives

Instructions to the preprocessor on how data is to be prepared for compiling.

The Standard C++ Library

The ANSI and ISO committees responsible for designing and approving the Standard C++ specification have approved the Standard C++ Library. Each compiler vendor must supply its own implementation of the Standard C++ Library (or an implementation purchased from someone else).

This just means, "Use the `cout` object and insert the text `Using C++\n` to the screen." You may be wondering what the `\n` is doing in the quotation marks. The `\n` is a special character combination, called an *escape sequence*, that represents the newline character, which causes the cursor to drop to the next line on the screen. The backslash character (\\) tells the compiler that a special character follows.

The compiler sees an escape sequence as a single character. You can use escape sequences to send commands like carriage returns and tab movements to the screen. You can also use them to send nonprinting characters or characters that may confuse the compiler, such as the double quotation mark ("). For example, the compiler would choke on the following statement:

```
cout << "He said, "See you tomorrow.""
```

The compiler would attempt to end the string at `"He said, "`, which is obviously not the desired output. To create the correct output to the screen, we must use escape sequences for the literal double quotation marks, like this:

```
cout << "He said, \"See you tomorrow.\""
```

Table 1.3 shows several of the most common escape sequences.

Escape Sequence

A character combination consisting of a (/) followed by a letter or combination of digits used to provide literal representations of non-printing characters, characters with special meanings and actions like carriage returns and tab movements.

TABLE 1.3 Escape Sequences Commonly Used When Writing Text to the Screen

Escape Sequence	Description
\a	Alert (bell, beep)
\b	Backspace
\n	New line
\r	Carriage return
\t	Horizontal tab
\v	Vertical tab
\'	Single quotation mark
\"	Double quotation mark
\\	Backslash
\?	Question mark

Let's alter the program from Listing 1.1 to make it actually do something, such as writing some text to the screen. We'll write the title of this book: *Using C++*. Listing 1.2 shows the complete source code needed to do it.

LISTING 1.2   A Program That Uses the Standard Output Stream to Display a Simple Message Onscreen

```
1: ///////////////////////////////////////////////////////////
2: //   Module  : second.cpp
3: //
4: //   Purpose : Demonstration of standard output using cout
5: ///////////////////////////////////////////////////////////
6:
7: #include <iostream.h>
8:
9: void main()
10: {
11:     // Write "Using C++" to the screen
12:     cout << "Using C++\n";
13: }
```

The output of the program is as follows:

```
Using C++
```

In this program, lines 1 through 5 are again comments making up a simple program description. Line 7 uses the #include preprocessor directive to give the program access to the input/output stream library. Line 9 begins the main() function, and line 10 begins the code block that makes up the body of main(). Line 11 is a simple comment, and line 12 uses the cout object to write Using C++ to the screen. Finally, line 13 ends the program by closing the main() block.

Listing 1.3 is a more complex example that writes several lines of text to the screen. Note that although there are several cout statements listed in the code, the actual text displayed onscreen is broken into separate lines only where the newline escape sequence is used.

LISTING 1.3   A Program That Uses *cout* to Display Several Lines of Text Onscreen

```
 1: ///////////////////////////////////////////////////////////
 2: //   Module  : third.cpp
 3: //
 4: //   Purpose : Demonstration of standard output using cout
 5: ///////////////////////////////////////////////////////////
 6:
 7: #include <iostream.h>
 8:
 9: void main()
10: {
11:     // Write some stuff to the screen
12:     cout << "Using C++ ";
13:     cout << "is the only way ";
14:     cout << "to really learn C++\n";
15:     cout << "\n";
16:     cout << "So practice, practice, practice.\n";
17: }
```

The output from this program is as follows (notice the blank line in the middle of the text):

```
Using C++ is the only way to really learn C++

So practice, practice, practice.
```

In Listing 1.3, lines 1 through 10 perform the same function as they have in the previous programs, so I won't describe them again. Line 11 is a simple comment, and lines 12 through 16 use the cout object to write text to the screen. Note that only lines 14, 15, and 16 contain newline characters, and that line 14 contains **only** a newline character, creating a blank line on the screen. Finally, line 17 ends the program by closing the main() block.

You can use the insertion operator multiple times in a single cout statement to display several separate character strings one after another, as shown here:

```
cout << "This is a single " << "character string."
```

Listing 1.4 is a slight modification of the program from Listing 1.3, showing how this works in a real program.

LISTING 1.4   A Program That Uses the Standard Output Stream to Display a Simple Message Onscreen

```
 1: ///////////////////////////////////////////////////////////////
 2: //  Module  : fourth.cpp
 3: //
 4: //  Purpose : Demonstration of standard output using cout
 5: ///////////////////////////////////////////////////////////////
 6:
 7: #include <iostream.h>
 8:
 9: void main()
10: {
11:    // Write some stuff to the screen
12:    cout << "Using C++ " << "is the only way "
13:    cout << "to really learn C++\n\nSo practice, ";
14:    cout << "practice, practice.\n";
15: }
```

This slightly rearranged program has the same output as the program in Listing 1.3.

You can also use multiple insertion operators in a single cout statement to combine text and numbers, like this:

```
// Display text and numbers to the screen
cout << "There are " << 7 << " days in a week.";
```

This code results in the output you might expect:

```
There are 7 days in a week.
```

The Standard Input Stream

Okay, it's nice to be able to write data to the screen, but what about getting some user input? This is where things begin to get a little more interesting—and fun. The standard input stream cin is the easiest way to get input from a user.

The cin object uses the extraction operator (>>) to extract information from a stream, in this case the standard input stream, which is the keyboard. When you extract input, you need to have a place to store the information the user provides. C++ uses *variables* to store data in computer memory.

SEE ALSO

➤ *To learn more about variables, see page 45*

Listing 1.5 shows a program that uses cin to read in the user's first name. The cin object stores the name in a variable called name, and then displays the contents of the name variable on the screen using cout.

LISTING 1.5   A Program That Uses the Standard Input Stream to Get a User's First Name

```
 1: //////////////////////////////////////////////////////
 2: //  Module  : fifth.cpp
 3: //
 4: //  Purpose : Demonstration of standard input/output using
 5: //            cin and cout
 6: //////////////////////////////////////////////////////
 7:
 8: #include <iostream.h>
 9:
10: void main()
11: {
12:    // Ask the user a question
13:    cout << "Hello, what's your first name?\n>";
14:
15:    // Create a place to store up to 25 characters for a name
16:    char name[25];
17:
18:    // Get the user's name
19:    cin >> name;
20:
21:    // Use the name, writing it to the screen
22:    cout << "Welcome to the world of C++, " << name << "!";
23: }
```

LISTING 1.5

1 Line 13: Use the cout object to display a question

2 Line 16: Create a character string variable

3 Line 19: Use the cin object to get the user's first name

The only thing in this program that might be unfamiliar to you is the declaration of the name variable:

```
char name[25];
```

This statement just tells the compiler that name is a variable that can contain up to 25 characters (you'll learn all about variables in Chapter 2, "Exploring C++ Data Types, Variables, and Constants").

When I type my first name (Rob) in response to the prompt, we get the following program output:

```
Hello, what's your first name?
>Rob
Welcome to the world of C++, Rob!
```

Just as the cout object can use multiple insertion operators in a single statement, the cin object can use multiple extraction operators in a single statement. Suppose that we want to get not only the user's first name, but his or her last name as well. We can modify the program from Listing 1.5 to do this by simply providing another name variable and using multiple extraction operators for cin, as shown in Listing 1.6.

LISTING 1.6

① Line 13: Use the cout object to display a question

② Lines 16-17: Create two character string variables

③ Line 20: Use the cin object to get the user's first and last names

LISTING 1.6   A Program That Uses the Standard Input Stream to Get a User's First Name *and* Last Name

```
 1: //////////////////////////////////////////////////////////
 2: //  Module  : sixth.cpp
 3: //
 4: //  Purpose : Demonstration of standard input/output using
 5: //            cin and cout
 6: //////////////////////////////////////////////////////////
 7:
 8: #include <iostream.h>
 9:
10: void main()
11: {
12:     // Ask the user a question
13:     cout << "Hello, what's your name?\n>";          ①
14:
15:     // Create places to store up to 25 characters for a name
16:     char fname[25];      ┐
17:     char lname[25];      ┘                           ②
18:
19:     // Get the user's name
20:     cin >> fname >> lname;          ③
```

```
21:
22:     // Use the name, writing it to the screen
23:     cout << "Welcome to the world of C++, "
24:         << fname << " " << lname << "!";
25: }
```

The cin object is "smart enough" to know how to extract separate words from the keyboard input by the whitespace typed between words. In this program, the cin object gets two words from the keyboard and stores them in the variables fname and lname using this line of code:

```
cin >> fname >> lname;
```

When I type my first and last names as input, we get the following program output:

```
Hello, what's your name?
>Rob McGregor
Welcome to the world of C++, Rob McGregor!
```

You may wonder what would happen if you typed three separate words in response to the question, "Hello, what's your name?" For example, if you typed Joe Van Goma as three separate words, each separated by a space character, the program output would look like this:

```
Hello, what's your name?
>Joe Van Goma
Welcome to the world of C++, Joe Van!
```

There are ways around these sorts of problems, as you'll see throughout this book.

The Standard Error Stream

The standard error stream object, cerr, uses the same syntax that the cout object uses. You can use the standard error stream to output messages to the screen when an error occurs in a program, while still sending cout statements to the standard output device (which can also be a printer or a file on disk).

Exploring C++ Data Types, Variables, and Constants

Explore the fundamental data types

Get acquainted with derived data types

Learn to use variables and constants

Discover how to resolve the scope of variables and constants

Understand declarations and definitions

See how to cast data types

Understanding C++ Data Types

At its most basic level, a computer program performs an operation on some data and produces a result. Because C++ is a *strongly typed* language, each piece of data—that is, each data element—must have a specific data type. Technically speaking, a *data type* describes a set of values and the operations that can be applied to that set. In layman's terms, a data type determines how the data is represented in the computer and the kinds of data processing that can be performed on it.

There are two kinds of data types in C++:

- Fundamental data types
- Derived data types

We'll look at these kinds of data types in some detail in the following sections, often creating and using *variables* to do so (variables are thoroughly discussed later in this chapter). Because variables and data types are quite interrelated, you really need to understand one concept to understand the other. This is the classic "chicken or the egg" scenario. For now, you should simply know that variables can hold values and are declared using the following syntax:

```
DataType  VariableName;
```

This statement tells the compiler that the variable `VariableName` has the data type `DataType`. You can also assign a value to initialize a variable when you declare it, like this:

```
DataType  VariableName = SomeValue;
```

SEE ALSO

➤ *For more information about variables and variable declarations, see page 45*

Exploring the Fundamental Data Types

The fundamental data types used in C++ fall into these categories:

- Integer type
- Character type

- Boolean type
- Floating-point type
- Double-precision type

Each of these data types has its own characteristics, and each uses a predetermined amount of memory. Unfortunately, different computer systems use different numbers of bytes to store these data types. This can mean trouble for C++ programmers who want the code to work on various platforms. An integer data type may be 2 bytes long on one platform, such as DOS, but 4 bytes long on another platform, such as UNIX. Be careful; the byte size of a data type can be very important at times.

The Integer Type

The set of integers includes positive and negative whole numbers and the number zero; integers have no fractional parts. This is a basic mathematical concept. Integers have an optional sign and one or more digits, as in these examples:

+134

−48

+349

−4838

0

31847

If an integer has no sign, you can assume it's a positive number. Notice that the number 31847 uses no comma to format the number. For one thing, commas aren't allowed in integers because they aren't a number. More importantly, the C++ language specification allows only numeric digits of the number itself. C++ makes things more interesting (and more perplexing) by defining several types of integers. Specifically, there are *signed integers* (positive and negative integers) and *unsigned integers* (positive integers only), and there may be different byte-storage sizes for each, which allows the set of possible values to differ greatly. Table 2.1 shows the integral types, along with typical byte sizes (byte sizes are operating-system dependent—for more information about byte sizes, read on).

Bit

The smallest component of computer memory.

Byte

A set of eight bits.

Signed Integer

The set of positive and negative integers.

Unsigned Integers

The set of positive integers.

What Are Integral Data Types?

The word *integral* literally means "whole," or in the case of computer data types, "not fractional." Any simple data type that doesn't use floating-point numbers (a decimal point) is an integral type.

TABLE 2.1   **Integral Data Types and Common Byte Sizes**

Integral Type	Byte Size
char	1
bool	1
short	2
int	2 or 4
long	4 or 8

Byte Size

The number of bytes an object takes up in computer memory.

Integers in C++ are made up of several different categories, based on the number of bytes each type uses. Table 2.2 gives the range of values permissible for each integer of a particular byte size.

TABLE 2.2   **The Possible Ranges of Values for Signed and Unsigned Integral Data Types of Various Byte Sizes**

Size	Sign	Minimum Value	Maximum Value
1	signed	–128	127
1	unsigned	0	255
2	signed	–32,768	32,767
2	unsigned	0	65,535
4	signed	–2,147,483,648	2,147,483,647
4	unsigned	0	4,294,967,295

Never make assumptions about the size of a data type. Use the C++ sizeof operator to let the compiler get accurate data type byte sizes for you. The sizeof operator returns the number of bytes used by a data type. For example, you can discover the byte size of an int on your computer system like this:

```
int IntBytes = sizeof(int);
```

You can find the byte size of a char data type like this:

```
int CharBytes = sizeof(char);
```

I run on Windows NT; when I enter these sizeof statements, they return these values: 8 for sizeof(int) and 1 for sizeof(char).

The Character Type

Characters are important; we use characters every day. This book is (for the most part) made up of sequences (*strings*) of characters. The data type char is used to represent a single character of data. A char can use single quotes to specify a value, as in this example:

```
char ch = 'A';
```

A char is an integral data type, so you can also define the same character value A using an integral ASCII code as a value. Because the uppercase letter *A* is represented by the integer 65 in the ASCII character table, you can assign the uppercase A to the char variable ch like this:

```
char ch = 65;
```

As you can see from Table 2.1, a char takes 1 byte (8 bits). Because most character sets contain 256 characters, using an unsigned char allows access to character codes 0 through 255. Characters are usually stored in *arrays* to form character strings, like this:

```
char ch[] = "GUITAR";
```

SEE ALSO

➤ *To get an in-depth understanding of arrays, see page 133*

Internally, the computer stores each character as a binary code, each having a unique pattern of ones and zeros. These codes can be represented in your source code using character, decimal, hexadecimal, octal, or binary notation—the compiler translates each as needed to the appropriate char type. Table 2.3 shows how the ASCII characters that make up the string GUITAR look in each of these notation schemes.

SEE ALSO

➤ *For more information about decimal numbers, see page 405*
➤ *For more information about binary numbers, see page 407*
➤ *For more information about octal numbers, see page 409*
➤ *For more information about hexadecimal numbers, see page 417*

String

A group of characters stored in a computer as a single unit of data.

Character Sets

The set of characters you find on a computer keyboard changes from country to country because of fundamental language differences such as spelling, accents, and punctuation. This is why different countries often use different *character sets.*

Array

A collection of data, all of the same type. Each array element is accessed by an index number.

Binary

A number system based on two rather than ten. There are only two symbols used in binary, 0 or 1, resulting in two possible alternatives..

Decimal Numeration System

A number system based on groups of ten.

Hexadecimal Numeration System

A number system based on groups of 16.

TABLE 2.3   Numeric Values of ASCII Codes for Some Uppercase Letters in the English Alphabet

Character	Decimal	Hexadecimal	Octal	Binary
G	71	0x47	0107	01000111
U	85	0x55	0125	01010101
I	73	0x49	0111	01001001
T	84	0x54	0124	01010100
A	65	0x41	0101	01000001
R	82	0x52	0122	01010010

Because each character takes one byte, the character string GUITAR uses six bytes, right? Wrong—it uses seven bytes. Why? Because a character string like this has the null character (0x00 or '\0') appended to terminate the string (this is called a *null-terminated string*). Literally translating the array into individual characters gives us the following set of seven distinct characters that actually make up the string:

```
{ 'G', 'U', 'I', 'T', 'A', 'R', '\0' }
```

These characters are stored in memory in seven contiguous 1-byte memory addresses, as shown in Figure 2.1.

FIGURE 2.1

A character array in contiguous memory addresses.

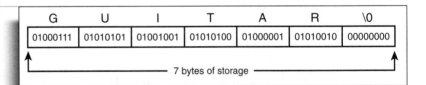

One interesting thing about character data is that it can be represented not only as a character, but also in any of several different ways as an integer using the character's numeric (ASCII) value. This set of seven characters might just as easily be written using hexadecimal numbers, like this:

```
{ 0x47, 0x55, 0x49, 0x54, 0x41, 0x52, 0x00 }
```

In Listing 2.1, all three styles of character arrays are used to store and output the character string GUITAR.

LISTING 2.1   **Three Different Ways of Representing a Character String**

```
1: ////////////////////////////////////////////////////////
2: //   Module  : char.cpp
3: //
4: //   Purpose : Demonstrates three different ways of
5: //             representing a character string
6: ////////////////////////////////////////////////////////
7:
8: #include <iostream.h> ─────────────── 1
9:
10: void main()
11: {
12:     char ch1[] = "GUITAR";
13:     char ch2[] = {'G', 'U', 'I', 'T', 'A', 'R', '\0'};     2
14:     char ch3[] = {0x47, 0x55, 0x49, 0x54, 0x41, 0x52, 0x00};
15:
16:     cout << "ch1 = " << ch1 << '\n';
17:     cout << "ch2 = " << ch2 << '\n';     3
18:     cout << "ch3 = " << ch3 << '\n';
19: }
```

LISTING 2.1

1 Line 8: Provides access to cout

2 Lines 12-14: Assigns the word GUITAR to three character arrays using three different data formats

3 Lines 16-18: Displays the data

Here, as you might expect, is the output from the program shown in Listing 2.1:

```
ch1 = GUITAR
ch2 = GUITAR
ch3 = GUITAR
```

The Boolean Type

A relative newcomer to the built-in data types provided by C++ is the Boolean data type, specified by the `bool` keyword. A `bool` can store only two possible values: `true` and `false`. We use Boolean variables to test conditions in a program to help the computer make decisions. Booleans are very useful for keeping track of the various states a code block might be in at any given time during program execution. For example, a Boolean variable might be declared like this:

```
bool NeedToSave = false;
```

Elsewhere in the program code, this variable could be used to see whether the program should save some files. By checking the

Boolean

Consisting of only two values: `true` or `false`

Boolean Logic

The term *Boolean* was derived from the name of the British mathematician George Boole (1815–1864). Boole designed a system of logic that used only true and false, which turned out to be perfect for use with computers.

value of NeedToSave to see whether it's true or false, the program will "know" what to do. You'll see a lot more bool usage later in this book.

SEE ALSO

➤ *For more information about the use of Boolean data, see page 78*

Floating-Point and Double-Precision Types

Floating-point numbers consist of an integer part and a fractional part, with a decimal point in between. Floating-point numbers are important for a myriad of computer applications, from checkbook balancing to Internet commerce to rocket science. Double-precision numbers are floating-point numbers with a high degree of decimal place accuracy. You can choose from three different types of floating-point numbers, depending on the level of numeric precision you need:

- float
- double
- long double

The typical byte sizes of these data types are shown in Table 2.4. Again, actual byte sizes vary depending on the operating system you use.

TABLE 2.4   Typical Byte Sizes for Floating-Point and Double-Precision Data Types

Data Type	Number of Bytes
float	4
double	8
long double	12 or 16

When you use a floating-point number in a program, you must provide at least one digit to the right of the decimal point, even if that digit is 0. Also, if the data type is float, you should specify this by appending an f to the end of the number. For example, if the number 42 is to be represented as a float, it must be written as 42.0f. As a double, the number is simply 42.0.

Take a look:

```
float   MyFLoat  = 42.0F;  // or 42.0f
double MyDouble = 42.0;
```

If the data type is `long double`, you should specify this by appending an L to the end of the number, like this:

```
long double MyLongDouble = 42.0L;
```

The floating-point types are most commonly used for mathematical operations and to store the results of these operations. Consider the following simple math problem as an example:

```
float cx = 12.0f, cy = 2.3f;
float cz = cx * cy;
```

Translated, this means: `cz = 12.0 * 2.3`, which is `27.6`.

Introducing Derived Data Types

A *derived data type* is any data type constructed from one or more of the fundamental types. Here are some common derived data types:

- Arrays
- Pointers
- References
- Structures
- Unions
- Classes

Because these types are so flexible and can be combined in innumerable ways, there are really an infinite number of possible derived data types. These common data types are covered in detail in other chapters of this book, so I won't go into them in much detail now, although we'll take a cursory look at each.

Arrays

An *array* is a collection of similar objects; a grouping of like data types that reside in a contiguous block of bytes in memory. You use an index number to access each *element* of the array, similar to the way in which you can find a certain post office box by number in a post office.

Derived Data Type

A data type that inherits functionality from an ancestor.

Element

A component part of an array.

Arrays can be built using different "shapes." There are three general shapes of arrays, each corresponding to the structure of an individual array:

- One-dimensional arrays
- Two-dimensional arrays
- Multi-dimensional arrays

You already saw a simple one-dimensional character array in the GUITAR string example, earlier in this chapter. Each element in a character array takes up one byte of storage space—one character. Other types of arrays can be made up of floats, doubles, or some other data type, so each array element would take up a much larger amount of storage space.

SEE ALSO

➤ *For an in-depth look at one-dimensional arrays, see page 133*

➤ *For an in-depth look at two-dimensional arrays, see page 144*

➤ *For more information about multi-dimensional arrays, see page 156*

Pointers and References

A *pointer* is a variable that points to a specific location in memory; a pointer gives you the actual memory address of a specific object. A *reference* is an alias for an object; references are similar to pointers but have less functionality and stricter usage rules. Pointers and references are covered thoroughly in Chapter 10, "Using Pointers and References."

SEE ALSO

➤ *For more information about pointers, see page 246*

➤ *For more information about memory addresses, see page 247*

➤ *For more information about references, see page 266*

Structures, Unions, and Classes

A *structure* is a data type that groups other data types together into a single, compound data type. Structures make it easy to keep variables logically related within source code by making each logically related variable a *member* of a structure.

Pointer

A data type that indicates the location (address) of a variable.

Reference

An alias for an object, similar to a pointer, used to pass an object by reference rather than by value.

Structure

A user defined data type that groups together logically related data.

Member

A component variable of a structure, union or class.

A *union* is similar to a structure. Unlike a structure, however, only one of the members of a union can be used at any one time. Unions give you a powerful and compact way to represent data.

A *class* is an enhanced structure that provides the object-oriented features of C++. Classes are discussed and demonstrated at length in Parts III, "Object-Oriented Programming," and IV, "Using the Standard C++ Library."

SEE ALSO

➤ *For more information about structures, see page 214*

➤ *For more information about unions, see page 236*

➤ *For an introduction to classes, see page 480*

Introducing the Standard String

Character *strings* are among the most used data structures in computer programming. You use strings when working with text files, generating report data, interacting with users, and a myriad other common activities. The Standard C++ library provides a string object that's efficient and easy to use.

To use a standard string object, you must include the standard string header file <string> within your program using the #include preprocessor directive, like this:

```
#include <string>
```

Notice that the <string> header file doesn't use the conventional .h file extension (or any other extension). The Standard C++ library header files use no file extensions at all.

SEE ALSO

➤ *To learn more about standard strings, see page 740*

Using Variables

Back in the days before high-level programming languages existed, memory addresses were used to store and retrieve all the data in a computer program. *Variables* are actually just aliases for memory locations; that is, they are named storage locations in

---

Union

A user defined data type similar to a structure that may contain several members. Members of a union can only be accessed one at a time.

Class

A user-defined data type that consists of data members and functions.

Declaring and Defining Variables

Before you can use a variable, function, class, or any other piece of program data (object), you must declare and define it. The distinction between declaration and definition is significant. A *declaration* simply introduces a name of some sort into a program, letting the compiler know that a function or some data exists. A declaration also spells out the expected format by specifying storage class, data type, and linkage for an object or function.

Conversely, a *definition* actually reserves (allocates) new storage, creating a function or an identifier (some piece of data) for use within a program. It's important to keep in mind that declarations can also be definitions (most of them are), but only if they cause storage to be reserved. In addition, declarations are used to designate class templates and to specify new namespaces (these topics are covered thoroughly in later chapters).

You must declare a variable in a program before you can use it (if you don't, the compiler will remind you by complaining). There is sometimes confusion between declaring and defining variables in C++, so remember this:

- A variable *declaration* simply associates a name (an identifier) with a specific variable.

- A variable *definition* tells the compiler to actually reserve storage space in memory for the variable's data—to actually create a specific variable.

A variable takes up some amount of memory—how much depends on the variable's data type. Variable declarations can also act as variable definitions, and usually do. Here are some examples of variable declarations that are also definitions:

```
float   f;
int     x;
char    ch;
string str;
```

Note that whether variables are initialized with some values or not, the compiler still sets aside storage space in memory for these variables at compile time. (If you're a little fuzzy about this, don't worry—it'll become clearer as you read on.)

Declaration

A statement associating an identifier with an object or process so the user can refer to the object or process by name.

Storage Class

Determines how the C++ compiler reserves storage space for program identifiers.

Identifier Definition

A declaration does not automatically reserve storage space for an identifier; a definition does reserve storage space for an identifier.

Constant

An identifier with a fixed value at compile time that cannot be changed during program execution.

Almost all real-world programs are composed of multiple source files (modules), with corresponding header files for each module. A variable or constant declaration that is a declaration **only** simply tells the compiler that a name is defined *somewhere* in the program, but not here. For example, if the preceding variables are defined in one module, that module's header file might declare them so that other modules can use them, like this:

```
extern float  f;
extern int    x;
extern char   ch;
extern string str;
```

The extern keyword is a dead giveaway that these are declarations only. Using the extern keyword is the only way to declare a variable without also defining it. You typically put variable declarations like these in a header file to make them available to multiple modules, and you put the corresponding definitions in a source file. The extern keyword allows other modules that use this header file to access the external variables.

SEE ALSO

➤ *To better understand the* extern *keyword, see page 56*

Initializing Variables

You can initialize a variable when you declare it, or you can initialize the variable in a separate statement sometime after it's declared. For example, declaration and initialization of variables in one step looks something like this:

```
float  f  = 5.0f;
int    x  = 10;
char   ch = 'A';
string str = "Dream Theater";
```

Declaration in one place followed by initialization in a separate statement would look something like this:

```
float  f;
int    x;
char   ch;
string str;
f    = 5.0f;
```

```
x   = 10;
ch  = 'A';
str = "Dream Theater";
```

Neither method holds any real advantage over the other, but the one-step version is more concise, which is always a plus.

Using Named Constants

A *constant* is a value that never changes. All numbers, whether integer or floating-point, are constants. The number 45 is always the number 45—it's constantly the same value. Likewise, characters and strings of characters are also constants. Consider these constant values:

```
45

49.8

'X'

"A literal string"
```

These constant values are known as *literals*, actual values of a data element that can never change. You can create a *named constant* in C++ to store a specific, unchanging literal value. In C++, a variable can accept the values of many different literals during program execution, but a named constant can't. A named constant is like a variable that cannot vary—the value of a named constant, once assigned, can never change during program execution.

Declaring and Initializing Named Constants

Creating a named constant is a lot like creating a variable, with the exception that you *must* initialize the constant when you declare it, unlike a variable (which you can initialize anytime after you declare it). Programmers often refer to named constants as either *named constants* or *constants*, and to literals as either *literals* or *constant values*, so be aware that these terms are often used interchangeably.

Lining Up Source Code in Columns

Perhaps you've noticed my penchant for lining up data in columns. When multiple lines of code contain similar statements such as the preceding variable declarations and associated assignment values, lining things up in columns is a good idea. The compiler doesn't care about the extra whitespace, and it makes reading the source code easier. (Several third-party code editors are available for various platforms that help with this type of thing.)

Named Constant

A meaningful identifier that acts as an alias for a literal value. Once assigned, the value can never change during program execution.

Literals

The actual values stored in memory for constants and variables.

The Uppercase Constant Tradition

Traditionally, constant identifiers are declared in all uppercase letters, although you don't have to declare them this way. Using this technique makes it easy to know at a glance which elements of the source code are constants.

You declare a constant just like you declare a variable—with the addition of the const keyword, using this syntax:

```
const DataType ConstantIdentifier = SomeValue;
```

For example, to create two constants representing the value of pi (π) and the number of hours in a day, you might use these declarations:

```
const double PI = 3.14159;
const int HOURS_IN_DAY = 24;
```

Types of Constants

Like variables, constants have specific data types that are strictly enforced by the compiler. There are four major types of constants:

- Integer
- Character
- Floating-point
- String literals

Let's take a look at each of these types of constants to get an idea of what each can do for you.

Integer Constants

Integral Constant

A constant data element declared as some signed or unsigned integral data time containing a valid integral value.

An *integer constant* is a constant data element declared as some signed or unsigned integral data type that contains some valid integral value. Here are some examples of integer constants:

```
const bool  PRINTSTATE = false;
const short OCTAVE     = 12;
const int   MAXNODES   = 3498;
const long  MAXAMOUNT  = 12934924;
```

Character Constants

Character Constant

A constant that holds a literal character value or character escape sequence.

A *character constant* contains a character or a character escape sequence. The value of the constant is specified by surrounding the character with single quotation marks (´). Here are some examples of character constants:

```
// Character literals
const char FIRST_LOWER_ALPHA = 'a';
const char LAST_LOWER_ALPHA  = 'z';

// Character escape sequences
const char ALERT = '\a';
const char TAB   = '\t';
```

Floating-Point Constants

A *floating-point constant* contains a floating-point value. Here are a couple examples of floating-point constants:

```
const float  BODYTEMP  = 98.6f;
const double FREQUENCY = 90.7;
```

String Literals

A *string literal* contains zero or more characters surrounded by double quotation marks (") and acts as a constant for a null-terminated string of characters. Here are a couple examples of string literals:

```
const char APPNAME    = "My Application";
const char APPVERSION = "Version 1.0";
```

Using Named Constants in Source Code

When working with literal data in a program, it's preferable to use a named constant in your source code instead of the literal value, whenever possible. The use of constants makes source code easy to read and to maintain. Imagine the agony of using the literal value 42 in 500 places in your source code, only to discover that you should have used 43 instead; you'd have to find every occurrence of 42 and replace it with 43. By using a named constant to represent the literal value in the program, you'd only have to change the 42 to 43 in one place—the constant declaration!

Listing 2.2 demonstrates using a named constant instead of a literal in source code. In this example, you could change the literal value in only one place (if needed), which effectively changes the value throughout the program.

Floating-Point Number

A number containing an integer part and a fractional part separated by a decimal point.

Floating-Point Constant

A constant containing a floating-point literal value.

String Literal

A string literal contains zero or more characters surrounded by double quotation marks (") that act as a constant for a null-terminated string.

LISTING 2.2   **Using a Named Constant Instead of a Literal in Source Code**

```
 1: ///////////////////////////////////////////////////////////
 2: //   Module  : const.cpp
 3: //
 4: //   Purpose : Demonstration of using a named constant
 5: //                    instead of a literal value
 6: ///////////////////////////////////////////////////////////
 7:
 8: #include <iostream.h>
 9:
10: void main()
11: {
12:     const int THE_ANSWER = 42;  ─────────────── ①
13:
14:     cout << "The first answer to the ultimate question is "
15:        << THE_ANSWER << ".\n";
16:
17:     cout << "The second answer to the ultimate question is "
18:        << THE_ANSWER << ".\n";
19:
20:     cout << "The third answer to the ultimate question is "
21:        << THE_ANSWER << ".\n";
22:
23:     // imagine five hundred more times...yikes!
24: }
```

Resolving the Scope of Variables and Constants

A prime goal of programmers is to restrict the visibility of information to only those areas in which it needs to be seen. C++ programs are built from blocks of code, and each block has its own scope of influence over the code within. A variable is visible within the code block in which it is defined. Here's a code block A that contains another code block B:

```
// Block A
{
    // Block B
```

memory. Each specific data type stores information using a specific number of bytes in memory. For example, on a 32-bit operating system, the size of an integer is four bytes.

The computer needs only a starting address for a variable. It can then read as many bytes from memory as required for a given data type, starting at this location. A computer program operates on data, which is stored in memory. During program execution, the same memory location may contain different values at different times. This fact is why this type of memory location is called a *variable*.

Here are a few variables of different types that might be used for test results in a school:

```
char    grade;
short   score;
float   average;
```

Using variables makes programming much easier than it would be if you had to use memory addresses directly. One of the fundamental aspects of most modern programming languages is the ability to create variables for use within your programs, thus hiding the nastiness of raw memory addresses from the programmer. Of course, C++ gives you the ability to declare and define as many type-specific variables as you need for any given task. Figure 2.2 shows how the test-results variables declared in the preceding example might be stored in computer memory.

FIGURE 2.2

Creating named storage locations in memory.

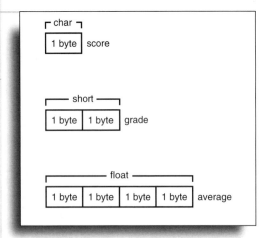

```
      {
      }
   }
```

The preceding example shows a *nested block*, with one block nested within another. Here's the nested block with two different `MyInt` variables defined and initialized:

```
// Block A
{
   int MyInt = 5;

   // Block B
   {
      int MyInt = 10;
   }
}
```

Once execution exits a code block, most objects within the block are destroyed and their values lost—they go *out of scope*. Some variables retain their values throughout the life of a program—they never go out of scope. These types of variables are called *static variables*, and they're discussed later in this chapter in "Specifying Storage Class."

When you have nested blocks of code, any objects defined in the outer blocks are ordinarily visible in the inner blocks. The exception is when an object in an inner block uses a name defined in an outer (parent) block. When this happens, the outer name is hidden from the inner block, as if it doesn't exist. When the inner block variable goes out of scope, the program again "sees" the outer object of the same name. The program in Listing 2.3 demonstrates this concept.

Nested Block

A code block that exists inside another code block.

Out of Scope

Can no longer be interpreted by the code compiler.

LISTING 2.3   **Like-Named Variables and Constants Can Exist in Different Scopes**

```
1: //////////////////////////////////////////////////////////////
2: //  Module  : scope.cpp
3: //
4: //  Purpose : Demonstration of like-named variables and
5: //            constants existing in different scopes
6: //////////////////////////////////////////////////////////////
7:
```

continues...

LISTING 2.3

Select an action you want to Undo from the list of most recent actions.

1 Line 12: Define ch at Level 1

2 Line 15: Define a second ch at Level 2

3 Line 18: Define a third ch at Level 3

LISTING 2.3 **Continued**

```
 8: #include <iostream.h>
 9:
10: void main()
11: {
12:     char ch = 'A';                              1
13:     cout << "Level 1, ch = " << ch << '\n';
14:     {
15:         char ch = 'B';                          2
16:         cout << "Level 2, ch = " << ch << '\n';
17:         {
18:             char ch = 'C';                      3
19:             cout << "Level 3, ch = " << ch << '\n';
20:         }
21:         cout << "Level 2, ch = " << ch << '\n';
22:     }
23:     cout << "Level 1, ch = " << ch << '\n';
24: }
```

Output from the program in Listing 2.3 is as follows:

```
Level 1, ch = A
Level 2, ch = B
Level 3, ch = C
Level 2, ch = B
Level 1, ch = A
```

Interface and Implementation Files

Function and class declarations are usually found in header (interface) files—typically having an `.h` or `.hpp` file extension. Function and class definitions (implementations) are usually found in source (implementation) files—typically having a `.cpp` file extension.

Understanding Declarations and Definitions

Variable declarations are often definitions as well, but functions must be separated into an interface part and an implementation part. A function declaration is merely a prototype for a function that declares its format (interface) to the compiler. For example, a function that takes a `float` value argument and returns a `float` value might be declared like this:

```
float MyFunc(float);
```

Here is one possible function definition (implementation) for the preceding declaration:

```
float MyFunc(float f) { return f/2.0f; }
```

The fact that the function has a body means that it's a definition for that function. Although in C you get away without using a function prototype, in C++ you must provide both the interface and the implementation.

By using the `enum` keyword, you can make declarations associate a name with a constant value. For example, here's an `enum` declaration for the four suits used with common playing cards:

```
enum CardSuits{ Hearts, Diamonds, Clubs, Spades };
```

No variable exists, only the declaration of the new data type `CardSuits`. To create a variable of type `CardSuits`, you must define one, like this:

```
CardSuits cs;
```

Thereafter, you can assign only a valid `CardSuits` value to the variable `cs`, as in:

```
cs = Diamonds;
```

The following doesn't work though, because `King` isn't an enumerated `CardSuits` type:

```
cs = King;
```

Declarations can also introduce new derived data types, including structures, unions, and classes. For example, here's a structure that describes a triangle:

```
struct Triangle
{
    float Angle1;
    float Angle2;
    float Angle3;
}
```

Again, no variable exists, only the declaration of the `Triangle` data type values. To create a variable of type `Triangle`, you must define one, like this:

```
Triangle tri;
```

SEE ALSO

➤ *For more information about structures, see page 214*

Type Definition

An alias declared for an existing data type through the use of the `typedef` keyword.

A declaration can also declare an alias for an existing data type, a process known as *type definition*. Using the keyword `typedef`, you can create as many aliases as you like for existing data types:

```
typedef unsigned long ULONG;
typedef unsigned char BOOL;
```

Using typedefs can make long, unwieldy data types easier to read and use (not to mention easier to type). In these examples, ULONG actually means unsigned long, and BOOL actually means unsigned char.

Declaration Specifiers and Declarators

Decl-specifier

The type name portion of a declaration.

The first part of a declaration is the declaration-specifier, or *decl-specifier* part of the declaration. This portion of the declaration specifies the data type of an identifier.

Declarator

Determines whether an item will be global, private, or protected within the scope of a program.

The portion of a declaration that specifies the name to be introduced into a program is the *declarator*. Take a look at the following examples:

```
char ch;
bool IsTrue(int i, int j);
```

In these simple examples, the decl-specifiers are char and bool. The declarators are ch and IsTrue.

Specifying Linkage

Many programmers use both C and C++ code to develop an application—and the various idiosyncrasies of the languages in question can cause unexpected problems at link time. To link C functions and C++ functions, you must define a linkage specification to ensure that all the functions will work together as intended. This is necessary because of the differences in the internal architectures of C and C++.

The extern keyword specifies external linkage and is typically used when C functions must be used in C++ programs. Because of the way C++ handles function name translation during the compile process, C functions must be declared using C linkage.

You can declare functions to use C linkage by using the `extern` `"C"` linkage specifier individually in each function declaration, like this:

```
extern "C" int Func1(int);
extern "C" int Func2(float);
extern "C" int Func3();
```

Or you can declare a group of C functions to use C linkage by using the `extern` `"C"` linkage specifier in a code block, like this:

```
extern "C"
{
    int Func1(int);
    int Func2(float);
    int Func3();
}
```

These techniques are equivalent, so it depends on programmer preference for which is used.

Specifying Storage Class

Storage class determines the duration and visibility of an object or function and where an object should be stored. Storage-class specifiers tell the compiler which storage class an object or function should have. There are four storage-class specifiers, as listed in Table 2.5.

TABLE 2.5   **Types of C++ Storage-Class Specifiers**

Specifier	Description
auto	Specifies that a variable has local (automatic) extent. This is the default storage class.
register	Specifies that, if possible, a variable should be stored in a machine register.
static	Specifies that a variable has static duration, existing for the duration of program execution. Using `static` initializes a variable to zero by default. When `static` is used with variables or functions at the file scope level (within a module), it specifies that a variable or function has internal linkage and isn't visible from outside the file in which it's defined.

continues...

TABLE 2.5   **Continued**

Specifier	Description
extern	Specifies that a variable or function has external linkage, thus allowing its name to be seen from files other than the one in which it's defined.

Typecast

To convert from one data type to another data type.

Casting Data Types

Sometimes, it's necessary to change some information from one data type to another; coercing a data element from one type to another is called *typecasting*. For example, you may want to convert a short integer into a long integer to make your data fit the data type expected by some function you want to call. There are two different ways to do this:

- Casting implicitly
- Casting explicitly

Let's take a closer look at both of them.

Casting Implicitly

By definition, C++ automatically promotes integral and floating-point data types to their next level of byte size, without any extra coding on your part. For example, converting a short integer to a long integer can be automatically performed by the compiler because the compiler implicitly assumes that you want to perform this conversion:

```
short MyShort = 5;
long MyLong = MyShort;
```

Converting from a float to a double can also be automatically performed by the compiler because the compiler implicitly assumes that you want to perform this conversion:

```
float MyFloat = 5.5f;
double MyDouble = MyFloat;
```

Typecasts tell the compiler how to store some bit values. Data types with smaller byte sizes can easily fit into data types with larger byte sizes. For example, promotion from char to short is easy, because a short has plenty of room available to store a char:

```
char ch = 'A';
short s = ch;
```

These statements convert the char A into the short integer 65. The other way around is a different story, however. Casting from a larger data type to a smaller data type—such as from a short to a char—doesn't work well. It's like trying to fit five gallons of gasoline into a one-gallon gas can. Here's what can happen:

```
short s = 3043;
char ch = s;
```

In this scenario, the short integer 3043 is converted into a char value, but because a char can only store one byte, it can only store values ranging from -128 to 127 (refer to Table 2.2). A short stores two bytes, and can range from -32,768 to 32,767 (again, refer to Table 2.2). The preceding statements convert the short value 3043 into the char value -29 (and we all know that 3043 does **not** equal -29). A good compiler will warn you about improper, "wrong-way" conversions like these so that you can decide if that's really what you want the source code to do. A typical wrong-way conversion warning looks something like this:

```
Warning, 'initializing' :
conversion from 'short' to 'char', possible loss of data
```

Casting Explicitly

Sometimes, it's necessary to explicitly tell the compiler how to cast certain data types—if only to silence annoying compiler warnings about automatic type conversion. Explicit casts can also be more meaningful and instructive to readers of the code.

For example, the same typecasts described in the preceding section can be (and often are) typecast explicitly. The short to long cast would look like this:

```
short MyShort = 5;
long MyLong = (long)MyShort;
```

The float to double cast would look like this:

```
float MyFloat = 5.5f;
double MyDouble = (double)MyFloat;
```

SEE ALSO

➤ *For more information about these kinds of typecasts, see page 666*

Examining Expressions and Statements

Syntax

The formal rules that govern how valid instructions are written in a programming language.

Semantics

The set of rules that provides the meaning of instructions written in a programming language.

Operand

An item on which an operation is performed.

Operator

Designates an operation to be per-formed on an operand.

Expression

A set of symbols that form a unit to which meaning or value is assigned.

Overview

A compiler isn't very smart—it can't think. It needs a formal set of rules that exactly describes the C++ language so that it knows what we mean by each symbol and combination of letters in our source code. This formal set of rules about how C++ must be written is called C++ *syntax*. The set of rules that determines meaning and application of these syntax rules is called C++ *semantics*.

Although the syntax and semantics of C++ largely determine your source code, your code also reflects your programming style. Because C++ is so flexible in nature, it allows you to write functionally equivalent code in numerous ways. Expressions and statements in your source code tell the compiler exactly what you want your program to do, and in this sense, they **are** the program.

Understanding Expressions

An *expression* is any combination of operands and operators that produces a value. This definition is quite broad, encompassing many areas. *Operands* can be names, numbers, constants, and variables (among other things), and there are numerous *operators* that act on operands. In fact, the most common problems in C++ programs stem from not fully grasping the full implications of the relationships between the operands and operators in an expression. There are several common types of expressions, as summarized in Table 3.1.

TABLE 3.1   Common C++ Expression Types

Expression Type	Description
Primary	A primary expression is an entity that acts as a component for building composite expressions.
Postfix	A postfix expression consists of an expression fol-lowed by a postfix operator (see Table 3.2).
Unary operator	A unary operator acts on a single operand in an expression.
Binary operator	A binary operator acts on two operands in an expression.

Expression Type	Description
Conditional operator	A conditional operator acts on three operands in an expression.
Explicit cast	An explicit cast expression explicitly converts one data type to another.
Pointer-to-member operator	A pointer-to-member operator expression returns the value of a specified class member.

Using Operators and Operands

Operators and operands are the building blocks of expressions. Operands include constants, variables, strings, and function calls, among other things. Operands are program entities that are manipulated by operators. Operators act on operands, manipulating them in some way (you'll learn more about the various types of operators later in this chapter). For now, let's look at a few examples of operands and operators in action. In the following code fragment, the operands are named op1, op2, and op3; the operators are the symbols that manipulate them:

```
// Assign 12 to op1
int op1 = 12;

// Assign 100 to op2
int op2 = 100;

// Add 12 and 100, and assign resulting value to op3
int op3 = op1 + op2;
```

A C++ program evaluates Boolean expressions based on the *precedence* of the operators involved. Subexpressions using operators with higher precedence are evaluated first, followed by those with lower priority, until the entire expression is evaluated.

Precedence

The order in which operations are performed.

In this case, the plus operator (+) acts on the two operands op1 and op2, adding them together, left to right. The equals sign (=) then assigns the resulting value, right to left, to the operand op3. The operations occur in this order because of *operator precedence*, meaning that some operations are always performed before others.

SEE ALSO

➤ *For more information about operator precedence, see page 91*

Primary Expressions

A *primary expression* is a name, a literal (constant), any name
explicitly qualified by the scope resolution operator (::), a class
destructor (~), or a this pointer.

SEE ALSO

➤ *To learn about scope resolution, see page 528*

➤ *For information about class destructors, see page 494*

➤ *For information about* this *pointers, see page 496*

Primary expressions include the following:

- Integer constants
- Character constants
- Float constants
- String literals
- Identifiers
- Operator function names
- Conversion function names
- this pointers

Postfix Operators and Postfix Expressions

A *postfix operator* is an operator that follows a primary expression.
When a postfix operator follows a primary expression, the result
is a *postfix expression*. The postfix operators have the highest
level of precedence in expression evaluation and are listed in
Table 3.2.

TABLE 3.2   Postfix Operators

Operator Type	Operator Notation
Explicit type conversion operator	type-name(*value*)
Function-call operator	( )
Member-selection operator	. or ->)

Operator Type	Operator Notation
Postfix decrement operator	--
Postfix increment operator	++
Array subscript operator	[ ]

Following are some examples of these types of operators as used in postfix expressions:

```
int(MyFloat)        // Explicit type conversion operator
MyFunc()            // Function-call operator
pMyStuct->Member    // Member-selection operator
i--                 // Postfix decrement operator
i++                 // Postfix increment operator
MyArray[0]          // Subscript operator
```

Note that the pre- and post-increment operators increase a value by one, and the pre- and post-decrement operators decrease a value by one. For example:

```
int x = 0;
x++;  // x now equals 1
x--;  // x equals zero again
```

Unary Operator Expressions

As its name indicates, a *unary operator* deals with a single operand in an expression. After the postfix operators, the unary operators have the highest level of precedence in expression evaluation; they are listed in Table 3.3.

Unary Operator

A unary operator deals with a single operand in an expression.

TABLE 3.3 **Unary Operators**

Operator Type	Description
Indirection operator (*)	Converts a *pointer* operand to the actual data pointed to.
Address-of operator (&)	Furnishes a pointer to its operand by getting the operand's *memory address*.
Unary plus operator (+)	Performs an integral promotion on its operand.
Unary negation operator (–)	Gives the negative of its operand.

continues…

TABLE 3.3   **Continued**

Operator Type	Description
Logical NOT operator (!)	Negates the value of its operand, resulting in an integer that is either 0 or 1.
One's complement operator (~)	Performs a bitwise one's complement on its operand, changing each 1 bit to 0 and each 0 bit to 1.
Prefix increment operator (++)	Increments the value of its operand by 1.
Prefix decrement operator (--)	Decrements the value of its operand by 1.
sizeof operator	Furnishes the size of its operand in terms of type char.
new operator	Tries to dynamically allocate an object of its operand's type. If not enough memory is available, new will fail.
delete operator	Deallocates an object created using the new operator.

SEE ALSO

➤ *For an in-depth look at pointers, see page 246*

➤ *To learn about using memory addresses, see page 247*

➤ *For more information about the* new *and* delete *operators, see page 277*

Take a look at Listing 3.1. Although I don't expect you at this point to fully understand the code in the listing, the fragments give some examples of the operators in action. For now, just look at the syntax used for each operator in the code. As you progress through this book, the meaning of each of these statements will become clear.

LISTING 3.1

1 Line 2: Allocate a new integer (see Chapter 11)

2 Lines 5-6: Use the in-direction operator (see Chapter 10)

LISTING 3.1   **Some Examples of Unary Operator Usage**

```
1:    // new operator
2:    int* pInt = new int; // allocate an int        1
3:
4:    // Indirection operator (*)
5:    *pInt = 5;                                      2
6:    int i = *pInt;   // i == 5
7:
8:    // delete operator
```

```
 9:    delete pInt;      // deallocate the int  ──── ③
10:
11:    // Address-of operator (&)
12:    pInt = &i;        // get the address of i ──── ④
13:
14:    // Unary plus operator (+)
15:    char c = 'A';  ──────────────────────────┐
16:    int z = +z;       // promote from char to int ─┘ ⑤
17:
18:    // Unary negation operator (-)
19:    i = -i;  // negate i, i == -5  ──── ⑥
20:
21:    // Logical NOT operator (!)
22:    i = !i;  // i == 0 ──┐
23:    i = !i;  // i == 1 ──┘ ⑦
24:
25:    // Prefix increment operator (++) ──┐
26:    ++i;  // i == 2
27:                                         ⑧
28:    // Prefix decrement operator (--)
29:    --i;  // i == 1  ──┘
30:
31:    // sizeof operator
32:    i = sizeof(short);  // i == 2 (32-bit OS) ──┐
33:    i = sizeof(int);    // i == 4 (32-bit OS) ──┘ ⑨
```

LISTING 3.1 CONTINUED

③ Line 9: Delete the allocated integer (see Chapter 11)

④ Line 12: Get the memory address of a variable (see Chapter 10)

⑤ Lines 15-16: Promote a char to an int using the plus operator

⑥ Line 19: Negate an operand with the negation operator

⑦ Lines 22-23: Toggle values with the logical NOT operator (see Chapter 4)

⑧ Lines 25-30: Use the prefix increment and decrement operators to adjust a variable value

⑨ Lines 32-33: Use the sizeof operator

Binary Operator Expressions

A *binary operator* acts on two operands in an expression. The order of operations within an expression is determined both by operator grouping and precedence. Table 3.4 lists the binary operators.

The Useless Unary Plus Operator

Most unary operators provide important facilities for C++ programmers. The exception is the unary plus operator, which is almost useless. C++ supports automatic data type promotion, so the use of the unary plus operator is rarely (if ever) explicitly needed.

Binary Operator

A binary operator acts on two operands in an expression.

TABLE 3.4 **The Binary Operators**

Category	Operators
Multiplicative operators	Multiplication (*), Division (/), Modulus (%)
Additive operators	Addition (+), Subtraction (-)
Shift operators	Right-Shift (>>), Left-Shift (<<)

continues...

TABLE 3.4   **Continued**

Category	Operators
Relational and equality operators	Less Than (<), Greater Than (>), Less Than or Equal to (<=), Greater Than or Equal to (>=) Equal to (==), Not Equal to (!=)
Bitwise operators	Bitwise AND (&), Bitwise exclusive OR (^), Bitwise inclusive OR (¦), Logical AND (&&), Logical OR (¦¦)

Even in complex expressions, there can never be more than two operands acted on at a time with the binary operators. For complex expressions, the compiler internally combines two operands to yield a single operand used in further expression evaluation. Consider the following expression:

```
int i = 5 * 4 / 2;
```

The compiler evaluates the value of i as two binary operations. The first binary operation uses the multiplication operator (*). Evaluation is from left to right, following standard mathematical rules, multiplying 5 and 4. This, of course, results in the value 20. The second binary operation uses the division operator (/). Evaluation is again from left to right, dividing 20 by 2, resulting in 10 as the final value of the expression. This assignment of the value 10 to the variable i forms a complete expression statement, and is consequently terminated by a semicolon—but you'll learn more about that later in this chapter.

Pointer-to-Member Operator Expressions

Similar to the indirection operator (*), the pointer-to-member operators convert a pointer operand to the actual data pointed to, but the pointer-to-member operators are special types of binary operators.

There are two pointer-to-member operators, and these are used to get the value of a specific class member. These operators dereference a class member-pointer operand. The operators use the following notation: .* and ->*.

Before you can fully grasp what pointer-to-member means, you must become familiar with object-oriented programming concepts and the workings of C++ classes and class members. Part III of this book provides in-depth information about these topics.

SEE ALSO

➤ *To get a good grasp of pointer-to-member operator usage, see page 253*

Conditional Operator Expressions

The conditional operator (?:) uses three operands and takes the following form:

```
x > 0 ? x : y
```

If the expression to the left of the ? is true, then the expression evaluates to x, else the expression evaluates to y. For example:

```
bool b = (5 > 3) ? true : false;
```

Because (5 > 3) evaluates to true, the expression uses the first operand following the ? symbol. The value of the identifier b after expression evaluation is, of course, true.

SEE ALSO

➤ *For more information on the conditional operator, see page 91*

Explicit Cast Expressions

If an expression contains two or more operands of different data types acted on by a binary arithmetic operator (+, -, *, /, or %), the compiler usually performs automatic type conversion for you. For example, consider the following code fragment:

```
float f = 2.5f;
int   i = 3;
float result = f * i;
```

Given the float value f and the integer value i used in this simple expression, the integer i is converted to the equivalent float value 3.0f, yielding a result of 7.5f.

When you have to ensure a conversion from one data type to another, you can explicitly cast the value to the desired data type. This conversion is commonly known as *casting* or *typecasting*. The cast operator is of the form (data-type) and ensures a proper conversion if possible within the context of a given expression.

For example, an explicit cast of the operand i in the preceding fragment would look like this:

```
float f = 2.5f;
int   i = 3;
float result = f * float(i);
```

Likewise, you can use the cast operator to coerce entire compound expressions to a desired data type by enclosing the compound expression in parentheses. For example, the following expression first converts integers to floats, and then converts the resulting float expression to a double:

```
int n1 = 3, n2 =4;
float f = 3.5;
double dbl = double(f / float(n1) * float(n2));
```

SEE ALSO
➤ *To learn more about typecasting, see page 58*

Using Statements

Statements

Statements make up a program, controlling how the computer reacts during program execution.

Statements control how a program flows during execution. Statements can be generally categorized as follows:

- Expression statements
- Compound statements
- Label statements
- Selection statements
- Iteration statements
- Declaration statements
- Jump statements

In this chapter, you've seen several basic statements. Let's take a look at each of these statement categories for an overview of what each represents within a C++ program.

Expression Statements

Most *expression statements* are used to assign values or call functions. It should come as no surprise that most statements are expression statements; earlier in this chapter, we covered expressions in some detail. A complete expression statement is terminated by a trailing semicolon:

```
cout << "This is the life...\n";
```

Other types of expression statements generate or assign values using the assignment operator (=), commonly known as the equals sign. The value of the expression on the right of the equals sign is often called the *r-value*; the value of the expression on the left side of the equals sign is often called the *l-value*. The assignment of the r-value to the l-value in an expression makes it an assignment statement, like this one that assigns 100 (the r-value) to the integer variable i (the l-value):

```
int i = 5 * 20;
```

A further example might be the calculation of an employee's pay for the week, using a series of expression statements to accomplish the task:

```
float fPayRate = 20.65f;
float fHoursWorked = 35.32f;
float fGrossPay = fHoursWorked * fPayRate;
cout << "Employee gross pay is: " << fGrossPay << '\n';
```

Of course, this is a simplistic view of payroll calculation, but it demonstrates several types of expression statements. The first and second lines in the code fragment are assignment statements that both use floating-point literals as the r-value. The third line is an assignment statement that uses a calculated expression as the r-value, and the fourth line is an expression statement that manipulates the cout object to display the result of the calculations.

Compound Statements

A *compound statement*, as its name suggests, combines several expression statements into a group, forming a block of code. A block is surrounded by braces { }, with individual statements

Expression Statements

Statements used to assign values or call functions.

L-Value

The value of the expression on the left hand side of an assignment operator.

R-Value

The value of the expression on the right hand side of an assignment operator.

Compound Statement

A compound statement combines several expression statements into a group, forming a block of code.

falling between the opening and closing braces. For example, the body of the following simple function definition is a compound statement that contains two expression statements:

```
long Square(int n)
{
    long j = long(n1) * long(n1);
    return j;
}
```

Selection Statements

Selection Statement

A selection statement provides conditional execution within a program using the `if` and `switch` statements.

A *selection statement* provides conditional execution within a program using the `if` and `switch` statements. Conditional execution simply means that if a specified condition is met, a corresponding statement will execute. The valid selection statements are as follows:

- The `if` statement
- The `else if` statement
- The `else` statement
- The `switch` statement

Using Nested Selection

The use of selection statements within selection statements creates a situation called a *nested selection operation*. Nested selection is very useful at times, but code can easily become confusing and convoluted if the nesting gets too deep.

These statements use a Boolean expression to determine the condition. The Boolean expression determines whether the statement that follows should execute. This statement can be any type of statement, including blocks and other selection statements.

Switching Directions

In practice, the `switch` statement uses two or more `case` labels to determine which course of execution to take.

The `switch` statement differs from the other selection statements in that it allows a program to determine a specific course of execution based on an expression value, allowing a program to decide to choose one of several alternatives. You'll learn the details about using all these selection statements in Chapter 4, "Using Conditional Expressions and Selection Statements."

SEE ALSO

➤ *For more information about making decisions in your programs, see page 92*

Iteration Statements

Iteration statements provide your programs with the ability to execute statements in a repeating loop. The valid iteration statements are shown in Table 3.5.

TABLE 3.5 The C++ Iteration Statements

Statement	Description
for	Allows a program to iterate through a code block a specified number of times.
while	Allows a program to iterate through a code block indefinitely, until some Boolean condition eventually breaks the loop.
do	Allows a program to iterate through a code block indefinitely, until some Boolean condition eventually breaks the loop.

SEE ALSO

➤ *To learn more about iteration and looping, see page 103*

Declaration Statements

As you've already seen in this chapter, a *declaration statement* associates a name with an identifier. A declaration statement introduces a name, or declarator, within its current level of scope, no matter whether this scope is the program, file, or code block level of scope. If you create a variable using *automatic* or *register storage class*, the variable is initialized each time code execution enters the block. If the variable uses the static storage class, the variable is initialized only the first time execution enters the block, giving the block a "memory" of sorts.

SEE ALSO

➤ *To learn more about declarations, see page 54*
➤ *To learn more about storage class, see page 57*

Iteration Statements

Iteration statements provide your programs with the ability to execute statements in a repeating loop.

Differentiating Between while **and** do

The difference between the while and do statements is that do always executes the corresponding statement at least once; the while statement might not execute at all. This is because the evaluation expression for a do loop comes *after* the execution statement; in a while loop, the evaluation expression comes *before* the execution statement.

Register

An area of the central processing unit (CPU) that is used to store binary digits while they are being processed.

Storage Class

Determines how the C++ compiler reserves storage space for program identifiers.

Automatic Storage Class

Declares a variable to be automatic, visible only in the block in which it is declared.

Declaration Statement

Associates a name with an identifier.

Jump Statements

Jump statements transfer control away from the current point of execution.

Jump Statements

Jump statements transfer control away from the current point of execution. There are four keywords used to create jump statements, as shown in Table 3.6.

TABLE 3.6   **The Keywords Used in Jump Statements**

Keyword	Purpose
break	Terminates an iteration statement and passes control to the code point after the terminated statement.
continue	In an iteration statement, terminates the execution of the current loop and jumps back to the loop-continuation point.
return	Exits a function, returning control to the caller of the function, along with the function return value (if any).
goto	Unconditionally transfers control to a local label statement.

Label Statements

Label Statement

A label statement is an identifier that names an execution point in your code.

A *label statement* is an identifier that names an execution point in your code. The syntax is a label name followed by a colon, like this:

```
LabelName:
```

The Stigma of goto

In the early days of programming, code was written haphazardly, without much structure or flow control. Early programs used conditional statements to make decisions, and execution would go to some other execution point, someplace else in the code. This type of programming is particularly frustrating to follow while reading the source code because execution jumps around so unexpectedly. Code written like this became known as "spaghetti code." The C++ goto statement is a holdover from those pasta-filled pioneering days of spaghetti code.

Label statements are the targets of goto statements; label statements provide a destination for unconditional transfer of program execution. To jump to the label declared in the preceding example, you would simply use this statement:

```
goto LabelName;
```

The use of goto statements is generally frowned on, but it does have its uses. Listing 3.2 demonstrates a common use for label statements: jumping to a generic error label to handle an unanticipated error.

LISTING 3.2   **A Demonstration of a Label Statement**

```
1:  bool SomeFunction()
2:  {
3:      // Some stuff here...
4:
```

```
 5:        if (FAILED(SetQuality(quality)))
 6:        {
 7:            Msg("Failed to set quality.\n");
 8:            goto generic_error;
 9:        }
10:
11:        if (FAILED(Resolve(0)))
12:            goto generic_error;
13:
14:        // Some more stuff here...
15:        return true;
16:
17:    generic_error:
18:        Msg("An error has occured.\n");   // user-defined function
19:        return false;
20:    }
```

LISTING 3.2

1 Line 5: Test a condition

2 Line 8: If the tested condition is true, the goto statement executes, jumping to line 17

3 Line 11: Test another condition

4 Line 12: If the tested condition is true, the goto statement executes, jumping to line 17

5 Line 17: The target of the goto statements

This is obviously not a complete program; it's just the shell of a hypothetical function to demonstrate the use of the label statement. The FAILED() function on lines 5 and 11 isn't part of the C++ language; it's just a hypothetical addition. Basically, this code just jumps the program execution point to the label generic_error: on line 17 if either of the calls to FAILED() returns a value of true, indicating failure. If this happens, the code in the generic_error: section is executed. If not, the function returns before reaching the generic_error: code.

This chapter has introduced a number of new concepts, and the next several chapters expand on the introductory material presented here to give you a working knowledge of C++ in action.

CHAPTER

4

Using Conditional Expressions and Selection Statements

Learn to use Boolean conditions and expressions

Make decisions using selection statements

Understand the logical *AND*, *OR*, and *NOT* operators

Gain insight into the nature of truth by using truth tables

See how to create and use enumerated data types

Using Boolean Conditions and Expressions

George Boole was a nineteenth century mathematician who thought in terms of computer science long before there *was* such a thing as computer science. It was Boole who created Boolean algebra and formalized Boolean logic. The Boolean condition expresses either truth or falsehood. You can find analogies for this condition in many ways. You can think of the condition as *on* or *off*, *zero* or *not zero* (as in C and C++), *positive* or *negative*, or simply as *true* or *false*. Any way you look at it, a Boolean condition is a binary situation—a dichotomy.

You use expressions that evaluate the Boolean condition to allow your programs to make decisions—to become flexible and autonomous. In this chapter, you'll see a variety of ways to use Boolean variables, conditions, and expressions to write more complex programs allowing you to solve more complex problems.

Understanding Boolean Expressions

Boolean

Consisting of only two values: true or false. Derived from the Boolean algebraic system developed by George Boole, which uses logical operations instead of arithmetic operations.

By definition, a Boolean expression resolves to either true or false. There is no middle ground in Boolean logic. C++ uses Boolean expressions to accomplish many things. A Boolean expression in C++ is enclosed within parentheses, often comparing the relationship between two or more operands.

Because C++ sees the value of zero as false and the value of non-zero as true, sometimes a single operand is all you need. A single-operand Boolean expression evaluates to false if the value within the Boolean expression is false. Consider the Boolean evaluation in the following statement:

```
bool MyBool = (0);
```

Because the expression (0) is false in Boolean logic, the variable MyBool becomes false. This is equivalent to saying:

```
bool MyBool = (false);
```

Likewise, a single-operand Boolean expression evaluates to `true` if the value within the Boolean expression is true, as in the following statement:

```
bool MyBool = (100);
```

Because `100` is non-zero, the expression `(100)` evaluates to `true` (in cases like this, the literal value of `100` is demoted from type `integer` to type `bool`). This is equivalent to saying:

```
bool MyBool = (true);
```

More commonly, Boolean expressions compare the relationship between two operands. The relational operators perform the comparison, which can be something as simple as this one:

```
bool MyBool = (4 == 5)
```

This expression uses the C++ equality operator, which is composed of two equal signs (`==`). The expression is obviously false; we know intuitively that 4 *does not* equal 5. Here's a statement that evaluates to `true`:

```
bool MyBool = (5 == 5)
```

This is so because 5 *does* equal 5. Simple enough—the equality operator seems easy enough to use, doesn't it? Be careful though; the equality operator is an operator that gets many new C++ programmers into trouble. To see what I mean, take a look at the following example, which complicates matters a bit by introducing variables into the mix:

```
int   x = 3;

bool MyBool1 = (x == 4);   // Evaluates to false: x equals 3
bool MyBool2 = (x = 5);    // Evaluates to true: now x equals 5
```

A problem exists in this code fragment, but it isn't readily noticeable to many new C++ programmers—it's just the sort of thing that causes hard-to-find bugs. In the first Boolean expression, the variable `MyBool1` becomes `false` because the Boolean condition `(x==4)` is `false` (x equals 3). The second Boolean expression is a different matter altogether. Although the expression in the parentheses is meant to *compare* x and 5 to see

Beware of the Assignment Operator

The assignment operator (=) is sometimes mistakenly used in place of the equality operator (==), which can cause elusive bugs in your programs. Be very careful about checking that your code uses the correct operator for a given situation.

whether they're equal, it actually *assigns* the value 5 to the variable x; when you use an assignment as a Boolean expression, it *always* evaluates to true, so MyBool2 becomes true.

Of course, Boolean expressions aren't restricted to the equality operator. Boolean expressions can use any of the relational operators, which are described in Table 4.1.

TABLE 4.1   Relational Operators Used in Boolean Expressions

Operator	Description
==	The equality operator. Both operands must equate for the expression to be true.
<=	The less-than-or-equal-to operator. The left operand must be less than or equal to the right operand for the expression to be true.
<	The less-than operator. The left operand must be less than—but not equal to—the right operand for the expression to be true.
>==	The greater-than-or-equal-to operator. The left operand must be greater than or equal to the right operand for the expression to be true.
>	The greater-than operator. The left operand must be greater than—but not equal to—the right operand for the expression to be true.
!=	The inequality operator. The expression is true only if the operands do not equate.

The program in Listing 4.1 gives some examples of Boolean expressions that use each of the relational operators to compare two integer values.

LISTING 4.1   Using the Relational Operators to Compare Two Integer Values in Boolean Expressions

```
1: /////////////////////////////////////////////////////
2: // Module : bool.cpp
3:
4: void main()
5: {
6:     int num1 = 5;
```

```
 7:    int num2 = 10;
 8:
 9:    bool MyBool1 = (num1 == num2);    // false
10:    bool MyBool2 = (num1 <= num2);    // true
11:    bool MyBool3 = (num1 <  num2);    // true
12:    bool MyBool4 = (num1 >= num2);    // false
13:    bool MyBool5 = (num1 >  num2);    // false
14:    bool MyBool6 = (num1 != num2);    // true
15: }
```

This program produces no output; it merely demonstrates the relational operators at work. Lines 5 and 6 set up two integer variables, num1 and num2, assigning to them the respective values 5 and 10. Each of the lines 9 through 14 creates a Boolean variable and assigns it a value based on the evaluation of the Boolean expression at the end of the statement. These six statements evaluate to true or false as indicated in Table 4.2.

TABLE 4.2 The Evaluation of Six Boolean Expressions Using Relational Operators, Where _num1 = 5_ and _num2 = 10_

Expression	Value	Explanation
(num1 == num2)	false	5 is _not_ equal to 10, so this expression is false.
(num1 <= num2)	true	5 _is_ less than 10, so this expression is true.
(num1 < num2)	true	5 _is_ less than 10, so this expression is true.
(num1 >= num2)	false	5 is _not_ less than 10, so this expression is false.
(num1 > num2)	false	5 is _not_ less than 10, so this expression is false.
(num1 != num2)	true	5 is _not_ equal to 10, so this expression is true.

A good way to get a handle on how a Boolean expression evaluates is to step through your source code a line at a time in a debugger, watching the values of your variables change as each statement executes. Figure 4.1 shows the program from Listing 4.1 running in the Visual C++ debugger. The bottom pane is the Watch window, which allows you to see the values of any variables you specify. The top pane displays the source code as you step through the program. The figure shows the state of the six MyBool variables as program execution reaches the closing brace of the main() function.

FIGURE 4.1

Using the Visual C++ debugger to watch the values of Boolean variables during program execution helps to understand Boolean expression evaluation.

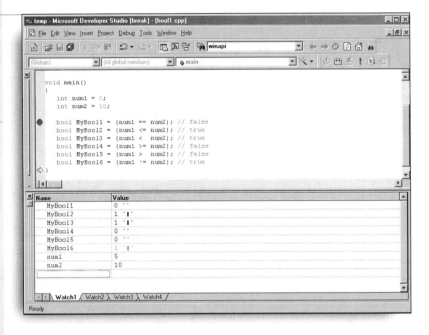

Using the Logical Operators

C++ provides three logical operators that are used in combination with the relational operators to form complex Boolean expressions. These three logical operators are listed here:

- Logical AND (&&)
- Logical OR (¦¦)
- Logical NOT (!)

These logical operators make it possible for you to write programs that can manage multiple scenarios by evaluating intricate Boolean expressions. For right now, we'll just look at the logical operators to see how they're used. In later chapters, you'll see how they can add some effective decision-making functionality to your C++ programs when combined with selection statements.

Logical *AND*

The logical AND operator is used to combine multiple relational or equality expressions into more comprehensive compound expressions. Its use is straightforward, as in this example:

```
(true && false)
```

This expression evaluates to false because something can't be both true AND false. In place of the keywords true and false in the preceding expression, we can substitute simple Boolean expressions, resulting in a compound Boolean expression. Take a look at this expression:

```
((5 < 10) && (10 > 20))
```

The first simple expression is (5 < 10), which evaluates to true. The second simple expression is (10 > 20), which evaluates to false. Substituting the values of each simple expression into the original expression brings us back to the original true AND false expression, which you've already seen is false. These two statements are therefore equivalent—they evaluate the same way:

```
( true   &&   false )
((5 < 10) && (10 > 20))
```

To handle complex situations, you can chain together multiple expressions to act as subexpressions within a complex Boolean expression. Take a look at the program in Listing 4.2, which uses the logical AND operator to create some complex expressions.

LISTING 4.2   **Using the *AND* Operator to Create Complex Boolean Expressions**

```
 1: /////////////////////////////////////////////////
 2: // Module : andbool.cpp
 3:
 4: void main()
 5: {
 6:     int x = 10;
 7:     int y = 20;
 8:     char ch1 = 'A';
 9:     char ch2 = 'Z';
10:
11:     bool MyBool1 = ((x < y) && (ch1 == ch2));   // false
12:     bool MyBool2 = ((x < ch1) && (ch1 != ch2)); // true
13:     bool MyBool3 = ((x != y) && (ch1 != ch2));  // true
14:     bool MyBool4 = ((x < y) && (ch1 == ch2) &&
15:        (x < ch1) && (y > ch2));                 // false
16: }
```

Note

The expression (x<ch1) in Listing 4.2 compares the integral value of the integer variable x (which is 10) to the integral value of the character variable ch1 (which is 65). That is, the ASCII character 'A' is equivalent to the integer value 65 (which is its ASCII code).

As does Listing 4.1, the program in Listing 4.2 produces no output; it merely demonstrates the logical AND operator at work. Lines 6 through 10 declare some variables that are used in the expressions that follow. Lines 11 through 15 actually evaluate the complex expressions, assigning the result to the Boolean variables `MyBool1`, `MyBool2`, `MyBool3`, and `MyBool4`.

SEE ALSO

➤ *For a more in-depth look at how* AND *expressions are evaluated, see page 86*

Logical *OR*

Like the logical AND operator, the logical OR operator is used to combine multiple relational or equality expressions into more comprehensive compound expressions. Its use is straightforward, as in this example:

```
(true || false)
```

This expression evaluates to `true` because something *must* be either true OR false. An OR expression is false only if ***all*** simple expressions involved are false. In place of the keywords `true` and `false` in the preceding expression, we can substitute Boolean expressions, resulting in a compound Boolean expression. For example, take a look at this expression:

```
((5 < 10) || (10 > 20))
```

The first simple expression is `(5 < 10)`, which evaluates to `true`. The second simple expression is `(10 > 20)`, which evaluates to `false`. Substituting the values of each simple expression into the original compound expression brings us back to the original `true` OR `false` expression, which you've already seen is `true`. These two statements are equivalent, and they evaluate the same way:

```
( true    || false )
((5 < 10) || (10 > 20))
```

We can rewrite the program from Listing 4.2 to use OR instead of AND, and the results are quite different. Take a look at the program in Listing 4.3, which uses the logical OR operator to create complex expressions.

LISTING 4.3   Using the *OR* Operator to Create Complex Boolean Expressions

```
 1: ////////////////////////////////////////////////////
 2: // Module : orbool.cpp
 3:
 4: void main()
 5: {
 6:     int x = 10;
 7:     int y = 20;
 8:     char ch1 = 'A';
 9:     char ch2 = 'Z';
10:
11:     bool MyBool1 = ((x < y) || (ch1 == ch2));   // true
12:     bool MyBool2 = ((x < ch1) || (ch1 != ch2)); // true
13:     bool MyBool3 = ((x != y) || (ch1 != ch2));  // true
14:     bool MyBool4 = ((x < y) || (ch1 == ch2) ||
15:         (x < ch1) || (y > ch2));                // true
16: }
```

As does Listing 4.2, this program produces no output; it merely demonstrates the logical OR operator at work. Because at least one of the simple expressions within each complex expression evaluates to true, all the MyBoolX variables take on the value of true during program execution.

SEE ALSO

➤ *For a more in-depth look at how OR expressions are evaluated, see page 87*

Logical *NOT*

The logical NOT operator is easy to conceptualize—it simply negates the value of its operand. For example, if the operand is true, the negation is false, and vice versa. Consider the following example:

```
bool MyBool = true; // MyBool is true
MyBool = !MyBool;    // MyBool is false
MyBool = !MyBool;    // MyBool is true
```

The first statement sets the variable MyBool equal to true. The second statement sets MyBool to the negation of MyBool, from true to NOT-true (false). The third statement is the same as the second, except that this time, the negation is from false to

The OR Rule

Remember this rule of thumb: An OR expression is false only if *all* simple expressions involved are false.

Boolean Toggling

The negation of a Boolean variable, which toggles it from true to false, or from false to true.

Truth Table

A truth table defines the outcomes of all possible logical combinations of simple Boolean expressions.

NOT-false (true). This type of negation of a Boolean variable is called *Boolean toggling*, or simply *toggling* the variable. Toggling is used frequently in real-world programs to alternate the state of Boolean flags during program execution.

Evaluating Boolean Conditions with Truth Tables

The Boolean condition of truth or falsehood is a binary situation—there are only two possibilities. The result of a logical operation on a simple Boolean expression can be easily determined through the use of a simple mathematical tool called a *truth table*.

Traditionally in mathematics, the logical elements being compared are named p and q, and I'll follow that convention here. Of course, p and q can stand for any valid Boolean expression, whether simple or complex. In the following sections, you'll see the truth tables for the logical operators. These truth tables have two entries (true and false) for each operand. For example, Table 4.3 identifies the operands p and q and gives the possible combinations of values for each. The easiest way to generate these combinations is to write true-false-true-false under the q column, and true-true-false-false under the p column.

TABLE 4.3 A Simple Truth Table for Operands *p* and *q*

p	q
true	true
true	false
false	true
false	false

A Truth Table for the *AND* Operator

The AND operator evaluates Boolean expressions according to a given pattern of logic. The AND rule of thumb can be summed up as *it's true only if it's always true*. In other words, if the two operands being compared are both true, then the result is true; otherwise the result is false. Table 4.4 is the truth table for a logical AND operation, using p and q as the operands. For example, using Table 4.4, the first row means that if p=true and q=true, then (p&&q)=true.

TABLE 4.4 A Simple Truth Table for a Logical *AND* Operation

p	q	(p && q)
true	true	true
true	false	false
false	true	false
false	false	false

A Truth Table for the *OR* Operator

Like the AND operator, the OR operator also evaluates Boolean expressions according to a given pattern of logic. The OR rule of thumb can be summed up as *it's false if it's always false, otherwise it's true*. That is, if the two operands being compared are both false, then the result is false; otherwise the result is true. Table 4.5 is the truth table for a logical OR operation, again using p and q as the operands.

TABLE 4.5 A Simple Truth Table for a Logical *OR* Operation

p	q	(p || q)
true	true	true
true	false	true
false	true	true
false	false	false

A Truth Table for the *NOT* Operator

The NOT operator simply negates the value of its operand. Table 4.6 is the truth table for a logical NOT operation, using p and !p as the operands. The value in the !p column is simply a negation of the value in the p column.

TABLE 4.6   A Simple Truth Table for a Logical *NOT* Operation

p	!p
true	false
false	true

Truth tables can get much more complex as the expressions get more complex. Let's take a look at some more complex expressions as they relate to truth tables.

Creating More Complex Truth Tables

To figure out the proper evaluation of a complex Boolean expression, you must identify each element of the expression in a truth table column. After the simple elements have been identified and evaluated, the logical operations are easy to evaluate using the simple rules of thumb for each operator. Table 4.7 identifies p and q in the first two columns, and NOT-p and NOT-q in the second two columns. The final two columns show the values that result from their respective operations.

TABLE 4.7   A Truth Table Showing The Relationships Between Several Logical Operations

p	q	!p	!q	(p¦¦q)	!(!p&&!q)
true	true	false	false	true	true
true	false	false	true	true	true
false	true	true	false	true	true
false	false	true	true	false	false

De Morgan's Law

The expressions (p¦¦q) and !(!p&&!q) are synonymous. This duality of expression sums up De Morgan's law of logic. This law was discovered (proved mathematically) by the British logician Augustus De Morgan.

Notice that the last two columns in Table 4.7 are the same. This indicates that certain complex logical operations are equivalent, even though they may look completely different. To verify that all these calculations are correct, we can write a C++ program. Listing 4.4 is a program that generates a truth table equivalent to the one in Table 4.7.

LISTING 4.4   Creating a Truth Table in C++

```
1: ///////////////////////////////////////////////////
2: // Module  : truth.cpp
3: //
4: // Purpose : Generates a truth table for p, q, !p, !q,
5: //               (p||q), and !(!p&&!q)
6:
7: #include <iostream.h>
8:
9: // Define a macro that means "Put nine spaces here"
10: #define S9  "         "
11:
12: // Function prototype
13: void DisplayTruthTableRow(bool p, bool q);
14:
15: ///////////////////////////////////////////////////
16: // DisplayTruthTableRow()
17:
18: void DisplayTruthTableRow(bool p, bool q)
19: {
20:     // Display a single row of the truth table
21:
22:     cout << p << S9 << q << S9 << !p << S9 << !q
23:         << S9 << (p || q) << S9 << !(!p && !q) << '\n';
24: }
25:
26: ///////////////////////////////////////////////////
27: // Driver — main()
28:
29: void main()
30: {
31:     // Print a header for the truth table, nicely spaced
32:     cout << "p        q         !p       !q       "
33:         << "(p||q) !(!p&&!q)\n";
34:     cout << "-----------------------------------"
35:         << "---------------\n";
36:
```

LISTING 4.4

① Line 10: Define a spacing macro

② Line 13: Declare the display function

③ Lines 22-23: Evaluate expressions and output results

④ Lines 32-35: Output column headings

continues…

LISTING 4.4   **Continued**

```
37:    // First line: True True
38:    DisplayTruthTableRow(true, true);
39:
40:    // Second line: True False
41:    DisplayTruthTableRow(true, false);
42:
43:    // Third line: False True
44:    DisplayTruthTableRow(false, true);
45:
46:    // Fourth line: False False
47:    DisplayTruthTableRow(false, false);
48: }
```

⑤

The output from the program in Listing 4.3 produces a truth table that looks like this:

p	q	!p	!q	(p¦¦q)	!(!p&&!q)
1	1	0	0	1	1
1	0	0	1	1	1
0	1	1	0	1	1
0	0	1	1	0	0

Notice that the values 1 and 0 in this program's output equate to the true and false values in Table 4.7.

The program begins by including the <iostream.h> header because cout is used for the output. This statement is followed by the macro definition on line 10, which lets us use the identifier S9 as an alias for nine space characters—this helps to make the program code more readable, and it formats the truth table columns to line up properly. Line 13 declares the prototype for the function DisplayTruthTableRow(), which actually uses cout to display the output for a row. This statement is followed by the definition for the function, starting on line 18.

DisplayTruthTableRow() takes two bool parameters, p and q. These parameters are used in expressions whose results are printed to the screen by cout on lines 22 and 23. In the main() function, the program simply displays headers for each column of the truth table (lines 31 through 35). The program then fills in the appropriate values for each of the four rows by calling `DisplayTruthTableRow()` four times (lines 38, 41, 44, and 47), sending the corresponding values of p and q for each row.

Using the Conditional Operator

The conditional operator (`?:`) takes three operands and allows you to succinctly make decisions within your code based on the outcome of a conditional Boolean expression. The operator uses the following syntax:

```
(conditional_expression) ?  expression1 : expression2;
```

The `conditional_expression` acts as a test. There are two possible outcomes: `expression1` or `expression2`. If `conditional_expression` evaluates to `true`, then `expression1` is used. If `conditional_expression` evaluates to `false`, then `expression2` is used. The best way to understand this syntax is with a few examples. Consider this simple example:

```
int x = (a == b) ? 10 : 20;
```

If a happens to be equal to b, then x=10, otherwise x=20. Let's try another one. Consider the following, where you need to make a decision about which of two values to assign to a string based on some condition in your program:

```
string str =
   (x <= y) ? "less than or equal to" : "greater than";
```

If x is less than or equal to y, then str="Less than or equal to", otherwise str="Greater than".

Understanding Operator Precedence

A C++ program evaluates Boolean expressions based on the *precedence* of the operators involved. Subexpressions using operators with higher precedence are evaluated first, followed by those with lower priority, until the entire expression is evaluated.

The NOT operator has the highest precedence, so it is always performed first. Relational operators come next, followed by the AND and OR operators (evaluated in left-to-right order). Finally comes

Precedence

The order in which operations are performed.

the conditional operator, which has the lowest precedence. Consider this example:

```cpp
int a = 5;
int b = 5;
int y = 0;
char ch = (a==b && !y) ? 'A' : 'Z';
```

In this code fragment, the last line is evaluated according to the rules of operator precedence just described. The NOT operation !y is performed first; the equality operation a==b comes next, followed by the AND operation (a==b && !y). Finally, the conditional operator (?:) uses these values to determine the appropriate character to assign to ch (in this case, 'A').

Using Selection Statements

Selection statements give you the power to make complex decisions in your programs. Selection statements are often used in combination with Boolean expressions such as the ones you've seen in this chapter. There are two types of selection statements in C++:

- if statements
- switch statements

Let's look at each to see how they work.

Using the *if* Statement

The if statement is similar to the conditional operator, but it allows you to expand the scope of your decision making by providing much more flexibility. The if statement uses a Boolean expression to determine the condition. The most general format of the if statement is as follows:

```cpp
if (expression)
    statement;
```

The if statement's Boolean expression determines whether or not the statement following the expression should execute. For example:

```
int x = 5;
if (x == 5)
    cout << "x equals 5";
```

In this case, the phrase x equals 5 would be printed on the screen. Complex Boolean expressions can be used as well, as in the following if statement:

```
int x = 5;
int y = 10;
if ((x == 5) && (y < x))
    cout << "x equals 5 AND y is less than x";
```

In this case, the cout statement would not execute because y is *not* less than x, and the if test condition evaluates to false.

The *else* Clause

Extensions to the if statement introduce some real power into your C++ programming tool kit. These extensions involve the else clause, which includes the else if clause. The general format of the else clause is shown here:

```
if (expression)
    statement;
else
    statement;
```

The general format of the else if clause is as follows:

```
if (expression)
    statement;
else if (expression)
    statement;
```

You can handle all other situations by appending a final else clause:

```
if (expression)
    statement;
else if (expression)
    statement;
else
    statement;
```

In each of these cases, statement can be any type of valid C++ statement, including blocks and other selection statements. Take a look at the program in Listing 4.5, which uses if statements to make some decisions based on user input.

LISTING 4.5

① Line 14: Get user input

② Line 17: Use the if statement

③ Line 23: Use an else if statement

④ Line 27: Use the else statement

LISTING 4.5   **Using an *if* Statement to Make a Decision Based on User Input**

```cpp
1: //////////////////////////////////////////////////////
2: // Module  : if.cpp
3: //
4: // Purpose : Demonstrates the if statement
5:
6: #include <iostream.h>
7:
8: void main()
9: {
10:    int num;
11:
12:    // Get a number from the user
13:    cout << "Enter a number from 1 to 5 >";
14:    cin >> num;
15:
16:    // Make a decision based on the number
17:    if (1 == num)
18:       cout << "You chose the number ONE.\n";
19:    else if (2 == num)
20:       cout << "You chose the number TWO.\n";
21:    else if (3 == num)
22:       cout << "You chose the number THREE.\n";
23:    else if (4 == num)
24:       cout << "You chose the number FOUR.\n";
25:    else if (5 == num)
26:       cout << "You chose the number FIVE.\n";
27:    else
28:    {
29:       cout << "Your number wasn't 1, 2, 3, 4, or 5!\n";
30:       cout << "You should follow instructions...\n";
31:    }
32: }
```

This program simply requests a number from the user and stores it in the variable num (line 14). A series of if statements occur from lines 17 through 28. The conditional expression in each of these statements compares a literal value to the value of num; based on the outcome of each comparison, the appropriate cout statement is printed. Notice that if the value provided by the user isn't within the requested range of 1 through 5, the final else clause on line 27 tells the user that the input was invalid. Notice also that this else clause uses a code block (lines 28 through 31) to process more than one statement in response to the clause.

Nesting *if* Statements

To provide even more complex decision making in your programs, if statements can be *nested* one inside another. The basic syntax of nested if statements is as follows:

```
if (expression)
{
   if (expression)
      statement;
}
```

The syntax for nested if statements is straightforward, but it can get complex if taken too far. Here is a more complex example of the nested if syntax:

```
if (expression)
{
   if (expression)
   {
      if (expression)
      {
         if (expression)
            statement;
      }
      else
         statement;
   }
   else if
   {
      if (expression)
         statement;
```

Minimize Nested if Statement Levels

You should strive to keep nested **if** statements to the minimum number of nested levels you really need; otherwise, the source code becomes hard to read and maintain.

```
        }
        else
            statement;
    }
```

It's easy to see how this type of nesting can become confusing, so be careful when nesting `if` statements.

Using the *switch* Statement

The `switch` statement allows a program to determine the best course of execution based on an expression value. The general format of the `switch` statement is shown here:

```
switch (expression)
    statement;
```

In practice, the `switch` statement uses two or more `case` labels to determine which course of execution to take. A `case` label uses this format:

```
case constant-expression: statement;
```

Statements following `case` labels typically use the `break` keyword to prevent execution from "falling through" to the next `case` label statement. The abstract format for a typical `switch` statement is shown here:

```
switch (expression)
{
    case constant-expression-1: statement; break;
    case constant-expression-2: statement; break;
    ...
    case constant-expression-N: statement; break;
    default: statement;
}
```

`case` **Labels Are Literals**

`case` labels must be literal values such as numbers or single characters. Strings of characters won't work, but constant expressions representing literal values will.

The optional `default` label acts as a catch-all, handling anything that isn't specified by a `case` label. Listing 4.6 is a simple, concrete example that revises the program from Listing 4.4 to use `switch` instead of `if` statements.

LISTING 4.6   Using the *switch* Statement to Make Decisions

```
1: ////////////////////////////////////////////////////
2: // Module  : switch.cpp
3: //
4: // Purpose : Demonstrates the switch statement
5:
6: #include <iostream.h>
7:
8: void main()
9: {
10:    int num;
11:
12:    // Get a number from the user
13:    cout << "Enter a number from 1 to 5 >";
14:    cin >> num;
15:
16:    // Make a decision based on the number
17:    switch (num)
18:    {
19:       case 1:
20:          cout << "You chose the number ONE.\n";
21:          break;
22:       case 2:
23:          cout << "You chose the number TWO.\n";
24:          break;
25:       case 3:
26:          cout << "You chose the number THREE.\n";
27:          break;
28:       case 4:
29:          cout << "You chose the number FOUR.\n";
30:          break;
31:       case 5:
32:          cout << "You chose the number FIVE.\n";
33:          break;
34:       default:
35:          cout << "Your number wasn't 1, 2, 3, 4, or 5!\n";
36:          cout << "You should follow instructions...\n";
37:    }
38: }
```

LISTING 4.6

① Line 17: Use the `switch` statement to make a decision

② Line 19: Use a `case` label

③ Line 34: Use the `default` label

Mutual Use of `if` and `switch`

You can use `if` statements within `switch` statements, and `switch` statements within `if` statements.

This program prints a sentence on the screen that corresponds to the number entered by the user. On line 17, the `switch` statement begins, using `num` as the expression. The `case 1` through `case 5` statements provide the output strings for each possible match with `num`. On line 34, the `default` clause provides a catch-all for invalid user input. Notice that the `break` keyword is used to prevent execution from falling through into other `case` labels. When the `break` statement is executed, program control jumps to the first statement past the `switch` statement.

Using Enumerations

Enumeration is the process of numbering something. In C++, an enumeration does just that: associates a name with a number to make program code more meaningful for the reader. You create an enumerated type by using the `enum` keyword followed by a list of named constants called *enumerators*. By default, the compiler assigns values to enumerators, beginning with zero and incrementing by 1 for each name in the set. You can also designate the enumerators to have specific values; these values don't have to be unique (but the names *must* be unique). The general format of an `enum` statement is as follows:

```
enum [tag] { name1, name2, ... };
```

The `tag` part of the statement is optional, but it is recommended for creating an alias for the enumeration set. Here's an example of an enumeration listing some types of coins:

```
enum Coins { penny, nickel, dime, quarter };
```

These enumerated values equate to `penny=0`, `nickel=1`, `dime=2`, and `quarter=3`. The program shown in Listing 4.7 gives a more complete example of how to use enumeration, displaying a day of the week that corresponds with an enumerated value.

LISTING 4.7   **An Example That Uses Enumeration**

```
1: /////////////////////////////////////////////////////
2: // Module  : enum.cpp
3: //
4: // Purpose : Demonstrates the use of enumeration
```

```
 5:
 6: #include <iostream.h>
 7:
 8: enum WEEKDAYS
 9: {
10:     Sun, Mon, Tues, Wed, Thurs, Fri, Sat
11: };
12:
13: void main()
14: {
15:     WEEKDAYS wd;
16:     wd = Mon;
17:
18:     switch (wd)
19:     {
20:         case Sun:
21:             cout << "Sunday";
22:             break;
23:         case Mon:
24:             cout << "Monday";
25:             break;
26:         case Tues:
27:             cout << "Tuesday";
28:             break;
29:         case Wed:
30:             cout << "Wednesday";
31:             break;
32:         case Thurs:
33:             cout << "Thursday";
34:             break;
35:         case Fri:
36:             cout << "Friday";
37:             break;
38:         case Sat:
39:             cout << "Saturday";
40:             break;
41:     }
42: }
```

LISTING 4.7 CONTINUED

1 Lines 8-11: Define weekdays as enumerated values

2 Lines 15-16: Create and initialize a WEEKDAYS variable

3 Line 18: Determine which day of the week wd represents

This program doesn't allow for any user input. Instead, it declares an enumerated type called WEEKDAYS on lines 8 through 11. Line 15 declares the variable wd of type WEEKDAYS, and line 16 assigns to it the value Mon. A switch statement beginning on line 18 checks the value of wd and displays a day of the week that corresponds to the enumerated value.

Enumerations aren't integer values, although they can easily be converted to integer values by using an explicit typecast. For example, the following statement won't work on most C++ compilers:

```
if (wd == 2) { // do something }
```

This is because wd is of type WEEKDAYS, and 2 is an integer. To ensure that this will work as expected you can provide an explicit typecast, like this:

```
if (int(wd) == 2) { // do something }
```

An enum Is Not an Integer

The variable wd in Listing 4.7 is *not* an integer. It's a variable of type WEEKDAYS, although it can be promoted to an integer with an explicit cast.

SEE ALSO

➤ *For a refresher on basic typecasting, see page 58*

CHAPTER 5

Building Iteration Loops

Learn why loops are important for repetitive tasks

Learn how to use C++ iteration statements

Understand the concepts behind loop design

Understand the flow of control in iteration

Discover how you can fine-tune your loops

Why Use Loops?

Loop

A method of structuring programming statements so they are repeated as long as certain conditions
are met.

Interation

One pass through the body of a
loop.

Looping and Iteration

The act of iterating through a section
of code over and over again is called
looping, and the section of iterated
code is called a *loop*.

Many programming tasks are repetitive, having little variation
from one item to the next. The process of performing the same
task over and over again is called *iteration*, and C++ provides
built-in iteration functionality. A *loop* executes the same section
of program code over and over again, as long as a loop condition
of some sort is met with each iteration. This section of code can
be a single statement or a block of statements (a compound
statement). Now that we've got that out of the way, let's see why
you might need to use an iteration loop in a C++ program.

Suppose that you have to write a program that calculates equivalent temperatures in both Fahrenheit and Celsius. You could
write the code for each possible calculation, but that would be
time-consuming and prone to error (not to mention foolish).
C++ offers built-in support for automating iterative tasks; in this
chapter, you'll see just how easy it is to use iteration loops to
automate repetitive tasks.

Using a bit of program design shorthand called *pseudocode*, we
can lay out a basic algorithm that specifies what we want the
computer to do. The pseudocode just specifies, in everyday language, a generalization of the task at hand. Suppose that we have
to create a table showing equivalent Fahrenheit and Celsius temperatures for the range of 32 to 75 degrees Fahrenheit. We can
use a loop to apply the conversion algorithm for each degree
within this range. The process would look something like the
following basic algorithm:

For each degree in the specified range (32 to 75 degrees
Fahrenheit), do the following:

1. Calculate equivalent Celsius temperature.

2. Write the equivalent temperatures to the screen.

In the sections that follow, I'll present three versions of a temperature conversion program using three kinds of loops. When
implemented in a real program, the preceding two steps could
become functions of their own, or they could be coded directly
into main(). For the instructional purposes of a simple program

like this, coding directly into `main()` makes the code more self-explanatory, so these programs just perform all their processing in `main()`.

There are several ways to write the code for this algorithm, using any of the three looping statements C++ provides:

- The `for` statement
- The `while` statement
- The `do` statement

Phases of Loop Execution

The statement part of a loop is called the *body* of the loop. This loop body has several phases of execution:

- *Loop entry*, which occurs when the flow of execution reaches the first statement within the loop body.
- *Iteration*, which is an individual pass through the body of a loop.
- *Conditional test*, which is the point of execution at which the Boolean expression is evaluated and the decision is made to either terminate the loop or begin a new iteration.
- *Loop exit*, which occurs when execution passes out of the loop to the next statement following the loop.
- *Termination condition*, which is the condition that causes the loop to be terminated.

Examining Iteration Statements

The C++ iteration statements provide your programs with the capability to execute statements zero or more times within a loop. You set up a loop by using a `for`, `while`, or `do` statement; each of these three iteration statements performs its task a little differently. Each statement iterates until a termination expression evaluates to `false`, or until the loop is explicitly terminated by using a `break` statement (we'll look at the `break` statement as it applies to loops later in this chapter). Now let's look at each of the iteration statements to see how they're used.

What Is Pseudocode?

Pseudocode is an algorithmic shorthand that lays out, in everyday language, the steps to solving a problem. Pseudocode often serves as the basis for program comments.

Using the *for* Statement

The for statement lets a program execute some statement (including a compound statement) a specified number of times. This means that a for statement is most often used when there are a specified number of items to iterate through (such as the range of degrees for the temperature conversion mentioned earlier). The general format of the for statement is as follows:

```
for (initializing-list; expression; altering-list)
statement;
```

The flow of control for a for statement is determined by the components within the parentheses. Figure 5.1 shows this flow of control.

FIGURE 5.1

The flow of control within a `for` statement.

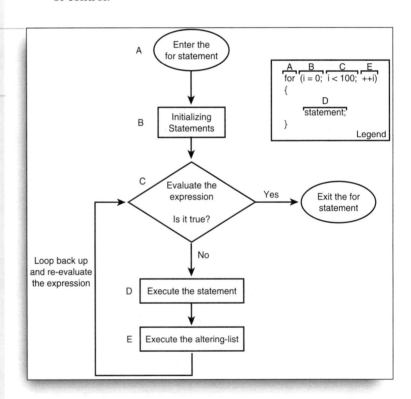

The `initializing-list` allows you to initialize some data. This initialization is performed just once, when execution first enters the for statement. The Boolean `expression` evaluates to `true` or false, and the loop continues as long as this expression is true. The altering-list allows you to modify the data initialized in the initializing-list, allowing your code to break out of the loop when conditions are right. The statement portion is the code that is executed for the specified number of iterations. This statement can be a simple statement or a compound statement (a block). When the statement is a block, the general format looks something like this:

```
for (initializing-list; expression; altering-list)
{
    statement1;
    statement2;
    // other statements
    statement n;
}
```

Here's a comparison between code that uses a loop and code that doesn't. Suppose that I want to write the numbers 1 through 10 to the screen. I could do this (the hard way):

```
short i = 0;
cout << ++i << " ";   // writes 1
cout << ++i << " ";   // writes 2
cout << ++i << " ";   // writes 3
cout << ++i << " ";   // writes 4
cout << ++i << " ";   // writes 5
cout << ++i << " ";   // writes 6
cout << ++i << " ";   // writes 7
cout << ++i << " ";   // writes 8
cout << ++i << " ";   // writes 9
cout << ++i << " ";   // writes 10
```

The variable i is incremented using the preincrement operator (++), which adds 1 to the value of i before it's used for anything else. Preincrementing the variable i causes its value to increase by 1 at each line. Here's how you can achieve the same result with far fewer lines of code by using a for loop (the easy way):

```
for (short i = 1; i < 11; ++i)
    cout << i << " ";   // write each number
```

In this case, the loop begins with i initialized to 1, and the loop writes the value of i with each iteration as long as i is less than 11.

As another simple example of a `for` loop, Listing 5.1 shows a complete program that uses a `for` loop to iterate through all the uppercase letters of the alphabet, using a simple statement to output the letters to the screen.

LISTING 5.1   A Program That Uses a *for* Loop to Iterate Through All the Uppercase Letters of the Alphabet

```
 1: ///////////////////////////////////////////////////////
 2: // Module: for1.cpp
 3:
 4: #include <iostream.h>
 5:
 6: void main()
 7: {
 8:    // List all uppercase letters of the alphabet (ASCII)
 9:    for (char ch = 'A'; ch < 'Z' + 1; ++ch)
10:       cout << ch << " ";
11: }
```

The output of this program is as follows:

A B C D E F G H I J K L M N O P Q R S T U V W X Y Z

Because the program uses the `cout` object to display the letters, the program includes the input/output stream header (`<iostream.h>`) on line 4. The `for` loop is the only thing in the `main()` function; it begins on line 9. This `for` statement's `initializing-list` consists of a single item: the `char` variable `ch` (initialized to the character A). The Boolean expression `ch < 'Z' + 1` acts as the test to check whether the loop has iterated enough times. The `altering-list` consists of a single item, `++ch`, which increments the value of `ch` by one with each iteration. Because a `char` variable is an integral type, the `++ch` statement in the `altering-list` advances `ch` through the alphabet one letter at a time (the character A is the same as ASCII code 65, the character B is the same as ASCII code 66, and so on).

Let's take a closer look at what's happening during loop execution (a good way to see this in real time is to step through the loop code one line at a time in a debugger).

Stepping through *for1.cpp*

1. Program execution enters `main()` and reaches the `for` statement.

2. When execution first enters the `for` statement, the `char` variable `ch` is created and assigned the value `A` (ASCII value 65).

3. The test expression uses `'Z' + 1` to iterate one past `Z` (ASCII code 90), otherwise the character `Z` would never print to the output device. The test expression therefore checks to see whether `ch` is less than `'Z' + 1` (ASCII code 91). If not, the loop terminates.

4. The `cout` statement displays the character `ch`, followed by a space.

5. The variable `ch` is incremented by one.

6. Go back to step 3.

Using a *for* Loop for Temperature Conversion

To create a temperature conversion program such as the one discussed earlier, we can follow steps similar to the ones used in Listing 5.1. We must set up the `for` loop to initialize a degree counter at 32 degrees; the test expression must check to see whether this counter has exceeded 75 degrees (which happens at 76, of course). The `for` statement to accomplish this task looks something like this:

```
for (int degree = 32; degree < 76; ++degree)
{
    // calculate and display degrees here
    ;
}
```

To actually convert from degrees Fahrenheit to degrees Celsius, we use the following simple formula:

```
Celsius = 0.55 * (Fahrenheit - 32)
```

Take a look at Listing 5.2, which puts it all together into a complete program.

LISTING 5.2   **Using a *for* Loop to Generate a Table of Fahrenheit-to-Celsius Temperature Conversions Ranging from 32 to 75 Degrees Fahrenheit**

```
1: ///////////////////////////////////////////////////////
2: // Module  : for2.cpp
3: //
4: // Purpose : Displays equivalent temperatures in both
5: //           Fahrenheit and Celsius (range 32-75 F).
6:
7: #include <iostream.h>
8:
9: void main()
10: {
11:    // Write a table title
12:    //
13:    cout << "Temperature Equivalents in Fahrenheit"
14:       << " and Celsius\n\n";
15:
16:    // Write a heading for each column
17:    //
18:    cout << "Fahrenheit\tCelsius\n";
19:    cout << "----------\t-------\n";
20:
21:    // Use a for loop to generate the table
22:    //
23:    float degreeC;   // Degrees in Celsius
24:    for (int degreeF = 32; degreeF < 76; ++degreeF)
25:    {
26:       // Convert from F to C
27:       //
28:       degreeC = 0.55f * (degreeF - 32);
29:
30:       // Display the current conversion row
31:       //
32:       cout << degreeF << "\t\t" << degreeC << '\n';
33:    }
34: }
```

The output for the program in Listing 5.2 displays the temperature equivalents in two-column format:

```
Temperature Equivalents in Fahrenheit and Celsius
Fahrenheit    Celsius
----------    -------
32            0
33            0.55
34            1.1
35            1.65
36            2.2
37            2.75
38            3.3
39            3.85
40            4.4
41            4.95
42            5.5
43            6.05
44            6.6
45            7.15
46            7.7
47            8.25
48            8.8
49            9.35
50            9.9
51            10.45
52            11
53            11.55
54            12.1
55            12.65
56            13.2
57            13.75
58            14.3
59            14.85
60            15.4
61            15.95
62            16.5
63            17.05
64            17.6
65            18.15
66            18.7
67            19.25
68            19.8
69            20.35
70            20.9
71            21.45
```

72	22
73	22.55
74	23.1
75	23.65

Needless to say, the use of the `for` loop saves a lot of typing when compared with the alternative of hard-coding the conversion and output statements within the source code for each conversion!

Okay, let's take a look at how the program works. First, the `main()` function writes out a table title (lines 13 and 14) and headings for two columns (lines 18 and 19), separated by a tab character (`\t`). The first column is for Fahrenheit, the second is for Celsius. Line 23 declares the `float` variable `degreeC` (degrees in Celsius). This variable's purpose is to store the converted temperature value. Line 24 begins the `for` loop, using the `initializing-list`, Boolean `expression`, and `altering-list` described earlier. The integer variable `degreeF` (degrees in Fahrenheit) is declared and initialized with the value `32`, the first Fahrenheit value to be converted. The `expression` tests that the value is less than 76, and the `altering-list` increments `degreeF` by 1 at the end of each iteration. Line 28 performs the actual calculation of the Celsius value, storing this value as a `float` in `degreeC`. The table rows are output to the screen on line 32, where two tab characters separate the `degreeF` and `degreeC` variables to force the columns to line up properly with the column headers.

Creating Infinite Loops Using the *for* Statement

Here's a final note about `for` loops: A `for` loop doesn't require that values be specified for the `initializing-list`, `expression`, or `altering-list`—these semicolon-separated items within parentheses are all optional. In fact, it's a common practice to leave them all out, resulting in an infinite loop, like this:

```
for (;;) statement;
```

Note that program execution can exit this type of `for` statement only by using a `break` or `goto` statement.

SEE ALSO

➤ *For more information about the* goto *and* break *statements, see page 74*

Note

The variable **degreeC** is declared outside the loop instead of inside the loop. This is because, if it were declared within the loop, processor time would be wasted creating and destroying the variable with each iteration.

The Dreaded goto Statement

The **goto** statement jumps program execution to a label statement, without any way of returning. In general, use of **goto** is frowned on because overuse of **goto** creates what many programmers refer to as "spaghetti code"; that is, code that becomes so tangled it's hard to follow from end to end.

Using the *while* Statement

The while statement is similar to the for statement. It also uses an initializer, evaluates an expression, and uses an altering mechanism to eventually break out of the loop. With the while statement, however, only the expression part is built in (the initializing and altering statements are left up to the programmer to provide). The general format of the while statement is as follows:

```
while (expression) statement;
```

The statement can be a single statement or a compound statement within a code block. The flow of control for a while statement is determined by the evaluation of the test expression. Figure 5.2 shows the flow of control in a while statement.

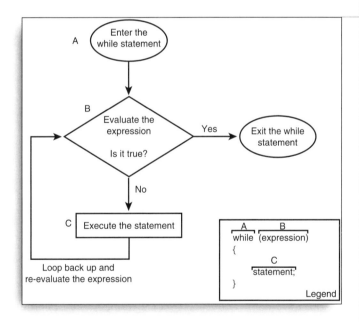

FIGURE 5.2

The flow of control within a while statement.

If the expression in parentheses evaluates to true, the statement is executed. This continues until some alteration occurs within the statement to make the expression false, or until the statement explicitly breaks out of the loop using the break keyword.

Listing 5.3 is a modified version of the alphabet program previously used to demonstrate the for loop (refer to Listing 5.1). In Listing 5.3, the code iterates through all the uppercase letters of the alphabet using a while loop.

LISTING 5.3   **A Program That Uses a *while* Loop to Iterate Through All the Uppercase Letters of the Alphabet**

```
 1: //////////////////////////////////////////////////
 2: // Module   : while1.cpp
 3:
 4: #include <iostream.h>
 5:
 6: void main()
 7: {
 8:     // List all uppercase letters of the alphabet (ASCII)
 9:     //
10:     char ch = 'A';        1
11:     while (ch < 'Z' + 1)  2
12:     {
13:         cout << ch << " ";
14:         ++ch;        // increment to the next letter   3
15:     }
16: }
```

As expected, the output for this program is the same as that generated by the program in Listing 5.1:

A B C D E F G H I J K L M N O P Q R S T U V W X Y Z

The main difference between Listing 5.3 and Listing 5.1 is the loop construction. The while statement's initializer consists of the char variable ch, which is initialized to the character A on line 10. The Boolean expression in the while statement ch < 'Z' + 1 on line 11 acts as the test to check whether the loop has iterated enough times. The altering mechanism for this loop consists of the statement ++ch on line 14, which increments the value of ch by one with each iteration.

Note that lines 13 and 14 in this listing could be consolidated into a single statement by postincrementing the `ch` variable, like this:

```
cout << ch++ << " ";
```

This would accomplish the same thing—a good example of how C++ allows you to write concise code. By postincrementing `ch` (`ch++`) we arrive at the desired result, but preincrementing (`++ch`) would increment the initialized value *before* the `cout` object writes its value to the screen, which would erroneously produce this output:

```
B C D E F G H I J K L M N O P Q R S T U V W X Y Z [
```

Using a *while* Loop for Temperature Conversion

The `while` loop can be used in place of the `for` loop you saw in Listing 5.2 to create the temperature conversion program discussed earlier. The main difference is the construction of the loop. The program must explicitly initialize and increment the degree being converted, something like this:

```
short degreeF = 32;
while (degreeF < 76)
{
    // calculate and display degrees here
    ++degreeF;  // increment
}
```

Listing 5.4 provides the complete program source code needed to accomplish the temperature conversion task with a `while` loop.

LISTING 5.4   **Using a *while* Loop to Generate a Table of Fahrenheit-to-Celsius Temperature Conversions Ranging from 32 to 75 Degrees Fahrenheit**

```
1: ////////////////////////////////////////////////////////
2: // Module  : while2.cpp
3: //
4: // Purpose : Displays equivalent temperatures in both
5: //           Fahrenheit and Celsius (range 32-75 F).
6:
7: #include <iostream.h>
8:
```

continues...

LISTING 5.4

1 Lines 13-14: Create a table title

2 Lines 18-19: Create headings for the temperature columns

3 Line 24: Initialize the Fahrenheit degree counter

4 Line 26: Test to see whether the loop is finished

5 Lines 27-36: The compound statement that is iterated

LISTING 5.4 **Continued**

```
 9: void main()
10: {
11:    // Write a table title
12:    //
13:    cout << "Temperature Equivalents in Fahrenheit"          ─┐
14:       << " and Celsius\n\n";                                ─┘  ──①
15:
16:    // Write a heading for each column
17:    //
18:    cout << "Fahrenheit\tCelsius\n";                         ─┐
19:    cout << "----------\t------\n";                          ─┘  ──②
20:
21:    // Use a while loop to generate the table
22:    //
23:    float degreeC;
24:    int   degreeF = 32;  // initialize to 32 degrees  ──③
25:
26:    while (degreeF < 76)  ──④
27:    {                                                         ─┐
28:       // Convert from F to C                                 │
29:       //                                                     │
30:       degreeC = 0.55f * (degreeF - 32);                      │
31:                                                              ├──⑤
32:       // Display the conversion row                          │
33:       //                                                     │
34:       cout << degreeF << "\t\t" << degreeC << '\n';          │
35:       degreeF++;                                             │
36:    }                                                         ─┘
37: }
```

The output for this program displays the temperature equivalents in two-column format, just as the program in Listing 5.2 did.

The differences between Listing 5.4 and Listing 5.2 are few, relevant only to the way the while statement's looping mechanism works. The programs are identical up to line 24. Here, the integer variable degreeF is explicitly created and initialized to 32 before the while loop begins. degreeF is the variable used as the while loop's test condition, so the loop "knows" when to stop iterating. The expression on line 26 tests that the value is less than 76; if so, the code block that follows is executed. Line 30 performs the actual calculation of the Celsius value, storing this value as a float in degreeC. The table rows are output to the screen on line 34, where two tab characters separate the degreeF and degreeC variables to force the columns to line up properly. Line 35 increments degreeF, ensuring that the loop will eventually terminate when this value reaches 76.

Creating Infinite Loops Using the *while* Statement

Here's a final note about while loops: Just as you can with the for statement, you can generate an endless loop with the while statement, simply by ensuring that the evaluation expression is always true. For both of the following examples, the test condition is always true:

```
while (1) statement;

while (true) statement;
```

Using the *do* Statement

The do statement is very similar to the while statement. It too takes an initializer, evaluates an expression, and uses an altering mechanism to eventually break out of the loop. The do statement will always execute the corresponding statement at least once—the while loop might not (if the condition is false on the first iteration). With the do loop, the evaluation expression comes after the execution statement. The general format of the do statement is as follows:

```
do statement;
while (expression);
```

The flow of control for a do statement is determined by the evaluation of the test expression. Figure 5.3 shows the flow of control in a do statement.

If the expression in parentheses evaluates to true, the loop iterates again, executing the statement until the expression evaluates to false. This continues until some alteration occurs within the statement to make the expression false, or until the statement explicitly breaks out of the loop using the break keyword.

FIGURE 5.3

The flow of control within a do statement.

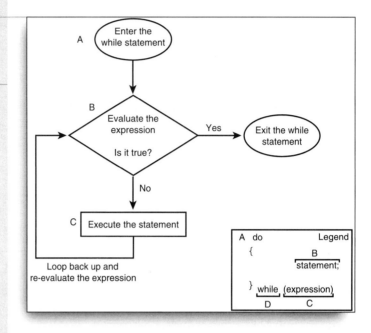

Listing 5.5 shows another modified version of the alphabet program, this time iterating through all the uppercase letters of the alphabet using a do loop.

LISTING 5.5   A Program That Uses a *do* Loop to Iterate Through All the Uppercase Letters of the Alphabet

```
 1: //////////////////////////////////////////////////////
 2: // Module  : do1.cpp
 3:
 4: #include <iostream.h>
 5:
 6: void main()
 7: {
 8:     // List all uppercase letters of the alphabet (ASCII)
 9:     //
10:     char ch = 'A';
11:     do
12:     {
13:         cout << ch << " ";
```

```
14:        ++ch;  // increment to the next letter
15:    }
16:    while (ch < 'Z' + 1);
17: }
```

As expected, the output for this program is the same as that generated by the programs in Listings 5.1 and 5.3:

A B C D E F G H I J K L M N O P Q R S T U V W X Y Z

The main difference between Listing 5.5 and Listing 5.3 is (again) how the loop is constructed. The do statement's initializer consists of the char variable ch, which is initialized to the character A on line 10. The Boolean expression in the while statement ch < 'Z' + 1 on line 16 acts as the test to check whether the loop has iterated enough times. The altering mechanism for this loop consists of the statement ++ch on line 14, which increments the value of ch by one with each iteration.

Using a *do* Loop for Temperature Conversion

The do loop can be used in place of the while loop you saw in Listing 5.4 to create yet another version of the temperature conversion program. Again, the main difference between these programs is the construction of the loop, which is something like this:

```
do
{
    // calculate and display degrees here
    degreeF++;}
while (degreeF < 76);
```

Listing 5.6 reveals the source code needed to accomplish this task.

LISTING 5.6 **Using a *do* Loop to Generate a Table of Fahrenheit-to-Celsius Temperature Conversions Ranging from 32 to 75 Degrees Fahrenheit**

```
1: /////////////////////////////////////////////////////
2: // Module  : do2.cpp
3: //
```

continues…

LISTING 5.4

1 Lines 13-14: Create a table title

2 Lines 18-19: Create headings for the temperature columns

3 Line 24: Initialize the Fahrenheit degree counter

4 Line 26: Begin the do loop

5 Lines 27-36: The compound statement that is iterated

6 Line 37: Test to see whether the loop is finished

LISTING 5.6 **Continued**

```
4:  // Purpose : Displays equivalent temperatures in both
5:  //                Fahrenheit and Celsius (range 32-75 F).
6:
7:  #include <iostream.h>
8:
9:  void main()
10: {
11:    // Write a table title
12:    //
13:    cout << "Temperature Equivalents in Fahrenheit"        — 1
14:        << " and Celsius\n\n";
15:
16:    // Write a heading for each column
17:    //
18:    cout << "Fahrenheit\tCelsius\n";                        — 2
19:    cout << "----------\t------\n";
20:
21:    // Use a do loop to generate the table
22:    //
23:    float degreeC;
24:    int   degreeF = 32;  // initialize to 32 degrees        — 3
25:
26:    do        — 4
27:    {
28:       // Convert from F to C
29:       //
30:       degreeC = 0.55f * (degreeF - 32);
31:
32:       // Display the conversion row                        — 5
33:       //
34:       cout << degreeF << "\t\t" << degreeC << '\n';
35:       degreeF++;
36:    }
37:    while (degreeF < 76);        — 6
38: }
```

The output for this program displays the temperature equivalents in two-column format, just as the programs in Listings 5.2 and 5.4 do.

The main difference between Listing 5.6 and Listing 5.4 is the construction of the loop. The programs are identical up to line 26 where the do loop begins. The code block that begins on line 27 is always executed at least once. Line 30 performs the actual calculation of the Celsius value, storing this value as a float in degreeC. The table rows are output to the screen on line 34, where two tab characters separate the degreeF and degreeC variables to force the columns to line up properly. Line 35 explicitly increments degreeF, ensuring that the loop will eventually terminate when this value reaches 76. Line 37 performs the test to see whether the loop should terminate.

Creating Infinite Loops Using the *do* Statement

Here's a final note about do loops: Just as you can with the for and while statements, you can generate an endless loop with the do statement, simply by ensuring that the evaluation expression is always true. In the following two examples, the evaluation expression is always true:

```
do statement;
while (1);
```

```
do statement;
while (true);
```

Designing Loops

Getting loops to work correctly is sometimes an arduous task for beginning C++ programmers, but with a little practice, it becomes second nature (like most things in life). Loops are often used to provide interactivity to programs. For example, operating systems that make extensive use of a *graphical user interface* (GUI, pronounced "gooey") such as Microsoft's Windows NT, the Macintosh OS, or Sun's Solaris use loops to control almost everything that happens within a program. These loops typically sense keyboard and mouse movement and respond appropriately, creating a programming paradigm known as *event-driven programming*. Let's take a look at how simple loops can be used to create a basic interactive program environment.

Graphical User Interface

A set of graphics and icons that replaces the character type menu used by many machines. A GUI interface can float on top of an operating system such as DOS or UNIX to allow for ease of operator use.

Event-Driven Programming

A programming model that relies on and responds to user input, usually from within a program event-loop.

Designing the Flow of Interactive Program Control

To design a program that uses loops to interactively respond to user input, you must anticipate the many things a user might do. Let's design and implement a program that wraps program execution inside a loop, iterating through the execution cycle until the user requests that the program terminate.

Thinking through the loop cycle

1. Begin main program loop.

2. Perform program tasks.

3. Check to see whether the user wants to continue.

4. If the user wants to continue, loop back to step 2.

The first order of business is deciding which type of looping structure to use. Because we don't know when the user will want to quit, a for loop is a poor choice. The user wants to perform some program task or he or she wouldn't be running the program, so the do looping structure seems appropriate. This decision should give us enough information to design a preliminary program loop, something like the following pseudocode:

```
void main()
{
    do
    (
        // do something
    )
    while (user wants to continue)
```

With this as a basis, there are two questions you must answer to make this pseudocode into real code you can compile and run:

1. What is the "something" that the program will do?

2. What is the test that determines whether the user wants to continue?

The something the program can do is, for the moment, unimportant. The test, however, is critical to the proper functioning of the loop. A common test is to check a Boolean variable that determines whether the program should terminate. Another method is to use an equality test to see whether the user has asked the program to end. An example of this type of loop is shown here:

```cpp
char quit; // Determines if user wants to quit

// Begin program loop
//
do
{
   //
   // Do something...
   //
   // See if the user wants to quit
   //
   cout << "Enter Q to quit >";
   cin >> quit;   // Get user input

// Quit only if user picked 'q' or 'Q'
//
while ((quit != 'q') && (quit != 'Q'));
```

In this example, the char variable quit is used to determine whether the program should end. The while statement checks for the character Q (both uppercase and lowercase), and loops if this character isn't specified by the user. You'll see an incarnation of this program later in this chapter—as a simple implementation of the shell game.

Using *break* and *continue* for Greater Loop Control

Sometimes it's necessary to break out of a loop, or to stop the current loop iteration and continue execution with the next iteration. These actions are possible in C++ thanks to the break and continue statements. The break statement (as you've seen before) is used to continue program execution at the statement following a switch statement or at the statement following one of the looping statements (for, while, or do).

The break statement can be used to exit a loop if some special event occurs, such as a variable attaining a certain value.

For example, assume that if some integer variable (`MyInt`) reaches the value of `100` within a loop, the program should exit (`break`) the loop. Using an endless `for` loop, you could something like this:

```
int MyInt = 0;

for (;;)
{
   cout << MyInt++ << " ";
   if (MyInt > 100)
      break;
}
cout << "\nThe loop has ended.\n";
```

The condition of `MyInt` being greater than 100 causes the endless loop to terminate.

The `continue` statement is used to continue execution at the start of the next loop iteration, skipping whatever might be left in the current iteration. For example, a Boolean condition within a loop might evaluate to `true`, indicating that the rest of the current loop iteration should not execute. The following code snippet demonstrates this by using a `while` loop to display all positive, odd integers having a value less than `1000`:

```
int MyInt = 0;

while (++MyInt < 1000)
{
   if ((MyInt % 2) == 0)
      continue;
   cout << "Odd number: " << MyInt++ << "\n";
}
```

The `while` statement's test expression preincrements the `MyInt` variable with each loop iteration; the `if` statement uses the modulus operator (`%`) to see whether the current value of `MyInt` is perfectly divisible by 2. If it *is* perfectly divisible by 2, it's an even number and the loop continues with the next iteration without displaying this number. Otherwise, the loop executes normally, displaying the value of `MyInt` (which must be odd because program execution reached the `cout` statement).

Infinite Loops Can End

A loop is infinite when its structure has no exit condition. Internally, however, loop code can terminate an endless loop by evaluating an exit condition. This exit condition then uses the **break** statement to break out of the loop.

The Modulus Operator

The modulus operator gets the remainder of a division operation, returning zero if the division has no remainder.

Using Nested Loops

It's often useful to place one loop inside another—sometimes several. This process is called *nesting loops*. A nested loop iterates through its entire cycle with each iteration of its parent loop. The program in Listing 5.7 demonstrates how a simple nested loop works.

Nested Loops

The process of placing one loop, or several, inside another loop(s).

LISTING 5.7 **A Demonstration of a Simple Nested Loop**

```
1: /////////////////////////////////////////////////////
2: // Module : nested.cpp
3:
4: #include <iostream.h>
5:
6: void main()
7: {
8:    int i = 1;
9:    while (i <= 3)
10:    {
11:       int j = 1;
12:       while (j <= 3)
13:       {
14:          cout << "i = " << i << ", j = " << j << '\n';
15:          j++;
16:       }
17:       cout << '\n';
18:       i++;
19:    }
20: }
```

LISTING 5.7

1 Lines 9-19: The outer while loop increments i

2 Line 12-16: The inner while loop increments j

The output for this program looks like this:

```
i = 1, j = 1
i = 1, j = 2
i = 1, j = 3

i = 2, j = 1
i = 2, j = 2
i = 2, j = 3

i = 3, j = 1
```

```
i = 3, j = 2
i = 3, j = 3
```

As you can see from this output, the inner loop increments j three times for every iteration of the outer loop (which increments i).

Putting It All Together

Now that you've seen how the various looping statements work and understand nested loops, let's write that interactive shell game I mentioned earlier in this chapter. The shell game is an old gambling game that uses three shells and one pea. The pea is hidden under one of three shells. The object of the game is to guess which shell the pea is under. If you get it right, you win some cash (in the simplistic version I present here, money isn't used).

The program design is conceptually simple. An outer loop controls the rest of the program. Within this loop, the shell game is played. Various inner loops perform basic error checking to validate user input. The following pseudocode shows the general form of the program:

```
main()
{
   // Begin main loop
   do
   (
      Get a random number from 1 to 3
      (This is the shell the pea is under).

      // Begin the input loop
      do
      {
         Get a guess from the user
      }
      while (input is invalid)

      Announce the winner

      do
```

```
        {
            Ask user if he wants to continue or quit
        }
        while (input is invalid)
    )
    while (user wants to continue)


    User has quit, end program
}
```

Normally, program tasks such as getting a random number, checking the winner, seeing whether the user wants to quit, and so on are performed by individual program functions. In this program, the entire process occurs in main(). The complete program code that spells out all the details missing in this pseudocode is shown in Listing 5.8.

LISTING 5.8 A Simple Guessing Game That Provides Interactive Program Loops, Letting the User Decide Whether to Continue

```
 1: /////////////////////////////////////////////////////
 2: //  Module  : ShellGame.cpp
 3: //
 4: //  Purpose : A simple guessing game that provides
 5: //            some interactive program loops, letting
 6: //            the user decide whether to continue.
 7: /////////////////////////////////////////////////////
 8:
 9: #include <iostream>
10: #include <cstdlib>    // For random numbers
11: #include <ctime>      // To seed random number
12: #include <string>     // For standard strings
13:
14: using namespace std;
15:
16: void main()
17: {
18:     // Some variables
19:     //
20:     short UserNum;    // Number the user chooses
21:     short ProgNum;    // Random number the program chooses
22:     char  quit;       // Determines if user wants to quit
```

continues...

LISTING 5.8

1 Lines 9-12: Include necessary Standard C++ Library headers

2 Lines 20-22: Declare variables used by the program

LISTING 5.8 CONTINUED

3 Line 25: Prepare (seed) the random number generator

4 Line 29: Begin the main program loop

5 Lines 32-34: Pick a random number using the library function rand()

6 Line 38: Begin the input loop

7 Line 43: Get the user's guess

8 Lines 48-53: Scold the user if input is invalid

9 Line 57: Validate the user's guess

10 Lines 61-62: Find out who won

LISTING 5.8 **Continued**

```
23:
24:    // Seed the random number generator
25:    srand((unsigned)time(0));   ──3
26:
27:    // Begin program loop
28:    //
29:    do   ──4
30:    {
31:       // Pick a random number from 1 to 3
32:       ProgNum    = rand();
33:       float fMap = float(2.0f / RAND_MAX);   ──5
34:       ProgNum    = ProgNum * fMap + 1.5F;
35:
36:       // Begin input loop
37:       //
38:       do   ──6
39:       {
40:          cout << "I have 3 shells and 1 pea. " <<
41:             "Which shell is the pea under?\n";
42:          cout << "Pick a number from 1 to 3 >";
43:          cin >> UserNum;      // Get user input   ──7
44:          cout << '\n';
45:
46:          // See if the user entered a valid number
47:          //
48:          if ((UserNum < 1) || (UserNum > 3))
49:          {
50:             cout << "I said a number from 1 to 3! ";
51:             cout << UserNum << " is NOT from 1 to 3...";   ──8
52:             cout << "\nPlease try again...\n\n";
53:          }
54:       }
55:       // Loop only if input was invalid
56:       //
57:       while ((UserNum < 1) || (UserNum > 3));   ──9
58:
59:       // See who won
60:       //
61:       string winner = (UserNum == ProgNum) ?
62:          "You WIN!\n" : "You LOSE...\n";   ──10
63:
```

```
64:        // Let the user know the outcome
65:        //
66:        cout << "The pea is under shell number "
67:            << ProgNum << ", you picked " << UserNum          ⑪
68:            << "--" << winner;
69:
70:        // See if the user wants to continue or quit
71:        //
72:        do
73:        {
74:            cout << "Enter C to continue, Q to quit >";
75:            cin >> quit;   // Get user input  ⑫
76:            cout << '\n';
77:        }
78:        // Loop only if input was invalid
79:        //
80:        while ((quit != 'q') && (quit != 'Q') &&
81:            (quit != 'c') && (quit != 'C'));          ⑬
82:    }
83:    // Quit only if user picked 'q' or 'Q'
84:    //
85:    while ((quit != 'q') && (quit != 'Q'));  ⑭
86:
87:    // User has quit, say goodbye
88:    //
89:    cout << "Thanks for playing, bye!\n";
90: }
```

Sample output for a run of the game looks like this:

```
I have 3 shells and 1 pea. Which shell is the pea under?
Pick a number from 1 to 3 >1

The pea is under shell number 3, you picked 1--You LOSE...
Enter C to continue, Q to quit >c

I have 3 shells and 1 pea. Which shell is the pea under?
Pick a number from 1 to 3 >2

The pea is under shell number 2, you picked 2--You WIN!
Enter C to continue, Q to quit >c
```

```
I have 3 shells and 1 pea. Which shell is the pea under?
Pick a number from 1 to 3 >56

I said a number from 1 to 3! 56 is NOT from 1 to 3...
Please try again...

I have 3 shells and 1 pea. Which shell is the pea under?
Pick a number from 1 to 3 >3

The pea is under shell number 2, you picked 3--You LOSE...
Enter C to continue, Q to quit >q

Thanks for playing, bye!
```

Okay, let's go over the code in some detail to see what's happening here. The first thing you might notice are the unfamiliar headers included in lines 9 through 12. These are Standard C++ library headers (the Standard C++ Library is covered in Part III, "Object-Oriented Programming"). Line 14 contains a curious looking statement. This tells the compiler to use the Standard C++ Library namespace. Namespaces are covered in Chapter 16, "Exploring Namespaces"—for now, just take my word for it that this statement is useful (and ignore it).

Lines 20 through 22 declare three variables that the program uses throughout: UserNum, ProgNum, and quit. As the comments suggest, UserNum stores the number of the shell the user guesses the pea to be under, ProgNum is the shell the pea is actually under, and quit is a Boolean flag used to terminate the program loop when the user requests to quit.

Line 25 calls the standard library function srand() to seed the random number generator with a value. The value sent to the function is the current system time, returned from the standard library function time(). These two function calls are the reason the cstdlib and ctime header files are included in the program.

Line 29 begins the main program loop, which only terminates when the user requests to quit. Lines 32 through 34 use the standard library function rand() to actually pick a random number. Because rand() returns a number from zero to RAND_MAX (a number defined by whatever implementation of C++ you use—typically quite large), the random number must be massaged a bit. This massaging maps the random value into the range of 1, 2, or 3 by performing some floating-point division and converting the result to an integer that must be either 1, 2, or 3.

At this point, the computer knows where the pea is hiding, so it's up to the user to try to pick the right shell. Line 43 gets the user's guess, and lines 48 through 52 chide the user if it's invalid input (that is, the user does not enter 1, 2, or 3). Line 57 loops back up to line 38 if the input is invalid, giving the user a chance to enter a valid number. Lines 61 and 62 use the conditional operator to compare the user's and computer's numbers, assigning the appropriate string to the variable winner. Lines 65 through 68 write the results of the game to the screen, revealing the winner.

The do loop from lines 72 through 81 asks the user whether he or she wants to continue or quit, and validates that the answer is either a C or a Q (uppercase and lowercase characters are valid). If the user selects C, the program loops back up to line 38 to start a new game; if the user selects Q, the game ends. Line 89 simply prints a good-bye message.

Using Arrays

Learn how to define and initialize an array

Learn how to access array elements

See how to use loops with arrays

Investigate the use of parallel arrays

Learn to use multi-dimensional arrays

Why Use Arrays?

With the exception of character strings, the data types and variables you've seen up to this point have been simple data types that store only a single value. Consider these two variables:

```
char ch = 'B';
int num = 134;
```

Variables like these are called *scalar* variables. They can contain only a single value at a time, and you can't subdivide them further; they are elemental. An *array* is a group of variables having the same data type.

In writing efficient programs, it's often convenient to have an array of variables (all having the same data type) that act together as a logical group. Arrays are immediately useful for many types of activities, such as creating the grocery list you might use when shopping, or developing the safety checklist used by airline pilots before takeoff. Arrays are often used to store related information as a list. Because people use lists for almost everything, the list is a familiar concept. Lists of related *elements* like this can be stored as *one-dimensional arrays*.

As an example of how an array would be useful, think of the programming task of reversing a string of characters. Because the last character in the sequence must be the first character in the reversed sequence, each character has to be known before the reversal process can occur. Given a string of five hundred characters, it would be a daunting task to declare all the variables needed for the task. Of course, programming them with the correct values without errors popping up somewhere along the line is quite a chore, too, and a tedious one. To assign characters to each of the variables would require some 500 lines of code, one for each variable. Imagine the nightmarish code that could result from something like this:

```
char ch1   = 'T';
char ch2   = 'h';
char ch3   = 'e';
char ch4   = ' ';

. . .
```

```
char ch500 = '?'

// Print all of the characters
//
cout << ch1 << ch2 << ch3 << ch4 <<

  . . .

  << ch500;
```

Here, there are 500 or so variables named ch1, ch2, ch43, ch450, and so on; the entire process of declaring and working with this many variables having similar names gets out of control rather quickly. Arrays make this same task easy, even elegant.

Understanding One-Dimensional Arrays

A one-dimensional array is stored as a contiguous block of memory, with each element of the array taking up some portion of that memory as shown in Figure 6.1.

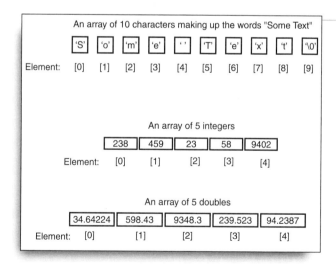

FIGURE 6.1

Array elements occupy contiguous space in computer memory.

One-dimensional arrays are structured variables, with *one name* used by *all* the variables in the array. These variables can share a common name and data type, but each lives in its own unique little section of computer memory, in line with all the others, like houses along a street. Like a house, each array element must have a unique address, and the *element index* of the array makes this possible. A specific array element can be singled out for use by calling it by its name (the array name) followed by the index of the element within the array, like this:

```
char ch[450];
```

This statement accesses character number 451 in the array. The statement accesses character number 451 (and not character number 450) because all C++ arrays are zero-based. For example, if you have an array with 500 elements, the element indexes run from zero (0) for the first element to 499 for the 500th element.

Now consider a character string such as you've seen in several programs in this book:

```
char name[] = "Tara the Dog";
```

The identifier name is the name of the character array, and the set of brackets [ ] is the array index operator. Each character in the string makes up a single scalar variable, a single array element. To identify a specific character in the string, you can use an index into the array. The string seems to contain 12 characters—but don't forget the hidden termination character you learned about back in Chapter 2: the null character \0. Counting the null character, the array contains 13 characters, and each of them lives as a separate scalar variable within the array character variable called name.

Defining an Array

You define an array in the same way you define a singular variable, only different. The difference is that you must identify how many variables you want in the array—you must decide how many elements. The basic syntax for creating a one-dimensional array is as follows:

```
data-type array-name[index-count];
```

For example, the following declaration defines an array of five float values named fnum:

```
float fnum[5];
```

Remember the part about C++ arrays being zero-based? Don't forget! This is one of the most common mistakes novice C++ programmers make. Take a look at this common mistake:

```
float fnum[5];
fnum[5] = 328.5f
```

If I tried to use this snippet of code in a program, the compiler might accept it, but the program would cause unpleasant things to happen in computer memory because the array ranges from fnum[0] to fnum[4]! The variable fnum[5] does not point to the fifth location in the array; it points to the next contiguous location in memory (the nonexistent sixth location in the array). This memory might be occupied by some other system process on your computer at runtime, perhaps your operating system. See how C++ gives you just enough rope to hang yourself? (Or, in this case, it may be just enough to hang your system.) Metaphors aside, here's a look at how you *should* access the elements of an array.

Accessing Array Elements

As you've seen, you access an array element by its index within the array. You've also seen why, if you are not careful with arrays, strange bugs can occur in your program or your computer (or worse, in your customer's computer). So that you can see the specifics of how to access an array, the program in Listing 6.1 demonstrates creating and using an array of integers.

LISTING 6.1   **A Program That Demonstrates Creating and Manipulating an Array of *float* Values**

```
1: /////////////////////////////////////////////////////
2: //  Module  : array1.cpp
3: //
4: //  Purpose : Shows the simple usage of a
5: //            one-dimensional array
6: /////////////////////////////////////////////////////
7:
8: #include <iostream.h>
9:
```

continues…

LISTING 6.1   Continued

```
10: void main()
11: {
12:    // Create an array of five floats
13:    //
14:    float num[5];
15:
16:    // Initialize the array elements with float values
17:    //
18:    num[0] = 3.4f;
19:    num[1] = 7.88f;
20:    num[2] = 29.5f;
21:    num[3] = 56.9f;
22:    num[4] = 34.2f;
23:
24:    // Display the initialized array elements
25:    //
26:    cout << "num[0] == " << num[0] << '\n';
27:    cout << "num[1] == " << num[1] << '\n';
28:    cout << "num[2] == " << num[2] << '\n';
29:    cout << "num[3] == " << num[3] << '\n';
30:    cout << "num[4] == " << num[4] << '\n';
31: }
```

LISTING 6.1

1 Line 14: Declare a float array with five elements

2 Lines 18-22: Assign values to the array elements by index to initialize the array

3 Lines 26-30: Iterate through each array element by index, displaying the result

The output of this program is as expected, displaying the values of all the array elements:

```
num[0] == 3.4
num[1] == 7.88
num[2] == 29.5
num[3] == 56.9
num[4] == 34.2
```

Line 14 of this program shows how you create an array of five floating-point values. Lines 18 through 22 initialize the array by assigning values to its elements. The code from lines 26 through 30 iterates through each array element by index, displaying the result to the screen using cout.

Accessing Array Elements Through Iteration

Elements can be accessed in any order within the given range of an array. The most common way of running through an entire array is with an iteration loop, using a counting variable of some sort to act as the index into the array. Take a look at the following example, in which an array of integers is iterated in a loop:

```
int MyIntArray[5];
for (int i = 0; i < 5; i++)
    MyIntArray[i] = i * 2.25f;
```

The variable i acts as a counting variable, giving access to each array element in a loop. The array index is 0 on the first iteration, 1 on the second, and so on. The program in Listing 6.2 shows this array in action, storing the results of a series of math equations.

LISTING 6.2   A Program That Demonstrates Iterating Through an Array of Five *float* **Values with a Loop**

```
 1: ///////////////////////////////////////////////////
 2: //  Module  : array2.cpp
 3: //
 4: //  Purpose : Shows the simple usage of loops with a
 5: //              one-dimensional array
 6: ///////////////////////////////////////////////////
 7:
 8: #include <iostream.h>
 9:
10: void main()
11: {
12:     // Create an array of five integers
13:     //
14:     float num[5];
15:
16:     // Iterate through the array elements, initializing
17:     // them with float values
18:     //
19:     for (int i = 0; i < 5; i++)
20:         num[i] = i * 2.25f;
21:
```

①

②

LISTING 6.2

① Line 14: Declare a float array with five elements.

② Lines 19-20: Assign values to the array elements using a for loop to initialize the array

continues…

LISTING 6.2 CONTINUED

3 Lines 25-26: Iterate through each array element using a for loop

LISTING 6.2 **Continued**

```
22:    // Iterate through the array elements,
23:    //    displaying their values...
24:
25:    for (i = 0; i < 5; i++)
26:       cout << "num[" << i <<"] == " << num[i] << '\n';    ──┐
                                                                 ├─ 3
27: }                                                         ──┘
```

The output of this program shows the incrementing multiples of 2.25:

```
num[0] == 0
num[1] == 2.25
num[2] == 4.5
num[3] == 6.75
num[4] == 9
```

Like the program in Listing 6.1, the program in Listing 6.2 uses an array of five floating-point values, declared on line 14. Lines 19 and 20 initialize the array by assigning values to each array element using indexes generated in a for loop. The for loop on line 25 and its accompanying output statement on line 26 iterate through each array element again, displaying the results of the earlier multiplication for each element.

Initializing One-Dimensional Arrays During Declaration

Note

If you declare an array of five elements but supply only four initializing values, the fifth element isn't initialized, and so contains some garbage value.

You can initialize the elements of an array at the same time you declare the array. The following code snippet declares a float array of five elements and initializes the elements with five floating-point values:

```
float num[5] = { 3.4f, 7.88f, 29.5f, 56.9f };
```

An interesting side effect of supplying initializers for array elements during declaration is that the compiler knows how many elements the code specifies for initialization. Because of this, you can leave out the numeric specifier for the array, letting the compiler discover it at compile time. For example, the preceding num array can be declared and initialized like this instead:

```
float num[] = { 3.4f, 7.88f, 29.5f, 56.9f };
```

This can be useful when you don't really know (or care to find out) how many elements are in an array. A good example of this is declaring a character array and initializing it with a long string of characters:

```
char text[] = "I don't care how long this text is...";
cout << text;
```

The program in Listing 6.3 demonstrates both of these declaration styles and iterates through the values.

LISTING 6.3   A Program That Demonstrates Creating and Initializing Arrays Simultaneously

```
 1: ////////////////////////////////////////////////////
 2: //  Module  : array3.cpp
 3: //
 4: //  Purpose : Shows the declaration and initialization
 5: //            of a one-dimensional array
 6: ////////////////////////////////////////////////////
 7:
 8: #include <iostream.h>
 9: #include <string.h>
10:
11: void main()
12: {
13:     // Create and initialize two arrays
14:     //
15:     float num[5] = { 3.4f, 7.88f, 29.5f, 56.9f, 34.2f };
16:     char space[] = "I'm spacing out...";
17:
18:     // Iterate through the array elements,
19:     //    displaying their values...
20:
21:     for (int i = 0; i < 5; i++)
22:         cout << "num[" << i <<"] == " << num[i] << '\n';
23:
24:     // Space out a little
25:     //
26:     cout << '\n' << space << '\n';
27:
28:     for (i = 0; i < int(strlen(space)); i++)
29:         cout << space[i] << " ";
30: }
```

LISTING 6.3

1 Lines 15-16: Define and initializes two arrays, an array of floats and an array of chars

2 Lines 21-22: Display each element of the num array individually

3 Lines 28-29: Display each element of the space array individually, adding an extra space between each element

This initialization technique is compact and works well, as the output of the program makes quite clear:

```
num[0] == 3.4
num[1] == 7.88
num[2] == 29.5
num[3] == 56.9
num[4] == 34.2

I'm spacing out...
I ' m   s p a c i n g   o u t . . .
```

This program uses a few simple for loops to iterate through each element of the arrays num and space. The float array num is defined and initialized on line 15; the char array space is defined and initialized on line 16. On lines 21 and 22, you can see the first for loop, used to iterate through the num array, displaying each element and its corresponding value on the screen.

Line 28 begins the for statement used to loop through the space array. The conditional test expression used by this for statement is a comparison between the current iteration value (variable i) and the number of characters in the space array:

```
i < int(strlen(space))
```

This expression uses the Standard C Library function strlen() to get the number of characters in the space array. This function returns a value of type size_t, an alias for unsigned int. The int() wrapper around strlen() explicitly casts the strlen() return value to a signed integer type and then compares this value to the signed integer variable i.

Using Parallel Arrays

Arrays can work in parallel to contain some data that might be related. Parallel arrays can use iterative indexing to access the data from several arrays using a single index. Suppose that Caesar, owner of Caesar's Exotic Bazaar, needs a program to store information about the items in his catalog. The information he needs to store includes an item code, a price, and a description. These three pieces of information could easily coexist in arrays that run parallel to form a basic record containing three items (fields):

```
string ItemCode[5];
double Price[5];
string Description[5];
```

Consider the information presented in Table 6.1. This table shows three columns of items from the catalog. Each of these columns would make a good candidate for storage as arrays. Because the column data is all related, the data in each array would run parallel to the next, as shown in Figure 6.2.

TABLE 6.1 The Data in Each of These Three Columns Can Be Stored in an Array

Item Code	Price ($)	Description
HW-832	12.99	Hammer of Thor (replica)
H-234	5.99	Flower Basket, small
H-584	29.99	Crystal Goblet
H-452	35.99	Wind Chimes
U-235	129.99	Dragon Sculpture

	Item Code	Price ($)	Description
[0] ⟶	HW-832	12.99	Hammer of Thor (replica)
[1] ⟶	H-234	5.99	Flower Basket, small
[2] ⟶	H-584	29.99	Crystal Goblet
[3] ⟶	H-452	35.99	Wind Chimes
[4] ⟶	U-235	129.99	Dragon Sculpture

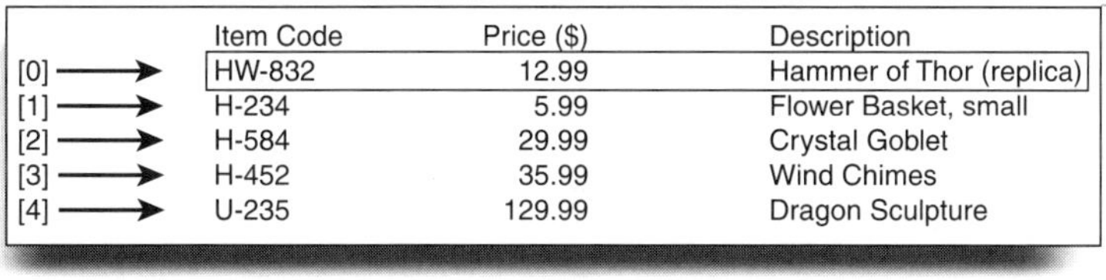

FIGURE 6.2

Columns of related data make good candidates for parallel arrays.

The information for each array can be manipulated in several ways. In general, the same index (whatever its value may be) is used to access elements in each of the three arrays. According to Table 6.1, a hammer costs $12.99 and its item code is HW-832. Using parallel arrays, you could store this related data in the first element of each array like this:

```
ItemCode[0]    = "HW-832";
Price[0]       = 12.99;
Description[0] = "Hammer of Thor (replica)";
```

You could even go so far as to use named constants to make the code even more explicit:

```cpp
const int HAMMER = 0;

ItemCode[HAMMER]    = "HW-832";
Description[HAMMER] = "Hammer of Thor (replica)";
Price[HAMMER]       = 12.99;
```

These both mean the same thing, of course, because HAMMER means zero. The program in Listing 6.4 demonstrates the use of these very same parallel arrays in a bit more depth, storing and displaying some of Caesar's catalog information.

LISTING 6.4   A Program That Uses Parallel Arrays to Handle Related Data

```cpp
 1: /////////////////////////////////////////////////////////
 2: //  Module  : array4.cpp
 3: //
 4: //  Purpose : Shows the simple use of parallel arrays
 5: /////////////////////////////////////////////////////////
 6:
 7: #include <iostream>
 8: #include <string>
 9:
10: using namespace std;
11:
12: const char NL  = '\n';
13: const char TAB = '\t';
14:
15: void main()
16: {
17:     // Declare and initialize the three arrays (the data
18:     // would typically be read from a file on disk...)
19:     //
20:     string ItemCode[5] =
21:     {
22:         "HW-832", "H-234", "H-584", "H-452", "U-235"
23:     };
24:
25:     double Price[5] =
26:     {
27:         12.99, 5.99, 29.99, 35.99, 129.99
28:     };
```

LISTING 6.4

1 Lines 12-13: Define constants for the newline and tab characters

2 Lines 20-23: Define and initializes the array of item codes

3 Lines 25-28: Define and initialize the array of prices

```
29:
30:     string Description[5] =
31:     {
32:         "Hammer of Thor (replica)",
33:         "Flower Basket, small",
34:         "Crystal Goblet",
35:         "Wind Chimes",
36:         "Dragon Sculpture"
37:     };
38:
39:
40:     // Print a little report
41:     //
42:     cout << "Caesar's Exotic Bazaar\n\n";
43:     cout << "Item Code" << TAB
44:         << "Price" << TAB << TAB
45:         << "Description" << NL << NL;
46:
47:     for (int i = 0; i < 5; ++i)
48:     {
49:         cout << ItemCode[i]  << TAB << TAB
50:             << "$" << Price[i] << TAB << TAB
51:             << Description[i] << NL;
52:     }
53: }
```

LISTING 6.4 CONTINUED

4 Lines 30-37: Define and initialize the array of descriptions

5 Lines 42-45: Display a report-header on the screen

6 Lines 47-52: Loop through the arrays, displaying each element in the report

The compact declare-and-initialize technique works well for these array declarations. The output of the program looks like this:

```
Caesar's Exotic Bazaar

Item Code       Price           Description

HW-832          $12.99          Hammer of Thor (replica)
H-234           $5.99           Flower Basket, small
H-584           $29.99          Crystal Goblet
H-452           $35.99          Wind Chimes
U-235           $129.99         Dragon Sculpture
```

Let's take a closer look at how this works. Lines 12 and 13 define constants for the newline and tab characters, which are used to format the output for the report. Lines 20 through 23 define and initialize the ItemCode array with the values from Table 6.1. Likewise, the Price and Description arrays are defined and initialized with the values from Table 6.1 in lines 25 through 28 and lines 30 through 37, respectively.

A header for the report is written to the screen using cout on lines 42 through 45. Finally, the for loop running from lines 47 through 52 iterates through all three arrays simultaneously, in parallel. The current element in each array, as specified by the loop index i, displays each array element to the screen for the report.

As you can see, one-dimensional arrays are a powerful tool for your C++ arsenal, but there are other types of arrays that can be even more useful for certain things. The most-often used of these is the two-dimensional array.

Understanding Two-Dimensional Arrays

A two-dimensional array is an extension of the concepts you've just learned; it literally adds another dimension to your programming power. A one-dimensional array can be thought of as a row of element variables that has only length. You can think of a two-dimensional array as a grid that has both rows **and** columns, both length **and** width. Figure 6.3 shows the difference between the two kinds of arrays.

A two-dimensional array is the perfect vehicle for representing chessmen on a chessboard, formulas in a spreadsheet, or maybe keeping track of a virtual hero as he blasts his way through a labyrinth of alien-infested caverns.

You create a two-dimensional array just like you create a one-dimensional array but with an additional, second set of index brackets. The element arrangement shown in Figure 6.3 is a five-by-five grid. Here's the code needed to create a five-by-five grid of integer variables:

```
int grid[5][5];
```

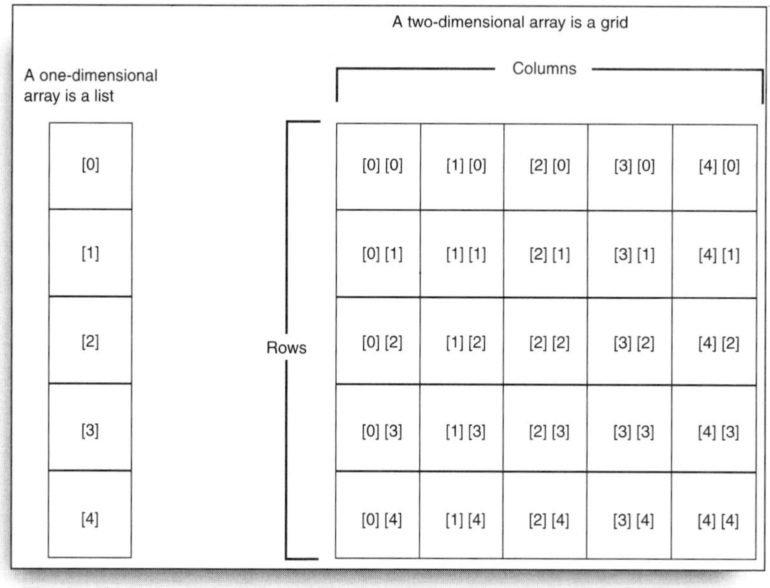

A two-dimensional array is a grid

A one-dimensional array is a list

Columns

Rows

FIGURE 6.3

A one-dimensional array is a row that has only length; a two-dimensional array has both rows and columns—both length and width.

This type of grid structure requires a little additional work from you to set up and maintain, but its ease of use makes it great. The grid is divided into columns and rows, one set of brackets controlling each, as shown in Figure 6.3. This row/column metaphor makes it easy to visualize which array element is being accessed at all times.

Processing Two-Dimensional Arrays

A two-dimensional array uses a pair of array indexes, one for the columns and another for the rows. Figure 6.4, later in this chapter, shows how these rows and columns form a grid that can be used programmatically to represent data that can be displayed in a table of values. A good example of this is a multiplication table: a grid whose values directly relate to the positions those values hold within the grid. For example, at column position 7 and row position 7, the value should be 49. In C++ code, the declaration of the array (the multiplication table) and the assignment of a value looks like this:

```
int MyGrid[10][10];
MyGrid[6][6] = 7 * 7;
```

The first statement allocates space for a ten-by-ten grid of integers. Don't forget that because the array is zero-based, column seven and row seven must be identified with array index 6.

Working with Columns

The columns in a two-dimensional array can be represented by *either* of the pair of indexes used by the array. Because of this, you should take care to be consistent in your use of the index pairs. Whichever of the pair you chose to represent columns, you must obviously use the other to represent rows. The choice boils down to one of two configurations:

- `MyArray[column][row]`
- `MyArray[row][column]`

To display the values of the elements in column number one of a three-by-three array using the `[column][row]` configuration for the index pairs, you use these indexes:

```
int MyArray[3][3];

cout << MyArray[0][0];
cout << MyArray[0][1];
cout << MyArray[0][2];
```

Remember that C++ uses zero-based arrays, so column number one is really `MyArray[0][x]`. The program in Listing 6.5 defines and initializes a two-dimensional array and then sums all the values in a column. This program uses the `[column][row]` configuration for the index pairs, and uses the data in Table 6.2 to fill the array.

TABLE 6.2   Numeric Data Needed to Initialize a Two-Dimensional Array

	Column0	Column1	Column2
Row0	10	40	70
Row1	20	50	80
Row2	30	60	90

LISTING 6.5   A Program That Totals the Column Values in a Two-Dimensional Array

```
1: ////////////////////////////////////////////////////
2: //  Module  : columns.cpp
3: //
4: //  Purpose : Shows the simple use of a 2D array
5: ////////////////////////////////////////////////////
6:
7: #include <iostream>
8: #include <string>
9:
10: using namespace std;
11:
12: ////////////////////////////////////////////////////
13: //  Define some constants
14:
15: const int MAXCOL = 3;
16: const int MAXROW = 3;
17:
18: ////////////////////////////////////////////////////
19: //  main()
20:
21: void main()
22: {
23:    // Define and initialize the 2D array
24:    //
25:    int Array2d[MAXCOL][MAXROW] =
26:    {
27:       {10, 20, 30},  // Column1
28:       {40, 50, 60},  // Column2
29:       {70, 80, 90}   // Column3
30:    };
31:
32:    // Add column #1
33:    //
34:    int sum = 0;
35:    cout << "Column #1 sum total:\n\n";
36:
37:    for (int i = 0; i < MAXROW; ++i)
38:    {
```

❶ Lines 15-16

❷ Lines 25-30

❸ Line 35

❹ Line 37

LISTING 6.5

❶ Lines 15-16: Define two integer constants

❷ Lines 25-30: Define a two-dimensional array and initializes its elements with values

❸ Line 35: Display a description of what's to follow

❹ Line 37: Set up a `for` loop to iterate through row elements

continues...

LISTING 6.5   **Continued**

```
39:        sum += Array2d[0][i]; // total as we iterate ────5
40:
41:        cout << "Array2d[0][" << i << "] == " <<      ⎤
42:            Array2d[0][i] << '\n';                    ⎦── 6
43:    }
44:    cout << "\nColumn Total  == " << sum; ────7
45: }
```

The output for this program shows the result of summing the values in column number one from Table 6.2:

```
Column #1 sum total:

Array2d[0][0] == 10
Array2d[0][1] == 20
Array2d[0][2] == 30


Column Total  == 60
```

The program code is really quite simple. Using constants in place of literal values is a good idea whenever possible in your programs. Lines 15 and 16 define two integer constants: MAXCOL and MAXROW, each of them equal to 3 (in this case). Lines 25 through 30 define the two-dimensional array itself and initialize its elements with the values from Table 6.2. Line 34 then defines the variable sum, which holds the running sum total of all row values in the column.

To display a header of sorts—a description of what's to follow—line 35 uses cout. On line 37, the for loop begins, designed to iterate through row elements 0 through 2. Line 39 actually sums the row element values with each iteration, and lines 41 and 42 display the current row element to the screen. When the loop terminates after processing Array2d[0][2], line 44 displays the sum total of the row values in column number one, stored in the variable sum.

Working with Rows

Like columns, the rows in a two-dimensional array can be
represented by *either* of the pair of indexes used by the array.
The program in Listing 6.6 is a modified version of the one
in Listing 6.5. This program defines and initializes a two-
dimensional array and then sums all the values in a row. This
program also uses the `[column][row]` configuration for the index
pairs and uses the data in Table 6.2 to fill the array.

The only difference is the loop section of the program. Compare
the loops in Listing 6.5 and Listing 6.6 to see the difference.
The loop to sum the values in *column number one* looks like this:

```
for (int i = 0; i < MAXROW; ++i)
{
   sum += Array2d[0][i]; // total as we iterate

   cout << "Array2d[0][" << i << "] == " <<
      Array2d[0][i] << '\n';
}
```

The loop to sum the values in *row number one* looks like this:

```
for (int i = 0; i < MAXCOL; ++i)
{
   sum += Array2d[i][0]; // total as we iterate

   cout << "Array2d[" << i << "][0] == " <<
      Array2d[i][0] << '\n';
}
```

The array indexes are used differently to access either a column
or a row. To display the values of the elements in row number
one of a three-by-three array using the `[column][row]` configuration for the index pairs, you use these indexes:

```
int MyArray[3][3];


cout << MyArray[0][0];
cout << MyArray[1][0];
cout << MyArray[2][0];
```

Remember that C++ uses zero-based arrays, so row number one is really `MyArray[x][0]`. Listing 6.6 presents the entire row-adding program.

LISTING 6.6   A Program That Totals the Row Values in a Two-Dimensional Array

```
 1: ///////////////////////////////////////////////////////
 2: //  Module  : rows.cpp
 3: //
 4: //  Purpose : Shows the simple use of a 2D array
 5: ///////////////////////////////////////////////////////
 6:
 7: #include <iostream>
 8: #include <string>
 9:
10: using namespace std;
11:
12: ///////////////////////////////////////////////////////
13: //  Define some constants
14:
15: const int MAXCOL = 3;
16: const int MAXROW = 3;
17:
18: ///////////////////////////////////////////////////////
19: //  main()
20:
21: void main()
22: {
23:    // Declare and initialize the 2D array
24:    //
25:    int Array2d[MAXCOL][MAXROW] =
26:    {
27:       {10, 20, 30},  // Column1
28:       {40, 50, 60},  // Column2
29:       {70, 80, 90}   // Column3
30:    };
31:
32:    // Add row #1
33:    //
```

LISTING 6.6

1 Lines 15-16: Define two integer constants

2 Lines 25-30: Define a two-dimensional array and initialize its elements with values

```
34:    int sum = 0;
35:    cout << "Row #1 sum total:\n\n";────3
36:
37:    for (int i = 0; i < MAXCOL; ++i) ────4
38:    {
39:       sum += Array2d[i][0]; // total as we iterate ────5
40:
41:       cout << "Array2d[" << i << "][0] == " <<
42:           Array2d[i][0] << '\n';
43:    }
44:    cout << "\nRow Total    == " << sum; ────7
45: }
```

LISTING 6.5 CONTINUED

3   Line 35: Display a description
    of what's to follow

4   Line 37: Set up a for loop to
    iterate through row elements

5   Line 39: Sum the row elements

6   Lines 41-42: Display the current
    column element

7   Line 44: Display the sum total

The output of this program looks like this:

```
Row #1 sum total:

Array2d[0][0] == 10
Array2d[1][0] == 40
Array2d[2][0] == 70

Row Total    == 120
```

Implementing a Multiplication Table

Multiplication tables can have varying numbers of columns and rows, depending on how high you need to multiply. To perform multiplication in a table, you can set up a nested loop to iterate through all the elements of the table, assigning each a value as the loops progress. I like to use named constants when working with arrays to keep literal values out of the source code as much as possible, so I'll again use the named constants MAXCOL and MAXROW, this time initialized to 10:

```
const int MAXCOL = 10;
const int MAXROW = 10;
```

By using the named constants MAXCOL and MAXROW in source code instead of literals, the maximum values of the columns and rows (which define its size) are defined in one place: where they're declared. This arrangement allows you to change the size of the array by changing the constant values of MAXCOL and MAXROW at compile time.

I'll create a 10-by-10 array to use as the multiplication grid, using the constants MAXCOL and MAXROW to predefine, at compile time, the number of columns and rows to allocate. You can create a MAXCOL-by-MAXROW grid for the multiplication table like this:

```
int grid[MAXCOL][MAXROW];
```

You can then iterate through the array, populating the array elements by multiplying the values of the current column and current row at each iteration, like this:

```
int col, row;

for (row = 0; row < MAXROW; row++)
{
   for (col = 0; col < MAXCOL; col++)
   {
      if ((row == 0) && (col == 0))
         grid[col][row] = 0;

      else
         grid[col][row] = col * row;
   }
}
```

This can be a little confusing to understand at first glance; take a look at Figure 6.4, which shows the column and row layout for the multiplication grid.

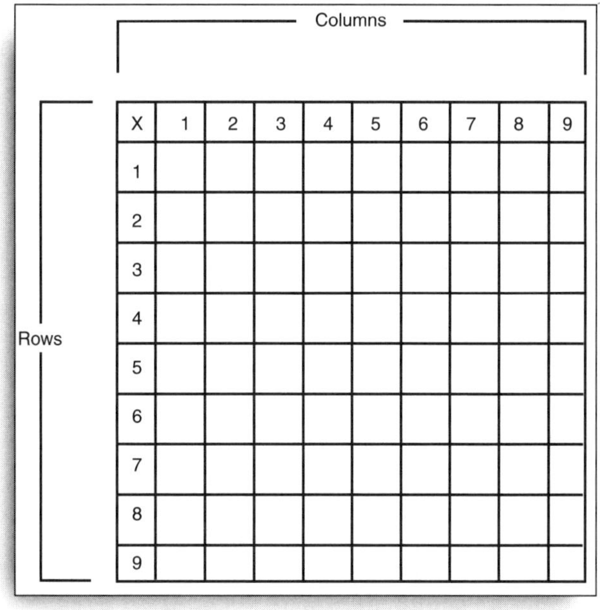

FIGURE 6.4

The column and row layout for the multiplication grid.

Now look at the code in Listing 6.7. This program creates a two-dimensional array representing a multiplication table. The program uses the array to track the values for the table.

LISTING 6.7   A Program That Demonstrates Using a Two-Dimensional Array to Create a Multiplication Table

```
 1: /////////////////////////////////////////////////
 2: //   Module  : MultTable.cpp
 3: //
 4: //   Purpose : Creating a multiplication table from a
 5: //             two-dimensional array
 6: /////////////////////////////////////////////////
 7:
 8: #include <iostream.h>
 9:
10: void main()
```

continues…

LISTING 6.7 **Continued**

```
11: {
12:     const int MAXCOL = 10;
13:     const int MAXROW = 10;
14:
15:     // Create a 10x10 grid for the multiplication table
16:     //
17:     int grid[MAXCOL][MAXROW];
18:     int row, col;
19:
20:     // Iterate and populate the array elements,
21:     //
22:     for (row = 0; row < MAXROW; row++)
23:         for (col = 0; col < MAXCOL; col++)
24:             grid[col][row] = col * row;
25:
26:     // Iterate through the array elements,
27:     //   displaying their values...
28:
29:     for (row = 0; row < MAXROW; row++)
30:     {
31:         for (col = 0; col < MAXCOL; col++)
32:         {
33:             if ((row == 0) && (col == 0))
34:                 cout << 'x';
35:
36:             else if (col == 0)
37:                 cout << row;            // Column header
38:
39:             else if (row == 0)
40:                 cout << col;            // Row header
41:
42:             else
43:                 cout << grid[col][row]; // Product
44:
45:             if (col != MAXCOL - 1)      // Last col: no tab
46:                 cout << '\t';
47:
48:         }
49:         cout << "\n\n";  // Next row, space it nicely
50:     }
51: }
```

The output of this program shows the resulting multiplication table:

x	1	2	3	4	5	6	7	8	9
1	1	2	3	4	5	6	7	8	9
2	2	4	6	8	10	12	14	16	18
3	3	6	9	12	15	18	21	24	27
4	4	8	12	16	20	24	28	32	36
5	5	10	15	20	25	30	35	40	45
6	6	12	18	24	30	36	42	48	54
7	7	14	21	28	35	42	49	56	63
8	8	16	24	32	40	48	56	64	72
9	9	18	27	36	45	54	63	72	81

Let's go over some of the high points of this program. Take a look at program lines 12 and 13, which define the two integer constants MAXCOL and MAXROW. These are used again in the array definition on line 17. Line 18 introduces the col and row variables, used to access the array elements. (Using these variable names when accessing the array elements is less prone to error than using variable names such as x and y.)

The nested for loops running from lines 22 through 24 iterate through the array elements, calculating the table values while iterating. The actual multiplication used to get the display value occurs on line 24.

The rest of the program, lines 29 through 50, displays the multiplication table. The display of the table is accomplished with another nested for loop. Lines 33 and 34 handle the case of row 1, column 1 (grid[0][0]), outputting a single character x to the display. The else-if statements from lines 36 through 40 display row and column headers, 1 though 9. If none of the first three clauses in this long `if` statement is true, the `else` clause kicks in by default, displaying the pre-multiplied contents of the current column and row (`grid[col][row]`).

Lines 45 and 46 use a tab character to space the columns evenly during the iterated output of the table to the screen (for all columns except the last one—it doesn't need another tab character). The inner loop runs once for each column. When a column is complete, the inner loop terminates (line 48) and two newline characters are written to the screen to drop down two lines on the screen, ready for the next row.

Multi-Dimensional Arrays

Even a two-dimensional array sometimes isn't enough. You can add another dimension to create a multi-dimensional array such as a three-dimensional array or a four-dimensional array. Multi-dimensional arrays can go to much higher dimensions than four dimensions, but most programmers can't successfully cope with that level of dimensional complexity—I'm one of them. Multi-dimensional arrays with more than four dimensions tax my common sense a bit, so I tend to stay away from them (most programmers do). In fact, you'll rarely find a need to go beyond the fourth dimension with arrays.

I'll stick to an example that should be easy for everyone (even me!) to conceptualize. Remember that a grid uses columns and rows, which could just as easily be called length and width. Now imagine a stack of grids, gaining volume: The array has not only length and width, but height as well. This is a three-dimensional array, logically forming a box-like structure to hold your data, as shown in Figure 6.5.

This box metaphor is useful in visualizing the locations of individual elements in a 3D array. The three array dimensions can each represent anything you want in terms of the real world. You aren't constrained to thinking in terms of length, width, and height. As an example, Listing 6.8 uses a three-dimensional array to represent a calendar, or more specifically, a five-year log of daily activities for a temporal physicist. The program uses the three array dimensions as day, month, and year.

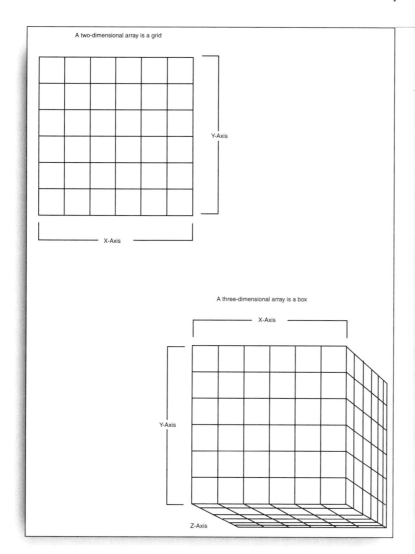

A two-dimensional array is a grid

Y-Axis

X-Axis

A three-dimensional array is a box

X-Axis

Y-Axis

Z-Axis

FIGURE 6.5

A three-dimensional array is formed from a stack of grids.

LISTING 6.8   Using a Three-Dimensional Array to Keep a Five-Year Log of Daily Activities

```
1: ////////////////////////////////////////////////
2: //  Module  : array5.cpp
3: //
4: //  Purpose : Shows the use of a three-dimensional
5: //            array
6: ////////////////////////////////////////////////
7:
```

continues...

LISTING 6.8   **Continued**

```
 8: #include <iostream>
 9: #include <string>
10:
11: using namespace std;
12:
13: //////////////////////////////////////////////////////
14: // Define five journal entries as macros
15:
16: #define LogEntry1 "Jan 1, Year 1.\nI feel a certain \
17: sense of apprehension in this place. Almost \
18: everyone seems to \nbe gone now..."
19:
20: #define LogEntry2 "Mar 10, Year 1.\nMy view of the  \
21: secret world has improved with the new \
22: phase-modulator...";
23:
24: #define LogEntry3 "Aug 16, Year 2.\nThe natives of \
25: the cliff area have vanished this time, but \
26: shockwaves from the \nvalley are...";
27:
28: #define LogEntry4 "Dec 25, Year 4.\nChristmas again. \
29: I haven't seen a hint of snow for over two years...";
30:
31: #define LogEntry5 "Jun 7, Year 5.\nI can't believe my \
32: eyes, my team's found the wormhole, coming any day...";
33:
34: //////////////////////////////////////////////////////
35: // Some constants to make the program more readable
36:
37: const char NL   = '\n';        ❶
38:
39: const short MAXDAY   = 31;  ⎤
40: const short MAXMONTH = 12;  ⎬ ❷
41: const short MAXYEAR  = 5;   ⎦
42:
43: const short JAN = 0;   ⎤
44: const short FEB = 1;   ⎟
45: const short MAR = 2;   ⎟
46: const short APR = 3;   ⎟
47: const short MAY = 4;   ⎟
48: const short JUN = 5;   ⎬ ❸
49: const short JUL = 6;   ⎟
50: const short AUG = 7;   ⎟
51: const short SEP = 8;   ⎟
52: const short OCT = 9;   ⎟
53: const short NOV = 10;  ⎟
54: const short DEC = 11;  ⎦
```

```
55:
56: //////////////////////////////////////////////////////
57: // main()
58:
59: void main()
60: {
61:     // Declare and initialize the array with the five
62:     // macro entries (the data would typically be read
63:     // from a file on disk...)
64:     //
65:     string DailyLog[MAXDAY][MAXMONTH][MAXYEAR];    ──4
66:     string LogEntry;
67:
68:     DailyLog[0][JAN][0]  = LogEntry1;
69:     DailyLog[10][MAR][0] = LogEntry2;
70:     DailyLog[16][AUG][1] = LogEntry3;   ──5
71:     DailyLog[25][DEC][3] = LogEntry4;
72:     DailyLog[7][JUN][4]  = LogEntry5;
73:
74:     // Print a log header
75:     //
76:     cout << "Log Entries:" << NL << NL;   ──6
77:
78:     // Print all log entries
79:     //
80:     short day, month, year;   ──7
81:
82:     for (year = 0; year < MAXYEAR; ++year)
83:     {
84:         for (month = 0; month < MAXMONTH; ++month)
85:         {
86:             for (day = 0; day < MAXDAY; ++day)      ──8
87:             {
88:                 LogEntry = DailyLog[day][month][year];
89:                 if (LogEntry.size() != 0)
90:                     cout << LogEntry << NL << NL;
91:             }
92:         }
93:     }
94: }
```

LISTING 6.8 CONTINUED

4 Line 65: Declare the 3D array

5 Lines 68-72: Write the log entries to the log in the specified locations

6 Line 76: Output a log header

7 Line 80: Define variables for day, month, and year

8 Lines 82-93: Iterate through the log array, displaying only log entries that contain data

The output of this program shows the resulting log entries from the array, as you can see in Figure 6.6.

FIGURE 6.6

The console output of the five-
year log program in Listing 6.8.

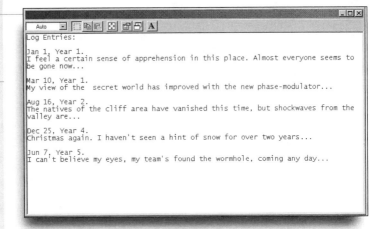

```
Log Entries:

Jan 1, Year 1.
I feel a certain sense of apprehension in this place. Almost everyone seems to
be gone now...

Mar 10, Year 1.
My view of the  secret world has improved with the new phase-modulator...

Aug 16, Year 2.
The natives of the cliff area have vanished this time, but shockwaves from the
valley are...

Dec 25, Year 4.
Christmas again. I haven't seen a hint of snow for over two years...

Jun 7, Year 5.
I can't believe my eyes, my team's found the wormhole, coming any day...
```

This program declares five macros to hold the long strings used as log entries (lines 16 through 32); lines 39 through 41 specify constants for the maximum values of day, month, and year in the log. Lines 43 through 54 name and number the 12 months of the year as constant values (adding a lot of readability to the code).

The 3D array `DailyLog` is defined on line 65; lines 68 through 72 write the log entries to the log in the specified `DailyLog[day][month][year]` index locations. Line 80 defines three variables for day, month, and year, used in the iteration of the array. Lines 82 through 93 encompass a `for` loop with two nested levels, running from year to month to day. These loops iterate through the log array, displaying only log entries that contain data.

Line 88 gets the log entry string from the current array element. Line 89 uses the standard string member function `size()` to see whether the string is empty. Only if the string has a size greater than zero does the program display the log entry (line 90).

As you've seen in this chapter, arrays can certainly add programming power to your programs. Next up—a look at functions.

Creating and Using Functions

Learn about various types of functions

Understand function return types and values

Find out how to create your own functions

Discover how to use command-line arguments

Find out how to use variable-argument lists

See how to make functions reusable with modules

Why Use Functions?

Interface

A connecting link that allows independent systems, such as a user and a computer, to meet and communicate.

Functions are extremely important in C++, and any real C++ program will have at least one custom function designed to perform some of the program's work. By creating your own functions, you open the door to an endless world of possibilities. In this chapter, you'll see how to conceptualize and write your own functions. You'll also see how to pass data to the functions, process this data, and return a useful result to the caller of the function.

Information Hiding

Functions should not modify any global data because this can easily lead to side effects (also known as bugs). By passing in function arguments for any outside data a function needs, you can help minimize the risk of side effects.

When you create a function of your own design, you must think carefully about what you want the function to do, and how it should interface with the rest of the program. Choose a descriptive function name and think about the *interface* between your new function and the outside world. A robust function interface is extremely important. As a general rule, a function shouldn't modify any global data. It should only perform its task using its own internal data, along with any data passed into the function as function parameters. Figure 7.1 identifies the basic syntax of a function call.

FIGURE 7.1

The basic syntax of a function call—passing data to the function using parameters.

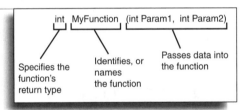

```
int  MyFunction  (int Param1,  int Param2)
```
Specifies the function's return type

Identifies, or names the function

Passes data into the function

Calling functions is easy—you just use the function name followed by a pair of parentheses enclosing the parameter list. A function is always called by another function (with the exception of `main()`, which is called by the operating system). The **called** function must often be able to receive data from the **calling** function. This data is passed to the called function through its *parameters*, its interface to the world outside the function. How a called function works internally isn't really important to the calling function—that's the called function's own secret inner world. All the calling function really needs to know is the following:

■ The type of data the called function expects to receive as parameter data

■ The type of data the called function returns

Various Types of Functions

There are three general kinds of functions:

■ Void functions

■ Functions that return a value

■ Inline functions

Each of these types of function has the same basic structure and syntax, with a few differences. Let's take a closer look at all three types of functions.

Void Functions

A void function is a function that returns no value. A void function uses the C++ keyword `void` as the return type in its function declaration and definition. Void functions are subroutines you call to perform processing of some sort, without the need to return any value. Consider the following void function declaration:

```
void About();
```

As its name hints, this function should print information about something to the screen. To create a function that does this, we could simply use the following function definition:

```
void About()
{
    cout << "You'd put real information here...\n"
    cout << "and possibly here...\n"
}
```

Then, by just calling the `About()` function in your code, whatever text the function specifies is printed to the screen. As a concrete example, the program in Listing 7.1 does just that.

LISTING 7.1   **A Program Showing the Use of a Simple Function**

```
1: /////////////////////////////////////////////////////
2: //  Module  : func1.cpp
3: //
4: //  Purpose : Shows the usage of a simple function
5: /////////////////////////////////////////////////////
6:
7: #include <iostream.h>
8:
9: // Global constants
10: //
11: const char *PROGNAME = "Function Sample Program #1";
12: const char *AUTHOR   = "Rob McGregor";
13:
14: // Function prototype
15: //
16: void About();
17:
18: /////////////////////////////////////////////////////
19: //  About()
20:
21: void About()
22: {
23:    cout << PROGNAME;
24:    cout << "\n   From \"Using C++\"\n   by " <<
25:       AUTHOR <<'\n';
26: }
27:
28: /////////////////////////////////////////////////////
29: //  Driver : main()
30:
31: void main()
32: {
33:    // Call the sole function...
34:    //
35:    About();
36: }
```

The output from this program is shown here:

```
Function Sample Program #1
   From "Using C++"
   by Rob McGregor
```

The program itself is quite simple, making only a single function call. On lines 11 and 12, two global constants are declared: PROGNAME and AUTHOR. These two constants are used as strings for the About() function, whose prototype appears on line 16.

Lines 21 through 26 provide the definition for the About() function, using the cout object to display some text, including PROGNAME and AUTHOR. The main() function, defined from lines 31 through 36, simply calls the About() function to display its message before terminating execution.

Functions That Return a Value

Functions that don't specify void as the return type must return a value of some sort to the function caller. An example of this is a simple function that squares a number, returning the value of the number times itself:

```
long Square()
{
    return num * num;
}
```

A function like this needs only one piece of information from the outside—the number to square. What is the value of num? This information can be sent into the function as a *function parameter*. Parameters are the interface to a function, allowing code outside a function to provide it with information, to communicate with that function.

To send a specific number to the Square() function, you simply add a parameter variable to the function declaration, like this:

```
long Square(const long num)
{
    return num * num;
}
```

The declaration const long num inside the function call parentheses is the parameter declaration. This means that the function expects to receive a long integer as a parameter. The const modifier places a restriction on the parameter: It guarantees that the function can't modify the value num behind your back—that it will remain constant within the function.

Function Parameter

A variable local to a function which takes on the value of an argument passed to the function.

Use const for Protection

You should use the const modifier for any function parameter that shouldn't change value within a function. This protects you from unwelcome bugs resulting from parameter data that has unexpectedly changed value within a function.

Naturally, functions aren't limited to a single parameter. Functions can have as many parameters as needed, but fewer parameters make for a friendlier function interface. How about a function that extends the functionality provided by the Square() function? By adding a second parameter, you can create a similar function that raises a number to **any** power—not just to the second power, as Square() does. One possible implementation of this is the Power() function shown here:

```
long Power(const long num, const int pow)
{
    long RetVal = num;

    if (num == 1) return 1;

    for (int i = 1; i < pow; i++)
        RetVal *= num;

    return RetVal;
}
```

This function uses a for loop to multiply the value provided by the num parameter repeatedly, until it reaches the desired power. The program in Listing 7.2 shows both the Square() and Power() functions in action.

LISTING 7.2   **Using Function Parameters to Perform Some Useful Math Operations**

```
 1: /////////////////////////////////////////////////////////
 2: //  Module  : func2.cpp
 3: //
 4: //  Purpose : Shows the usage of functions that use
 5: //            parameters
 6: /////////////////////////////////////////////////////////
 7:
 8: #include <iostream.h>
 9:
10: // Function prototype
11: //
```

```
12: long Square(const long num);
13: long Power(const long num, const int pow);
14:
15: /////////////////////////////////////////////////
16: //   Square()
17:
18: long Square(const long num)
19: {
20:     return num * num;
21: }
22:
23: /////////////////////////////////////////////////
24: //   Power()
25:
26: long Power(const long num, const int pow)
27: {
28:     long RetVal = num;
29:     if (num == 1) return 1;
30:     for (int i = 1; i < pow; i++)
31:        RetVal *= num;
32:
33:     return RetVal;
34: }
35:
36: /////////////////////////////////////////////////
37: //   Driver : main()
38:
39: void main()
40: {
41:     // Use the Square() and Power() functions...
42:     //
43:     cout << "3 * 3 = " << Square(3);
44:     cout << "\n6 * 6 = " << Square(6);
45:     cout << "\nTwo to the fourth power is "
46:        << Power(2, 4);
47:     cout << "\nEight to the third power is "
48:        << Power(8, 3);
49:     cout << "\nFive to the third power is "
50:        << Power(5, 3);
51:}
```

LISTING 7.2

1 Lines 12-13: Prototypes for the Square() and Power() functions

2 Lines 18-21: The Square() function

3 Lines 26-34: The Power() function

4 Lines 43-44: Invoke the Square() function

5 Lines 45-50: Invoke the Power() function

This program uses the function parameters for the Square() and Power() functions to perform some useful math operations. The output from the program looks like this:

```
3 * 3 = 9
6 * 6 = 36
Two to the fourth power is 16
Eight to the third power is 512
Five to the third power is 125
```

Lines 12 and 13 provide the function prototypes for both Square() and Power(). Lines 18 through 21 provide the definition for the Square() function, and lines 26 through 34 provide the definition for the Power() function.

The main() function runs from lines 39 through 51 and calls the Square() and Power() functions, sending various arguments to the functions and displaying the values on the screen.

Inline Functions

Inline Function

Inline functions tell the compiler to replace every inline function call in the source code with the function body code.

Calling a function takes a bit of time. First, the caller has to call the function. The program locates the function, and program execution enters the function. Then the function does its work. Next, the return value is sent back to the caller, and execution leaves the function, returning it to the caller. Conversely, *inline functions* tell the compiler to replace every inline function call in the source code with the function body code, avoiding the overhead of the function call altogether.

When you declare a function to be an inline function, you're telling the compiler to try to substitute the function definition for every corresponding function call. However, the compiler doesn't always inline a function, especially if it's too large to inline—you should only inline small functions.

Remember the Square() and Power() functions from Listing 7.2? An inline version of the Square() function looks like this:

```
inline long Square(const long num)
{
    return num * num;
}
```

Recall that the original function call to Square() in the source code looks like this:

```
cout << "6 * 6 = " << Square(6);
```

The inline version of this function after compiler translation would replace the function call with the function body, giving you this:

```
cout << "6 * 6 = " << 6 * 6;
```

An inline version of the Power() function looks like this:

```
inline long Power(const long num, const int pow)
{
   long RetVal = num;

   for (int i = 0; i < pow; i++)
      RetVal *= num;

   return RetVal;
}
```

Recall that the original function call to Power() in Listing 7.2 looks like this:

```
cout << "\nEight to the third power is "
   << Power(8, 3);
```

The compiler translation for an inline version of the Power() function looks something like this:

```
cout << "\nEight to the third power is " <<
{
   RetVal = 8;
   for (int i = 0; i < 3; i++)
      RetVal *= 8;
};
```

The inline function will execute faster because no processor time is wasted by jumping to the function, executing it, and returning a value—everything's done inline.

SEE ALSO

➤ *For more information on function call efficiency, see page 209*

Only Inline Small Functions

The inline modifier is a request to the compiler to expand the function code within the calling code—to "inline the function." The compiler can choose to ignore this request if the performance cost of inlining the function becomes greater than the performance cost of the function call itself.

The larger the function, the less likely it is that the compiler will inline it. Functions that use the inline keyword should be simple, without too many lines of code. Unfortunately, various compilers use various means to measure where this inline threshold of too many lines lies, so it's difficult to generalize about how many is too many lines of code.

Components of a Function

Functions can have various components, including these:

- Function return types and values
- Function parameters
- Default parameters

You've already seen examples that use almost all these components, but the next sections look at each component in more detail.

Function Return Types and Values

Return Type

A function's *return type* specifies the type of value that function should return to its caller.

Return Value

The value which is returned by a function.

A function's *return type* specifies the type of value that function should return to its caller. The final statement that executes in a function returning a value is the `return` statement, which specifies the *return value*. Consider this function declaration:

```
int GetNumber();
```

Based on this declaration, the function would return an integer value, maybe like this:

```
int GetNumber()
{
    return 100;
}
```

or like this:

```
int GetNumber()
{
    int retval = 100;

    // Do something with retval...
    // ...

    return retval;
}
```

Now consider this function declaration:

```
float GetNumber();
```

Based on this declaration, the function would return a `float` value to the caller, maybe like this:

```
float GetNumber()
{
    return 100.0f;
}
```

or like this:

```
float GetNumber()
{
    float retval = 100.0f;

    // Do something with retval...
    // ...

    return retval;
}
```

Function Parameters

Function *parameters* are extremely important for the purposes of data hiding and abstraction. By making your functions use parameters instead of using shared global variables, you make code more robust and less prone to error. Function parameters make it possible for a function to perform the processing required by its caller. Function parameters must be made up of a `type-specifier` (the data type part) and a `declarator` (the identifier part), like this:

```
return-type-specifier
FunctionDeclarator(param-type-specifier ParamDeclarator);
```

Multiple parameters are passed to a function as a comma-separated list of type-specifier/declarator pairs. Here's a sample function that calculates the average value of three integers:

```
float AverageThreeInts(int Num1, int Num2, int Num3)
{
    return float(Num1 + Num2 + Num3) / 3.0f;
}
```

You could then call the function like this, storing the average value in the variable avg:

```
float avg = AverageThreeInts(5, 12, 16);
```

It's important to remember that a function can **receive many** parameter values, but it can **return only one** value. Figure 7.2 shows this concept. The value returned from the body of the function must be of the same data type as the function return type specified in the function header.

FIGURE 7.2

The basic syntax of a function call—passing data to the function using parameters.

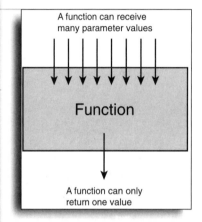

A function can receive many parameter values

Function

A function can only return one value

Default Parameters

C++ allows you to specify default values for function parameters, making it even easier to call a function by reducing the number of parameters it may be necessary to pass. If you supply a default parameter, all other parameters following that parameter in the parameter list must have defaults too. For example, given the following enumerated type, this ShowMessage() function prototype uses a default parameter correctly:

```
enum MessageStyle { msLowercase, msUppercase, msNormal };
int ShowMessage(char *msg, MessageStyle ms = msLowerCase);
```

A lot of functions have parameters that aren't often used, so default values provide argument data for these automatically. Here's an example: Suppose that I want to show a message using the ShowMessage() function. All I have to do is this:

```
ShowMessage("My message...");
```

By sending only one argument to the function, the default value of `msLowerCase` is assigned to the second argument. Notice that the argument is a string literal. C++ regards the first character of the string as the first element of a character array, because these two expressions are equivalent:

```
char *msg  = "Text";
char msg[] = "Text";
```

You'll see more about this in Chapter 10, "Using Pointers and References," as you read about pointers.

Creating Your Own Functions

So far, you've seen a lot of function activity going on in this chapter. Each function used in the sample programs has a declaration and a definition. The declaration, called a *prototype*, is the function's interface to the rest of the code in a program. You must abide by this interface because C++ is highly type safe, and because the compiler is very picky about proper data types in function arguments.

In the function definition, the function header must be the same as the function declaration's interface in the prototype, but the body of the function can be whatever you need it to be.

Declaring a Function

You create a function prototype by deciding what types of data the function needs from the outside world. You create a parameter list for the function based on this data. You then decide on a descriptive name for the function and create a prototype for the function.

Consider a function that adds together all the numbers in a range of numbers. This function would return a value representing the sum of these numbers. The function would also need a few pieces of data to use in processing the required information (the sum of all the numbers). The function might be called `SumRange()`, and it sums all numbers in the range specified by two

Prototype

Consists of the function's name, parameter list, and return type.

parameters, perhaps called `NumStart` and `NumEnd`. A preliminary prototype for the function might look like this:

```
SumRange(NumStart, NumEnd);
```

The type of numeric data to provide is an important consideration that can change depending on the design goals of the program. For this example, I've chosen to use `long` integer data. With this decision made, the completed function prototype looks like this:

```
long SumRange(long NumStart, long NumEnd);
```

Defining a Function

Implement

To write the source code that defines the body of the declaration.

Given the specification provided by the function prototype for `SumRange()`, you can now *implement* the function—create its function definition. The first task is to write the skeleton for the function definition, using the prototype as a model:

```
long SumRange(long NumStart, long NumEnd)
{
    // Do something
}
```

Using Local Variables

Global

An identifier that is available to all levels of a program.

Variables you define outside any function are considered *global*. These variables can be seen and modified by any function—and this is where bugs can easily crop up. Function parameters are a much better way to pass data to functions to see and modify.

Local Variables

Identifiers created within a function body that exist only within that function.

Variables created within a function body exist only within that function; they are called *local variables*. The `SumRange()` function must return a value of type `long`, so let's get that out of the way. By creating the local variable `retval` as type `long`, I can safely store a value for the function to return, like this:

```
long SumRange(long NumStart, long NumEnd)
{
    long retval = 0;
    //
    // Do something to alter retval
    //
    return retval;
}
```

The life span for `retval` is short; this variable goes out of scope as soon as program execution leaves the `SumRange()` function.

The third and final incarnation of the function uses a `for` loop to iterate through the number range, adding numbers throughout, and storing the value in `retval`, like this:

```
long SumRange(long NumStart, long NumEnd)
{
    int retval = 0;

    for (int i = NumStart; i < NumEnd + 1; i++)
        retval += i;

    return retval;
}
```

Using Command-Line Arguments

Command-line arguments make programs much more user friendly. They allow a user to specify several options on the command line—or more commonly, in batch or script files. A good program should always explain what these parameters are, a task that has traditionally been done with a `Usage()` function that displays the directions for the program.

Command-line arguments are passed to a program from the operating system through the use of two parameters added to the `main()` function. Understanding these two parameters is key to command-line processing. The first parameter is an integer value that traditionally has been called `argc`. Although you can name this parameter anything you want, I'll stick with tradition and use `argc`. The second parameter is an array of character strings traditionally called `argv[]`.

The first command-line argument is always implicitly present, sent from the operating system when the program runs. This first parameter is the fully qualified path to the executable that's running. I often use a make file called `test.mak` to compile and link simple programs. Assuming that the program compiles and links successfully, I get a `test.exe` file that I can run.

This means that the path to the executable is the first element of the argument array (that is, it is argv[0]), which may look like this:

```
K:\RWM\BOOKS\USINGCPP\SOURCE\CHAP7\TEST.EXE
```

Getting the Number of Arguments

The function argument argc tells how many parameters have been passed to the program. If argc is equal to 1, no parameters have been passed. A simple check on the value of argc can quickly let your program know whether to process command-line arguments or not. Assume that the value of argc is less than 2 and that the program expects at least one command-line argument. A simple check can see whether the user forgot the parameter and tell the user so, like this:

```
if (argc < 2)
{
    cout << "Error, no command line arguments.\n"
    cout << "Terminating program execution...\n"
    return;
}
```

Getting and Using the Arguments

As I said earlier, there is always at least one argument sent to a program: the fully qualified path to the executable, which is stored in the argv array at element zero:

```
char *program_path = argv[0];
```

You can display all command-line arguments on the screen with a simple for loop, using values from 0 to argc-1 as element indexes into the argv[] array, like this:

```
for (int i = 0; i < argc; ++i)
{
    cout << "argv[" << i << "] is: "
        << argv[i] << '\n';
}
```

Take a look at the program in Listing 7.3, which displays all command-line arguments using this type of loop.

LISTING 7.3   A Program That Displays All Command-Line Arguments Sent to It

```
1: /////////////////////////////////////////////////////
2: //  Module  : func3.cpp
3: //
4: //  Purpose : Shows the usage of command line
5: //            parameters
6: /////////////////////////////////////////////////////
7:
8: #include <iostream.h>
9:
10: void main(int argc, char *argv[])
11: {
12:     // Display all command line arguments
13:     //
14:     for (int i = 0; i < argc; ++i)
15:     {
16:        cout << "argv[" << i << "] is: "
17:            << argv[i] << '\n';
18:     }
19: }
```

LISTING 7.3

1 Line 10: The main() function accepting command-line arguments

2 Lines 14-17: Loop through the arguments, accessing each with the index variable i

Here's the command line I used for a test run of the program:

```
test.exe /? /h /H /Q /s a_word_or_two
```

The output of the program displays all items sent from the command line as arguments to the program. Using the preceding command line, the output from the program in Listing 7.3 looks like this:

```
argv[0] is: K:\RWM\BOOKS\USINGCPP\SOURCE\CHAP7\TEST.EXE
argv[1] is: /?
argv[2] is: /h
argv[3] is: /H
argv[4] is: /Q
argv[5] is: /s
argv[6] is: a_word_or_two
```

This program uses a simple for loop to iterate through all the command-line arguments it receives, displaying each to the screen. On line 14, the value of argc is used as the loop termination condition in the for loop. For each iteration, the variable i holds the index of the current command-line argument being processed, which is the index of a string in the argv[] array or strings.

So how do you use the information that this process makes available to you? All you really have to do is analyze the arguments the user sends from the command line and have your program respond appropriately for each argument. One way to do this is with a modified version of the loop you saw in Listing 7.3. The modifications involve checking each command-line argument in the argv[] array to see whether the item is a command-line argument (or *switch*) your program recognizes. Such a loop would look like this:

```
for (int i = 0; i < argc; ++i)
{
   // Check for /?
   //
   if (!strcmp(argv[i], "/?")) // User wants help
   {
      Usage();
      return;
   }

   //
   // Check for other switches...
   //
}
```

The ANSI C function strcmp() is used to compare two character strings. The resulting return value is zero if the strings are the same.

A Command-Line Argument-Processing Program

Now let's develop a program that uses command-line switches to set internal program options. Let's make the program display a line of text in various ways, depending on the command-line arguments provided. The program takes all code out of main() except calls to other functions. Six custom functions defined within the program perform all the work for the program. These six functions are as follows:

- LCase()

- UCase()

- DisplayText()

- ProcessArgs()

- TryBail()

- Usage()

All program functionality is broken into these functions, whose prototypes look like this:

```
void char* LCase(char *str);
void char* UCase(char *str);
void DisplayText(short style);
void ProcessArgs(int argc, char *argv[]);
void TryBail(int argc);
void Usage();
```

The text displayed by the program can be displayed in all upper-case characters, all lowercase characters, or normal characters, depending on the argument sent to the DisplayText() function. Command-line argument processing is handled in the ProcessArgs() function. The TryBail() function just checks to see whether any command-line arguments are present. The Usage() function displays the syntax and usage of all command-line parameters supported by the program. Listing 7.4 gives the details for each of these functions.

LISTING 7.4 **A Program That Uses Command-Line Arguments to Set Program Options**

```
 1: //////////////////////////////////////////////////////
 2: //  Module  : func4.cpp
 3: //
 4: //  Purpose : Shows the usage of command line
 5: //            arguments
 6: //////////////////////////////////////////////////////
 7:
 8: #include <iostream.h>
 9: #include <ctype.h>
10: #include <stdlib.h>
11: #include <string.h>
```

LISTING 7.4

1 Lines 8-11: Include all header files needed by the program

continues…

LISTING 7.4 CONTINUED

2 Lines 15-20: List prototypes for custom functions defined in the program

3 Lines 24-26: List global constants for specifying a sentence style

4 Lines 31-40: Usage() instructs the user about valid command-line switches

5 Lines 45-54: UCase() modifies a string to use all uppercase letters

LISTING 7.4   **Continued**

```
12:
13: // Function prototypes
14: //
15: char* LCase(char *str);
16: char* UCase(char *str);
17: void DisplayText(short style);
18: void ProcessArgs(int argc, char *argv[]);
19: void TryBail(int argc);
20: void Usage();
21:
22: // Sentence style module-level constants
23: //
24: const short NORMAL    = 0;
25: const short UPPERCASE = 1;
26: const short LOWERCASE = 2;
27:
28: ////////////////////////////////////////////////////
29: //   Usage()
30:
31: void Usage()
32: {
33:    cout << "Usage:\n\n";
34:    cout << "    TEST [/?][/N][/U][/L]\n\n";
35:    cout << "Valid command line switches are:\n\n";
36:    cout << "/?  \tDisplays this usage message.\n";
37:    cout << "/N  \tDisplays text normally.\n";
38:    cout << "/U  \tDisplays text all uppercase.\n";
39:    cout << "/L  \tDisplays text all lowercase.\n";
40: }
41:
42: ////////////////////////////////////////////////////
43: //   UCase()
44:
45: char* UCase(char *str)
46: {
47:    // Convert each char in the string to uppercase
48:    //
49:    int len = strlen(str);
50:    for (int i = 0; i < len; i++)
51:        str[i] = toupper(str[i]);
52:
53:    return str;
54: }
```

```
55:
56: /////////////////////////////////////////////////////
57: //   LCase()
58:
59: char* LCase(char *str)
60: {
61:     // Convert each char in the string to lowercase
62:     //
63:     int len = strlen(str);
64:     for (int i = 0; i < len; i++)
65:         str[i] = tolower(str[i]);
66:
67:     return str;
68: }
69:
70: /////////////////////////////////////////////////////
71: //   DisplayText()
72:
73: void DisplayText(short style)
74: {
75:     char MyText[] =
76:         "Alter this text using Command Line Switches.\n";
77:
78:     switch (style)
79:     {
80:       case NORMAL:
81:         cout << "NORMAL:\n" << MyText;
82:         break;
83:
84:       case UPPERCASE:
85:         cout << "UPPERCASE:\n" << UCase(MyText);
86:         break;
87:
88:       case LOWERCASE:
89:         cout << "LOWERCASE:\n" << LCase(MyText);
90:         break;
91:     }
92: }
93:
94: /////////////////////////////////////////////////////
95: //   TryBail()
96:
```

LISTING 7.4 CONTINUED

6 Lines 60-68: LCase()
modifies a string to use all
lowercase letters

7 Lines 73-92: DisplayText()
uses a parameter to specify
how to display some text

continues…

Listing 7.2 Continued

⑧ Lines 97-104: TryBail() checks the number of command-line arguments and bails out of the program if there are less than two

⑨ Lines 109-141: ProcessArgs() performs simple processing of command-line arguments

LISTING 7.4   **Continued**

```cpp
97: void TryBail(int argc)
98: {
99:    if (argc < 2)
100:   {
101:       Usage();       // User error-no command line arguments
102:       exit(0);       // bail out...
103:   }
104: }
105:
106: ////////////////////////////////////////////////////////
107: //   ProcessArgs()
108:
109: void ProcessArgs(int argc, char *argv[])
110: {
111:    // Process any command line arguments
112:    //
113:    for (int i = 0; i < argc; ++i)
114:    {
115:       // Check for /?
116:       //
117:       if (!strcmp(argv[i], "/?"))
118:       {
119:          Usage();       // User wants help
120:          return;        // bail out...
121:       }
122:
123:       // Check for /N
124:       //
125:       else if ((!strcmp(argv[i], "/N"))
126:          ||   (!strcmp(argv[i], "/n")))
127:          DisplayText(NORMAL);
128:
129:       // Check for /U
130:       //
131:       else if ((!strcmp(argv[i], "/U"))
132:          ||   (!strcmp(argv[i], "/u")))
133:          DisplayText(UPPERCASE);
134:
135:       // Check for /L
136:       //
137:       else if ((!strcmp(argv[i], "/L"))
138:          ||   (!strcmp(argv[i], "/l")))
139:          DisplayText(LOWERCASE);
140:    }
141: }
```

```
142:
143: /////////////////////////////////////////////////////////
144: //   main()
145:
146: void main(int argc, char *argv[])
147: {
148:     // Bail out if the user didn't supply arguments
149:     //
150:     TryBail(argc);
151:
152:     // Process all the command line arguments
153:     //
154:     ProcessArgs(argc, argv);
155:
156:     // Do other program stuff
157:     // ...
158:     // ...
159: }
```

The output for this program depends on the command-line switch used. If no arguments are specified on the command line, or if the argument is /?, the program displays the following usage information:

```
Usage:

    TEST [/?][/N][/U][/L]


Valid command line switches are:

/?      Displays this usage message.
/N      Displays text normally.
/U      Displays text all uppercase.
/L      Displays text all lowercase.
```

If the command-line switch is /N (or /n), the program displays this line of text:

```
Alter this text using Command Line Switches.
```

If the command-line switch is /U (or /u), the program displays the line of text like this, in all uppercase characters:

```
ALTER THIS TEXT USING COMMAND LINE SWITCHES.
```

And if the command-line switch is /L (or /l), the program displays the line of text like this, in all lowercase characters:

```
alter this text using command line switches.
```

Seeing how these switches work should help you implement command-line processing in your own programs. Let's take a closer look at the program's functions, to see how they all work.

Analyzing the Program Code

This program begins by including four standard header files that provide access to the functions and objects needed by the program (lines 8 through 11). The prototypes for the six user-defined functions are listed on lines 15 through 20. The three constant values on lines 24 through 26 provide style identifiers used to decide how to display the output text.

The Usage() function runs from lines 31 through 40 and instructs the user about valid command-line switches by using the cout object to display its text.

The workings of the UCase() function were described earlier in this chapter. The function runs from lines 45 through 54 and modifies a string to use all uppercase letters. Likewise, the LCase() function, running from lines 60 through 68, modifies a string to use all lowercase letters.

The DisplayText() function begins on line 73 and immediately creates the local variable MyText on lines 74 and 75. The function parameter style specifies one of the global constants defined earlier (NORMAL, UPPERCASE, or LOWERCASE). The function uses a switch statement to decide on the proper way to display the text; it calls LCase() or UCase() as appropriate.

In lines 97 through 104, the TryBail() function checks the number of command-line arguments. If there are less than two arguments, the function bails out of the program by calling the ANSI C function exit().

The ProcessArgs() function on lines 109 through 141 performs simple processing of command-line arguments by using the strcmp() function to compare strings, a technique you saw earlier in this chapter. The main() function simply calls the TryBail() and ProcessArgs() functions to perform all the program's tasks.

The exit() Function

Because Standard C is part of Standard C++, all the tried and true functions C programmers know and love are available in C++. The exit() function is used to terminate the program with an exit code for the operating system. To use the exit() function, include the header <stdlib.h> in your source file.

Using Variable-Argument Lists

On occasion, you'll run across a function that uses a *variable-argument list*, indicated by the ellipsis operator (...). The ellipsis means that more function parameters can be used than are specified in the function header, but that the number can vary and the data types are unknown.

You access the argument list using three macros provided by the Standard C Library headers <stdio.h> and <stdarg.h>. These three macros are listed in Table 7.1

SEE ALSO

➤ *For more information on macros, see page 310*

TABLE 7.1   **The Three Variable-Argument Lists**

Macro	Description
va_arg	Returns the current argument.
va_start	Sets a pointer to the beginning of the list of optional arguments.
va_end	Resets the argument pointer.

The variable argument macros use the following syntax:

```
type va_arg(va_list arg_ptr, type);
void va_end(va_list arg_ptr);
void va_start(va_list arg_ptr);               // UNIX version
void va_start(va_list arg_ptr, prev_param); // ANSI version
```

Remember the AverageThreeInts() function presented earlier in this chapter? By using a variable-length argument list, you can rewrite the function to work with any number of integers. The code in Listing 7.5 demonstrates the AverageInts() function, an updated version of the AverageThreeInts() function that uses a variable-argument list to average a varying number of integer values.

Variable-Argument Lists and Type Safety

The ellipsis operator isn't used very often in C++ because a variable-length list isn't type safe and violates the fundamental C++ principle of enforcing strict type checking.

Two Versions of va_start

There are UNIX and ANSI versions of the **va_start** macro. Because these versions are slightly different, be sure to use the one appropriate for your system. The ANSI version takes an additional argument.

LISTING 7.5   A Program That Demonstrates Using a Variable-Argument List

```
 1: //////////////////////////////////////////////////////
 2: //   Module  : func5.cpp
 3: //
 4: //   Purpose : Demonstrates a variable-argument list
 5: //////////////////////////////////////////////////////
 6:
 7: #include <iostream.h>
 8: #include <stdio.h>
 9: #include <stdarg.h>
10:
11: // Function prototype
12: //
13: float AverageInts(int num1, ...);          1
14:
15: //////////////////////////////////////////////////////
16: //   AverageInts()
17:
18: float AverageInts(int num1, ...)           2
19: {
20:     // Some local variables
21:     //
22:     int sum    = 0;
23:     int count  = 0;                  3
24:     int curNum = num1;
25:
26:     // Initialize variable arguments
27:     va_list loc;
28:     va_start(loc, num1);             4
29:
30:     // 0 is used as the argument-list terminator
31:     //
32:     while (curNum != 0)
33:     {
34:         sum += curNum;              // Add the numbers
35:         count++;                    // increment count       5
36:         curNum = va_arg(loc, int); // update current num
37:     }
38:
39:     // Reset variable arguments
40:     //
41:     va_end(loc);                  6
```

```
42:
43:     return sum ? (float(sum) / float(count)) : 0.0f ;
44: }
45:
46: /////////////////////////////////////////////////////////
47: //  main()
48:
49: void main()
50: {
51:     // Call the AverageInts() function several times
52:     //
53:     cout << "Average: "   << AverageInts(1, 2, 3, 4, 0);
54:     cout << "\nAverage: " << AverageInts(2, 3, 4, 0);
55:     cout << "\nAverage: " << AverageInts(3, 4, 0);
56:     cout << "\nAverage: " << AverageInts(4, 0) << '\n';
57: }
```

LISTING 7.5 CONTINUED

7 Lines 53-56: Invoke the AverageInts() function with different numbers of arguments

The output for this program is as follows:

```
Average: 2.5
Average: 3
Average: 3.5
Average: 4
```

Let's analyze the important sections of this program. On line 13, you can see the prototype for the AverageInts() function, which uses the ellipsis to specify a variable-argument list. On line 18 is the AverageInts() function header, which also uses the ellipsis.

Lines 22 through 24 take care of declaring some local variables for the AverageInts() function, and lines 27 through 28 initialize the variable-argument list. The variable loc keeps track of the current location within the argument list, giving us access to the items in the list. Each invocation of the va_arg() macro retrieves the next item in the argument list; the call on line 36 assigns the result to the variable curNum, the current number in the argument list. Line 41 cleans up, resetting the variable-argument pointer. Note that zero is used as the argument-list terminator for the function, so it isn't included in any of the averages.

The main() function calls the same function several times, using a different number of arguments for each function call. Lines 53 through 56 list four calls to the AverageInts() function with different numbers of arguments each time.

Getting Modular with Functions

Some functions are generic enough to be used in many programs. You can make these functions available to any program if you separate the function declarations into a header file, and put the function definition in the source file. After compiling your module, you'll have a stand-alone object (.obj) file you can then link into your programs. By including the header file for your function module in a source file, your programs will "know about" your functions.

Now I'll take two functions that would be useful for any number of programs and put them into their own module. Doing this makes them available when I need them for other programs. The two functions are UCase() and LCase(), functions developed for the program back in Listing 7.4.

The module, which I'll code-name module1, is composed of the header file (the interface) and the source file (the implementation). The header file is module1.h, shown in Listing 7.5. The source file is module1.cpp, shown in Listing 7.6.

LISTING 7.5

① Lines 7 and 8: Preprocessor directives for single inclusion

LISTING 7.5   **The Header File for *module1: module1.h***

```
 1: /////////////////////////////////////////////////////////
 2: //   Module  : module1.h
 3: //
 4: //   Purpose : Interface for module1.cpp
 5: /////////////////////////////////////////////////////////
 6:
 7: #ifndef __MODULE1_H_
 8: #define __MODULE1_H_
 9:
10: #include <stdlib.h>
11: #include <ctype.h>
12: #include <string.h>
13:
14: // Function prototypes
```

```
15: //
16: extern char* LCase(char *str);
17: extern char* UCase(char *str);
18:
19: #endif //__MODULE1_H__        2
```

LISTING 7.5 CONTINUED

2 Line 19: End of single inclusion

Like a source file, the module1.h header file begins with some comments about what the file is for (lines 1 through 5). I always provide these comments so that I know at a glance what a module is for—even months or years after creating the code. Lines 7 and 8 are some preprocessor directives that you haven't yet seen used in this book, so I'll take a moment to explain them.

On line 7, the preprocessor directive #ifndef asks the question, "Has the preprocessor identifier __MODULE1_H__ been defined?" If not, line 8 defines the identifier, and everything in the file until the #endif directive is included. The #endif directive marks the end of the preprocessor code block that starts on line 7. If the symbol __MODULE1_H__ **has** already been defined, file inclusion jumps from the #ifndef directive to the #endif directive, skipping the code within the preprocessor block completely.

In this case, the code within the preprocessor block includes three header files: <stdlib.h>, <ctype.h>, and <string.h>. When included in module1.cpp, these files give the LCase() and UCase() functions access to the Standard C Library functions they need to get their jobs done. This code block also contains the prototypes for these functions, the interface to the module's functionality.

SEE ALSO

➤ *For more information about preprocessing and single inclusion, see page 302*

The source code in Listing 7.6 lists the same two functions you saw back in Listing 7.4; nothing's changed except that the functions are now isolated in their own module for easier reuse. By placing these functions in a separate file, we can compile them into a separate object file. Because it links separately into the main program file (see Listing 7.7), this separate module file is known as a *translation unit*.

LISTING 7.6

1 Line 7: The function interface file

2 Lines 9-35: These functions are isolated because they are in a file separate from any other functions—a different translation unit

LISTING 7.6   **The Source File for *module1: module1.cpp***

```
1: ////////////////////////////////////////////////////
2: //   Module   : module1.cpp
3: //
4: //   Purpose : Shows the usage of modular functions
5: ////////////////////////////////////////////////////
6:
7: #include "module1.h"          1
8:
9: ////////////////////////////////////////////////////
10: //  UCase()
11:
12: char* UCase(char *str)
13: {
14:     // Convert each char in the string to uppercase
15:     //
16:     int len = strlen(str);
17:     for (int i = 0; i < len; i++)
18:         str[i] = toupper(str[i]);
19:
20:     return str;
21: }
22:
23: ////////////////////////////////////////////////////
24: //  LCase()
25:
26: char* LCase(char *str)                                2
27: {
28:     // Convert each char in the string to lowercase
29:     //
30:     int len = strlen(str);
31:     for (int i = 0; i < len; i++)
32:         str[i] = tolower(str[i]);
33:
34:     return str;
35: }
```

To test module1, I created the simple test program shown in Listing 7.7 to "drive" the module1 functions LCase() and UCase().

LISTING 7.7   A Simple Driver Program to Test the *module1* Functions

```
 1: //////////////////////////////////////////////////////
 2: //   Module  : main.cpp
 3: //
 4: //   Purpose : Shows the usage of modular functions
 5: //////////////////////////////////////////////////////
 6:
 7: #include <iostream.h>
 8: #include "module1.h"
 9:
10: void main()
11: {
12:     cout << "This is a test\n";
13:     cout << UCase("This is a test of UCase\n");
14:     cout << LCase("This is a test of LCase\n");
15: }
```

This is the output of the test program:

```
This is a test
THIS IS A TEST OF UCASE
this is a test of lcase
```

As you can see, after including the module1 header file in line 8, the module1.cpp module "knows" about LCase() and UCase() and can use the functions freely on lines 12 through 14. This approach to programming is called *modular design*, and it keeps data in the modules where it belongs. In Chapter 21, "Understanding C++ Classes," you'll see how a similar technique is used in object-oriented programming to separate class interfaces from class implementations.

Specifying Function Linkage

C and C++ code are deeply related (after all, C is part of C++), but various idiosyncrasies in the languages can cause unexpected problems at link time. Because of differences in the internal architecture of C and C++, you must link C functions and C++ functions using the extern "C" linkage specification to ensure that all the functions will work together as intended.

Modular Design

A method of programming that separates program components into well-defined modules that can be used to hide data and promote code reuse.

Because of the way C++ handles function name translation during the compile process, C functions must be declared using C linkage to prevent "name mangling." You declare functions to use C linkage by using the extern "C" linkage specifier individually in each function declaration, like this:

```
extern "C" int Func1(int);
extern "C" int Func2(float);
extern "C" int Func3();
```

You can also declare a group of C functions to use C linkage by using the extern "C" linkage specifier on a code block, like this:

```
extern "C"
{
    int Func1(int);
    int Func2(float);
    int Func3();
}
```

SEE ALSO

➤ *For more information about name mangling, see page 208*

Beyond the Basics

Overloading Functions

See how function overloading works

Understand why the compiler mangles function names

Learn about function calls and their use of the stack

See how to change the numbers and types of function parameters

Why Use Function Overloading?

In Chapter 7, "Creating and Using Functions," you saw how functions can make your life much easier by allowing you to break complex programming tasks into bite-size chunks. Using functions reduces the amount of code you have to write and maintain because you can create a single function definition and use it in multiple places. In a language like C, when you have several functions that perform similar tasks but work with different data types, each of the functions requires a unique name.

As an example, think about multiplying two numbers to yield a third (the product). Although it seems like a simple enough exercise, think of the possibilities when you are faced with the different data types available in C++. Some of the possibilities are demonstrated in the following function prototypes:

```
float  Mult2Floats(float num1, float num2);
int    Mult2Ints(int num1, int num2);
long   Mult2Longs(long num1, long num2);
double Mult2Doubles(double num1, double num2);
float  MultFloatInt(float num1, int num2);
float  MultFloatLong(float num1, long num2);
double MultDoubleInt(double num1, int num2);
double MultDoubleLong(double num1, long num2);
```

As you can see, there are several ways to multiply two numbers. Not only are the parameter types different among these functions, the return types are different, too. The worst part about using functions like these is trying to remember which function to call, given a certain set of data.

The program in Listing 8.1 shows the tedium of defining and using all these similar function names. The program simply calls each function to generate a return value and then displays the result to the screen.

LISTING 8.1   **A Program Demonstrating the Confusion and Inconvenience of Using Multiple Unique, Yet Similar, Function Names**

```
1: ///////////////////////////////////////////////////////
2: // Module  : tedious.cpp
3: //
4: // Purpose : Demonstrates the tedious naming of
```

```
 5: //                 similar functions
 6: //////////////////////////////////////////////////
 7:
 8: #include <iostream.h>
 9:
10: const char NL = '\n';
11:
12: //////////////////////////////////////////////////
13: // Function prototypes
14:
15: int    Mult2Ints(int num1, int num2);
16: long   Mult2Longs(long num1, long num2);
17: float  Mult2Floats(float num1, float num2);
18: double Mult2Doubles(double num1, double num2);
19: float  MultFloatInt(float num1, int num2);
20: float  MultFloatLong(float num1, long num2);
21: double MultDoubleInt(double num1, int num2);
22: double MultDoubleLong(double num1, long num2);
23:
24: //////////////////////////////////////////////////
25: // Mult2Ints()
26:
27: int Mult2Ints(int num1, int num2)
28: {
29:    return num1 * num2;
30: }
31:
32: //////////////////////////////////////////////////
33: // Mult2Longs()
34:
35: long Mult2Longs(long num1, long num2)
36: {
37:    return num1 * num2;
38: }
39:
40: //////////////////////////////////////////////////
41: // Mult2Floats()
42:
43: float Mult2Floats(float num1, float num2)
44: {
45:    return num1 * num2;
46: }
```

LISTING 8.1

1 Line 10: Define a newline constant

2 Lines 15-22: Declare eight distinct multiplication functions

3 Lines 27-30: Multiply two ints to return an int

4 Lines 35-38: Multiply two longs to return a long

5 Lines 43-46: Multiply two floats to return a float

continues...

LISTING 8.1   **Continued**

```
47:
48: /////////////////////////////////////////////////////
49: // Mult2Doubles()
50:
51: double Mult2Doubles(double num1, double num2)  ─┐
52: {                                                │ 6
53:     return num1 * num2;                          │
54: }  ──────────────────────────────────────────────┘
55:
56: /////////////////////////////////////////////////////
57: // MultFloatInt()
58:
59: float MultFloatInt(float num1, int num2)  ─┐
60: {                                           │ 7
61:     return num1 * float(num2);              │
62: }  ─────────────────────────────────────────┘
63:
64: /////////////////////////////////////////////////////
65: // MultFloatLong()
66:
67: float MultFloatLong(float num1, long num2)  ─┐
68: {                                             │ 8
69:     return num1 * float(num2);                │
70: }  ───────────────────────────────────────────┘
71:
72: /////////////////////////////////////////////////////
73: // MultDoubleInt()
74:
75: double MultDoubleInt(double num1, int num2)  ─┐
76: {                                              │ 9
77:     return num1 * double(num2);                │
78: }  ────────────────────────────────────────────┘
79:
80: /////////////////////////////////////////////////////
81: // MultDoubleLong()
82:
83: double MultDoubleLong(double num1, long num2)  ─┐
84: {                                                │ 10
85:     return num1 * double(num2);                  │
86: }  ───────────────────────────────────────────────┘
87:
```

```
88:  ////////////////////////////////////////////////////////
89:  // main()
90:
91:  void main()
92:  {
93:      // Calculate the values
94:      //
95:      int i     = Mult2Ints(10, 20);
96:      long l    = Mult2Longs(30, 40);
97:      float f1  = Mult2Floats(5.6f, 6.2f);
98:      double d1 = Mult2Doubles(6.93, 1.52);
99:      float f2  = MultFloatInt(25.2f, 6);
100:     float f3  = MultFloatLong(2.4f, 3);
101:     double d2 = MultDoubleInt(6.65, 4);
102:     double d3 = MultDoubleLong(5.25, 2);
103:
104:     // Display the values
105:     //
106:     cout << "Mult2Ints(10, 20)        == " << i << NL;
107:     cout << "Mult2Longs(30, 40)       == " << l << NL;
108:     cout << "Mult2Floats(5.6f, 6.2f)  == " << f1 << NL;
109:     cout << "Mult2Doubles(6.93, 1.52) == " << d1 << NL;
110:     cout << "MultFloatInt(25.2f, 6)   == " << f2 << NL;
111:     cout << "MultFloatLong(2.4f, 3)   == " << f3 << NL;
112:     cout << "MultDoubleInt(6.65, 4)   == " << d2 << NL;
113:     cout << "MultDoubleLong(5.25, 2)  == " << d3 << NL;
114: }
```

LISTING 8.1 CONTINUED

11 Lines 95-102: Call the appropriate functions to get various return values

12 Lines 106-113: Display the results using cout

The output from this program looks like this:

```
Mult2Ints(10, 20)        == 200
Mult2Longs(30, 40)       == 1200
Mult2Floats(5.6f, 6.2f)  == 34.72
Mult2Doubles(6.93, 1.52) == 10.5336
MultFloatInt(25.2f, 6)   == 151.2
MultFloatLong(2.4f, 3)   == 7.2
MultDoubleInt(6.65, 4)   == 26.6
MultDoubleLong(5.25, 2)  == 10.5
```

As you can probably see, it would be almost painful at times to remember which specific data types you're passing as arguments and to use the correct function name with those types. This is the restriction that C places on programmers. Wouldn't it be nice if you could just forget about the various types and function names and just call a `Multiply()` function to handle every case presented in Listing 8.1? Thankfully, C++ allows you to use a technique called *function overloading* to do just that!

So, what does it mean to "overload" a function? This just means that you create multiple functions that all have the same function name. Internally, the C++ compiler keeps track of all the function parameters and return types for overloaded functions. When you call an overloaded function, the compiler matches up the data type(s) used in your function call with the type(s) used by the appropriate overloaded function. If no overloaded function exists that uses the data type your function call specifies, the compiler generates an error telling you so. At that point, you can decide to either change your function call arguments or write a new overloaded function to handle the situation.

Types of Function Overloading

Overloading functions is a great C++ language feature that makes programming much easier. Overloaded functions can make your code flexible, allowing it to respond appropriately in many different situations. You will want to overload functions in two general cases, when you want to

- Change a function's parameter information
- Change the function's operation

Overloading by Parameter Type

Each overloaded function must have a unique set of return types and parameters. When overloading a function by parameter type, you're changing the function's parameter information, and you have three choices. You can combine these choices in many ways:

- Change the data types of existing function parameters
- Change the number of function parameters
- Change the return data type

Changing the Data Types of Function Parameters

You can overload a function by changing the types of data the function receives as parameter data. When you overload functions in this way, you provide flexibility in your program. For example, these two functions are overloaded only by parameter data type:

```
int Multiply(int num1, int num2)
{
    return num1 * num2;
}


int Multiply(float num1, float num2)
{
    return (int(num1 * num2 + 0.5f);
}
```

Both versions return an integer value, but the second uses an explicit cast operation to convert each floating-point parameter value into an integer value. In the case of the second function, the value `0.5f` is added to the product resulting from the `float` parameter multiplication. This technique ensures that the value will round off properly. You would use both functions in the same way within your code, not worrying about type casting parameter values every time a function is called:

```
int MyInt1 = Multiply(5, 10);
int MyInt2 = Multiply(5.25, 10.5);
```

Changing the Number of Function Parameters

You can also overload a function by changing the number of parameters it receives. For example, these two functions are overloaded only by the number of parameters they receive:

```
int Multiply(int num1, int num2)
{
    return num1 * num2;
}


int Multiply(int num1, int num2, int num3)
{
    return num1 * num2 * num3;
}
```

Both versions return an integer value, but the first takes two parameters, while the second takes three parameters. You could use either function, as needed; the compiler resolves the function call to the appropriate version of the function using the internal mangled name to find the correct function address. (You learn about name mangling later in this chapter.) Using these functions in your code is as easy as this:

```
int MyInt1 = Multiply(5, 10);
int MyInt2 = Multiply(5, 10, 2);
```

Changing the Number of Function Parameters and Their Data Types

The final twist on function overloading by changing function parameters is when you change both the types and the numbers of the parameters. This is no problem in C++, making it easy for you to provide all these overloaded functions:

```
int Multiply(int num1, int num2)
{
    return num1 * num2;
}

int Multiply(float num1, float num2)
{
    return (int(num1 + 0.5f) * int(num2 + 0.5f));
}

int Multiply(int num1, int num2, float num3)
{
    return num1 * num2 * int(num3 + 0.5f);
}
```

Changing a Function's Return Data Type

When you overload a function by changing the return data type, you can add a lot of flexibility to a program. For example, these two functions are overloaded only by return data type:

```
int Multiply(int num1, int num2)
{
    return num1 * num2;
}
```

```
float Multiply(int num1, int num2)
{
    return float(num1 * num2);
}
```

The version returning a `float` value uses an explicit cast operation to convert an integer value into a floating-point value. Again, this technique allows you to use both functions in the same way within your code, so that you don't have to worry about type-casting return values every time a function is called:

```
float MyFloat = Multiply(5, 10);
int   MyInt = Multiply(5, 10);
```

Overloading Functions by Operation

In addition to overloading functions by parameter or return type, overloading a function by its intended operation is another important consideration. When you overload by operation, you must still provide a declaration that differs somehow from other functions with the same name, but the purposes of the various overloaded functions can be completely different. Suppose that you are writing a card game of some sort. The rules of the game require the following:

- For each turn, each player must draw a card from a deck of standard playing cards.
- The program will graphically draw to the screen the image of whichever card the player drew from the deck.

The use of the word *draw* in each of these steps refers to completely different activities. When coded as functions, the names for both of these activities are the exactly same, yet the activities themselves are totally different. Assuming that `PlayingCards` is an enumerated type defining a deck of playing cards, the function declarations for each might look like this:

```
PlayingCards Draw();        // "Draws" a new card from the deck
Draw(PlayingCards card); // "Draws" the card to the screen
```

Even though the data types used are the same in each, without a doubt, these two functions each have a unique purpose.

Operator Overloading

A particularly useful derivative of *function overloading* is called *operator overloading* and is discussed in Chapter 14, "Overloading Operators." Operator overloading allows you to define your own custom operators that act like built-in C++ operators.

The function prototypes in Listing 8.1 all use different parameter types and different return values; in C programming, you'd be forced to use those types of function declarations. C++ function overloading can streamline your code and make your life easier. Here are the same functions from Listing 8.1, rewritten as overloaded `Multiply()` functions:

```
int    Multiply(int num1, int num2);
long   Multiply(long num1, long num2);
float  Multiply(float num1, float num2);
double Multiply(double num1, double num2);
float  Multiply(float num1, int num2);
float  Multiply(float num1, long num2);
double Multiply(double num1, int num2);
double Multiply(double num1, long num2);
```

As you can see, the parameter and return types are the same as before, but each declaration overloads the single function name `Multiply()`, eliminating the tedious function names used previously. To see the newly overloaded `Multiply()` functions in action, take a look at the program in Listing 8.2.

LISTING 8.2

1 Line 10: Define a newline constant

LISTING 8.2   **A Program Demonstrating Function Overloading to Eliminate Similar Function Names**

```
 1: //////////////////////////////////////////////////////
 2: //  Module  : overload1.cpp
 3: //
 4: //  Purpose : Demonstrates the convenience of
 5: //            overloaded function names
 6: //////////////////////////////////////////////////////
 7:
 8: #include <iostream.h>
 9:
10: const char NL = '\n';
11:
12: //////////////////////////////////////////////////////
13: // Overloaded function prototypes
14:
```

```
15: int    Multiply(int num1, int num2);
16: long   Multiply(long num1, long num2);
17: float  Multiply(float num1, float num2);
18: double Multiply(double num1, double num2);
19: float  Multiply(float num1, int num2);
20: float  Multiply(float num1, long num2);
21: double Multiply(double num1, int num2);
22: double Multiply(double num1, long num2);
23:
24: //////////////////////////////////////////////////////
25: // Multiply()
26:
27: int Multiply(int num1, int num2)
28: {
29:    return num1 * num2;
30: }
31:
32: //////////////////////////////////////////////////////
33: // Multiply()
34:
35: long Multiply(long num1, long num2)
36: {
37:    return num1 * num2;
38: }
39:
40: //////////////////////////////////////////////////////
41: // Multiply()
42:
43: float Multiply(float num1, float num2)
44: {
45:    return num1 * num2;
46: }
47:
48: //////////////////////////////////////////////////////
49: // Multiply()
50:
51: double Multiply(double num1, double num2)
52: {
53:    return num1 * num2;
54: }
```

LISTING 8.2 CONTINUED

2 Lines 15-22: Declare eight distinct multiplication functions

3 Lines 27-30: Multiply two `int`s to return an `int`

4 Lines 35-38: Multiply two `long`s to return a `long`

5 Lines 43-46: Multiply two `float`s to return a `float`

6 Lines 51-54: Multiply two `double`s to return a `double`

continues…

LISTING 8.2 CONTINUED

7 Lines 59-62: Multiply a
float and an int to
return a float

8 Lines 67-70: Multiply a
float and a long to
return a float

9 Lines 75-78: Multiply a
double and an int to
return a double

10 Lines 83-86: Multiply a
double and a long to
return a double

LISTING 8.2 **Continued**

```
55:
56: /////////////////////////////////////////////////////
57: // Multiply()
58:
59: float Multiply(float num1, int num2)
60: {
61:     return num1 * float(num2);
62: }
63:
64: /////////////////////////////////////////////////////
65: // Multiply()
66:
67: float Multiply(float num1, long num2)
68: {
69:     return num1 * float(num2);
70: }
71:
72: /////////////////////////////////////////////////////
73: // Multiply()
74:
75: double Multiply(double num1, int num2)
76: {
77:     return num1 * double(num2);
78: }
79:
80: /////////////////////////////////////////////////////
81: // Multiply()
82:
83: double Multiply(double num1, long num2)
84: {
85:     return num1 * double(num2);
86: }
87:
88: /////////////////////////////////////////////////////
89: // main()
90:
91: void main()
92: {
93:     // Calculate the values
```

```
94:    //
95:    int i     = Multiply(10, 20);
96:    long l     = Multiply(30, 40);
97:    float f1  = Multiply(5.6f, 6.2f);
98:    double d1 = Multiply(6.93, 1.52);
99:    float f2  = Multiply(25.2f, 6);
100:   float f3  = Multiply(2.4f, 3);
101:   double d2 = Multiply(6.65, 4);
102:   double d3 = Multiply(5.25, 2);
103:
104:   // Display the values
105:   //
106:   cout << "Multiply(10, 20)      == " << i << NL;
107:   cout << "Multiply(30, 40)      == " << l << NL;
108:   cout << "Multiply(5.6f, 6.2f) == " << f1 << NL;
109:   cout << "Multiply(6.93, 1.52) == " << d1 << NL;
110:   cout << "Multiply(25.2f, 6)    == " << f2 << NL;
111:   cout << "Multiply(2.4f, 3)     == " << f3 << NL;
112:   cout << "Multiply(6.65, 4)     == " << d2 << NL;
113:   cout << "Multiply(5.25, 2)     == " << d3 << NL;
114: }
```

LISTING 8.2 CONTINUED

11 Lines 95-102: Call the overloaded functions to get various return values

12 Lines 106-113: Display the results using cout

The output from this program looks like this:

```
Multiply(10, 20)      == 200
Multiply(30, 40)      == 1200
Multiply(5.6f, 6.2f) == 34.72
Multiply(6.93, 1.52) == 10.5336
Multiply(25.2f, 6)    == 151.2
Multiply(2.4f, 3)     == 7.2
Multiply(6.65, 4)     == 26.6
Multiply(5.25, 2)     == 10.5
```

As you can see, it's much easier, once the functions are defined, to call Multiply() every time, not worrying about the parameter or return types to figure out which function to call. So, how does C++ accomplish this wondrous feat? Let's take a look under the hood.

Examining the Internals of Function Overloading

Internally, your computer does a lot of work when it runs a program. At compile time, the C++ compiler reserves all the memory space the program needs to run properly. When your computer's central processing unit (CPU) loads a program's binary code into memory, each code element (functions, variables, constants, and so on) loads into some arbitrary memory address. To make sure that the computer executes everything correctly, the compiler generates unique names for each function name in a program. In this way, there can be no mistaking which function is which.

Mangling Function Names for Type-Safe Linkage

C++ compilers use a technique called *name mangling*, or *name decorating*, to ensure that all function names are unique. This is how C++ enforces some of its strict type-safety rules. Name mangling involves generating a unique function name for all functions, notably overloaded functions. Different compiler vendors use different techniques to mangle function names, but it typically involves adding the return type and parameter types to a function name, or something similar. Consider these three overloaded function declarations:

```
int Mult(int, int);
int Mult(int, float);
float Mult(float, long);
```

The compiler eliminates any doubt about which overloaded function is really being called at any given time by using internal names to identify each function uniquely. These three functions (all named Mult()) might end up having internal mangled names like these:

```
__INT_MULT_INT_INT()
__INT_MULT_INT_FLOAT()
__FLOAT_MULT_FLOAT_LONG()
```

Name Mangling Can Prevent Linkage

Modern C++ compilers mangle every function name, overloaded or not, to provide type-safety for programs. Functions to be used in both C and C++ must not use mangled function names. To prevent name mangling, you must use the extern "c" linkage specification, as described back in Chapter 2.

Function Calls and the Stack

As mentioned earlier, program elements such as variables, constants, and functions are loaded into memory at runtime and exist there, each located at some arbitrary memory address. When you make a function call in a program, the function return value and any parameters the function needs are placed into a special area of memory reserved for use by the program. This memory region is called the *stack* because it behaves much like a physical stack of items. Imagine a stack of dishes being put into a cabinet one at a time—the first one in is the last one out. This first-in/last-out (FILO) arrangement is used extensively by function calls as a program runs.

When you make a function call, the function return variable and any parameter data are created on the stack. The arguments sent into the function go into the parameter stack space for the function. Function parameters are simply local variables to that function. When the function returns, the return value of the function (if any) is stored in the stack in the function return variable. The parameters are "popped" off the stack, going out of scope. The function return variable pops off the stack last, and the function evaluates to that return value.

When functions call other functions that call still more functions, the stack can get rather deep. Imagine this series of function calls:

```
float func1(float f)
{
    return f * 2;
}

float func2(float f1, float f2)
{
    float f = func1(f1);
    return func3(f2, f);
}

float func3(float f1, float f2)
{
```

```
    float f = func1(f1) + func1(f2);
}

float func4(float f)
{
    return func2(f, f);
}
```

The players in this game of "push and pop the stack" are as follows:

- `func1()` return variable
- `func1()` float parameter
- `func2()` return variable
- `func2()` float parameter 1
- `func2()` float parameter 2
- `func3()` return variable
- `func3()` float parameter 1
- `func3()` float parameter 2
- `func4()` return variable
- `func4()` float parameter

If you call `func4()`, the stack would reflect the following steps as the function calls proceed.

Stepping through the stack of function calls

1. The return variable for `func4()`, along with the `func4()` float parameter, are pushed onto the stack.

2. The `func4()` function calls `func2()`. The return variable for `func2()`, along with the two `func2()` float parameters, are pushed onto the stack.

3. The `func2()` function creates the local float variable f and pushes it onto the stack. The `func2()` function then calls `func1()`.

4. The `func1()` return variable and float parameter are pushed onto the stack (see Figure 8.1). Because `func1()` calls no other functions, its float parameter and function address pop off the stack, returning the value to its caller, `func2()`.

5. The `func2()` function then calls `func3()`. The `func3()` return variable and two `float` parameters are pushed onto the stack.

6. The `func3()` function creates the local `float` variable f and pushes it onto the stack. The `func3()` function then calls `func1()` twice in a single expression (see Figure 8.2).

7. The `func1()` return variable and `float` parameter are pushed onto the stack. Because `func1()` calls no other functions, its `float` parameter and function `return` variable pop off the stack, returning the value to its caller, `func3()`. (This is done twice.)

8. Because `func3()` has completed its task, its local variable, `float` parameters, and function `return` variable all pop off the stack, returning a value to its caller, `func2()`.

9. The `func2()` function has also completed its task, so its local variable, `float` parameters, and function `return` variable all pop off the stack, returning a value to its caller, `func4()`.

10. Finally, `func4()` has the `return` value from `func2()`, so its `float` parameter and function `return` variable pop off the stack, returning the result to the original caller.

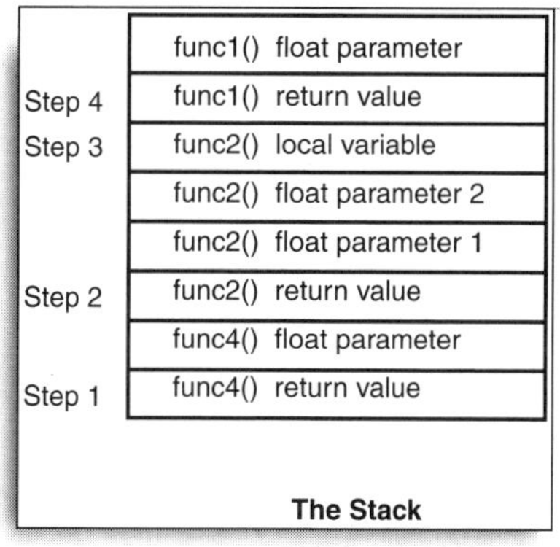

	func1()	float parameter
Step 4	func1()	return value
Step 3	func2()	local variable
	func2()	float parameter 2
	func2()	float parameter 1
Step 2	func2()	return value
	func4()	float parameter
Step 1	func4()	return value

The Stack

FIGURE 8.1

A view of the stack after step 4.

This chapter has demonstrated the power of C++ function overloading. In the remainder of this book, you'll see function overloading used considerably, expanding on the basic examples presented in this chapter. Next up, a look at creating user-defined data types.

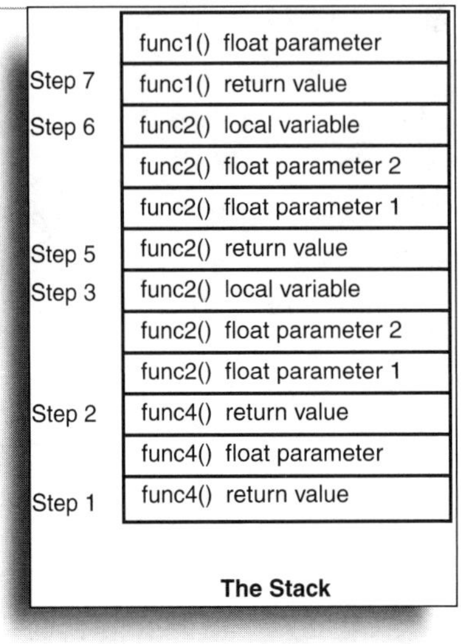

FIGURE 8.2

A view of the stack after step 7.

	func1() float parameter
Step 7	func1() return value
Step 6	func2() local variable
	func2() float parameter 2
	func2() float parameter 1
Step 5	func2() return value
Step 3	func2() local variable
	func2() float parameter 2
	func2() float parameter 1
Step 2	func4() return value
	func4() float parameter
Step 1	func4() return value

The Stack

Using Structures and Unions

Learn to create new data types with structures

See how to create arrays of structures

Use functions as structure members

Learn to create new data types with unions

Creating New Data Types with Structures

As you learned briefly back in Chapter 2, "Exploring C++ Data Types, Variables, and Constants," a *structure* is a data type that groups other data types together into a single, compound data type. Structures make it easy to keep variables logically related within source code by making them *members* of a common structure.

Structure

A user-defined data type that groups together logically related data.

Everything in the real world is made up of component parts—everything has some sort of structure. A personal computer has structure, for example. It's made up of an assemblage of basic components including a keyboard, a mouse, a monitor, and a CPU. Each of these items in turn has its own components that give it a unique structure. Even if we get down to the most fundamental parts of the computer (such as the ball within the mouse that rolls around on the desktop to provide cursor movement), we know that there is still structure within, down to the molecular, atomic, and subatomic levels.

The concept of grouping things together to form other things is the fundamental concept of structure. By definition, the word *structure* refers to the organization or arrangement of individual elements within a group. In programming, it's virtually impossible to create anything more than a simple program without creating derived data types to group your program data in some semblance of logical organization. Structures are user-defined types that make your programming task easier by keeping your code organized and grouped.

Think about the individual yet related pieces of data in your mailing address—there are several pieces of information involved in providing a full mailing address. In the United States, a typical mailing address has these components:

```
Name
Street Address
City
State
Zip Code
```

Imagine a mailing list program that contains thousands of such addresses in a database of some sort. Without a custom data structure to logically group these items, it would be very cumbersome to keep names and addresses for different individuals (that is, different *records*) from getting mixed up. The obvious solution is to create a structure to organize the data, giving each address a unique, cohesive framework.

Each of the components of the address item just listed is an individual entity, but when they are used together as a mailing address, they form a single unit. To create a C++ structure that contains these entities, we must first identify their symbolic names (identifiers), data types, and arrangement within the proposed structure. This is actually pretty easy in most cases, as you'll soon see.

Adding Data Types as Structure Members

A C++ structure uses the following general syntax:

```
struct   StructTag
{
    data-type member1;
    data-type member2;
    // more members
    data-type memberN;
};
```

Just as you must when declaring stand-alone variables in a program, you must supply a data type and an identifier for each *data member* in a structure. By providing a name for the structure, you can easily use it in your programs. Note that the closing brace *must* be followed by a terminating semicolon to mark the end of the structure.

The struct keyword marks the beginning of a structure; the StructTag tag is an optional (but very advantageous) name for the structure. This optional name is useful if you need to create more than one instance of a structure object. For example, if you declare a structure without a tag, you need to create a variable of that unnamed structure type at the same time, like this:

Data Member

A class-level variable; a data component of a class that consists of a valid data type.

```
struct
{
    int x, y;
}
Demo;
```

In this case, `Demo` is a variable that contains x and y data members. By giving the structure a name, you can create as many variables of that structure type (identified by the name) as you want, for example:

```
struct Demo
{
    int x, y;
};
```

In this case, `Demo` isn't a variable; it's a new data type. You can then use the new data type-name `Demo` to create variables of type `Demo`, like this:

```
Demo demo1, demo2;
```

To create a custom data structure for a mailing address, you could define the structure in any number of ways. Here's one I decided on:

```
struct MailingAddress
{
    string Name;
    string StreetAddress;
    string City;
    string State;
    string Zip;
};
```

Don't Confuse Data Members with Data

It's important to note that a structure's data members themselves are where data is stored. But the data members shouldn't be confused with the ***contents*** of the data members—the data itself.

This structure uses identifiers derived from the entity names listed earlier. The structure tag is (appropriately) `MailingAddress`, and all of its members use Standard C++ strings to store the data.

As I said before, declaring a new structure requires you to specify the names of the members, their data types, and their arrangement within the structure. To use a structure, you must declare a variable that uses the structure as its type specifier. The compiler reserves enough storage space to store each of the data members in the structure.

Assigning values to the structure's data members is referred to as *filling*, or *populating*, the data structure. You access each data member by name, separating the structure variable name from the data member with the *dot operator* (.). The syntax of accessing data members with the dot operator is shown here:

```
struct-variable.data-member-identifier
```

To make this abstract discussion more concrete, take a look at the program in Listing 9.1, which defines the `MailingAddress` structure, creates a variable of type `MailingAddress`, populates the structure with address data, and displays the data on the screen by retrieving the strings from the data members.

Dot Operator

An operator used to separate a structure, union, or class name from a class member.

LISTING 9.1   A Program That Demonstrates Creating and Using a Simple Data Structure

```
 1: //////////////////////////////////////////////////////
 2: //  Module   : MailingAddress.cpp
 3: //
 4: //  Purpose : An example of creating and using a
 5: //            simple data structure
 6: //////////////////////////////////////////////////////
 7:
 8: #include <iostream>   // For cout
 9: #include <string>     // For standard strings
10:
11: using namespace std;  // Use the standard namespace
12:
13: // Create a mailing address data structure
14: //
15: struct MailingAddress
16: {
17:    string Name;
18:    string Street;
19:    string City;
20:    string State;
21:    string Zip;
22: };
23:
24: void main()
25: {
```

LISTING 9.1

1 Lines 8-9: Include Standard C++ library headers

2 Lines 15-22: Declare the `MailingAddress` structure

continues…

LISTING 9.1 **Continued**

```
26:    // Declare a variable of type MailingAddress
27:    //
28:    MailingAddress ma;  ──3
29:
30:    // Populate the structure with some data
31:    //
32:    ma.Name   = "John Galt";
33:    ma.Street = "14 Golden Lane";
34:    ma.City   = "Atlantis";
35:    ma.State  = "AZ";
36:    ma.Zip    = "44342-0489";
37:
38:    // Access the data stored in the structure
39:    //
40:    cout << "The contents of the MailingAddress \n"
41:       << "data structure is:\n\n";
42:
43:    cout << ma.Name   << '\n';
44:    cout << ma.Street << '\n';
45:    cout << ma.City   << '\n';
46:    cout << ma.State  << '\n';
47:    cout << ma.Zip    << '\n';
48: }
```

The output of the program looks like this:

```
The contents of the MailingAddress
data structure is:

John Galt
14 Golden Lane
Atlantis
AZ
44342-0489
```

Lines 15 through 22 of the program declare the MailingAddress structure. Line 28 declares the identifier ma, a variable of type MailingAddress. Lines 32 through 36 populate the structure by assigning string literals to the various data members. Lines 43 through 47 retrieve the stored data from the structure and print it to the screen using the cout object.

Now let's take a look at another structure, one that's often used in the field of computer graphics. Examine the following simple data structure, which defines the location of a point in three-dimensional space by providing a floating-point coordinate for the x-axis, y-axis, and z-axis:

```
struct Point3d
{
    float x;
    float y;
    float z;
};
```

Because C++ is so flexible in how code is formatted, the Point3d structure could just as easily be written like this:

```
struct Point3d { float x; float y; float z; };
```

As you saw in Listing 9.1 you can initialize a data structure's member variables after declaring an instance of the structure. You can also populate data members when you create a structure instance by providing default values in braces, like this:

```
Point3d pt = { 3.0f, 3.5f, -5.0f };
```

This syntax assigns the values you've specified to the data members of the structure corresponding to the order in which they appear. The code in Listing 9.2 is very similar to that in Listing 9.1; it demonstrates the concept of declaring and initializing a structure in a single step.

Structure Instances

When you declare a variable of some structure type, you create an *instance* of that structure.

LISTING 9.2 Declaring and Initializing a Data Structure Simultaneously

```
 1: ////////////////////////////////////////////////////
 2: //  Module  : Point3d.cpp
 3: //
 4: //  Purpose : An example of creating and using a
 5: //            simple data structure
 6: ////////////////////////////////////////////////////
 7:
 8: #include <iostream.h>
 9:
10: // Create a 3d point structure
11: //
```

continues...

LISTING 9.2   **Continued**

LISTING 9.2

1 Lines 12-17: Declare the Point3d structure

2 Line 23: Declare and initialize a structure variable in a single step

3 Lines 30-32: Retrieve and display the structure data

```
12: struct Point3d
13: {
14:    float x;
15:    float y;
16:    float z;
17: };
18:
19: void main()
20: {
21:    // Declare and initialize a Point3d variable
22:    //
23:    Point3d pt = { 2.1f, 1.2f, 3.4f };
24:
25:    // Access the data stored in the structure
26:    //
27:    cout << "The contents of the Point3d \n"
28:         << "data structure is:\n\n";
29:
30:    cout << "x: " << pt.x << '\n';
31:    cout << "y: " << pt.y << '\n';
32:    cout << "z: " << pt.z << '\n';
33: }
```

The output of this program looks as you might expect:

```
The contents of the Point3d
data structure is:

x: 2.1
y: 1.2
z: 3.4
```

Creating Arrays of Structures

A single structure can be very useful, but the real value of structures becomes apparent when you are dealing with large quantities of data in multiple structure instances. By creating an array of structure variables, you can have as many complete structures as you need (structure array elements are often called *records*). You create an array of structures just like you create an array of a simple data type. For example, an array of 100 `Point3d` structures might be declared like this:

```
Point3d pt[100];
```

As you'll recall from Chapter 6, "Using Arrays," an array in C++ is always zero-based. Although we might declare 100 data elements for an array, those 100 elements are indexed from 0 to 99. To access the members of the array, you must use a combination of structure data member and array element syntax as shown in Figure 9.1.

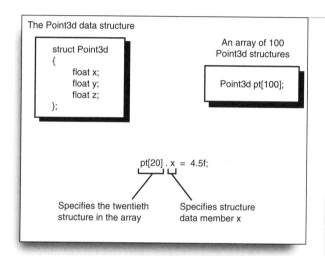

FIGURE 9.1

Accessing the twenty-first element of a `Point3d` structure array.

A good example of the use of a `Point3d` structure array is to store the coordinates of three-dimensional objects in a 3D computer graphics program. In this type of data representation, a set of 3D coordinates makes up the "faces" of an object. These faces are usually just triangles assembled to look like some real-world object. The set of 3D points (called *vertices*, in computer graphics lingo) that make up an object can often be generated mathematically by a program.

Interactive graphics systems often draw (called *rendering* in computer graphics lingo) these triangles by playing connect-the-dots—using simple lines to connect the vertices. Drawing a 3D object using just the 3D points and lines is called *wireframe rendering*. Okay, now that I've got the ten-cent computer-graphics terminology lesson out of the way, let's see the end result of an array of structures used to store some useful Point3d data. Take a look at the diamond-like wireframe image in Figure 9.2.

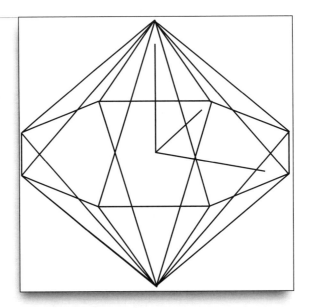

This simple wireframe rendering is the result of performing some mathematical calculations on a set of three original 3D points. The points are mathematically rotated around a virtual axis, generating several more points traversing 360 degrees. When the points are assembled into a series of triangles, they look like the image in Figure 9.2.

When rendered by a photo-realistic ray-tracing program, this same data set becomes quite realistic, as you can see in Figure 9.3. The math involved in generating these images is well beyond the scope of this book and isn't the issue at hand, so I'm not going to go into it here. The important issue is that these images—and most of the special animated effects you see in the latest blockbuster science-fiction movies—are created using programs that store and manipulate sets of 3D points. In the case of the diamond, the set is an array of Point3d structures.

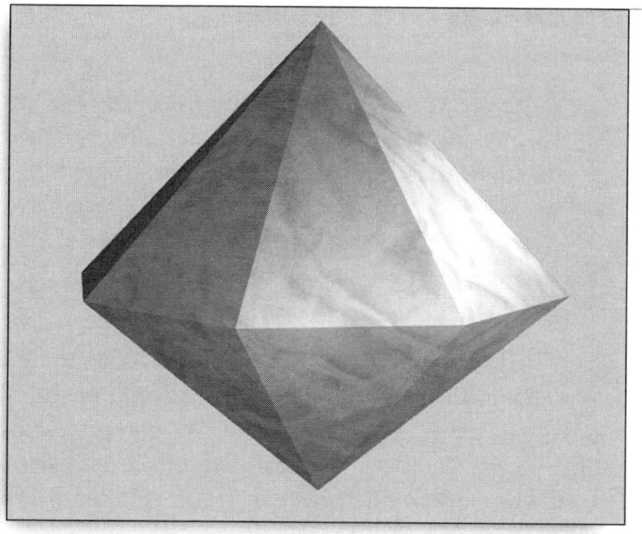

FIGURE 9.3
A ray-traced rendering of three-dimensional data stored in an array of structures.

To get an idea of how large these types of data sets can get, take a look at the rendering of data defining a mountain in Figure 9.4. This is a much more complex wireframe image that was generated mathematically by a program I wrote in C++, which uses arrays of `Point3d` structures to hold the `Point3d` data.

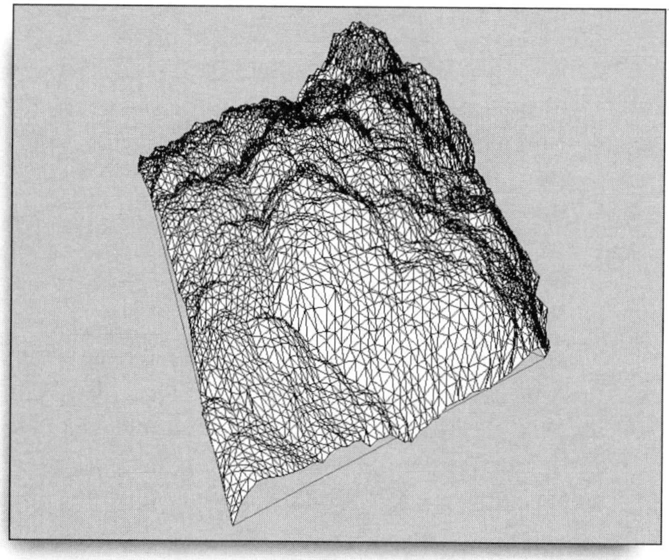

FIGURE 9.4
An array of more than 8,000 `Point3d` structures was used for this wireframe rendering of a mountain.

Try Ray Tracing for Yourself

Ray tracing is an advanced method of generating photo-realistic computer images; the image in Figure 9.3 was generated using a ray tracer. If you'd like to try your hand at it, or just want to learn more, visit `http://www.povray.org` and download the ***totally free*** ray tracer POVRAY, available as freeware for every major operating system and hardware platform.

Structures as Data Members

As you've seen, when you declare a structure within a program, you create a new data type, and this data type is immediately available for use in creating variables. Because the data members of a structure are variables themselves, it stands to reason that you can use a structure variable as a data member of some other structure. Using structures as data members of other structures is a great way to model complex data, and this type of data model is called a *hierarchical structure*.

Now I'll introduce a more complex example to tie this all together in a program. Suppose that you have to calculate payroll for the employees of the ACME company's three key departments: the anvil department, the explosives department, and the rocketry department. You could use the following data structure to define the data for each department:

```
struct Dept
{
    string Name;        // Department name
    short  CostCenter;  // Cost center
};
```

Likewise, you could define employee data in a structure like this one:

```
struct EmpPayroll
{
    string Name;        // Employee name
    short  EmpNum;      // Employee number
    bool   Exempt;      // Can earn overtime?
    float  Rate;        // Rate of pay
    float  Hours;       // Hours worked
    Dept   Department;  // Structure as a member
};
```

Notice that the Department member of the EmpPayroll structure is the Dept structure. When using structures as data members in this way, each substructure is accessed using a dot operator to get at the members. For example, to access the CostCenter for an employee of type EmpPayroll, you have to use one dot to access the employee variable's Department member, and another dot to access the Department member's CostCenter member, like this:

```
EmpPayroll MyEmployee;
MyEmployee.Department.CostCenter = 200;
```

Presenting a Payroll Processing Program

Of course, when you process payroll data for a company like ACME, you will have more than one employee. This is a case in which an array of structures comes in handy. The program in Listing 9.3 uses arrays of structures to illustrate basic payroll processing for the ACME company's three departments. As you examine the code, note that this program reads employee data out of a text file using a standard file stream, filling the employee array with this data.

SEE ALSO

➤ For more information about file streams, see page 805

LISTING 9.3 Using Arrays of Structures to Model Employee Payroll Data

```
 1: ////////////////////////////////////////////////////
 2: //   Module  : acme.cpp
 3: //
 4: //   Purpose : Shows the usage of arrays of structures
 5: ////////////////////////////////////////////////////
 6:
 7: #include <iostream>    // For cout
 8: #include <string>      // For standard strings
 9: #include <fstream>     // For standard file access
10:
11: using namespace std;   // Use the standard namespace
12:
13: const int MAX_EMPLOYEES = 9;
14:
15: // Create a department structure
16: //
17: struct Dept
18: {
19:     string Name;        // Department name
20:     short  CostCenter;  // Cost center
21: };
```

LISTING 9.3

1 Lines 17-21: Create a department structure

continues...

LISTING 9.3 CONTINUED

2 Lines 25-33: Create a payroll
structure

LISTING 9.3 **Continued**

```
22:
23: // Create an employee payroll structure
24: //
25: struct EmpPayroll
26: {
27:    string Name;        // Employee name
28:    short  EmpNum;       // Employee number
29:    bool   Exempt;       // Can earn overtime?
30:    float  Rate;         // Rate of pay
31:    float  Hours;        // Hours worked
32:    Dept   Department;   // Structure as a member
33: };
34:
35: // Global arrays of structures
36: //
37: Dept        dept[3];
38: EmpPayroll  ep[MAX_EMPLOYEES];
39:
40: // Function prototypes
41: //
42: void DisplayReportHeader();
43: bool LoadEmpData(string sFilename);
44: void Usage();
45:
46: /////////////////////////////////////////////////////////
47: //  DisplayReportHeader()
48:
49: void DisplayReportHeader()
50: {
51:    // Display a report header
52:    //
53:    cout << "EmpName" << "\t\t";
54:    cout << "EmpNum" << '\t';
55:    cout << "Dept Name" << '\t';
56:    cout << "CCtr" << '\t';
57:    cout << "Hours" << '\t';
58:    cout << "Pay" << "\n\n";
59: }
60:
61: /////////////////////////////////////////////////////////
62: //  LoadEmpData()
```

```
63:
64: bool LoadEmpData(const char *filename)
65: {
66:     // Fill the department "database"
67:     //
68:     dept[0].Name = "Anvils";
69:     dept[0].CostCenter = 100;
70:
71:     dept[1].Name = "Explosives";
72:     dept[1].CostCenter = 200;
73:
74:     dept[2].Name = "Rocketry";
75:     dept[2].CostCenter = 300;
76:
77:     // Fill the employee "database." Note that these
78:     // items are read from a text file...
79:     //
80:     ifstream in(filename);
81:     if (!in)
82:         return false;  // failed to open file
83:
84:     int i = 0;
85:
86:     char buf[100];
87:     while (i < MAX_EMPLOYEES)
88:     {
89:         in.getline(buf, 20, '\t');
90:         ep[i].Name = buf;
91:
92:         in.getline(buf,20, '\t');
93:         ep[i].EmpNum = atoi(buf);
94:
95:         in.getline(buf,20, '\t');
96:         ep[i].Exempt = (buf == "true");
97:
98:         in.getline(buf, 20, '\t');
99:         ep[i].Rate = atof(buf);
100:
101:         in.getline(buf, 20, '\t');
102:         ep[i].Hours = atof(buf);
103:
104:         in.getline(buf, 20, '\n');
```

continues…

LISTING 9.3 CONTINUED

 Line 80: Open an external data file

LISTING 9.3 CONTINUED

④ Line 133: Open an external
data file

LISTING 9.3   **Continued**

```
105:         ep[i].Department = dept[atoi(buf)];
106:
107:      i++;
108:    }
109:    return true;
110: }
111:
112: //////////////////////////////////////////////////
113: //  Usage()
114:
115: void Usage() {
116:    cout << "\nUsage:\n\n   ACME.EXE DataFile\n\n";
117:    cout << "Example:\n   ACME.EXE acme.txt\n\n";
118: }
119:
120: //////////////////////////////////////////////////
121: //  Driver : main()
122:
123: int main(int argc, char *argv[])
124: {
125:    if (argc < 2)
126:    {
127:       Usage();
128:       exit(0);
129:    }
130:
131:    char filename[] = argv[1];
132:
133:    if (!LoadEmpData(filename))  ──④
134:       return 1;
135:
136:    DisplayReportHeader();
137:
138:    // Calculate and display the payroll
139:    //
140:    for (int i = 0; i < MAX_EMPLOYEES; i++)
141:    {
142:       // Calc current employee pay
143:       //
144:       float CurPay = ep[i].Hours * ep[i].Rate;
145:
```

```
146:        // Check for overtime
147:        //
148:        if ((!ep[i].Exempt) && (ep[i].Hours > 40.0))
149:        {
150:            // Calc overtime at half the regular rate...
151:            //
152:            float ot =
153:                (ep[i].Hours - 40.0) * (ep[i].Rate / 2.0);
154:
155:            // ...and add it to the regular pay
156:            //
157:            CurPay += ot;
158:        }
159:
160:        // Ensure that the columns line up right
161:        //
162:        string tabs =
163:            (ep[i].Department.Name == "Anvils") ?
164:            "\t\t" : "\t";
165:
166:        // Make the decimal output look nice
167:        //
168:        cout.flags(ios::fixed);
169:        cout.precision(2);
170:
171:        // Display report line
172:        //
173:        cout << ep[i].Name << '\t';
174:        cout << ep[i].EmpNum << '\t';
175:        cout << ep[i].Department.Name << tabs;
176:        cout << ep[i].Department.CostCenter << '\t';
177:        cout << ep[i].Hours << '\t';
178:        cout << CurPay << '\n';
179:    }
180:    return 0;
181: }
```

LISTING 9.3 CONTINUED

5 Line 153: Calculate overtime pay

6 Lines 168-169: Use format flags for uniform output

The input data for this program comes from a simple text file that contains the items listed in Table 9.1. The data for each employee is stored on a separate line of the text file, and each data element in the file is *tab-delimited* by a tab (\t) character. Each line in the file ends with a newline (\n) character.

TABLE 9.1   The Fields of the Input File Used by the Program in Listing 9.3

Name Code	Cost Center	Exempt	Pay Rate	Hours	Dept
Jack Hammer	101	true	12.55	55.25	0
Bob Goddard	110	true	15.95	35.15	1
Johnny Fuse	233	true	22.33	44.75	2
Bill Jones	434	false	7.55	40.25	0
Sue Smith	221	false	7.27	40.54	0
Tim Ross	711	false	10.43	45.75	1
Mike Mull	232	false	11.78	51.32	1
Phil Space	123	false	16.85	35.58	2
Aldo Cella	113	false	17.52	38.16	2

The output from the program in Listing 9.3 is as follows:

```
EmpName         EmpNum  Dept Name   CCtr   Hours   Pay

Jack Hammer     101     Anvils      100    55.25   789.08
Bob Goddard     110     Explosives  200    35.15   560.64
Johnny Fuse     233     Rocketry    300    44.75   1052.30
Bill Jones      434     Anvils      100    40.25   304.83
Sue Smith       221     Anvils      100    40.54   296.69
Tim Ross        711     Explosives  200    45.75   507.16
Mike Mull       232     Explosives  200    51.32   671.22
Phil Space      123     Rocketry    300    35.58   599.52
Aldo Cella      113     Rocketry    300    38.16   668.56
```

To run the program and get the desired results, you must specify the data file as a command-line parameter, like this:

```
ACME.EXE acme.txt
```

Examining the Payroll Processing Program

This is the most complex program you've seen yet in this book, so I'll take some extra time to explain what's going on. The program begins by including three Standard C++ Library headers on lines 7 through 9. These headers provide access to the cout object, standard strings, and standard file access (for reading the input data file). The using namespace std statement on line 11 tells the compiler to make the Standard C++ library namespace the default namespace (see Chapter 16, "Exploring Namespaces," for details about namespaces).

On line 13, the integer constant MAX_EMPLOYEES is set to 9 for three reasons: there are nine employees in the input file, there are nine EmpPayroll array elements used by the program, and each employee uses an array element.

The department structure you saw earlier (Dept) is declared on lines 17 through 22; the employee payroll structure (EmpPayroll) is declared on lines 25 through 33. These declarations are followed by the creation of two arrays of structures. On line 37, an array of three Dept structures is defined, one for each of the three departments mentioned earlier. On line 38, an array of nine (MAX_EMPLOYEES) EmpPayroll structures is defined, one for each employee. In a real application, this number would be dynamically allocated depending on the number of employees in the data file—for the purposes of this program, the number is hard coded.

SEE ALSO

➤ *To learn more about dynamic memory allocation, see page 275*

Lines 42 through 44 declare function prototypes for the three user-defined functions resident in this program. The DisplayReportHeader() function just outputs the payroll report's column headers to the screen. The LoadEmpData() function takes care of reading the information out of the input data file and filling the EmpPayroll array with data. The Usage() function simply displays a message about the command-line parameter expected by the program (the data file). Let's look at each of these functions.

Lines 49 through 59 define the DisplayReportHeader() function. This function just uses the cout object to display the report column headers, using tab characters to space the columns appropriately.

The LoadEmpData() function is defined on lines 64 through 110 and contains file stream code that uses the standard input file stream ifstream. This function begins by filling the department array with data, setting the Name and CostCenter fields of each structure in the dept array (lines 68 through 75). This is pretty straightforward.

The LoadEmpData() function takes a single parameter: the character array filename, which contains the name of the input data file. On line 80, the ifstream object attempts to open this file using the file alias in. If the file doesn't open successfully, the function returns false, indicating failure (lines 81 and 82). Assuming that the file is successfully opened, execution continues. On line 86, the character array buf (buffer) is defined. This buffer is used to temporarily hold the input data as it's read from the file.

A while loop begins on line 87, using the expression (i<MAX_EMPLOYEES) as its conditional test. The loop iterates for each employee, loading data into the EmpPayroll array. The body of the loop runs from lines 88 through 108; the ifstream function getline() is used to grab a single data element from the input file for each member of the EmpPayroll structure. Basically, getline() reads data from the current file position until it finds a tab or newline character, and then stores what it has read into buf. Typically, the getline() call looks like this:

```
in.getline(buf, 20, '\t');
```

This statement specifies the buf array as the target for the input data, that a maximum of 20 characters will be read in, and that the tab character \t should be used as the delimiter between data elements in the file. The department code is the last item on each data line in the input file, so a newline character acts as the delimiter for this data element instead of a tab character (line 104). After each data element has been read from the file, it's converted (if necessary) from text to the appropriate data type before being stored in an EmpPayroll structure member. The while loop continues until all data has been read from the file. The ANSI C functions atoi() (alpha to integer) and atof() (alpha to float) are used for the type conversions, as you can see in this sample statement from line 93:

```
ep[i].EmpNum = atoi(buf);
```

The Usage() function just displays a message that tells the user to use a command-line argument to specify the input data filename.

The `main()` function uses command-line arguments, which you learned about in Chapter 7, "Creating and Using Functions." It begins by checking that the number of command-line parameters is at least 2 (line 125). If not, the `Usage()` function is called to explain the expected command-line parameters and the program exits using the ANSI C function `exit()` (line 128); otherwise the command-line parameter `argv[1]` (the input data filename) is assigned to the character array variable `filename` (line 131).

Line 133 calls the `LoadEmpData()` function; if the function call fails (meaning that the function couldn't open the file), line 134 returns a value of `1` to the operating system (indicating that something went wrong). If all goes well, the global arrays are now populated with data and the `DisplayReportHeader()` function is called on line 136.

The final portion of `main()` consists of a `for` loop running from line 140 to line 179. This loop iterates through each element of the `EmpPayroll` array, `ep`. The current pay for an employee is calculated on line 144. To see whether an employee is eligible for overtime pay, we check the `EmpPayroll` members `Exempt` and `Hours`. If `Exempt` is `false` **and** `Hours` is greater than 40 (line 148), overtime pay is calculated (lines 152 and 153) and added to the regular pay (line 157).

Line 162 declares the string variable `tabs`, which is used to ensure proper alignment of the data in the department column of the output. Because of tab/column-alignment problems with the shortest department name `Anvils`, lines 162 through 164 provide proper column formatting with two tab characters for the department name `Anvil`, and one tab character for the rest.

Lines 168 and 169 call the `iostream` functions `flags()` and `precision()` to manipulate the `cout` object's decimal number output. This causes `cout` to use fixed decimal places truncated and rounded at two decimal places. Finally, lines 173 through 178 display the columns of data for an employee, using the `tabs` variable as the delineator for output of the department name on line 175.

Adding Functions as Members

In addition to data members, structures in C++ can use functions as members. This is where C++ differs greatly from C, introducing object-oriented programming capabilities into the language —C doesn't allow member functions. To declare a function as a member of a structure, the function prototype must be included in the structure definition. As an example, take a look at the following basic rectangle structure:

```
struct Rectangle
{
    int Left;
    int Top;
    int Right;
    int Bottom;
};
```

You could create a function to calculate the width of a Rectangle, like this (see Figure 9.5):

```
int Width(Rectangle rect) { return rect.Right - rect.Left; }
```

FIGURE 9.5

Calculating the width of a Rectangle.

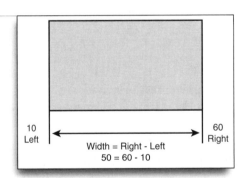

Likewise, you could create a function to calculate the height of a Rectangle, like this (see Figure 9.6):

```
int Height(Rectangle rect) { return rect.Bottom - rect.Top; }
```

C++ allows you to simplify your code by incorporating functions like these into your structures. By including these two functions as members of the Rectangle structure, you can eliminate the need for the function parameters because the Rectangle uses its internal data members to perform the calculations. Take a look at this revised `Rectangle` structure declaration, which includes the member functions:

```
struct Rectangle
{
    int Left;
    int Top;
    int Right;
    int Bottom;

    int Width() { return Right - Left; };
    int Height() { return Bottom - Top; };
};
```

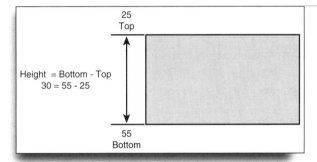

FIGURE 9.6

Calculating the height of a `Rectangle`.

The `Width()` and `Height()` functions are now a part of the structure declaration, a basic concept of object-oriented programming. Just as you use the dot operator to access data members, you use the dot operator to access member functions. You can access the `Width()` and `Height()` member functions like this:

```
Rectangle rect;

rect.Left   = 10;
rect.Top    = 25;
rect.Right  = 60;
rect.Bottom = 55;

int width  = rect.Width();   // In this case: 50
int height = rect.Height();  // In this case: 30
```

These examples should give you some inkling about what's going on under the hood when you call `iostream` functions for the `cout` object, as in this statement, which was used on line 169 of Listing 9.3:

```
cout.precision(2);
```

You can make calls like these in C++ but not in C because a C++ structure is really a *class*. You'll see a lot more about classes later in this book, beginning in Chapter 20, "Introducing Object-Oriented Programming." Now let's take a look at unions.

Using Unions for Efficient Storage

A *union* is similar to a structure, but unlike a structure, only one member of a union can be used at any one time. This is because a union reserves the same area of memory for each data member. This gives you a powerful and compact way to represent data. A union uses the same syntax as a structure, except that the keyword `union` is used instead of `struct`:

```
union UnionTag
{
    type-specifier DataMember1;
    type-specifier DataMember2;
    // Other members
    type-specifier DataMemberN;
};
```

A union can contain any data type as a member, so a union variable having several data types can take on values of several different types. If a union has both `int` and `float` data members, you can assign either of these types to the union. This means that a union can act as a variant data type, allowing you to store multiple types of data within a single variable—although the union can hold only one value in memory at a time. Here's an example:

```
union MyUnion
{
    int    num;
    float  flt;
};
```

Class

A user-defined data type that consists of data members and functions. A class's default access is private.

Union

A user-defined data type, similar to a structure, that may contain several members. Members of a union can only be accessed one at a time.

Accessing Union Members

To access a union member, you use the dot operator, just as you do for a structure. Take a look at the union in Listing 9.4, which shows off its multiple data-type capabilities.

LISTING 9.4   A Union Showing Off Its Multiple Data-Type Capabilities

```
 1: /////////////////////////////////////////////////
 2: //  Module  : union.cpp
 3: //
 4: //  Purpose : Shows the usage of unions
 5: /////////////////////////////////////////////////
 6:
 7: #include <iostream>    // For cout
 8: #include <string>      // For standard strings
 9:
10: using namespace std;  // Use the standard namespace
11:
12: // Create a union
13: //
14: union MyUnion
15: {
16:    int   num;
17:    float flt;
18: };
19:
20: /////////////////////////////////////////////////
21: //  main()
22:
23: void  main()
24: {
25:    MyUnion mu; // A MyUnion variable
26:
27:    // Use each of the data types within MyUnion
28:    //
29:    mu.num = 5000;
30:    cout << "As an int value:\n";
31:    cout << "  mu.num == " << mu.num << "\n\n";
32:
33:    mu.flt = 123.456f;
34:    cout << "As a float value:\n";
35:    cout << "  mu.flt == " << mu.flt << "\n";
36:
37: }
```

The output for the program looks like this:

```
As an int value:
  mu.num == 5000

As a float value:
  mu.flt == 123.456
```

What if line 33 immediately followed line 29? Could the union store both int and float values and retrieve them separately? The answer is no. If the code were to look like this,

```
mu.num = 5000;
mu.flt = 123.456f;
cout << "As an int value:\n";
cout << "  mu.num == " << mu.num << "\n\n";

cout << "As a float value:\n";
cout << "  mu.flt == " << mu.flt << "\n";
```

the int value would not be available, only the float value. The compiler will still display a value for mu.num, but not the value 5000. Instead, the output would look like this, converting the value 123.456f into an integer:

```
As an int value:
  mu.num == 1123477881

As a float value:
  mu.flt == 123.456
```

This is the big difference between a structure and a union.

Defining Structures as Union Members

Structures can also be union members. This allows a single union variable to behave as any structure it has as a member. For example, Listing 9.5 declares a union that contains a new Point2d structure and a Point3d structure (which you saw earlier).

LISTING 9.5   **A Union That Contains Two Structures: *Point2d* and *Point3d***

```
1: // Create a union with two structure members
2: //
3: union MyUnion2
4: {
5:     struct Point2d
6:     {
7:         float x;
8:         float y;
9:     };
10:
11:     struct Point3d
12:     {
13:         float x;
14:         float y;
15:         float z;
16:     };
17: };
```

> **Scope Resolution Operator**
>
> An operator used to specify the scope of an object within a specific class or namespace.

The members of this union are structures, nested directly within the union. Because the structures don't have variable identifiers, you can't access the member functions of the MyUnion2 structure. You can get to data members though, by using the *scope resolution operator* (::) to access the nested structure members. Using a variable mu of type MyUnion2, you can access Point3d data members to assign and retrieve values, like this:

```
MyUnion2 mu;

mu.Point3d::x = 1.0f;
mu.Point3d::y = 2.0f;
mu.Point3d::z = 3.0f;
```

By using this notation, you can specify the Point3d member you want to access by using the scope resolution operator, as in Point3d::z. Because the Point3d structure is wrapped within the union, you must qualify the statement with the union variable identifier (mu), as in mu.Point3d::z.

Listing 9.6 shows an altered version of this union, which adds variable identifiers to the end of each structure.

LISTING 9.6 A Union That Contains Two Structures with the Respective Variable Identifiers *pt* and *rect*

```
 1: // Create a union
 2: //
 3: union MyUnion3
 4: {
 5:    struct Point3d
 6:    {
 7:       float x;
 8:       float y;
 9:       float z;
10:    }
11:    pt;
12:
13:    struct Rectangle
14:    {
15:       int Left;
16:       int Top;
17:       int Right;
18:       int Bottom;
19:
20:       int Width()  { return Right - Left; };
21:       int Height() { return Bottom - Top; };
22:    }
23:    rect;
24: };
```

Now that there's a `rect` variable identifier for the `Rectangle` structure, the compiler reserves storage space that allows the use of its member functions, like this:

```
mu.rect.Left   = 10;
mu.rect.Top    = 25;
mu.rect.Right  = 60;
mu.rect.Bottom = 55;
int width  = mu.rect.Width();
int height = mu.rect.Height();
```

Listing 9.7 demonstrates the new and improved `MyUnion2` union in action. Note that this program uses the same basic techniques as Listing 9.1, assigning values to data members and displaying them with the `cout` object.

Note

The advantage of a union with nested structures over a structure with nested structures is that of lower memory usage. The union uses only enough memory for its largest member, so it's a better choice when you need access to only one member at a time.

LISTING 9.7   **Using a Union with Nested Structures as Members**

```cpp
 1: /////////////////////////////////////////////////////
 2: //  Module  : union2.cpp
 3: //
 4: //  Purpose : Shows the usage of a union with nested
 5: //            structures as members.
 6: /////////////////////////////////////////////////////
 7:
 8: #include <iostream>    // For cout
 9: #include <string>      // For standard strings
10:
11: using namespace std;  // Use the standard namespace
12:
13: // Create a union
14: //
15: union MyUnion2
16: {
17:    struct Point3d
18:    {
19:       float x;
20:       float y;
21:       float z;
22:    }
23:    pt;
24:
25:    struct Rectangle
26:    {
27:       int Left;
28:       int Top;
29:       int Right;
30:       int Bottom;
31:
32:       int Width()  { return Right - Left; };
33:       int Height() { return Bottom - Top; };
34:    }
35:    rect;
36: };
37:
38: /////////////////////////////////////////////////////
39: //  main()
40:
```

continues…

LISTING 9.7 **Continued**

```
41: void main()
42: {
43:    MyUnion2 mu; // A MyUnion variable
44:
45:    // Assign some values to the Point3d members
46:    //
47:    mu.Point3d::x = 1.0f;
48:    mu.Point3d::y = 2.0f;
49:    mu.Point3d::z = 3.0f;
50:
51:    // Display the values
52:    //
53:    cout << "Union as a Point3d value:\n";
54:
55:    cout << "    mu.Point3d::x == " <<
56:       mu.Point3d::x << "\n";
57:
58:    cout << "    mu.Point3d::y == " <<
59:       mu.Point3d::y << "\n";
60:
61:    cout << "    mu.Point3d::z == " <<
62:       mu.Point3d::z << "\n\n";
63:
64:    // Assign some values to the Rectangle members
65:    //
66:    mu.Rectangle::Left   = 10;
67:    mu.Rectangle::Top    = 25;
68:    mu.Rectangle::Right  = 60;
69:    mu.Rectangle::Bottom = 55;
70:
71:    // Calculate and display the width and height
72:    //
73:    cout << "Union as a rectangle value:\n";
74:
75:    cout << "    mu.rect.Left    == "
```

```
76:          << mu.rect.Left << '\n';
77:
78:     cout << "   mu.rect.Top       == "
79:          << mu.rect.Top << '\n';
80:
81:     cout << "   mu.rect.Right     == "
82:          << mu.rect.Right << '\n';
83:
84:     cout << "   mu.rect.Bottom    == "
85:          << mu.rect.Bottom << "\n\n";
86:
87:     cout << "   mu.rect.Width()   == "
88:          << mu.rect.Width() << '\n';
89:
90:     cout << "   mu.rect.Height() == "
91:          << mu.rect.Height() << '\n';
92: }
```

The output for this program looks like this:

```
Union as a Point3d value:
    mu.Point3d::x == 1
    mu.Point3d::y == 2
    mu.Point3d::z == 3

Union as a rectangle value:
    mu.rect.Left     == 10
    mu.rect.Top      == 25
    mu.rect.Right    == 60
    mu.rect.Bottom   == 55

    mu.rect.Width()  == 50
    mu.rect.Height() == 30
```

Defining Unions as Structure Members

In a similar manner, unions can also be members of structures. This allows for very flexible structures. For example, the following `MyStruct2` structure contains a union member that uses the data member name `mu2`:

```
struct MyStruct2
{
    int   Num1;
    float Num2;
    union
    {
        int   Mem1;
        float Mem2;
    }
    mu2;
};
```

As you can see, structures and unions are powerful, flexible programming tools that can make your programs much more organized.

Using Pointers and References

Declare, dereference, and assign pointers

Use pointers to structures

Use pointers as function parameters

Use pointer arithmetic

Declare and initialize a reference

Use references as function parameters and return values

Overview

Software is, at its heart, lots of binary code—a slew of 1s and 0s flipping about, turning on and off. As programming languages have progressed and evolved over the years, the abstraction separating the programmer from the binary fiddling going on in the underlying hardware has dramatically increased.

This abstraction is complete in the case of some modern programming languages. Many contemporary programmers don't even understand the notion of memory addressing —it's a foreign concept to them. Luckily, C++ allows you to use as high a level of abstraction as you're comfortable with, or to get down to the bare metal if you need to. Pointers and references are what allow C++ programmers to get down to that bare metal, directly working with memory addresses as needed.

Understanding Pointers

Pointer

A data type consisting of an unbound set of values that indicates the location (memory address) of a variable.

A *pointer* is a special type of variable that stores a memory address. The actual value of the address is usually not important to the programmer. Pointer variables have names like any other variable, so you can use the name of the pointer as an alias for the actual memory address stored in the variable. Because the name represents the address, it is said to *point* to the address, thus the name *pointer*.

Why Use Pointers?

A pointer to a memory address is the mechanism provided by C++ to let you manipulate memory addressing and take complete control of your program's destiny. Pointer variables, or pointers, play a huge role in C++, as do *references* (discussed later in this chapter). Pointers are variables used to store memory addresses; they allow you to access the fundamental storage structure of the computer.

Each identifier you declare in a program takes up a certain amount of memory that's set aside by the compiler at compile time. At runtime, an identifier is loaded into memory somewhere, into some memory address determined by the computer that executes the program. It's usually not important exactly *where* in memory a variable is located, but by using a pointer, you can find out *exactly* where that variable is in memory and manipulate it. You can also allocate chunks of memory dynamically as you need it, using pointers to keep track of what you've allocated—in fact, pointers are **required** for dynamic memory allocation (the topic of Chapter 11, "Allocating Memory in C++").

SEE ALSO

➤ *For more information about using pointers for dynamic memory allocation, see page 277*

Memory Addressing

Each object and function in a program takes up some portion of computer memory when the program runs. For example, objects such as the following three intrinsic data types are stored in computer memory—arbitrarily—at runtime:

```
char    grade;
short   score;
float   average;
```

There's no way to know into what address a particular object will load, and that's where pointers become important. Take a look at Figure 10.1, which shows these three objects as they might look when loaded into computer memory somewhere, each starting at some specific (although arbitrary) address and having some certain length (as determined by its data type).

Declaring a Pointer

To declare a pointer to a specific data type, you use the indirection operator (*) between the data type and the variable name, using this syntax:

```
DataType * VariableName;
```

I like to use a lowercase p as a prefix for a pointer variable name because this naming convention makes it easy for me to identify pointer variables in my source code. For example, you can define some variable Var as an integer and declare another variable pVar as a pointer to an integer, like this:

```
int Var = 50;
int *pVar;
```

Note

The memory addresses shown in Figure 10.1 are arbitrary—it's impossible to know at what address a variable will be stored at runtime.

Note

A pointer to an object must have the same data type as the object it points to.

FIGURE 10.1

Three intrinsic C++ objects as they might look when loaded into computer memory addresses.

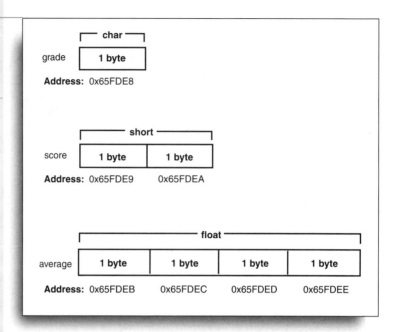

grade

┌─── char ───┐

| 1 byte |

Address: 0x65FDE8

score

┌─────── short ───────┐

| 1 byte | 1 byte |

Address: 0x65FDE9   0x65FDEA

average

┌─────────────── float ───────────────┐

| 1 byte | 1 byte | 1 byte | 1 byte |

Address: 0x65FDEB   0x65FDEC   0x65FDED   0x65FDEE

The first line of this code says, "Define the integer Var and set it equal to 50"; the second line says, "Declare the integer pointer pVar." You can then make pVar point to Var by getting the memory address of Var and storing it in pVar, using the address-of operator (&), like this:

```
pVar = &Var;
```

Dereference

The process of getting the actual object pointed to by a pointer.

The address-of operator returns the actual starting memory address of an object. The memory address of Var is now stored in pVar. To get the actual data pointed to by pVar, you must use the indirection operator (*) to *dereference* the pointer, as follows:

```
cout << "The variable pointed to by pVar = " << *pVar;
```

This dereferencing gets the actual object pointed to by the pointer. A common mistake of programmers first using pointers is forgetting to use the address-of operator when assigning the address of a variable to a pointer variable. Failure to use this operator will result in an error. For example, this is incorrect:

```
*pVar = Var; // Var is an object, can't assign to a pointer
```

The correct statement assigns the address of Var, not Var itself, like this:

```
*pVar = &Var; // &Var is an address
```

A small program to demonstrate this process is shown in Listing 10.1. Figure 10.2 shows the Microsoft Visual C++ debugger with both pVar and *pVar in the watch window, showing that a pointer value (pVar) is an actual memory address and that the object the pointer points to (*pVar) is an integer. The value of pVar is a hexadecimal memory address, whereas the value of Var is the integer stored at that address.

LISTING 10.1 **A Program Demonstrating Simple Pointer Use**

```
1: ///////////////////////////////////////////////////////
2: //   Module   : pointer1.cpp
3: //
4: //   Purpose : A simple demonstration of using a pointer
5: ///////////////////////////////////////////////////////
6:
7: #include <iostream.h>
8:
9: void main()
10: {
11:    int Var = 50;
12:    int *pVar;
13:    pVar = &Var;
14:    cout << "The variable Var, pointed to by pVar, is "
15:       << *pVar << ".\nVar is located at address: "
16:       << pVar << endl;
17: }
```

LISTING 10.1

① Lines 12-13: Create and initialize a pointer variable

The output from this program looks like this:

```
The variable Var, pointed to by pVar, is 50.
Var is located at address: 0x0068FDF4
```

This program creates an integer variable (Var) on line 11 and initializes it to the value 50. Line 12 declares a pointer to an integer (pVar), and line 13 assigns the address of the object Var to the pointer pVar.

On line 15, the pointer pVar is dereferenced to get the actual object pointed to (Var), displaying its value on the screen. On line 16, the value of the pointer pVar itself is used to display the memory address of Var.

Object Size and Pointers

Because the compiler knows what data type a pointer points to, it knows how many bytes of data to retrieve from memory beyond the starting address of the pointer when dereferencing.

FIGURE 10.2

The Microsoft Visual C++ debugger with both pVar (address) and *pVar (object) in the Watch window.

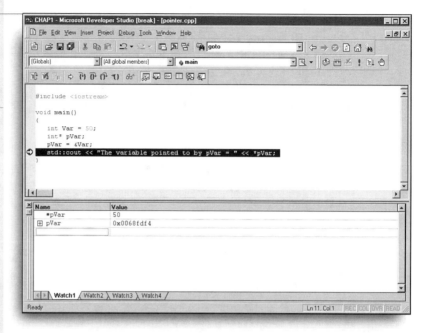

Remember the variables shown in Figure 10.1? If we define these variables and, additionally, define a pointer to each variable, we get something like this:

```
char    grade;
short   score;
float   average;

char*   pGrade    = &grade;     // pointer to grade
short*  pScore    = &score;     // pointer to score
float*  pAverage  = &average;   // pointer to average
```

Regardless of what the value is for grade, score, or average, the pointers pGrade, pScore, and pAverage are always going to point at the memory address of the corresponding variable.

Figure 10.3 shows these objects in memory, each starting at some specific memory address. Each object has a specific length that's determined by its data type, and each object has a pointer pointing to it.

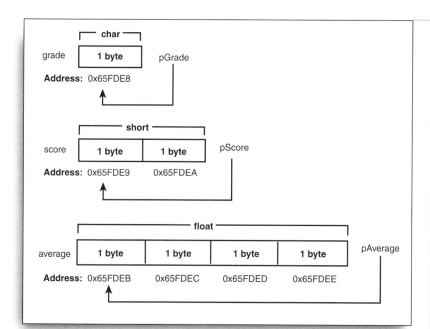

FIGURE 10.3
How pointers relate to computer memory.

Dereferencing a Pointer

A pointer references an object's address—it's not the object itself. To get the actual object pointed to by a pointer, you have to dereference the pointer. By using the indirection operator, you can get the object that the pointer points to. Here's an example of the difference between these two uses of a pointer variable:

```
float MyFloat = 1.5f;  // define a float variable
float *pFloat;         // declare a pointer to a float

pFloat = &MyFloat;
```

In this code snippet, the *pointer* is pFloat, but the object *pointed to* is *pFloat. This is a very important distinction—you must fully understand the difference between pFloat and *pFloat. This is a difficult concept to come to terms with in the beginning. By dereferencing pFloat with the dereference operator (*) you come up with the actual object pointed to. Reread the first part of this chapter until you understand these concepts fully, because understanding pointers and memory addresses is critical to advancing to higher levels of using C++. Make sure you fully comprehend the following points:

- The object `myFloat` is the same as the dereferenced pointer to that object, which is `*pFloat`.

- The pointer `pFloat` is the same as the address of `myFloat`, which is `&myFloat`.

Getting Pointers to Structures

You can have a pointer to a structure just as easily as you can have a pointer to an `int` or a `float`. To set a pointer to a structure, just use the address-of operator to get the starting address of the structure and assign this address to a pointer, which then references the actual structure object. For example, here's a structure called `Image`:

```
typedef struct
{
    int        width;
    int        height;
    unsigned *pbits;
}
Image;
```

Assume that the `Image` structure holds the data for a color picture (notice that the third member of this structure is a pointer itself). Now let's declare two `Image` objects, `Picture1` and `Picture2`, and a pointer to an `Image` structure:

```
Image Picture1;
Image Picture2;
Image *pImage;
```

To point the `pImage` pointer to `Picture1`, just do this:

```
pImage = &Picture1;
```

Likewise, to point the `pImage` pointer to `Picture2`, just do this:

```
pImage = &Picture2;
```

Using Pointer-to-Member Notation

When you use a pointer to a structure, class, or union, you must use a special type of notation to access structure, class, or union members. This notation uses the pointer-to-member operator (->) to provide member access. The following example uses the Image structure, first assigning to the pImage pointer the address of the Picture1 object, like this:

```
Image  Picture1;
Image *pImage = &Picture1;
```

To access the width member of the Picture1 object directly, you use the dot operator (.) to specify the member, like this:

```
Picture1.width = 100;
```

To access the width member of the Picture1 object by pointer, you use the pointer-to-member operator (->) to specify the member, like this:

```
pImage->width = 100;
```

You can also access the width member of the Picture1 object directly using pointer dereferencing: You use the dot operator to specify the member, like this (the parentheses are required to tell the compiler to dereference the pointer before trying to access the width member):

```
(*pImage).width = 100;
```

Finally, you can use the pointer-to-member operator to access the width member of the Picture1 object by way of the pointer by using the address-of operator on the Picture1 object itself, which yields a pointer, like this (again, the parentheses are required to tell the compiler to get the address of the object before trying to access the width member):

```
(&Picture1)->width = 100;
```

All four of these statements accomplish the same thing, each using a slightly different syntax to set the value of the width member. Each form has its place, but the `Picture1.width` and `pPicture1->width` forms are the most common.

Listing 10.2 puts all this together into a complete program.

LISTING 10.2   A Program That Demonstrates Several Ways to Access a Structure Member Using Pointer-to-Member Operators

```
1: ////////////////////////////////////////////////////
2: //  Module  : pointer2.cpp
3: //
4: //  Purpose : Demonstrates several ways to access a
5: //            structure member using the indirection
6: //            and dot operators.
7: ////////////////////////////////////////////////////
8:
9: #include <iostream.h>
10:
11: const char NL = '\n';
12:
13: // The Image structure
14: //
15: typedef struct
16: {
17:     int      width;
18:     int      height;
19:     unsigned *bits;
20: }
21: Image;
22:
23: ////////////////////////////////////////////////////
24: // main()
25:
26: void main()
27: {
28:     Image  Picture1;
29:     Image *pImage = &Picture1;
30:
31:     Picture1.width = 100;
32:
33:     cout << "Picture1.width      == "
34:         << Picture1.width << NL;
35:
```

```
36:    cout << "pImage->width      == "
37:       << pImage->width << NL;
38:
39:    cout << "(*pImage).width    == "
40:       << (*pImage).width << NL;
41:
42:    cout << "(&Picture1)->width == "
43:       << (&Picture1)->width << NL;
44: }
```

The output from this program is as follows:

```
Picture1.width      == 100
pImage->width       == 100
(*pImage).width     == 100
(&Picture1)->width == 100
```

This program uses the Image structure declared from lines 15 through 21 to demonstrate data member access using a pointer. The first task of the main() function is to create an instance of an Image structure (Picture1) on line 28. Line 29 defines a pointer to an Image object (pImage) and initializes it with the address of the Picture1 object (&Picture1).

On line 31, the value of the Picture1.width member is initialized to the value 100. The remaining statements in the main() function show various ways of accessing the width member. Line 34 uses the Picture1.width member directly.

Line 37 uses the pointer pImage to access the width member, using the pointer-to-member operator (->).

Line 40 uses the dereferenced pImage pointer (*pImage) with the dot operator (.) to access the width member.

Line 43 uses the address of the Picture1 object (&Picture1) with the pointer-to-member operator to access the width member.

Using Pointers as Function Parameters

Passing a structure to a function by value is inefficient because the entire structure must be copied. Each member of the structure must be pushed onto the stack, copied, and later popped back off the stack. This approach uses extra processor cycles. Imagine the performance hit when using structures containing hundreds of members—this Polygon structure, for example:

```
Struct Polygon
{
    int BorderColor;
    int FillColor;
    Point2d pt[1000];
};
```

This imaginary structure represents a polygon composed of up to 1,000 vertices. If you sent this structure directly into a function as an argument, the program would have to copy each of these vertices to the stack when the function is called. This approach would be downright foolish. Here's a prototype for a function that demonstrates this foolishness:

```
void Draw(Polygon MyPolygon);
```

When passing a structure to a function, a better way is to use pointers. Passing a pointer to a structure as a function argument simply tells the function the address of the structure so that the function can do what it needs to do by accessing the actual structure, not a copy of it. Declaring a function to use pointer parameters is easy—just use the indirection operator, like this:

```
void Draw(Polygon *pMyPolygon);
```

Of course, when you send a pointer to a structure into a function, you must use the pointer-to-member operator to access the structure's members. For example, the Draw() function declared above might use the pMyPolygon parameter like this (assuming that the value for BLACK had been defined somewhere in the program):

```
void Draw(Polygon *pMyPolygon)
{
    // ...
    pMyPolygon->BorderColor = BLACK;
    // ...
}
```

Using Arrays as Pointers

The first element of an array holds the address of the array itself, and as such, is a pointer of sorts. This is why both of the following statements perform the same task:

```
char *Phrase  = "Some text";
char Phrase[] = "Some text";
```

To get a pointer to the entire array, the array name itself, without the braces, is used (for example, Phrase). You can also create a pointer to an array explicitly, like this:

```
void main()
{
   char Phrase[] = "Some text";
   char *pPhrase = Phrase;

   cout << pPhrase << endl;

   for (int i =0; i<strlen(pPhrase); ++i)
      cout << pPhrase[i];
}
```

You can also get explicit pointers to array elements by using the address-of operator on a given element. For example, to get a pointer to the sixth element of the Phrase array ('t'), you could do this:

```
char *p5 = &Phrase[5];  // sixth element, zero-based array
```

Passing Arrays to Functions

Because the first element of an array is actually a pointer to the array, you must send arrays directly into functions as reference arguments rather than by value.

Take a look at this array:

```
int MyIntArray[100];
```

You can get a pointer to the array by taking the address of its first element, like this:

```
int *pInt = &MyIntArray[0];
```

```
for (int i = 0; i < 100; i++)
    MyIntArray[i] = Square( &(MyIntArray[i]) );
```

Notice the parentheses around the array and its element index: `&(MyIntArray[i])`. The parentheses ensure that the compiler can correctly resolve this expression.

If the element being passed to the function is a complex structure instead of an integer, then the use of the pointer parameter greatly speeds up the operation.

Passing an Entire Array

To pass an entire array into a function, you can just send the array name (a pointer to the array). Because the function will likely need access to all array elements, you must also pass an argument to tell the function how many elements the array contains. Here's another overloaded `Square()` function; this time, it takes an array pointer and an element count as parameters to square every array element with a single function call:

```
void Square(int *pArray, int count)
{
    for (int i = 0; i < count; i++)
        pArray[i] = pArray[i] * pArray[i];
}
```

To square every array element, just pass the array address and element count into the new function, like this:

```
int MyIntArray[100];

// Populate the array
//
for (int i = 0; i < 100; i++)
    MyIntArray[i] = i;

// Square each array element
//
Square(MyIntArray, 100);
```

The program in Listing 10.3 demonstrates the use of arrays and pointers with functions.

Another, more economical way to write this statement is to use just the array name, with no element brackets, like this:

```
int *pInt = MyIntArray;
```

These two statements are equivalent, but the second is obviously more concise. Along the same lines, you can pass individual array elements or their addresses into a function, or you can pass the entire array.

Passing Array Elements

Here's a simple function, called `Square()`, that simply multiplies its argument by itself and returns the result:

```
long Square(int num) { return num * num; }
```

This function expects to receive an integer as a parameter. The array elements of `MyIntArray[]`, when passed by value, fit this description. To square each member of `MyIntArray[]`, you might do this:

```
int MyIntArray[100];

// Populate the array
//
for (int i = 0; i < 100; i++)
   MyIntArray[i] = i;

// Square each array element
//
for (int i = 0; i < 100; i++)
   MyIntArray[i] = Square(MyIntArray[i]);
```

Suppose that we define an overloaded `Square()` function that takes a pointer to an integer as an argument instead, like this:

```
long Square(int *pNum) { return *pNum * *pNum; }
```

This version of the function uses the indirection operator to get the actual integer pointed to (`*pNum`), and multiplies it by itself. Using this function with the `MyIntArray[]` array in a function call would look like this:

```
// Square each array element
//
```

LISTING 10.3   **A Program That Demonstrates Using Arrays and Pointers with Functions**

```
1: //////////////////////////////////////////////////////
2: //  Module  : array.cpp
3: //
4: //  Purpose : Shows three ways of using arrays and
5: //                pointers with functions
6: //////////////////////////////////////////////////////
7:
8: #include <iostream.h>
9:
10: const char NL = '\n';
11:
12: // Overloaded function prototypes
13: //
14: long Square(int num);
15: long Square(int *pNum);
16: void Square(int *pArray, int count);
17:
18: //////////////////////////////////////////////////////
19: //  main()
20:
21: void main()
22: {
23:     const int MAX = 5;
24:
25:     int Array1[MAX];
26:     int Array2[MAX];
27:     int Array3[MAX];
28:
29:     // Populate the arrays
30:     //
31:     for (int i = 0; i < MAX; i++)
32:     {
33:         Array1[i] = i;
34:         Array2[i] = i;
35:         Array3[i] = i;
36:     }
37:
38:     // Display each Array1 element, squared
39:     //
```

```
40:     for (i = 0; i < MAX; i++)
41:        cout << i << " squared is "
42:           << Square(Array1[i]) << NL;
43:
44:     // Display each Array2 element, squared
45:     //
46:     cout << NL;
47:     for (i = 0; i < MAX; i++)
48:        cout << i << " squared is "
49:           << Square( &(Array1[i]) ) << NL;
50:
51:     // Display each Array3 element, squared
52:     //
53:     cout << NL;
54:     Square(Array3, MAX);
55:     for (i = 0; i < MAX; i++)
56:        cout << i << " squared is "
57:           << Array3[i] << NL;
58: }
59:
60: ///////////////////////////////////////////////////
61: //  Square()
62:
63: long Square(int num)
64:    { return num * num; }
65:
66: ///////////////////////////////////////////////////
67: //  Square()
68:
69: long Square(int *pNum)
70:    { return *pNum * *pNum; }
71:
72: ///////////////////////////////////////////////////
73: //  Square()
74:
75: void Square(int *pArray, int count)
76: {
77:    for (int i = 0; i < count; i++)
78:       pArray[i] = pArray[i] * pArray[i];
79: }
```

LISTING 10.3 CONTINUED

3 Lines 40-57: Square and display all array elements using three overloaded Square() functions

This program provides the following output:

```
0 squared is 0
1 squared is 1
2 squared is 4
3 squared is 9
4 squared is 16

0 squared is 0
1 squared is 1
2 squared is 4
3 squared is 9
4 squared is 16

0 squared is 0
1 squared is 1
2 squared is 4
3 squared is 9
4 squared is 16
```

This program begins by declaring function prototypes for three overloaded Square() functions. The first two versions of this function each square a number, but the third version, declared on line 16, squares the elements of an entire array. To demonstrate each of these functions, the main() function begins by defining the integer constant MAX with a value of 5 (line 23). This constant is subsequently used with array operations in the rest of the main() function to represent the upper bound of an array.

Lines 25 through 27 declare three arrays of integers, each having MAX (5) elements. The for loop running from lines 31 through 36 populates the arrays by assigning the loop iteration value (i) to each array element.

The for loop running from line 40 through line 42 uses the first version of the Square() function, sending array elements to the function *by value*. This approach is acceptably efficient with an integer array, but the elements of an array of structures would be better off being passed *by reference*, using a pointer. The for loop running from line 47 through line 49 calls the second version of Square(), which does just that, passing each array element by address instead of by value. Line 54 calls the third version of the

`Square()` function, which squares each array element. The final `for` loop runs from line 54 through line 57, displaying the altered values of each array element.

Using Pointer Arithmetic

An interesting use of pointers is *pointer arithmetic*. You can use the increment (++) and decrement (- -) operators on a pointer to move the pointer in memory. The number of bytes the pointer moves depends on the size of the object pointed to. For example, in the case of a `char` pointer, an increment operation moves the pointer one byte past where it previously pointed (because a `char` is one byte long). Likewise, an `int` pointer would move `sizeof(int)` bytes (because an `int` is `sizeof(int)` bytes long). The program in Listing 10.4 shows the use of pointer arithmetic on a character string to display the string in both forward and reverse order.

LISTING 10.4 A Program That Uses Pointer Arithmetic to Display a Character String in Both Forward and Reverse Order

```
1: /////////////////////////////////////////////////////
2: //  Module  : Arithmetic.cpp
3: //
4: //  Purpose : Shows basic use of pointer arithmetic
5: /////////////////////////////////////////////////////
6:
7: #include <iostream.h>
8: #include <string.h>
9:
10: const char NL = '\n';
11:
12: // Function Prototype
13: //
14: char * ReverseString(char *pStr);
15:
16: /////////////////////////////////////////////////////
17: //  main()
18:
19: void main()
20: {
21:     char *str = "This is a test string.";
```

continues…

LISTING 10.4 CONTINUED

① Lines 24-25: Display a character string using pointer arithmetic

② Lines 42-53: Use pointer arithmetic to reverse characters in a string

LISTING 10.4 **Continued**

```
22:     char *ch  = &str[0];
23:
24:     for (unsigned i = 0; i < strlen(str); ++i) ────────┐
25:        cout << *ch++; // increment to next character ──┤──── ①
26:
27:     cout << NL << ReverseString(str);
28: }
29:
30: /////////////////////////////////////////////////////
31: //  ReverseString()
32:
33: char * ReverseString(char *pStr)
34: {
35:     // Use pointer arithmetic to reverse the string
36:     //
37:     int  len = strlen(pStr);     // Number of chars
38:     char *s  = &(pStr[0]);       // Get ptr to start char
39:     char *e  = &(pStr[len-1]);   // Get ptr to end char
40:     char temp;                   // buffer char
41:
42:     do ──────────────────────────────────────────┐
43:     {                                             │
44:        // Swap outer digits                       │
45:        temp = *s;   // temp  = start              │
46:        *s   = *e;   // start = end                │
47:        *e   = temp; // end   = temp               │──── ②
48:                                                   │
49:        // Move inward, into the string from both ends │
50:        ++s;                                       │
51:        --e;                                       │
52:     }                                             │
53:     while (s < e);   // repeat until midpoint ────┘
54:
55:     return pStr;
56: }
```

The output from this program looks like this:

```
This is a test string.
.gnirts tset a si sihT
```

As you can see, the string is reversed. The program begins by including <string.h> on line 8, providing access to the ANSI C library function strlen(), used in the string reversal function ReverseString(), which is declared on line 14.

Line 21 defines and initializes the character string str, and line 22 defines a pointer (ch) to the first character of the string. The for loop in lines 24 and 25 demonstrates accessing each character in the string with pointer arithmetic. Line 25 is the key to this operation, sending the dereferenced ch pointer (*ch) to the cout object for display, while simultaneously post-incrementing ch to point to the next character in the string. With each iteration of the loop, the next character is displayed.

Line 27 concludes the main() function by calling the ReverseString() function to display the string in reverse order. The ReverseString() function itself uses pointer arithmetic to reorder the characters in the string.

Line 37 uses the strlen() function to get the number of characters in the string, assigning this value to the variable len. Line 38 assigns the address of the first character in the string to the character pointer s (s is for start).

Because the character string is zero-based, the expression len-1 gives the location of the last character in the string. Line 39 assigns the address of the last character in the string to the character pointer e (e is for end). Line 40 declares the character object temp, used as temporary storage while shuffling character positions.

The actual reversal is accomplished in the do loop that runs from lines 42 through 53. In this loop, on line 45, the temp object is assigned the value pointed to by s (*s). On line 46, the value pointed to by s (*s) is then assigned the value pointed to by e (*e). Finally, on line 47, the value pointed to by e (*e) is assigned the value stored in temp. These three statements achieve the swapping of two characters.

Line 50 pre-increments the value of pointer s, pointing it one character *forward* in the string. Likewise, line 51 pre-decrements the value of pointer e, pointing it one character *backward* in the string. As the loop iterates, these pointers move inward, toward the middle, away from the ends of the string. When the value of pointer s is equal to or greater than the value of pointer e, the middle of the string has been reached and all the characters have been swapped, so the loop terminates, returning the value of the reversed string on line 55.

Understanding References

Reference

An alias for an object, similar to a pointer, used to pass an object by reference rather than by value.

A *reference* is an alias for an object and is closely related to a pointer. References are used mainly for passing values to functions and for avoiding messy pointer notation (such as accessing a structure member like this: `(*myPointer).myMember`). You specify a reference by using the reference operator (`&`), which is the same symbol as is used for the address-of operator (`&`).

Realize that although pointers and references have a lot in common, a reference is **not** a pointer. A reference must reference an existing object, and you tell the reference which object when you declare the reference. After the reference is declared, anything you do *with* it or *to* it is actually being done to the object being referenced—imagine a reference as acting as a kind of C++ voodoo doll. Once declared, a reference can't be changed to reference some other object.

Declaring and Initializing a Reference

Unlike a pointer, which is a variable itself (one that holds a memory address), a reference must have an associated object that it references: You can't declare a reference without specifying its associated object. As an example, the following code fragment creates a reference to a `float` variable:

```
float  f  = 2.5f;
float& fr = f;   // fr now references f
```

If you change the value of the reference `fr`, you're really changing the value of `f` because `fr` is **really** `f`, referenced as another name:

```
fr += 2.5f;   // now f == 5.0, because fr is really f
```

References can also be declared as a constant (const), meaning that the object referenced can't be altered in any way, for example:

```
const float& f = 5.5f;
```

In this case, the object f always has a value of 5.5f throughout the object's lifetime.

Using References as Function Parameters

If you want to pass a reference to a function, you simply declare the function to use a reference, like this:

```
long Square(const int&);
```

When a function parameter is declared const, it specifies that the function cannot change its value in any way. The function definition then uses the reference parameter, like this:

```
long Square(const int& i) { return i * i; }
```

Then, when you send an argument to the function, you can simply do it as if you are passing the argument by value:

```
int num = 5;
int n = square(num);
```

If we rewrite the function using a pointer parameter instead of a reference parameter we'd have this:

```
long Square(int *i) { return (*i) * (*i); }
```

Notice that the pointer has to be dereferenced for each operand in the multiplication operation. Then, when you send an argument to the function, you'd have to use the address-of operator to send the address of num as an argument, like this:

```
int num = 5;
int n = square(&num);
```

The use of references can really clean up your code, making it easier to read and maintain. Also, if you use references instead of pointers as often as possible, you'll eliminate the possibility of hard-to-spot pointer-related bugs. Suppose that you are passing a large data structure into a function. As you know, passing the structure by value is inefficient because the entire structure must

Tip

You should normally pass a reference to a function only as a **const** parameter. Doing so avoids the possibility of inadvertently changing the data being referenced. If you need to change data passed as a parameter, use a pointer instead of a reference.

be copied. Passing by pointer can sometimes get a bit messy, notation-wise (depending on what you're trying to do). Passing a reference to the structure makes your code clean and efficient.

Using References as Function Return Values

Because a reference can modify the object it references, you can create a function for the sole purpose of modifying the object by way of the reference. Although I prefer to pass a reference to a function as a const parameter—to avoid the possibility of inadvertently changing the object being referenced—sometimes it's convenient to use a reference to change the object, and it's perfectly legal to do so. Consider the following Point3d data structure:

```
typedef struct
{
    float x, y, z;
}
Point3d;
```

The following sample function, named Increment(), increments the members of the structure by reference:

```
void Increment(Point3d& p, float f)
{
    p.x += f;
    p.y += f;
    p.z += f;
}
```

A const reference, in contrast, won't even compile when used in this way. For example, the following function, Increment2(), won't compile because the const reference is unalterable, yet the code insists that the members be altered:

```
void Increment2(const Point3d& p, float f)
{
    p.x += f;    // this won't compile
    p.y += f;    // this won't compile
    p.z += f;    // this won't compile
}
```

This contradiction in terms causes a compiler error, so never attempt to modify const reference objects. Also, you should always use the const modifier when you want to avoid inadvertent changes to the data, eliminating side effects. For demonstration purposes only, the program in Listing 10.5 shows the use of a reference parameter in a function whose purpose is to increment the value of all Point3d structure members by some specified amount.

LISTING 10.5   **A Program That Demonstrates Altering an Object by Using a Reference Parameter**

```
1: ///////////////////////////////////////////////////
2: //   Module   : reference.cpp
3: //
4: //   Purpose : Demonstrates passing a function return
5: //             value by reference parameter.
6: ///////////////////////////////////////////////////
7:
8: #include <iostream.h>
9:
10: typedef struct
11: {
12:     float x, y, z;
13: }
14: Point3d;
15:
16: // Function prototype
17: //
18: void Increment(Point3d& p, float f);
19:
20: ///////////////////////////////////////////////////
21: //   main()
22:
23: void main()
24: {
25:     Point3d pt = {1.0f, 1.0f, 1.0f};
26:     cout << "Initial Values of pt members:\n";
27:     cout << "  pt.x == " << pt.x << endl;
28:     cout << "  pt.y == " << pt.y << endl;
29:     cout << "  pt.z == " << pt.z << endl;
30:
```

continues...

LISTING 10.5

1 Lines 10-14: Declare a Point3d structure

LISTING 10.5 CONTINUED

2 Line 32: Pass a structure
  by reference

3 Lines 45-48: A non-
  const structure
  reference parameter
  allows the structure to
  be altered

LISTING 10.5 **Continued**

```
31:     const float INC = 5.0f;
32:     Increment(pt, INC); ─────────────────────────────── 2
33:     cout << "\nIncremented Values (++" << INC
34:         << ") of pt members:\n";
35:     cout << "   pt.x == " << pt.x << endl;
36:     cout << "   pt.y == " << pt.y << endl;
37:     cout << "   pt.z == " << pt.z << endl;
38: }
39:
40: //////////////////////////////////////////////////////////
41: //  Increment()
42:
43: void Increment(Point3d& p, float f)
44: {
45:     p.x += f;
46:     p.y += f;                                             3
47:     p.z += f;
48: }
```

The output from this program is as follows:

```
Initial Values of pt members:
   pt.x == 1
   pt.y == 1
   pt.z == 1

Incremented Values (++5) of pt members:
   pt.x == 6
   pt.y == 6
   pt.z == 6
```

The program begins by declaring the structure type Point3d from lines 10 through 14. This is followed on line 18 by the declaration of the Increment() function, which takes a reference to a Point3d structure as a parameter. On line 25, the main() function creates and initializes an instance of a Point3d object (pt). This is followed by several cout statements that display the initial values of the pt data members.

On line 31, the floating-point constant INC is defined to have the value 5. This value is used on line 32 in a call to the Increment() function, along with pt, specifying how much each member should be incremented. This is followed by several more cout statements that display the incremented values of the pt data members.

The Increment() function itself simply takes a reference to a Point3d object (p), and increments the x, y, and z data members by the amount specified in the f parameter. The result is direct modification of the object referenced by parameter p.

Allocating Memory in C++

Understand the differences between allocating memory statically and dynamically

Learn about the stack and the free store

Discover the *new* and *delete* operators

See how you can dynamically allocate arrays

Learn to handle dynamic memory allocation errors

Find out how you can create your own *new* and *delete* operators

Allocating Static Memory

When you declare a predesignated number of variables for a program to use during its execution, you are working with *static memory*. Static memory is reserved by the compiler at compile time. Let's say you are planning to use an array of structures to represent employee data in a program, for example:

```
struct Employee
{
    char  FirstName[15];
    char  LastName[20];
    float PayRate;
    int   EmpNum;
    int   CostCenter;
};
```

You might declare the employee array like this:

```
const int MAX_EMPLOYEES = 1000
Employee emp[MAX_EMPLOYEES];
```

In some cases, the size of this array will be adequate; in most cases, however, it won't be. If the company has less than one thousand employees, the program is reserving memory it will never use—a waste of computer resources. If it's possible that more than one thousand employees may be needed at some point during program execution, the program won't function properly. When an array element with the index 1000 is used, the program will fail because it has only reserved room for one thousand employees (indexes 0 through 999):

```
emp[1000].PayRate = 8.25f;  // error, this is employee 1001
```

You might think to write some code that will let the user specify how many employees will be needed for a run of the program, something like this:

```
int EmpCount = 0;

cout << "How many employees in the company?";
cin >> EmpCount;

Employee emp[EmpCount];
```

It's a nice idea, and on the right track, but this code won't work. Trying to compile this code results in a compiler error such as this one:

```
Error: Constant expression expected
```

This occurs because the compiler needs a *constant* value inside the array brackets to reserve the number of employees statically at compile time. How do you work around this annoyance? *Dynamic memory* is the answer.

Allocating Dynamic Memory

When you use dynamic memory, you're not constrained to any fixed number of array elements. If you allocate the memory for the array at run time instead of at compile time, you make the program both flexible and efficient, using only as much memory as the program requires.

Two basic areas of computer memory are available for use by your programs:

- The stack
- The free store

These areas of memory serve completely different purposes and are used in different ways.

The Stack

With C++, you can use objects that have a specified scope, that have lifetimes limited to a certain code block. In the case of global objects, the scope (lifetime) of the objects is the same as the lifetime of the program. Objects local to a code block such as a function body have a lifetime as long as the function executes. These kinds of *stack-based objects* have a predetermined lifetime.

Suppose that you define an object local to a code block, such as a function, like this:

```
void func()
{
   int x = 5;
}
```

Dynamic Memory

Memory allocated by a program during program execution.

The variable is reserved on the stack by the compiler at compile time. What this really means is that the compiler generates the machine code needed to create enough storage space on the stack to hold an integer, and to store the value 5 in that space.

Every time func() is called within a program, memory is automatically allocated for its local variable x. The compiler statically reserves the required program memory at compile time.

The Free Store (The Heap)

The free store, traditionally known as *the heap*, is a pool of computer memory that's available for use by a program in creating dynamic objects—this is dynamic memory. With C++, you can create objects that have an unknown life span—objects that are not restricted by the scope in which they're created. These are called *heap-based objects*, and because they have no predetermined life span, they don't go out of scope until you destroy them.

Memory Leak

Memory dynamically allocated at runtime that is never released, even after program termination.

When you need to allocate a new object dynamically at run time, you just grab some memory from the free store for the object to use. The object then lives on the free store until you explicitly kill it (don't worry, it's not as violent as it sounds), and the memory returns to the free store. The tricky part is that if you don't *explicitly* kill the object, the memory dynamically allocated for it is never deallocated. Even after the program terminates, the dynamic object is out there in memory somewhere, taking up space. If this happens, you get the dreaded side effect of improper dynamic memory usage called a *memory leak*.

Using the *new* and *delete* Operators

Memory you dynamically allocate must be explicitly deallocated to prevent memory leaks from occurring. This cycle of dynamic allocation and deallocation is achieved in C++ through the use of two very important operators:

- The new operator
- The delete operator

The ANSI C library contains the `malloc()` and `realloc()` functions to allocate memory from the free store, and the `free()` function to release allocated memory. To allocate memory dynamically in C++, you use the `new` operator. To deallocate memory previously allocated with `new`, you use the `delete` operator. In the next sections, you'll take a look at the use of each of these operators so that you can get a feel for the cycle of dynamic memory allocation and deallocation.

Using the *new* Operator

The `new` operator opens the door to a new way of thinking about programming and gives some real meaning to the existence of pointers in the language. To create a dynamic object, such as an object of type `Employee` such as you saw in an earlier chapter, you must create a pointer to the data type and assign to it a new object of that type, like this:

```
Employee *emp = new Employee;
```

Compare this C++ code with the equivalent allocation of dynamic memory in C, where you would use the ANSI C library function `malloc()`:

```
Employee *emp = (Employee*)malloc(sizeof(Employee));
```

The syntax for using `new` is quite intuitive and is far superior to its equivalent in C. To get a better idea of how to use `new`, let's take a look at a few more examples.

The following statement allocates an integer and returns a pointer to it:

```
int *pInt = new int;
```

The following statement allocates a character, initializes it to `'X'`, and returns a pointer to it:

```
char *pChar = new char('X');
```

Using the *delete* Operator

As you've learned, when you allocate an object in the free store memory, it's your job to deallocate it as well, to prevent memory

---

Garbage Collection

Some object-oriented programming languages (for example, Java) contain a feature known as garbage collection, which means that the language automatically cleans up any allocated memory for you. C++ has no garbage collection feature—it's up to you to clean up after your objects.

leaks. The delete operator disposes of any objects allocated using new, and uses the following syntax:

```
delete ObjPointer
delete [] ArrayPointer
```

In the first syntax statement shown for delete, ObjPointer is the pointer to some data type that points to the object previously allocated using new. The second syntax statement deletes dynamic arrays, and the ArrayPointer is the pointer to the first array element of an array previously allocated using new. The entire cycle of using new and delete is pretty simple really, but there are a couple of pitfalls to be aware of:

- You should always set your pointers equal to zero after deleting an associated object. In this way, you can be sure that the pointer isn't pointing to anything.

- Major problems can arise if you try to delete an object that doesn't exist. This can occur when you delete an object associated with a pointer and then try to delete it again. This can happen more easily than you might think, if the deallocation occurs in a function that might be called in more than one place in your code. You should always check to see whether a pointer is set to zero before attempting to delete an object that you *think* is associated with it.

The program in Listing 11.1 shows the process of allocating, using, and deallocating objects on the free store. The program declares six pointers to six different data types. Two functions, CreateObjects() and DestroyObjects(), perform the allocation and deallocation of the objects.

Be aware that this program purposefully contains a bug that can cause problems. The program tries to delete the same objects twice in a row. The first delete statement destroys the objects, but the second delete statement finds no objects left in existence to delete. This little error can overwrite memory that the program no longer controls, possibly wreaking havoc on the end user's system. To avoid the memory bug, leave off line 87 of the code.

LISTING 11.1   A Program That Demonstrates Dynamic Allocation of Various Types of Built-In C++ Objects

```
1:  ////////////////////////////////////////////////////
2:  //   Module   : dynamic1.cpp
3:  //
4:  //   Purpose : Demonstrates creating, using, and
5:  //               destroying dynamic variables.
6:  ////////////////////////////////////////////////////
7:
8:  #include <iostream.h>
9:  const char NL = '\n';
10:
11: // Global pointers for dynamic allocation
12: //
13: char   *c = 0;
14: short  *s = 0;
15: int    *i = 0;
16: long   *l = 0;
17: float  *f = 0;
18: double *d = 0;
19:
20: // Function prototypes
21: //
22: void CreateObjects();
23: void DestroyObjects1();
24: void InitializeObjectValues();
25:
26: ////////////////////////////////////////////////////
27: // CreateObjects()
28:
29: void CreateObjects()
30: {
31:     // Allocate the objects associated with the pointers
32:     //
33:     c = new char;
34:     s = new short;
35:     i = new int;
36:     l = new long;
37:     f = new float;
38:     d = new double;
39: }
40:
```

LISTING 11.1

❶ Lines 33-38: Dynamically allocate the six objects

continues…

LISTING 11.1 **Continued**

```
41:  ////////////////////////////////////////////////////
42:  // DestroyObjects1()
43:
44:  void DestroyObjects1()
45:  {
46:      // Kill the objects associated with the pointers
47:      //
48:      delete c;
49:      delete s;
50:      delete i;
51:      delete l;
52:      delete f;
53:      delete d;
54:  }
55:
56:  ////////////////////////////////////////////////////
57:  // InitializeObjectValues()
58:
59:  void InitializeObjectValues()
60:  {
61:      // Initialize the objects to some value
62:      //
63:      *c = 'R';
64:      *s = 255;
65:      *i = 303030;
66:      *l = 40404040;
67:      *f = 34.78f;
68:      *d = 92384.42958;
69:  }
70:
71:  ////////////////////////////////////////////////////
72:  // main()
73:
74:  void main()
75:  {
76:      CreateObjects();
77:      InitializeObjectValues();
78:
79:      cout << "Object *c == " << *c << NL;
80:      cout << "Object *s == " << *s << NL;
81:      cout << "Object *i == " << *i << NL;
```

```
82:    cout << "Object *l == " << *l << NL;
83:    cout << "Object *f == " << *f << NL;
84:    cout << "Object *d == " << *d << NL;
85:
86:    DestroyObjects1(); // OK, objects are allocated
87:    DestroyObjects1(); // Oops! Objects already dead!
88: }
```

The output from this program shows that the objects are being correctly allocated and assigned values:

```
Object *c == R
Object *s == 255
Object *i == 303030
Object *l == 40404040
Object *f == 34.78
Object *d == 92384.4
```

This program begins by declaring six global pointers to six built-in C++ data types (lines 13 through 18). Lines 22 though 24 give the function declarations for the three helper functions CreateObjects(), DestroyObjects1(), and InitializeObjectValues(). As their names suggest, these functions do the actual work of creating, initializing, and destroying the dynamic objects.

The CreateObjects() function runs from lines 29 through 39, and dynamically allocates the six types of objects by using the new operator for each object. The corresponding DestroyObjects1() function runs from lines 44 through 54, deallocating the six objects by using the delete operator. The InitializeObjectValues() function runs from lines 59 through 69, initializing each of the objects with a value appropriate to its type.

The main() function ties everything together; it begins by calling the helper functions CreateObjects() and InitializeObjectValues() to create and initialize the six objects. Lines 79 through 84 simply display the values of the objects, and line 86 calls DestroyObjects1() to destroy the objects. Line 87 again calls DestroyObjects1(), attempting to delete the objects again. Because the objects being pointed to have already been destroyed, the pointers are now pointing to the memory addresses where each object used to be. Deallocating this memory again can cause a problem—not always immediately, but eventually.

Imagine the following scenario: The objects are deleted, releasing their memory back into the free store. Each pointer still points to the starting address of the dead object. Now suppose that one or more of the memory addresses that the six pointers point to is grabbed up by some other dynamic allocation; later on in your code, the DestroyObjects1() function is called again. The function would attempt to delete memory that's now in use by another object! Depending on the actual situation, your implementation of C++, your hardware, and your compiler, any of several disastrous things could result from a bungle like this. This is why you should always set a pointer equal to zero after you delete its associated object.

You may wonder why the deallocation function is named DestroyObjects1(). This is because I wrote two versions of the function. The second version, DestroyObjects2(), is shown in Listing 11.2; the second version of this function checks for null pointers before wantonly deallocating memory.

LISTING 11.2

Lines 6,12,18,24,30,36:
Check for non-pull
pointers

LISTING 11.2   **A Revised Deallocation Function: *DestroyObjects2()***

```
 1:  ////////////////////////////////////////////////////
 2:  // DestroyObjects2()
 3:
 4:  void DestroyObjects2()
 5:  {
 6:      if ———①
 7:      {
 8:          delete c;
 9:          c = 0;
10:      }
11:
12:      if (s) ———①
13:      {
14:          delete s;
15:          s = 0;
16:      }
17:
```

```
18:     if (i) ——————①
19:     {
20:         delete i;
21:         i = 0;
22:     }
23:
24:     if (l) ——————①
25:     {
26:         delete l;
27:         l = 0;
28:     }
29:
30:     if (f) ——————①
31:     {
32:         delete f;
33:         f = 0;
34:     }
35:
36:     if ——————①
37:     {
38:         delete d;
39:         d = 0;
40:     }
41: }
```

On lines 6, 12, 18, 24, 30, and 36 in this revised function, the
pointers are checked for non-zero values before deleting the
dynamic memory they point to. The pointers are each then set
to zero to ensure that these checks will work properly if the
function is called again before memory is allocated for the
pointers.

Allocating Arrays

So far in this book, you've only seen arrays that exist on the
stack and that have a limited scope. Arrays of this type are ideal
when you know exactly how many elements the array needs. For
example, the assignment of the following string literal to a character array of unspecified size works beautifully:

```
char str[] = "A character string";
```

The compiler figures out how many characters are in the string at compile time and reserves the correct amount of space. A pointer to a string can be used in the same way, like this:

```
char *str = "A character string";
```

Again, the compiler figures out how many characters are in the string at compile time and reserves the correct amount of space. When you don't know how many characters a string might consist of, the compiler can't reserve a specified amount of storage for the array of characters. This is where dynamic memory allocation comes in quite handy.

To allocate a specified number of characters for a dynamic array, you use the new operator to allocate as many characters as a given string requires, like this:

```
int count = 100;
char *str = new char[count];
```

This code fragment dynamically creates an array of 100 characters. But note that the variable count can contain any valid integer value, such as a value specified by the user. The program in Listing 11.3 demonstrates how a dynamic character array might be used.

Static Allocation vs Dynamic Allocation of Arrays

During static array allocation the number of elements specified in the array brackets **must** be a constant value. Dynamic allocation with new allows you to use a variable instead, although a constant will work just as well.

LISTING 11.3   **A Program That Demonstrates Dynamically Allocating a Character Array**

```
 1:  ///////////////////////////////////////////////////
 2:  //   Module  : char.cpp
 3:  //
 4:  //   Purpose : Demonstrates creating, using, and
 5:  //             destroying a dynamic character array.
 6:  ///////////////////////////////////////////////////
 7:
 8:  #include <iostream.h>
 9:  #include <string.h>
10:
11:  const char NL = '\n';
12:
13:  ///////////////////////////////////////////////////
14:  // main()
15:
```

```
16:  void main()
17:  {
18:      char *str = 0;
19:      char word[128];
20:
21:      cout << "Please type a word > ";
22:      cin >> word;
23:
24:      str = new char[strlen(word) + 1];
25:      strcpy(str, word);
26:
27:      cout << "word == " << word << NL;
28:      cout << "str  == " << str << NL;
29:
30:      delete [] str;
31:  }
```

LISTING 11.3

❶ Lines 18-19: Declare a character pointer and a character array

A sample run of this program produced the following output:

```
Please type a word > ThisIsn'tReallyAWord
word == ThisIsn'tReallyAWord
str  == ThisIsn'tReallyAWord
```

This program contains only a `main()` function and begins by declaring the character pointer `str` on line 18. This statement is followed by the declaration of the character array `word[]` on line 19. The `word[]` array is just a buffer used to hold the text input by the user, which is gathered on line 22.

On line 24, a dynamic character array is allocated to be the exact size needed to store the user's word by using the ANSI C library function `strlen()` (explicitly adding `+1` to account for the string's zero-terminator). In the same statement, the starting address of the new array is assigned to the pointer `str`. The statement on the following line (line 25) uses the ANSI C library function `strcpy()` to copy the contents of `word[]` to the character array pointed to by `str`.

Lines 27 and 28 simply display the strings stored in each array; line 30 deletes the array pointed to by `str`. Note that because the program ends here (and we won't access any memory pointed to by `str` again), there's no need to set `str` equal to zero.

Creating Dynamic Arrays of Structures

Creating dynamic arrays of other types, including structures, is just as easy as creating an array of a built-in data type. Going back to the original example of the Employee array discussed earlier in this chapter, you now have the knowledge you need to create a dynamic array that can be whatever size the user specifies (assuming that there is enough memory available, of course). The program in Listing 11.4 shows the uncompilable code you saw earlier (that attempted to use a variable to allocate static memory), revised to compile correctly by using dynamic memory allocation.

LISTING 11.4   **Using *new* and *delete* to Dynamically Create and Destroy an Array of Structures**

```
 1:  //////////////////////////////////////////////////////
 2:  //   Module  : employee.cpp
 3:  //
 4:  //   Purpose : Demonstrates creating a dynamic array
 5:  //////////////////////////////////////////////////////
 6:
 7:  #include <iostream.h>
 8:
 9:  struct Employee
10:  {
11:     char  FirstName[15];
12:     char  LastName[20];
13:     float PayRate;
14:     int   EmpNum;
15:     int   CostCenter;
16:  };
17:
18:  //////////////////////////////////////////////////////
19:  //   main()
20:
21:  void main()
22:  {
23:     int EmpCount = 0;
24:
25:     // Find out how many employees the array should hold
```

```
26:     //
27:     cout << "How many employees in the company? ";
28:     cin >> EmpCount;
29:
30:     // Create the employee array dynamically
31:     //
32:     Employee *emp = new Employee[EmpCount];
33:
34:     // Initialize EmpNum for each employee in the array
35:     //
36:     for (int i =0; i < EmpCount; ++i)
37:         emp[i].EmpNum = i + 1;
38:
39:     // Display the employee number for each element
40:     for (i =0; i < EmpCount; ++i)
41:         cout << "emp[" << i << "].EmpNum == "
42:         << emp[i].EmpNum << NL;
43:
44:     // Kill the array
45:     //
46:     delete [] emp;
47: }
```

The output from this program shows that the array of Employee structures is allocated as expected:

```
How many employees in the company? 10
emp[0].EmpNum == 1
emp[1].EmpNum == 2
emp[2].EmpNum == 3
emp[3].EmpNum == 4
emp[4].EmpNum == 5
emp[5].EmpNum == 6
emp[6].EmpNum == 7
emp[7].EmpNum == 8
emp[8].EmpNum == 9
emp[9].EmpNum == 10
```

Resizing Dynamic Arrays

One of the benefits of dynamic memory is that we can create an array of ten `Employee` structures on the fly, but resizing a dynamic array is a bit trickier than creating it. To come back and "stretch" that array to hold the five new employees that need to be added to it is possible, though. To see how you might accomplish this take a look at the program presented in Chapter 24, "Implementing Dynamic Storage in C++" (`IntArray.cpp`).

This program begins by declaring the data structure `Employee` on lines 9 through 16; the structure contains five data members. Again, the `main()` function is the only function defined in the program, and it starts out by asking the user to supply the number of `Employee` objects to allocate (lines 27 and 28). The value the user specifies is placed into the local variable `EmpCount`.

Earlier in this chapter I explained that static allocation using the `EmpCount` variable wouldn't work, but here's the fix for this: line 32 actually allocates the `Employee` array, using the value stored in `EmpCount` to specify how many employees to allocate dynamically. The `for` loop on lines 36 and 37 initializes the `EmpNum` member of each array element to the value `i+1`, where `i` is incremented with each iteration. Another `for` loop runs from lines 40 through 42, displaying the `EmpNum` member of array element `i` with each iteration. Finally, line 46 deletes the dynamic array, returning allocated memory to the free store.

Before I leave the subject of dynamic arrays, a few words about dynamic multidimensional arrays are in order. When dynamically allocating a multidimensional array, the first dimension can be variable, but any additional dimensions must be constant expressions. The following statement allocates a two-dimensional array of floats, with the array being of size `NumFloats*100`:

```
int NumFloat = 50;
char (*pFloat)[100] = new float[NumFloat][100];
```

Dealing with Allocation Errors

So far, the examples you've seen treat the free store as an unlimited supply of memory, using no error trapping whatsoever. Unfortunate as it may seem, sometimes there just isn't enough memory available in the free store to do what a program needs to do. When a program attempts to dynamically allocate memory and the allocation fails, your programs should gracefully handle the situation. Failing to trap a failed allocation results in disaster for the program—and possibly for the computer the program is running on.

Detecting Memory Allocation Failures

After you dynamically create a new object on the free store, the pointer used in the assignment of the new object contains the starting address of that new object. There are times (unfortunately) when the computer system on which a program is running just doesn't have enough free memory to accomplish a given task.

One way to check for an allocation failure is by examining the return value from the new operator—it returns zero if there's insufficient memory available. If the address contained in the pointer is zero (null), the allocation has failed (miserably) because of insufficient memory in the free store. You can detect an insufficient memory condition by checking the pointer after an attempted allocation to see whether it contains a null memory address, as in this example:

```
int *pMyIntArray = new int[500];
if (pMyArray == 0)
{
    cerr << "Error: pMyArray allocation failed.\n";
    // Gracefully handle the error here...
    // ...
}
```

If the value of the pointer is zero, there was insufficient memory to grant your allocation request. As you can imagine, a simple test like this can save you a lot of grief. This is only one way to check for an allocation failure. Another way is with the C++ set_new_handler() function.

Using the *set_new_handler()* Function

C++ programs use an internal new_handler pointer to point to the address of a function that will handle memory allocation failures. To set the pointer to a user-defined function that will handle these errors, use the C++ set_new_handler() function. By default, the new_handler pointer is zero, causing the new operator to return zero.

Available Free Store Memory

The free store consists of whatever system memory is available for dynamic allocation. The amount of memory available for the free store varies depending on the type of machine and the number of programs that are running on it—it **cannot** be expanded.

By assigning a function to act as an error condition handler, you can centralize your response to allocation failures. The set_new_handler() function overrides the default behavior of the new operator to provide this response. This function uses the following syntax:

```
set_new_handler(FunctionName);
```

In this syntax, FunctionName is the name of the function you want to use to handle the out-of-memory condition. The program in Listing 11.5 demonstrates the use of the set_new_handler() function by depleting the free store and responding to the resulting error condition.

SEE ALSO

➤ For more information about function pointers, see page 325

LISTING 11.5

① Line 10: Gain access to the set_new_handler() function

LISTING 11.5   A Program That Deletes the Free Store and Calls a Function to Handle the Error Condition

```
 1: ///////////////////////////////////////////////////////
 2: //   Module  : deplete.cpp
 3: //
 4: //   Purpose : Demonstrates using the set_new_handler()
 5: //             function
 6: ///////////////////////////////////////////////////////
 7:
 8: #include <iostream.h>
 9: #include <stdlib.h>
10: #include <new.h>
11:
12: const char BEEP = '\a';
13: const int  DEPLETE_VAL = 32000;
14:
15: ///////////////////////////////////////////////////////
16: // RespondToNewFailure()
17:
18: static void RespondToNewFailure()
19: {
20:    cerr << "Whoa!! Out of memory!!\n" << BEEP;
21:    exit(1);
22: }
23:
```

```
24:  //////////////////////////////////////////////////////
25:  // main()
26:
27:  void main()
28:  {
29:     #ifdef _MSC_VER
30:        _set_new_handler((int (__cdecl *)
31:           (unsigned int))RespondToNewFailure);
32:     #else
33:        set_new_handler(RespondToNewFailure);
34:     #endif
35:
36:     long count = DEPLETE_VAL;
37:     for (;;)
38:     {
39:        char *deplete = new char[DEPLETE_VAL];
40:
41:        cout << "So far, I've depleted " << count
42:           << " bytes of memory...\n";
43:
44:        count += DEPLETE_VAL;
45:     }
46:  }
```

LISTING 11.5 CONTINUED

2 Lines 37-45: Deplete the free store just for fun

When compiled with Borland C++ and run under Windows 98 in DOS mode, the program in Listing 11.5 gives the following output:

```
So far, I've depleted 32000 bytes of memory...
So far, I've depleted 64000 bytes of memory...
So far, I've depleted 96000 bytes of memory...
So far, I've depleted 128000 bytes of memory...
So far, I've depleted 160000 bytes of memory...
So far, I've depleted 192000 bytes of memory...
So far, I've depleted 224000 bytes of memory...
So far, I've depleted 256000 bytes of memory...
So far, I've depleted 288000 bytes of memory...
So far, I've depleted 320000 bytes of memory...
So far, I've depleted 352000 bytes of memory...
So far, I've depleted 384000 bytes of memory...
So far, I've depleted 416000 bytes of memory...
So far, I've depleted 448000 bytes of memory...
So far, I've depleted 480000 bytes of memory...
```

```
So far, I've depleted 512000 bytes of memory...
Whoa!! Out of memory!!
```

The program includes the header file `<new.h>` on line 10; this header provides the interface needed to use the `set_new_handler()` function. This statement is followed on lines 12 and 13 by some constant definitions. The first is used to generate a beep, and the second to specify how many objects to allocate with each use of the `new` operator.

The function `RespondToNewFailure()` is defined from lines 18 through 22; all it does is display a message telling the user that the free store is out of memory and then exit the program with an error code for the operating system. This static function is called automatically if the `new` operator fails.

In the `main()` function, on lines 29 through 34, the `new_handler` pointer is adjusted by calling `set_new_handler()`, or the unconventional `set_new_handler()` for Microsoft compilers (the Microsoft version doesn't use the Standard C++ declaration for the function). Preprocessor directives are used to handle the Microsoft quirkiness.

SEE ALSO

➤ *For more information about these preprocessor directives, see page 302*

Line 36 defines the variable `count`, which keeps track of how many bytes have been allocated by the `for` loop running from lines 37 through 45. This `for` loop repeatedly allocates memory to the same pointer, causing memory leaks and running until the free store is depleted. Note that this is *extremely* bad behavior for a program, done here only to simulate an out-of-memory condition. When the free store is finally exhausted, the `RespondToNewFailure()` function is called, displaying the error message you saw in the sample output shown earlier.

Creating Your Own *new* and *delete* Operators

Although the default global `new` and `delete` operators provided by your compiler are fine for use in most situations, you may run across a situation in which you need more control over the

Caution

The program in Listing 11.5, when compiled under certain operating systems, will use all the free store available in actual computer memory (RAM) and will continue to deplete any free store that exists as virtual memory on a disk file. To be safe, you may want to just to look at the program here in the book, and not try compiling and running it.

allocation process. On the rare occasion when you need this control (perhaps while debugging a program), you can overload the default new and delete operators, much as you can overload any other function. The difference here is that you're overloading a global operator—the same one used by the compiler's runtime library. If you do overload these operators, be aware that overloading the global new and delete operators has far-reaching implications with other code that the program may include or link with.

Here's an example of an overloaded new operator. This version of new allocates memory using the ANSI C library function malloc() and initializes all memory to zero using the ANSI C library function memset():

```
void * operator new(size_t size)
{
   void *pRet;

   pRet = malloc(nSize);
   if (pRet == NULL)
      return pRet;

   memset(pRet, 0, size);
   return pRet;
}
```

This new operator checks for a NULL return value from malloc(), which indicates failure. If this returned pointer is not NULL, the memset() function initializes the memory and returns the pointer.

Creating an overloaded delete operator is just as easy:

```
void operator delete(void *p) { free(p); }
```

This version of delete simply calls the ANSI C library function free() to release the allocated memory.

As you have seen, dynamic memory allocation is a powerful, flexible tool for you to use in your programs, allowing you to create programs capable of using any memory available on the end-user's computer system. Later, in Chapter 24, "Implementing Dynamic Storage in C++," you'll see how to overload the new and delete operators for individual object types—a much more useful application of overloaded new and delete operators.

Understanding the Preprocessor

Understand the phases of preprocessing

See why custom macros can simplify your source code

Learn to use the preprocessor operators and directives

See how conditional compilation can make your code more versatile

Understand the problem of international keyboard character sets

Learn to use predefined macros

Preprocessor Macro

A special expression that defines a symbolic name for an expression or value by utilizing the `#define` preprocessor directive.

Linking

As you'll recall from Chapter 1, the linker takes any object code files compiled from your source code and links them with any C++ library code required by your program. The end result is an executable file, having an `.exe` file extension, that your target computer platform's operating system can load and run.

Note

As your programs get more complex, you'll see a need to split logically related areas of functionality into separate source files. This is especially true of object-oriented programming in C++, where putting classes into separate modules promotes reusable code (see Chapter 20).

Linking Incrementally

When you want to create a new executable file, but you want to translate and relink only the source files that have changed since the last program build, the process is known as *incremental linking*. Linking incrementally can be a big time saver when building large programs containing many source files.

External Linkage

Identifiers having external linkage are sometimes referred to "global" identifiers. For example:

```
extern int x;
```

Introducing the Preprocessor

The *preprocessor* is a program that processes and manipulates the text of a source file, usually invoked by the compiler as the first step of the compilation process. The process of preprocessing is called *translation*, and the preprocessor's job is to break up source file text into *tokens*. These tokens are used to locate and follow any preprocessor directives within the text.

The preprocessor, and specifically the use of its several directives, is often confusing for programmers new to C/C++. Code that's heavily laden with preprocessor directives and *preprocessor macros* is often baffling to new C/C++ programmers. The problem is that you need to understand some facets of the preprocessor before others become clear in your mind. This confusion is common, and hard to avoid. If you find yourself scratching your head in bewilderment, read through this chapter a few times until it all becomes clear (and it will, in time).

A common example of a preprocessor directive that you've seen used throughout this book is the `#include` directive. All preprocessor directives begin with a pound (#) symbol, which is the token the preprocessor is on the lookout for. These directives give the C++ programmer a lot of power, providing conditional compilation, user-defined preprocessor macros, and predefined ANSI preprocessor macros that perform specialized tasks.

Each source file that makes up a program is run through the preprocessor. The text of each source file, together with any files included using the `#include` directive, make up what the compiler sees as a *translation unit*. Each translation unit is compiled into its own binary object module that is then used by the linker to create executable files.

Translation units must communicate with each other often. This is what makes it possible for an identifier defined in one module to be used by another module. This communication occurs mainly through calls to objects, functions, and functions that use external linkage.

Understanding Preprocessing Phases

The preprocessor runs through the following four phases when preparing a source file for compilation:

1. **Character Mapping**   Maps all source file characters, converting any special character sequences to an internal representation.

2. **Line Splicing**   Any line ending in a backslash character (\) followed immediately by an end-of-line character (a hard return) is spliced together with the line that follows it in the source file, forming a single line. This means that there must be **no whitespace** between the backslash and the hard return at the end of a line splice.

3. **Tokenization**   The preprocessor next identifies each character in a source file as either a preprocessing token or a whitespace character and removes all program comments from the source file.

4. **Preprocessing**   The preprocessor executes any preprocessor directives and expands macros into their literal values within the source file (see the section "Expanding Macros" later in this chapter for an explanation of macro expansion). If an #include statement is encountered in this phase, any text in the include file goes through the preceding preprocessing steps.

Understanding Preprocessor Directives

Preprocessor directives make it possible for you to write a single set of source files that will compile correctly on several operating systems and hardware platforms. The preprocessor is the key to the portability of both C and C++ (for example, macros are often used to create aliases for data types that use different byte sizes on different platforms). The preprocessor follows directives it encounters in a source file and performs whatever tasks those directives specify.

When Preprocessor Directives Are Ignored

Preprocessor directives are carried out before macro expansion occurs; preprocessor directives that appear within a macro are ignored.

The preprocessor recognizes the 12 ANSI directives listed in Table 12.1, along with the defined() operator, which evaluates to true if a preprocessor symbol has been defined.

TABLE 12.1   The C++ Preprocessor Directives

Directive	Description
#include	Causes the preprocessor to include the contents of a specified file as if those contents had been typed into the source file in place of the directive.
#define	Defines a preprocessor symbol in a program. A preprocessor symbol is a special identifier that the preprocessor can recognize.
#undef	Undefines an existing preprocessor symbol from your program.
#if	Used with the defined() operator. Corresponds to the C++ if statement, but must be terminated by a matching #endif directive.
#ifdef	A Boolean directive that evaluates to true if a specified preprocessor symbol has already been defined.
#ifndef	A Boolean directive that evaluates to true if a specified preprocessor symbol has not yet been defined.
#elif	Used with the defined() operator, and in combination with the #if directive, this directive corresponds to the C++ else-if clause in an if statement.
#else	Used in combination with the #if directive, this directive corresponds to the C++ else clause in an if statement.
#endif	Terminates a corresponding #if directive.
#error	Generates a compile-time error message.
#line	Tells the preprocessor to change the line number and filename used internally by the compiler to some other specified line number and filename.
#pragma	A directive that specifies compiler-specific instructions to the compiler, allowing it to offer machine-specific and operating-system-specific features, yet still retain compatibility with C and C++.

With the exception of whitespace characters, the pound sign (#) **must** be the first character on a line containing a preprocessor directive. Between the pound sign and the directive itself, you can put any number of whitespace characters. For example, the following are all valid #include directives (which you've already seen many times in this book):

```
#include <iostream>
    #include <iostream>
#        include <iostream>
```

Lines containing preprocessor directives can be continued by immediately preceding the end-of-line marker with a backslash (\), for example:

```
#include  \
   <iostream>
```

You'll probably never have cause to write an include statement in this way, but it illustrates the point that you **can** split preprocessor directive lines if you want to. Lines are usually only broken up like this when the line is longer than the space available onscreen for a single line in your source file editor.

Okay, let's see some examples of how to use preprocessor directives in a source file.

Including Files

Probably the most often-used preprocessor directive is the `#include` directive. This directive tells the preprocessor to take any text that exists within a specified include file and copy it into your source file at the very point that the `#include` directive is located, replacing the directive. Suppose that you have a header file that looks like this:

```
///////////////////////////////////////////////////
// Some header file : MyStuct.h

typedef struct MyStruct
{
   int member1;
   float member2;
};
```

A source file that includes this header might look like this:

```
///////////////////////////////////////////////////
// Some source file : source.cpp

#include "MyStruct.h"
```

Placement of Preprocessor Directives

You can use preprocessor directives anywhere in a source file, but a directive only affects the code that appears *after* that directive in the file.

```
void main()
{
   MyStruct *pms = new Mystruct[100];
   //
   // ...
   //
   delete [] pms;
}
```

Note

In the `source.cpp` example, the
`*` symbol in front of the identifier
`pms` marks it as a pointer, which is
then used for dynamic allocation of
100 `MyStruct` structures. The
array is cleaned up with the
`delete` statement at the end of
`main()`.

The entire contents of the header file is merged with the source
file during preprocessing, resulting in a fully preprocessed intermediate file ready for the compiler to translate into object code.
Here's what this intermediate file would look like, merged and
stripped of comments by the preprocessor:

```
struct MyStruct
{
   int member1;
   float member2;
}
void main()
{
   MyStruct *pms = new Mystruct[100];

   delete [] pms;
}
```

Defining and Undefining Symbols

You define new preprocessor symbols in your source code using
the `#define` directive. This directive is the most versatile; it
allows you to define standalone identifiers, identifiers used for
literal text substitutions, and identifiers that represent powerful
macro functions.

Standalone, name-only identifiers are often used as flags in
source code; defining one is as easy as this:

```
#define BEEN_HERE
```

This directive defines a symbol called BEEN_HERE. This symbol is
just a name that has been defined, but it has no value associated
with it. Identifiers like this are often used to conditionally
compile source code, as you'll soon see.

In addition to name-only identifiers, you can also use the #define directive to create identifiers used for simple text substitution macros, as in this example:

```
#define PI        3.14159
#define MCCURB   \
    "Margin Content Control and Utilization Review Board"
```

If you use these defined symbols, called macros, in a program, the symbolic name is replaced by its associated literal value during preprocessing. Note that the backslash character is used here to splice the lines defining the MCCURB symbol. After you've defined a symbol, you can use it in a program, like this:

```
cout << "The value of the irrational number PI is roughly "
    << PI << '\n';
cout << "\nI'm not sure how this relates to the "
    << MCCURB << " ruling...\n";
```

These statements will expand during preprocessing into the following fully expanded statements:

```
cout << "The value of the irrational number PI is roughly "
    << 3.14159 << '\n';
cout << "\nI'm not sure how this relates to the "
    << "Margin Content Control and Utilization Review Board"
    << " ruling...\n";
```

A common use of these simple replacement macros is to give an alias to an operator symbol, making the code more readable. For example, here are the exclusive or operator and the modulus operator, aliased as XOR and MODULUS, respectively:

```
#define XOR        ^
#define MODULUS  %
```

You'll often see C programs using #define directives to represent a constant value, such as this macro SCREENWIDTH, which represents the width of a standard DOS video display:

```
#define SCREENWIDTH  640    // Width of the display in DOS is
                            // 640 pixels
```

Of course, the more sensible thing to do in this case is to define the screen width as a C++ constant of some type to maintain C++ type-safety, as in this example:

```
const short SCREENWIDTH = 640;
```

C++ Constants Versus Macro Literals

It's always preferable to use C++ typed constants instead of typeless macro literals because C++ is a strongly typed language. Using macros to define identifiers defeats the C++ type-checking mechanism, and can lead to hard-to-detect coding errors.

Typeless Parameters

Macro parameters are called typeless because no data type is specified when sending parameters to a macro.

You can also define simple macros to represent function calls, creating an alias for the function, like this WAIT_FOR_KEYPRESS macro:

```
#define WAIT_FOR_KEYPRESS  getch();
```

Even more complex, you can define macros that take typeless parameters, making it convenient to write tight, fast code. Here are a few sample macros of this sort, each of them quite useful in certain situations:

```
#define MIN(a,b) (>) ? :
#define MAX(a,b) (>) ? :
#define SQUARE(n) (n)*(n)
```

For a better grip on what macros like these do, see the section entitled "Exploring Macros" later in this chapter.

You'll see more about these types of macros later in this chapter.

Compiling Conditionally

Conditional compiling is one of the most useful C++ tricks you can learn. The basic idea is to define a symbol somewhere, then use preprocessor directives wherever you need them in your source code to determine whether the symbol has already been defined. For example, when using the typedef keyword to create type aliases, you can prevent compiler errors by "protecting" the typedef statement with a conditional compilation block. A block of code like this defines a name-only symbol as a flag to tell the preprocessor that the alias exists. Here's an example that protects a typedef for an unsigned char:

```
#ifndef __BYTE
#define __BYTE
typedef unsigned char BYTE;
#endif
```

In the preceding code snippet, the name-only flag __BYTE is defined at the same time the type alias is defined. After this has been done once, it won't be done again. This is because the #ifndef __BYTE directive will see that __BYTE has already been defined and will skip down to the statement following the corresponding #endif directive.

Another common scenario is the use of multiple compilers to compile the same set of source files. When you need to be completely portable among two or more compilers, you must isolate any compiler-specific pieces of code within conditional compilation blocks. As a common example, the two dominant C++ compilers for the PC are from Borland and Microsoft. Like all compilers, each of these popular compilers internally defines macros that it uses to do its job. By finding a symbol that is unique to a specific compiler, you can test to see whether that is the compiler that's currently compiling the source code.

For example, the Borland C++ compiler defines the symbol __BORLANDC__, which is unique to Borland. Microsoft Visual C++ defines the symbol _MSC_VER, which is unique to Microsoft. With this in mind it's easy to write code that will compile on either compiler, for example:

```
#ifdef __BORLANDC__          // Borland C++
    #include <mem.h>
#elif defined (_MSC_VER)      // Microsoft C++
    #include <memory.h>
#endif
```

The `#elif` directive uses the `defined()` operator to test for the existence of the identifier `_MSC_VER`. The `defined()` operator is equivalent to the `#ifdef` directive when used like this,

```
#if defined(SYMBOL)
    // do something
#endif
```

which is the same as this:

```
#ifdef SYMBOL
    // do something
#endif
```

Likewise, the `defined()` operator is equivalent to the `#ifndef` directive when used like this,

```
#if !defined(SYMBOL)
    // do something
#endif
```

Keeping Track of Defined Symbols

If you have got several source files, keeping track of symbols you've defined can be difficult (if not impossible). By using the `#ifdef` and `#ifndef` directives you can assure that a symbol that's already defined doesn't get redefined.

which is the same as this:

```
#ifndef SYMBOL
    // do something
#endif
```

The `defined()` operator has an advantage over the `#ifdef` and `#ifndef` directives because it can be used in more ways, such as in logical expressions. Here's an example, using the `defined()` operator to introduce multiple expressions into the mix:

```
#if defined(MATH_CO) && !defined(__BORLANDC__)
    #define ACOS    acosl
    #define SQRT    sqrtl
    #define POW     powl
    #define COS     cosl
    #define SIN     sinl
    #define EPSILON 1.0e-15
#else
    #define EPSILON 1.0e-5
#endif
```

In this example, the `defined()` operator is used twice in a logical AND (`&&`) operation. If the symbol `MATH_CO` **is** defined **AND** the symbol `__BORLANDC__` is **not** defined, then the symbols `ACOS`, `SQRT`, `POW`, `COS`, `SIN`, and `EPSILON` are then defined. Otherwise, only the symbol `EPSILON` is defined.

Getting Platform Independent

You can use the same technique of conditional compilation to ensure that code specific to a given hardware platform is compiled into your executable file correctly. Because various operating systems and hardware platforms have specific features, functionality, and needs, you may want to specify certain code be compiled into a build targeting one platform, but not another. Conditional compilation like this can improve program performance by taking advantage of some specific hardware feature, or can allow your code to access specific operating system functionality. The program in Listing 12.1 shows how you might conditionally compile for the Digital Alpha, Intel x86, MIPS, and PowerPC hardware platforms.

LISTING 12.1   A Code Segment That Demonstrates Compiling Conditionally for Multiple Hardware Platforms

```
 1: #if defined(_M_ALPHA) // DEC Alpha
 2:
 3:    //
 4:    // Alpha stuff here...
 5:    //
 6:
 7: #elif defined(_M_IX86)  // Intel x86
 8:
 9:    //
10:    // Intel (and clone) x86 stuff here...
11:    //
12:
13: #elif defined(_M_MRX000)   // MIPS
14:
15:    //
16:    // MIPS stuff here...
17:    //
18:
19: #elif defined(_M_PPC)   // Apple PowerPC
20:
21:    //
22:    // PowerPC stuff here...
23:    //
24:
25: #else
26:
27:    #error Must define a target architecture.
28:
29: #endif
```

Single-File Inclusion

Header files define interfaces for functions, structures, unions, and classes; they also define preprocessor macros and external variables, among other things. If an entity is defined in a header included by one module, and the same entity is defined again in another module, the linker will choke, claiming duplicate identifiers in two or more modules. You can use the #ifdef and #define directives to prevent this duplication in a technique called *single-file inclusion*, or a *one-time include*.

The traditional way of preventing multiple-file inclusion is simple and works really well. Conceptually, it works like this:

- Using the name of the header file as a basis, you choose a preprocessor identifier to use for single inclusion. By manually mangling the filename somewhat, you can make sure that the identifier is unique within your program (see the "Implementing Single-File Inclusion in a Header File" steps that follow for details).

- Place an #include directive in a source file to tell the preprocessor to include the specified header file into that source file. If the identifier doesn't yet exist when the preprocessor reaches that header file, then the identifier is defined and the header file is included in the source file.

- If the same header file is included again, perhaps by another module, the preprocessor looks to see whether the single-inclusion identifier exists yet. If the identifier already exists, the header has already been included, so the preprocessor bypasses the header file contents altogether, resulting in a single-file inclusion.

Although this may sound complicated, the process is really very easy to implement.

Implementing single-file inclusion in a header file

1. Create an identifier name, usually derived from the header filename (for example, mystruct.h). A typical single-include identifier begins with one or two underscore characters before the filename. So far, this gives you this identifier: __

2. Follow the underscores with the filename in all uppercase letters:

   __MYSTRUCT

3. Add an underscore character to replace the dot character in the filename:

   __MYSTRUCT_

4. Now add the file extension, in uppercase characters, followed by two more underscore characters to wrap it up, giving you the final identifier:

```
__MYSTRUCT_H__
```

5. Using the preprocessor directive `#ifndef` and your new identifier, add this statement to the beginning of your header file:

```
#ifndef __MYSTRUCT_H__
```

6. Follow this statement in the header file with the `#define` directive, to define your new identifier, like this:

```
#define __MYSTRUCT_H__
```

7. At the end of the header file, end the `#ifndef` directive by inserting a corresponding `#endif` directive.

If you apply these steps to the `MyStruct.h` header file you saw earlier in this chapter, the resulting header file would look like this:

```
///////////////////////////////////////////////////
// Some header file : MyStuct.h

#ifndef __MYSTRUCT_H__
#define __MYSTRUCT_H__

typedef struct MyStruct
{
    int member1;
    float member2;
}

#endif // __MYSTRUCT_H__
```

Excluding Debug Code

You can sprinkle special code for debugging purposes liberally throughout your source code, having it call special debug functions to give you diagnostic and other important debugging information. Then, only when you're creating a debug build of your program, you can include the debug code that is already present in the executable file. You do this by defining a symbol

Always Use Single-Inclusion for Header Files

You should always use a single-inclusion block to protect the contents of header files from being included more than once.

that tells your conditional compilation code that you're debugging. All debugging code in your source files can be conditionally included or excluded from a build simply by adding or commenting out the following line of code:

```
#define _DEBUG
```

There's always a possibility that the symbol might be already defined, so it's safer to wrap a conditional block around it, like this:

```
#ifndef _DEBUG
#define _DEBUG
#endif
```

This syntax is equivalent to using the following `defined` operator:

```
#if !defined(_DEBUG)
#define _DEBUG
#endif
```

You can then use the `_DEBUG` symbol in a conditional compilation block wherever you need to in your source code, for example:

```
#ifndef _DEBUG
    //
    // Debugging is off, just production code...
    //
#else
    //
    // Debugging is on, do some debug thing...
    //
#endif // _DEBUG
```

A Compiler-Generated Debug Symbol

Many modern compilers (such as Microsoft Visual C++) allow you the choice of creating either a debug or a release build of your program, defining a debug symbol for you when you choose a debug build.

If your compiler doesn't automatically generate a debug symbol for you by giving you the option of creating a debug or release build, you can create a debug header file that you include before including any other headers in your source. This will assure that your debug symbol is defined for all included source files.

Outputting Errors

Sometimes, you'll want to output special diagnostic messages to the screen while compiling—perhaps to remind you that you've forgotten to do something or to give you some clue about what's going wrong with a build, as in this example:

```
#if !defined(_WIN32)
    #error ERROR: This code was written exclusively for Win32
#endif
```

In this example, if the symbol _WIN32 is undefined, the error message prints to the screen. Here's another possibility:

```
#ifndef __cplusplus
    #error "ERROR: This code intended only for C++!"
#endif
```

In this example, if you're using a C compiler, then the standard symbol __cplusplus will be undefined, and the error message prints to the screen. Most modern compilers will automatically define the symbol _cplusplus for you when compiling a .cpp file (if your compiler doesn't do this, you can easily define the symbol yourself). Likewise, a Win32 compiler will define a symbol like _WIN32 in some header that's standard to the specific operating system. In the case of 32-bit Microsoft Windows applications, _WIN32 is defined when you include the header <windows.h>.

Understanding Pragmas

A *pragma* is a feature, workaround, or shortcut that's specific to a hardware platform and compiler. Each compiler defines its own set of pragmas, letting the compiler do things in the best way possible for its environment, while still retaining compatibility with the language standard. The basic syntax for using a pragma is shown here:

```
#pragma PragmaString
```

In this syntax, PragmaString is a series of characters sent to the pragma, subject to the rules of macro expansion (discussed in the next section). Pragmas aren't supported by all compilers, and they are generally used only by advanced programmers in headers and source files that ship with your compiler. Refer to your compiler's documentation to find out what pragmas it supports.

Exploring Macros

In C++, a macro is a useful tool that's also a bit confusing at times. Programmers often use macros to create aliases for lengthy statements that are tedious to type, making them short and descriptive instead. As you've already seen, a macro begins with the #define preprocessor directive. This directive is followed by the declarator for the macro and the expression or statement the declarator aliases. The basic syntax is like this:

```
#define MACRO_NAME [expression/statement]
```

Defining Macros

Consider the following two macros:

```
#define STR    "The sky is blue on "
#define PRN    std::cout
```

These are simple macros that act as symbolic constants, but they offer the advantage of saving keystrokes and making code more readable. Macros can be very useful, but it's easy to go overboard with them. Because the compiler doesn't know what type of data a macro stands in for, macros can undermine the strong type-checking that C++ performs, so be careful when using them.

A lengthy macro can extend across several lines if each line is terminated with a backslash (\) character followed immediately by a hard return. The macro in Listing 12.2 demonstrates this kind of continuation, making a macro out of an entire main() function and using the simple macros just defined.

When to Use Macros

Macros can be useful for eliminating tedious, repetitive typing, and they are very important in C programming, but they have much less usefulness in C++ programming. Because macros reorganize source code text before the compiler sees it, they can cause problems that aren't readily apparent. In short, it's good to know how to create and use a macro, but don't use one unless you think you have to.

LISTING 12.2   A Sample Program Using Simple Macros

```
 1:  /////////////////////////////////////////////////////////
 2:  //  Module  : macro.cpp
 3:  //
 4:  //  Purpose : Shows the use of simple replacement
 5:  //            macros
 6:  /////////////////////////////////////////////////////////
 7:
 8:  #include <iostream.h>
 9:
```

```
10: enum WEEKDAYS
11: {
12:     Sun, Mon, Tues, Wed, Thurs, Fri, Sat
13: };
14:
15: // Some simple macros
16: //
17: #define STR   "The sky is blue on "
18: #define PRN   cout
19:
20: // Define main() as a macro
21: //
22: #define MAIN  void main() {               \
23:     WEEKDAYS wd;                          \
24:     wd = Mon;                             \
25:     switch (wd)                           \
26:     {                                     \
27:        case Sun:                          \
28:            PRN << STR << "Sunday";        \
29:            break;                         \
30:                                           \
31:        case Mon:                          \
32:            PRN << STR << "Monday";        \
33:            break;                         \
34:                                           \
35:        case Sat:                          \
36:            PRN << STR << "Saturday";      \
37:            break;                         \
38:     }                                     \
39: }
40:
41: // Run the main() function as a macro
42: //
43: MAIN
```

LISTING 12.2

1 Lines 10-13: Define days of the week as enumerated values

2 Lines 17-18: Define two simple replacement macros

This program produces the output string The sky is blue on Monday through the use of macro replacement. Lines 10 through 13 define seven enumerated values representing days of the week. Line 17 defines the symbol STR as a macro to represent the string literal "The sky is blue on". The simple replacement macro on line 18 uses the symbol PRN to represent the cout object. These types of macros are especially useful because you can define short symbols to stand in for long expressions. The entire main() function of this program is defined as a macro. Admittedly, this is a bit overboard, but it does show the extent of what you can do with a macro, using it to replace text in source files.

The macro MAIN begins on line 22, and uses the backslash character at the end of each line, 22 though 38 to splice the lines into a single macro. Within the MAIN macro, the macros PRN and STR are used to output a string to the screen based on the matching enumerated WEEKDAYS value initialized on line 24.

More complex macros can create aliases for function pointers, shorten complex data type declarations to a more manageable size, and even take parameters to return a value like a function. Here is a more complex macro that calculates the number of elements in an array:

```
#define ARRAY_SIZE (sizeof / sizeof([0]))
```

The macro ARRAY_SIZE is a macro function that calculates the number of elements in an array. Whatever parameter A is sent into the macro the source code is expanded to the actual value when the preprocessor kicks in at compile time. For example, given an array like this,

```
double val[] = { 12.3, 34.5, 6.4, 7.0 };
```

The ARRAY_SIZE macro can calculate the number of elements the array contains, like this:

```
int ElementCount = ARRAY_SIZE(val);
```

When the preprocessor *expands* the macro, the preceding line looks like this:

```
int ElementCount = (sizeof(val) / sizeof((val)[0]));
```

Expanding Macros

Macros are expanded in the preprocessor's final phase, generating a fully preprocessed text file that's ready for the compiler to translate into binary object code. When the preprocessor expands macros, it replaces the symbolic macro identifier with the fully preprocessed literal text of the macro. For example, given an integer array named `MyIntArray[]`, here's how you would use the `ARRAY_SIZE` macro defined at the end of the preceding section:

```
int MyIntArray[100];
int size = ARRAY_SIZE(MyIntArray);
```

The `ARRAY_SIZE` macro as used here would expand like this in the fully preprocessed source file:

```
int size = sizeof(MyIntArray) / sizeof(MyIntArray[0]));
```

When macros use arguments, you should always use parentheses around each argument to prevent unwanted side effects from occurring. Here's a macro that takes two arguments (a and b):

```
#define TEST_MACRO(a, b)  a / b * 2
```

Using this macro in your code would be asking for trouble. Because of the way this macro is defined, it will work as expected—sometimes. Here are two examples of using the macro:

```
cout << TEST_MACRO(12, 3);
cout << TEST_MACRO(5 + 7, 1 + 2);
```

The first statement gives the expected result, evaluating (as it should) to 8, because the expanded macro yields this expression:

```
cout << 12 / 3 * 2;
```

Although at first glance, the second example looks the same as the first, the second example expands to a result different than expected. Although 5+7 equals 12, and 2+1 equals 3, this usage of `TEST_MACRO` evaluates, wrongly, to 16 instead of 8—a substantial difference! This happens because the expanded macro yields the following expression:

```
cout << 5 + 7 / 1 + 2 * 2;
```

The order of operator precedence comes into play when evaluating this expression, and the wrong answer results. (The division—7/1—and multiplication—2 * 2—operations are performed first, and the expression is evaluated in this way: 5 + 7 + 4.) To prevent this sort of problem, because you don't know how the macro will be used, enclose the arguments in parentheses. This simple step causes macros to evaluate correctly even when the arguments passed to a macro are expressions that use multiple operands themselves. Here's the revised TEST_MACRO definition, using parentheses:

```
#define TEST_MACRO(a, b)   /   * 2
```

The previous two examples of using this macro now expand to the following equivalent (and correctly evaluated) expressions:

```
cout << (12) / (3) * 2;
cout << (5 + 7) / (1 + 2) * 2;
```

Using Preprocessor Operators

There are three ANSI preprocessor operators. The first is defined, which you've seen before. The second and third are used in conjunction with the #define directive. The three preprocessor operators are as follows:

1. **The defined operator**   Tests to see whether an identifier has been defined.
2. **The "stringizing" operator (#)**   Converts pre-expanded macro arguments into string literals.
3. **The token-pasting operator (##)**   Allows tokens used as actual arguments to be concatenated to form other tokens.

Using the # Operator

Stringizing

The term *stringizing* refers to the conversion of macro arguments into string literals.

The pound sign (#) is the "stringizing" operator; it converts pre-expanded macro parameters into string literals. You can use this operator only with macros that take arguments because this operator tells the preprocessor to wrap quotation marks around the actual argument being sent to the macro—stringizing the argument. Here's a sample macro that takes a single argument:

```
#define PRINT  cout << #a << '\n'
```

Any whitespace characters to the left and right of the argument are ignored. Here are a few examples of how you could use the PRINT macro just defined:

```
void main()
{
    PRINT(   A few words and some extra whitespace.   );
```

```
    PRINT("A few words in quotes");
    PRINT(5 * 5);
}
```

Whatever appears inside the parentheses is converted, character for character, into a string. These PRINT statements yield the following results at runtime:

```
A few words and some extra whitespace.
"A few words in quotes"
5 * 5
```

The first PRINT statement won't even compile without the macro that uses the stringizing # operator. It would be like saying this:

```
cout <<    A few words and some extra whitespace.    << '\n';
```

Without quotes around the sentence, the compiler will choke. In the second PRINT statement, the quotes print because the # operator converts the quotes in the original string to literal quotes in the output string.

Using the ## Operator

The double pound sign (##) operator is the "token-pasting" operator (sometimes called the *merge operator* or the *concatenation operator*). It merges separate tokens into a single, combined token. As such, you can't use this operator on the first or last token in a macro definition. Concatenation of tokens occurs before macro expansion and is useful for generating unique names. For example, here's a macro that concatenates two arguments:

```
#define CONCAT(a, b) a##b
```

You could use the CONCAT macro to concatenate two tokens, like this:

```
float CONCAT(TestFloat, 1) = 0.0f;
```

This snippet produces the following expanded statement:

```
float TestFloat1 = 0.0f;
```

Here's a complete program that shows the use of the token-pasting operator:

```
#include <iostream>

#define DEF     int Test##a
#define PRINT   std::cout << Test##a << '\n'

void main()
{
   DEF(1) = 5;
   DEF(2) = 10;
   PRINT(1);
   PRINT(2);
}
```

After preprocessor substitution and macro expansion, the code for the main function looks like this:

```
void main()
{
   int Test1 = 5;
   int Test2 = 10;
   cout << Test1 << '\n';
   cout << Test2 << '\n';
}
```

Using the macro DEF to define DEF(1) and DEF(2) actually creates the integer variables Test1 and Test2, which can then be used anywhere within the main() function. This type of macro usage is rarely (if ever) needed, but it's an interesting trick. Remember, only use macros if you need to.

Considering Internationalization Issues

Most countries around the world use keyboard character sets that are much different than what is used in the United States. In many countries, certain characters that are essential parts of C++ programming—such as the opening and closing braces that make up a code block—aren't even present on the keyboard!

To work around this difficulty, digraph sequences, trigraph sequences, and keyword sequences were developed to allow programmers from around the world to write and exchange portable C++ solutions to real-world problems. Let's take a quick look at these sequences.

Digraph Sequences

A *digraph* is a pair of characters used to represent a single character (for example, using the character pair <% to represent a { character). The C++ digraph sequences are specific pairs of matched characters that programmers can use when important keys aren't available on the keyboard—a common occurrence when using non-English character sets. The digraph sequences defined in standard C++ are listed in Table 12.2.

TABLE 12.2 **The Digraph Sequences Provided by Standard C++**

Symbol	Digraph Sequence
{	<%
}	%>
[	<:
]	:>
#	%:
##	%:%:

When used in source code, digraphs look a bit peculiar. Here's a `main()` function that uses digraphs for the function body braces:

```
void main()
<%
    cout << "Hello digraphs!\n";
%>
```

Here's the declaration of a 50-character array using digraphs:

```
char ch<:50:>;
```

Trigraph Sequences

A *trigraph* is a set of three characters used to represent a single character (for example, using the character-trio ??< to represent a { character). The C++ trigraph sequences are specific trios of matched characters that programmers can use when important keys aren't available on the keyboard—a common occurrence when using non-English character sets. The trigraph sequences defined in standard C++ are listed in Table 12.3.

Digraph

A specific pair of matched characters that programmers can use when important keys aren't available on their keyboard.

Trigraph

A specific set of three matched characters that programmers can use when important keys aren't available on their keyboard.

TABLE 12.3   **The Trigraph Sequences Provided by Standard C++**

Symbol	Trigraph Sequence
#	??=
[	??(
{	??<
\	??/
]	??)
}	??>
^	??'
¦	??!
~	??-
?	???

When used in source code, trigraphs look very peculiar. Here's a main() function that uses trigraphs for the function body braces:

```
void main()
??<
    cout << "Hello trigraphs!\n";
??>
```

Here's the declaration of a 50-character array using trigraphs:

```
char ch??(50??);
```

Keyword Sequences

In addition to digraphs and trigraphs, several keyword sequences are defined by C++—for the same reasons the digraphs and trigraphs were defined. Table 12.4 shows these keyword sequences.

TABLE 12.4   **The C++ Keyword Sequences That Alias the Logical and Bitwise Operators**

Keyword	Symbol Sequence
and	&&
and_eq	&=
bitand	&

Keyword	Symbol Sequence
bitor	¦
compl	~
not	!
or	¦¦
or_eq	¦=
xor	^
xor_eq	^=
not_eq	!=

Examining Predefined Macros

The standard ANSI C specification predefines six macros. As a superset of C, C++ also includes these predefined macros. These predefined macros are listed in Table 12.5.

TABLE 12.5 **The Six ANSI C Predefined Macros**

Macro	Description
__DATE__	The compilation date of the current source file.
__FILE__	The name of the current source file.
__LINE__	The line number in the current source file.
__STDC__	Specifies complete conformance to the ANSI Standard C specification. Not defined for most C++ compilers.
__TIME__	The most recent compilation time of the current source file.
__TIMESTAMP__	The date and time of the last modification of the current source file.

Note

Although Standard C++ is a superset of Standard C, and Standard C includes these six macros, not all implementations of C++ support all these macros. This is because not all C++ implementations are hosted implementations (which fully implement Standard C++)—many C++ compilers use freestanding implementations (that only partially implement the Standard C++ language). Check your compiler's documentation to make sure it supports the standard macros.

The program in Listing 12.3 demonstrates the use of conditional compilations, blocks, simple macros, and predefined macros. The program attempts to use each of the six predefined macros. Because not all implementations of C++ support all these macros, each is wrapped with a conditional compilation block.

LISTING 12.3 **A Program That Uses the Six Predefined ANSI C Macros**

```
 1: /////////////////////////////////////////////////
 2: //  Module  : predefined.cpp
 3: //
 4: //  Purpose : Uses the predefined ANSI C macros
 5: /////////////////////////////////////////////////
 6:
 7: #include <iostream.h>
 8:
 9: #define NL '\n'
10:
11: void main()
12: {
13:    // __DATE__
14:    //
15:    #ifdef __DATE__
16:       cout << "The __DATE__ macro says: " << __DATE__
17:          << NL;
18:    #else
19:       cout << "This compiler doesn't support __DATE__."
20:          << NL;
21:    #endif
22:
23:    // __FILE__
24:    //
25:    #ifdef __FILE__
26:       cout << "The __FILE__ macro says: " << __FILE__
27:          << NL;
28:    #else
29:       cout << "This compiler doesn't support __FILE__."
30:          << NL;
31:    #endif
32:
33:    // __LINE__
34:    //
35:    #ifdef __LINE__
36:       cout << "The __LINE__ macro says: " << __LINE__
37:          << NL;
38:    #else
39:       cout << "This compiler doesn't support __LINE__."
40:          << NL;
41:    #endif
```

```
42:
43:    // __STDC__
44:    //
45:    #ifdef __STDC__
46:       cout << "Amazing! This compiler supports "
47:          "the __STDC__ macro " << NL;
48:    #else
49:       cout << "This compiler doesn't support __STDC__."
50:          << NL;
51:    #endif
52:
53:    // __TIME__
54:    //
55:    #ifdef __TIME__
56:       cout << "The __TIME__ macro says: " << __TIME__
57:          << NL;
58:     #else
59:       cout << "This compiler doesn't support __TIME__."
60:          << NL;
61:    #endif
62:
63:        // __TIMESTAMP__
64:    //
65:    #ifdef __TIMESTAMP__
66:       cout << "The __TIMESTAMP__ macro says: "
67:          << __TIMESTAMP__ << NL;
68:     #else
69:       cout << "This compiler doesn't support "
70:          "__TIMESTAMP__." << NL;
71:     #endif
72: }
```

LISTING 12.3 CONTINUED

5 Line 56: Use the __TIME__ macro

6 Line 66: Use the __TIMESTAMP__ macro

When I ran this code through my Microsoft compiler and executed the resulting program, it produced this output:

```
The __DATE__ macro says: Jun  5 1998
The __FILE__ macro says: f:\rwm\cpp\predefined.cpp
The __LINE__ macro says: 35
This compiler doesn't support __STDC__.
The __TIME__ macro says: 07:23:23
The __TIMESTAMP__ macro says: Fri Jun  5 07:23:22 1998
```

This program begins by defining the simple substitution macro NL on line 9 to stand in for the newline character. Then, several #ifdef preprocessor blocks check each of the standard macro symbols to see if they are defined by the implementation of C++ doing the compiling. For example, line 15 checks to see if the __DATE__ macro is defined by the compiler's C++ implementation. If so, line 16 compiles into the object code of the source file, otherwise, line 19 compiles into the object code of the source file. The same is true for the other preprocessor blocks that test for the remaining predefined macros.

Creating and Using Function Pointers

Understand how a function can have a pointer

See why pointers to functions can be valuable

Create function pointer data types

Declare and use function pointers

Create arrays of function pointers

Function Address

A function address is the memory location marking the starting address of the memory segment that a function's executable code loads into at runtime.

How Can a Function Have a Pointer?

When a function is compiled into an executable program, storage is reserved for the function's executable code to reside in memory at runtime. When the program runs, the function loads into memory somewhere. The address marking the beginning of the function in memory is called the *function address*.

By using a function name without the parentheses you can obtain the starting address of the function, much as using an array name without the braces gives you the starting address of the array. Here's an example: Given the function Func(), the address of the function is Func. Simple, right?

It stands to reason that if you have an address for a function, you should be able to store that address in a pointer variable, just as you can any other memory address. The tricky part is that the compiler needs to know what type of object a pointer points to. The usual solution is to create an alias for a function pointer, as you'll see shortly.

Some Reasons for Declaring Pointers to Functions

Why would you want to use a pointer to a function? Here are a few common uses for function pointers that should give you an idea of what a function pointer is good for:

- **To simplify code**   Using pointers to functions can simplify your programming by eliminating redundant code. The use of typedef function pointers often results in elegant, easy-to-understand source code.

- **Dynamic tables of functions**   Sometimes it's convenient to create dynamic tables of functions at runtime, using function pointers to call the functions in the table.

- **Callback functions**   Modern operating systems use a technique known as a *callback*, which lets the operating system call a function in a program that it's running. A *callback function* is a program function that the operating system calls.

Callback functions are often used for real-time, interactive systems. The operating system calls the callback function by using its function address.

- **Object-oriented system design**   Function pointers form the underlying mechanism used by C++ that makes object-oriented programming possible, and you can extend your own programming by using them, too.

Declaring and Using Function Pointers

If you have a pointer to an integer, the data type pointed to is int. What kind of data type is pointed to when you have a pointer to a function? The data type is based on the parameters and return type of the function. These items identify the function signature, and that's all you need to create a function pointer. To demonstrate how a function pointer is just like any other pointer, let's create two pointers: one to an integer, another to a function.

You declare the pointer to an integer like this:

```
int *pInt;
```

Now let's declare the simple function Func(), so you know what function signature you need a pointer to. Here's the Func() prototype:

```
void Func(int i);
```

To declare a pointer to a function you follow this syntax:

```
ReturnType (*Name)(ParameterList);
```

where ReturnType is the function return data type, Name is the name of the pointer to create, and ParameterList is the list of function parameters. This means that a pointer to Func() would look like this:

```
void (*pFunc)(int i);
```

The arbitrary identifier pFunc now represents a pointer to a function having the same signature as Func(). A function pointer can be assigned to any function that has the same signature, and this makes function pointers quite versatile. After you assign a function address to the pointer, you can invoke the function through the pointer, like this:

```
pFunc = Func;   // Assign function address to pointer
pFunc();        // Invoke the function using the pointer
```

In C++ you can have either a pointer to an object or a pointer to a function. Although these two pointer types both hold addresses, be aware that you *can't* use pointer arithmetic with a pointer to a function like you can with a pointer to an object. The function pointer points to the code segment where the function's executable code resides in memory—that place where execution goes when the function is called.

Sometimes a function pointer is used as a parameter for a function, and this can lead to some exotic looking code. For example, a function pointer having the following declaration:

```
void (*pfnFunc)(int);
```

represents a pointer to a function that has a return type of void, and that takes an integer argument. When used in the prototype of a function that expects this type of pointer as a parameter, you get this sort of function declaration:

```
void Test(void (*pfnFunc)(int));
```

A simple example of using a function pointer as a function argument like this is shown in the program given in Listing 13.1.

Exotic Code

Using function pointers in function calls can produce some bizarre-looking (confusing) source code. By using a **typedef** for the function pointer, you can make the code much cleaner (less confusing).

LISTING 13.1   **A Program That Demonstrates the Simple Usage of a Function Pointer**

```
 1   //////////////////////////////////////////////////////
 2   //   Module  : FunctionPointerFun1.cpp
 3   //
 4   //   Purpose : Demonstrates the use of a function
 5   //             pointer.
 6   //////////////////////////////////////////////////////
 7
 8   #include <iostream.h>
 9
10   // Function prototypes
11   //
12   void Func(int i);
```

```
13   void Test(void (*pfnFunc)(int));
14
15   /////////////////////////////////////////////////////////
16   //  main()
17
18   void main()
19   {
20      Test(Func);
21   }
22
23   /////////////////////////////////////////////////////////
24   //  Func()
25
26   void Func(int i)
27   {
28      cout << "Inside Func(), i == " << i << endl;
29   }
30
31   /////////////////////////////////////////////////////////
32   //  Test()
33
34   void Test(void (*pfnFunc)(int))
35   {
36      // Dereference the function pointer explicitly
37      //
38      (*pfnFunc)(101);
39
40      // Dereference the function pointer implicitly
41      //
42      pfnFunc(102);
43   }
```

LISTING 13.1

1 Line 13: Declare a function that uses a function pointer as a parameter

2 Lines 38-42: Call the function pointed to by explicit dereference and by implicit dereference

The output for this program shows that both forms of dereferencing the function pointer work equally well:

```
Inside Func(), i == 101
Inside Func(), i == 102
```

This program declares two functions on lines 12 and 13: Func() and Test(). Not coincidentally, the function Test() takes a function pointer parameter that is the same as the function signature used by Func(). By sending the Test() function the argument Func on line 20, the address of Func() is sent to Test().

The Test() function uses this function address to call Func() via its function address. On line 38, the function pointer is dereferenced explicitly, sending the argument 101 to Func(). On line 42 the function pointer is dereferenced implicitly, sending the argument 102 to Func(). The Func() function simply displays a text string that contains the value sent to it (line 28).

Declaring a New Data Type

As you can see from Listing 13.1, the syntax used for functions that have pointers to functions as parameters is a bit obtuse:

```
void Test(void (*pFunc)(int));
```

A nice way to make the code more readable, and to prevent careless typing mistakes that can lead to bugs, is to create an alias for the function pointer by using the C++ keyword typedef. For example, to create the alias PFUNC you can just do this:

```
typedef void (*PFUNC)(int);
```

Using a Function Pointer Type

Using the new syntax you just created, you can revise the program shown in Listing 13.1, resulting in the program given in Listing 13.2. This version of the program uses the following type definition:

```
typedef void (*pfnFunc)(int);
```

With the typedef alias incorporated into the code, the program is much more readable, and the code looks less exotic.

LISTING 13.2   **A Program That Demonstrates the Simple Usage of a Function Pointer as a Type Definition**

```
1   //////////////////////////////////////////////////////////
2   //  Module  : FunctionPointerFun2.cpp
3   //
4   //  Purpose : Demonstrates the use of a function
5   //            pointer.
6   //////////////////////////////////////////////////////////
7
8   #include <iostream.h>
```

```
9
10   // Function prototypes
11   //
12
13   typedef void (*pfnFunc)(int);
14
15   void Func(int i);
16   void Test(pfnFunc pfn);
17
18   /////////////////////////////////////////////////////
19   //  main()
20
21   void main()
22   {
23      Test(Func);
24   }
25
26   /////////////////////////////////////////////////////
27   //  Func()
28
29   void Func(int i)
30   {
31      cout << "Inside Func(), i == " << i << endl;
32   }
33
34   /////////////////////////////////////////////////////
35   //  Test()
36
37   void Test(pfnFunc pfn)
38   {
39      // Dereference the function pointer explicitly
40      //
41      (*pfn)(101);
42
43      // Dereference the function pointer implicitly
44      //
45      pfn(102);
46   }
```

LISTING 13.2

① Line 13: Create a type definition for a function pointer

② Line 16: Use the new function pointer type

③ Lines 41-46: Call the function pointed to by explicit dereference and by implicit dereference

The output of this version of the program is exactly the same as the first incarnation (as you might expect):

```
Inside Func(), i == 101
Inside Func(), i == 102
```

The only change to this program from its predecessor is the use of a type definition (line 13) that is used to simplify the Test() function interface. The change is most evident in the Test() function declaration (line 16) and implementations (line 37).

By comparing the two versions of the Test() function (the original version and the typedef version) you can see how a type definition can eliminate confusing code when working with function pointers. The original Test() function declaration from Listing 13.1 looked like this:

```
void Test(void (*pfnFunc)(int));
```

while the typedef version in Listing 13.2 is cleaner, looking like this:

```
void Test(pfnFunc pfn);
```

The Test() function calls Func() via its function address. On line 41, the function pointer is dereferenced explicitly, sending the argument 101 to Func(). On line 45 the function pointer is dereferenced implicitly, sending the argument 102 to Func(). The Func() function simply displays a text string that contains the value sent to it (line 31).

You can use function pointers to communicate with some system that exists outside the confines of a program. This system can be another program that is running simultaneously, or even the operating system itself. When you provide a function address to a system, and the system later calls your function in response to some program event that occurs at runtime, you are providing a callback function.

The Standard C++ Library contains several functions that work using function pointers for callbacks. For example, here's the declaration of the Standard C++ Library terminate_handler type used in exception handling:

```
typedef void (*terminate_handler)();
```

This `terminate_handler` type specifies a pointer to a function, having a `void` return type and no parameter list, that you want to install as a terminate handler.

Creating Arrays of Function Pointers

Creating a function pointer is one thing, but creating an array of these pointers is a convenient way to access a table of functions. Most implementations of C++ use this technique internally to store the addresses of overloaded functions.

The program in Listing 13.3 shows how to create and use a simple array of function pointers. The program uses the general concept of shapes. Each function, pointed to by a function pointer in the array, draws a different shape of some random color. If this were an actual graphics program it would, of course, actually draw these shapes. Because it's not an actual graphics program, the "drawing" as far as this program is concerned is just a text message that *says* it's drawing some colored shape.

To implement the choosing of random colors, some enumerated colors are set up:

```
enum colors { BLACK = 0, YELLOW = 1, BLUE = 2,
   GREEN = 3, RED = 4, ORANGE = 5, MAGENTA = 6,
   WHITE = 7 };
```

The random color can be chosen using the Standard Library function `rand()`, declared in `<stdlib.h>`. The following function, `GetRand()`, uses lower and upper bounds to specify a range for the random number:

```
int GetRand(int lower, int upper)
{
   return rand() % (upper + 1 - lower) + lower;
}
```

The program uses a simple `for` loop to iterate through each function pointed to by the array elements.

LISTING 13.3

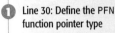

Line 30: Define the PFN
function pointer type

LISTING 13.3   **A Program That Uses an Array of Function Pointers**

```
1  /////////////////////////////////////////////////////
2  //   Module   : FunctionPointerArray.cpp
3  //
4  //   Purpose : Demonstrates the use of an array of
5  //             function pointers.
6  /////////////////////////////////////////////////////
7
8  #include <iostream.h>
9  #include <stdlib.h>
10 #include <string.h>
11 #include <time.h>
12
13 // Colors
14 enum colors { BLACK = 0, YELLOW = 1, BLUE = 2,
15    GREEN = 3, RED = 4, ORANGE = 5, MAGENTA = 6,
16    WHITE = 7 };
17
18 // Prototypes
19 //
20 bool DrawTriangle(int clr);
21 bool DrawSquare(int clr);
22 bool DrawPentagon(int clr);
23 bool DrawHexagon(int clr);
24 bool DrawOctagon(int clr);
25 bool DrawCircle(int clr);
26 char * GetColor(int clr);
27 int GetRand(int lower, int upper);
28
29 // Function pointer type
30 typedef bool (*PFN)(int clr);
31
32 char str[10];   // Global string for colors
33 /////////////////////////////////////////////////////
34 //   main()
35
36 void main()
37 {
38    // Initialize the random number generator
39    //
40    srand((unsigned)time(NULL));
41
```

```
42     // Declare and initialize an array of
43     // function pointers
44     //
45     PFN pfn[6] = { DrawTriangle, DrawSquare,
46        DrawPentagon, DrawHexagon, DrawOctagon,
47        DrawCircle };
48
49     // Call the functions via the pointers
50     //
51     for (int i = 0; i < 6; ++i)
52        pfn[i](GetRand(1, 8));
53  }
54
55  //////////////////////////////////////////////////////
56  //  GetRand()
57
58  int GetRand(int lower, int upper)
59  {
60     return rand() % (upper + 1 - lower) + lower;
61  }
62
63  //////////////////////////////////////////////////////
64  //  GetColor()
65
66  char * GetColor(int clr)
67  {
68     char *str;
69
70     switch (clr)
71     {
72        case BLACK:
73           strcpy(str, "a black");
74           break;
75        case YELLOW:
76           strcpy(str, "a yellow");
77           break;
78        case BLUE:
79           strcpy(str, "a blue");
80           break;
81        case GREEN:
82           strcpy(str, "a green");
83           break;
```

LISTING **13.3** CONTINUED

2 Lines 45-47: Declare and initialize an array of function pointers

3 Lines 51-52: Use the function pointers to call the functions

continues...

LISTING 13.3 **Continued**

```
84      case RED:
85          strcpy(str, "a red");
86          break;
87      case ORANGE:
88          strcpy(str, "an orange");
89          break;
90      case MAGENTA:
91          strcpy(str, "a magenta");
92          break;
93      case WHITE:
94          strcpy(str, "a white");
95          break;
96      }
97      return str;
98  }
99
100 ///////////////////////////////////////////////////////
101 //  Drawing functions
102
103 bool DrawTriangle(int clr)
104 {
105     cout << "Drawing " << GetColor(clr)
106         << " triangle...\n";
107     return true;
108 }
109
110 bool DrawSquare(int clr)
111 {
112     cout << "Drawing " << GetColor(clr)
113         << " square...\n";
114     return true;
115 }
116
117 bool DrawPentagon(int clr)
118 {
119     cout << "Drawing " << GetColor(clr)
120         << " pentagon...\n";
121     return true;
122 }
123
124 bool DrawHexagon(int clr)
```

```
125  {
126      cout << "Drawing " << GetColor(clr)
127          << " hexagon...\n";
128      return true;
129  }
130
131  bool DrawOctagon(int clr)
132  {
133      cout << "Drawing " << GetColor(clr)
134          << " octagon...\n";
135      return true;
136  }
137
138  bool DrawCircle(int clr)
139  {
140      cout << "Drawing " << GetColor(clr)
141          << " circle...\n";
142      return true;
143  }
```

A sample run of this program produced the following output:

```
Drawing a red triangle...
Drawing a white square...
Drawing a magenta pentagon...
Drawing a blue hexagon...
Drawing a green octagon...
Drawing an orange circle...
```

Lines 20 through 25 declare the prototypes for the "draw" functions, each taking an `int` parameter and returning a `bool` value. Line 30 provides the `typedef` alias `PFN` for the function pointer type `bool(*PFN)(int)`. A global character array is declared on line 32, and this is used by the `GetColor()` function to return the descriptive string corresponding to an enumerated color value (defined from lines 14 through 16).

The main function begins on line 36, and it starts out by seeding the random number generator using the ANSI C Library function `srand()`. Next, the array of six function pointers (`pfn[]`) is declared and initialized with the function addresses of the six shape-drawing functions.

The srand() and rand() Functions

The `srand()` and `rand()` functions are ANSI C functions declared in the header `<stdlib.h>`. The `srand()` function "seeds" the random number generator using an unsigned integer value. The `rand()` function returns a pseudo-random integer value based on the seed value. Initializing the `srand()` using the same seed value every time will produce the same series of random numbers from `rand()` every time. For this reason, the computer's system time is usually used as the seed value, guaranteeing a different set of random numbers every time.

Lines 51 and 52 use a `for` loop to iterate through all the pointers in the array, calling the functions they point to. Each function is sent a random number between one and eight, inclusive, using the `GetRand()` function discussed earlier.

Each shape-drawing function uses the `GetColor()` function to translate the numeric color value (given in the enumeration from lines 14 through 16) into a string that represents the color. The `GetColor()` function runs from lines 66 through 98, and uses a `switch` statement to match up a numeric value with the correct string, using the ANSI C `strcpy()` function (declared in the header `<string.h>`) to assign a string to the global character array `str`. All the shape-drawing functions print a text message using `cout`, and all return `true`.

Using Pointers to Overloaded Functions

Pointers to overloaded functions are just as easy to work with as ordinary function pointers. Assuming three overloaded functions exist, each named `Overload()`, which one of the three gets pointed to when you assign the function address `Overload` to a function pointer?

The compiler uses the function parameter and function return types to determine which function to point to in a case like this. Using type definitions to alias a long function pointer declaration really makes it easier to work with overloaded function pointers, by reducing the amount of exotic code. The program in Listing 13.4 demonstrates using pointers to three overloaded functions.

LISTING 13.4   **A Program That Demonstrates the Use of Pointers to Overloaded Functions**

```
1  //////////////////////////////////////////////////////////
2  // Module  : OverloadedFunctionPointer.cpp
3  //
4  // Purpose : Demonstrates the use of pointers to
5  //           overloaded functions.
6  //////////////////////////////////////////////////////////
7
```

```
8    #include <iostream.h>
9
10   // Prototypes
11   //
12   int Overload(int i, float f);
13   double Overload(double d, float f);
14   float Overload(float f, char c);
15
16   // Function pointer types
17   //
18   typedef int (*PFN_OVERLOAD1)(int i, float f);
19   typedef double (*PFN_OVERLOAD2)(double d, float f);
20   typedef float (*PFN_OVERLOAD3)(float f, char c);
21
22   ///////////////////////////////////////////////////////
23   //   main()
24
25   void main()
26   {
27       // Declare and initialize the function pointers
28       //
29       PFN_OVERLOAD1 pfn1 = Overload;
30       PFN_OVERLOAD2 pfn2 = Overload;
31       PFN_OVERLOAD3 pfn3 = Overload;
32
33       // Call the functions via the pointers
34       //
35       pfn1(1, 1.5f);
36       pfn2(1.5, 2.5f);
37       pfn3(1.5f, 'X');
38   }
39
40   ///////////////////////////////////////////////////////
41   //   Overloaded functions
42
43   int Overload(int i, float f)
44   {
45       cout << "Calling Overload(int " << i
46           << ", float " << f << ")\n";
47       return i;
48   }
49
```

LISTING 13.4

1 Lines 12-14: Prototypes for three overloaded functions

2 Lines 18-20: Function pointer type definitions for each overloaded function

3 Lines 28-31: Declare and initialize the function pointers

4 Lines 35-37: Use the function pointers to call their functions

continues…

LISTING 13.4   **Continued**

```
50 double Overload(double d, float f)
51 {
52    cout << "Calling Overload(double " << d
53       << ", float " << f << ")\n";
54    return d;
55 }
56
57 float Overload(float f, char c)
58 {
59    cout << "Calling Overload(float " << f
60       << ", char '" << c << "')\n";
61    return f;
62 }
```

The output from this program is as follows:

```
Calling Overload(int 1, float 1.5)
Calling Overload(double 1.5, float 2.5)
Calling Overload(float 1.5, char 'X')
```

This program begins by declaring three overloaded functions, all named Overload(), from lines 12 through 14. The function pointer type definitions for these functions are given on lines 18 through 20, and these typedefs are used to declare and initialize three function pointers on lines 29 through 31. The compiler matches the parameter types given by the typedefs to determine the correct overloaded function to assign to each pointer.

The pointers are used to call the functions on lines 35 through 37; each overloaded function is sent the appropriate argument types. Each overloaded function simply writes a text message onscreen, displaying its function signature with the actual arguments.

Using Pointers to Member Functions

Creating and using pointers to member functions is a little more complex than creating and using pointers to global functions. A member function pointer must be qualified by the structure name when it's declared. As an example, here's a Box structure that contains length, width, and height data members, and a CalcVolume() member function:

```
struct Box
{
    float length;
    float width;
    float height;

    float CalcVolume()
        { return length * width * height; }
};
```

To create a pointer to `Box::CalcVolume()` you can either use the direct method to get the address of the function in one step, like this:

```
float (Box::*PFN)() = &Box::CalcVolume;
```

or you can use the `typedef` method you saw earlier, to keep the code a little cleaner:

```
typedef float (Box::*PFN)();
```

In this case the alias for the declaration is `PFN`. To assign an address to a pointer of this type, simply declare a pointer of type `PFN` and assign the member function address, like this:

```
PFN pfn = &Box::CalcVolume;
```

The use of these two styles is a bit different. With either of them an object of the type the member function belongs to must exist *before* you can reference the function. With the first method, you must access the member function using the pointer name `PFN`, like this:

```
Box cube = { 2.0f, 2.0f, 2.0f };
float volume = (cube.*PFN)();
```

With the second method, you must access the member function using the pointer name `pfn` (of type `PFN`), like this:

```
Box cube = { 2.0f, 2.0f, 2.0f };
float volume = (cube.*pfn)();
```

Notice that the `typedef` version aliases the type of the pointer as `PFN`. The actual pointer is `pfn`. The direct version uses the name given as the function pointer (`PFN`). The program in Listing 13.5 puts it all together for you, showing both methods of creating member function pointers.

LISTING 13.5   **A Program That Demonstrates the Use of Pointers to Member Functions**

```
1    /////////////////////////////////////////////////////////
2    //   Module  : MemberFunctionPointer.cpp
3    //
4    //   Purpose : Demonstrates the use of pointers to
5    //             member functions.
6    /////////////////////////////////////////////////////////
7
8    #include <iostream.h>
9
10   struct Box
11   {
12      float length;
13      float width;
14      float height;
15
16      float CalcVolume()
17         { return length * width * height; }
18   };
19
20   // Function pointer types
21   //
22   float (Box::*PFN1)() = &Box::CalcVolume;
23   typedef float (Box::*PFN2)();
24
25   /////////////////////////////////////////////////////////
26   //   main()
27
28   void main()
29   {
30      Box cube = { 2.0f, 2.0f, 2.0f };
31
32      // Declare and initialize the function pointer
33      //
34      PFN2 pfn = &Box::CalcVolume;   // using the typedef
35
36      // Call the function via the pointer
37      //
38      cout << "\nPFN1: Cube volume is " << (cube.*PFN1)();
39      cout << "\nPFN2: Cube volume is " << (cube.*pfn)();
40   }
```

The output from this program shows that both methods of deriving and using a pointer to a member function work equally well:

```
PFN1: Cube volume is 8
PFN2: Cube volume is 8
```

This program begins by defining the Box structure (lines 10 through 18), which contains the sole member function CalcVolume(). Line 22 directly derives a new pointer (PFN1) for the Box::CalcVolume() function and assigns the function address to this pointer in a single statement. Line 23 derives a new function pointer type and uses the typedef statement to create the pointer type alias PFN2.

The first task in the main() function is to create an instance of a Box (cube), in this case providing the length, width, and height values at 2.0 each. After the cube object exists, the Box::CalcVolume() function can be accessed. Line 34 uses the pointer type PFN2 derived on line 23 to create a pointer called pfn. This pointer is then assigned the address of the Box::CalcVolume() function. Lines 38 and 39 use the two function pointers to call the Box::CalcVolume() member function, using the appropriate pointer name for each call.

Overloading Operators

Discover reasons for overloading operators

Learn how an operator is like a function call

Find out how to overload operators

See some examples of operator overloading

Why Overload Operators?

Operators form the basis of many expressions in C+ statements, working with the built-in C++ data types to aid us in writing code that's easy to understand, modify, and maintain. Remember the overloaded Multiply() functions back in Chapter 8? Those functions were written to demonstrate how function overloading works, but they aren't really very useful for real-world code. Imagine if you actually had to use functions like this to perform multiplication:

```
// z = x * y
//
int x = 5, y = 10;
int z = Multiply(x, y);
```

This works, but it's not very convenient—and how about when you need to multiply three operands instead of two, as in this example:

```
// a = x * y * z
//
int x = 5, y = 10, z = 20;
int a = Multiply(Multiply(x, y), z);
```

You can see that this could quickly get out of hand. How far out of hand? Suppose that, in addition to the Multiply() function, you've also defined overloaded Add(), Subtract(), and Divide() functions for a program to use, and you need to write this formula in source code:

```
a = (b + c) / d * (e - f)
```

Coding this equation using nested function calls (in a manner similar to that used by the previous couple of examples) would give you this confusing mess of code:

```
// a = (b + c) / d * (e - f)
//
int b = 5, c = 10, d = 15, e = 20, f = 25;
int a = Multiply(Divide(Add(b, c), d), Subtract(e, f));
```

How's that for counterintuitive? Luckily, C++ predefines the math operators for us, so we can just write this instead:

```
// a = (b + c) / d * (e - f)
//
int b = 5, c = 10, d = 15, e = 20, f = 25;
int a = (b + c) / d * (e - f);
```

This makes a lot more sense. You can see at a glance, without deciphering a bunch of function calls, what the code is doing. This is what makes operators so valuable. Now, suppose that you have a structure, like the `Point2d` structure you saw back in Chapter 9. To refresh your memory, here's its structure declaration:

```
struct Point2d
{
    float x;
    float y;
};
```

To alter a point, moving it from one position to another, you must modify each structure member to reflect its new position, in this case members x and y.

Figure 14.1 shows three points plotted on a grid. Assume that you have to calculate the distances between each of these positions. Because the built-in C++ operators only work with the simple data types provided by C++, you'd be forced to write some function to calculate the distance from one point to another (the length of the line which connects two points would be the distance).

To calculate the distance from Point B to Point C, just subtract each member of Point B from each corresponding member of Point C, like this:

```
DistX = PointC.x - PointB.x;
DistY = PointC.y - PointB.y;
```

This might lead you to write a function like this:

```
Point2d Subtract(const Point2d& a, const Point2d& b)
{
    Point2d pt;
    pt.x = b.x - a.x;
    pt.y = b.y - a.y;
    return pt;
}
```

FIGURE 14.1

Three points on a two-dimensional grid, located at positions (0,0), (8,7), and (10,16).

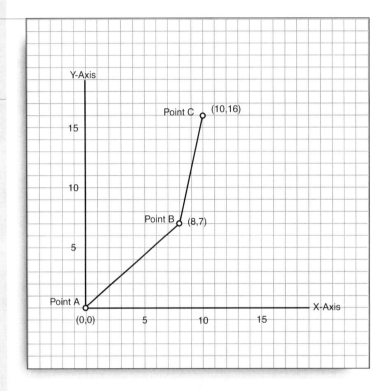

You could then use this function to calculate the distance between two points, like this:

```
Point2d ptB = { 8.0f, 7.0f };
Point2d ptC = { 10.0f, 16.0f };

Point2d ptDist = Subtract(ptB, ptC);
```

This looks suspiciously like the code we decided earlier was unintuitive—except that now we're using a Subtract() function instead of a Multiply() function—bringing us full circle back to where we started. Imagine the convoluted code that would result if other point manipulation functions were written and used on several points in a single complex expression, for example:

```
Point2d ptDist = Multiply(Divide(Add(ptA, ptC), ptD),
    Subtract(ptE, ptF));
```

In short, this code uses function calls to perform tasks much better suited to operators. If only you could define operators for your user-defined data types to make them look as though they are a part of the C++ language.... As it turns out, C++ is so flexible and extensible that it lets you do exactly that!

An Operator Is a Function Call

To define an operator for your new data type, you must overload an existing C++ operator (just like you can overload a function). The overloaded operator takes the form of a function, and the C++ operator syntax makes the operator behave just like a built-in operator for a simple data type. Using the `Point2d` example from the preceding section, you could define a subtraction operator in place of the subtraction function. The resulting syntax for use of the operator in your source code then becomes much more intuitive, as you can see here:

```
Point2d ptB = { 8.0f, 7.0f };
Point2d ptC = { 10.0f, 16.0f };

Point2d ptDist = ptC - ptB;
```

The expression `ptC - ptB` assumes that some overloaded subtraction operator already exists that knows how to subtract one `Point2d` structure from another. The operator must first be declared as a function using the `operator` keyword. The general syntax for creating an operator is as follows:

```
ReturnType operator OpSymbol();
```

In this syntax, `ReturnType` specifies the data type returned by the function, and `OpSymbol` refers to the operator symbol you want to overload. The operators that C++ allows you to overload are listed in Table 14.1. With few exceptions, an operator must be either unary or binary, taking one or two arguments, respectively. Table 14.1 also shows, for each operator symbol, whether the default operator type is unary or binary.

Overloaded Operator

A function that executes when a specified operator is encountered in an expression.

TABLE 14.1   **The Built-In C++ Unary and Binary Operators That Can Be Overloaded**

Symbol	Operator Name	Type
–	Subtraction	Binary
–	Unary negation	Unary
– –	Decrement1	Unary
!	Logical NOT	Unary
!=	Inequality	Binary
%	Modulus	Binary
%=	Modulus/assignment	Binary
&	Bitwise AND	Binary
&	Address-of	Unary
&&	Logical AND	Binary
&=	Bitwise AND/assignment	Binary
*	Multiplication	Binary
*	Pointer dereference	Unary
*=	Multiplication/assignment	Binary
,	Comma	Binary
/=	Division/assignment	Binary
–=	Subtraction/assignment	Binary
->	Member selection	Binary
->*	Pointer-to-member selection	Binary
/	Division	Binary
^	Exclusive OR	Binary
^=	Exclusive OR/assignment	Binary
¦	Bitwise inclusive OR	Binary
¦¦	Logical OR	Binary
¦=	Bitwise inclusive OR/assignment	Binary
~	One's complement	Unary

Symbol	Operator Name	Type
+	Addition	Binary
+	Unary plus	Unary
++	Increment1	Unary
+=	Addition/assignment	Binary
<	Less than	Binary
<<	Left shift	Binary
<<=	Left shift/assignment	Binary
<=	Less than or equal to	Binary
=	Assignment	Binary
==	Equality	Binary
>	Greater than	Binary
>=	Greater than or equal to	Binary
>>	Right shift	Binary
>>=	Right shift/assignment	Binary

In addition to the unary and binary operators, there are a few special operators that you can overload. Table 14.2 lists those special C++ operators that are neither unary nor binary yet can be overloaded.

> **Note**
>
> Several of the operator symbols in Table 14.1 are basically over-loaded already. The compiler knows from the context (the operators being used) which internal operation to perform.

TABLE 14.2   Special C++ Operators That Can Be Overloaded

Symbol	Operator Name
( )	Function call
[ ]	Array subscript
delete	delete
new	new

Now that you've seen the operators you *can* overload, take a look at Table 14.3, which lists the built-in C++ operators that *cannot* be overloaded.

TABLE 14.3   **The Built-In C++ Operators That Cannot Be Overloaded**

Symbol	Operator Name
#	"Stringizing" preprocessor operator
##	Concatenation preprocessor operator
.	Member selection
.*	Pointer-to-member selection
::	Scope resolution
? :	Conditional

Overloading an Operator

As an example of overloading an operator, let's define the currently hypothetical subtraction operator for the `Point2d` structure. To do this, you must write an operator function that overloads the built-in C++ subtraction operator. Because this subtraction operation needs two operands, it is declared as a binary `operator-()` that takes two `Point2d` references, like this:

```
Point2d operator-(const Point2d& v1, const Point2d& v2);
```

The parameters are declared as `const` references, guaranteeing that the operands used with the operator won't be altered in any way. Once the declaration is in place, it's a simple matter to create a function body for the operator, like this:

```
Point2d operator-(const Point2d& p1, const Point2d& p2)
{
    Point2d pt;
    pt.x = p1.x - p2.x;
    pt.y = p1.y - p2.y;
    return pt;
}
```

Compare this with the `Subtract()` function you saw earlier:

```
Point2d Subtract(const Point2d& a, const Point2d& b)
{
    Point2d pt;
```

```
      pt.x = b.x - a.x;
      pt.y = b.y - a.y;
      return pt;
}
```

They're almost identical, aren't they? They should be—they both perform exactly the same task. Again, the benefit of creating the operator-() function instead of the Subtract() function is that you can then invoke the operator function using this intuitive syntax:

```
Point2d ptDist = ptA - ptB;
```

This intuitive syntax is much more desirable than explicitly calling a function, like this:

```
Point2d ptDist = Subtract(ptA, ptB);
```

To test the new Point2d operator operator-(), the program in Listing 14.1 creates three Point2d objects and assigns to one of them the result of the subtraction operation performed on the other two. The program uses both the Subtract() function and the operator-() function to show the difference in usage between the two.

LISTING 14.1   A Program to Test the New Overloaded *operator-()* Function

```
 1: ///////////////////////////////////////////////////
 2: //  Module  : subtract.cpp
 3: //
 4: //  Purpose : Demonstrates the creation and use of a
 5: //            global subtraction operator for a
 6: //            user-defined type.
 7: ///////////////////////////////////////////////////
 8 :
 9: #include <iostream.h>
10:
11: const char NL = '\n';
12:
13: ///////////////////////////////////////////////////
14: //  The Point2d structure
15:
```

continues...

LISTING 14.1 **Continued**

```
16: struct Point2d
17: {
18:    float x;
19:    float y;
20: };

21:
22: /////////////////////////////////////////////////////////
23: //  Module function prototypes
24:
25: Point2d operator-(const Point2d& p1,
26:    const Point2d& p2);
27: Point2d Subtract(const Point2d& p1,
28:    const Point2d& p2);
29:
30: /////////////////////////////////////////////////////////
31: //  operator-()
32:
33: Point2d operator-(const Point2d& p1, const Point2d& p2)
34: {
35:    Point2d pt;
36:    pt.x = p1.x - p2.x;
37:    pt.y = p1.y - p2.y;
38:    return pt;
39: }
40:
41: /////////////////////////////////////////////////////////
42: //  Subtract()
43:
44: Point2d Subtract(const Point2d& p1,
45:                     const Point2d& p2)
46: {
47:    Point2d pt;
48:    pt.x = p1.x - p2.x;
49:    pt.y = p1.y - p2.y;
50:    return pt;
51: }
52:
53: /////////////////////////////////////////////////////////
54: //  main()
55:
56: void main()
```

```
57:  {
58:      Point2d pt1 = { 10.0f, 16.0f };
59:      Point2d pt2 = {  8.0f,  7.0f };
60:
61:      // Use the Subtract function to calc pt3
62:      //
63:      Point2d pt3 = Subtract(pt1, pt2);
64:
65:      cout << "Using Subtract():\n";
66:      cout << "pt1.x = " << pt1.x << "\tpt1.y = "
67:          << pt1.y << NL;
68:      cout << "pt2.x = " << pt2.x << "\tpt2.y = "
69:          << pt2.y << NL;
70:      cout << "pt3.x = " << pt3.x << "\tpt3.y = "
71:          << pt3.y << NL << NL;
72:
73:      // Use the operator-() function to calc pt3
74:      //
75:      pt3 = pt1 - pt2;
76:
77:      cout << "Using operator-():\n";
78:      cout << "pt1.x = " << pt1.x << "\tpt1.y = "
79:          << pt1.y << NL;
80:      cout << "pt2.x = " << pt2.x << "\tpt2.y = "
81:          << pt2.y << NL;
82:      cout << "pt3.x = " << pt3.x << "\tpt3.y = "
83:          << pt3.y << NL;
84:  }
```

LISTING 14.1 CONTINUED

⑥ Lines 58-59: Define two points

⑦ Line 63: Use the Subtract()
function

⑧ Line 75: Use the operator-()
function

⑥ (marker at lines 58-59)

⑦ (marker at line 63)

⑧ (marker at line 75)

The output of this program verifies that the Subtract() and
operator-() functions both work correctly and arrive at the same
result, as you can see here:

```
Using Subtract():
pt1.x = 10      pt1.y = 16
pt2.x = 8       pt2.y = 7
pt3.x = 2       pt3.y = 9

Using operator-():
pt1.x = 10      pt1.y = 16
pt2.x = 8       pt2.y = 7
pt3.x = 2       pt3.y = 9
```

Lines 16 through 21 describe a `Point2d` structure and the `operator-()` function, which overloads the subtraction operator for `Point2d` objects, is declared on lines 25 and 26. Likewise, the original `Subtract()` function is declared on lines 27 and 28. The actual bodies for these functions are identical, as you can see in their definitions. The `operator-()` body block runs from line 34 through line 39, and the `Subtract()` body block runs from line 47 through line 51.

On line 63 the `Subtract()` function returns a new point (`pt3`) that represents the length of the line from `pt1` to `pt2`, and lines 65 through 71 output the member data for all three points to the screen.

On line 75 the `operator-()` function calculates `pt3` again using operator syntax instead of an explicit function call, and lines 77 through 83 output the member data for all three points to the screen.

Some Examples of Operator Overloading

The `operator-()` example you just saw is typical of how you go about overloading an operator. As you saw in Tables 14.1 and 14.2, there are a lot of C++ operators you're allowed to overload. In the following sections, I'll show a few additional examples of overloading other operators, including these:

- The assignment operator
- Some relational operators
- An overloaded function-call operator

Overloading the Assignment Operator

The syntax for the assignment operator is the same as that used for the subtraction operator, a binary situation of two operands:

```
op1 = op2
op1 - op2
```

The assignment operator is an unusual creature. You can override it, but not as a binary operator as you might expect. Binary operands aren't changed during expression evaluation, but unary operands are. Because op1 receives the value of op2, this means that the assignment operation is unary.

C++ does place a restriction on overloading the assignment operator: It must be a member function (as opposed to a global function). The addition of an operator=() function as a member of the Point2d structure would make the structure declaration look like this:

Member Function

A function that's contained (encapsulated) within a structure or class, having direct access to the data members of that structure or class.

```
struct Point2d
{
    float x;
    float y;

    void operator=(const Point2d& p);
};
```

To actually overload the assignment operator for a Point2d structure, you would simply define a unary operator function, qualifying it to be within the scope of the Point2d structure, like this:

```
void Point2d::operator=(const Point2d& p)
{
    x = p.x;
    y = p.y;
}
```

The values of the parameters of the reference object p are assigned directly to the internal x and y members of the structure. Although C++ provides a default assignment operator for structures, by using this technique, you can create an overloaded assignment operator for any structure you design. By overloading the operator, you can fully control the assignment operation of each member, perhaps excluding certain members from the overall assignment if some special condition exists. Here's an example of such filtering, where the members copy normally except when y is greater than 1,000:

```
void Point2d::operator=(const Point2d& p)
{
    x = p.x;
    y = (p.y > 1000) ? 0.0f : p.y;
}
```

Binary operator functions must be declared at file scope. Unary operator functions can be declared either at file scope or as member functions of a structure or class.

Overloading Relational Operators

The relational operators return Boolean values, and an overloaded relational operator can be either binary (as a global function), or unary (as a member function). To add some relational capabilities to aid in the use of the `Point2d` structure, I'll show you the less-than (<), greater-than (>), equal-to (==), and not-equal-to (!=) operators, implemented both as standalone operator functions and as member operator functions.

The standalone versions of these functions, declared at file scope (globally) are all binary, taking two arguments. Here are the declarations for all four global versions of these operators:

```
bool operator<(const Point2d& p1, const Point2d& p2);
bool operator>(const Point2d& p1, const Point2d& p2);
bool operator==(const Point2d& p1, const Point2d& p2);
bool operator!=(const Point2d& p1, const Point2d& p2);
```

Each of these operators is quite similar to the others, and they're all quite easy to implement—so easy that you might want to declare them as `inline` functions.

Here are the definitions for each of these operators:

```
bool operator<(const Point2d& p1, const Point2d& p2)
    { return ((p1.x < p2.x) && (p1.y < p2.y)); }

bool operator>(const Point2d& p1, const Point2d& p2)
    { return ((p1.x > p2.x) && (p1.y > p2.y)); }

bool operator==(const Point2d& p1, const Point2d& p2)
    { return ((p1.x == p2.x) && (p1.y == p2.y)); }

bool operator!=(const Point2d& p1, const Point2d& p2)
    { return ((p1.x != p2.x) && (p1.y != p2.y)); }
```

Overloading these operators as member functions of the `Point2d` structure is just as easy. First, you add the operator declarations to the structure, giving you the following declaration:

```
struct Point2d
{
```

```
    float x;
    float y;

    // Operator members
    //
    void operator=(const Point2d& p);
    bool operator<(const Point2d& p);
    bool operator>(const Point2d& p);
    bool operator==(const Point2d& p);
    bool operator!=(const Point2d& p);
};
```

Each of these operators is identical to its global counterpart, in declaration and definition, except that the first argument is no longer needed because the data members of the structure are used instead. Here are the definitions for each of these member operators:

```
bool Point2d::operator<(const Point2d& p)
    { return ((x < p.x) && (y < p.y)); }

bool Point2d::operator>(const Point2d& p)
    { return ((x > p.x) && (y > p.y)); }

bool Point2d::operator==(const Point2d& p)
    { return ((x == p.x) && (y == p.y)); }

bool Point2d::operator!=(const Point2d& p)
    { return ((x != p.x) && (y != p.y)); }
```

Overloading the Function Call Operator

The function call operator is used internally by C++ whenever you make a function call. You can overload this operator to make an instance of some user-defined type look like a function call. This is called a *function object*, and is an essential part of how the Standard Template Library (STL)—a large part of the Standard C++ Library—does things. A function object can be used in place of a function pointer, and has more uses (as you'll see in Part IV, "Using the Standard C++ Library," of this book).

Function Object

An instance of a structure or class that defines an overloaded function call operator: operator().

As a demonstration of how function call overloading works, take a look at the program in Listing 14.2. This program demonstrates the process of overloading the function call operator for a structure.

SEE ALSO

➤ *For more information about the Standard Template Library, see page 684*

➤ *For more information about the function objects, see page 694*

LISTING 14.2   A Program That Demonstrates One Possible Use for Overloading a Function Call Operator

LISTING 14.2

① Line 19: The two-dimensional array uses the Grid structure

② Lines 25-26: Declare an overloaded function call operator

```
1:  /////////////////////////////////////////////////////
2:  //   Module  : FunctionOp.cpp
3:  //
4:  //   Purpose : Demonstrates the creation and use of an
5:  //             overloaded function call operator for a
6:  //             user-defined type.
7:  /////////////////////////////////////////////////////
8:
9:  #include <iostream.h>
10:
11: const char NL = '\n';
12:
13: /////////////////////////////////////////////////////
14: //   The Grid structure
15:
16: struct Grid
17: {
18: private:
19:    int grid[5][5];
20:
21: public:
22:    void SetValue(int row, int column, int value)
23:       { grid[row][column] = value; }
24:
25:    int operator()(int row, int column)
26:       { return grid[row][column]; }
27: };
28:
29: /////////////////////////////////////////////////////
30: //   main()
```

```
31:
32: void main()
33: {
34:     Grid g;
35:
36:     // Set the values of the squares
37:     //
38:     for (int r = 0; r < 5; ++r)
39:         for (int c = 0; c < 5; ++c)
40:             g.SetValue(r, c, r * c);
41:
42:     // Get the value of some specified squares
43:     //
44:     cout << "g.grid[0][0] == " << g(0, 0) << NL;
45:     cout << "g.grid[1][1] == " << g(1, 1) << NL;
46:     cout << "g.grid[2][2] == " << g(2, 2) << NL;
47:     cout << "g.grid[3][3] == " << g(3, 3) << NL;
48:     cout << "g.grid[4][4] == " << g(4, 4) << NL;
49: }
```

LISTING 14.2 CONTINUED

3 Lines 38-40: Fill the Grid array with values

4 Lines 44-48: Use the overloaded function call operator to retrieve array elements

The output from this program shows that the array elements specified in the function call operator's parameter list are returned to the caller as expected:

```
g.grid[0][0] == 0
g.grid[1][1] == 1
g.grid[2][2] == 4
g.grid[3][3] == 9
g.grid[4][4] == 16
```

In lines 15 through 27, this program declares a Grid structure. This structure contains a private grid, which is a two-dimensional array defining a logical 5-by-5 grid. The structure also defines a SetValue() member function on lines 22 and 23, and an overloaded function call operator operator()() as a member function on lines 25 and 26. In this case the overloaded function call operator operator()() for object g is returning g.grid[row][column], which allows you to use the more intuitive syntax g(row, column).

Because the array is private, the access function `SetValue()` is used to place a value into a specific array element. The `operator()()` function is used to get a value from an array element. A `for` loop, running from lines 38 through 40 in the `main()` function, populates the array elements with data. The overloaded function call operator is used in lines 44 through 48 to access specific array elements, using the syntax `g(row,col)`.

Bulletproofing Programs with Assertions and Exceptions

Examine error-handling strategies

Learn to handle programming and runtime errors

Discover how assertion macros can help you detect programming errors

Learn to handle anomalous situations with exception handling

Devising Error Handling Strategies

Like it or not, bugs crop up in programs. An elusive bug can cause errors to occur that crash the program—or worse, the user's computer. You can usually categorize an error as a *programming error* or as a *runtime error* that's beyond the programmer's control. To prevent catastrophe, you should use error-handling mechanisms to help detect programming errors in your source code and to deal with runtime errors, too.

Handling Runtime Errors

The C++ *exception-handling* mechanism is the preferred way to deal with runtime errors and any unanticipated program behavior. Exceptions offer the C++ programmer an efficient and well-structured way of trapping errors that crop up at runtime. Later in this chapter, you learn how C++ exception handling works and how you can use it to bulletproof your code.

Handling Programming Errors

The preferred way to handle programming errors is through the use of *assertions*. An assertion is used to alert you of a condition that should never be able to occur in a program. For example, if you've written a library of functions and one of these functions should never be able to accept an value greater than 100, you should assert that the argument being passed is less than 100, like this:

```
assert(x < 100);
```

The following sections take a look at assertions, including how they work and how you should use them.

Using Assertions

Assertions protect you from yourself. During program testing, assertions warn you about—and point out—careless programming mistakes. An assertion is a macro that alerts you to programming errors when it sees them at runtime in a debug build of a program. Because it's a macro, an assertion can be conditionally compiled to be present in a program only when a debugging preprocessor flag (for example, _debug) is defined.

Because assertions can slow program execution somewhat, debug program builds are often slower than nondebug builds, but the information assertions can provide is worth the performance hit.

Understanding the *assert()* Macro

An assertion has traditionally been implemented as a macro called assert() or ASSERT(). The ANSI C standard defines an assert() macro that's used to identify logic errors during program development. The ANSI C assert() macro is declared in the assert.h header file like this:

```
void assert(int expression);
```

Although it's an integer, expression is used as a Boolean value. When the expression argument evaluates to false, the ANSI C assert() macro prints a message that helps you diagnose what went wrong. The macro then rudely calls abort() to abruptly terminate program execution. The message provides diagnostic information that reveals the name of the source file and the line number at which the assertion failed; the information also includes the expression that caused the assertion to fail. The actual implementation of the ANSI assert() macro is unique for each implementation of C++, but the result is consistent across platforms and compilers.

The ANSI C assert() macro is often inappropriate because it aborts execution. Sometimes, the ANSI macro just doesn't provide enough information—or perhaps you want your program to continue execution after an assertion fails instead of terminating immediately with an abort(). The solution to these problems with assert() is to define a custom assertion macro that's more user friendly than the ANSI version. You can create your own macro and make it as user friendly and feature filled as you want. I prefer to define my own assertion macros. For example, here's one way a custom assert() macro can be defined:

Note

In general, any part of ANSI C is also part of Standard C++ by default, since C++ is a superset of C. In Standard C++, the assert() macro is declared in the Standard header <cassert>, although the Standard C header <assert.h> can be used as well.

Note

The assert() macro serves the same basic purpose on every hardware platform, for every compiler. The implementation of the macro may vary, but the end result remains the same.

```
#define assert                              \
  if (!)                                    \
  {                                         \
    cerr << "\nAssertion Failed: " << #a    \
       << "\nFailure occurred on line "     \
       << __LINE__ << " of source file:"    \
       << "\n   \"" << __FILE__ << "\"\n"; \
  }
```

This macro replaces the ANSI C `assert()` macro, and it works only in C++ because it uses the `cerr` object (which doesn't exist in C). The new macro makes use of the predefined ANSI macros `__LINE__` and `__FILE__`.

SEE ALSO

➤ *For more information about custom macros, see page 310*

➤ *For more information about predefined ANSI macros, see page 319*

Some Guidelines for Using Assertions

Assertions are great for debugging and can save you countless hours you might otherwise waste tediously searching for elusive bugs. An assertion tells you exactly which line of code—in which specific source file—contains a programming or logic error. Here are some common situations in which you should use assertions:

- **To check for valid function arguments and values.** Invalid arguments sent to your functions can crash your program, so if there's a doubt about a value an argument should or should not have, assert this in your code. For example, if a pointer argument should never be 0 (null), assert it.

- **To validate array indexes.** As you do with function argument values, you should assert the use of an array index to verify that it's within the range of the array.

- **To check assumptions you've made in your code.** If you've made an assumption in your code, assert the assumption. For example, if you assume that a function can never return a value greater than 10, assert that it doesn't.

- **To detect functions that are not yet implemented or tested.** If you have functions with declarations and empty bodies in your source code as placeholders, put an assertion in there to show that the function exists but isn't yet implemented.

- **To verify that code is portable.** If you're working on code that has to run on multiple hardware platforms or operating systems, assert any code that you suspect might not be fully portable.

Demonstrating Assertions

Okay, enough theory—now it's time to define some assertion macros of our own and then write a driver program to test them out. The header file MyAssert.h, shown in Listing 15.1, defines two custom assertion macros: assert() and ASSERT(). These macros can be used by any program that includes the MyAssert.h header file.

LISTING 15.1 A Header File That Defines the *assert()* and *ASSERT()* Macros

```
 1: /////////////////////////////////////////////////////
 2: // Module  : MyAssert.h
 3: //
 4: // Purpose : Custom assert() and ASSERT() macros
 5: /////////////////////////////////////////////////////
 6:
 7: #ifndef __MYASSERT_H__
 8: #define __MYASSERT_H__
 9:
10: // Replace any existing assert and ASSERT with the
11: // macros in this file
12:
13: #ifdef assert
14:     #undef assert
15: #endif
16:
17: #ifdef ASSERT
18:     #undef ASSERT
19: #endif
```

LISTING 15.1

1 Lines 13-19: Undefine assert() and ASSERT() if already defined

continues…

LISTING 15.1   **Continued**

```
20:
21: // Define assert and ASSERT for debug and
22: // release builds
23:
24: #if defined(_DEBUG)
25:
26:     // Define the debug macros
27:
28:     #define assert                                \
29:         if (!)                                    \
30:         {                                         \
31:             cerr << "\nAssertion Failed: " << #a  \
32:                 << "\nFailure occurred on line "  \
33:                 << __LINE__ << " of source file:" \
34:                 << "\n    \"" << __FILE__ << "\"\n"; \
35:         }
36:
37:     #define ASSERT(a, str)                        \
38:         if (!)                                    \
39:         {                                         \
40:             cerr << "\nAssertion Failed: " << #a  \
41:                 << " " << #str                    \
42:                 << "\nFailure occurred on line "  \
43:                 << __LINE__ << " of source file:" \
44:                 << "\n    \"" << __FILE__ << "\"\n"; \
45:         }
46: #else
47:
48:     // Define the release macros as nothing
49:     //
50:     #define assert
51:     #define ASSERT(a, str)
52:
53: #endif // #if defined(_DEBUG)
54:
55: #endif // __MYASSERT_H__
```

This header file provides two macros: assert() and ASSERT(). These macros both use the predefined ANSI macros __LINE__ and __FILE__ to display the current line number and filename of the offending source file. The program in Listing 15.2 demonstrates how you can put these macros to use.

LISTING 15.2   **A Driver Program to Test the Custom *assert()* and *ASSERT()* Macros Defined in *MyAssert.h***

```
1: //////////////////////////////////////////////////////
2: //   Module  : assert.cpp
3: //
4: //   Purpose : A driver program to demonstrate the
5: //             assert() and ASSERT() macros defined in
6: //             MyAssert.h
7: //////////////////////////////////////////////////////
8:
9: #include <iostream.h>
10: #include "MyAssert.h"
11:
12: // Constant definitions
13: //
14: const int hearts   = 0;
15: const int diamonds = 1;
16: const int clubs    = 2;
17: const int spades   = 3;
18:
19: // Function prototypes
20: //
21: void Print(char *str);
22: void PrintSuit(int suit);
23: int NotYetImplemented();
24:
25: //////////////////////////////////////////////////////
26: //   main()
27:
28: void main()
29: {
30:     assert(false);    // Always fails ─────────────┐
31:                                                     │
32:     int x = 5;                                      │
33:     assert(x == 5);   // this one's okay            │
34:     assert(x == 10);  // this one's an error        │──── ❶
35:                                                     │
36:     ASSERT(x == 10, "x should be 5!");              │
37:     assert("This will fail" == 0); // Always fails ─┘
38:
39:     char *str1 = 0;
40:     char *str2 = "\nA test string\n\n";
```

continues…

LISTING 15.2

❶ Lines 30-37: Assert several different expressions

LISTING 15.2 CONTINUED

2 Line 57: Check for a null
pointer

LISTING 15.2 **Continued**

```
41:
42:    Print(str1);
43:    Print(str2);
44:
45:    PrintSuit(hearts);
46:    PrintSuit(spades);
47:    PrintSuit(10);
48:
49:    int y = NotYetImplemented();
50: }
51:
52: //////////////////////////////////////////////////
53: //   Print()
54:
55: void Print(char *str)
56: {
57:    ASSERT(str == 0, "String should not be null");
58:    if (str != 0)
59:       cout << str;
60: }
61:
62: //////////////////////////////////////////////////
63: //   PrintSuit()
64:
65: void PrintSuit(int suit)
66: {
67:    switch (suit)
68:    {
69:       case hearts:
70:          cout << "Hearts\n";
71:          break;
72:
73:       case diamonds:
74:          cout << "Diamonds\n";
75:          break;
76:
77:       case clubs:
78:          cout << "Clubs\n";
79:          break;
80:
81:       case spades:
```

```
82:            cout << "Spades\n";
83:            break;
84:
85:        default:
86:            // Invalid suit detected
87:            //
88:            assert("Invalid suit detected" == 0);
89:    }
90: }
91:
92: ///////////////////////////////////////////////////////
93: // NotYetImplemented()
94:
95: int NotYetImplemented()
96: {
97:    assert("Function not yet implemented" == 0);
98:    return 0;
99: }
```

The output from this program shows how the custom assertion macros make debugging easier, helping you catch programming errors in the early stages of program testing:

```
Assertion Failed: false
Failure occurred on line 30 of source file:
    "assert.cpp"


Assertion Failed: x == 10
Failure occurred on line 34 of source file:
    "assert.cpp"


Assertion Failed: x == 10 "X should be 5!"
Failure occurred on line 36 of source file:
    "assert.cpp"


Assertion Failed: "This will fail" == 0
Failure occurred on line 37 of source file:
    "assert.cpp"


Assertion Failed: str == 0 "String should not be null"
Failure occurred on line 57 of source file:
    "assert.cpp"
```

```
A test string

Hearts
Spades

Assertion Failed: "Invalid suit detected" == 0
Failure occurred on line 88 of source file:
    "assert.cpp"

Assertion Failed: "Function not yet implemented" == 0
Failure occurred on line 97 of source file:
    "assert.cpp"
```

Lines 14 through 17 define four constants used to represent playing card suits. These constants come into play in the PrintSuit() function, which runs from lines 65 through 90.

The main() function starts out by asserting several different expressions (lines 30 through 37). The assertion on line 30 always fails because an assertion must be true (or else it fails). The assertion on line 33 succeeds because x is equal to 5 (line 32 makes this so). Since we already know that (x==5) is true, then the assertion on line 34 must fail—x can't equal both 5 **and** 10. The assertion on line 36 fails for the same reason, and gives a string description of why the assertion failed. The assertion on line 37 fails because the description string doesn't (and can't possibly) equal zero.

These assertions are followed by calls to the functions Print(), PrintSuit(), and NotYetImplemented(). The Print() function runs from lines 55 through 60 and asserts that the character pointer sent as an argument is not zero (null). If it is, the assertion tells you right where to go to fix the problem.

The PrintSuit() function runs from lines 65 through 90; on line 88, the function asserts that the value received is invalid if the default clause is chosen.

The NotYetImplemented() function runs from lines 95 through 99; the assertion on line 97 reminds the programmer that this function is just a placeholder and is not yet implemented in the source code.

Assertion macros can be as complex as you need them to be and can easily fit in with today's GUI operating systems. For example, here's an ASSERT macro for Microsoft Win32 that uses a system message box to display the assertion message, moving beyond simple console output:

```
#define assert                                   \
  if (!)                                          \
  {                                               \
     char _buf[256];                              \
     sprintf(_buf, "\nAssertion Failed: %s"       \
        "\n\nFailure occurred on line %d "        \
        " of source file: \"%s\" ", #a,           \
        __LINE__, __FILE__);                      \
     MessageBox(0, _buf, "Assertion Failure",     \
        MB_OK ¦ MB_ICONINFORMATION);              \
  }
```

The result of this macro executing in a debug build of a Windows program is shown in Figure 15.1, displaying an assertion message in a system message box.

FIGURE 15.1

An assertion message as displayed by a program running under Microsoft Windows.

Although assertions are useful debugging tools, they're no replacement for robust error handling—that's where exception handling comes into play.

Handling Exceptions

Although assertions are a great way to find logic and programming errors during the debugging process, they aren't useful beyond the debugging phase because in release builds, the macros expand to nothing. To handle runtime errors such as failed memory allocation and unanticipated disk file problems (for example, if the disk is full), you need to turn to *exception handling*.

Exception

A runtime error that occurs in a program.

Exception Handling

A C++ mechanism that allows you to gracefully handle runtime errors that might occur in a program.

When unexpected errors occur in your program, you can trap and deal with them using exceptions. A function can return using the C++ exception handling mechanism instead of its normal return mechanism. When this happens, we say that the function has "thrown" an exception. Code wrapped in a try block is granted the ability to throw exceptions, and the exceptions are caught by catch exception handlers that deal with the situation.

You can bulletproof your programs using the C++ exception handling keywords try, catch, and throw to trap and respond to errors in a logical, robust way. When an anomaly occurs, you throw an exception. A corresponding exception handling routine can then catch the exception. In the next sections, you learn how to set up and use exception handlers in your own programs.

The *try* Block

A try block protects any code within the block—including functions called from within the block—either directly or indirectly. A try block is like a sentinel that guards some section of code, shielding it from errors. You set up a try block like this:

```
try
{
    // Here you put C++ code you want to protect
}
```

Only the code inside a try block can detect or handle exceptions. As you can with other C++ code blocks, you can nest try blocks as needed.

The *catch* Exception Handler

A catch clause is an exception handler, catching (handling) an exception thrown by a throw statement and providing code that actually attempts to handle an error. You specify the type of error to handle by passing a parameter to the catch handler, like this:

```
catch(Parameter)
{
    // Handle errors here
}
```

The parameter, which can be named or unnamed, denotes the type of exception the clause handles. This parameter can be any valid C++ data type, including a structure or a class, and the `catch` handler is known by the data type given in the parameter. You can define a `catch` handler to catch any type of exception object. For example, here's a `catch` handler that catches character strings:

```
catch(char *str)
{
   cerr << str;
}
```

Often, programmers define custom data types to represent possible exceptions and pass these objects in their exception handlers. For example, here's a structure that can represent an exception:

```
struct DivideByZero { };
```

This structure exists only for use as an exception type, to be used as a parameter to an exception handler. A special function called the *default constructor* is generated by the compiler for this structure (unless you explicitly define this member function yourself). A constructor function has the same name as the structure and has no return type (not even `void`). For example, the constructor for the `DivideByZero` structure would be declared like this:

```
DivideByZero();
```

The structure can contain an explicit constructor that takes a parameter—which can be useful for an exception object. For example, this revised `DivideByZero` structure contains the character pointer `_msg` and a `DivideByZero()` constructor function that takes a character pointer as a parameter:

```
struct DivideByZero
{
   char *_msg;
   DivideByZero(char *msg) { _msg = msg; }
};
```

This string can be used to output a message similar to an assertion.

SEE ALSO

➤ *For more information about constructors, see page 494*

The *throw* Statement

The throw statement actually throws an exception of the specified type (this is sometimes called *raising an exception*), using the following general syntax:

```
throw Argument;
```

In this syntax, Argument is sent to the corresponding catch handler. Here's an example in which an exception is thrown if an expected condition isn't met, sending a character string as the argument:

```
if (x != 10)
    throw "Error: x != 10";
```

Using Exception Handling

Usually, a program will have exception handlers defined for several types of errors that might occur. Here's an example of the layout of a typical try block and its associated catch clauses:

```
try
{
    // code to protect
}

catch(int x)
{
    // handle int errors
}

catch(char *str)
{
    // handle char* errors
}
```

This try block has two catch handlers: one that catches integer exceptions and one that catches character pointer exceptions. You can define as many catch handlers as you need to cover all the bases.

The program in Listing 15.3 uses exception handling to trap a simple divide-by-zero error. In combination with the function

ErrInfo(), which (similar to an assertion) displays the line and file where an error occurred, the program uses the DivideByZero structure (presented earlier) as an exception type.

LISTING 15.3 A Program That Uses Exception Handling to Trap a Divide-by-Zero Error

```
1: //////////////////////////////////////////////////////
2: //  Module  : exception.cpp
3: //
4: //  Purpose : Demonstrates the use of C++ exception
5: //            handling.
6: //////////////////////////////////////////////////////
7:
8: #include <iostream.h>
9: #include <stdio.h>
10:
11: struct DivideByZero
12: {
13:    char *_msg;
14:    DivideByZero(char *msg) { _msg = msg; }
15: };
16:
17: char * ErrInfo(char *b);  // function prototype
18:
19: //////////////////////////////////////////////////////
20: //  main()
21:
22: void main()
23: {
24:    float denom;
25:    char buf[256];
26:
27:    try
28:    {
29:       do
30:       {
31:          cout
32:             << "Enter a number from 0-10, inclusive: ";
33:          cin >> denom;
34:       }
35:       while ((denom < 0) || (denom > 10)) ;
```

continues…

LISTING 15.3 **Continued**

```
36:
37:        if (denom == 0)
38:            throw DivideByZero(ErrInfo(buf));
39:
40:        float x = 10.0f / denom;
41:        cout << "x == " << x;
42:    }
43:
44:    catch(DivideByZero dbz)
45:    {
46:        cerr << "Attempted division by zero!\n";
47:        cerr << dbz._msg << '\n';
48:    }
49: }
50:
51: ////////////////////////////////////////////////////
52: //  ErrInfo()
53:
54: char * ErrInfo(char *b)
55: {
56:    sprintf(b, "   The error occurred in file \"%s\" "
57:        "near line %d", __FILE__, __LINE__);
58:    return b;
59: }
```

① → (points to lines 44-49)

② → (points to lines 54-59)

The output from this program shows that if a divide-by-zero exception is detected, the catch handler uses the DivideByZero structure to display an error message:

```
Enter a number from 0-10, inclusive: 0
Attempted division by zero!
   The error occurred in file "exception.cpp" near line 57
```

This program begins by defining the DivideByZero structure you saw earlier (lines 11 through 15), which is used as an exception type. On line 17, the function ErrInfo() is declared. This function is used to display an assertion-like message and is defined starting on line 54. The function uses the variable buf[] (a character array declared on line 25) to store a message that displays the line and file where the error occurred. The ErrInfo() function uses the ANSI C Library function sprintf() to format the string with the predefined macros __FILE__ and __LINE__.

The `main()` function wraps all its code in a `try` block, so that any divide-by-zero anomalies that occur in the program—anywhere—can be trapped by the `catch` handler beginning on line 44. This handler displays an exception message that includes the `DivideByZero` structure's `ErrInfo()`-formatted string (lines 46 and 47).

A `do` loop, beginning on line 29, ensures that the user picks a valid number (from 0 through 10, inclusive). The check on line 37 determines whether an exception should be thrown. If so, line 38 throws an exception of type `DivideByZero`, sending the `ErrInfo()` string as the structure's exception message.

Creating custom exception types like the `DivideByZero` structure is the preferred way of handling exceptions (as opposed to using a standard type, like an `int`). Because each structure is a distinct data type, a `catch` clause can be explicit about exactly what type of error it traps.

Catching Unexpected Exceptions

You can't possibly trap for every type of exception that might occur in a program, but C++ exception handling provides a way to generically handle unexpected exceptions. You can catch unexpected exceptions by using an ellipsis (. . .) as the parameter for a `catch` clause. An exception handler that uses the ellipsis parameter handles any type of exception, but a handler like this must be the last handler for its `try` block. Here's an example of a simple unexpected exception handler:

```
catch(...)
{
    cerr << "Handling an unknown exception!\n";
}
```

The program in Listing 15.4 demonstrates the use of an unexpected exception handler, throwing exceptions in response to user input. The program loops until an unexpected exception is thrown by the user's input.

LISTING 15.4

1 Lines 31-44: Use a switch
statement to throw different
types of exceptions

LISTING 15.4   **A Program That Demonstrates Handling Unknown Exceptions**

```
1: /////////////////////////////////////////////////////
2: //   Module   : unknown.cpp
3: //
4: //   Purpose : Demonstrates the use of C++ exception
5: //             handling.
6: /////////////////////////////////////////////////////
7:
8: #include <iostream.h>
9: #include <stdio.h>
10:
11: struct Unknown { };
12: const char NL = '\n';
13:
14: /////////////////////////////////////////////////////
15: //   main()
16:
17: void main()
18: {
19:    bool quit = false;
20:    do
21:    {
22:       try
23:       {
24:          int pick;
25:          cout << "\nPick an exception to throw:\n";
26:          cout << "   1) Integer\n";
27:          cout << "   2) Float\n";
28:          cout << "   3) Character String\n\n>";
29:          cin >> pick;
30:
31:          switch (pick)
32:          {
33:             case 1:
34:                throw pick;
35:                break;
36:             case 2:
37:                throw float(pick);
38:                break;
39:             case 3:
40:                throw "Cool, I'm picked!";
41:                break;
42:             default:
43:                throw Unknown();
44:          }
```

```
45:        }
46:
47:        catch(int i)
48:        {
49:           cerr << "\nInteger exception: " << i << NL;
50:        }
51:
52:        catch(float f)
53:        {
54:           cerr << "\nFloat exception: " << f << NL;
55:        }
56:
57:        catch(char *str)
58:        {
59:           cerr << "\nCharacter string exception: "
60:              << str << NL;
61:        }
62:
63:        catch(...)
64:        {
65:           cerr << "Handling an unknown exception!\n";
66:           cerr << "Quitting!\n";
67:           quit = true;
68:        }
69:     }
70:    while (!quit);
71: }
```

Here's the output from a sample run of the program, showing that each thrown exception is caught by the appropriate type of catch handler, even when the exception type has no explicit handler defined:

```
Pick an exception to throw:
    1) Integer
    2) Float
    3) Character String


>2


Float exception: 2
```

```
Pick an exception to throw:
   1) Integer
   2) Float
   3) Character String

>3

Character string exception: Cool, I'm picked!

Pick an exception to throw:
   1) Integer
   2) Float
   3) Character String

>5
Handling an unknown exception!
Quitting!
```

This program provides a little three-item menu from which the user can choose to throw an exception. A do loop iterates through the selection process until the user generates an unknown exception by picking a number that's not on the menu.

The default constructor for the Unknown structure (defined on line 11) is called on line 43, throwing an Unknown exception object that's caught by the unexpected exception handler defined from lines 63 to 68. Once this handler is called, the quit flag (used as the loop termination condition) is set to true and the program terminates.

Throw Site

A throw site is the point in a program at which a **throw** statement is executed.

Exception Stack Frame

An exception stack frame is the stack used by an exception handling block to store automatic objects. This stack automatically unwinds if an exception is thrown.

Cleaning Up Allocated Resources

When an exception is thrown, C++ cleans up all local objects constructed before the exception was thrown. A special context exists between the location of the throw statement (the *throw site*) and its corresponding catch clause. This context is called the *exception stack frame*.

The exception stack frame contains all local objects created during the execution of the guarded code, including any functions called from the guarded code, either directly or indirectly. When an exception is thrown, this stack is "unwound," destroying all automatic objects local to the stack. This automatic cleanup can prevent other exceptions from being thrown as side effects of a previous exception.

**Unhandled Exceptions in a
try Block**

If an exception occurs and no catch handler can be found that corresponds with the exception type, then the Standard C++ Library function `terminate()` is called. By default, this function calls `abort()` to terminate program execution.

16

Exploring Namespaces

- Learn what namespaces are and what they can do for you

- See how to declare and define namespaces

- Discover how to use unnamed namespaces

- Learn about the *using* declaration and the *using* directive

- Find out about namespace aliases and composite namespaces

- Understand the global namespace

What Is a Namespace?

Namespace

A C++ declaration area that lets you add a secondary name to an identifier, helping to insure that no duplicate global identifier names exist in a program.

A *namespace* is a C++ declaration area that lets you add a secondary name to an identifier, helping to ensure that no duplicate global identifier names exist in a program. The namespace is just a name that acts as a wrapper for the identifiers within it. Why would you need something like this in C++?

Imagine two identifiers, both declared at file scope (globally), but in separate header files that will compile into the same program. Now imagine that these two identifiers have the same name:

```
// module1.h
//
struct Pencil
{
    float length;
    int   color;
    bool  eraser;
};


// module2.h
//
struct Pencil
{
    float  price;
    char * manufacturer;
    int    code;
};
```

These two `Pencil` structures are very different, and they are meant to serve different purposes. The `Pencil` declared in `module1.h` models the physical pencil itself. The `Pencil` declared in `module2.h` represents retail information about the pencil. What happens if you try to use both of these headers in a single program? Take a look at this program:

```
#include "module1.h"
#include "module2.h"

void main()
{
    Pencil p;
}
```

Including both files into a program build causes a problem because the first module the compiler encounters (`module1.h`) will define *its* version of a `Pencil`, globally. When the compiler encounters the `Pencil` in the second module (`module2.h`), it generates an error such as this one:

```
module2.h : error : 'Pencil' : 'struct' type redefinition
Error executing linker.
```

This error occurs because the compiler can't have two global structures with the same name. These global structures are declared in the global namespace. If you need to use both of these `Pencil` types in a single program, you can do it by defining your own custom namespaces for the structures to "live in." In the same way, if you compiled these structures into separate translation units, the linker would have the same problem as the compiler did and would generate a "duplicate name" error when trying to link the object files.

Declaring a Namespace

A namespace is to a `Pencil` structure what an area code is to a phone number. Imagine that the Smith family and the Jones family live in different parts of the country, hundreds of miles apart, but they have the same phone number: 555-3843. By simply adding an area code to the phone number, the Smith family, at phone number (234)555-3843, can be easily differentiated from the Jones family, at phone number (789)555-3843. A namespace works the same way, adding the extra identifier needed to differentiate two identifiers that have the same name.

The syntax for declaring a namespace is as follows:

```
namespace Name { MemberList }
```

In this syntax, `Name` is the name of the namespace and `MemberList` is the list of functions and data in the namespace. To make both of the `Pencil` structure declarations you saw earlier work within a single program, you create a namespace for each. Let's call one namespace `Physical`, like this:

```
// module1.h
//
```

```
namespace Physical
{
   struct Pencil
   {
      float length;
      int   color;
      bool  eraser;
   };
}
```

Let's call the other namespace `Retail`, like this:

```
namespace Retail
{
   struct Pencil
   {
      float  price;
      char * manufacturer;
      int    id;
   };
}
```

By using a namespace identifier with the scope resolution operator (`::`) to fully qualify which `Pencil` you're talking about at any given time, you can use *both* `Pencil` structures in a single program, like this:

```
void main()
{
   Physical::Pencil p1;
   Retail::Pencil   p2;

   // Use the pencils for something...
   // ...
}
```

A namespace definition is where the implementations of members are defined. A definition can also be spread across a source file, or multiple source files, as needed. Let's begin with the following simple namespace example:

```
namespace Demo
{
   void func1();
```

```
    void func2();
    void func3();

    void func1()
        { cout << "Demo::func1()" << NL; }
    void func2()
        { cout << "Demo::func2()" << NL; }
    void func3()
        { cout << "Demo::func3()" << NL; }
}
```

You can put these functions, wrapped by the namespace Demo, into a header file to make them accessible to any program, like this:

```
// Demo.h
//
#ifndef __DEMO_H__
#define __DEMO_H__

namespace Demo   // Declaration
{
    void func1();
    void func2();
    void func3();
}


#endif //__DEMO_H__// Demo.h
```

The implementation for the Demo namespace could be placed in a single definition block in a source file, like this:

```
// Demo.cpp
//

// ...

namespace Demo   // Definition
{
    void func1()
        { cout << "Demo::func1()" << NL; }
    void func2()
        { cout << "Demo::func2()" << NL; }
```

```
        void func3()
            { cout << "Demo::func3()" << NL; }
    }
```

This simply adds a new level of scope to the functions in the namespace. The implementation for the Demo namespace could also be scattered throughout a source file, like this:

```
// Demo.cpp
//

// ...

namespace Demo   // First part of definition
{
    void func1()
        { cout << "Demo::func1()" << NL; }
}

// other code...

namespace Demo   // Second part of definition
{
    void func2()
        { cout << "Demo::func2()" << NL; }
    void func3()
        { cout << "Demo::func3()" << NL; }
}
```

Unnamed Namespaces

A namespace doesn't always need to have a name. If you want to prevent name clashes with other modules, but want data to remain private to a module, like a static identifier, you can declare an unnamed namespace. Internally, each unnamed namespace uses a unique identifier preventing the possibility of name clashes. This makes an unnamed namespace a better choice than static storage class for identifiers that you want to keep local to a module but that you don't want anything outside that module to see. Consider this unnamed namespace:

Name Spaces and Namespaces

Don't confuse the C-language concept of a *name space* with the C++-language concept of a *namespace*. A name space (two words) is a limited C construct that is totally different from a C++ namespace (one word).

```
namespace
{
    void func1();
    void func1()
        { cout << "<unnamedNS>::func1()" << NL; }
}
```

The function `func1()` defined in this unnamed namespace can only be used within the module in which it's defined. There is no way to explicitly qualify an unnamed namespace, so other modules won't be able to see the members of the unnamed namespace.

When you use more than one unnamed namespace in a module, you must take care not to use duplicate identifiers. The compiler can't resolve the ambiguity of duplicate names within the two unnamed namespaces—they will clash. The same applies to duplicate identifiers defined at file scope and unnamed namespace scope, as in this example:

```
namespace
{
    void func1();
    void func1()
        { cout << "<unnamedNS>::func1()" << NL; }
}

// Global function
//
void func1();
void func1() { cout << "::func1()" << NL; }
```

In this case, the compiler can't resolve the duplicate identifier `func1()` and will generate an error such as this one:

```
Error: Ambiguity between:
'<unnamedNS>::func1()' and '::func1()'
```

The program in Listing 16.1 demonstrates the use of two unnamed namespaces in a module.

LISTING 16.1

① Lines 14-17: Declare an unnamed namespace having one function

② Lines 19-24: Define the Demo namespace containing function func2()

③ Lines 28-29: Declare and defines a global function func2()

④ Lines 33-37: Define the function func1() for the first unnamed namespace

LISTING 16.1 **A Program That Demonstrates the Use of Unnamed Namespaces**

```
 1: ////////////////////////////////////////////////////
 2: //   Module  : unnamed1.cpp
 3: //
 4: //   Purpose : Demonstrates the use of unnamed
 5: //             namespaces
 6: ////////////////////////////////////////////////////
 7:
 8: #include <iostream.h>
 9:
10: const char NL = '\n';
11:
12 : // Unnamed namespace declarations
13: //
14: namespace
15: {
16:     void func1();
17: }
18:
19: namespace Demo
20: {
21:     void func2();
22:     void func2()
23:        { cout << "Demo::func2()" << NL; }
24: }
25:
26: // Global function func2()
27: //
28: void func2();
29: void func2() { cout << "::func2()" << NL; }
30:
31: // Unnamed namespace definition
32: //
33: namespace
34: {
35:     void func1()
36:        { cout << "<unnamedNS>::func1()" << NL; }
37: }
38:
39: ////////////////////////////////////////////////////
40: //   main()
41:
```

```
42:  void main()
43:  {
44:     func1();
45:     Demo::func2();
46:     func2();
47:  }
```

The output from this program is simply:

```
<unnamedNS>::func1()
Demo::func2()
::func2()
```

In this program, the declaration and definition of the unnamed namespace are split into different code blocks. The unnamed namespace declares its sole member function func1() on lines 14 through 17. The namespace Demo is declared and defined from lines 19 through 24 and contains one function: func2().

On line 28, the global function func2() is declared, and this function is defined on line 29. The definition of the unnamed namespace runs from lines 33 through 37, providing a definition for function func1(). In the main() function, the namespace functions func1() and func2() are called, along with the global function func2(). Notice that the compiler sees the ::func2() and the Demo::func2()functions as completely separate constructs (because they are).

Getting Explicit Access to Namespaces

As you've already seen, when working with multiple namespaces, it's necessary to qualify identifiers with explicit names that use the scope resolution operator. There are two other ways you can access namespace members. C++ provides two uses of the namespace-related keyword using so that you can access namespace members in two ways:

- The using declaration
- The using directive

The *using* Declaration

The using declaration tells the compiler that you're going to use some member of some namespace, eliminating the need for explicit qualification within the scope of the declaration. A using declaration has the following syntax:

```
using Name::Member;
```

In this syntax, Name refer to the name of a namespace, and Member refers to the member of the namespace you're planning to use. Here's an example of accessing a member variable of a namespace with the using declaration:

```
namespace temp { int x = 1; }

int x = 0;

void main()
{
    using temp::x;
    cout << x;
}
```

In this snippet, the cout object displays the number 1 (and not 0) because the default x now uses temp::x. To access the global x, you must explicitly specify global scope, as in ::x. Listing 16.2 shows a complete program that demonstrates how to access identifiers with explicit qualification and the using declaration.

using Declarations for
Namespace Functions

If the member of a namespace you intend to access is a function, you must use *only* the function name in the using declaration—no function call parentheses or parameters can be specified.

LISTING 16.2 **A Program That Demonstrates Access Using Explicit Qualification and the *using* Declaration**

```
 1:  /////////////////////////////////////////////////////////
 2:  //   Module  : access1.cpp
 3:  //
 4:  //   Purpose : Demonstrates the namespace access using
 5:  //                explicit qualification and the
 6:  //                using declaration.
 7:  /////////////////////////////////////////////////////////
 8:
 9:  #include <iostream.h>
10:
```

```
11:  const char NL = '\n';
12:
13:  // namespace declarations
14:  //
15:  namespace first
16:  {
17:     void func1();
18:     void func1()
19:        { cout << "first::func1()" << NL; }
20:  }
21:
22:  namespace second
23:  {
24:     void func1();
25:     void func1()
26:        { cout << "second::func1()" << NL; }
27:  }
28:
29:  // Global function
30:  //
31:  void func1();
32:  void func1() { cout << "::func1()" << NL; }
33:
34:  /////////////////////////////////////////////////////////
35:  //  main()
36:
37:  void main()
38:  {
39:     // Explicit access
40:     //
41:     cout << "Explicit access:\n";
42:
43:     ::func1();        // global
44:     first::func1();   // first
45:     second::func1();  // second
46:
47:     // using-declaration access
48:     //
49:     cout << "\nusing-declaration access:\n";
50:     using first::func1;
51:     func1();
```

LISTING 16.2

1 Lines 15-20: Define the `first` namespace

2 Lines 22-27: Define the second namespace

3 Lines 30-31: Declare and defines a global function

4 Lines 43-45: Call functions explicitly

5 Lines 50-51: Use a `using` declaration to call a function implicitly

LISTING 16.2   Continued

```
52:    {
53:        using second::func1; // only valid in this block ─────┐  6
54:        func1();─────────────────────────────────────────────┘
55:    }
56:    func1();                    // back to first::func1() ─── 7
57: }
```

The output from this program looks like this:

```
Explicit access:
::func1()
first::func1()
second::func1()

using-declaration access:
first::func1()
second::func1()
first::func1()
```

This program declares and uses the namespaces first (lines 15 through 20) and second (lines 22 through 27); both of these namespaces contain a function named func1(). In addition, the global function func1() is declared on line 31 and defined on line 32. There are three separate instances of the func1() function in this program.

The main() function begins by explicitly calling the three func1() functions using explicit qualification. Line 43 calls the global ::func1() function; line 44 calls first::func1(); and line 45 calls second::func1(). The using declaration on line 50 specifies that any unqualified func1() call in the current block actually refers to first::func1(); line 51 provides this unqualified func1() call, outputting the text first::func1().

Within the sub-block that runs from line 52 through 55, the using declaration on line 53 specifies that any unqualified func1() call in this block actually refers to second::func1(); line 54 provides this unqualified func1() call, outputting the text second::func1().

As execution leaves this code block, the `using second::func1` declaration goes out of scope, so the call to `func1()` on line 56 refers once again to `first::func1()`, outputting the text `first::func1()`.

The *using* Directive

The `using` declaration allows you to use certain members of a namespace—but only those you specify—without explicitly qualifying them. In contrast, the `using` directive allows you to use *all* the members of a namespace without explicitly qualifying them. The `using` directive uses the following syntax:

```
using namespace Name;
```

In this syntax, `Name` refers to the name of a namespace. All members of the `Name` namespace are now available without explicit qualification. To demonstrate the difference between a `using` declaration and the `using` directive, take a look at the following example. Assume namespace `Name` contains two members:

```
namespace Name { int x = 1; int y = 2; }
```

With two `using` declarations you can gain access to both members without fully qualifying them, like this:

```
using Name::x;
using Name::y;

void main()
{
   // Access both members without explicit quialification
   //
   cout << x << endl << y << endl;
}
```

If a namespace has a thousand members, you'd need a thousand `using` declarations to access them all without explicit qualification. With a single `using` directive you can gain access to all members (no matter how many there are) without fully qualifying them, like this:

```
using namespace Name;
```

```
void main()
{
   // Access both members without explicit qualification
   //
   cout << x << endl << y << endl;
}
```

Listing 16.3 shows a complete program that demonstrates how to access identifiers with the using directive.

LISTING 16.3

① Lines 14-19: Define the first namespace

② Lines 21-26: Define the second namespace

LISTING 16.3 **A Program That Demonstrates Access with a _using_ Directive**

```
 1:  //////////////////////////////////////////////////////
 2:  //   Module   : access2.cpp
 3:  //
 4:  //   Purpose : Demonstrates the access to namespace
 5:  //                members with a using directive.
 6:  //////////////////////////////////////////////////////
 7:
 8:  #include <iostream.h>
 9:
10:  const char NL = '\n';
11:
12:  // namespace declarations
13:  //
14:  namespace first
15:  {
16:     void func1();
17:     void func1()
18:        { cout << "first::func1()" << NL; }
19:  }
20:
21:  namespace second
22:  {
23:     void func1();
24:     void func1()
25:        { cout << "second::func1()" << NL; }
26:  }
27:
28:  //////////////////////////////////////////////////////
29:  //   main()
30:
31:  void main()
```

① ②

```
32: {
33:     // using-directive access for namespace second
34:     //
35:     using namespace second;
36:
37:     first::func1();  // explicitly qualified
38:     func1();         // using-directive qualified
39: }
```

LISTING 16.3 CONTINUED

3 Line 35: Declare implicit access for all of namespace *second*

4 Lines 37-38: Make explicit and implicit function calls

The output from this program looks like this:

```
first::func1()
second::func1()
```

Like the program in Listing 16.2, this program declares and uses the namespaces `first` (lines 14 through 19) and `second` (lines 21 through 26). Both of these namespaces contain a function named `func1()`.

The `main()` function begins by applying a `using` directive to namespace `second` on line 35, and then explicitly calls `first::func1()` on line 37, outputting the text `first::func1`. This statement is followed by an unqualified call to `func1()` on line 38, resulting in the screen output `second::func1()`, which shows how the `using` directive has made the members of namespace `second` available.

Note that if the global `func1()` function from Listing 16.2 had been present in Listing 16.3, it would have caused a name clash, resulting in an ambiguous, unresolvable function call to the unqualified `func1()`. This is because when you use `func1()` the compiler doesn't know whether you mean `::func1()` or `second:func1()`. In this case, even with the `using` directive for namespace second in effect, you would still need to explicitly qualify each of the functions as either `::func1()` or `second:func1()`.

Using Namespace Aliases

When working with namespaces, its good to design descriptive names for them. However, using explicit qualification of identifiers that have a long namespace name can make code more difficult to read than necessary. For example, here's a namespace definition:

```
namespace ThisIsAReallyLongNamespaceMoniker
{
    int x;
    void func1()
    {
        cout << "ThisIsAReallyLongNamespaceMoniker::func1()"
    }
}
```

Imagine having to use `ThisIsAReallyLongNamespaceMoniker::func1()` throughout your code. Instead, you could define a macro that refers to and replaces this long identifier, like this:

```
#define ThisIsAReallyLongNamespaceMoniker   Shorter
```

Then you could use the macro to make the code more readable, like this:

```
Shorter::func1();
```

After preprocessing, the preceding statement would expand back to the original name:

```
ThisIsAReallyLongNamespaceMoniker::func1()
```

A namespace alias allows you to accomplish the same thing as the macro, but you accomplish it by using the `namespace` keyword to create an alias for an existing namespace, like this:

```
namespace Shorter = ThisIsAReallyLongNamespaceMoniker;
```

You might consider this a nickname for the namespace (consider my name—Robert Wayne McGregor—but most people just call me Rob).

Using Composite Namespaces

You can nest one namespace within another, and you can *only* declare a namespace at file scope or nested within another namespace. When you nest one namespace within another, you get a *composite namespace*. Member namespaces of a composite namespace require more qualification than those declared at file scope—you need one qualifier for each level of nesting in the composite namespace. Take a look at this composite namespace named, appropriately, `composite`:

```
namespace composite
{
   namespace outer
   {
      namespace inner
      {
         void func1() { }   // inner
      }
      void func1() { }      // outer
   }
   void func1() { }         // composite
}
```

The `composite` namespace contains the nested namespaces `outer` and `inner`. Each of these namespaces contains its own `func1()` function. To access these three functions, you must fully qualify them by namespace (or by nested namespace) name. The `func1()` functions would be explicitly accessed like this:

```
void main()
{
   composite::func1();                  // composite
   composite::outer::func1();           // outer
   composite::outer::inner::func1();  // inner
}
```

The Global Namespace

C++ provides a single global namespace for all programs to use. As you've seen, this namespace is explicitly accessed using the scope resolution operator with no qualifier. For example, `::func1()` refers to the global `func1()` function. The global namespace is implicitly specified for any identifier not wrapped in a namespace.

The `namespace temp` example you saw earlier is a good example. Here's a revised version that uses functions and variables:

```
namespace temp
{
   func1() { cout << "temp::func1()\n"; }
   int x = 1;
}

func1() { cout << "::func1()\n"; }
int x = 0;

void main()
{
   using temp::x;
   using temp::func1;

   cout << x << '\n';
   cout << ::x << '\n';
   func1();
   ::func1();
}
```

This example makes use of using declarations for namespace members and uses global scope resolution to access the global variable and function. The program's output is, of course, this:

```
1
0
temp::func1()
::func1()
```

The Standard Namespace

The Standard C++ library provides a special namespace, called std, that wraps the entire standard library. All identifiers in the standard C++ header files are defined in this std namespace. When using standard C++ library objects, you must qualify them with the std:: prefix to specify the standard namespace.

A common example is the use of the standard C++ library object cout, which must be fully qualified as std::cout when you include the standard library header <iostream> (as opposed to the old header <iostream.h>—it's not wrapped in the Standard namespace). To use the standard `cout` object without explicit qualification, you could use a `using` declaration, like this:

```
using std::cout;
```

You could also use a `using` directive to clarify the use of the standard library object, like this:

```
using namespace std;
```

SEE ALSO

➤ *For more information about the standard namespace, see page 682*

Analyzing the Mathematics of Memory

Examine numeration systems and bases

Review the decimal numeration system

Learn to use the binary, octal, and hexadecimal
numeration systems

Understand how to convert from one numeration system
to another

Binary Digit

The smallest component of computer memory. A binary digit is more commonly called a *bit*.

Bit

A binary digit. The smallest component of computer memory.

Overview

At its most basic level, a computer is just a simple machine that processes sequences of 1s and 0s—called *binary digits*, or *bits*. That's all the computer really knows. A compiler must translate the high-level source code to low-level machine code before the computer can execute it.

This chapter explains the concepts behind the numbering systems used in computer science and shows you how to convert from one system to another. In a high-level language like C++ you can still (and often must!) access these binary digits, manipulating them at will—but only if you know how. In this chapter, you'll learn about the immensely important mathematical subject of base numeration systems and base conversions. A firm grounding in these numbering systems is important for understanding how to manipulate individual bits within the computer's memory, the subject of Chapter 18, "Manipulating Bits."

Because a computer does everything in binary, you, as a programmer, should learn to think in binary too—at least to a certain extent. Understanding how the computer uses memory is the only way you can take full advantage of the bitwise operators provided as part of C++. As a serious programmer, you should be familiar with these four number systems:

- Decimal
- Binary
- Octal
- Hexadecimal

The Binary/Hexadecimal Connection

Binary and hexadecimal are more useful than octal for a few reasons. First, binary is the native language of the computer, so it is immensely useful for understanding the bits and bytes under the hood. Hexadecimal is a compact and direct translation of binary that's easier for humans to deal with.

The first one's easy; you've no doubt been using it all your life. The other three are probably a different story. Each of these number systems has its advantages, but you'll find binary and hexadecimal to be the most useful in your programs. Before these number systems can empower you as a programmer, you have to understand the number systems themselves—and for that you'll need to grasp the fundamentals of how to think in bases other than base 10.

You've most likely been exposed to bases other than 10 at some point in your life. For the benefit of those who have only distant recollections of it, let's brush off the cobwebs and take a look at the mathematics involved (don't worry, it's pretty easy stuff).

Examining Bases of Numeration Systems

Let's begin by talking about numeration systems and bases. A numeration system is just a system of counting. The *base* of a numeration system is simply a number you use to group numbers when doing the counting. The base lets you know how many symbols are used in any given numeration system, giving you the information you need for grouping. For example, base 10 uses these 10 symbols:

0, 1, 2, 3, 4, 5, 6, 7, 8, 9

Look familiar? It should—these are the symbols used in the decimal system of numeration, which you probably use every day. It's based on groups of 10, so it's called base 10, or decimal (the prefix *deci* means 10). Fundamental to understanding bases other than 10 is conceptualizing what's happening in base 10 itself. People are so conditioned in using base 10 that they don't usually think about what's going on under the hood.

Base

The radix, or basis, of a numeration system.

Reviewing the Decimal Numeration System (Base 10)

What happens if you start at zero and count up to nine? In base 10, you have only ten symbols (0 through 9) and now you've used them all. As you'll remember from elementary school, these digits take up what's called the *ones-place*. Where do you go from here? How do you count higher? How do you "spell" the number ten using the symbols provided? Simple—you move to the next place—the *tens-place*. By dropping a 1 into the tens-place, you can start all over again in the ones-place. Pretty basic, eh? Suppose that you see the number 247 and extract the bases from it. You have a 2 in the hundreds-place, a 4 in the tens-place, and a 7 in the ones-place.

Base Numeration Symbols

The rule for using symbols to represent digits in any base is that you start with the symbol 0 and increment by 1 until you have as many symbols as the base number. In the case of decimal numeration, the symbols are 0 through 9. Note that there's no symbol for ten. *Ten,* the base, is represented by the two symbols 1 and 0, placed side by side, like this: 10.

In the decimal system, we're used to seeing numbers like 124, 53, and 1842. We instantly think of these numbers as meaning "one hundred and twenty-four," "fifty-three," and "one thousand eight hundred and forty-two." That's perfectly true—but only if we're talking about base 10! These same numbers mean something completely different in other numeration systems. Take a look at Table 17.1, which shows what these numbers actually represent in several other numeration systems.

TABLE 17.1   **Various Numbers Represented in Several Numeration Systems**

Base 10	Base 7	Base 5	Base 2
53	104	203	110101
124	235	444	1111100
1842	5241	24332	11100110010

The numbers in the first column of Table 17.1 fall into places of 10 when you write them out column-wise, like this:

```
1000  100   10    1
- - - - - - - - - - - - - - - - - -
0     0     5     3
0     1     2     4
1     8     4     2
```

Notice that the columns, or "places," are all of powers of 10, like this:

$$10^3 \quad 10^2 \quad 10^1 \quad 10^0$$

This is how *all* numeration systems work. The columns are determined by the powers of the base, whatever that base may be. The way we discover the true meaning of the number represented by the symbols used is by extracting the bases from it. For example, given the number 53 (base 10), we can easily see the extracted bases by writing the number in expanded form, like this:

```
53 = (5 * 10) + (3 * 1)
```

Likewise, we can see the extracted bases in the number 124 (base 10) by writing the number in expanded form, like this:

```
124 = (1 * 100) + (2 * 10) + (4 * 1)
```

Okay, enough base 10; you have already have a good understanding of that one. Now let's go binary.

Analyzing the Binary Numeration System (Base 2)

The binary system of numeration is the native language of computers. Because binary is based on groups of two, it uses base 2. This equates to place columns derived from the following powers of 2:

2^8 2^7 2^6 2^5 2^4 2^3 2^2 2^1 2^0

Recall that in base 10, there are ten symbols available to represent numbers (0 through 9). In base 2, there are only two symbols: 0 and 1. Using these two symbols, you can represent any number in binary, and that's what computers do. In computer memory, each symbol takes up a single byte. The place-columns for base 2, as derived from the powers of 2 listed before, are as follows:

128 64 32 16 8 4 2 1

As it turns out, that's eight places (bits). Just enough to fill one byte.

Converting Binary to Decimal

If given the binary number 101010, how would you convert it to decimal? Just fill in the place-columns, multiply, and add. The answer turns out to be 42, as shown in Table 17.2.

TABLE 17.2 **The Decimal Number 42 in Binary: (128*0) + (64*0) + (32*1) + (16*0) + (8*1) + (4*0) + (2*1) + (1*0)**

128	64	32	16	8	4	2	1
0	0	1	0	1	0	1	0

Using this same logic, you can easily calculate the binary number that has 1s in all eight columns (11111111). It turns out to be 255 in decimal. That's why a one-byte integral value like a char can have only 256 possible values (0 through 255). So, now you can convert from binary to decimal, but what about the other way around?

Converting Decimal to Binary

To represent a decimal number in binary, you must convert it by doing the opposite of what you just saw; you must extract the bases. To make it easy to convert from one base to another, you can use a conversion algorithm. To convert a number from decimal to binary, you simply apply the algorithm.

Assume that you have the number 53 (base 10) and want to convert it to binary. Basically, you look at the binary place-columns and, starting on the left side, do a little base 10 division. To find the starting place-column, find the first column that's numerically smaller than the number you're converting. Follow these algorithm steps:

The algorithm for converting from decimal to binary

1. "How many times will 128 go into 53?" The answer is, of course, zero. Okay, that's not the starting column, so a 0 goes in the 128 column. Move to the next column.

2. "How many times will 64 go into 53?" The answer is, again, zero, so that's not the starting column either. A 0 goes in the 64 column. Move to the next column.

3. "How many times will 32 go into 53?" The answer this time is 1. Okay, a 1 goes in the 32 column. But in this case, you've just used 32 and have only 21 left to play around with (53 - 32 = 21). Move to the next column.

4. "How many times will 16 go into 21?" The answer is 1, so a 1 goes in the 16 column. Now you've used 16 more and only have 5 left (21 - 16 = 5). Move to the next column.

5. "How many times will 8 go into 5?" The answer is zero, so a 0 goes in the 8 column. Move to the next column.

6. "How many times will 4 go into 5?" The answer is 1, so a 1 goes in the 4 column. Now you've only got 1 left to play around with (5 - 4 = 1). Move to the next column.

7. "How many times will 2 go into 1?" The answer is zero, so a 0 goes in the 2 column. Move to the last column.

8. "How many times will 1 go into 1?" The answer is 1, so a 1 goes in the 1 column. Now you're done because you're out of columns and have used all of the "bits" of the number 53.

This process reveals that 53 (base 10) is the same as 110101 (base 2). The end result of the process is shown in Table 17.3.

TABLE 17.3 **The Decimal Number *53* Converted to Binary: (128*0) + (64*0) + (32*1) + (16*1) + (8*0) + (4*1) + (2*0) + (1*3)**

128	64	32	16	8	4	2	1
0	0	1	1	0	1	0	1

Analyzing the Octal Numeration System (Base 8)

The octal system of numeration is based on groups of eight, so it uses base 8. This equates to place columns derived from the following powers of 8:

8^4 8^3 8^2 8^1 8^0

Similar to base 10, which has ten symbols available to represent numbers (0 through 9), base 8 has only eight symbols (0 through 7). Using these eight symbols, you can represent any number in octal. The place-columns for base 8, as derived from the five powers of eight just listed, are as follows:

32768 4096 512 64 8 1

Converting Octal to Decimal

Octal numbers in C++ are specified by a prefixed zero, so if given the octal number 0623, what does it represent in decimal? Like binary, you can just fill in the columns, multiply, and add. The answer turns out to be 403 (base 10), as shown in Table 17.4.

Use the Powers of a Base as Columns

To find the starting place-column when converting from decimal to some other base, first identify the columns by calculating powers of the base, largest powers on the left. Then find the first column that's numerically smaller than the number you're converting.

TABLE 17.4   **The Decimal Number *403* in Octal: (512*0) + (64*6) + (8*2) + (1*3)**

512	64	8	1
0	6	2	3

Converting Decimal to Octal

Just as you converted a decimal number to binary, you can convert a decimal number to octal, using the same algorithm. Assume that you have the number 123 (base 10) and want to convert it to octal. You must first identify the columns used by the base 8 numbering system. To find the starting place-column, find the first column that's numerically smaller than the number you're converting—in this case, 123. Then, as before, do a little base 10 division, working from left to right.

The algorithm for converting decimal to octal

1. "How many times will 64 go into 123?" The answer is, of course, once. So you put 1 in the 64 column. Now you've used 64 bits and have only 59 left (123 - 64 = 59). Move to the next column.

2. "How many times will 8 go into 59?" The answer is 7, so a 7 goes in the 8 column. This round you've used 56 (7 * 8) for a total of 120. There are only 3 bits left (59 - 56 = 3). Move to the next column.

3. "How many times will 1 go into 3?" Of course the answer is 3, and you've run out of bits, so you're done.

The end result of this process is shown in Table 17.5, which shows that 123 (base 10) is the same as 173 (base 8) as shown here:

(64*1) + (8*7) + (1*3) = 123

TABLE 17.5   **The Decimal Number *123* Converted to Octal is *173***

512	64	8	1
0	1	7	3

Okay, before we move on to hexadecimal, let's look at a program that converts decimal numbers into numbers of any base 2 though 10.

A Base Conversion Program: *CONVERT*

The CONVERT program shown in Listing 17.1 uses an algorithm similar to the one you've seen used in the last few sections to convert decimal numbers into numbers of some other base. For clarity, this program uses minimal error checking.

LISTING 17.1 **A Program to Illustrate Base Conversion**

```
 1: ///////////////////////////////////////////////////////
 2: //  Module  : convert.cpp
 3: //
 4: //  Purpose : Converts numbers from decimal (base 10) to
 5: //            some number base (2-10).
 6: ///////////////////////////////////////////////////////
 7:
 8: #include <iostream>
 9: #include <string>
10: #include <cstdlib>
11:
12: using namespace std;
13:
14: ///////////////////////////////////////////////////////
15: // Function Declarations
16:
17: string Convert(const int& num, const int& newbase);
18: string ReverseStr(const string& str);
19:
20: ///////////////////////////////////////////////////////
21: // Convert()
22:
23: string Convert(const int& num, const int& newbase)
24: {
25:    string str;
26:    char   ch;
27:    int    remainder = 0;
28:    int    quotient  = num;
```

LISTING 17.1

1 Lines 8-10: Include the Standard C++ Library files the program needs to perform its work

2 Lines 17-18: Declare function prototypes

continues…

LISTING 17.1 CONTINUED

③ Lines 32-33: Calculate the remainder and the quotient

④ Lines 57-60: Declare variables used for the string reversal

⑤ Lines 62-73: Reverse the string using a do loop and some pointer arithmetic

LISTING 17.1 **Continued**

```
29:
30:     while (quotient > 0)
31:     {
32:         remainder = quotient % newbase;
33:         quotient  = quotient / newbase;
34:
35:         // Convert remainder to a char and add it to string
36:         itoa(remainder, &ch, 10);
37:         str += ch;
38:     };
39:
40:     // Because the bits in the number are converted from
41:     // low to high, we must reverse it to get the proper
42:     // order.
43:
44:     str = ReverseStr(str);
45:     return str;
46: }
47:
48: //////////////////////////////////////////////////////////
49: // ReverseStr()
50:
51: string ReverseStr(const string& s1)
52: {
53:     string str = s1;
54:
55:     // Use pointer arithmetic to reverse the string
56:
57:     int  last = str.size();   // Number of chars in string
58:     char *s   = &str[0];       // Get pointer to start char
59:     char *e   = &str[last-1]; // Get pointer to end char
60:     char temp;
61:
62:     do
63:     {
64:         // Swap outer digits
65:         temp = *s;  // temp = start
66:         *s = *e;    // start = end
67:         *e = temp;  // end = temp
68:
69:         // Move inward into the string from both ends
70:         ++s;
71:         --e;
72:     }
73:     while (s < e);   // repeat until midpoint
```

```
74:
75:    return str;
76: }
77:
78: //////////////////////////////////////////////////////////
79: // Driver
80:
81: void main()
82: {
83:    int  num;
84:    int  base;
85:    char quit;
86:
87:    do
88:    {
89:        do
90:        {
91:           cout << "In what base shall we work "
92:              << "(2-10)? >";
93:           cin >> base;
94:        }
95:        while ((base < 2) || (base > 10));
96:
97:        do
98:        {
99:           cout << "Enter a positive decimal integer "
100:              << "for conversion >";
101:           cin >> num;
102:        }
103:        while (num < 0);
104:
105:        // Convert bases
106:        string answer = Convert(num, base);
107:
108:        // Write output
109:        cout << num << " = " << answer << " in base "
110:           << base << '\n';
111:        cout << '\n';
112:
113:        // See if the user wants to continue or quit
114:        cout << "Enter Q to quit, C to continue >";
115:        cin >> quit;
116:        cout << '\n';
117:    }
118:    while ((quit != 'Q') && (quit != 'q'));
119: }
```

Analyzing the *CONVERT* Program

Most of the work in this program is done by the Convert() function, which performs the actual conversion algorithm. The Convert() function returns a Standard C++ Library string and takes two integer references as its parameters, as declared in line 17:

```
string Convert(const int& num, const int& newbase);
```

The Convert() function starts at line 20, and the bulk of this function's work is performed in a while loop. Before the loop begins, the value of the number to convert (num) is assigned to the variable quotient in line 28:

```
int quotient = num;
```

Within the loop, two calculations are performed: One to get the quotient of the amount remaining divided by the base, the other to get the remainder. On line 32, the integer portion of the remainder is calculated first, using the modulus operator (%):

```
remainder = quotient % newbase;
```

On line 33, the quotient is the amount remaining divided by the base:

```
quotient  = quotient / newbase;
```

On lines 36 and 37, the Standard C Library function itoa() (integer to alphanumeric) converts the current digit from an int to a char and concatenates this char to the result string using the std::string += operator:

```
itoa(remainder, &ch, 10);
str += ch;
```

Because of the way this algorithm works, the Convert() function produces the digits of the number conversion string in reverse order. For example, to convert the decimal number 123 to the octal number 173 as we did earlier (refer to Table 17.5), the algorithm goes through several steps, as shown in Figure 17.1. (Study this figure for a while and you'll get the hang of it.) Let's walk through the loop for this conversion to see why this is so.

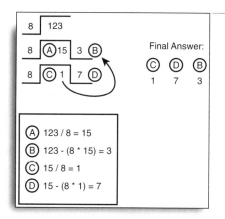

FIGURE 17.1

The mathematical steps used in the CONVERT algorithm.

Iteration #1: The number to be converted (quotient = num = 123) is divided by the base (8), saving off the remainder (3) and the new quotient (15). The remainder (3) is stored in the result string (currently: 3).

Iteration #2: The quotient (15) is divided by the base (8), saving off the remainder (7) and the new quotient (1). The remainder (7) is stored in the result string (currently: 37).

Iteration #3: The quotient (1) is divided by the base (8), saving off the remainder (1) and the new quotient (0). The remainder (1) is stored in the result string (currently: 371).

The loop iterates until the quotient reaches zero, giving, as shown in lines 28 through 38, the following full cycle:

```
int quotient = num;

while (quotient > 0)
{
    remainder = quotient % newbase;
    quotient  = quotient / newbase;

    // Convert remainder to a char and add it to string
    itoa(remainder, &ch, 10);
    str += ch;
};
```

As you can see from the preceding iterations, the result string holds the value 371—but you saw earlier that the correct answer is 173. The characters in the string holding the digits must be reversed (refer to Figure 17.1). The ReverseStr() function performs this reversal process, taking a standard string as a parameter and returning the reversed string:

```
str = ReverseStr(str);
```

The ReverseString() function begins on line 48 and uses pointer arithmetic to access the members of the string's character array. The first and last elements of the character array are identified and stored as character pointers (lines 57 through 60):

```
int  last = str.size();     // Number of characters in the
                            // string
char *s   = &str[0];        // Get a pointer to the start
                            // character
char *e   = &str[last-1];   // Get a pointer to the end
                            // character
char temp;
```

Then a do loop iterates through the array, working from the outside in until it reaches the middle, swapping front and back all along the way (lines 62 through 73):

```
do
{
    // Swap outer digits
    temp = *s;  // temp = start
    *s = *e;    // start = end
    *e = temp;  // end = temp

    // Move inward into the string from both ends
    ++s;
    --e;
}
while (s < e);    // repeat until midpoint
```

The driver function, main(), just runs through a few do loops to provide some basic interactivity (in the same way you saw back in Chapter 5, "Building Iteration Loops"). The main() function gets the number to convert and the base to convert it to, and calls Convert() to get the answer as a standard string.

Analyzing the Hexadecimal Numeration System (Base 16)

The hexadecimal (hex) system of numeration is based on groups of sixteen, so it's called base 16, or hexadecimal (the prefixes `hexa` means 6 and `deci` means 10—6 + 10 = 16). This equates to place columns derived from the following powers of 16:

16^4 16^3 16^2 16^1 16^0

Base 16 has sixteen symbols that can be used for counting, and each equates to four bits, acting as a sort of shorthand for tedious binary codes, as shown in Table 17.6.

The Power of Hexadecimal

Many commercial C++ programs make extensive use of hexadecimal because it empowers the programmer with a convenient notation for bit manipulation.

TABLE 17.6   **The Hexadecimal Numeration System with Equivalent Bit Pattern and Decimal Values**

Hex Value	Bit Pattern	Decimal Value
0	0000	0
1	0001	1
2	0010	2
3	0011	3
4	0100	4
5	0101	5
6	0110	6
7	0111	7
8	1000	8
9	1001	9
A	1010	10
B	1011	11
C	1100	12
D	1101	13
E	1110	14
F	1111	15

At first sight, hexadecimal might seem trickier than the other numeration systems. This is because, in addition to the digits 0 through 9, it uses the letters A through F. It does take some getting used to, but as it turns out, when you have to manipulate bits, hexadecimal is wonderful (you just have to get comfortable with the system). Using these sixteen symbols, you can represent any number in hexadecimal. The place-columns for base 16, as derived from the five powers of 16 listed before, is as follows:

1048576   65536   4096   256   16   1

Converting Hexadecimal to Decimal

Hexadecimal numbers in C++ are specified by the prefix 0x. Take the number 0x35FF0F, for example. What does it represent in decimal? Like the other systems, you can just fill in the columns, multiply, and add. The answer turns out to be 3,538,703 (base 10), as shown in Table 17.7.

TABLE 17.7   **The Decimal Number *3,538,703* in Hexadecimal: (1048576*3) + (65536*5) + (4096*15) + (256*15) + (16*0) + (1*15)**

1048576	65536	4096	256	16	1
3	5	F	F	0	F

This means that hex 0x35FF0F translates to binary 001101011111111100001111.

An Exercise for the Reader

Try your hand at modifying the CONVERT program in Listing 17.1 to handle bases larger than 10.

Converting Decimal to Hexadecimal

To convert a decimal number to a hex number, you follow the same algorithm you did when converting from decimal to octal, earlier in this chapter. The only difference is that the letters A through F must be added to the mix.

Assume that you have the decimal number 123 and want to convert it to a hex number. You must first identify the columns used by the base 16 numbering system. To find the starting place-column, find the first column that's numerically smaller than the number you're converting (123)—in this case, the place column would be 16. Then, as before, do a little base 10 division, working from left to right.

The algorithm for converting decimal to hexadecimal

1. "How many times will 16 go into 123?" The answer turns out to be 7. So you put 7 in the 16 column. Now you've used 112 bits (16 * 7 = 112) and have only 11 left (123 - 112 = 11). Move to the next column.

2. "How many times will 1 go into 11?" The answer is obviously 11, so a B goes in the 1 column (remember that in hex, you spell *eleven* as the symbol B). Now you've run out of bits, so you're done.

The end result of this process is shown in Table 17.8, which demonstrates that 123 (base 10) is the same as 0x7B (base 16) as shown here:

(16*7) + (1*11) = 123

TABLE 17.8   **The Decimal Number *123* Converted to Hex Is *0x7B***

256	16	1
0	7	B

So, how would you write the decimal 22 in hex? That's 16 + 6, which is the same as 0x10 + 0x6, or 0x16.

Converting Hexadecimal to Binary

Using the information in Table 17.6, it's easy to convert from hex to binary. Use the shorthand described in this table and substitute the four-digit binary sequence that corresponds to each hex digit. For example, 0x37BF converts to binary as follows:

3 = 0011, 7 = 0111, B = 1011, F = 1111

This gives us the binary number 0011011110111111.

Converting Binary to Hexadecimal

To convert this number to hexadecimal, you could convert the binary back to decimal and then convert the decimal to hex—but that's the hard way. Using the reverse of the process described earlier, you can write the entire binary number simply by substituting the four bits that correspond to each hex digit.

It's a common practice to break up large binary numbers into groups of four characters, so that they correspond to one of the hex numbers shown in Table 17.6. For example, binary 00000000 is the same as 0000 0000, which is hex 0x00. Binary 11111111 is the same as 1111 1111, which translates to hex 0xFF; and binary 10110101 is 1011 0101, which is hex 0xB5.

At this point, you should be ready to put the information you've learned in this chapter to good use. The foundation has been laid for you to learn how to manipulate individual bits in computer memory, the subject of the next chapter.

Manipulating Bits

Learn about bit numbering

Find out how to declare and use bit fields

Discover the bit operators

Learn how to manipulate bits within variables

Explore bit-shifting and the bit-shift operators

Working with Bits

In Chapter 17, "Analyzing the Mathematics of Memory," you learned the inner workings of binary and hexadecimal numeration. In this chapter, you'll build on that knowledge and learn how to adjust individual bits as you see fit. The shroud of mystery that surrounds this low-level world of bits and bytes will fall away, revealing to you the elegance of bit operations.

As you'll recall, there are eight bits in a byte; the C++ bit operators let you manipulate the individual bits within a byte as you see fit. This is power! Using bit operators, you can get down to the bare metal, controlling the values of the bits.

Understanding Bit Numbering

Most-Significant Bit

The bit to the left-most position of an integer.

Least-Significant Bit

The bit in the right-most position of an integer.

The most common way of looking at computer memory is as a hierarchy of bits. The bits in a byte are numbered from 7 to 0, left to right, as shown in Figure 18.1. Bit 7 is the *most-significant bit* (also called the *high-order bit*). Bit 0 is the *least-significant bit* (also called the *low-order bit*). Eight bits make up a byte, two bytes make up a word (16 bits), and two words make up a double word (32 bits).

FIGURE 18.1

Bit numbering and the corresponding bit values in a byte.

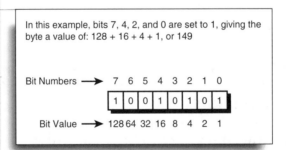

In this example, bits 7, 4, 2, and 0 are set to 1, giving the byte a value of: 128 + 16 + 4 + 1, or 149

Bit Numbers → 7 6 5 4 3 2 1 0

| 1 | 0 | 0 | 1 | 0 | 1 | 0 | 1 |

Bit Value → 128 64 32 16 8 4 2 1

Understanding Bit Fields

Bit Field

A structure member that uses a specified number of bits.

A special type of structure (or union) data member contains a specified number of bits. This structure is called a *bit field*. You use bit fields to make the best possible use of space in a structure. A bit field's length is specified by a positive integer value.

Because the compiler considers a bit field an integral type, the data member must be of one of three integer types: `unsigned int`, `signed int`, or `int`.

Declaring a Bit Field

You declare a bit field as a data member by using the following syntax:

```
DataType Name : Size;
```

In this syntax, `DataType` is the data type specifier for the bit field, `Name` is an optional declarator for the bit field, and `Size` is the number of bits in the bit field. Consider the following structure:

```
struct
{
    unsigned short member1 : 5;   // 5 bits
    unsigned short member2 : 3;   // 8 bits
    unsigned short member3 : 6;   // 14 bits
    unsigned short member4 : 2;   // 16 bits
}
```

Each of the members of this structure makes up a certain number of bits of a single `unsigned short` integer. Because `member1` gets only five of the 16 bits, the maximum possible value `member1` can contain is `31`, as shown here:

```
16 + 8 + 4 + 2 + 1 = 31
```

Likewise, `member2` gets only three of the 16 bits, so the maximum possible value `member2` can contain is `7`, as shown here:

```
4 + 2 + 1 = 7
```

Following this line of reasoning, it's easy to see that `member3` gets six of the 16 bits, so the maximum possible value `member3` can contain is `63`:

```
32 + 16 + 8 + 4 + 2 + 1 = 63
```

The final member, `member4`, gets the remaining two bits, so the maximum possible value `member4` can contain is `3`:

```
2 + 1 = 3
```

Unnamed Bit Fields

Unnamed bit fields are rare. They are used mainly to align structure byte sizes on integer boundaries to increase program speed.

Using a Bit Field

Using a bit field is just as easy as using any other data member. The program in Listing 18.1 shows how you can save memory by using bit fields to store 16 Boolean values in a single unsigned short integer (assumed to be 16 bits, or 2 bytes).

LISTING 18.1

❶ Line 10: Define USHORT as a new data type

❷ Lines 12–31: Define 16 1-bit bit fields to use as Boolean variables

LISTING 18.1 **Using Bit Fields to Pack 16 Boolean Variables into the Byte Space of 2 *bools***

```
 1: ////////////////////////////////////////////////////
 2: //  Module  : bitfield.cpp
 3: //
 4: //  Purpose : Demonstration of bit fields
 5: ////////////////////////////////////////////////////
 6:
 7: #include <iostream>
 8: using namespace std;
 9:
10: typedef unsigned short USHORT;  ────────❶
11:
12: struct MyBitBools ─────────────────────────────────┐
13: {                                                   │
14:     // Some bit fields to use as Boolean variables  │
15:     USHORT b1  : 1;                                 │
16:     USHORT b2  : 1;                                 │
17:     USHORT b3  : 1;                                 │
18:     USHORT b4  : 1;                                 │
19:     USHORT b5  : 1;                                 │
20:     USHORT b6  : 1;                                 │
21:     USHORT b7  : 1;                              ───┼──❷
22:     USHORT b8  : 1;                                 │
23:     USHORT b9  : 1;                                 │
24:     USHORT b10 : 1;                                 │
25:     USHORT b11 : 1;                                 │
26:     USHORT b12 : 1;                                 │
27:     USHORT b13 : 1;                                 │
28:     USHORT b14 : 1;                                 │
29:     USHORT b15 : 1;                                 │
30:     USHORT b16 : 1;                                 │
31: }; ─────────────────────────────────────────────────┘
32:
```

```
33: void main()
34: {
35:     MyBitBools mbb;
36:
37:     mbb.b1  = true;
38:     mbb.b2  = false;
39:     mbb.b3  = true;
40:     mbb.b4  = false;
41:     mbb.b5  = true;
42:     mbb.b6  = false;
43:     mbb.b7  = true;
44:     mbb.b8  = false;
45:     mbb.b9  = true;
46:     mbb.b10 = false;
47:     mbb.b11 = true;
48:     mbb.b12 = false;
49:     mbb.b13 = true;
50:     mbb.b14 = false;
51:     mbb.b15 = true;
52:     mbb.b16 = false;
53:
54:     cout << "sizeof(MyBitBools) = "
55:         << sizeof(MyBitBools) << "\n\n";
56:     cout << "mbb.b1  = " << mbb.b1  << '\n';
57:     cout << "mbb.b2  = " << mbb.b2  << '\n';
58:     cout << "mbb.b3  = " << mbb.b3  << '\n';
59:     cout << "mbb.b4  = " << mbb.b4  << '\n';
60:     cout << "mbb.b5  = " << mbb.b5  << '\n';
61:     cout << "mbb.b6  = " << mbb.b6  << '\n';
62:     cout << "mbb.b7  = " << mbb.b7  << '\n';
63:     cout << "mbb.b8  = " << mbb.b8  << '\n';
64:     cout << "mbb.b9  = " << mbb.b9  << '\n';
65:     cout << "mbb.b10 = " << mbb.b10 << '\n';
66:     cout << "mbb.b11 = " << mbb.b11 << '\n';
67:     cout << "mbb.b12 = " << mbb.b12 << '\n';
68:     cout << "mbb.b13 = " << mbb.b13 << '\n';
69:     cout << "mbb.b14 = " << mbb.b14 << '\n';
70:     cout << "mbb.b15 = " << mbb.b15 << '\n';
71:     cout << "mbb.b16 = " << mbb.b16 << "\n\n";
72: }
```

LISTING 18.1 CONTINUED

3 Lines 37–52: Assign Boolean values to the bit fields

Line 10 of this program defines the type name ULONG as an unsigned short. Lines 12 through 31 define the MyBitBools structure, which contains 16 1-bit bit fields that we use as Boolean variables. Line 35 declares the MyBitBools variable mbb, and lines 37 through 52 assign alternating true and false values to each member of the mbb structure. Lines 54 and 55 display the size (in bytes) of the MyBitBools structure. Finally, lines 56 through 71 display the values of the bit fields, verifying their single-bit Boolean nature.

The output of this program proves that, by using bit fields, we can squeeze 16 Boolean variables into the same number of bytes in which only 2 normal bool variables can fit:

```
sizeof(MyBitBools) = 2

mbb.b1  = 1
mbb.b2  = 0
mbb.b3  = 1
mbb.b4  = 0
mbb.b5  = 1
mbb.b6  = 0
mbb.b7  = 1
mbb.b8  = 0
mbb.b9  = 1
mbb.b10 = 0
mbb.b11 = 1
mbb.b12 = 0
mbb.b13 = 1
mbb.b14 = 0
mbb.b15 = 1
mbb.b16 = 0
```

Figure 18.2 shows the locations of the bit field members within the single unsigned short they occupy.

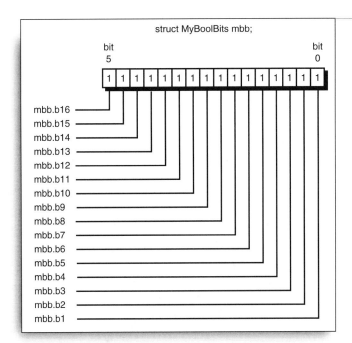

FIGURE 18.2

A structure of 16 1-bit bit fields and their corresponding locations within the unsigned short they occupy.

Using Bit Operators

Six operators are used in C++ programs to manipulate bits, as listed in Table 18.1.

TABLE 18.1   **The C++ Bit Operators**

Description	Operator	Purpose
AND	&	Provides a bit-by-bit comparison between two operands—if the two bits being compared are both 1, the result is 1, otherwise the result is 0.
Inclusive OR	¦	Provides a bit-by-bit comparison between two operands—if the two bits being compared are both 0, the result is 0, otherwise the result is 1.
Exclusive OR (XOR)	^	Provides a bit-by-bit comparison between two operands—if the two bits being compared are both 0, the result is 0; if they're both 1, the result is still 0.

The Unary Bit Operator

All the operators in Table 18.1 are binary operators except for the one's complement (NOT) operator, which is unary.

continues…

TABLE 18.1   Continued

Description	Operator	Purpose
		Only the case of a 0 and a 1 gives the result of 1.
NOT (one's complement)	~	Changes each 0 to a 1, and each 1 to a 0.
Left-shift	<<	Shifts bits to the left.
Right-shift	>>	Shifts bits to the right.

You'll examine all six of these operators in the following sections to see exactly what they're good for, and you'll see some concrete examples along the way.

The Bitwise *AND* Operator

The AND (&) operator performs a bit-by-bit comparison of its two operands. The AND rule of thumb can be summed up as *it's true only if it's always true*. In other words, if the two bits being compared are both 1, the result is 1, otherwise the result is 0.

A bit in one operand is always compared to the corresponding bit occupying the same bit position in the other operand. Each comparison is independent of any of the others. Here's an example:

```
  1 1 0 1 0 1 0 1
& 1 0 1 0 1 1 0 1
-----------------
  1 0 0 0 0 1 0 1
```

The binary number 11010101 is the same 0xD5 (decimal 213), and the binary number 10101101 is the same 0xAD (decimal 173). The binary value 100000101 resulting from this AND operation is 0x85 (decimal 133). Take a look at the following code, which uses the AND operator and the C library function printf() to demonstrate in code the comparison operation just shown, using the same numbers.

```
#include <stdio.h>

void main()
{
```

Why Use printf()?

The Standard C Library is a part of the Standard C++ Library, and using C library functions is sometimes the most efficient way to get job done. The printf() function is a part of the Standard C Library, and it has a lot of flexibility in formatting output for the screen. In this example, the Standard C printf() function is more concise than a corresponding C++ statement using the cout object.

```
        int n1 = 0xD5;
        int n2 = 0xAD;
        int n3 = n1 & n2;

        printf("0x%X & 0x%X = 0x%X, or %i\n", n1, n2, n3, n3);
    }
```

As expected, the output of the program is as follows:

```
0xD5 & 0xAD = 0x85, or 133
```

AND operations are used mainly for *masking* (filtering) specified
bits from an operand. For example, if you need to reserve a
range of numbers that will be considered valid for some purpose
(such as a message identifier to be used by one of your programs), you can specify a range of valid values using a mask. The
mask makes it easy to test whether the ID is valid with a single
comparison for all numbers within the mask range. Listing 18.2
gives an example of this use of the AND operator for masking.

LISTING 18.2   **An Example Using the *AND* Operator to Test a Range of Values
with a Mask**

```
 1: //////////////////////////////////////////////////
 2: // and.cpp
 3:
 4: #include <iostream>
 5: #include <string>
 6:
 7: using namespace std;
 8:
 9: bool IsGoodID(int id);
10:
11: //////////////////////////////////////////////////
12: // Constants
13:
14: // Restrict range of good IDs to < 16 (0x0010)
15: const int mask = 0x000F; ────────────────────── 1
16:
17: // Some IDs to test
```

LISTING 18.2

1 Line 15: The mask constant

continues…

LISTING 18.2 CONTINUED

2 Lines 18-23: The GoodID and
BadID constants

3 Line 30: Using the AND
operator to mask an ID

LISTING 18.2   **Continued**

```
18: const int GoodID1 = 0x0001;   // 1
19: const int GoodID2 = 0x0004;   // 4
20: const int GoodID3 = 0x0008;   // 8
21: const int GoodID4 = 0x000F;   // 15
22: const int BadID1  = 0x0010;   // 16
23: const int BadID2  = 0xFC10;   // 64528
24:
25: //////////////////////////////////////////////////////
26: // IsGoodID()
27:
28: bool IsGoodID(int id)
29: {
30:     int result = (id & mask);
31:     return (result == id);
32: }
33:
34: //////////////////////////////////////////////////////
35: // Driver()
36:
37: void main()
38: {
39:     string str;
40:
41:     // Find the BadID...
42:     str = IsGoodID(GoodID1) ? "GoodID" : "BadID";
43:     cout << str << endl;
44:
45:     str = IsGoodID(GoodID2) ? "GoodID" : "BadID";
46:     cout << str << endl;
47:
48:     str = IsGoodID(GoodID3) ? "GoodID" : "BadID";
49:     cout << str << endl;
50:
51:     str = IsGoodID(GoodID4) ? "GoodID" : "BadID";
52:     cout << str << endl;
53:
54:     str = IsGoodID(BadID1) ? "GoodID" : "BadID";
55:     cout << str << endl;
56:
57:     str = IsGoodID(BadID2) ? "GoodID" : "BadID";
58:     cout << str << endl;
59: }
```

2

3

The output from the program in Listing 18.2 is as follows:

```
GoodID
GoodID
GoodID
GoodID
BadID
BadID
```

For any number within the mask range (0 through 15), the result of the AND operation with the mask value (0x000F) returns that same number. The values 0x0010 (BadID1) and 0xFC10 (BadID2) fail the mask test because the result of the AND operation mask isn't the same as the original value. Let's take a closer look at how this program works.

The program begins by including the standard iostream and string headers, followed by the using namespace std declaration (lines 4 through 7). Line 15 declares the constant mask, which acts as the mask when ANDing ID values in the IsGoodID() function. Lines 18 through 23 declare the IDs to be tested. The meat of the program occurs in lines 28 through 32, where we define the function IsGoodID(). This function receives an ID as a parameter and tests to see whether it falls within the allowable range by using the AND operator with the mask and the ID as operands (line 30).

The driver function main() simply sends each of the ID constants to the IsGoodID() function to determine whether the ID falls within the range allowed by the mask. Depending on the return value of this function call, the program writes to the screen the corresponding string GoodID or BadID.

The Bitwise Inclusive *OR* Operator

The inclusive OR (¦) operator performs a bit-by-bit comparison of its two operands, similar to the comparison performed by the AND operator. The OR rule of thumb can be summed up as *it's false if it's always false, otherwise it's true*. That is, if the two bits being compared are both 0, the result is 0, otherwise the result is 1.

A bit in one operand is always compared to the corresponding bit occupying the same bit position in the other operand.

Use a Debugger to Study the Code

You can get a much better understanding of the AND operation described in Listing 18.2 by watching and comparing the values of the result and id variables in the IsGoodID() function while the program runs in a debugger.

Each comparison is independent of any of the others. Here's an OR example using the same numbers previously used for the AND example:

```
  1 1 0 1 0 1 0 1
¦ 1 0 1 0 1 1 0 1
- - - - - - - - - - - - - - - - -
  1 1 1 1 1 1 0 1
```

The binary number 11010101 is the same as 0xD5 (decimal 213), and the binary number 10101101 is the same as 0xAD (decimal 173). The binary value 111111101 resulting from this OR operation is 0xFD (decimal 253). Take a look at the following code, which uses the OR operator and the Standard C Library function printf() to demonstrate in code the comparison operation just shown, using the same numbers.

```c
#include <stdio.h>

void main()
{
    int n1 = 0xD5;
    int n2 = 0xAD;
    int n3 = n1 ¦ n2;

    printf("0x%X ¦ 0x%X = 0x%X, or %i\n", n1, n2, n3, n3);
}
```

The program produces the expected output:

```
0xD5 ¦ 0xAD = 0xFD, or 253
```

Inclusive OR operations are extremely useful for *combining* specified bits. You can use OR to pack bits into a message or style that might be used by one of your programs. As an example of this usage, suppose that you have the values 1, 2, 4, and 8. In hex, the same values are 0x1, 0x2, 0x4, and 0x8; in binary, they're 0001, 0010, 0100, and 1000. Watch what happens when you OR them:

```
0001 ¦ 0010 ¦ 0100 ¦ 1000 = 1111
```

All these values were "packed" into a single value. Now, what do you suppose will happen if you AND the value 0010 with the packed value 1111? Take a look:

```
0010 & 1111 = 0010
```

You get what you started with. This can be very useful if you create identifiers and use these numbers as flags. You could do something like this:

```
const int Style1 = 0x0001;  //  0001
const int Style2 = 0x0002;  //  0010
const int Style3 = 0x0004;  //  0100
const int Style4 = 0x0008;  //  1000
```

Then you could combine them, like so:

```
int pack = Style1 | Style2 | Style3 | Style4;
```

Creative use of hex values allows you to do all kinds of useful things with the bit operators. Now you can check to see whether Style2 exists in pack,

```
bool exists = ((Style2 & pack) == style);
```

which it does, so exists turns out to be true.

The Bitwise Exclusive *OR* Operator (*XOR*)

Like its counterparts, the exclusive OR (^) operator (XOR) performs a bit-by-bit comparison of its two operands. The XOR rule of thumb can be summed up as *if they're different, it's true; otherwise, it's false*. That is, if the two bits being compared are both 0, the result is 0; if the bits are both 1, the result is still 0. Only the case of a 0 and a 1 gives the result of 1.

As with the other bit operators, a bit in one operand is always compared to the corresponding bit occupying the same bit position in the other operand. Each comparison is independent of any of the others. Here's an XOR example using the same numbers previously used for AND and OR:

```
  1 1 0 1 0 1 0 1
^ 1 0 1 0 1 1 0 1
- - - - - - - - - - - - - - - - - -
  0 1 1 1 1 0 0 0
```

The resulting binary number 01111000 is the same as 0x78 (decimal 120). Take a look at the following code, which uses the XOR operator and the Standard C Library function printf() to demonstrate in code the comparison operation just shown, using the same numbers.

```
#include <stdio.h>

void main()
{
    int n1 = 0xD5;
    int n2 = 0xAD;
    int n3 = n1 ^ n2;

    printf("0x%X ^ 0x%X = 0x%X, or %i\n", n1, n2, n3, n3);
}
```

The program produces the expected output:

```
0xD5 ^ 0xAD = 0x78, or 120
```

Exclusive OR operations are extremely useful for data encryption and computer graphics, among other things. You can also use XOR to unpack bits from a packed message or style like the one you saw earlier. Remember Style1, Style2, and so on from a few paragraphs back? As an example of this usage, take a look at the program in Listing 18.3, which uses the AND, OR, and XOR operators to combine, check, and remove "styles."

LISTING 18.3   An Example Using the *AND*, *OR*, and *XOR* Operators to Combine, Check, and Remove "Styles"

```
 1: ////////////////////////////////////////////////////////
 2: // AndOrXor.cpp
 3:
 4: #include <iostream>
 5: #include <string>
 6:
 7: using namespace std;
 8:
 9: bool IsStylePresent(int num, int style);
10:
11: ////////////////////////////////////////////////////////
12: // Constants
13:
14: // Some styles to combine
```

```
15: const int Style1 = 0x0001;  //   1
16: const int Style2 = 0x0002;  //   2
17: const int Style3 = 0x0004;  //   4
18: const int Style4 = 0x0008;  //   8
19: const int Style5 = 0x0010;  //  16
20: const int Style6 = 0x0020;  //  32
21:
22: //////////////////////////////////////////////////////
23: // IsStylePresent()
24:
25: bool IsStylePresent(int num, int style)
26: {
27:     // If style is found return true, else return false
28:     bool result = ((num & style) == style);
29:     return result;
30: }
31:
32: //////////////////////////////////////////////////////
33: // Driver()
34:
35: void main()
36: {
37:     string str;
38:     int style;
39:
40:     // Combine styles 1 & 2
41:     style = Style1 | Style2;
42:     str = IsStylePresent(style, Style3) ? "Yes" : "No";
43:     cout << str << endl;  // should be "No"
44:
45:     // Add in style 3
46:     style |= Style3;
47:     str = IsStylePresent(style, Style3) ? "Yes" : "No";
48:     cout << str << endl;  // should be "Yes"
49:
50:     // Add in styles 4 & 5
51:     style |= Style4 | Style5;
52:     str = IsStylePresent(style, Style5) ? "Yes" : "No";
53:     cout << str << endl;  // should be "Yes"
54:
55:     // Verify that style 2 is still here
56:     str = IsStylePresent(style, Style2) ? "Yes" : "No";
```

LISTING 18.3

1 Lines 15–20: Define style constants

2 Line 28: Use the AND operator to test for a style

3 Lines 41–42: Combine styles with the OR operator and checks the result

continues…

LISTING 18.3 CONTINUED

4 Lines 60–61: Remove
a style with the NOT
operator and checks
the result

LISTING 18.3   **Continued**

```
57:     cout << str << endl;  // should be "Yes"
58:
59:     // Remove style 2
60:     style ^= Style2;
61:     str = IsStylePresent(style, Style2) ? "Yes" : "No";
62:     cout << str << endl;  // should be "No"
63:
64:     // Add in style 6
65:     style |= Style6;
66:     str = IsStylePresent(style, Style6) ? "Yes" : "No";
67:     cout << str << endl;  // should be "Yes"
68: }
```

The output from the program in Listing 18.3 is as expected:

```
No
Yes
Yes
Yes
No
Yes
```

The program begins by including the standard `iostream` and `string` headers, followed by the `using namespace std` declaration (lines 4 through 7). Lines 15 through 20 declare the style constants, which we combine in various ways throughout the program. Lines 25 through 30 define the Boolean function `IsStylePresent()`. This function receives two integer parameters: `num` and `style`. The parameter `num` represents the combined styles to look in for the particular style specified by the `style` parameter. Using the AND test on line 28, we can determine if the style represented by `style` is present in `num`. If so, `IsStylePresent()` returns `true`, otherwise it returns `false`.

The driver function `main()` sets up a variety of test cases, combining styles in various ways and then checking the result using the `IsStylePresent()` function and printing the result to the screen. For example, line 41 combines `Style1` and `Style2` using an OR operation, and line 42 assigns either a `"Yes"` or a `"No"` string to the variable `str` depending on the return value of the `IsStylePresent()` function. Line 60 uses the NOT operator (~) to remove a style from the `style` variable (I cover this concept in the next section).

The One's Complement (*NOT*) Operator

The one's complement operator (~), or NOT operator, is a unary operator that toggles every bit in its operand, changing every 0 to a 1, and every 1 to a 0. This operation is called the *one's complement*. If you have the binary number 0001 (0x1) and you take its complement, the result is 1110 (0xE). When you combine these two values with the AND operator, the complement becomes quite useful in clearing bits. For example:

```
0001 & 1110 = 0000
```

In C++ code, this operation would look something like this:

```
int flag1 = 0x01;        // 0001, set bit 1
flag1 = flag1 & ~0x01;   // clear bit 1
```

A more concise way of writing the same thing is shown here:

```
flag1 &= ~0x01;   // clear bit 1
```

You can selectively set and clear bits by using the OR, AND, and NOT operators, as shown in Listing 18.4.

LISTING 18.4   A Program That Selectively Sets and Clears Bits by Using the *OR*, *AND*, and *NOT* Operators

```
 1: ////////////////////////////////////////////////////
 2: // not.cpp
 3:
 4: #include <stdio.h>
 5:
 6: void main()
 7: {
 8:     int flag1 = 0x01; // 0001, bit 1 is set
 9:     int flag2 = 0x02; // 0010, bit 2 is set
10:     int flag3 = 0x04; // 0100, bit 3 is set
11:     int flag4 = 0x08; // 1000, bit 4 is set
```

continues...

LISTING 18.4

1 Lines 8–11: Define some flags to play with bit operations

LISTING 18.4 **Continued**

```
12:
13:     printf("flag1 = 0x%X \n", flag1);
14:     printf("flag2 = 0x%X \n", flag2);
15:     printf("flag3 = 0x%X \n", flag3);
16:     printf("flag3 = 0x%X \n\n", flag4);
17:
18:     flag1 = flag1 & ~0x01;    // clear bit 1
19:     flag2 &= ~0x02;           // same thing, clear bit 2
20:     flag3 &= ~0x04;           // same thing, clear bit 3
21:     flag4 &= ~0x08;           // same thing, clear bit 4
22:
23:     printf("flag1 = 0x%X \n", flag1);
24:     printf("flag2 = 0x%X \n", flag2);
25:     printf("flag3 = 0x%X \n", flag3);
26:     printf("flag4 = 0x%X \n\n", flag4);
27:
28:     flag1 | 0x01;             // set bit 1
29:     flag2 |= 0x02 | 0x04;     // set bits 2 & 3
30:     flag3 |= 0x04;            // set bit 3
31:     flag4 |= 0x04 | 0x08;     // set bits 3 & 4
32:
33:     printf("flag1 = 0x%X \n", flag1);
34:     printf("flag2 = 0x%X \n", flag2);
35:     printf("flag3 = 0x%X \n", flag3);
36:     printf("flag4 = 0x%X \n\n", flag4);
37:
38:     flag1 &= ~0x02;  // set bit 2
39:     flag2 &= ~0x04;  // clear bit 3, leave bit 2
40:     flag3 &= ~0x04;  // clear bit 3
41:     flag4 &= ~0x08;  // clear bit 4, leave bit 3
42:
43:     printf("flag1 = 0x%X \n", flag1);
44:     printf("flag2 = 0x%X \n", flag2);
45:     printf("flag3 = 0x%X \n", flag3);
46:     printf("flag4 = 0x%X \n", flag4);
47: }
```

LISTING 18.4 CONTINUED

2 Lines 13–16: Display the initial values of the flags

3 Lines 18–21: Clear the bits that are currently set in each flag

4 Lines 23–26: Display the modified flag values

5 Lines 28–31: Manipulate the bits in each flag

6 Lines 33–36: Display the modified flag values

7 Lines 38–41: Manipulate the bits in each flag again

8 Lines 43–46: Display the modified flag values

The output from the program in Listing 18.4 is as follows:

```
flag1 = 0x1
flag2 = 0x2
flag3 = 0x4
flag3 = 0x8

flag1 = 0x0
flag2 = 0x0
flag3 = 0x0
flag4 = 0x0

flag1 = 0x0
flag2 = 0x6
flag3 = 0x4
flag4 = 0xC

flag1 = 0x0
flag2 = 0x2
flag3 = 0x0
flag4 = 0x4
```

Because this program uses the Standard C Library function
`printf()` to display formatted data on the screen, line 4 includes
the Standard C input/output library header `<stdio.h>`, which
gives us access to this function. The rest of the program listing
consists of the implementation of `main()`.

The `main()` function begins by declaring four flag variables and
assigning to them hex values that set bits 1, 2, 3, and 4, respectively (lines 8 through 11). The values of each flag are then
printed to the screen with `printf()`, using the hexadecimal format specifier `%X` prefaced by the string `0x` (the `0x%X` combination
forces the flags to print correctly as hex numbers, for instance:
`0x003FA`). Line 18 clears bit 1 from `flag1` (which has only bit 1
set), resulting in zero. We clear the corresponding bits for the
other three flags in lines 19, 20, and 21. This results in all four
flags having the value of `0`, as shown by the output generated by
lines 23 through 26. The code performs a few other bit operations throughout the rest of the program, following the same
methodology.

Manipulating Bits in Signed and Unsigned Numbers

The sign of a number, which indicates whether the number is positive or negative, is stored in the leftmost bit of its data type. The number zero is treated as positive, that is, unsigned. This is why, when you take the absolute value of the extremes of a signed data range, negative values are one "higher" than the positive values.

Consider the value range of a signed char, from –128 to 127. A char typically uses 8 bits of storage. If the char is signed and positive, the leftmost bit is 0, as in 127 (binary 01111111). Its counterpart at the opposite end of the unsigned char range is -128 (binary 10000000). If this were an unsigned char, the 10000000 would represent decimal 128, one higher than allowed by the signed char. This indicates that when you are *bit twiddling* (that is, manipulating individual bits in memory), you should always be aware of the data type you're working with.

Exploring Bit-Shifting

In addition to the AND, OR, XOR, and NOT operators, there are the shift operators, which actually shift bits left or right within a variable. When you shift bits left or right, you change the bit patterns, resulting in a completely different value.

Using the Left-Shift Operator

The left-shift operator (<<) shifts bits to the left, as its name implies. For example, if you have the binary number 1101001011010010 and you left-shift by four bits, you end up with 0010110100100000. Figure 18.3 shows this left-shifting process. This C++ statement accomplishes the shift:

```
var = var << 4;
```

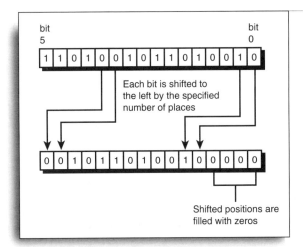

FIGURE 18.3
Left-shifting by four bits.

For unsigned integers, each position shifted represents a multi-plication by 2 (this is a *very* fast way to multiply by two), because each bit position represents a power of 2. As all the bits shift to the left by four places, the bits on the far-left side "fall off" and are lost. The vacated bits on the right are filled with zeros.

Using the Right-Shift Operator

The right-shift operator (>>) shifts bits to the right, as its name implies. Signed numbers use the leftmost bit to indicate the sign of the number. When bits of a signed number are shifted right, most computers duplicate the sign of the leftmost bit in the vacated bits. For example, if you have the signed binary number 1101001011010010 and you right-shift by four bits, you end up with 1111110100101101 (see Figure 18.4).

For unsigned numbers, the vacated bit positions are filled with zeros. The same bit sequence in an unsigned number would become 0000110100101101 (see Figure 18.5). This C++ statement accomplishes the shift:

```
var = var >> 4;
```

FIGURE 18.4

Right-shifting a signed number by four bits.

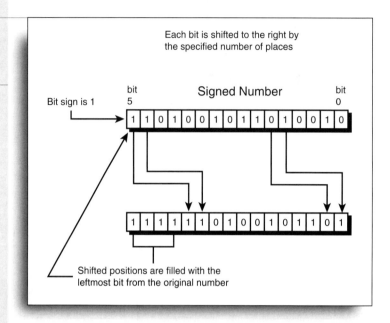

FIGURE 18.5

Right-shifting an unsigned number by four bits.

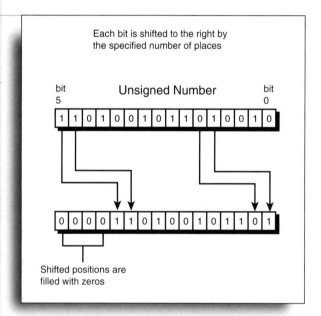

Listing 18.5 demonstrates the use of the bit-shift operators.

LISTING 18.5 **Examining Left-Shifting and Right-Shifting Operations**

```
1: ///////////////////////////////////////////////////
2: // shift.cpp
3:
4: #include <stdio.h>
5:
6: typedef unsigned int UINT;
7: typedef int INT;
8:
9: ///////////////////////////////////////////////////
10: // Driver()
11:
12: void main()
13: {
14:     // Left-shift
15:     printf("Left-Shifting by 2\n\n");
16:
17:     UINT var1 = 3; // 0011, or 0x03, or 3
18:     printf("var1 = 0x%X, or %i \n", var1, var1);
19:
20:     var1 = var1 << 2;
21:     printf("var1 = 0x%X, or %i \n", var1, var1);
22:
23:     var1 = var1 << 2;
24:     printf("var1 = 0x%X, or %i \n\n", var1, var1);
25:
26:     INT var2 = -3; // 11111101, or 0xFD, or -3
27:     printf("var2 = 0x%X, or %i \n", var2, var2);
28:
29:     var2 = var2 << 2;
30:     printf("var2 = 0x%X, or %i \n", var2, var2);
31:
32:     var2 = var2 << 2;
33:     printf("var2 = 0x%X, or %i \n\n", var2, var2);
34:
35:     // Right-shift
36:     printf("Right-Shifting by 2\n\n");
37:
38:     var1 = 128; // 0011, or 0x03, or 3
39:     printf("var1 = 0x%X, or %i \n", var1, var1);
40:
```

LISTING 18.5 Continued

```
41:    var1 = var1 >> 2;
42:    printf("var1 = 0x%X, or %i \n", var1, var1);
43:
44:    var1 = var1 >> 2;
45:    printf("var1 = 0x%X, or %i \n\n", var1, var1);
46:
47:    var2 = -128;
48:    printf("var2 = 0x%X, or %i \n", var2, var2);
49:
50:    var2 = var2 >> 2;
51:    printf("var2 = 0x%X, or %i \n", var2, var2);
52:
53:    var2 = var2 >> 2;
54:    printf("var2 = 0x%X, or %i \n", var2, var2);
55: }
```

The output from the program in Listing 18.5 is as follows:

```
Left-Shifting by 2

var1 = 0x3, or 3
var1 = 0xC, or 12
var1 = 0x30, or 48

var2 = 0xFFFFFFFD, or -3
var2 = 0xFFFFFFF4, or -12
var2 = 0xFFFFFFD0, or -48


Right-Shifting by 2

var1 = 0x80, or 128
var1 = 0x20, or 32
var1 = 0x8, or 8

var2 = 0xFFFFFF80, or -128
var2 = 0xFFFFFFE0, or -32
var2 = 0xFFFFFFF8, or -8
```

As does Listing 18.4, the program in Listing 18.5 uses the Standard C Library function `printf()`. Line 20 performs a left-shift by two places, and line 23 shifts another two places.

The `printf()` statements write the results to the screen after each operation. The rest of the program is similar to lines 20 and 23, except that they use different shifting operations.

Right-shifting is the opposite of left-shifting, and since left-shifting multiplies by two, right-shifting divides by two. If the number being divided isn't a multiple of two, then the resulting fractional part is truncated. To better understand this, take a look at the program in Listing 18.6.

LISTING 18.6   A Program Demonstrating Left-and Right-Shifting on Sequences of Numbers

```
 1: ////////////////////////////////////////////////////
 2: // Module  : shift2.cpp
 3: //
 4: // Purpose : Shows the result of left and right
 5: //           shifting operations.
 6: ////////////////////////////////////////////////////
 7:
 8: #include <iostream.h>
 9:
10: ////////////////////////////////////////////////////
11: // main()
12:
13: void  main()
14: {
15:    int num;
16:
17:    for (int i = 0; i < 10; ++i)
18:    {
19:       num = 10 << i;
20:       cout << "10 << " << i << " == " << num << endl;
21:    }
22:    cout << endl;
23:
24:    for (i = 0; i < 10; ++i)
25:    {
26:       num = 100 >> i;
27:       cout << "100 >> " << i << " == " << num << endl;
28:    }
29: }
```

This program generates the following results from the shift operations:

```
10 << 0 == 10
10 << 1 == 20
10 << 2 == 40
10 << 3 == 80
10 << 4 == 160
10 << 5 == 320
10 << 6 == 640
10 << 7 == 1280
10 << 8 == 2560
10 << 9 == 5120

100 >> 0 == 100
100 >> 1 == 50
100 >> 2 == 25
100 >> 3 == 12
100 >> 4 == 6
100 >> 5 == 3
100 >> 6 == 1
100 >> 7 == 0
100 >> 8 == 0
100 >> 9 == 0
```

As you can see, the left-shift loop doubles the resulting value with each iteration. Similarly, the right-shift loop halves the resulting value with each operation, truncating any fractional parts.

CHAPTER

19

Compiling, Linking, and Debugging

Understand how compilers work

Resolve compiler errors

Understand how linkers work

Resolve linker errors

Automate builds using make files

Find and fix buggy code

Build Process

You must go through the build process (the process of compiling and linking a C++ program) to create an executable file.

Exploring the Compiler

After you have written the source code for a program, you must *build* an executable file by compiling your source files and linking the resulting object modules with any other object modules or libraries needed by the program. Chapter 1, "Getting Started with C++," introduces you to the compiler, and by now, you've undoubtedly had some hands-on experience building programs. Let's consider the compiler. Generally speaking, compiling is the process of converting your text files (source code) into binary object code files (machine code).

Understanding How Compilers Work

Compiling consists of several steps, including the following:

1. Preprocessing
2. Parsing
3. Compiling
4. Optimizing
5. Assembling

Before the compiler begins the compilation process, the preprocessor runs through the source code. The preprocessor expands macros, includes files, and processes any other preprocessor directives, writing the resulting source code to a temporary file.

The compiler then takes over, often running two or more passes over the temporary file created by the preprocessor. The compiler's first pass breaks the code into its basic elements, analyzing the syntax and storing each distinct program element into a collection structure called a *tree*. This process is called *parsing*. The parser then writes the tree data to another temporary, intermediate file.

Generated Object Code

In the next pass, a code generator reads the tree data and generates either assembly language or machine code. If assembly language code is the result (which it usually is), the compiler usually makes one or more passes over the assembly language files, looking for any code that can be optimized. Finally, an assembler assembles the machine code. The end result is an object file (usually having a `.obj` or `.o` extension) for each module used by your program.

Resolving Compiler Errors

It's rare to write a program that compiles properly the first time. You usually have small typographical errors, such as a misspelled object name or a missing semicolon. The compiler finds these syntax errors in your source code and displays corresponding warning and error messages. Sometimes, these messages are cryptic or don't really mean what they seem to mean. The best course of action to take when you get a compiler error that doesn't make sense is to refer to the error number in your compiler's reference manual.

Often, fixing a single compiler error can eliminate all the remaining errors. Listing 19.1 shows the source code for a program with a simple typographical error—a single missing semicolon—that causes a stream of compiler errors.

LISTING 19.1   A Simple Program That Shows How a Single Error in the Source Code Can Trigger a String of Compiler Errors

```
 1: //////////////////////////////////////////////////////
 2: //   Module  : compile.cpp
 3: //
 4: //   Purpose : Demonstrates a string of compiler errors
 5: //             caused by a single typo in the code.
 6: //////////////////////////////////////////////////////
 7:
 8: #include <iostream.h>
 9:
10: void main()
11: {
12:    for(int x = 0, x < 10; ++x)
13:        cout << "x == " << x;
14: }
```

LISTING 19.1

1 Line 12: This comma should be a semicolon

Note

The sample compiler errors shown here were generated by Microsoft Visual C++. Your compiler may give similar, but completely different, error messages.

Modern compilers provide output of what they're doing and list any errors they find during the compile process. Compiler error messages generally tell you where the error occurred, including which source file and line number. The output from the compiler for the erroneous code in Listing 19.1 might look like the following, displaying several error messages:

```
Compiling...
compile.cpp
compile.cpp(12) :
    error C2086: 'x' : redefinition
compile.cpp(12) :
    error C2143: syntax error : missing ';' before '<'
compile.cpp(12) :
    error C2143: syntax error : missing ';' before '<'
compile.cpp(12) :
    error C2143: syntax error : missing ')' before '<'
compile.cpp(12) :
    error C2143: syntax error : missing ';' before '<'
compile.cpp(12) :
    error C2059: syntax error : ')'
compile.cpp(13) :
    error C2143: syntax error : missing ';' before 'tag::id'

compile.exe - 7 error(s), 0 warning(s)
```

By looking up the first error code (C2086) in the compiler reference manual, it becomes plain that the "redefinition" that's taking place on line 12 is the x in the for loop. The compiler thinks the given identifier is defined more than once, because the erroneous comma creates an initializer list. The comma should be a semicolon. By changing the comma in the for clause,

```
for(int x = 0, x < 10; ++x)
    std::cout << "x == " << x;
```

to the semicolon it **should** be,

```
for(int x = 0; x < 10; ++x)
    std::cout << "x == " << x;
```

all seven compiler errors promptly vanish, giving this compiler output:

```
Compiling...
compile.cpp
Linking...

compile.exe - 0 error(s), 0 warning(s)
```

Exploring the Linker

As you learned way back in Chapter 1, a *linker* is a program that works hand-in-hand with the compiler to produce executable files. The linker takes any object code files compiled from your source code and links them with special execution code and with any library code required by your program. The code in a library consists of several object modules grouped together logically and combined by a special *librarian* program into a single library file (usually having a `.lib` extension). The end result is an executable file, typically having an `.exe` file extension, that your target computer platform's operating system can load and run.

Resolving Linker Errors

The linker's job of connecting various modules into an executable program is an important one, but often the linker will find errors that the compiler can't. The most common of these errors is probably duplicate identifiers found in different modules. Here's a very simple example of how this might occur. Assume we have two source files used to build an executable: `temp.cpp` and `temp1.cpp`. For example, here's the complete listing for `temp.cpp`:

```
//////////////////////////////////////////////////////
//   Module  : temp.cpp
//
//   Purpose : Demonstrates linker errors.
//////////////////////////////////////////////////////

#include <iostream.h>

int a = 3;
int b = 4;
```

> **Librarian**
>
> The librarian is a program that links object modules into a static library. A static library contains all the functionality of the combined object modules, and this library code can be linked into your executable files.

```
void main()
{
   cout << a << endl << b << endl;
}
```

Now, here's the complete listing for `temp1.cpp`:

```
/////////////////////////////////////////////////////////
// Module  : temp1.cpp
//
// Purpose : Demonstrates linker errors.
/////////////////////////////////////////////////////////

int a = 1;
int b = 2;
```

Both of these source files will compile without error. The problem arises when you try to link both modules into a single executable program. Since the variables a and b are declared at file scope in both modules, the linker doesn't know which a or b to use in any given situation, resulting in errors such as these (again, generated by Microsoft Visual C++—your linker errors may vary):

```
temp.cpp
Linking...
temp1.obj : error LNK2005:
   "int  b" (?b@@3HA) already defined in temp.obj
temp1.obj : error LNK2005:
   "int  a" (?a@@3HA) already defined in temp.obj
temp.exe : fatal error LNK1169:
   one or more multiply defined symbols found
```

Like compiler errors, linker errors are best resolved by looking up the error message in your linker documentation. It may take several attempts to figure out what the problem is, especially with the cryptic error messages many linkers generate. Perseverance does pay off though, and eventually you'll discover the problem and the program will link, giving you an executable file ready for debugging and testing.

Automating Builds Using Make Files

As you learned in Chapter 1, the make utility automates the compiling and linking process (the build process). In general, the make utility can use directives similar to preprocessor directives and can have comments and macros as well. Typically, a make file coordinates the combination of the compiler, linker, and other tools to create the executable file.

As an example, let's look at a simple make file that automates the build of an executable by coordinating the actions of the compiler and linker. The following make file tells the compiler to build the object files test1.obj and test2.obj, using the source files test1.cpp, test2.cpp, header1.h, header2.h, header3.h, and header4.h. The make file then tells the linker to use the object files test1.obj and test2.obj to build the executable file test.exe. Here's the make file:

```
#
# A simple Make file for Microsoft nmake
#

# Set compiler and linker command line switches
#
CSwitch  = /c /Zpil /G2 /Ox
LnkSwitch = /CO /MAP

# Tell the compiler which files to use to build test1.obj
#
test1.obj: test1.c header1.h header2.h
   cl $(CSwitch) test1.c

# Tell the compiler which files to use to build test2.obj
#
test2.obj: test2.c header3.h header4.h
   cl $(CSwitch) test2.c

# Tell the linker the object files needed to build test.exe
#
test.exe: test1.obj test2.obj
   link $(LnkSwitch) test1+test2
```

Consult Your Make Utility Documentation

Each make utility has its own set of commands and options, so you'll need to check your compiler's documentation for details about the one you use.

Note that make file comments are preceded by the pound symbol (#). This make file sets some compiler and linker command-line switches with the `CSwitch` and `LnkSwitch` statements. The two object files needed for building the `test.exe` program (`test1.obj` and `test2.obj`) are compiled, and then they are linked together to create `test.exe`.

Finding and Fixing Buggy Code

Most compilers do a good job of alerting you to syntax errors in your code, but even after a program compiles and links with no errors and no warnings, you may have potential time bombs waiting to go off. These types of bugs aren't always easy to find—sometimes they're almost impossible to locate. That's why using assertions and handling exceptions, as discussed in Chapter 15, "Bulletproofing Programs with Assertions and Exceptions," can really make a difference in your code, making it much more robust than it might be otherwise.

Adding Debug Code

The process of building a robust program is made much easier by adding debug code to your source code. The debug code can give you all sorts of insights into programming errors, logic errors, and just plain bad program design. Most debug code is handled using macros that expand to nothing when a release version of a program is built. The use of debug code relies on the preprocessor to conditionally compile the debug code into a module only when it is needed.

SEE ALSO

➤ *For more information about preprocessing and conditional compilation, see page 302*

Using the Preprocessor for Debugging

Debug Build

A build that defines a debug symbol, including all supplemental code needed for debugging a program. This debug code can considerably increase program size and reduce performance.

By using preprocessor directives that rely on some debugging symbol (such as `_DEBUG`), you can conditionally compile your programs to either contain the debug code (a *debug build*) or not contain the debug code (a *release build*). By creating a header file that contains any custom macros you want to use for debugging, you provide a reusable way to easily introduce debug code into all your programs.

For example, by defining the debugging symbol _DEBUG in a header file, you can enable debug code in all source files that include that header:

```
#ifndef _DEBUG
    #define _DEBUG
#endif
```

The header file shown in Listing 19.2 is such a file, containing several custom macros used for debugging. This header file provides several macros in both debug and release versions. Table 19.1 gives descriptions of these macros.

Release Build

A build that doesn't define a debug symbol, excluding all debug code from the resulting executable file. Because the debug code is not present, a release build is usually much smaller and faster than a debug build.

TABLE 19.1   **The Macros Provided by *debug.h***

Macro	Description
pause	A macro that uses the DOS command pause to temporarily halt program execution at runtime.
assert	A macro that stringizes and displays as an error message the expression passed in as a parameter if that expression evaluates to false.
ASSERT	A macro that displays an explicit error message sent as a parameter if the expression, also passed in as a parameter, evaluates to false.
ASSERT_MB	The same as the ASSERT macro, but using the Win32 system function MessageBox() to display the error message instead of using cerr.
VERIFY	A macro that verifies that a pointer contains a non-zero address.
CATCH_FLOAT_PTR	A macro that implements a catch handler for floats.
CATCH_INT_PTR	A macro that implements a catch handler for integers.
DELETE	A macro that deletes a valid pointer and then sets it to zero.

LISTING 19.2

1 Line 21: A pause macro for DOS systems

LISTING 19.2   A Header File That Contains Customized Macros Useful for Debugging

```
 1: //////////////////////////////////////////////////////////
 2: //   Module   : debug.h
 3: //
 4: //   Purpose : Supplies useful debugging macros
 5: //////////////////////////////////////////////////////////
 6:
 7: #ifndef __DEBUG_H__
 8: #define __DEBUG_H__
 9:
10: #include <iostream.h>
11: #include <stdlib.h>
12: #include <stdio.h>
13:
14: // Define the debug symbol (comment this out for
15: // release builds)
16:
17: #ifndef _DEBUG
18:    #define _DEBUG
19: #endif
20:
21: #define pause   system("pause") ──────1
22:
23: // Replace existing assert and ASSERT with the
24: // macros in this file
25:
26: #ifdef assert
27:    #undef assert
28: #endif
29:
30: #ifdef ASSERT
31:    #undef ASSERT
32: #endif
33:
34: #ifdef ASSERT_VALID
35:    #undef ASSERT_VALID
36: #endif
37:
38: // Define assert and ASSERT for debug and
39: // release builds
40:
```

```
41: #if defined(_DEBUG)
42:
43:    // Define the debug macros
44:
45:    // The stock assert macro, sans exit()
46:    //
47:    #define assert                                    \ ─┐
48:      if (!)                                          \  │
49:      {                                               \  │
50:         cerr << "\nAssertion Failed: " << #a          \  │
51:            << "\nFailure occurred on line "          \   ➋
52:            << __LINE__ << " of source file:"         \  │
53:            << "\n   \"" << __FILE__ << "\"\n";        \  │
54:      } ───────────────────────────────────────────────┘
55:
56:    // The ASSERT macro takes a string argument
57:    //
58:    #define ASSERT(a, str)                            \ ─┐
59:      if (!)                                          \  │
60:      {                                               \  │
61:         cerr << "\nAssertion Failed: " << #a          \  │
62:            << " " << #str                            \   ➌
63:            << "\nFailure occurred on line "          \  │
64:            << __LINE__ << " of source file:"         \  │
65:            << "\n   \"" << __FILE__ << "\"\n";        \  │
66:      } ───────────────────────────────────────────────┘
67:
68:    // The ASSERT_MB macro takes a string argument
69:    //
70:    #ifdef _WIN32
71:      #define ASSERT_MB                               \ ─┐
72:        if (!)                                        \  │
73:        {                                             \  │
74:           char _buf[256];                             \  │
75:           sprintf(_buf,                               \  │
76:              "\nAssertion Failed: %s"                 \  │
77:              "\n\nFailure occurred on line %d "       \   ➍
78:              " of source file: \"%s\" ", #a,          \  │
79:              __LINE__, __FILE__);                      \  │
80:           MessageBox(0, _buf,                          \  │
81:              "Assertion Failure",                     \  │
82:              MB_OK | MB_ICONSTOP);                     \  │
83:        } ─────────────────────────────────────────────┘
```

LISTING 19.2 CONTINUED

➋ Lines 47-54: Define the debug assert macro

➌ Lines 58-66: Define the debug ASSERT macro

➍ Lines 71-83: Define the debug ASSERT_MB macro for Win32

continues...

LISTING 19.2 **Continued**

```
84:
85:    #else
86:       #define ASSERT_MB
87:    #endif // ifdef _WIN32
88:
89:    #define VALIDATE(ptr)                              \
90:       if (!(ptr))                                     \
91:       {                                               \
92:          cerr << "\nValidation Failed: Pointer '"  \
93:             << #ptr << "' is null.\n"                 \
94:             << "Failure occurred on line "           \
95:             << __LINE__ << " of source file:"        \
96:             << "\n   \"" << __FILE__ << "\"\n";       \
97:          throw(ptr);                                  \
98:       }
99:
100: #else
101:
102:    // Define the release macros
103:    //
104:    #define assert
105:    #define ASSERT(a, str)
106:    #define ASSERT_MB
107:
108:    #define VALIDATE(ptr)    if (!ptr) throw(ptr)
109:
110: #endif // #if defined(_DEBUG)
111:
112: #define CATCH_FLOAT_PTR                             \
113: catch(float *)                                      \
114: {                                                   \
115:    cerr << "Invalid float pointer.\n"              \
116:       << "Failure occurred on line "               \
117:       << __LINE__ << " of source file:"            \
118:       << "\n   \"" << __FILE__ << "\"\n";           \
119: }
120:
121: #define CATCH_INT_PTR                               \
122: catch(int *)                                        \
123: {                                                   \
124:    cerr << "Invalid int pointer.\n"                \
125:       << "Failure occurred on line "               \
126:       << __LINE__ << " of source file:"            \
127:       << "\n   \"" << __FILE__ << "\"\n";           \
128: }
```

```
129:
130: #define DELETE(p)  if (p) delete p; p = 0
131:
132: #endif //__DEBUG_H__
```

Strategies for Testing and Debugging

As you write your source code, use assertions liberally. This single strategy can save you countless hours of time that might be otherwise wasted searching for elusive bugs. The use of assertions can quickly weed out any logic errors or programming mistakes. Assertions also help to make your code more readable by providing code that is self-documenting.

The next strategy is a thorough testing of all program features with various types of data a user might input into the program at runtime. You can never know what a user might try to do with a program, so you've got to be prepared for anything—users often input some oddball data, so make sure that you check for a wide variety of error conditions. This type of "thinking like a user" can alert you to areas that need better exception handling or revised program logic.

With a debugger, step through every line of source code you write. Never assume that your code will work, even if it looks correct, because a simple typo can cause unexpected results. After you're confident that a section of code works as you intended, you can move on, writing and debugging new code. Set breakpoints in the source code to allow you to isolate problems quickly. By adding *watches* to objects, you can see their values as you step through the code.

By executing a program up to a breakpoint, then stepping through the code one line at a time while watching object values, it's usually fairly easy to find and eliminate bugs. Figure 19.1 shows several watches set in the Microsoft Visual C++ debugger (in the lower pane) and a breakpoint allowing line-by-line analysis of some troublesome source code.

Watch Variables

A watch variable is a symbol you create in a debugger to watch the value of the variable as the program runs in the debugger. Used in combination with breakpoints, watches are powerful debugging tools.

Breakpoint

A breakpoint is a marker you create in a debugger to temporarily halt (break) execution at some point in your code as the program runs in the debugger. Used in combination with watch variables, breakpoints are powerful debugging tools.

FIGURE 19.1

Microsoft Visual C++ at runtime, with a breakpoint and several watches set in the debugger.

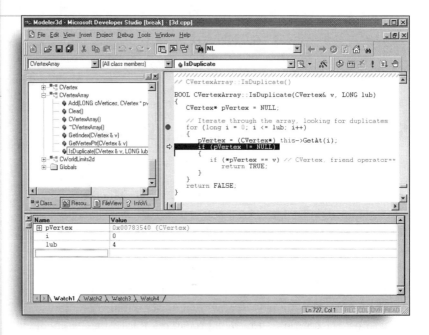

The program in Listing 19.3 is a simple driver program that tests the functionality of the debug.h header file shown in Listing 19.2.

LISTING 19.3

① Line 11: Begin a try block to enable exception handling

LISTING 19.3   A Driver Program to Test the Functionality of *debug.h*

```
 1: //////////////////////////////////////////////////////////
 2: //  Module : driver.cpp
 3: //
 4: //  Purpose : Testing the debugging header: debug.h
 5: //////////////////////////////////////////////////////////
 6:
 7: #include "debug.h"
 8:
 9: void main()
10: {
11:     try ————①
12:     {
13:         double *array = new double[1000];
14:
15:         for (int i = 0; i < 1000; ++i)
```

```
16:      {
17:          cout << "Validating &array[" << i << "]\n";
18:          VALIDATE(&array[i]); ——————②
19:      }
20:
21:      delete [] array;
22:
23:      float *pf = new float;
24:      VALIDATE(pf);
25:      *pf = 5.5f;
26:
27:      DELETE(pf); ——————③
28:      VALIDATE(pf);
29:      *pf = 5.5f;
30:
31:  }
32:  CATCH_FLOAT_PTR ——————
33:  CATCH_INT_PTR ——————④
34: }
```

LISTING 19.3 CONTINUED

② Line 18: Use the VALIDATE macro to validate the address of each array element

③ Line 27: Use the DELETE macro to delete the object a pointer points to

④ Lines 32-33: Use the CATCH_FLOAT_PTR and CATCH_INT_PTR macros as catch handlers

The output from this driver program is as follows:

```
Validating &array[0]
Validating &array[0]
Validating &array[1]
Validating &array[2]
...
Validating &array[996]
Validating &array[997]
Validating &array[998]
Validating &array[999]

Validation Failed: Pointer 'pf' is null.
Failure occurred on line 28 of source file:
    "F:\Using C++\source\chap19\driver.cpp"
Invalid float pointer.
Failure occurred on line 32 of source file:
    "F:\Using C++\source\chap19\driver.cpp"
```

The problem is that the validation of pointer pf fails. Let's take a look at what's going on here.

The program begins by creating an array of 1,000 integers on line 13. Lines 15 through 20 then run the elements of the array through the VALIDATE() macro to validate that the address for each element is non-zero. As you can see from the program output, the elements of the array successfully pass the VALIDATE() test. Line 21 deletes the array, preventing a memory leak.

Line 23 creates a pointer to a float (pf) and assigns to it the address of a newly allocated float object. The VALIDATE() macro on line 24 validates the address stored in the pointer, and on line 27, the float object is deleted. Line 28 attempts to validate the pointer again, but the validation fails because the pointer's value is zero. Line 29 throws a float exception because pf is invalid and can't be assigned a float value. This exception triggers the catch handler macro CATCH_FLOAT_PTR on line 32.

It's interesting to look at the fully preprocessed source file, comparing the results when the preprocessor symbol _DEBUG *is* defined and when it *is **not*** defined. Most compilers allow you to view the fully preprocessed source files; Listing 19.4 shows what the main() function looks like when it is fully preprocessed ***without*** defining _DEBUG (the release version).

LISTING 19.4

1 Line 9: The expanded release version of the VALIDATE macro

2 Line 16: The expanded release version of the DELETE macro

LISTING 19.4   **The Fully Preprocessed Release Version of *main()***

```
 1: void main()
 2: {
 3:    try
 4:    {
 5:        double *array = new double[1000];
 6:        for (int i = 0; i < 1000; ++i)
 7:        {
 8:           cout << "Validating &array[" << i << "]\n";
 9:           if (!&array[i]) throw(&array[i]);    ———①
10:        }
11:        delete [] array;
12:        float *pf = new float;
13:        if (!pf) throw(pf);
14:        *pf = 5.5f;
15:
16:        if (pf) delete pf; pf = 0;    ———②
17:        if (!pf) throw(pf);
```

```
18:        *pf = 5.5f;
19:     }
20:     catch(float *)
21:     {
22:        cerr << "Invalid float pointer.\n"
23:           << "Failure occurred on line " << 32
24:           << " of source file:" << "\n   \""
25:           << "F:\\Using C++\\source\\chap19\\driver.cpp"
26:           << "\"\n";
27:     }
28:     catch(int *)
29:     {
30:        cerr << "Invalid int pointer.\n"
31:           << "Failure occurred on line " << 33
32:           << " of source file:" << "\n   \""
33:           << "F:\\Using C++\\source\\chap19\\driver.cpp"
34:           << "\"\n";
35:     }
36: }
```

LISTING 19.4 CONTINUED

3 Lines 20-27: The expanded release version of the CATCH_ FLOAT_PTR macro

4 Lines 28-35: The expanded release version of the CATCH_INT_PTR macro

By defining _DEBUG in debug.h and recompiling, the main() function becomes much different because the debug code is compiled in. Listing 19.5 shows what the main() function looks like when it is fully preprocessed *with* _DEBUG defined (the debug version).

LISTING 19.5   **The Fully Preprocessed Debug Version of *main()***

```
1: void main()
2: {
3:     try
4:     {
5:        double *array = new double[1000];
6:        for (int i = 0; i < 1000; ++i)
7:        {
8:           cout << "Validating &array[" << i << "]\n";
9:           if (!(&array[i]))
10:          {
11:             cerr << "\nValidation Failed: Pointer '"
12:                << "&array[i]" << "' is null.\n"
13:                << "Failure occurred on line " << 20
14:                << " of source file:" << "\n   \""
15:                << "driver.cpp" << "\"\n";
16:             throw(&array[i]);
17:          };
```

LISTING 19.5

1 Lines 9-17: The expanded debug version of the VALIDATE macro

continues...

LISTING 19.5 CONTINUED

2 Line 34: The expanded debug version of the DELETE macro

3 Lines 45-51: The expanded debug version of the CATCH_FLOAT_PTR macro

4 Lines 52-58: The expanded debug version of the CATCH_INT_PTR macro

LISTING 19.5   Continued

```
18:         }
19:         delete [] array;
20:         int *pi = 0;
21:
22:         float *pf = new float;
23:         if (!(pf))
24:         {
25:            cerr << "\nValidation Failed: Pointer '"
26:               << "pf" << "' is null.\n"
27:               << "Failure occurred on line " << 28
28:               << " of source file:" << "\n    \""
29:               << "driver.cpp" << "\"\n";
30:            throw(pf);
31:         };
32:         *pf = 5.5f;
33:
34:         if (pf) delete pf; pf = 0;
35:         if (!(pf)) {
36:            cerr << "\nValidation Failed: Pointer '"
37:               << "pf" << "' is null.\n"
38:               << "Failure occurred on line " << 32
39:               << " of source file:" << "\n    \""
40:               << "driver.cpp" << "\"\n";
41:            throw(pf);
42:         };
43:         *pf = 5.5f;
44:      }
45:   catch(float *)
46:   {
47:      cerr << "Invalid float pointer.\n"
48:         << "Failure occurred on line " << 36
49:         << " of source file:" << "\n    \""
50:         << "driver.cpp" << "\"\n";
51:   }
52:   catch(int *)
53:   {
54:      cerr << "Invalid int pointer.\n"
55:         << "Failure occurred on line " << 37
56:         << " of source file:" << "\n    \""
57:         << "driver.cpp" << "\"\n";
58:   }
59: }
```

By using the macros defined in debug.h, along with any macros you write yourself—along with exception handling, you're well on your way to creating robust, bug-free programs.

PART

III

Object-Oriented Programming

Introducing Object-Oriented Programming

Learn the fundamentals of object-oriented programming (OOP)

See the differences between procedural programming and OOP

Understand the concept of objects

Find out about polymorphism and virtual methods

Find out about the relationship of objects to classes in C++

Examine the benefits of code reuse

Fundamentals of Object-Oriented Programming

Your ability to quickly develop robust applications is directly related to your ability to create reusable software modules (classes). C++ allows you to fully realize the potential of object-oriented programming (OOP); in this chapter, you'll gain insight into how to unleash the OOP power C++ offers.

C++ can allow you to take advantage of code reuse through the development of new object classes and code libraries. In particular, this chapter provides a discussion of object-oriented programming techniques as applied to C++. These techniques are used in subsequent chapters to show you how to develop robust object-oriented programs in C++. In the following sections, we'll discuss these essential object-oriented programming concepts:

- How OOP simplifies the development process through inheritance and polymorphism
- The benefits of writing reusable object classes and code
- Why OOP cuts development and debugging time
- How class libraries can make software construction easier

Moving from Procedural Programming to OOP

Whether you're a novice C++ programmer, a C programmer, or a programmer moving to C++ from some other procedural language who is trying to get a better handle on object-oriented programming, this section should shed a little light on the benefits and concepts of OOP.

In the late 1960s, the concept of procedural programming arose from the need to increase programmer productivity. Procedural programming made program construction easier than coding directly in assembly language. Procedural languages like Pascal and C provided a higher level of abstraction and made this greater productivity possible. The concept of reusable functions made procedural programming possible. With the advent of procedures, functions, and high-level languages, programmers could produce code much faster than ever before.

After a short time, with new methodologies of modularization and data hiding, procedural programming evolved into structured programming. Structured programming made larger programs easier to design and maintain. Almost everything you've seen in this book so far has been procedural/structured programming.

Not long after structured programming came into vogue, the idea of object-oriented programming (OOP) came about as a natural evolutionary extension of the concepts and methodology used in procedural/structured programming.

Although, for many people, the concept of OOP is a new way of thinking about program design and construction, OOP has actually been around for nearly 30 years. Smalltalk, the first object-oriented programming language, was developed at the famous Palo Alto Research Center (PARC) labs in the early 1970s. C++ borrows many of its object-oriented ideas from Smalltalk. After almost two decades, the OOP paradigm (or model) has finally caught on and has moved into the mainstream of computer programming—it's become not only accepted, but even fashionable. But OOP isn't about jumping on the bandwagon—OOP is both an art and a science, the technique of creating programs that are collections of objects that know how to interact with each other to accomplish a program's design goals.

Black Boxes and Bugs

In procedural programming, chunks of program code are broken into modules and functions that are built as "black boxes." These black boxes hide from the programmer the complexity of what's inside them, and each box attempts to hide information within to prevent unwanted or unauthorized data access.

In theory, the black box doesn't write outside its boundaries. It's not supposed to change any data not under its jurisdiction, and it shouldn't introduce any side effects (bugs) into the program. Unfortunately, this is difficult to accomplish in real-world procedural programs, and the number of side effects introduced into the system usually grows proportionately with the size of the program. The larger a program gets, the more inclined programmers are to let data become global, easing their programming burden. Although the global data makes writing the program easier, more bugs are likely to appear in the code.

The Object Advantage

Procedural programming generally takes the route of converting real-world problems into computer-like terms to support the writing of a program. Object-oriented programming takes a different approach to solving problems by using a program model that mirrors the real-world problem. By thinking about the problem in real-world terms, you can often find a natural object-oriented solution.

You should identify items that can be broken out into computer data models and show the interrelationships naturally defined by the problem. These items may or may not actually exist in the real world, but are represented in the computer as new data types known as *objects*. Objects are defined in code by the data structures we call *classes*, and classes know how to perform specific actions by intercepting *messages* and acting on them with *methods*. If these OOP terms are new to you, just remember the following:

Runtime Instance

An object—a variable of some data type that is created at runtime.

- An ***object*** is simply a *runtime instance* of a class (the actual object created from the class specification when a program runs).

- ***Methods*** are class member functions contained within the object, as defined in the class specification.

- ***Messages*** are the actual function calls made to class member functions.

SEE ALSO

➤ *For more information about C++ classes, see page 486*

➤ *For more information about class member functions, see page 505*

Conceptualizing Objects

To help you visualize the relationship of a class to an object *of* that class, imagine a beautiful car with all the most expensive options. A car like this doesn't just magically appear—it has to be built by someone. The auto workers who build such a car can't just make it up as they go along and hope that a successful and safe car will result from their efforts. A skilled designer has to conceptualize and design the car, often from the ground up. Before the car is built, the designer must draw diagrams (schematics and blueprints) for every part of the car. These diagrams give the mechanical and electrical engineers the exact specifications they need to construct the car. In this example, the specification represents the class; the car is the actual object constructed to this specification (see Figure 20.1).

Class or Object?

In this book, the terms *class* and *object* are often interchangeably, but be aware that there *is* a difference. An object is a runtime instance of a class. The distinction between class and object is that you can use a class to build many objects, but an object can only have one class.

FIGURE 20.1

A class is the schematic diagram that gives the exact specifications for the construction of an object.

Of course, we realize that a car isn't the same as a drawing of a car, but on an abstract level, they *are* one and the same. All the details about the construction of the car are present in the specification, and everything that's in the specification can be found in the car. This is the relationship of class to object.

During program execution, a program creates an object to the exact specifications given by the class. The object contains its class data safely tucked away inside itself and relies on the class specification for its functionality. An object can manipulate itself through the use of its class methods. Object data is stored inside the object—not as global data. This storage of data within the object is referred to as *encapsulation*.

SEE ALSO

➤ *For more information on encapsulation, see page 487*

To provide access to its data and methods, an object exposes itself to other objects using its *class interface*. In addition to being able to control its own actions, if an object knows about other objects, it can manipulate those objects as well (using the other object's class interfaces). A C++ class interface is usually declared in a header (.h) file that specifies the class structure and functionality. The implementations of class methods are then defined in a source (.cpp) file.

SEE ALSO

➤ *To learn how to design class interfaces, see page 512*

➤ *To see how to implement a class interface, see page 516*

The C++ keywords private, protected, and public give you complete control over which objects have access to any given object's data. These keywords are how C++ lets you prevent the data access side-effects so often found in procedural programming languages like Pascal and C.

SEE ALSO

➤ *To learn how to use the access specifiers, see page 489*

Naming Classes

Classes used in examples and code listings in this book use the naming convention in which a class name always begins with an uppercase C. For example, a class that models an automobile might have the imaginative name **CAutomobile**, and a class that models a camera might have the name **CCamera**.

Inheritance

One of the things programmers new to OOP find most astonishing is that objects can inherit properties and functionality from other objects to form parent-child relationships and object hierarchies. What this means to the programmer is that code can be broken into several layers of functionality, and that this functionality can be built one layer at a time into different classes with various abilities—all from a common set of source code. This layering and sharing of code allows the design of class hierarchies, in which objects grow organically from each other, very much like things are organized in the real world.

The process of creating a new class from an existing class is called *inheritance*. Inheritance provides the new, derived (child) class with all the functionality contained in the base (parent, or ancestor) class, and allows you to extend the class's capabilities to provide solutions specific to the new class.

Let's go back to the example of a car. A car isn't the most basic type of vehicle—you would want to establish an abstract base class that defines the common characteristics and abilities of all types of transport vehicles. Assume that you design a base class and call it CVehicle. From this abstract base class, you can create various types of more specialized vehicle objects.

You could derive the classes CLandVehicle, CWaterVehicle, and CAirVehicle directly from CVehicle. Each derived class would inherit all the abstract capabilities of CVehicle but would have member variables and functions added to refine the class definition for each type of vehicle. These classes could be further refined by deriving new classes from these first-level derived classes. From CLandVehicle, for example, we could derive CTruck, CCar, and CMotorcycle. From CWaterVehicle, we could derive CShip, CBoat, and CJetSki. CAirVehicle could spawn CPlane, CGlider, and CHelicopter. These classes are all derived from the base class CVehicle to form the simple class hierarchy shown in Figure 20.2.

When working on a new project, the best thing to do is to analyze the problem at hand and begin designing a set of classes into just such a class hierarchy. Use inheritance extensively, but wisely. By keeping the classes small and focused at each level of the hierarchy, you can leverage more code for reuse in the new classes. The trick is to keep the attributes and operations common to all objects at any given level of an object hierarchy in the base classes, and to derive the more specialized classes from these.

FIGURE 20.2

A graphical representation of the fictional `CVehicle` class hierarchy.

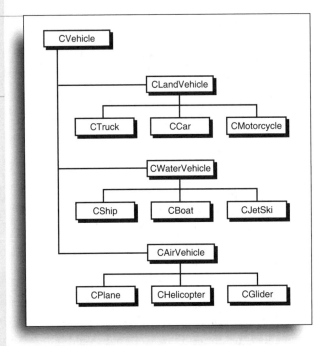

The base class `CVehicle` contains all properties common to land, water, and air vehicles: they all move under their own power (or whatever properties they are that these vehicles share). The `CLandVehicle` class narrows down the definition by defining properties common only to land vehicles. Remember that the `CLandVehicle` class inherits all the properties defined in its parent class, `CVehicle`, so it isn't necessary for the `CLandVehicle` class to re-specify the property of self-propulsion. However, the `CLandVehicle` class does have a property that neither the `CWaterVehicle` or `CAirVehicle` classes possess: land vehicles all have wheels. The number of wheels each land vehicle has is a property that can be specified in the even-more-specific classes `CTruck`, `CCar`, and `CMotorcycle`—and so on, as necessary.

Saving Time with OOP

OOP saves development time because classes that have already been written and debugged are sure to be free of side effects. When bugs manifest themselves in new, derived class code, the bugs can **only** be located in the derived class code.

Inheritance offers another useful feature that should be exploited whenever possible. This is the fact that small, efficient, focused classes that have been fully debugged are *reliable*. As you derive more complex classes from the debugged base classes, the only code you have to worry about is the *new* code that's been added to the derived class. Each iteration of class development and inheritance produces a small amount of code that is built on (and fully compatible with) the fully debugged code of its ancestor classes. Any bugs found in derived classes can be pin-pointed in the new code of the derived class. Keeping classes small and focused on specific goals makes debugging easier at each level of a class hierarchy.

SEE ALSO

➤ *To learn more about class inheritance, see page 522*

➤ *To learn more about class hierarchies, see page 523*

Introducing Polymorphism and Virtual Methods

Another great feature of OOP is the ability of different types of objects to react differently to the same function calls. Imagine two classes, one inherited from the other, that both contain a method called Draw(). Each class can respond differently to the Draw() message depending on just *what* the class is supposed to draw. The potential of different objects in a hierarchy to respond differently to the same message is known as *polymorphism*, which literally means many shapes, or shape-shifter.

Polymorphism is accomplished through the use of *virtual* methods, and is as important as inheritance in the realm of OOP. A virtual method in a base class allows a derived class to change the implementation of the method. The example of different classes exhibiting polymorphic responses to the Draw() method can occur only with virtual methods, with the derived class *overriding* the virtual Draw() method of its ancestor class.

Staying with the metaphor of a car, let's use the fictional CLandVehicle class introduced in the preceding section as an example. Suppose that CLandVehicle contains a Draw() method that, because CLandVehicle is very abstract, simply draws a box. The two classes CCar and CTruck are derived from the CLandVehicle class, which means that they inherit the Draw() function and know how to draw a box. Because these two derived classes aren't as abstract as their parent, however, they can each override the Draw() function differently to draw something more appropriate than a box (such as a car or a truck). Figure 20.3 shows a CLandVehicle object and the two derived objects all responding differently to the Draw() function.

Use Intermediary Classes

The vehicle hierarchy example is a bit sketchy, at best. In practice, the two classes CCar and CTruck wouldn't derive directly from the base class CLandVehicle, but from one or more intermediary classes; CFourWheel-LandVehicle, for instance.

FIGURE 20.3

Polymorphism allows related objects to respond differently to the same Draw() message.

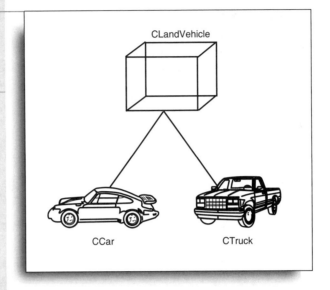

To get polymorphic

1. Create a base class with at least one virtual method.

2. Derive a new class or classes from the base class.

3. In the derived class, override the virtual method from the base class.

4. Respond differently to the virtual method in each derived class.

To put it simply, an ancestor class passes on all its virtual member functions and protected data members to its descendants. The descendants of the ancestor class can change (override) the implementation of any method that has been declared as virtual in the base class.

SEE ALSO

➤ *To learn more about polymorphism, see page 547*

Object-Oriented Software Strategies

The procedural and object-oriented approaches both work. When tackling a real-world problem, you have the choice of using either programming model. Although you can solve a problem using either the procedural or the object-oriented paradigm, you'll soon see how the object-oriented approach is more intuitive.

When using either approach, it's not good programming practice to just rush in and begin coding. You must first go through the basic analysis and design phases of software construction. The idea for a program usually begins as an abstract concept, such as "We need to keep better track of our inventory." At the start, there's no detailed plan, no clear-cut path to program design.

In commercial development, a software engineer is often at the helm of a project, so there is a skilled artisan who can create the conceptual model and design the class relationships and interfaces. In smaller development projects though, this isn't the case; more often than not, the programmer is also the software designer. When you're the software architect, **you** must decide on the best course of action.

In the procedural model, program design is completely function based, and you run through a series of statements and function calls, hopefully ending up with the data you need. The object-oriented design likely contains similar functions, but they are encapsulated into classes to make the design more logical and self-contained.

Virtual Functions, Inherited Data Members, and Code Bloat

As you derive more specialized classes from more general classes, you create an *inheritance chain*. The inheritance chain carries the code for all virtual functions and protected data members with it. The linker looks through the base class's compiled object (.obj) code to find the virtual functions and protected data members; it then links these items into each of the derived classes.

A derived object contains a lookup table called a *virtual function table* (also called a *v-table*, or *VTBL*). This table contains entries that point to the memory addresses of any virtual functions inherited from its ancestors. When an inherited function is called, the object looks into its v-table and uses the function pointer stored there to call the proper version of the function from its ancestor code.

Because of this inheritance chain, it's imperative to keep classes as tightly focused and abstract as possible. Each class from which you derive other classes should perform only the bare minimum it needs to do. Classes at the bottom of a class hierarchy can suffer from "code bloat" if the programmer isn't extremely careful and meticulous about keeping base classes trimmed to the bare bones. Keep classes abstract at the top of a hierarchy, making them more detailed and functional as you inherit.

Assume that a base class ClassA has four functions and four data members. Two of the functions are virtual, and two of the data members are protected. When you derive a new class ClassB from ClassA, the new class inherits both virtual functions and both protected members. If ClassB doesn't need some portion of ClassA's inherited functionality, you're propagating code bloat. Suppose that you now add four more member functions and six more data members to ClassB. Two of these member functions are virtual, and two are protected data members.

If you derive another class ClassC from ClassB, that third-level class gets not only the inherited code from ClassB, but the code from ClassA as well. Figure 20.4 demonstrates the concept of code bloat. The problem compounds itself when several classes in an inheritance chain contain members that their descendants won't ever use. This is an indication that more intermediate classes need to be defined to filter out commonality and to eliminate the code bloat.

Reuse Your Classes

You can reuse classes in any number of projects. Because of the self-contained nature of objects, classes can be reused in any programming project, saving countless hours of development time. Eliminate from your classes as many dependencies as you can to promote more robust reusability.

Understanding Objects and Classes in C++

C++ is a fully object-oriented language that improves programmer productivity with its object-oriented capabilities and class templates. It also improves code readability and maintenance by providing a clean interface to object data. Specifically, C++ allows you to do the following:

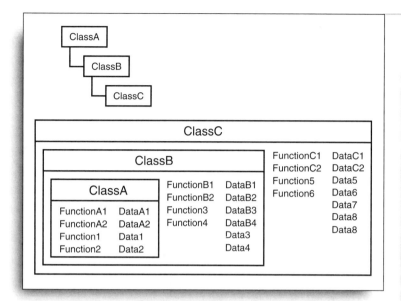

FIGURE 20.4

A representation of code bloat in a class inheritance chain.

- Create libraries of objects that can be reused freely

- Modify objects that don't quite suit the task at hand by using inheritance to extend the object's abilities, and by using polymorphism to change an object's response to an existing virtual method

- Maintain your source code more easily and to incrementally debug small sections of code one class at a time

C++ delivers the power of OOP into your hands. A class (the *code* side of the coin) defines the behavior and the public interface for an object (the *executable* side of the coin). In other words, a class defines, both conceptually and in code, the capabilities, data, properties, and actions of a runtime object. Of course, it can start to get confusing when you develop a program that contains lots of files and classes. When you're working with a large number of classes and files, it can be hard to find class member functions when you need them, or even which file a specific class was defined in.

Luckily, modern programming tools can really decrease application development time. Complete development environments such as Borland C++, Borland C++Builder, and Microsoft Visual C++ can make your life much easier by offering object browsers and class design tools. Figure 20.5 shows the Microsoft Visual C++ Class Browser, a tool that makes maintaining and working with classes, functions, and variables easy by focusing on the classes themselves, not on the files that declare and define the classes. In Figure 20.5, the class browser shows all the classes and class members used by the program at a glance.

FIGURE 20.5

The Microsoft Visual C++ Class Browser makes maintaining and working with classes easy.

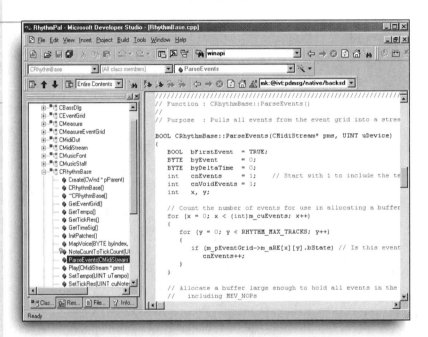

This level of abstraction makes it easier to focus on the overall structure of a program, not which files are involved. Class browsers are especially helpful when you are working with programs containing a large number of classes—you don't have to try to remember the source file in which a class, variable, or function resides. The browser remembers for you, so that you can concentrate on programming.

Examining the Benefits of Code Reuse

The idea of writing reusable code certainly isn't new—programmers have been doing it for years (or at least trying hard to do it for years). Electronics hardware manufacturers long ago discovered the benefits of the assembly line, designing and making components that can be used in countless electronic gadgets. For decades, computer programmers have struggled to reach the ideal of creating reusable software components that can be snapped into place in different programming projects.

Stop Reinventing the Wheel

You can save an incredible amount of development time by reusing code that has already been written and debugged. By using consistent interface and coding styles in your code, you can generate better code faster. With the proper interfaces in place, a class or class library can be seamlessly integrated into any project with a few `#include` statements. The knowledge that the reusable code has already been thoroughly debugged and tested lets you concentrate on creating new classes and code. This is, of course, highly preferable to wasting valuable development time debugging a buggy old cut-and-paste coding job that's been rehacked into any number of applications.

In its most basic terms, reusable code must present its interface to the outside world, usually in the form of a header (`.h`) file. Encapsulation of your code into C++ classes allows the code to be easily snapped into place in any C++ application that requires the functionality provided.

The moral: Stop reinventing the wheel! C++ allows you to create new objects from existing objects and to add to or override the methods and data within—even if the source code isn't available! Existing class libraries like the Microsoft Foundation Class (MFC) library and Borland's Visual Component Library (VCL) contain a plethora of classes that can be cultivated and extended through inheritance and polymorphism.

Component Software

With the advent of Microsoft's ActiveX components and Sun's JavaBeans, the holy grail of plug-in software is closer than ever before. The two big object-oriented development camps— the Component Object Model (COM) and the Common Object Request Broker Architecture (CORBA)—promise to give developers the benefits of object-oriented design and distributed programming, while supporting platform and language independence.

Simplify Your Overall Development Process with OOP

After base classes have been developed, new classes can be derived on demand to perform the additional operations you may need, without rewriting all the code or cutting and pasting code from one project to another (in which case the code would most likely have to be modified). Inheritance and polymorphism make quick work of deriving and modifying new classes.

If you concentrate on writing classes that promote code reuse, you'll save a lot of development time and a lot of money in long-term development costs. Class libraries speed the development process greatly by making it easy to quickly add features to your programs.

Using Code Libraries

C++ was designed to be an extensible language, and you should strive to create function libraries and class libraries you can reuse in any project. The C++ language is fast, portable, and powerful, providing the tools you need to perform any programming task and making the solutions you design available to all your programs, if the need arises.

SEE ALSO

➤ *To learn more about creating libraries, see page 542*

Understanding C++ Classes

Discover C++ classes and class design

Learn to encapsulate data and functions into C++ classes

Understand the *this* pointer

Discover how to use constructors and destructors

See how to specify access to class members

Creating C++ Classes

If there's one thing that truly sets C++ head and shoulders above C, it's got to be *classes*. C++ classes offer you an elegant, object-oriented solution to writing code that's easy to maintain and modify. In procedural programming languages, you typically create data structures and write functions to manipulate them, but in C++, you can bind the functions to the data that the functions act on. The class is the cornerstone of object-oriented programming in C++.

Thinking About Class Design

Back in Chapter 9, "Using Structures and Unions," you learned about structures. Unlike the structures allowed by a C compiler, structures in C++ are actually classes. The only difference between a struct and a class is the default access specification: By default, a struct uses public access, and a class uses private access (you'll see more about *access specifiers* later in this chapter). The bottom line is that everything you learned about structures in Chapter 9 applies to classes, and everything about classes in this chapter applies to structures—a structure is just a class with public access.

When creating a new class, you go through several phases of what's commonly called *class construction*. Generally, you follow steps similar the these:

Designing a class

1. Think about the class design. Try to conceptualize what the class should accomplish. Think about the class as a runtime object. What kind of properties and capabilities should that object have? How should it interact with other objects?

2. List any relevant data that should be encapsulated within the object as data members.

3. List the things the object knows or does, and encapsulate this data within the object as member functions.

4. Solidify the class interface. Write the class declaration and explore the relationships between data members and

Access Specifier

An access specifier defines the type of data access that class members make use of. The access specifier can specify public, private, or protected access to the class.

function members. Think about what data should be exposed to everyone, and what data should be hidden.

Classes don't often spring to life on the first attempt. I often find that my classes go through several changes as I work with them. You'll usually go through several iterations of class interface design. This is the normal course of things. When you add a new class to an existing program, you'll sometimes see new relationships that become possible, new ways of doing things with existing classes. It's at times like these that classes go through interface changes to accommodate the brilliant "new way" of interfacing the classes.

I often design a group of classes to work together, each relying somehow on another class's capabilities. This type of interaction between classes is called *coupling*. Coupling can be tight (usually considered to be a bad thing) or loose (usually considered to be a good thing). Loose coupling is preferable because, by definition, each class is more independent and therefore, more reusable.

Encapsulating Data

A class is like a "wrapper" you wrap around your data and the functions that manipulate that data. Classes *encapsulate* data through the use of member variables (data members) and member functions. A class binds them into a cohesive unit. When used properly, encapsulation makes complex processes easier by hiding the complexity from the user. In this case, the *user* in question is the user of the class, and this is usually you. The beauty of class creation is that once the class is complete, its complexity is hidden behind its interface to the outside world (its class declaration).

As a programmer, you'll often need to find solutions to many puzzling problems. Once you find a solution, you should make it reusable if possible. Making the manipulation of data *easy* is a prime goal of object-oriented programming. With C++ classes, you can extend the language as you see fit, adding the functionality you need by building your own libraries of code. This entire process starts with a single class.

Class Construction

Class construction is the act of designing and implementing a new class.

Coupling

To varying degrees, coupling is the amount of dependence one class has on another class in a set of classes designed to work together.

Encapsulation

The storage of data, and the operations to be performed on that data, within an object.

Class Instances

When you declare a variable of some class type, you create an *instance* of that class. This instance is called an *object*—a runtime object of a specified class type.

Declaring Classes

Class declaration is extremely important. The declaration is like a contract between the class and the user of the class (that's you, the programmer). The declaration is the well-defined interface to the class. Careful consideration in designing a class declaration makes using the class easier and more intuitive. When designing a class, you should consider these four member functions in most cases:

- Default constructor
- Destructor
- Copy constructor
- Copy assignment operator

At the end of this chapter, I present the CRect rectangle class, which demonstrates how to implement the big four member functions (constructor, destructor, copy constructor, and assignment operator) in a real class setting.

You declare a class in C++ by using the class keyword along with a pair of braces, terminated by a semicolon, like this empty class:

```
class MyClass { };
```

The basic idea is this: Put some data members into a class and then add some member functions to act on that data. Back in Chapter 9, you saw how structures use data members. Remember that structures are really classes in C++ (but not in C). Here is a simple structure declaration that groups together four variables used to describe a rectangle:

```
struct Rect
{
    int left;
    int top;
    int right;
    int bottom;
};
```

Note

Simple classes that are used mainly as private structures often don't need all, or any, of the big four member functions (constructor, destructor, copy constructor, and assignment operator).

The only thing you need to do to convert this structure into a class is to change the keyword struct to class, like this:

```
class Rect
{
    int left;
    int top;
    int right;
    int bottom;
};
```

That's all there is to it! Now it's a real C++ class—and the default access has changed from public to private. This means that these data members are no longer accessible outside the object, only internally. Later in this chapter, after a tour of the mechanics of class creation, you'll see the design and implementation of a useful rectangle class.

Specifying Access Control

By controlling access to class data members and member functions, you can greatly increase the integrity (robustness) of the software you create with C++. You can declare class members as having private, protected, or public access, as shown in Table 21.1. Access to class members is specified using three keywords: public, private, and protected.

TABLE 21.1 **The C++ Class Member Access Specifiers**

Access Specifier	Meaning
public	Class members are accessible by any object.
private	Class members are accessible only by the class itself.
protected	Class members are accessible by the class itself, and any classes derived from that class (see Chapter 22, "Implementing Class Inheritance," for information about derived classes).

Specifying Public Access

Any object defined in a program can see and manipulate the public data members and public member functions of a class. For example, the following is perfectly valid when using public access:

```
class CMyClass
{
public:
    int x;
};

void main()
{
    CMyClass myclass;
    myclass.x = 5;   // OK, public access
}
```

Because the data member x is public, the main() function can directly manipulate its value. On the other hand, the same thing with private or protected access doesn't work because x would not be available outside the class itself.

Specifying Private Access

Friend Function

A function external to a class that has full access to all class members, including protected and private members.

Friend Class

A class whose member functions are all friend functions of another class.

By specifying private access (the default for classes), class data can be used only by member functions and any friend classes or friend functions known to the class. If a member is private, it should be left alone. Use private access as protection to make your classes more robust.

```
class CMyClass
{
private:
    int x;
};

void main()
{
    CMyClass myclass;
    myclass.x = 5;   // Error! myclass.x is private
}
```

The preceding code *can't* work—the data is hidden within the object, in this case using the `private` access specifier. If you try to use this code, our old friend the compiler will generate an error similar to the following:

```
Error : 'x' :
cannot access private member declared in class 'CMyClass'
```

This is because `main()` can't access the private data member x. Private access promotes robustness of your code by preventing unauthorized access to such data members outside of the class itself.

Specifying Protected Access

By specifying protected access, the data member x is safely hidden away within the object. Only member functions and friends (classes or functions) of the class or a derived class can access the data. The following code starts with the same example used in the preceding two sections but uses the `protected` access specifier:

```
class CMyClass
{
protected:
   int x;
};

void main()
{
   CMyClass myclass;
   myclass.x = 5;  // Error! myclass.x is protected
}
```

Like the `private` access specifier, the `protected` access specifier hides data within the object; once again, the compiler will generate an error similar to the following if you try to use the preceding code:

```
Error : 'x' :
cannot access protected member declared in class 'CMyClass'
```

Applying Access Control

The same access control that's applicable to class member functions and data also applies to enumerations (enumerated data types) and nested classes.

Using Nested Classes

Like structures, classes can be nested one within another. The rules that apply to nested structures (see Chapter 9) apply to nested classes as well.

The difference between the protected and private specifiers is that the protected specifier makes members available to derived classes, and private doesn't.

SEE ALSO

➤ *For more information about derived classes, see page 522*

Defining Data Members

When defining a class, you'll likely begin with an empty class shell like this one, which declares a class to model a point in three-dimensional space (remember the Point3d structure from Chapter 9?):

```
class CPoint3d
{
};
```

Next, you add data members as variables local to the class. You can declare these member variables to have either automatic (non-static) storage class or static storage class.

Defining Non-Static Data Members

When you add data members to a class, the general idea is to add the data members within the brackets, just as you would do for a structure. In this example, I use the public keyword to specify public access for the members of the class, making the CPoint3d class equivalent to the Point3d structure from Chapter 9:

```
class CPoint3d
{
public:
    float x;
    float y;
    float z;
};
```

Non-static (automatic, or "regular") data members act just like the variables you've seen already in this book. You access them with the dot operator or the pointer-to-member operator, depending on whether you're working with an object (or object reference) or an object pointer. For example, given an object of type CPoint3d (or a reference to that object), you use this syntax to access the data members:

```
CPoint3d pt;

// Direct access, use the dot (.) operator
//
pt.x = 1.0f;
pt.y = 2.0f;
pt.z = 3.0f;
```

Given a pointer to an object of type CPoint3d, you would use this syntax to access the data members:

```
CPoint3d *pt = new CPoint3d;

// Pointer access, use the
//   pointer-to-member (->) operator
//
pt->x = 1.0f;
pt->y = 2.0f;
pt->z = 3.0f;
```

Defining Static Data Members

When you use the static keyword to modify a data member in a class declaration, you stipulate that all the instances of the class (objects of that class) share a single copy of that data member. Static data members are often used as a way to communicate between objects of like classes.

Let's add a static data member to the CPoint3d class. I'll call the new member count, because it will count the number of CPoint3d class instances that are running at any given time during a program's execution:

```
class CPoint3d
{
public:
    float x;
    float y;
    float z;
```

```
protected:
    static int count;
};
```

The count member uses protected access to keep count hidden from prying eyes, but visible to CPoint3d objects.

Using the count Member

The count member will come in handy later in this chapter, when we count the number of CPoint3d objects created at runtime in the sample program in Listing 21.1.

Using Constructors and Destructors

Constructors and destructors are different from anything you've seen so far. They are member functions that are called for you automatically by C++. A *constructor* is called when an object is being created. The *destructor* is called when an object is being destroyed (or goes out of scope). Constructor and destructor functions must have the same name as the class; unlike other functions, the constructor and destructor don't have return types—not even void.

Constructor Functions

Constructors can be overloaded to allow different approaches of object construction. There are several common types of constructors, including default constructors, copy constructors, and default-parameter constructors. You must be able to call a default constructor with no parameters—typically, a default constructor doesn't have any parameters. If the default constructor *does* have parameters, those parameters must all have default values. For the CPoint3d class, the default constructor looks like this:

```
CPoint3d::CPoint3d() :
    x(0.0f), y(0.0f), z(0.0f)
{
}
```

This syntax initializes all three non-static data members to zero, using something called the *initializer list*. This list is optional, but if it is present, it falls between the function call parentheses and the opening brace of the constructor body. A colon begins the list of comma-separated data members to initialize. Because static member initialization occurs in class scope, the variable count, declared in the preceding section, is visible to all objects of class Cpoint3d.

The initializer list uses function call syntax to initialize data members, as in x(0.0f). This statement accomplishes the same thing as explicitly assigning values to the members within the constructor body, although the initializer list syntax usually generates more efficient code than explicit assignment when compiled. Here's an example of explicit assignment within the constructor:

```
CPoint3d::CPoint3d()
{
    x = 0.0f;
    y = 0.0f;
    z = 0.0f;
}
```

Note that although non-static members should be initialized in the constructor's initializer list or function body, you can't initialize the count member in *either* of these areas. This is because it's against C++ rules to initialize static data members in the class declaration or implementation. The initialization of static data members must occur at file scope—globally—even if the data members use the private access specifier. In this example, the count member can be initialized at file scope, outside the class declaration, like this:

```
int CPoint3d::count = 0;
```

SEE ALSO

For more information about scope, see page 52

Another way to initialize class members is explicitly, by parameter. Default-parameter construction is a common practice because it adds a lot of flexibility to how the finished class can be used in source code. A default-parameter constructor for the CPoint3d class would typically give all three values (x, y, and z) default values, like this:

```
CPoint3d::CPoint3d(float cx = 0.0f, float cy = 0.0f,
    float cz = 0.0f)
{
    x = cx;
    y = cy;
    z = cz;
}
```

Initializer List

The initializer list is a list of values used by a class constructor to initialize data member values before the body of the constructor executes.

Using Multiple Constructors

A constructor must have the same name as its class. You can declare any number of constructors (as long as you follow the rules of function overloading).

This is a first step in creating a copy constructor and an assignment operator for the class (later in this chapter you'll see the remaining steps) .

SEE ALSO

➤ *For details on creating copy constructors, see page 500*

➤ *For details on creating copy assignment operators, see page 504*

The Destructor Function

The destructor receives no parameters, so it can't be overloaded. A class's destructor name is comprised of a tilde (~) followed by the name of the class, as in ~CPoint3d(). The destructor for the CPoint3d class looks like this:

```
CPoint3d::~CPoint3d()
{
}
```

Because the CPoint3d class doesn't require any cleanup, there is no code in the destructor function body. In this case, the destructor isn't really needed because the compiler supplies a default destructor for you if you don't include one in your code.

You should use the destructor to clean up whatever little messes the object has made during its lifetime, such as deleting any memory that it may have dynamically allocated. Using one or more constructors and a destructor make class initialization and cleanup completely transparent to the end user (the user of the class, that is).

Understanding the *this* Pointer

Each instance of a class (that is, each object) contains a const pointer to itself that member functions use to know which object instance has called a member function. This const pointer is called the this pointer, and its syntax is shown here:

```
this->ClassMember
```

or

```
*this
```

Only non-static member functions can use the `this` keyword because the `this` pointer doesn't exist for static members, only non-static ones. When a member function executes, the `this` pointer points to the object that's executing the function. For example, the `CPoint3d` class and its x, y, and z data members can be accessed within a member function using the `this` pointer like this:

```
this->x = 1.0f;
this->y = 1.0f;
this->z = 1.0f;
```

By using the indirection operator on the `this` pointer, you can effectively get the object itself, as in this example, assuming that this code is called from within a member function:

```
CPoint3d pt = *this;
```

For this sort of thing to work, a copy assignment operator function must exist for the class. This is a technique similar to that used by copy constructors, as you'll see later in this chapter.

Take a look at the program in Listing 21.1. This program demonstrates the use of a static data member used as an object counter. Because the constructor and destructor are non-static, the `this` pointer exists for these functions; the new static data member `count` is manipulated in these functions by explicitly using the `this` pointer.

The this Pointer

The **this** pointer is an internal pointer that yields the address of an object instance. It is used by member functions to identify a specific instance of a class.

LISTING 21.1   A Program That Demonstrates the Use of the *this* Pointer and a Static Data Member

```
 1: ////////////////////////////////////////////////////////
 2: //  Module  : static.cpp
 3: //
 4: //  Purpose : Shows the use of a static data member
 5: ////////////////////////////////////////////////////////
 6:
 7: #include <iostream>
 8:
 9: ////////////////////////////////////////////////////////
10: // Class declaration
11: ////////////////////////////////////////////////////////
12:
```

continues...

LISTING 21.1

❶ Line 13: Begin the CPoint3d class declaration

❷ Lines 19-20: Declare the constructor and destructor functions

❸ Lines 24-26: Declare public data members

❹ Line 31: Declare a private static data member

❺ Lines 41-48: Define the default constructor function

❻ Lines 50-56: Define the class destructor function

LISTING 21.1 **Continued**

```
13: class CPoint3d ──────❶
14: {
15: public:
16:
17:     // Constructor/destructor
18:     //
19:     CPoint3d();  ┐
20:     ~CPoint3d(); ┘──────❷
21:
22:     // Public data members
23:     //
24:     float x;  ┐
25:     float y;  ├──────❸
26:     float z;  ┘
27:
28: private:
29:     // Protected data members
30:     //
31:     static int count;  ──────❹
32: };
33:
34: ////////////////////////////////////////////////////////
35: // Class definition
36: ////////////////////////////////////////////////////////
37:
38: ////////////////////////////////////////////////////////
39: // Constructor/destructor
40:
41: CPoint3d::CPoint3d() :                          ┐
42:     x(0.0f), y(0.0f), z(0.0f)                   │
43: {                                               │
44:     // Display, then increment static member    │
45:     //                                          ├──❺
46:     std::cout << "Constructing : now "          │
47:        << ++(this->count) << " CPoint3d objects exist\n"; │
48: }                                               ┘
49:
50: CPoint3d::~CPoint3d()                           ┐
51: {                                               │
52:     // Display, then decrement static member    │
53:     //                                          ├──❻
54:     std::cout << "Destructing  : now "          │
55:        << --(this->count) << " CPoint3d objects exist\n"; │
56: }                                               ┘
```

```
57:
58: // Must initialize static data members at file scope!
59: //
60: int CPoint3d::count = 0;          ──7
61:
62: /////////////////////////////////////////////////////////
63: // main()
64:
65: void main()
66: {
67:     CPoint3d *ppt1 = new CPoint3d;
68:     CPoint3d *ppt2 = new CPoint3d;
69:     CPoint3d *ppt3 = new CPoint3d;          8
70:     CPoint3d *ppt4 = new CPoint3d;
71:
72:     delete ppt1;
73:     delete ppt2;
74:     delete ppt3;          9
75:     delete ppt4;
76: }
```

LISTING 21.1 CONTINUED

7 Line 60: Initialize the static data member at file scope

8 Lines 67-70: Allocating four CPoint3d objects causes the constructor for each to be called

9 Lines 72-75: Deallocating the four CPoint3d objects causes the destructor for each to be called

The output from this program looks like this:

```
Constructing : now 1 CPoint3d objects exist
Constructing : now 2 CPoint3d objects exist
Constructing : now 3 CPoint3d objects exist
Constructing : now 4 CPoint3d objects exist
Destructing  : now 3 CPoint3d objects exist
Destructing  : now 2 CPoint3d objects exist
Destructing  : now 1 CPoint3d objects exist
Destructing  : now 0 CPoint3d objects exist
```

This is the first full program you've seen in this book so far that defines and uses a C++ class. Line 13 of the program begins the CPoint3d class declaration. Lines 19 and 20 declare the constructor and destructor functions for the class.

The declaration of public class data members happens on lines 24 through 26; the declaration of the private static data member count occurs on line 31.

Lines 41 through 48 provide the default constructor function definition for the class; default values are initialized in the initializer list on line 42. The static count member is accessible to all instances of the class, so lines 46 and 47 use the `cout` object to display the current value of `count`. The `count` member stores the number of class instances running at any given moment. This member is pre-incremented because the constructor call indicates that a new object has just been created.

Likewise, on lines 54 and 55, in the class destructor definition, the `count` member is pre-decremented by 1 because the object is being destroyed. The `cout` object is again used to display the current value of `count`.

Because static data members must be initialized at file scope, not at class scope, line 60 takes care of this, initializing `CPoint3d::count` to 0. Finally, the `main()` function simply allocates four `CPoint3d` objects (lines 67 through 70), causing the constructor for each to be called. This results in four `count` statements being written to the screen. The four `CPoint3d` objects are then immediately destroyed (lines 72 through 75). This action causes the destructor and resulting object count to be written to the screen for each.

Creating Copy Constructors

A copy constructor is a constructor function designed to copy objects of the same class type. A copy constructor accepts a single argument (a reference to the same class type) and returns a copy of an object. The copy constructor is called whenever your code passes an object to a function by value instead of by reference. The copy constructor is also called if you initialize a new object with another object of the same type, as in this example:

```
CPoint3d pt1(1.0f, 2.0f, 3.0f);   // default constructor
CPoint3d pt2 new CPoint3d(pt1);   // copy constructor
```

The copy constructor initializes the values from an existing object to a new object having the same class type. To create a copy constructor for the `CPoint3d` class, you would first declare the function in the class declaration, like this:

```
CPoint3d(const CPoint3d& pt);
```

Notice that the parameter is a `const` reference to a `CPoint3d` object. We use the `const` keyword to ensure that the copy constructor does not alter the data of the object being passed into the function. Next, you define the actual copy constructor in the class definition, like this:

```
CPoint3d::CPoint3d(const CPoint3d& pt)
{
    this->x = pt.x;
    this->y = pt.y;
    this->z = pt.z;
}
```

Of course, it's not always this easy. If a class uses dynamic memory for any of its data members, the simple assignment of member values such as this isn't good enough. Assigning one pointer to another causes the second to point to the same memory location as the first. A copy constructor that does this is sure to cause problems.

The problems crop up when the original object goes out of scope before the copied object does. The destructor of this object frees the dynamic memory, but the copied object's pointer member still points to the newly freed address—a dangling pointer that's destined to cause weirdness. Consider the following simple class:

```
class MyClass
{
public:
    MyClass();
    MyClass(const MyClass& myclass);
    ~MyClass();

    float   myFloat;
    float *myFloatPtr;
};
```

The class has two data members: a `float` and a pointer to a `float`. The default constructor contains the code to dynamically allocate the actual float that `myFloatPtr` points to, like this:

```
MyClass::MyClass() : myFloat(0.0f)
{
```

```
    myFloatPtr = new float;   // allocate a float
    *myFloatPtr = 0.0f;       // initialize the float
}
```

In this constructor, a new `float` is allocated and assigned to `myFloatPtr`. The destructor automatically deletes this memory when the object is destroyed:

```
MyClass::~MyClass()
{
    if (myFloatPtr)
    {
        delete myFloatPtr;   // delete the float

        myFloatPtr = 0;      // reset the pointer
    }
}
```

Assuming the direct assignment of member values in the copy constructor, such as you saw earlier in this section, you'd get this condition:

```
MyClass::MyClass(const MyClass& mc)
{
    myFloat     = mc.myFloat;
    myFloatPtr = mc.myFloatPtr; // shallow copy of a pointer
}
```

Direct copying of a pointer like this leaves a dangling pointer when the reference object `mc` goes out of scope (which deletes the pointer). Imagine the class used in a program in a scenario like this one:

```
void main()
{
    MyClass *pmc = new MyClass;
    *pmc->myFloatPtr = 10.0f;

    MyClass mc(*pmc);

    std::cout << "The value of *myFloatPtr is: "
        << *mc.myFloatPtr << '\n';

    delete pmc;
```

```
        std::cout << "The value of *myFloatPtr is: "
            << *mc.myFloatPtr << '\n';
}
```

A program using this code on my computer produced the following output results:

```
The value of *myFloatPtr is: 10
The value of *myFloatPtr is: -1.9984e+018
```

As you can see, the first line is okay, but the second, pointing to the same place, is garbage. Obviously, the object was deleted—as was its pointer. When I ran this code, the act of accessing the dangling pointer threw an exception in the operating system. This was immediately followed by a nasty warning dialog box on my PC running Windows 98 (see Figure 21.1).

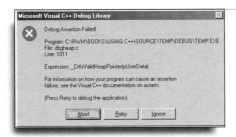

FIGURE 21.1

The result of accessing an invalid pointer because of a faulty copy constructor.

The proper way to write this copy constructor (to avoid memory access errors like the one shown in Figure 21.1) is to allocate the memory for the float pointer, just like the default constructor does, as you see here:

```
MyClass::MyClass(const MyClass& mc)
{
    myFloat    = mc.myFloat;
    myFloatPtr = new float;        // allocate a new float
    *myFloatPtr = *mc.myFloatPtr;  // assign by value
}
```

When I ran this program, the results were correct, as you'd expect, giving me the following output (without the scary warning box):

```
The value of *myFloatPtr is: 10
The value of *myFloatPtr is: 10
```

Creating Member Operators

Member operators are important in many classes, especially the copy assignment operator. Overloading an operator for a class is just like overloading an operator in a global module. Take a look at the following copy assignment operator for the CPoint3d class:

```
CPoint3d& CPoint3d::operator=(const CPoint3d& pt)
{
    x = pt.x;
    y = pt.y;
    z = pt.z;

    return *this;
}
```

The use of *this sends a reference to the object itself as the return value. In code, the operator is used like this:

```
CPoint3d p1(1.0f, 2.0f, 3.0f);  // construct and initialize
CPoint3d pt2 = pt1;             // copy assign
```

Other operators could be defined as well, such as this one that adds two CPoint3d objects together (that is, adds their member values):

```
CPoint3d& CPoint3d::operator+=(const CPoint3d& pt)
{
    x += pt.x;
    y += pt.y;
    z += pt.z;

    return *this;
}
```

Functions that are friends of the class can also overload operators, as does this declaration for a friend operator+():

```
friend CPoint3d operator+ (const CPoint3d& p1,
    const CPoint3d& p2);
```

The operator function definition for operator+() might look like this:

```
inline CPoint3d operator+ (const CPoint3d & p1,
    const CPoint3d & p2)
{
```

```
    return CPoint3d(p1.x + p2.x, p1.y + p2.y, p1.z + p2.z);
}
```

As you can see, this friend operator function uses the CPoint3d constructor CPoint3d::CPoint3d() to specify the return value of the addition operation.

SEE ALSO

➤ *To learn about friend functions, see page 536*

Defining Member Functions

You define member functions just like you do global functions, except that you define them within a class type. You've already seen some examples of member functions in constructors, destructors, and operator functions. By their very nature, these member functions are tightly bound to the class data members. Other member functions might perform tasks that have little or nothing to do with any class data members. For example, here's a CPoint3d member function definition that just displays information about the data members to the screen:

```
void CPoint3d::DumpToScreen()
{
    std::cout << "CPoint3d Data Members:\n\n";
    std::cout << "x == " << x << '\n'
        << "y == " << y << '\n' << "z == " << z << '\n';
    std::cout <<
        "Total number of CPoint3d objects in existence: "
        << count;
}
```

The corresponding declaration for this function must appear in the class declaration, and it would fit in like this:

```
class CPoint3d
{
public:
    ...
private:
    void DumpToScreen();
    ...
};
```

Defining Static Member Functions

Static member functions have class scope, but unlike a regular non-static member function, a static function doesn't have a `this` pointer. Because the function doesn't know about `this`, it can't access any non-static data. Interestingly, because a static member function doesn't use `this`, you can access it without creating an object of its corresponding class type. By adding a static member function `GetCount()` to the `CPoint3d` class declaration, you can give code outside the `CPoint3d` class access to the private static data member `count`. Take a look at this revised `CPoint3d` class declaration:

```
class CPoint3d
{
public:
    // Constructor/Destructor
    //
    CPoint3d()  { count++; }
    ~CPoint3d() { --count; }

    // Public member function
    //
    static int GetCount() { return count; }

    // Public data members
    //
    float x;
    float y;
    float z;

private:
    // Private member function
    //
    void DumpToScreen();

    // Private data members
    //
    static int count;
};
```

The new static `GetCount()` member function returns the value of the private static data member `count` to non-class members. Here's a little `main()` function you can use to test the new `GetCount()` function:

```
void main()
{
    std::cout << CPoint3d::GetCount() << '\n';
    CPoint3d *pt = new CPoint3d();
    std::cout << CPoint3d::GetCount() << '\n';
    delete pt;
    std::cout << CPoint3d::GetCount() << '\n';
}
```

The class `CPoint3d` now contains the static member function `GetCount()`. Although this function is a member of the `CPoint3d` class, it uses static storage class, so it's not necessarily affiliated with any given object of type `CPoint3d`. Because `GetCount()` is a static member function, you can call it without an existing object of class `CPoint3d`. All you need is the class name to provide the scope for `GetCount()`, as in `CPoint3d::GetCount()`. You can see this concept in action if you look at the first and last statements in the `main()` function in the preceding code snippet.

A static member function can't have the same name and parameter types as a non-static member function. When applied to class member functions, the `static` keyword specifies that the function accesses only static members. Static member functions have external linkage; because they don't have `this` pointers, they can't access non-static class data members, and they can't be declared as virtual.

Defining Non-Static Member Functions

Non-static member functions are just "regular" class member functions—the kind that have `this` pointers. Most member functions you'll write will be regular class member functions. You declare a class member function just as you would declare any other global function, with the exception that you declare it within a class. Like data members, member functions can have

Internal and External Linkage

Recall from Chapter 2 that linkage refers to how the names of objects and functions are shared between translation units, and that linkage can be either internal or external. Internal linkage means that names refer only to program elements inside their own translation units (they're not shared with other units). External linkage means that names refer to program elements in any translation unit in the program, elements that are shared, or "global."

public, private, or protected access. Here is a simple class definition that contains a single private data member and two member functions designed to provide access to the private member:

```
class MyClass
{
public:
    MyClass() : myColor(0) { }
    int GetColor() const { return myColor; }
    void SetColor(int clr) { myColor = clr; }

private:
    int myColor;
};
```

The constructor and both member functions are defined in the class declaration, providing a complete class definition at the same time. Because the GetColor() function uses the const modifier, you are guaranteed that the myColor member won't be modified by the function. The SetColor() member sets the value of myColor. In this way, outside influences never directly touch myColor.

Unlike global functions (but similar to functions defined within a namespace), you must use the class name to specify the function's scope. If the GetColor() and SetColor() functions were defined separately from the class declaration, they would look like this:

```
int MyClass::GetColor() const { return myColor; }
void MyClass::SetColor(int clr) { myColor = clr; }
```

Using Pointer-to-Member Operator Expressions

Similar to the indirection operator (*), the pointer-to-member operators convert a pointer operand to the actual *data pointed to*, but they are special types of binary operators.

There are two pointer-to-member operators you can use to access class members. These operators dereference a class member-pointer operand. The operators use the notation `.*` and `->*` and their basic syntax is shown here:

```
ClassObject .* ClassMemberPointer
ClassObjectPointer ->* ClassMemberPointer
```

The operator `.*` connects the operand to its left with the operand to its right. The left operand must be a class object, and the right operand must be a pointer to a member of the class type (pointer-to-member). Consider some class `mycls`, having some pointer `ptr` as a member. The expression `mycls.*ptr` dereferences class member `ptr`.

The operator `->**;pointer-to-member operator>` also connects the operand to its left with the operand to its right. In this case, however, the left operand must be a pointer to a class object, and the right operand must be a pointer to a member of the object's class type. Assuming that `MyClassPtr` is a pointer to a `mycls` object, the expression `MyClassPtr->*Ptr` yields the actual value of class member `ptr`.

You use the pointer-to-member operator by deriving a pointer type to a class member, like this (assuming that `mycls::member` is an `int`):

```
int mycls::*ptr = &mycls::member;
```

The program in Listing 21.2 demonstrates the use of both types of pointer-to-member operators and the standard dot (.) operator with both pointer and non-pointer members.

LISTING 21.2   A Program That Demonstrates Pointer-to-Member Operators

```
 1: /////////////////////////////////////////////////////////
 2: // Module  : MemberPtr.cpp
 3: //
 4: // Purpose : Demonstrates pointer-to-member operators
 5:
 6: #include <iostream.h>
 7: const char NL = '\n';
 8:
 9: /////////////////////////////////////////////////////////
10: // Class mycls
11:
```

continues…

LISTING 21.2

1 Lines 12-17: Declare the class mycls

2 Line 24: Create a mycls object

3 Line 29: Derive a new data type

4 Line 37: Get a pointer to the MyClass object

5 Lines 41-42: Assign the data members some values

6 Lines 46-54: Use the pointer-to-member operators to access the values in the data members

LISTING 21.2   **Continued**

```
12: class mycls
13: {
14: public:                              1
15:    int   member;
16:    int *ptr;
17: };
18:
19: //////////////////////////////////////////////////////
20: // main()
21:
22: void main()
23: {
24:    mycls MyClass;    // Create a class instance    2
25:
26:    // Derive a pointer type to the non-pointer
27:    //   class member
28:    //
29:    int mycls::*member = &mycls::member;         3
30:
31:    // Allocate a ptr member
32:    //
33:    MyClass.ptr = new int;
34:
35:    // Get a pointer to the class instance
36:    //
37:    mycls* pMyClass = &MyClass;        4
38:
39:    // Give the members values
40:    //
41:    pMyClass->*member = 5;                        5
42:    *MyClass.ptr     = 10;
43:
44:    // Get the member values using the (.), (->*),
45:    // and (.*) operators
46:    //
47:    cout << "pMyClass->*member = "
48:       << pMyClass->*member << NL;
49:    cout << "MyClass.*member   = "
50:       << MyClass.*member << NL;                  6
51:    cout << "*MyClass.ptr      = "
52:       << *MyClass.ptr << NL;
53:    cout << "*pMyClass->ptr    = "
54:       << *pMyClass->ptr << NL;
```

```
55:
56:     // Clean up
57:     //
58:     delete MyClass.ptr;
59: }
```

This program gives the following output:

```
pMyClass->*member = 5
MyClass.*member    = 5
*MyClass.ptr       = 10
*pMyClass->ptr     = 10
```

This program begins by declaring the simple class mycls from lines 12 though 17. The class has two integer data members: member and ptr. On line 24 we create an instance of class mycls, giving us the object MyClass. Line 29 derives a new data type—a pointer to the class member mycls::member.

On line 33 we allocate a new integer for the ptr data member, and on line 37 we get a pointer to the MyClass object. Lines 41 and 42 simply assign some values to the data members. Now we can use the pointer-to-member operators to access the values in the data members, which we do from lines 46 through 54. Finally, line 58 deletes the dynamically allocated integer to clean up.

Designing and Implementing a Rectangle Class

Now that you've seen a few simple classes, it's time to design and implement a complete, useful class. To that end, I now present the rectangle project. The idea is to design and implement a base class that models a simple rectangle object. Remember the four steps of class design from earlier in the chapter? Just in case you've forgotten, here they are again:

1. Think about the class design. Try to conceptualize what the class should accomplish. Think about the class as a runtime object. What kind of properties and capabilities should that object have? How should it interact with other objects?

2. List any relevant data that should be encapsulated within the object as data members.

3. List the things the object knows or does and encapsulate this data within the object as member functions.

4. Solidify the class interface by writing the class declaration or header files.

With this in mind, let's turn to the design of a rectangle class: CRect.

Designing the *CRect* Interface

The CRect class must follow these basic design criteria:

- The class must be fully reusable.

- The class must store a rectangle's bounds, representing the rectangle.

- The class must be able to calculate its own width and height for use by other objects.

- The class must be able to determine whether a point lies within its perimeter.

- For ease of use, the class should provide a default constructor, a default-parameter constructor, a copy constructor, and an assignment operator.

Sounds pretty easy, right? It is! To begin, the class needs to "know" the boundary of the rectangle it represents. The obvious data members for this are the four sides of the rectangle: left, top, right, and bottom (see Figure 21.2). I'll specify these data members as integers; this yields the following first-draft class declaration:

```
class CRect
{
public:
    int left;
    int top;
    int right;
    int bottom;
};
```

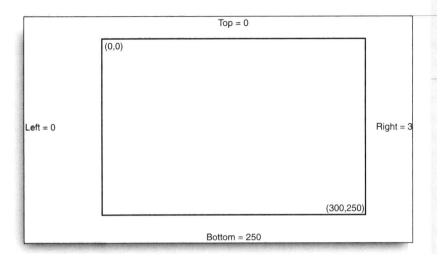

FIGURE 21.2

Defining a rectangle using the locations of its four sides.

So far, so good. Next, the functionality of the CRect class must be considered. The height and width of a rectangle can be derived from the data members already in the class. To find the width, just subtract the location of the left side from the location of the right side (see Figure 21.3). This calculation will be performed by a public member function called Width(). To find the height, just subtract the location of the top side from the location of the bottom side (see Figure 21.4). This calculation will be performed by a public member function called Height().

Determining whether a point falls within the perimeter of the rectangle is a simple matter of seeing whether the x coordinate falls within the bounds between the left and right of the rectangle, and whether the y coordinate lies within the bounds between the top and bottom of the rectangle. This will be the job of the public member function called PointWithin(). The rest of the member functions consist of the constructors and the copy assignment operator called for in the design specs. Table 21.2 lists all the proposed member functions for the CRect class.

FIGURE 21.3

Calculating the width of a rectangle from the locations of the left and right sides.

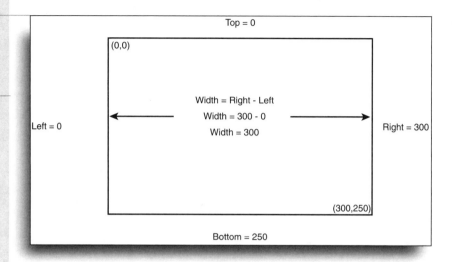

FIGURE 21.4

Calculating the height of a rectangle from the locations of the top and bottom sides.

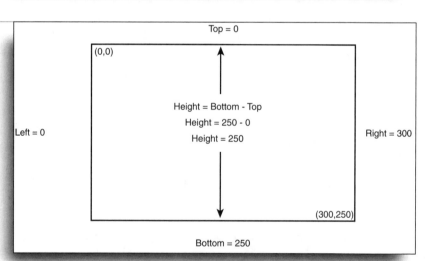

TABLE 21.2   The Member Functions of Class *CRect*

Function Name	Purpose
CRect()	Default constructor
CRect(int, int, int, int)	Default-parameter constructor
CRect(CRect&)	Copy constructor
CRect& operator=(const CRect&)	Copy assignment operator

Function Name	Purpose
bool PointWithin(int x, int y)	Returns true if the point defined by x and y lies within the rectangle's perimeter
int Height()	Returns the height of the rectangle
int Width()	Returns the width of the rectangle

By putting the class declaration in a header file separate from the implementation, you make the class accessible to any number of programs with a simple #include statement. The complete interface file for the CRect class is rect.h, shown in Listing 21.3.

LISTING 21.3   The Interface for the *CRect* Rectangle Class

```
 1: /////////////////////////////////////////////////////////
 2: //   Module   : rect.h
 3: //
 4: //   Purpose : Interface for the CRect class
 5: /////////////////////////////////////////////////////////
 6:
 7: #ifndef __RECT_H__
 8: #define __RECT_H__
 9:
10: /////////////////////////////////////////////////////////
11: // Class CRect
12:
13: class CRect
14: {
15: public:
16:
17:     CRect();
18:     CRect(int left, int top, int right, int bottom);
19:     CRect(CRect& rect);
20:     CRect& operator=(const CRect& rect);
21:
22:     // Public member functions
23:     //
24:     bool PointWithin(int x, int y);
25:     int Width();
26:     int Height();
27:
```

LISTING 21.3

1 Lines 7-8: Preprocessor directives for single inclusion of the header file

2 Lines 17-20: The declarations for the constructors and copy assignment operator

3 Lines 24-26: The public member functions of the class

continues…

LISTING 21.3 CONTINUED

4️⃣ Lines 30-33: The public data members of the class

5️⃣ Line 36: The end of the single inclusion #ifndef

LISTING 21.3 **Continued**

```
28:    // Public data members
29:    //
30:    int left;
31:    int top;
32:    int right;
33:    int bottom;
34: };
35:
36: #endif //__RECT_H__
```

This listing is a typical class header file; lines 7 and 8 ensure single file inclusion by using the #ifdef preprocessor directive. The declaration of the CRect class begins on line 13. All the members of the class are public in this implementation. The declarations for the constructors and copy assignment operator appear on lines 17 through 20; lines 24 through 26 give the declarations for the public member functions of the class. The public data members of the class are declared from lines 30 through 33, and the header file ends by terminating single file inclusion, matching up an #endif directive with the #ifndef directive at the beginning of the file.

Implementing the *CRect* Class

The implementation of the CRect class is straightforward and concise. When implementing a class, I usually start out by defining skeleton functions for all the class member functions. These skeleton functions consist of the declaration and a set of body braces, like this:

```
CRect& CRect::operator=(const CRect& rect)
{
    // Write code here... ;)
}
```

After these skeletons are coded, I then go back and work out the details for each function, sometimes realizing that other member functions might be needed to keep the code manageable. Often you'll find that the first draft goes through several

design iterations before you find the design that "feels right."
The complete CRect class implementation is shown in
Listing 21.4.

LISTING 21.4 **An Implementation of the *CRect* Rectangle Class**

```
 1: ///////////////////////////////////////////////////////
 2: //   Module  : rect.cpp
 3: //
 4: //   Purpose : Implementation of the CRect class
 5: ///////////////////////////////////////////////////////
 6:
 7: #include "rect.h"
 8:
 9: ///////////////////////////////////////////////////////
10: // Constructors
11:
12: // Default constructor
13: CRect::CRect()
14: {
15: }
16:
17: // Default-parameter constructor
18: CRect::CRect(int left = 0, int top = 0,
19:              int right = 0, int bottom = 0)
20: {
21:     this->left   = left;
22:     this->top    = top;
23:     this->right  = right;
24:     this->bottom = bottom;
25: }
26:
27: // Copy constructor
28: CRect::CRect(CRect& rect)
29: {
30:     this->left   = rect.left;
31:     this->top    = rect.top;
32:     this->right  = rect.right;
33:     this->bottom = rect.bottom;
34: }
35:
```

LISTING 21.3

1 Lines 7-8: Preprocessor directives for single inclusion of the header file

2 Lines 17-20: The declarations for the constructors and copy assignment operator

3 Lines 24-26: The public member functions of the class

continues...

LISTING 21.4   **Continued**

```
36: //////////////////////////////////////////////////////
37: // CRect::operator=()
38:
39: CRect& CRect::operator=(const CRect& rect)
40: {
41:     this->left   = rect.left;
42:     this->top    = rect.top;
43:     this->right  = rect.right;
44:     this->bottom = rect.bottom;
45:
46:     return *this;
47: }
48:
49: //////////////////////////////////////////////////////
50: // CRect::PointWithin()
51:
52: bool CRect::PointWithin(int x, int y)
53: {
54:     return ((x >= left) && (x <= right) &&
55:         (y >= top) && (y <= bottom));
56: }
57:
58: //////////////////////////////////////////////////////
59: // CRect::Width()
60:
61: int CRect::Width()
62:     { return right - left; }
63:
64: //////////////////////////////////////////////////////
65: // CRect::Height()
66:
67: int CRect::Height()
68:     { return bottom - top; }
```

④ ⑤ ⑥ ⑦

The constructors and copy assignment operator for class CRect are very similar to those you saw earlier in this chapter in class CPoint3d. The data members change, but the concept of these functions stays basically the same from class to class. The true worth of a class usually lies in its additional member functions, those beyond the constructors and operators. It is these additional member functions that provide the specialized services a class offers. In CRect, there are three public member functions that provide these specialized services: PointWithin(), Width(), and Height().

The CRect::PointWithin() function begins on line 52 and takes two arguments: x and y. If the values of x and y fall within the rectangle's perimeter, the function returns true; otherwise, it returns false. The compound Boolean expression on lines 54 and 55 handle the logic for this decision.

The CRect::Width() function begins on line 61, returning the calculated width on line 62. The CRect::Height() function begins on line 67, returning the calculated height on line 68.

Implementing Class Inheritance

Understand base and derived classes

See how to create class hierarchies

Discover how to override base class functions

Learn about friend classes and functions

See how to create binary class libraries

Understanding Base and Derived Classes

Inheritance

In C++ programming, inheritance is the ability of one class to derive characteristics from another class. The inherited class derives its characteristics from a base class, resulting in a derived class.

The object-oriented programming paradigm is based on the concept of object hierarchies that are created through *inheritance*. In this system, a simple base class acts as a foundation on which you can build more complex classes. The resulting classes can then act as the foundation for even more complex classes, and so on. A class that's built from an existing class, to extend its capabilities in some way, is called a *derived class*.

Obviously, before you can derive a class, you must have a base class to derive from. To create a derived class in C++, you must tell the compiler what base class your new derived class uses. Let's declare a minimal base class called CBase:

```
class CBase
{
protected:
    int myInt;
};
```

As you can see, class CBase has a single protected data member called myInt. Next, we can derive a new class CDerived from the base class CBase:

```
class CDerived : public CBase        // Derive from CBase
{
protected:
    float myFloat;
};
```

Because the myInt member in class CBase is declared as protected, the CDerived class actually has two data members: myFloat (declared in CDerived) and myInt (inherited from CBase). Look at the syntax used for the class declaration:

```
class CDerived : public CBase
```

This line tells us that CDerived inherits publicly from CBase. For extra security and data abstraction, you can also inherit privately, explicitly exposing inherited members as needed. You'll see more about private inheritance in Chapter 23, "Understanding Polymorphism."

Creating Class Hierarchies

When designing a class hierarchy, you should implement a base class that defines a common functionality on which derived classes can build. A class hierarchy is comprised of different levels of inheritance among a group of related classes that work together to provide solutions to programming problems. Imagine a base class CBase and its derived class CDerived1. Now imagine the class CDerived2 inheriting from CDerived1. These classes form a simple hierarchy that is often presented in tree format, as shown in Figure 22.1.

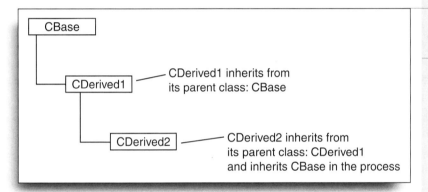

FIGURE 22.1
A simple class hierarchy.

Classes in a hierarchy usually have many things in common; the base class implements the basic functionality for this commonality. Any specialized class code should go into the derived classes. The base class should set the stage for all the derived classes, providing interface guidelines for its descendants by way of virtual functions and pure virtual functions.

SEE ALSO

➤ *To learn about virtual functions, see page 547*
➤ *To learn about pure virtual function, see page 549*

Designing Constructors and Destructors in a Hierarchy

Constructors and destructors are called for each class in an inheritance hierarchy. Derived class constructors are called only

Virtual and Pure Virtual Functions

Virtual functions ensure that the correct function is called for an object in an inheritance tree, no matter what expression is used to call the function. Pure virtual functions have no implementation in a base class—they are set equal to zero. A pure virtual function must be overridden and implemented in derived classes.

after all the inherited class constructors are called from the base class up through the derived class, giving each class in a hierarchy a shot at initializing and cleaning up its own portion of the derived class data.

For example, the constructor for a base class that allocates dynamic memory at run time should have a matching destructor that deallocates the memory automatically. Derived classes can each have their own dynamic allocations and deallocations to take care of in their own constructors and destructors. The program in Listing 22.1 provides a simple example of how this might look in a three-class hierarchy.

LISTING 22.1

① Lines 18-22: Allocate an array of 100 integers

LISTING 22.1   A Program Showing the Order of Constructor and Destructor Calls in a Simple Hierarchy

```
 1: /////////////////////////////////////////////////////
 2: //  Module    : hierarchy1.cpp
 3: //
 4: //  Comments : Shows the order of constructor and
 5: //             destructor calls in a simple hierarchy
 6: /////////////////////////////////////////////////////
 7:
 8: #include <iostream>
 9:
10: using namespace std;
11:
12: /////////////////////////////////////////////////////
13: // Class CBase
14:
15: class CBase
16: {
17: public:
18:    CBase()
19:    {
20:        myInt = new int[100];
21:        cout << "CBase::myInt[100], allocating.\n";
22:    }
```

①

```
23:
24:     ~CBase()
25:     {
26:         if (myInt)
27:         {
28:             delete [] myInt;
29:             myInt = 0;
30:             cout << "CBase::myInt[100], deallocating.\n";
31:         }
32:     }
33:
34: protected:
35:     int *myInt;
36: };
37:
38: //////////////////////////////////////////////////////
39: // Class CDerived1
40:
41: class CDerived1 : public CBase
42: {
43: public:
44:     CDerived1()
45:     {
46:         myFloat = new float[100];
47:         cout <<
48:             "CDerived1::myFloat[100], allocating.\n";
49:     }
50:
51:     ~CDerived1()
52:     {
53:         if (myFloat)
54:         {
55:             delete [] myFloat;
56:             myFloat = 0;
57:             cout <<
58:                 "CDerived1::myFloat[100], deallocating.\n";
59:         }
60:     }
61:
62: protected:
```

LISTING 22.1 CONTINUED

2 Lines 24-32: Delete the array of integers

3 Line 35: The protected int pointer myInt

4 Lines 44-49: Allocate an array of 100 floats

5 Lines 51-60: Delete the array of floats

continues…

LISTING 22.1 **Continued**

```
63:    float *myFloat;        6
64: };
65:
66: //////////////////////////////////////////////////////
67: // Class CDerived2
68:
69: class CDerived2 : public CDerived1
70: {
71: public:
72:    CDerived2()
73:    {
74:        myDouble = new double[100];
75:        cout << "CDerived2::myDouble[100], allocating.\n";
76:    }
77:
78:    ~CDerived2()
79:    {
80:        if (myDouble)
81:        {
82:            delete [] myDouble;
83:            myDouble = 0;
84:            cout <<
85:                "CDerived2::myDouble[100], deallocating.\n";
86:        }
87:    }
88:
89: protected:
90:    double *myDouble;        9
91: };
92:
93: //////////////////////////////////////////////////////
94: // main()
95:
96: void main()
97: {
98:    CDerived2 d2;
99: }
```

The constructors and destructors of the three classes generate the output for this program:

```
CBase::myInt[100], allocating...
CDerived1::myFloat[100], allocating...
CDerived2::myDouble[100], allocating...
CDerived2::myDouble[100], deallocating...
CDerived1::myFloat[100], deallocating...
CBase::myInt[100], deallocating...
```

As you can see, the constructor for each class in the hierarchy is called, starting with the base class and working through the hierarchy until the derived class constructor is called. The destructors are called in reverse order, destroying the derived classes first, and ending with the base class.

Overriding Base Class Functions

When you derive a new class from an existing class, you'll often want to *override* a base class function. Overriding a base class function allows you to provide a new implementation of the function that better suits the derived class or enhances the base class function in some way. If the derived class's override function enhances the base class version, the overriding function should call the overridden function to take care of any tasks it needs to perform.

You override a base class member function by creating a derived class containing a member function having the same function signature. Overriding functions can call their inherited counterparts to take care of any tasks the base object has to accomplish in the base class version of the member function. In the next section, the three classes CBase, CDerived1, and CDerived2 introduced in this example are used to provide an example of function overriding.

Override

When you override a function, you implement a function in a derived class that has the same function signature of an existing function in the base class.

Providing Scope Resolution for Base and Derived Classes

To explicitly access a member of a class in a hierarchy, you must resolve the scope to the desired class. You must specify the class name, followed by the scope resolution operator (`::`), followed by the class member—as shown in this syntax:

```
ClassName::Member
```

This method applies not only to member functions but to all class members, including enumerations and static members. As an example, I'll use the hierarchy shown in Figure 22.1. As you can see in this figure, the base class `CBase` is at the root of the hierarchy. The class `CDerived1` derives from `CBase`. The class `CDerived2` derives from class `CDerived1`. Assume that each class has a member function named `Draw()`. When calling `Draw()` for these classes, you can explicitly resolve the scope, specifying which specific class's `Draw()` function you mean. A `CDerived2` object inherits the `Draw()` functions from both of its ancestor classes, meaning that including its own `Draw()` function, it contains three different versions, explicitly accessed like this:

```
CBase1::Draw()
CDerived1::Draw()
CDerived2::Draw()
```

Calling `Draw()` without explicit scope resolution implicitly calls `CDerived2::Draw()`, because a `CDerived2` object is doing the calling.

Figure 22.2 shows the relation of a similar hierarchy of overridden member functions. This figure shows a three-tier hierarchy composed of `ClassA`, `ClassB`, and `ClassC`, where `ClassB` derives from (contains) `ClassA`, and `ClassC` derives from (contains) `ClassB`.

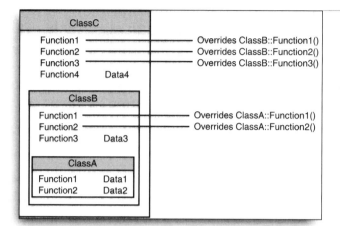

FIGURE 22.2

Overriding member functions in a simple three-tier hierarchy with several override functions.

Calling Base Class Functions

When a derived class member function overrides a base class member function, it is often necessary to call the base class function from within the derived class function. This arrangement allows each level of a class hierarchy to perform its own relevant work, resulting in a much better abstraction of the hierarchy.

Assume that the Draw() member in the CBase class hierarchy is a function that performs the work of drawing something graphically. Different computer systems have different initialization requirements for drawing graphics, but all of them need initialization of some sort. The Draw() function in the base class CBase could simply initialize the graphics subsystem of the computer, making sure that everything is set up and ready for drawing something by calling a helper function to initialize graphics:

```
bool CBase::Draw()
{
   // Initialize graphics
   return InitGraphics();
}
```

In this case, InitGraphics() is a system-dependent function that initializes graphics for a specific computer platform or compiler. The CDerived1 class should only concern itself with drawing whatever it is that CDerived1 objects are supposed to draw. The computer's graphics subsystem must be ready and waiting to draw the graphics. The beauty of inheritance is that the overriding CDerived1::Draw() function can let its inherited CBase::Draw() function do the work of initializing the computer's graphics subsystem.

Assume that the CDerived1 object is supposed to draw a color-filled rectangle. The CDerived1::Draw() function must first call the inherited CBase::Draw() function to initialize graphics, and then it can draw the rectangle. Assuming that DrawRect() is a function you've written to draw a rectangle, the CDerived1::Draw()function would look like this:

```
bool CDerived1::Draw()
{
    // Initialize graphics
    if (!CBase::Draw())
        return false;

    // Draw a rectangle
    DrawRect();
}
```

Let's further assume that the CDerived2 object is supposed to draw some text on top of the color-filled rectangle. The CDerived2::Draw() function should first call the inherited CDerived1::Draw() function to initialize graphics and draw the rectangle. Assuming that DrawText() is a function you've written to draw graphical text to the screen, the CDerived2::Draw() function would look like this:

```
bool CDerived2::Draw()
{
    // Initialize graphics and draw a rectangle
    if (!CDerived1::Draw())
        return false;
```

```
    // Draw some text
    DrawText();
}
```

In this scenario, `CDerived2::Draw()` first calls `CDerived1::Draw()` to draw the rectangle, and `CDerived1::Draw()` calls `CBase::Draw()` to initialize the graphics subsystem. After these tasks are performed by the base classes, the `CDerived2::Draw()` function can draw the text atop the rectangle. In this way, classes within a hierarchy can each perform their own small portion of the work.

Implementing a Class Hierarchy

The vehicle classes discussed in Chapter 20, "Introducing Object-Oriented Programming," are a good example of the object-oriented principles of encapsulation, inheritance, and polymorphism. The program in Listing 22.2 shows a very basic implementation of the `CLandVehicle` inheritance hierarchy. Each class defined in the program contains only a constructor, a destructor, and a `Draw()` member function. Each member function in each class simply writes a string to the standard output device to show the calling sequence of construction, execution, and destruction as the program runs.

LISTING 22.2   **A Program Showing the *CLandVehicle* Inheritance Hierarchy in Action**

```
 1: //////////////////////////////////////////////////////
 2: // Module  : vehicle.cpp
 3: //
 4: // Purpose : Demonstrates inheritance
 5: //////////////////////////////////////////////////////
 6:
 7: #include <iostream>
 8: using namespace std;
 9:
10: const char NL = '\n';
11:
12: //////////////////////////////////////////////////////
```

continues…

LISTING 22.2 **Continued**

```
13: // Base class: CVehicle
14:
15: class CVehicle
16: {
17: public:
18:    CVehicle()
19:       { cout << "Creating CVehicle." << NL; }
20:
21:    ~CVehicle()
22:       { cout << "Destroying CVehicle." << NL; }
23:
24:    void Draw()
25:       { cout << "Drawing CVehicle." << NL; }
26: };
27:
28: //////////////////////////////////////////////////////////
29: // Land vehicle base class: CLandVehicle
30:
31: class CLandVehicle : public CVehicle
32: {
33: public:
34:    CLandVehicle()
35:       { cout << "Creating CLandVehicle." << NL; }
36:
37:    ~CLandVehicle()
38:       { cout << "Destroying CLandVehicle." << NL; }
39:
40:    void Draw()
41:    {
42:       CVehicle::Draw();  // Call inherited member
43:       cout << "Drawing CLandVehicle." << NL;
44:    }
45: };
46:
47: //////////////////////////////////////////////////////////
48: // Truck base class: CTruck
49:
50: class CTruck : public CLandVehicle
51: {
52: public:
53:    CTruck()
54:       { cout << "Creating CTruck." << NL; }
```

```
55:
56:    ~CTruck()
57:      { cout << "Destroying CTruck." << NL; }
58:
59:    void Draw()
60:    {
61:       CLandVehicle::Draw();  // Call inherited member
62:       cout << "Drawing CTruck." << NL;
63:    }
64: };
65:
66: //////////////////////////////////////////////////////
67: // Car base class: CCar
68:
69: class CCar : public CLandVehicle
70: {
71: public:
72:    CCar()
73:      { cout << "Creating CCar." << NL; }
74:
75:    ~CCar()
76:      { cout << "Destroying CCar." << NL; }
77:
78:    void Draw()
79:    {
80:       CLandVehicle::Draw();  // Call inherited member
81:       cout << "Drawing CCar." << NL;
82:    }
83: };
84:
85: //////////////////////////////////////////////////////
86: // Motorcycle base class: CMotorcycle
87:
88: class CMotorcycle : public CLandVehicle
89: {
90: public:
91:    CMotorcycle()
92:      { cout << "Creating CMotorcycle." << NL; }
93:
94:    ~CMotorcycle()
95:      { cout << "Destroying CMotorcycle." << NL; }
96:
```

continues…

LISTING 22.2 CONTINUED

(8) Lines 56-57: Display a destruction message

(9) Lines 59-64: Call the base function and displays a drawing message

(10) Lines 72-73: Display a creation message

(11) Lines 75-76: Display a destruction message

(12) Lines 78-82: Call the base class function and displays a drawing message

(13) Lines 91-92: Display a creation message

(14) Lines 94-95: Display a destruction message

LISTING 22.2 CONTINUED

15 Lines 97-101: Call the base class function and displays a drawing message

16 Lines 110-112: Dynamically allocate vehicles

17 Lines 115-117: Call the Draw() function for each object

18 Lines 120-122: Delete the vehicle objects

LISTING 22.2 **Continued**

```
97:    void Draw()
98:    {
99:        CLandVehicle::Draw();  // Call inherited member
100:       cout << "Drawing CMotorcycle." << NL;
101:   }
102: };
103:
104: ///////////////////////////////////////////////////////
105: // Driver (pun intended)
106:
107: void main()
108: {
109:    // Create some vehicles
110:    CTruck      *pTruck = new CTruck;
111:    CCar        *pCar = new CCar;
112:    CMotorcycle *pMotorcycle = new CMotorcycle;
113:
114:    // Use the vehicles
115:    pTruck->Draw();
116:    pCar->Draw();
117:    pMotorcycle->Draw();
118:
119:    // Send 'em to the scrapyard
120:    delete pTruck;
121:    delete pCar;
122:    delete pMotorcycle;
123: }
```

The output for the program in Listing 22.2 clearly shows the class inheritance chain for the explicit construction and destruction of the objects *pTruck, *pCar, and *pMotorcycle. As you can see here, each of the base class constructors is called:

```
Creating CVehicle.
Creating CLandVehicle.
Creating CTruck.
Creating CVehicle.
Creating CLandVehicle.
```

```
Creating CCar.
Creating CVehicle.
Creating CLandVehicle.
Creating CMotorcycle.
Drawing CVehicle.
Drawing CLandVehicle.
Drawing CTruck.
Drawing CVehicle.
Drawing CLandVehicle.
Drawing CCar.
Drawing CVehicle.
Drawing CLandVehicle.
Drawing CMotorcycle.
Destroying CTruck.
Destroying CLandVehicle.
Destroying CVehicle.
Destroying CCar.
Destroying CLandVehicle.
Destroying CVehicle.
Destroying CMotorcycle.
Destroying CLandVehicle.
Destroying CVehicle.
```

The classes in this program display output messages using std::cout in the constructor, destructor, and Draw() member functions of each class. From within its own Draw() function, each class except CVehicle (the only non-derived class in the hierarchy) calls its inherited version of the Draw() function, ensuring that all levels of the hierarchy can perform properly.

For example, a truck is created on line 110, and the truck is "drawn" by calling the pTruck->Draw() method on line 115. The CTruck::Draw() method begins on line 59, and in turn calls its inherited CLandVehicle::Draw() method. The CLandVehicle::Draw() method begins on line 40, and in turn calls its inherited CVehicle::Draw() method, defined on lines 24 and 25. This chain of inherited calls allows each inherited object to perform some work specific to itself. Of course, the methods presented here do nothing except print a message to the screen, but they could perform actual drawing functions if graphics were actually being used.

Don't Forget to Call Inherited Functions

Because the derived member functions call their inherited counterparts first, the draw order proceeds from the top of the hierarchy down to the caller. You will usually call inherited functions in this fashion, ensuring that any work that must be performed by an ancestor is done. Hard-to-find bugs can arise from forgetting to call inherited member functions!

Using Friend Functions and Classes

You have seen how C++ provides access specifiers for class members, allowing you to hide class data as needed. When a class's members use public access, any runtime object can manipulate these public members at any time. C++ prevents any sort of possible misuse of class members by providing protected access for inherited classes, and private access for objects of the same class. All other non-related classes or functions are denied access to members that are public or protected.

You'll find that sometimes it's convenient—even necessary—to allow a function external to a class to access that class's protected or private members. Similarly, on occasion you'll need to give a class special access to some non-related class's protected or private members. This special access to the hidden parts of an object's life is granted to only those functions and classes that the object considers *friends*. Classes can declare friends as needed to simplify certain programming tasks, while keeping its class members hidden from non-friends (everyone else).

Using Friend Functions

Friend Function

A friend function is a function external to a class that has full access to all class members, including those that are protected and private.

A function that's declared within a class as a *friend function* has special access privileges for the class. Friend functions aren't class members, however; they are regular functions external to the class (that is, not found within the class scope).

Friend functions are often used to define operators. For example, you might want to write an operator function `operator+()` so that its usage syntax would be `c3 = c1 + c2`. Unfortunately, you can't do this as a class member function, because operators that are class members can take only a single argument (operand). The expression

```
c3 = c1 + c2
```

obviously has two operands: `c1` and `c2`. This means that `operator+()` with two explicit operands is out of the question as a class member because you'd have to supply two arguments to the operator function. The closest you can get to `operator+()` with an operator member is operator+=(). The second argument (operand) in this case is implicit—composed of the object's own data members. Using some class CPoint2d that represents a two-dimensional point, you'd have this as a member operator+=():

```
Class CPoint2d { int x, y };

CPoint2d& operator+=(const CPoint2d& p)
{
    this->x += p.x;
    this->y += p.y;
}
```

You could use this operator as follows:

```
CPoint2d p1 = { 2, 3 };
CPoint2d p2 = { 4, 5 };

p1 += p2;
```

The result of this would be: p1.x==6, and p1.y==8.

To correctly implement operator addition of two CPoint2d objects, you must instead define a global friend operator that takes two arguments. Although you're not confined to one argument for member functions other than operators, it's often just as convenient to define a global friend function to help out (for example, a function to find the midpoint between two given points). As a concrete example of friend operators and functions, Listing 22.3 shows the header file for a class CPoint2d that declares two friends: one an operator+() and the other a Midpoint() function. Note that this class is implemented inline, having no corresponding point2d.cpp file.

LISTING 22.3 A Class That Uses a Friend Operator and a Friend Function

```
1: ///////////////////////////////////////////////////
2: //  Module  : Point2d.h
3: //
4: //  Purpose : Class declaration and inline
5: //            implementation of a 2d point
6: ///////////////////////////////////////////////////
7:
```

continues…

LISTING 22.3

① Lines 8-9: Single header inclusion directives

② Lines 21-23: Default constructors for the CPoint2d class

③ Lines 32-33: Declare the external operator operator+() to be a friend

④ Lines 37-38: Declare the external function Midpoint() to be a friend

⑤ Lines 46-50: Prototypes for the external friend functions

LISTING 22.3   **Continued**

```cpp
 8: #ifndef __POINT2D_H__ ──────┐ ①
 9: #define __POINT2D_H__ ──────┘
10:
11: #include <iostream>
12:
13: //////////////////////////////////////////////////////////
14: // Class CPoint2d
15:
16: class CPoint2d
17: {
18: public:
19:     // Constructors
20:     //
21:     CPoint2d() : x(0.0f), y(0.0f) { } ────────┐
22:     CPoint2d(float NewX = 0.0f, float NewY = 0.0f)  │ ②
23:         { x = NewX; y = NewY; } ───────────────┘
24:
25:     // Member function
26:     //
27:     void dump() { std::cout << "X == " << x
28:         << ", Y == " << y << '\n'; };
29:
30:     // Friend operator
31:     //
32:     friend CPoint2d operator+ (const CPoint2d& p1, ──┐
33:         const CPoint2d& p2); ────────────────────┘  ③
34:
35:     // Friend function
36:     //
37:     friend CPoint2d Midpoint(const CPoint2d &p1, ──┐
38:         const CPoint2d &p2); ─────────────────────┘ ④
39:
40: protected:
41:     float x, y;
42: };
43:
44: // Friend prototypes
45: //
```

```
46: extern inline CPoint2d operator+ (const CPoint2d& p1,
47:    const CPoint2d& p2);
48:
49: extern CPoint2d Midpoint(const CPoint2d& p1,
50:    const CPoint2d& p2);
51:
52: #endif //__POINT2D_H__
```

LISTING 22.2 CONTINUED

5 Lines 46-50: Prototypes for the external friend functions

On lines 27 and 28 the `dump()` member function displays the values of class data members x and y. The friend operator (lines 32 and 33) and friend function (lines 37 and 38) are both external to the class and are totally unrelated, but they access the x and y data members of the CPoint2d class directly, with no trouble, because they're declared within the class as friends of the class. Listing 22.4 shows the code for the implementation of these friends of CPoint2d.

LISTING 22.4 **The Implementation of the Global Friends of the *CPoint2d* Class**

```
1: /////////////////////////////////////////////////////
2: // Module   : friends.cpp
3: //
4: // Comments : A global function and operator that
5: //              are friends of CPoint2d
6: /////////////////////////////////////////////////////
7:
8: #include "point2d.h"
9:
10: /////////////////////////////////////////////////////
11: // CPoint2d global friend operator+()
12:
13: inline CPoint2d operator+ (const CPoint2d& p1,
14:                            const CPoint2d& p2)
15: {
16:    return CPoint2d(p1.x + p2.x, p1.y + p2.y);
17: }
18:
19: /////////////////////////////////////////////////////
20: // CPoint2d global friend function
```

LISTING 22.4

1 Line 8: Includes the CPoint2d header file

2 Lines 13-17: Implement the operator+() function

continues...

LISTING 22.4 CONTINUED

③ Lines 22-31: Implements the Midpoint() function

LISTING 22.4   **Continued**

```
21:
22: CPoint2d Midpoint(const CPoint2d& p1,
23:                      const CPoint2d& p2)
24: {
25:    CPoint2d p;
26:
27:    p.x = (p1.x + p2.x) / 2;
28:    p.y = (p1.y + p2.y) / 2;
29:
30:    return p;
31: }
```

③

These implementations are straightforward and simple; they show quite nicely that the friends can access the CPoint2d protected members with no problems.

The driver program in Listing 22.5 shows the use of the CPoint2d class and its friends operator+() and Midpoint().

LISTING 22.5   **A Program That Demonstrates the Use of a Friend Operator and a Friend Function**

```
1: ///////////////////////////////////////////////////////
2: // Module   : FriendsMain.cpp
3: //
4: // Comments : Shows the use of friend functions
5: //              and operators for a 2d point class
6: ///////////////////////////////////////////////////////
7:
8: #include <iostream>
9: #include "point2d.h"
10:
11: using namespace std;
12:
13: ///////////////////////////////////////////////////////
14: // main()
15:
16: void main()
17: {
18:    // Create some points
19:    //
```

```
20:    CPoint2d pt1(1.5f, 2.5f);
21:    CPoint2d pt2(1.5f, 2.5f);
22:
23:    // Add them to get a third point
24:    //
25:    cout << "Add two points to get a third:\n\n";
26:    CPoint2d pt3 = pt1 + pt2;
27:
28:    // Dump the contents of the point data members
29:    //
30:    cout << "pt1: "; pt1.dump();
31:    cout << "pt2: "; pt2.dump();
32:    cout << "pt3: "; pt3.dump();
33:
34:    // Get the midpoint between pt1 and pt2 and
35:    //
36:    cout << '\n'
37:        << "Get the midpoint between pt1 and pt3:\n\n";
38:    CPoint2d pt4 = Midpoint(pt1, pt3);
39:
40:    // Dump the resulting midpoint to the screen
41:    //
42:    cout << "pt4: "; pt4.dump();
43: }
```

LISTING 22.5

1 Lines 20-21: Create and initializes two points

2 Line 26: Use the operator+() function

3 Lines 30-32: Call the dump() member of each point object

4 Line 38: Call the friend function MidPoint()

5 Line 42: Call the dump() member for the midpoint

The output of the program shows that the friends work correctly, as you can see here:

```
Add two points to get a third:


pt1: X == 1.5, Y == 2.5
pt2: X == 1.5, Y == 2.5
pt3: X == 3, Y == 5


Get the midpoint between pt1 and pt3:


pt4: X == 2.25, Y == 3.75
```

When the main() function reaches the expression on line 26, the compiler determines whether a suitable user-defined friend operator exists. In this case, the function signature for operator+() agrees with the use of the operator on line 26, so the operator function is called.

Declaring Friends

Friend declarations aren't affected by class access specifiers, so you can declare them anywhere within a class declaration.

From lines 30 through 31, the contents of the three `CPoint2d` objects are dumped to the screen to verify that everything is working as expected. The friend function `Midpoint()` then calculates the midpoint by directly accessing the x and y members of `Cpoint3d`; in line 42, the `dump()` member displays the results.

Using Friend Classes

Friend Class

A friend class is a class whose member functions are all friend functions of some class.

A *friend class* is a class whose member functions are all friend functions of some class. In other words, when class A declares another class B to be its friend, all the friend class B's member functions gain full access to class A's private and protected members.

Friendship and Inheritance

Friendship between classes isn't inherited, so friends of a parent class don't become friends of its children.

With friend classes, the friendship is a one-way street. Friend class B can access the class A's members, but class A can't reciprocate unless class B declares class A to be its friend as well. (If this happens, the classes automatically become best friends—just kidding.)

Now that you've seen how important family and friendship is in object-oriented C++ programming, let's take a look at how to package up the results of your efforts into binary libraries that promote class reuse.

Creating Class Libraries

Creating a binary library of your classes is a great programming productivity tool that can be indispensable for large development projects. Building libraries is easy—you just need some object files and a librarian program. Each compiler vendor supplies its own flavor of librarian, so refer to your compiler documentation to get specifics.

Using a librarian, you can build and modify your own libraries, and you can modify libraries provided by other programmers and commercial libraries you've purchased. For example, Borland C++ uses a librarian program called TLIB. In addition to creating static link libraries, librarians can perform many other useful library management tasks, such as:

- Adding object modules or additional libraries to an existing library
- Listing the contents of a library
- Extracting object modules from an existing library
- Removing object modules from an existing library
- Replacing object modules within an existing library

When you use libraries, large projects become much more manageable, requiring only the library file and any headers files used by the library.

Creating a Binary Library of Your Classes

If each of the vehicle classes introduced back in Listing 22.2 were pulled out into separate interface and implementation files (as they *should* be in the real world), each class would compile into a separate object file (module). This process might yield the following object files: vehicle.obj, landvehc.obj, car.obj, motorcyc.obj, and truck.obj.

Using the Borland librarian TLIB, these object modules can be linked together to form a library file called vehicle.lib with this simple command line:

```
tlib vehicle.lib +vehicle +landvehc +car +motorcyc +truck
```

Using the Library

The resulting library file vehicle.lib can then be linked with an application, but the compiler must know about the classes in the library before it can compile a module that uses the library. Modules using the library can only access its classes by including a header file for each library class used by the module.

A convenient solution to the pain of including a bunch of class headers in all your source files is to create a library header file. This is a header file that itself just includes every header needed by the library. By including a library header file with the header files for each object module, you can use all the classes in the library by using a single #include directive in a program source file. Listing 22.6 shows a sample header file for the vehicle.lib.

LISTING 22.6 The Header File for the Vehicle Library Includes All the Header Files Needed by the Library

```
 1: /////////////////////////////////////////////////////
 2: // Header  : VehicleLib.h
 3: //
 4: // Purpose : Header for the vehicle library vehicle.lib
 5: /////////////////////////////////////////////////////
 6:
 7: #ifndef __VEHICLELIB_H__
 8: #define __VEHICLELIB_H__
 9:
10: #include "vehicle.h"
11: #include "landvehc.h"
12: #include "car.h"
13: #include "motorcyc.h"
14: #include "truck.h"
15:
16: #endif // __VEHICLELIB_H__
```

Now, by simply including VehicleLib.h in a module and linking with vehicle.lib, all the functionality of the vehicle classes becomes available, as shown in this complete program:

```
#include "VehicleLib.h"

void main()
{
   CCar car;
   car.Draw();
}
```

In the next chapter, you'll learn about virtual functions and how classes in a hierarchy can use polymorphism to further ease your programming burdens.

Understanding Polymorphism

Learn to create abstract classes and define virtual functions

See how virtual functions work

Use pointers to classes in a hierarchy

Discover how to avoid the problem of class slicing

Realize the importance of using virtual destructors with polymorphism

What Is Polymorphism?

When I was a kid, I used to enjoy playing the game Dungeons and Dragons, and I still play it sometimes with my son. (He likes it, too.) The game allows you to choose one of several types of characters, such as a warrior or a wizard, and take on that character's role. In the game, I often choose to play the role of a wizard, working magic and casting spells to help fellow players as needed. One of my favorite spells is called *polymorph* because it lets the wizard change into any type of creature, such as a horse or a dragon.

Much like the wizard's spell (and using the same terminology), the game of C++ allows an object of one class to take on the role of one of several types of related classes. Under certain conditions, like a wizard, an object can polymorph, changing into any type of object derived from it. In C++, the potential of different objects in a class hierarchy to respond differently to the same message is known as *polymorphism*, which (as you learned briefly in Chapter 20, "Introducing Object-Oriented Programming") literally means "many shape," or "shape-shifter." You accomplish polymorphism in C++ through the use of *virtual* member functions.

Polymorph

Polymorphing is the act of changing from one class type to another, related class type.

Polymorphism

Polymorphism is the potential of different objects in a class hierarchy to respond differently to the same message.

`virtual`

The C++ keyword `virtual` enables the object-oriented features of polymorphism.

Getting Virtual

A virtual member function in a base class allows a derived class to change the implementation of the method. Like the wizard's spell, the virtual member function allows a base class object to polymorph into a derived object, actually becoming an object of the descended class. This is powerful stuff!

The path to polymorphism

1. Create a base class with at least one virtual member function.

2. Derive a new class (or classes) from the base class.

3. Override the virtual function (or functions) from the base class.

4. Respond appropriately to the virtual functions in each derived class.

By providing virtual functions in a base class, you open the door to the polymorphic capabilities of C++. The magic of virtual functions makes polymorphism possible. In the next sections, you'll see how to create and use virtual functions to give your programs extra flexibility (not to mention the ability to shape-shift).

Understanding Virtual Functions

Virtual functions are the key to polymorphism; the `virtual` keyword makes virtual functions possible. It's expected that virtual functions declared in a base class will be also declared in the derived class, with the same list of parameters. The version of the function in the derived class overrides the virtual function in the base class, so the function in the derived class *must* have the same signature as the virtual function it overrides. The `virtual` keyword is used only in the class interface for a member function, not in its implementation. The syntax for creating a virtual function is shown here:

```
virtual MemberFunction
```

As an example, here's the declaration of a class `CBase` containing one virtual function, specified as such by the `virtual` keyword:

```
class CBase
{
protected:
   virtual void func1();
};
```

However, you don't use the `virtual` keyword in the function implementation:

```
void CBase::func1() { }
```

If the overriding function in a derived class adds to or somehow relies on the functionality in the base class version, the derived class function should explicitly call its inherited base class version. For example, given class `CBase` containing the virtual function `func1()`, its derived class `CDerived` can override this virtual function with a `func1()` of its own. The derived class function `func1()` could explicitly call the base class `func1()` so that any work the base class version needs to perform can be executed.

Virtual Inheritance

An ancestor class passes on all its virtual member functions to its descendants. Descendants of the ancestor class can override the implementation of a base class's virtual function as long as the descendant uses the same function signature.

As with nonvirtual functions, the base class version of a function is called using the base class name (CBase), followed by the scope resolution operator (::), followed by the function call (func1()), as in CBase::func1(). This is the sort of thing that constructors and destructors do by default. Here's a look at this virtual inheritance scenario in code, where a class CDerived inherits from CBase a virtual func1():

```
class CBase
{
public:
    virtual void func1()
    {
        cout << "Calling CBase::func1()\n";
        // do other stuff here...
    }
};


class CDerived : public CBase // Derive from CBase
{
public:
    void func1()
    {
        CBase::func1(); // Call the inherited member function
        cout << "Calling CDerived::func1()\n";
        // do other stuff here...
    }
};
```

Abstract Base Class

An abstract base class is a C++ class that contains at least one pure virtual function.

Pure Virtual Function

A pure virtual function is a virtual function declaration in a base class that is set equal to zero. The base class provides no implementation for a pure virtual function, leaving this task up to the classes derived from the base class.

Creating Abstract Base Classes

When a base class is designed merely as a generic blueprint for more specialized classes, but is *not* meant to be used itself, it's called an *abstract base class*. An abstract base class can never have objects created from it—its purpose is to act only as the parent class for its child classes to build on. An abstract base class makes use of one or more *pure virtual functions* to specify a framework for derived classes to follow, but supplies no implementation of its own for these functions. Derived classes must supply their own implementations of the base class's pure virtual functions.

Defining Pure Virtual Functions

The one thing that marks a class as an abstract base class is the presence of a *pure virtual function*. This is a function that is set equal to zero in the class declaration. An abstract class must contain at least one pure virtual function. Pure virtual functions act as placeholders that prototype a function to be implemented in derived classes. As an example, the following is a class declaration for some new class CBase, which declares a pure virtual function Draw(). You don't supply a definition for a pure virtual function; just add = 0 to the end of the function declaration, like this:

```
class CBase
{
public:
    virtual void Draw() = 0;
};
```

Remember that you can use an abstract base class only as a base class for deriving other classes—you can't declare an instance of an abstract base class. If you try to instantiate an object of an abstract base class, the compiler will generate an error. To see this for yourself, type the program in Listing 23.1 and try to compile it.

LISTING 23.1   **A Program Demonstrating That You Can't Instantiate an Abstract Base Class**

```
 1: ///////////////////////////////////////////////////////
 2: //  Module    : Abstract.cpp
 3: //
 4: //  Comments : Demonstrates that an abstract class
 5: //             can't be instantiated (this program
 6: //             won't compile).
 7: ///////////////////////////////////////////////////////
 8:
 9: class CBase
10: {
11: protected:
12:    virtual void Draw() = 0;
13: };
```

continues...

LISTING 23.1   Continued

```
14:
15: void main()
16: {
17:     CBase b;      // Error! Can't instantiate abstract class!
18: }
```

On line 12 of this listing, the pure virtual function CBase::Draw() makes CBase an abstract base class. Line 17 attempts to instantiate an abstract base class object, which should cause the compiler to generate an error. When you try to compile this program, you'll get an error message similar to the following (if you *don't* get an error, you should get a new compiler):

```
Error: 'CBase'
Cannot instantiate abstract class due to following members:

'void CBase::Draw(void)' : pure virtual function not defined
```

Understanding Virtual Tables

Okay, you've seen how to write virtual functions, but how do they work? Various compilers implement virtual functions in various ways, but the most popular solution by far is the use of a virtual function table (also known as a VTABLE, a VTBL, or a v-table).

A VTABLE holds pointers to all the virtual functions in a class. A virtual function pointer (VPTR) is stored within each object. When a derived class accesses a virtual member function, the class looks in the VTABLE to find out which version of the function it should call. In the case of the CBase and CDerived classes defined earlier in this chapter, their relationship is as follows:

- A CDerived object *is* a CBase object.
- A CDerived object *contains* a CBase object.
- A CBase object *can become* a CDerived object.

The specifics of these relationships are easiest seen with a few examples. By creating a CBase object and calling func1(), the

VPTR points to the virtual func1() function in the CBase class (its only alternative because it's the only func1() function in the class), like this:

```
CBase *obj = new CBase;
obj->func1();  // The CBase VPTR points to CBase::func1()
```

Figure 23.1 presents this arrangement graphically.

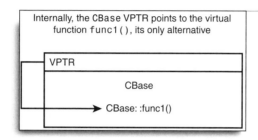

Internally, the CBase VPTR points to the virtual function func1(), its only alternative

VPTR

CBase

CBase::func1()

FIGURE 23.1

The virtual function pointer in the CBase class points to its only alternative, Cbase::func1().

By creating a CDerived object and calling func1(), the VPTR points by default to the func1() override function in the CDerived class, like this:

```
CDerived *obj = new CDerived;
obj->func1();  // CDerived VPTR points to CDerived::func1()
```

A CDerived object's VPTR can point to either the CBase or CDerived version of func1() at runtime, depending on the circumstances. For example, the CDerived object obj *could* call the CBase version of func1() by specifying that version explicitly, like this:

```
CDerived *obj = new CDerived;
obj->CBase::func1();  // calls the inherited CBase::func1()
```

In this case, the CDerived object looks into its class VTABLE, finds CBase::func1(), and then assigns the address of the inherited function to the CDerived VPTR. (Note that this works only if the inherited function is public because main() can access only public class methods.) Figure 23.2 presents this arrangement graphically.

FIGURE 23.2

The virtual function pointer in the CDerived class can point to either CBase::func1() or CDerived::func1().

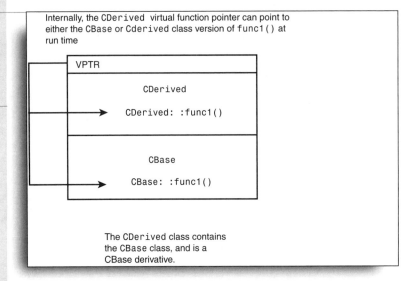

Internally, the CDerived virtual function pointer can point to either the CBase or Cderived class version of func1() at run time

VPTR

CDerived

CDerived: :func1()

CBase

CBase: :func1()

The CDerived class contains the CBase class, and is a CBase derivative.

Using Pointers to Classes in a Hierarchy

You've seen that a derived object actually contains the inherited object. Because a derived class actually contains and extends its base class, a pointer to the base class can assume the identity of a derived object. For example, with the base class CBase and its derived class CDerived1, a pointer to a CBase object can point to a CDerived1 object because CDerived1 *is* a CBase object—it inherits from and contains CBase:

```
CBase     *base;
CDerived1 derived1;

base = &derived1    // OK, CDerived1 is derived from CBase
```

Here's another, more concise way to dynamically accomplish this task:

```
CBase *base = new CDerived1; // Also OK: derived from CBase
```

Polymorphing with Pointers

A base object pointer that points to a derived object will call either the base class or the derived class version of a function, depending on whether the function is virtual in the base class. The program in Listing 23.2 demonstrates this, using both virtual and nonvirtual inheritance. This program shows the result of both using and *not* using the virtual keyword in a base class function declaration. This program defines two new simple class hierarchies: The base class CBase1 derives class CDerived1, and the base class CBase2 derives class CDerived2.

LISTING 23.2   **A Program Demonstrating How a Base Class Pointer That Points to a Descendant Can Polymorphically Handle Calls to Virtual and Nonvirtual Functions**

```
1: //////////////////////////////////////////////////////
2: //  Module  : virtual.cpp
3: //
4: //  Purpose : Demonstrates how a pointer to a base
5: //            class calls derived class functions for
6: //            virtual and nonvirtual base class
7: //            functions.
8: //////////////////////////////////////////////////////
9:
10: #include <iostream>
11:
12: //////////////////////////////////////////////////////
13: //  Class CBase1
14:
15: class CBase1
16: {
17: public:
18:    void Draw()
19:       { std::cout << "CBase1::Draw()\n"; }
20: };
21:
22: //////////////////////////////////////////////////////
23: //  Class CDerived1
24:
25: class CDerived1 : public CBase1 // Derive from CBase1
26: {
27: public:
28:    void Draw()
29:       { std::cout << "CDerived1::Draw()\n"; }
30: };
```

continues…

LISTING 23.2

❶ Lines 17-18: The CBase1 class declares Draw() as a nonvirtual member function

LISTING 23.2 CONTINUED

2 Lines 38-39: The CBase2 class declares Draw() as a virtual member function

3 Lines 59-62: Creates a CBase1 pointer and points it to a CDerived1 object

4 Lines 65-68: Draws base1 and derived1

LISTING 23.2   **Continued**

```
31:
32: /////////////////////////////////////////////////////
33: //  Class CBase2
34:
35: class CBase2  // Uses virtual Draw() function
36: {
37: public:
38:     virtual void Draw()
39:         { std::cout << "CBase2::Draw()\n"; }
40: };
41:
42: /////////////////////////////////////////////////////
43: //  Class CDerived2
44:
45: class CDerived2 : public CBase2 // Derive from CBase2
46: {
47: public:
48:     void Draw()
49:         { std::cout << "CDerived2::Draw()\n"; }
50: };
51:
52: /////////////////////////////////////////////////////
53: //  main()
54:
55: void main()
56: {
57:     // Create & use CBase1/CDerived1 object
58:     //
59:     CBase1    *base1;
60:     CDerived1  derived1;
61:
62:     base1 = &derived1;
63:
64:     std::cout << "base1->Draw() calls   : ";
65:     base1->Draw();
66:
67:     std::cout << "derived1.Draw() calls : ";
68:     derived1.Draw();
69:
70:     // Create & use CBase2/CDerived2 objects
71:     //
```

```
72:    CBase2     *base2;
73:    CDerived2  derived2;
74:
75:    base2 = &derived2;
76:
77:    std::cout << "\nbase2->Draw() calls    : ";
78:    base2->Draw();
79:    std::cout << "derived2.Draw() calls : ";
80:    derived2.Draw();
81: }
```

LISTING **23.2** CONTINUED

⑤ Lines 72-75: Creates a CBase2 pointer and points it to a CDerived2 object

The output from this program makes plain the internal differences between using virtual and nonvirtual functions in base classes:

```
base1->Draw() calls    : CBase1::Draw()
derived1.Draw() calls : CDerived1::Draw()


base2->Draw() calls    : CDerived2::Draw()
derived2.Draw() calls : CDerived2::Draw()
```

Notice that base2->Draw(), called on line 78, actually calls CDerived2::Draw() instead of CBase::Draw(). Because the base class CBase2 uses a virtual Draw() function, the base object pointer base2 (which actually points to the CDerived2 object derived2) uses polymorphism to appropriately call the derived class function CDerived2::Draw() instead of CBase2::Draw(). The base class CBase1 uses a nonvirtual Draw() function. Because nonvirtual functions can't be polymorphic, the base object pointer base1 (which actually points to the CDerived1 object derived1) calls the base class function CBase1::Draw().

The program in Listing 23.2 uses the address of an existing derived object to polymorph a base class pointer. As you saw earlier, a more convenient syntax uses dynamic allocation and direct polymorphism, directly assigning a newly allocated derived object to a base object pointer, like this:

```
CBase *obj = new CDerived;
```

The program in Listing 23.3 shows this entire process.

LISTING 23.3

① Line 24: Calls the derived class function

② Line 25: Calls the base class function

LISTING 23.3   **A Program That Demonstrates Polymorphism by Assigning a Base Class Pointer to a Derived Class Object**

```
 1: ////////////////////////////////////////////////////////
 2: // Module   : polymorph1.cpp
 3: //
 4: // Comments : Shows the use of polymorphic pointers
 5: ////////////////////////////////////////////////////////
 6:
 7: #include <iostream>
 8:
 9: class CBase
10: {
11: public:
12:    virtual void func1() { std::cout << "Base\n"; }
13: };
14:
15: class CDerived : public CBase
16: {
17: public:
18:    void func1() { std::cout << "Derived\n"; }
19: };
20:
21: void main()
22: {
23:    CBase *obj = new CDerived;
24:    obj->func1();
25:    obj->CBase::func1();
26:    delete obj;
27: }
```

The output from this program is simply this:

```
Derived
Base
```

On line 12 you define a public virtual function func1() in the base class CBase. On line 18 you define a public nonvirtual function in the derived class, which overrides the base class function CBase::func1(). On line 23, a base class pointer is polymorphed to reference a derived class object. Without explicit scope resolution, the statement on line 24 calls the derived class version of `func1()`.

Creating a Polymorphic Class Hierarchy

If a derived class *does not* provide an override function for a virtual function defined in a base class, the base class function will execute by default. If the derived class *does* provide an override function for a virtual function defined in a base class, the derived class function will execute by default.

To test polymorphic responses in a class hierarchy, let's create a basic hierarchy of classes representing some primitive three-dimensional geometric shapes. Classes for the following geometric shapes have to be defined:

- A box
- A cone
- A cylinder

The class names and inheritance relationships for these geometric primitives are presented in Table 23.1.

TABLE 23.1   **Classes to Represent Primitive Three-Dimensional Geometric Shapes**

Shape Type	Class	Base Class
Abstract	CShape3d	None
Box	CBox	CShape3d
Cone	CCone	CShape3d
Cylinder	CCylinder	CShape3d

The program in Listing 23.4 defines these classes. The code uses a single base class pointer to polymorphically call the member functions of all three descendant classes.

LISTING 23.4

Lines 18-33: The CShape3d class definition

LISTING 23.4   **A More Realistic Example of Polymorphism Using a Base Class, Three Derived Classes, and a Single Base Class Pointer**

```cpp
 1: /////////////////////////////////////////////////////////
 2: //   Module  : shapes.cpp
 3: //
 4: //   Purpose : Demonstrates base class pointer
 5: //             polymorphism
 6: /////////////////////////////////////////////////////////
 7:
 8: #include <iostream>
 9:
10: using namespace std;
11:
12: const char NL  = '\n';
13: const float PI = 3.14159f;
14:
15: /////////////////////////////////////////////////////////
16: // Class CShape3d
17:
18: class CShape3d
19: {
20: public:
21:     CShape3d() : myVolume(0.0f) { }
22:
23:     float Volume()
24:     {
25:        CalcVolume();
26:        return myVolume;
27:     }
28:
29: protected:
30:     virtual void CalcVolume() = 0;
31:
32:     float myVolume;
33: };
34:
35: /////////////////////////////////////////////////////////
36: // Class CBox
37:
```

```
38: class CBox : public CShape3d
39: {
40: public:
41:     // Constructor
42:     CBox(float l = 0.0f, float w = 0.0f, float h = 0.0f)
43:     {
44:         myLength = l;
45:         myWidth  = w;
46:         myHeight = h;
47:     }
48:
49: protected:
50:     void CalcVolume()
51:     {
52:         // Volume of a box: w * h
53:         myVolume = myWidth * myHeight;
54:     }
55:
56:     float myLength;
57:     float myWidth;
58:     float myHeight;
59: };
60:
61: /////////////////////////////////////////////////////
62: // Class CCylinder
63:
64: class CCylinder : public CShape3d
65: {
66: public:
67:     CCylinder(float r = 0.0f, float h = 0.0f)
68:     {
69:         myRadius = r;
70:         myHeight = h;
71:     }
72:
73: protected:
74:     void CalcVolume()
75:     {
76:         // Volume of a cylinder: PI * r*r * h
77:         myVolume = PI * myRadius * myRadius * myHeight;
78:     }
79:     float myRadius;
80:     float myHeight;
81: };
```

LISTING 23.4 CONTINUED

2 Lines 38-59: The CBox class definition

3 Lines 64-81: The CCylinder class definition

continues…

LISTING 23.4   **Continued**

```
82:
83: /////////////////////////////////////////////////////////
84: // Class CCone
85:
86: class CCone : public CShape3d
87: {
88: public:
89:    CCone(float r = 0.0f, float h = 0.0f)
90:    {
91:       myRadius = r;
92:       myHeight = h;
93:    }
94:
95: protected:
96:    void CalcVolume()
97:    {
98:       // Volume of a cone: 1/3 * PI * r*r * h
99:       myVolume = 0.333333f * PI * myRadius *
100:          myRadius * myHeight;
101:    }
102:    float myRadius;
103:    float myHeight;
104: };
105:
106: /////////////////////////////////////////////////////////
107: // main()
108:
109: void main()
110: {
111:    CShape3d *shape;
112:
113:    // A CShape3d pointer polymorphs into a CBox object
114:    //
115:    shape = new CBox(10.5f, 12.2f, 5.7f);
116:    std::cout << "Box Volume      : "
117:       << shape->Volume() << NL;
118:    delete shape;
119:
120:    // A CShape3d pointer polymorphs into a CCone object
121:    //
122:    shape = new CCone(1.2f, 3.4f);
```

④

⑤

```
123:     std::cout << "Cone Volume    : "
124:        << shape->Volume() << NL;
125:     delete shape;
126:
127:     // A CShape3d pointer polymorphs into a CCylinder
128:     //    object
129:     //
130:     shape = new CCylinder(1.2f, 4.5f);
131:     std::cout << "Cylinder Volume : "
132:        << shape->Volume() << NL;
133:     delete shape;
134: }
```

The output from this program is as follows, showing that the CShape3d pointer shape does indeed polymorph into other object types:

```
Box Volume      : 69.54
Cone Volume     : 5.12707
Cylinder Volume : 20.3575
```

The class declarations for the CShape3d, CBox, CCylinder, and CCone classes occurs from lines 18 through 104. Each class has Volume() and CalcVolume() virtual functions. Because of these virtual functions, the CShape3d pointer declared on line 111 can be used to polymorphically access the Volume() function of its derived classes, with the same pointer being used for each function call.

On line 115 you polymorph the CShape3d pointer into a CBox pointer, and the method call on line 117 actually calls the CBox::Volume() function.

On line 122 you polymorph the CShape3d pointer into a CCone pointer, and the method call on line 124 actually calls the CCone::Volume() function.

On line 130 you polymorph the CShape3d pointer into a CCylinder pointer, and the method call on line 132 actually calls the CCylinder::Volume() function.

Resolving Class Slicing

Polymorphism works only with pointers and references to objects. Serious problems can arise when passing polymorphic objects to functions by value instead of by reference or when copying one object to another. Passing a polymorphic object by value causes its copy constructor to be called; assigning one object to another causes its copy assignment operator function to be called. In either case, weird problems can crop up that are difficult to find and resolve. Here's an example of what might cause such a problem:

```
CShape3d *shape = new CCylinder;
CShape3d shape2 = *shape;
```

In this example, the shape2 object is assigned a CShape3d object, not a CCylinder object as you might expect. The reason for this is that the default copy assignment operator for an object such as CShape3d wouldn't know anything about the myRadius and myHeight members of the CCylinder class, so these members are "sliced off" (lost!) during the copy operation, which for a CShape3d object would look like this:

```
CShape3d& operator=(const CShape3d & shape)
{
    this->myVolume = shape.myVolume;
    return *this;
}
```

By modifying the CShape3d class to provide an empty implementation of CShape3d::CalcVolume() instead of a pure virtual function and then allocating some CCylinder objects assigned to CShape3d pointers, you can see the effects of class slicing for yourself. The modified CShaped3d class would look like this:

```
class CShape3d
{
public:
    CShape3d() : myVolume(0.0f) { }

    float Volume()
    {
        CalcVolume();
```

```
        return myVolume;
    }

protected:
    virtual void CalcVolume() { };

    float myVolume;
};
```

Next, add these three global functions to the program just before the main() function to experiment with class slicing:

```
void VolumeByAddress(CShape3d * shape);
void VolumeByReference(CShape3d & shape);
void VolumeByValue(CShape3d  shape);

void VolumeByAddress(CShape3d * shape)
    { std::cout << shape->Volume() << NL; }

void VolumeByReference(CShape3d & shape)
    { std::cout << shape.Volume() << NL; }

void VolumeByValue(CShape3d shape)
    { std::cout << shape.Volume() << NL; }
```

These three functions accept a CShape3d object by pointer address, by object reference, and by object value, respectively. The first two functions work with polymorphism; the third, passing the argument by value, does not. The VolumeByValue() function will slice the class, removing anything that's not part of the original CShape3d base class. To test this, replace the code in the main() function from Listing 23.4 with the code in Listing 23.5.

LISTING 23.5   A Modified *main()* Function to Test the Effects of Class Slicing

```
1: ////////////////////////////////////////////////////
2: // main()
3:
4: void main()
5: {
```

continues…

LISTING 23.5

1 Line 6: Declares a CShape3d pointer

2 Line 8: Polymorphs the CShape3d pointer into a CCylinder pointer

3 Line 10: Passes the polymorphed pointer by pointer address

4 Line 15: Passes the polymorphed pointer by object reference

5 Line 20: Passes the polymorphed pointer by value

LISTING 23.5   **Continued**

```
 6:    CShape3d *shape;  ————— 1

 7:

 8:    shape = new CCylinder(1.2f, 4.5f);  ————— 2
 9:    std::cout << "Cylinder Volume : ";
10:    VolumeByAddress(shape);  ————— 3
11:    delete shape;

12:

13:    shape = new CCylinder(1.2f, 4.5f);
14:    std::cout << "Cylinder Volume : ";
15:    VolumeByReference(*shape);  ————— 4
16:    delete shape;

17:

18:    shape = new CCylinder(1.2f, 4.5f);
19:    std::cout << "Cylinder Volume : ";
20:    VolumeByValue(*shape);  ————— 5
21:    delete shape;
22: }
```

The results of this little test are as follows:

```
Cylinder Volume : 20.3575
Cylinder Volume : 20.3575
Cylinder Volume : 0
```

As you can see, the third function call, `VolumeByValue()` on line 20, fails to produce the desired result thanks to the side effects of class slicing. Note that the `shape` pointer is assigned to a new `CCylinder` object just before each `VolumeBy*()` function call (on lines 8, 13, and 18) and is deleted just afterward. This approach ensures that the object being pointed to is freshly initialized before entering each test function (sort of like cleansing your palate with sherbet before moving to the next course of a fancy gourmet dinner).

Using Virtual Destructors

Problems can arise in your programs if the destructors for your classes don't clean up like they're supposed to. What would cause this to happen? Destructors are always called automatically, right? No, not always!

You see, if you polymorph a base class pointer into a derived class pointer, and the base class doesn't have a virtual destructor, the derived class destructor is never called. In many cases, this isn't a problem, but if the derived class destructor is supposed to do something really important, such as delete allocated memory, then you have a big problem: a hard-to-find memory leak.

The problem of destructors not being called properly occurs when you take a pointer to a base class, assign to it a pointer to a derived class, and then delete the object referenced by the pointer, as in this code snippet:

```
CBase *base = new CDerived;
delete base;
```

Although this code looks innocent enough (once you get used to the idea of polymorphism), a potentially devastating problem lurks in the shadows. The problem only arises if the base class destructor is nonvirtual. If this class definition is used for CBase, you're in trouble because the destructor is nonvirtual:

```
class CBase
{
public:
    CBase() : p(0) { std::cout << "CBase::CBase()\n"; }
    ~CBase() { std::cout << "CBase::~CBase()\n"; }

protected:
    int *p;
};
```

As an example of the dangerous nature of not using virtual destructors for base classes in a class hierarchy where polymorphism might be used, take a look at the program in Listing 23.6. This program generates a memory leak. It does so by allocating an array of 10,000 integers in a constructor that is never deleted. The integers in the array aren't deleted because, thanks to the polymorphism used in the program, the corresponding destructor is never called.

LISTING 23.6   A Program That Demonstrates the Importance of Virtual Destructors in Base Classes When Using Polymorphism

```
1: /////////////////////////////////////////////////////
2: // Module  : MemoryLeak.cpp
3: //
```

continues...

LISTING 23.6

① Lines 14-22: The definition for class CBase, improperly defining a nonvirtual destructor

② Lines 27-47: The definition for class CDerived

LISTING 23.6 **Continued**

```cpp
 4: //   Purpose : Demonstrates the importance of virtual
 5: //             destructors in base classes when using
 6: //             polymorphism.
 7: ////////////////////////////////////////////////////////
 8:
 9: #include <iostream>
10:
11: ////////////////////////////////////////////////////////
12: // Class CBase
13:
14: class CBase
15: {
16: public:
17:     CBase() : p(0) { std::cout << "CBase::CBase()\n"; }
18:     ~CBase() { std::cout << "CBase::~CBase()\n"; }
19:
20: protected:
21:     int *p;
22: };
23:
24: ////////////////////////////////////////////////////////
25: // Class CDerived
26:
27: class CDerived : public CBase
28: {
29: public:
30:     CDerived()
31:     {
32:         std::cout << "CDerived::CDerived(), allocating "
33:             "10,000 integers\n";
34:         p = new int[10000];
35:     }
36:
37:     ~CDerived()
38:     {
39:         std::cout << "CDerived::~CDerived(), "
40:             "deallocating 10,000 integers \n";
41:         if (p)
42:         {
43:             delete [] p;
44:             p = 0;
45:         }
46:     }
47: };
48:
```

```
49: ///////////////////////////////////////////////////////
50: // main()
51:
52: void main()
53: {
54:     CBase *base = new CDerived;
55:     delete base;
56:     std::cout << "Terminating program execution...\n";
57:     system("pause");
58: }
```

LISTING 23.6 CONTINUED

3 Lines 54-55: Creating and immediately deleting a polymorphic CDerived object

Although this program will compile, link, and run correctly, a serious memory leak exists that could wreak havoc on a user's computer. The output for this program shows that there is an enormous problem with the code:

```
CBase::CBase()
CDerived::CDerived(), allocating 10,000 integers
CBase::~CBase()
Terminating program execution...
```

Oops!! As you can see, the destructor for CDerived is never called! Those 10,000 integers are sitting out there in memory somewhere, lost forever, never having been deallocated (and the pointer to the integer array is long gone). Every time this program runs, a serious memory leak occurs. This is a *real danger* when using polymorphism!

How do you prevent this sort of problem? The answer is simple—if you plan on inheriting a new class from some existing class, the existing class should have its destructor declared as virtual. To eliminate the memory leak in this program, the proper thing to do is revise the base class destructor (on line 18 of Listing 23.6), declaring it as virtual, like this:

```
virtual ~CBase() { std::cout << "CBase::~CBase()\n"; }
```

This simple change allows the polymorphic nature of the program's CBase pointer base to call the destructors properly. By simply adding the keyword virtual to the CBase destructor, the destructors are called properly, and the memory leak vanishes, as you can see from the output of the revised program:

Use Virtual Destructors When Inheriting

It's important to declare a class's destructor as virtual if the class will ever act as a base class. Doing so can prevent undesirable memory leaks from occurring. When in doubt about whether you'll inherit from a class, default to using a virtual destructor.

```
CBase::CBase()
CDerived::CDerived(), allocating 10,000 integers
CDerived::~CDerived(), deallocating 10,000 integers
CBase::~CBase()
Terminating program execution...
```

Implementing Dynamic Storage in C++

Understand the benefits of container classes

Learn about dynamic arrays

Create a dynamic array class

Learn about linked lists

Create a linked list class

Container Classes

What do barrels, gas tanks, grocery bags, and milk cartons have in common? They're all containers, and people use containers to store things. When you design a program, it's often convenient to store similar data in containers of some sort. C++ classes are a great way to create dynamic containers that hold collections of objects while automatically handling memory management.

One common type of container is an *array*, a built-in feature of C++ you learned about in Chapter 6, "Using Arrays." Another common type of container is a *list*, which is a linear sequence of items. A list is a concept that's not directly supported by C++, but is easily created from C++ components. In this chapter, you'll see how to create classes that allow you to use dynamic arrays and lists of objects in your programs. Classes like these are called *container classes*, and they provide structured, dynamic storage in reusable modules that you can easily plug in to any program where they might be needed.

Creating Dynamic Arrays

The problem with ordinary C++ arrays is that they're static. To allocate the correct amount of storage space, you have to specify how many elements an array should have. Here's an example:

```
int MyIntArray[1000];
```

This statement statically reserves storage for 1000 integers, and the compiler sets aside this storage space at compile time. Many times, this isn't the best way to go about creating an array. You often just don't know how many elements are actually needed. When the number of elements isn't known at compile time, you can use the new operator to allocate storage dynamically at runtime, as shown in this example:

```
int count = 0;
cout << "How many integers in the dynamic array? ";
cin >> count;
int *pArray = new int[count];
```

This series of statements allows a user to specify how many elements should be dynamically allocated for the array. However, this approach still doesn't allow you to resize the array. It's stuck with the space you allocated. A *dynamic array* should expand and contract as needed.

Creating a Dynamic Array Class

The obvious solution for making dynamic arrays easy to use is to create a class that wraps an array, providing member functions to take care of the dirty work internally so that you don't have to reinvent the wheel every time you need a dynamic array. In this section, you create a container class that stores integers in a dynamic array. The array class should provide the ability to do the following:

- Add an item to the end of the array
- Insert an item into the array at a specified index
- Find an item within the array
- Delete a specific item from the array
- Automatically resize the array as items are added and deleted

In the following sections, you'll see how these items can be implemented for an array of integers by creating a class I'll call CIntArray. The foundation of this dynamic array class is an internal array that actually holds the integers. For the CIntArray class, let's create a pointer member (mypArray) that points to the start of the array. Another data member (mySize) will be useful for keeping track of how many elements are in the array. With these assumptions, we can create the following basic class declaration:

```
class CIntArray
{
protected:
    int *mypArray;
    int mySize;
};
```

In addition to these data members, several class methods are needed to provide the interface between the array and client programs that use the class. Table 24.1 describes these member functions.

Dynamic Array

A dynamic array expands and contracts dynamically, as needed, allocating only as much memory as is necessary.

Wrapper Classes

Wrapper classes typically encapsulate some set of global data and provide a set of functions to manipulate that data. Wrapping data and functions in a class allows you to use object-oriented techniques with the data.

TABLE 24.1   **The Class Methods to be Supported by the *CIntArray* Class**

Method	Description
Add()	Adds an item to the array.
Clear()	Clears all items from the array, reclaiming any allocated memory.
Insert()	Inserts an item at a specified array index.
Find()	Finds a specified integer value in the array.
Remove()	Removes a specified integer value from the array.
Size()	Returns the number of elements in the array.
operator=()	Copies the contents of one array to another array.
operator[]()	Provides access to the elements of the array.

First, we'll look at how these class methods might be implemented. Later in the chapter, you'll see the complete source code for the class interface and implementation.

SEE ALSO

➤ *For more information about operator functions, see page 347*

Adding an Item

To add a new item to the array, you must first allocate storage for the item. The CIntArray class will use dynamic allocation, reallocation, and deallocation to expand and contract the size of the array as needed. A reasonable name for a member function that adds an integer to the array is CIntArray::Add(). Because this CIntArray::Add() method will append an integer to the end of the array, the only parameter it needs is an integer. This gives us the following declaration for the CIntArray::Add() method:

```
bool Add(const int& i);
```

SEE ALSO

➤ *For more information about memory allocation and deallocation, see page 273*

The means used by the CIntArray class to resize the array as needed is simple.

Expanding an existing array

1. Each time an element is added, the class allocates a new array. The size of the new array accounts for any existing elements and the new element.

2. Copy the elements from the existing array into the new array, and add the new item.

3. Delete the original array and shift the mypArray pointer to point at the new array.

The key to allocating the correct number of elements when adding an item lies in the mySize member. When you are allocating the new array in step 1, the mySize member determines how many elements to allocate. By pre-incrementing the mySize member to account for the new element, you can allocate the new array like this:

```
int *pTemp = new int[++mySize];
```

Unfortunately, allocation might fail if there's no memory available, so it's always a good idea to check that the new pointer has a non-null value:

```
if (pTemp == 0)
{
   cerr << "New buffer memory allocation failed."
      << endl;
   --mySize;
   return false;
}
```

If the allocation succeeds (which it almost always will), then the existing array elements must be copied to the new array, as stated in step 2. The ANSI C library function memcpy() takes three arguments and copies bytes from one memory location to another. The first argument is a pointer to the target buffer, the second argument is a pointer to the source buffer, and the third argument is the number of bytes to copy. Using this function, copying the array is as easy as this:

```
if (mypArray)
   memcpy(pTemp, mypArray, mySize * sizeof(int));
```

Efficiency and Array Resizing

Adding and removing element in a dynamic array is usually quite efficient, since the elements are in contiguous memory blocks that can be copied from the old array to the new array by calling memcpy().

You can assign the value of the new element to the new array, using the array index `mySize-1` to account for the zero-based array, like this:

```
pTemp[mySize - 1] = i;
```

Once this is done, it's time for step 3. The existing array is easily deleted like this:

```
if (mypArray)
    delete [] mypArray;
```

The `mypArray` pointer can then be shifted to point to the newly allocated array, like this:

```
mypArray = pTemp;
```

Inserting an Item

Getting and Assigning Element Values

You can use the `CIntArray::opertor[]()` function to either get or set the value of an element in the array.

The `CIntArray::Insert()` method has to know two things to perform its task: the integer value to insert, and the array index into which it is to insert the value. This information gives us the following declaration for the `CIntArray::Insert()` function:

```
bool Insert(const int& i, const int& index);
```

Inserting an item into a specific array index means that all elements falling after the insertion point have to be shifted over to make room for the new element (see Figure 24.1).

FIGURE 24.1

Inserting a value means that other elements have to shift over to make room for the new element.

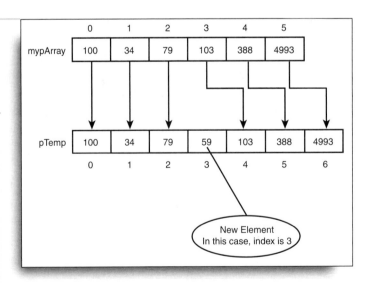

The insertion process is similar to the process used by CIntArray::Add() when you are adding a new element to the end of the array. The main difference is that the copying of the old array to the new array must be split into two steps to provide the empty element that will contain the new value. The first step copies all elements from element zero to the index specified for the insertion. Again using memcpy() to copy the elements, the first step of the copy looks like this,

```
memcpy(pTemp, mypArray, index * sizeof(int));
```

where index is the index of the new element. Figure 24.2 shows this process. The second step of the copy process copies the remaining elements to the rest of the new array, like this:

```
memcpy(pTemp + index + 1, &mypArray[index],
    (mySize - index + 1) * sizeof(int));
```

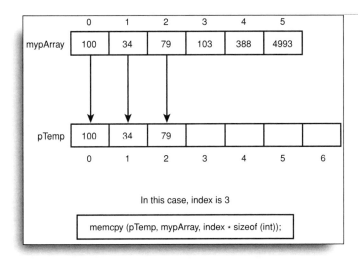

FIGURE 24.2

Copying the first section of the existing array to the new array.

Figure 24.3 shows this process.

By copying the existing array in two steps, we can leave an empty element for the insertion value, which is easily assigned with this statement:

```
pTemp[index] = i;
```

FIGURE 24.3

Copying the second section of the existing array to the new array.

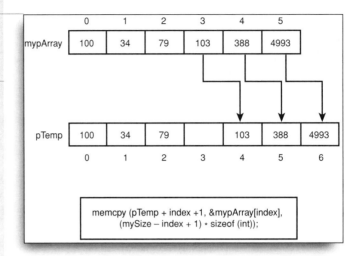

Again, the old array is deleted and the mypArray pointer is shifted to point to the newly allocated array, like this:

```
if (mypArray) delete [] mypArray;
mypArray = pTemp;
```

Finding an Item

Finding an item in an array is a simple matter of linearly iterating through the array, comparing each element to the value you're looking for. The function name CIntArray::Find() seems appropriate for this process. This function simply needs to know what value you're trying to find, and it returns the first element that contains that value. You pass this value as an argument to the function, as you can see in this prototype:

```
int Find(const int& i);
```

The act of iterating through the array and comparing each element to the search value is as easy as this:

```
for (int x = 0; x < mySize; ++x)
   if (mypArray[x] == i)
      return x;
return -1;
```

If the element isn't found, the value -1 is returned.

Deleting an Item

Deleting an item from the array requires that you know the index of the element you want to remove from the array. The function name `CIntArray::Remove()` is appropriate for this task. This function takes the target index as a parameter, giving the following declaration:

```
bool Remove(const int& index);
```

Removing an item means that the array will grow smaller. The technique used here is the same one you've seen before, only in reverse. A new array is allocated, but the new array is one element smaller than the old one. The `mySize` member must be pre-decremented to achieve this goal, like so:

```
int *pTemp = new int[--mySize];
```

The process of copying the old array to the new array must again be split into two steps, allowing us to avoid copying the element destined for demise. The copy operations again use the `memcpy()` function, and the first part of the copy looks like this:

```
memcpy(pTemp, mypArray, index * sizeof(int));
```

The second step of the copy is just a bit more cryptic. The expression `pTemp+index` uses pointer arithmetic to identify the element just *before* the item targeted for removal. The expression `&mypArray[index+1]` identifies the element just *after* the item targeted for removal:

```
memcpy(pTemp + index, &mypArray[index + 1],
   (mySize - index) * sizeof(int));
```

Clearing All Array Elements

A function to clear all elements from the array is useful, and can be called from the class destructor to automatically clean up when a `CIntArray` object goes out of scope. The function name `CIntArray::Clear()` is suitable, and its declaration is simply this:

```
void Clear();
```

All this function has to do is delete the array and reset the pointer and size values to zero, like this:

```
delete [] mypArray;
mypArray = 0;
mySize  = 0;
```

Creating an Array Assignment Operator

It's sometimes handy to be able to easily make a copy of an array. By providing an assignment operator for the CIntArray class, you can make a copy of an array by using a statement as simple as this:

```
CIntArray a1, a2;  // Create two empty, dynamic arrays

// ...
// Fill array a1 with data
// ...

a2 = a1;  // Assumes a1 already contains elements
```

In this case, the array a2 is the target container for all the elements in array a1. In a case like this the assignment operator must do several things, including:

- Clearing the target array of any data
- Allocating storage space for the target array, large enough to hold all source elements
- Copying the elements from the source array to the target array

The assignment operator function CIntArray::operator=() provides these capabilities, and uses a standard assignment operator syntax, like this:

```
CIntArray& operator=(const CIntArray& a);
```

This function begins by using the CIntArray::Clear() method to kill any elements that might currently exist in the target array. The allocation of a duplicate array is then accomplished with this statement:

```
mypArray = new int[a.mySize];
```

The size of the array is stored in CIntArray::mySize, and the array is completely copied using the memcpy() function, like this:

```
mySize = a.mySize;
memcpy(mypArray, a.mypArray, mySize * sizeof(int));
```

The Dynamic Array Class Interface

Putting together everything you've seen into a cohesive class declaration gives us the header file for the CIntArray class, shown in Listing 24.1.

LISTING 24.1   **The Header File for the *CIntArray* Class**

```
1: /////////////////////////////////////////////////////////
2: //   Module   : IntArray.h
3: //
4: //   Purpose : Interface for the CIntArray class
5: /////////////////////////////////////////////////////////
6:
7: #ifndef __INTARRAY_H__
8: #define __INTARRAY_H__
9:
10: class OutOfMemory { };   // for exception handling
11:
12: /////////////////////////////////////////////////////////
13: // Class CIntArray
14:
15: class CIntArray
16: {
17: public:
18:     // Constructors/Destructor
19:     //
20:     CIntArray() : mypArray(0), mySize(0) { }
21:     CIntArray(long size);
22:     virtual ~CIntArray() { this->Clear(); };
23:
24:     // Member functions
25:     //
26:     bool Add(const int& i);
27:     void Clear();
28:     bool Insert(const int& i, const int& index);
29:     int Find(const int& i);
30:     bool Remove(const int& index);
31:     int Size() const { return mySize; }
32:
```

LISTING 24.1

1 Line 10: Declare an exception type

2 Lines 26-31: Class member functions

continues...

LISTING 24.1 CONTINUED

❸ Lines 33-35: Class operator
member functions

LISTING 24.1   **Continued**

```
33:    CIntArray& operator=(const CIntArray& a);
34:    int& operator[](const int& index)
35:       { return mypArray[index]; }
36:
37: protected:
38:    // Protected data members
39:    //
40:    int *mypArray;
41:    int mySize;
42: };
43:
44: #endif //__INTARRAY_H__
```

On line 10, the class OutOfMemory is declared as an exception handler type that can be thrown if an allocation error occurs. The CIntArray::Size() method on line 31 is implemented inline to return the value of mySize. The CIntArray::operator[]() function (lines 34 and 35) is also implemented inline, returning the value of the array element for the index provided. This arrangement allows you to indirectly access the internal array elements using a syntax identical to a standard array.

Implementing the Dynamic Array Class

The implementation of the CIntArray class is given in Listing 24.2, which shows the complete versions of the member functions you've already examined.

LISTING 24.2   **The Implementation of the *CIntArray* Class**

```
 1: ////////////////////////////////////////////////////////
 2: //   Module   : IntArray.cpp
 3: //
 4: //   Purpose : The implementation of a dynamic
 5: //             integer array.
 6: ////////////////////////////////////////////////////////
 7:
 8: #include <iostream.h>
 9: #include <memory.h>      // for memcpy()
10: #include <assert.h>
```

```
11: #include "IntArray.h"
12:
13: //////////////////////////////////////////////////////
14: // Constructor
15:
16: CIntArray::CIntArray(long size)
17: {
18:     assert(size > 0);
19:     mypArray = new int[size];
20:     if (mypArray == 0)
21:     {
22:         cerr << "New buffer memory allocation failed."
23:             << endl;
24:         throw OutOfMemory();
25:     }
26:     mySize = size;
27: };
28:
29: //////////////////////////////////////////////////////
30: // CIntArray::operator=()
31:
32: CIntArray& CIntArray::operator=(const CIntArray& a)
33: {
34:     this->Clear();
35:     mypArray = new int[a.mySize];
36:     if (mypArray == 0)
37:     {
38:         cerr << "New buffer memory allocation failed."
39:             << endl;
40:         throw OutOfMemory();
41:     }
42:     mySize = a.mySize;
43:     memcpy(mypArray, a.mypArray, mySize * sizeof(int));
44:
45:     return *this;
46: }
47:
48: //////////////////////////////////////////////////////
49: // CIntArray::Add()
50:
51: bool CIntArray::Add(const int& i)
52: {
```

LISTING 24.2 CONTINUED

1 Lines 17-27: Array construction of a specific size

2 Lines 32-46: Define an assignment operator

continues…

LISTING 24.2 **Continued**

```
53:     // Allocate new array
54:     //
55:     int *pTemp = new int[++mySize];
56:     if (pTemp == 0)
57:     {
58:         cerr << "New buffer memory allocation failed."
59:             << endl;
60:         --mySize;
61:         return false;
62:     }
63:
64:     // Copy array bit for bit
65:     //
66:     if (mypArray)
67:         memcpy(pTemp, mypArray, mySize * sizeof(int));
68:
69:     // Set the new element's value
70:     //
71:     pTemp[mySize - 1] = i;
72:
73:     // Delete old array and point to new array
74:     //
75:     if (mypArray)
76:         delete [] mypArray;
77:     mypArray = pTemp;
78:
79:     return true;
80: }
81:
82: /////////////////////////////////////////////////////////
83: // CIntArray::Clear()
84:
85: void CIntArray::Clear()
86: {
87:     if (mypArray)
88:     {
89:         delete [] mypArray;
90:         mypArray = 0;
91:         mySize  = 0;
92:     }
93: }
```

```
94:
95: ///////////////////////////////////////////////////
96: // CIntArray::Find()
97:
98: int CIntArray::Find(const int& i)
99: {
100:    for (int x = 0; x < mySize; ++x)
101:       if (mypArray[x] == i)
102:          return x;
103:    return -1;
104: }
105:
106: ///////////////////////////////////////////////////
107: // CIntArray::Insert()
108:
109: bool CIntArray::Insert(const int& i, const int& index)
110: {
111:    // Make room for the insertion
112:    //
113:    int *pTemp = new int[++mySize];
114:    if (pTemp == 0)
115:    {
116:       cerr << "New buffer memory allocation failed."
117:          << endl;
118:       --mySize;
119:       rcturn false;
120:    }
121:
122:    // Move all elements, up to the insertion point,
123:    // into the new storage
124:    //
125:    if (mypArray)
126:    {
127:       memcpy(pTemp, mypArray, index * sizeof(int));
128:
129:       // Move all remaining elements into the new
130:       // storage
131:       //
132:       memcpy(pTemp + index + 1, &mypArray[index],
133:          (mySize - index + 1) * sizeof(int));
134:    }
135:
```

LISTING 24.2 CONTINUED

⑤ Lines 98-104: Find an item in the array

⑥ Lines 125-134: Copy data to the new array in two steps

⑤ (near lines 98-104)

⑥ (near lines 129)

continues…

LISTING 24.2 **Continued**

```
136:      // Insert the new element
137:      //
138:      pTemp[index] = i;
139:
140:      // Delete old array and point to new array
141:      //
142:      if (mypArray) delete [] mypArray;
143:      mypArray = pTemp;
144:
145:      return true;
146: }
147:
148: ///////////////////////////////////////////////////////
149: // CIntArray::Remove()
150:
151: bool CIntArray::Remove(const int& index)
152: {
153:      // Make the array smaller
154:      //
155:      int *pTemp = new int[--mySize];
156:      if (pTemp == 0)
157:      {
158:         cerr << "New buffer memory allocation failed."
159:            << endl;
160:         ++mySize;
161:         return false;
162:      }
163:
164:      // Move all elements up to the deletion point into
165:      // the new storage
166:      //
167:      if (mypArray)
168:      {
169:         memcpy(pTemp, mypArray, index * sizeof(int));
170:
171:         // Move all remaining elements into the new
172:         // storage
173:         //
174:         memcpy(pTemp + index, &mypArray[index + 1],
175:            (mySize - index) * sizeof(int));
176:
```

```
177:      // Delete old array
178:      //
179:      delete [] mypArray;
180:    }
181:    mypArray = pTemp; // point to new array
182:
183:    return true;
184: }
```

Line 9 includes the ANSI C library header `memory.h`, which provides access to the `memcpy()` function used throughout this class.
Line 10 includes the ANSI C library header `assert.h`, which
provides access to the `assert()` macro. The constructor running
from lines 17 through 27 preallocates an array to the value given
by the single parameter (`size`). If allocation fails during construction, the `OutOfMemory` exception is thrown on line 24. The rest of
the file contains the member functions you saw earlier.

Creating a Driver Program

To test the functionality of the `CIntArray` class, a driver program
is in order. The program should test all the features of the class;
the program in Listing 24.3 does just that.

LISTING 24.3   A Driver Program to Test the *CIntArray* Class

```
1: /////////////////////////////////////////////////////////
2: //  Module   : ArrayDriver.cpp
3: //
4: //  Purpose : A driver program to test the CIntArray
5: //            class.
6: /////////////////////////////////////////////////////////
7:
8: #include <iostream.h>
9: #include "IntArray.h"
10:
11: void DisplayArrayElements(CIntArray& ia);
12:
13: /////////////////////////////////////////////////////////
14: // main()
15:
```

continues...

LISTING 24.3

① Line 18: A *try* block to handle exceptions for the program

② Lines 24-28: Create, populate, and display the elements of an array

③ Lines 30-36: Insert and remove array elements

④ Line 39: Test the assignment operator

⑤ Line 48-51: Find an array item

LISTING 24.3 **Continued**

```
16: void main()
17: {
18:    try ──────── ①
19:    {
20:       const int INIT = 5;
21:       CIntArray ia1;
22:       CIntArray ia2;
23:
24:       cout << "\nCreating an array with " << INIT
25:          << " elements:\n";
26:       for (int i = 0; i < INIT; ++i)            ②
27:          ia1.Add(i);
28:       DisplayArrayElements(ia1);
29:
30:       cout << "\nInserting a 3 at element 1:\n";
31:       ia1.Insert(3, 1);
32:       DisplayArrayElements(ia1);
33:                                                 ③
34:       cout << "\nRemoving element 2:\n";
35:       ia1.Remove(2);
36:       DisplayArrayElements(ia1);
37:
38:       cout << "\nCopying array ia1 to ia2\n";
39:       ia2 = ia1; ──────────────────── ④
40:
41:       cout << "Clearing the first array (ia1)\n";
42:       ia1.Clear();
43:       DisplayArrayElements(ia1);
44:
45:       cout << "\nDisplaying the second array (ia2)\n";
46:       DisplayArrayElements(ia2);
47:
48:       int which = ia2.Find(2);
49:       if (which >= 0)                           ⑤
50:          cout << "\nThe number 2 is stored in element"
51:             " ia2[" << which << "]\n";
52:    }
```

```
53:    catch(OutOfMemory)
54:    {
55:       cerr << "Memory allocation failed!\n";
56:    }
57:    catch(...)
58:    {
59:       cerr << "Catching unknown exception!\n";
60:    }
61: }
62:
63: //////////////////////////////////////////////////////////////
64: // DisplayArrayElements()
65:
66: void DisplayArrayElements(CIntArray& ia)
67: {
68:    for (int i = 0; i < ia.Size() ; ++i)
69:       cout << "ia[" << i << "] == " << ia[i] << endl;
70: }
```

LISTING 24.3 CONTINUED

6 Line 53-60: Catch
OutOfMemory exceptions

7 Lines 57-62: Catch unknown
exceptions

8 Lines 66-70: Display all array
elements

This program provides the following output at run time:

```
Creating an array with 5 elements:
ia[0] == 0
ia[1] == 1
ia[2] == 2
ia[3] == 3
ia[4] == 4

Inserting a 3 at element 1:
ia[0] == 0
ia[1] == 3
ia[2] == 1
ia[3] == 2
ia[4] == 3
ia[5] == 4

Removing element 2:
ia[0] == 0
ia[1] == 3
ia[2] == 2
ia[3] == 3
ia[4] == 4
```

```
Copying array ia1 to ia2
Clearing the first array (ia1)

Displaying the second array (ia2)
ia[0] == 0
ia[1] == 3
ia[2] == 2
ia[3] == 3
ia[4] == 4


The number 2 is stored in element ia2[2]
```

The driver program uses a try block (starting on line 18) in the main() function to catch any exceptions that might occur. The corresponding catch handlers run from lines 53 through 60. The code within the try block performs several tests of the CIntArray class member functions.

Line 20 specifies that initially five elements will be added to array ia1, declared on line 21. Array ia2, declared on line 22, comes into play later in the block. Lines 26 and 27 add five items to the array using the CIntArray::Add() member function. Line 28 displays the items with a call to the DisplayArrayElements() function, which is defined from lines 66 through 70.

Line 31 inserts a new item, having a value of 3, at array element 1. Line 32 then displays the array elements again to verify that the item was added. Line 35 uses the CIntArray::Remove() member function to remove the item residing at array index number 2.

Line 39 uses the assignment operator to copy the elements from array ia1 to array ia2. On line 42, the ia1 array is killed off with a call to CIntArray::Clear(), and line 43 attempts to display the ia1 array elements. Because the array was just deleted, there are no elements to display, so nothing happens.

Line 46 attempts to display the ia2 array elements. Because the array was copied from ia1 before it was deleted, the elements originally placed into ia1 are displayed. The final test occurs on line 48, where the CIntArray::Find() method is invoked.

The argument sent into this function specifies that we're looking for a 2. As it happens, a 2 is found in element index 2, and this index is stored in the local variable which. Lines 50 and 51 display this information, wrapping up the test.

Creating Linked Lists

A *linked list* is a special collection structure that holds objects that are linked to other objects by pointers. The list is just a linear chain of objects, and these objects are called *nodes*. A *singly linked list* contains nodes that store some type of data, and each node has a pointer (the link) to the next node in the list. The first node in the list is called the *head*. The advantage of a linked list over an array is that while all array elements must be contiguous, the nodes in a list can reside anywhere in memory. Each node links to the next node using a pointer to that node. Figure 24.4 shows this concept.

Note

The destructor for `ia2` automatically cleans up the array when the `main()` function goes out of scope.

Singly Linked List

In a singly linked list, each node contains a link (pointer) to the next node in the list. A singly linked list can be traversed in only one direction.

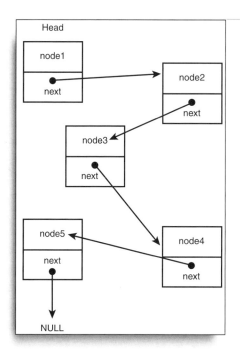

FIGURE 24.4

A singly linked list contains nodes; each node points to the next node in the list.

Doubly Linked List

In a doubly linked list each node contains links (pointers) to the previous node in the list **and** the next node in the list. A doubly linked list can be traversed both forward and backward.

Like a singly linked list, a *doubly linked list* also contains nodes that store some type of data, but each node has both a pointer to the next node in the list and a pointer to the previous node in the list. The first node in the list is called the *head* and the last node in the list is called the *tail*. The main advantage of a doubly linked list is that you can traverse the list both forward and backward; with a singly linked list, you can only traverse the list forward. Each node links to the next using a pointer (next) to that node, and each node links to the previous using a pointer (prev) to that node. Figure 24.5 shows this concept.

FIGURE 24.5

A doubly linked list contains nodes; each node points to both the next and the previous nodes in the list.

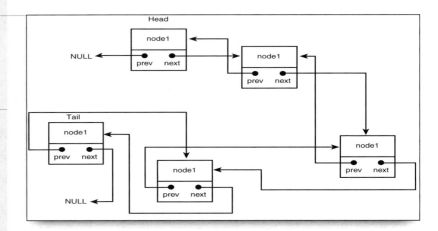

Note

If you only need to traverse a list from head to tail, use a singly linked list. Because each node in a singly linked list contains only a single link it uses less memory than a doubly linked list (where each node contains two links).

Like the dynamic array class you saw earlier, the obvious solution for making linked lists easy to use is to create a class that provides member functions to take care of most of the dirty work for you. In this section, you create a container class that stores integers in a doubly linked list. The linked list class should provide the ability to do the following:

- Add a node to the head or tail of the list
- Insert a node into the list at a specified location
- Find a node within the list
- Delete a specific node from the list
- Automatically resize the list as nodes are added and deleted

Creating a Linked List Class

In the following sections, you'll see how the previously listed linked list items can be implemented for a list of integers by creating a class I'll call CIntList. The following CIntList class declaration is a skeleton we can build on to add the features in the preceding list:

```
class CIntList
{
protected:
    CIntNode *mypHead;
    CIntNode *mypTail;
    CIntNode *mypCur;
    int mySize;
};
```

In addition to these data members, several class methods are needed to provide the interface between the list and client programs that use the class. Table 24.2 describes these member functions.

TABLE 24.2   **The Class Methods to be Supported by the *CIntArray* Class**

Method	Description
AddHead()	Adds a node to the head of the list.
AddTail()	Adds a node to the tail of the list.
Clear()	Removes all nodes from the list, deallocating all memory used by the list.
Current()	Returns a pointer to the current node.
Find()	Returns a pointer to the first node containing the specified integer value.
Head()	Returns a pointer to the first node in the list.
Insert()	Inserts a node into the list at a specified location.
Next()	Moves the current node along the list, toward the tail, and returns a pointer to the current node.
Prev()	Moves the current node along the list, toward the head, and returns a pointer to the current node.

continues…

TABLE 24.2   **Continued**

Method	Description
Remove()	Removes a specified node from the list.
Reset()	Resets the pointer to the current node to point at the head of the list.
Size()	Returns the number of nodes in the list.
Tail()	Returns a pointer to the last node in the list.

The foundation of this dynamic linked list class is a node class I call CIntNode. The list holds pointers to the head (mypHead) and tail (mypTail) of the list, and also provides a pointer to the current node (mypCur), which is used for traversing the list. The list will also keep track of how many nodes the list has (mySize). Before we can create a list of integer nodes, we need to define exactly what an integer node is.

Implementing a Node Class

Each node in the list must contain a pointer to the previous node and a pointer to the next node, as well as the data itself (in this case, an integer). To do this, we can declare the simple node class CIntNode. The skeleton for this class contains a pointer to the next node (mypNext), a pointer to the previous node (mypPrev), and the integer data itself (myInt) as protected members, like this:

```
class CIntNode
{
protected:
    CIntNode *mypPrev;   // Link pointer
    CIntNode *mypNext;   // Link pointer
    int myInt;           // the data
};
```

Notice that the mypPrev and mypNext pointers are members of—and pointers to—type CIntNode. This is where the fundamental power of the linked list comes into play—each node points to other nodes of the same type. Because the myInt value is protected, two overloaded Value() methods can be provided to allow programs to both get and set the value of this member.

The CIntList class, which I'll present shortly, holds pointers to the head and tail of the list. To allow the CIntList class direct access to the protected CIntNode class members, you can declare this class as a friend of CIntNode. This simplifies the list class and gives a performance boost over using access functions as intermediaries to the CIntNode protected members. This leads us to the final cut of the CIntNode class, as shown in Listing 24.4.

LISTING 24.4   **The Complete Code for the *CIntNode* Class**

```
 1: /////////////////////////////////////////////////////
 2: //   Module  : IntNode.h
 3: //
 4: //   Purpose : Interface for the CIntNode class
 5: /////////////////////////////////////////////////////
 6:
 7: #ifndef __INTNODE_H__
 8: #define __INTNODE_H__
 9:
10: /////////////////////////////////////////////////////
11: // Class CIntNode
12:
13: class CIntNode
14: {
15: public:
16:     CIntNode() : mypPrev(0), mypNext(0) { }
17:     int Value() const { return myInt; }
18:     void Value(const int& i) { myInt = i; }
19:
20:     friend class CIntList;
21:
22: protected:
23:     CIntNode *mypPrev;
24:     CIntNode *mypNext;
25:     int myInt;
26: };
27:
28: #endif //__INTNODE_H__
```

LISTING 24.4

1 Lines 16-18: Public member functions

2 Line 20: Declare the CIntList class as a friend

2 Lines 23-25: Protected data members

The constructor for the class (line 16) simply initializes the node pointers to zero. The Value() function on line 17 retrieves the value of myInt; the Value() function on line 18 sets the value of `myInt`. Line 20 declares the `CIntList` class to be a friend of `CIntNode`. Lines 23 through 25 declare the protected data members.

Adding a Node

To add a new node to the list, you must first allocate storage for it. The `CIntList` class will use dynamic allocation, reallocation, and deallocation to expand and contract the list as needed. A sensible name for a member function that adds an integer to the head of the list is `CIntList::AddHead()`. The `CIntList::AddHead()` function will allocate an integer node, assign an integer value to the node, and add the node to the head of the list. The only parameter needed is an integer, giving us the following declaration for the `CIntList::AddHead()` function:

```
bool AddHead(const int& i);
```

Adding an integer to the tail of the list is very similar, and the function `CIntList::AddTail()` fits the bill, using a similar declaration:

```
bool AddTail(const int& i);
```

Because the list's nodes can be anywhere in memory, all the nastiness required with the `CIntArray` class (creating new storage, copying existing data, and deleting the old storage) can be avoided completely. When adding a node, the address of the new node is assigned to a node pointer. Using a small amount of C++ code, if a node is deleted, any pointers pointing to that node are shifted to point to some other node.

The basic method of adding a node to the head or tail of the list is the same. The first step is to allocate a new node, like this:

```
CIntNode *pTemp = new CIntNode;
if (pTemp == 0)
{
    cerr << "New node memory allocation failed." << endl;
    return false;
}
```

Adding a node to the head of the list makes that node the new head. To achieve this, the pointers for the two nodes involved must be shifted. A new list that has no nodes (and, therefore, no head) must be considered as well. If the list is empty, you can just do this:

```
mypHead = pTemp;   // Assign as new head
mypTail = pTemp;   // Assign as new tail
mypCur  = pTemp;   // Assign as current node
```

In this case, all three pointers point to the same node. If the list contains one or more nodes, a different approach must be used:

```
pTemp->mypNext   = mypHead;
mypHead->mypPrev = pTemp;
mypHead = pTemp;   // Assign as new head
```

These three statements point the new node's mypNext pointer to the current head, and the current head's mypPrev pointer to the new node. The pTemp pointer is then set as the new head.

Adding a node to the tail of the list makes that node the new tail. To achieve this, the pointers for the two nodes involved must again be shifted. A new list that has no nodes (and therefore, no tail) is handled in the same way as when you add a node to the head—all three pointers are set to point at the new node.

If the list contains one or more nodes, a slightly different approach must be used to shift the pointers correctly:

```
mypTail->mypNext = pTemp;
pTemp->mypPrev   = mypTail;
mypTail = pTemp;   // Assign as new tail
```

These three statements point the existing tail's mypNext pointer to the new node, and the new node's mypPrev pointer to the existing tail. The pTemp pointer can then be set as the new tail. In either case—inserting at the head or inserting at the tail—the mySize member must be incremented to reflect the new size of the list.

Traversing the List

To allow a program to traverse the list either forward or backward, the friendly member functions CIntList::Next() and CIntList::Prev() are provided. To traverse the list in a forward direction (from head to tail), we can define the

`CIntList::Next()` function. Likewise, to traverse the list in a reverse direction (from tail to head), we can define the `CIntList::Prev()` function.

The `CIntList::Next()` function can be defined like this, pointing the `mypCur` pointer to the next node in the list to move its position one node forward along the list:

```
CIntNode * CIntList::Next()
{
    if (mypCur)
        mypCur = mypCur->mypNext;

    return mypCur;
}
```

Similarly, the `CIntList::Prev()` function can be defined like this, pointing the `mypCur` pointer to the previous node in the list to move its position one node backward along the list:

```
CIntNode * CIntList::Prev()
{
    if (mypCur)
        mypCur = mypCur->mypPrev;

    return mypCur;
}
```

Finding an Item

Finding an item that's already in the list is easy. You can start at either the head or the tail and traverse the list until the item is found or you run off one end of the list (indicating that the item you're seeking doesn't exist in the list). Starting at the head of the list, you can define a `CIntList::Find()` function like this:

```
CIntNode * CIntList::Find(const int& i)
{
    CIntNode *pTemp = mypHead;

    while (pTemp)
    {
        if (pTemp->myInt == i)
            return pTemp;
```

```
        pTemp = pTemp->mypNext;
    }
    return 0;
}
```

As long as the `pTemp` pointer is non-zero, it's considered a valid node. If the `pTemp` pointer equals zero, you've reached the end of the list. The `while` loop traverses the list, looking for a node that matches the item being sought. If the item is found, a pointer to that node is returned.

Inserting a Node

Inserting a node at a specific location requires two pieces of information: the integer value to insert and the address of the node where you want the insertion to occur (the new node inserts between the target and the node *after* the target). These requirements yield the following function declaration:

```
bool Insert(const int& i, CIntNode* pNode);
```

By using the `CIntList::Find()` function to locate the insertion point, you have the address you need.

The first step is to allocate a new node:

```
CIntNode *pTemp = new CIntNode;
```

Next, you can set the integer value for the node:

```
pTemp->myInt = i;
```

Then you have to shift the pointers for the affected nodes to link the new node into the list. Using extended pointer-to-member notation to access the next node's `mypPrev` member, assign to it the address of the new node, like this:

```
pNode->mypNext->mypPrev = pTemp;
```

Then set the new node's `mypPrev` member to point to the target node's `mypNext` member:

```
pTemp->mypNext = pNode->mypNext;
```

Finally, assign the address of the target node to the new node's `mypPrev` member, and assign the address of the new node to the target node's `mypNext` member, like this:

```
pTemp->mypPrev = pNode;
pNode->mypNext = pTemp;
```

Putting this all together, we get the following code:

```
pNode->mypNext->mypPrev = pTemp;
pTemp->mypNext = pNode->mypNext;
pTemp->mypPrev = pNode;
pNode->mypNext = pTemp;
```

Deleting All Nodes from the List

To delete all nodes from the list, effectively clearing it out, you can create a CIntList::Clear() function. This function uses a temporary node pointer to store the value of the head's mypNext pointer, like this:

```
CIntNode *pTemp;
```

In a while loop, the address of the head's next node is assigned to pTemp and the head is then deleted. The temporary node then becomes the new head, and the loop iterates until all the nodes are deleted, like this:

```
while (mypHead)
{
    pTemp = mypHead->mypNext;
    delete mypHead;
    mypHead = pTemp;
}
mySize = 0;
```

Deleting a Node

It's often necessary to delete an existing node from the list. By creating the CIntList::Remove() function, deleting a specific node is a snap. The function takes a pointer to a CIntNode object as a parameter, giving the following function declaration:

```
void Remove(CIntNode *pNode);
```

To make sure that pNode contains a non-zero address, you can use this simple test:

```
if (!pNode) return;
```

If there's only a single node in the list, and pNode contains a non-zero address, then that node *must* be the one to delete. Before doing anything else, check the mySize member so that you can clear the list using the CIntList::Clear() method if mySize is equal to 1:

```
if (mySize == 1)
{
    this->Clear();
    return;
}
```

To remove a node from a list with more than one node, you must determine whether the target node (the node you want to delete: pNode) is the head, the tail, or some node in between. You have to handle each of these cases differently because of the way the pointers must be shifted when deleting pNode.

If pNode is the head of the list, you have to make pNode->mypNext the new head before deleting pNode (which is really mypHead). If you don't do this, you'll lose the head of the list. This is a simple matter of swapping pointer values around, like this:

```
if (pNode == mypHead)
{
    mypHead = pNode->mypNext;
    mypHead->mypPrev = 0;
}
```

If pNode is the tail of the list, you have to make pNode->mypPrev the new tail before deleting pNode (which is really mypTail). This is also a simple matter of swapping pointer values around, like this:

```
if (pNode == mypTail)
{
    mypTail = pNode->mypPrev;
    mypTail->mypNext = 0;
}
```

If pNode isn't the head *or* the tail of the list, all you have to do is swap the pointers of the nodes on either side of the node you are deleting. You swap the pointers in two steps. First, using

extended pointer-to-member notation to access the next node's
`mypPrev` member, assign to it the address of the target node's
`mypPrev` member, like this:

```
pNode->mypNext->mypPrev = pNode->mypPrev;
```

Second, using extended pointer-to-member notation to access
the previous node's `mypNext` member, assign to it the address of
the target node's `mypNext` member, like this:

```
pNode->mypPrev->mypNext = pNode->mypNext;
```

All you have to do then is tidy up a bit: Delete the node (which
has now been unlinked from the list), reset the node's address to
zero, and decrement the `mySize` member by 1, like this:

```
delete pNode;
pNode = 0;
mySize--;
```

The Linked List Class Interface

Putting together everything in the preceding sections into a
cohesive class declaration gives us the header file for the
`CIntList` class, shown in Listing 24.5.

LISTING 24.5 **The Header for the *CIntList* Class**

```
 1: ///////////////////////////////////////////////////////
 2: //  Module  : IntList.h
 3: //
 4: //  Purpose : Interface for the CIntList class
 5: ///////////////////////////////////////////////////////
 6:
 7: #ifndef __INTLIST_H__
 8: #define __INTLIST_H__
 9:
10: #include "IntNode.h"
11:
12: ///////////////////////////////////////////////////////
13: // Class CIntList
14:
15: class CIntList
```

```
16: {
17: public:
18:    CIntList() : mypHead(0), mypTail(0), mypCur(0),
19:        mySize(0) { }
20:    virtual ~CIntList() { if (mypHead) Clear(); }
21:
22:    // Public Member functions
23:    //
24:    bool AddHead(const int& i);
25:    bool AddTail(const int& i);
26:    void Clear();
27:    CIntNode* Current() { return mypCur; }
28:    CIntNode* Find(const int& i);
29:    CIntNode* Head() { return mypHead; }
30:    bool Insert(const int& i, CIntNode* pNode);
31:    CIntNode* Next();
32:    CIntNode* Prev();
33:    void Remove(CIntNode *pNode);
34:    void Reset() { mypCur = mypHead; }
35:    int Size() const { return mySize; }
36:    CIntNode* Tail() { return mypTail; }
37:
38: protected:
39:    // Protected data members
40:    //
41:    CIntNode *mypHead;
42:    CIntNode *mypTail;
43:    CIntNode *mypCur;
44:    int mySize;
45: };
46:
47: #endif //__INTLIST_H__
```

LISTING 24.5

① Lines 18-19: Initialize class data members

② Lines 24-36: The public class member functions

③ Lines 41-44: The protected class data members

On lines 18 and 19, the class constructor initializes all the class data members to zero; the destructor calls the CIntList::Clear() function to delete the list when the object goes out of scope.

Lines 24 through 36 give the member function declarations for the class, and the protected data members are declared from lines 41 through 44. The CIntList::Current() method on line 27 returns a pointer to the current node. The `CIntList::Head()` method on line 29 returns a pointer to the first node in the list. The `CIntList::Reset()` method on line 34 resets the current item pointer to point at the head of the list. The `CIntList::Size()` method on line 35 returns the number of items in the list, and the `CIntList::Tail()` method on line 36 returns a pointer to the tail of the list.

Implementing the Linked List Class

The implementation of the `CIntList` class is shown in Listing 24.6. This code presents the complete versions of the member functions you already examined earlier in this chapter.

LISTING 24.6

① Lines 15-48: Add a node to the head of the list

LISTING 24.6   **The Implementation of the _CIntList_ Class**

```
 1: ///////////////////////////////////////////////////////
 2: //   Module  : IntList.cpp
 3: //
 4: //   Purpose : An implementation of a doubly linked
 5: //             integer list.
 6: ///////////////////////////////////////////////////////
 7:
 8: #include <iostream.h>
 9: #include <assert.h>
10: #include "IntList.h"
11:
12: ///////////////////////////////////////////////////////
13: // CIntList::AddHead()
14:
15: bool CIntList::AddHead(const int& i)
16: {
17:     // Allocate new node
18:     //
19:     CIntNode *pTemp = new CIntNode;
20:     if (pTemp == 0)
21:     {
22:         cerr << "New node memory allocation failed."
23:             << endl;
24:         return false;
25:     }
```

①

LISTING 24.6 CONTINUED

2   Lines 53-86: Add a node to
    the tail of the list

```
26:
27:     // Add the node to the head of the list
28:     //
29:     if (mypHead)
30:     {
31:        pTemp->mypNext   = mypHead;
32:        mypHead->mypPrev = pTemp;
33:        mypHead = pTemp;   // Assign as new head
34:     }
35:     else   // New list, head & tail are the same
36:     {
37:        mypHead = pTemp;   // Assign as new head
38:        mypTail = pTemp;   // Assign as new tail
39:        mypCur  = pTemp;
40:     }
41:     mySize++;
42:
43:     // Set the new node's value
44:     //
45:     mypHead->myInt = i;
46:
47:     return true;
48: }
49:
50: /////////////////////////////////////////////////////
51: // CIntList::AddTail()
52:
53: bool CIntList::AddTail(const int& i)
54: {
55:     // Allocate new node
56:     //
57:     CIntNode *pTemp = new CIntNode;
58:     if (pTemp == 0)
59:     {
60:        cerr << "New node memory allocation failed."
61:           << endl;
62:        return false;
63:     }
64:
65:     // Add the node to the tail of the list
66:     //
67:     if (mypTail)
```

1

2

continues...

LISTING 24.6 CONTINUED

3 Lines 91-102: Clear the list by deleting all nodes

LISTING 24.6 **Continued**

```
68:    {
69:        mypTail->mypNext = pTemp;
70:        pTemp->mypPrev   = mypTail;
71:        mypTail = pTemp;   // Assign as new tail
72:    }
73:    else
74:    {
75:        mypHead = pTemp;   // Assign as new head
76:        mypTail = pTemp;   // Assign as new tail
77:        mypCur  = pTemp;
78:    }
79:    mySize++;
80:
81:    // Set the new node's value
82:    //
83:    mypTail->myInt = i;
84:
85:    return true;
86: }
87:
88: /////////////////////////////////////////////////////////
89: // CIntList::Clear()
90:
91: void CIntList::Clear()
92: {
93:    CIntNode *pTemp;
94:
95:    while (mypHead)
96:    {
97:        pTemp = mypHead->mypNext;
98:        delete mypHead;
99:        mypHead = pTemp;
100:   }
101:   mySize = 0;
102: }
103:
104: /////////////////////////////////////////////////////////
105: // CIntList::Find()
106:
```

```
107: CIntNode * CIntList::Find(const int& i)
108: {
109:    CIntNode *pTemp = mypHead;
110:
111:    while (pTemp)
112:    {
113:       if (pTemp->myInt == i)
114:          return pTemp;
115:       pTemp = pTemp->mypNext;
116:    }
117:    return 0;
118: }
119:
120: //////////////////////////////////////////////////////////
121: // CIntList::Insert()
122:
123: bool CIntList::Insert(const int& i, CIntNode* pNode)
124: {
125:    assert(pNode != 0);
126:
127:    // Allocate a new node
128:    //
129:    CIntNode *pTemp = new CIntNode;
130:    if (!pTemp)
131:    {
132:       cerr << "Error allocating new node!\n";
133:       return false;
134:    }
135:    pTemp->myInt = i;       // set the value
136:
137:    // Shift pointers to link this node into the list
138:    //
139:    pNode->mypNext->mypPrev = pTemp;
140:    pTemp->mypNext = pNode->mypNext;
141:    pTemp->mypPrev = pNode;
142:    pNode->mypNext = pTemp;
143:
144:    mySize++;
145:    return true;
146: }
147:
148: //////////////////////////////////////////////////////////
```

LISTING 24.6 CONTINUED

4 Lines 107-118: Find an item in the list

5 Lines 123-146: Insert a new node into the list at a specific node

continues...

LISTING 24.6 CONTINUED

6 Lines 173-203: Remove a
specific node from the list

LISTING 24.6 **Continued**

```cpp
149: // CIntList::Next()
150:
151: CIntNode * CIntList::Next()
152: {
153:    if (mypCur)
154:        mypCur = mypCur->mypNext;
155:
156:    return mypCur;
157: }
158:
159: //////////////////////////////////////////////////////
160: // CIntList::Prev()
161:
162: CIntNode * CIntList::Prev()
163: {
164:    if (mypCur)
165:        mypCur = mypCur->mypPrev;
166:
167:    return mypCur;
168: }
169:
170: //////////////////////////////////////////////////////
171: // CIntList::Remove()
172:
173: void CIntList::Remove(CIntNode *pNode)
174: {
175:    if (!pNode)
176:        return;
177:
178:    if (mySize == 1)
179:    {
180:        this->Clear();
181:        return;
182:    }
183:
184:    if (pNode == mypHead)
185:    {
186:        mypHead = pNode->mypNext;
187:        mypHead->mypPrev = 0;
188:    }
189:    else if (pNode == mypTail)
```

6

```
190:    {
191:        mypTail = pNode->mypPrev;
192:        mypTail->mypNext = 0;
193:    }
194:    else
195:    {
196:        pNode->mypNext->mypPrev = pNode->mypPrev;
197:        pNode->mypPrev->mypNext = pNode->mypNext;
198:    }
199:
200:    delete pNode;
201:    pNode = 0;
202:    mySize--;
203: }
```

Creating a Driver Program

To test the functionality of the CIntList class, we have to create a driver program. The driver program in Listing 24.7 tests the major list functionality.

LISTING 24.7   A Driver Program to Test the *CIntList* Class

```
1: ////////////////////////////////////////////////////
2: // Module  : ListDriver.cpp
3: //
4: // Purpose : A driver program to test the CIntList
5: //            class.
6: ////////////////////////////////////////////////////
7:
8: #include <iostream.h>
9: #include "IntList.h"
10:
11: void DisplayListNodes(CIntList& list);
12:
13: ////////////////////////////////////////////////////
14: // main()
15:
16: void main()
17: {
18:     try
```

continues...

LISTING 24.7

1 Line 21-32: Create, populate, and
display a linked list, adding nodes
one at a time

2 Line 36-46: Remove each existing
node, one at a time

LISTING 24.7   **Continued**

```
19:    {
20:        CIntList list;   // Create a list
21:
22:        list.AddHead(1);
23:        DisplayListNodes(list);
24:
25:        list.AddHead(2);
26:        DisplayListNodes(list);
27:
28:        list.Insert(3, list.Find(2));
29:        DisplayListNodes(list);
30:
31:        list.AddTail(4);
32:        DisplayListNodes(list);
33:
34:        // Remove the nodes
35:        //
36:        list.Remove(list.Find(1));
37:        DisplayListNodes(list);
38:
39:        list.Remove(list.Find(2));
40:        DisplayListNodes(list);
41:
42:        list.Remove(list.Find(3));
43:        DisplayListNodes(list);
44:
45:        list.Remove(list.Find(4));
46:        DisplayListNodes(list);
47:    }
48:    catch(...)
49:    {
50:        cerr << "Catching unknown exception!\n";
51:    }
52: }
53:
54: /////////////////////////////////////////////////////////
55: // DisplayListNodes()
56:
57: void DisplayListNodes(CIntList& list)
58: {
```

```
59:    list.Reset();
60:
61:    if (list.Size() == 0)
62:    {
63:       cout << "\nThe list is empty...\n";
64:       return;
65:    }
66:
67:    cout << "\nList has " << list.Size()
68:       << " node(s):\n";
69:    CIntNode *pHead = list.Head();
70:    if (pHead)
71:       cout << "  list.Head()->Value() == "
72:          << pHead->Value() << endl;
73:
74:    CIntNode *pNode;
75:    for (int i = 1; i < list.Size() - 1 ; ++i)
76:    {
77:       pNode = list.Next();
78:       if (pNode)
79:          cout << "  list.Next()->Value() == "
80:             << pNode->Value() << endl;
81:    }
82:
83:    if (list.Head() == list.Tail()) return;
84:
85:    CIntNode *pTail = list.Tail();
86:    if (pHead)
87:       cout << "  list.Tail()->Value() == "
88:          << pTail->Value() << endl;
89: }
```

LISTING 24.7 CONTINUED

3 Lines 69-72: Display the head of the list

4 Lines 74-81: Display nonhead/nontail nodes

5 Lines 85-88: Display the tail of the list

The output from this program demonstrates the linked list class in action:

```
List has 1 node(s):
  list.Head()->Value() == 1

List has 2 node(s):
  list.Head()->Value() == 2
  list.Tail()->Value() == 1
```

```
List has 3 node(s):
  list.Head()->Value() == 2
  list.Next()->Value() == 3
  list.Tail()->Value() == 1

List has 4 node(s):
  list.Head()->Value() == 2
  list.Next()->Value() == 3
  list.Next()->Value() == 1
  list.Tail()->Value() == 4

List has 3 node(s):
  list.Head()->Value() == 2
  list.Next()->Value() == 3
  list.Tail()->Value() == 4

List has 2 node(s):
  list.Head()->Value() == 3
  list.Tail()->Value() == 4

List has 1 node(s):
  list.Head()->Value() == 4

The list is empty...
```

The driver program begins by declaring the DisplayListNodes() function on line 11. This function is defined from lines 57 through 89 and demonstrates traversing the list from head to tail, as well as using other CIntList methods.

Line 20 creates a list object, and line 22 adds an integer to the head of the list. Line 23 displays the contents of the list—currently a single node. Lines 25 and 26 perform the same task, adding a different integer value to the list and displaying the list, this time containing two nodes.

Line 28 uses a nested function call, first calling the CIntList::Find() function to locate the node containing the integer value 2. The object pointer returned from this function call is then sent to the CIntList::Insert() method to insert a new item just after the object retrieved by CIntList::Find().

Line 29 again displays the list, this time containing three nodes. Line 31 adds a new node to the tail of the list, and line 32 displays the list, which now contains four nodes.

Lines 36 through 46 remove each of the four nodes one at a time, displaying the list after each node is removed. The `CIntList::Remove()` method is used to do this, using a nested call to `CIntList::Find()` to find the node to delete. Lines 48 through 51 catch any unexpected exceptions that might occur.

Designing and Developing Object-Oriented Programs

Explore the development process

Understand the analysis of system requirements

Identify classes needed to build a system

Take a look at interface design

See how modularity improves reusability

Problem-Solving Techniques

Programs are written to perform some useful function for the end user. Whether a program is a graphics application meant to amuse and entertain or an accounting program designed to work with important financial data, the more complex the program becomes, the more difficult it is to reign in and control during development. Complex software is composed of multiple modules, classes, libraries, and other resources.

Breaking down a program's functional requirements into simple, solvable problems is the first step in system design. Each main problem must be solved to get a program to do what it needs to get done. By dividing these problems into subproblems that are easy to solve, you can arrive at an elegant solution. The solving of these subproblems is an iterative process that usually involves several phases of development.

Complex programs that use many modules and libraries form interrelated, complex software systems. Without an up-front plan and design, a large project is almost certainly doomed to fail. Today's object-oriented technology and plug-in component software make software construction easier, more manageable, and more robust than it's ever been. In this chapter, you'll look at some of the ways object-oriented programming makes the design and development of large software systems more manageable than anything programmers have had at their disposal in the past.

Exploring the Development Process

Each problem you face in the program design phase can be broken out into functional designs and class designs that work together to achieve the program's design goals. There are several phases to the development process:

- Analysis of system requirements
- Identification of classes needed to build the system
- Interface design

- Coding and debugging
- Testing

Analyzing System Requirements

A high-priced architect who's hired to design a house doesn't just start drawing. The architect consults with the client to find out what the client's expectations and needs are, and then draws up preliminary sketches for the client to approve. After the conceptual work and sketches are approved, the architect can begin the more detailed work of drawing up the blueprints, often using a computer program such as Autodesk's AutoCAD.

Software construction is very similar to the architect's approach to designing a house. By identifying the needs of the system and the expectations of the end users, the programmer is in a good position to begin the first steps of constructing the system. Like the architect, preliminary sketches of the systems are imperative. Before you can build a complex software system, you need to know all the facts—or as many as you can get your hands on. Determine—in as much detail as possible—what the system should do and develop a basic structure for the flow of data into and out of the system.

Once you've identified the detailed requirements of a system, you'll be prepared to begin designing the system. Just as the architect has computerized design tools such as AutoCAD at his or her disposal, programmers have computerized system and class design tools called CASE tools available. CASE tools allow you to draw your system graphically onscreen, specifying class interfaces and relationships. These tools generate the source code that corresponds to your system, saving you hours of coding and recoding as you redesign.

Undertaking a Project

Let's assume that you've been hired by a local entrepreneur, Mr. Smiley, to design an interactive application for his new restaurant. Mr. Smiley has gathered a preliminary list of items he has identified as features of the proposed new software package, code-named "Menu Maker." When you look at the list of the

CASE Tools

Computer Aided Software Engineering (CASE) programs offer data-modeling tools for object-oriented analysis, design, and multi-language implementation of classes, making the job of creating and maintaining classes and class hierarchies graphical, intuitive, and relatively painless. A variety of software companies offer CASE programs.

specifications for the project, you notice that they're rather generalized. The requirements he's provided are as follows:

- Menu Maker must have a polished graphical user interface (GUI).

- Users must be able to create and edit recipes for the dishes the restaurant serves.

- The recipes determine what type of foods the restaurant needs to purchase for stock.

- The program must track all sales and, using the food quantities in the recipes, estimate the usage of stock.

- The program must generate and print reports that estimate how much, and what type, of food to reorder to keep stock up to desired levels.

- Users must be able to use the recipes to design a menu that can be printed for use in the restaurant. In addition to actually printing the menu, the program must provide some way of previewing the menu layout on the screen.

- The program must calculate suggested prices for each menu item (recipe) based on the actual cost of the items used in the recipe.

This list is detailed enough to get you started, but each bullet point listed here can be broken out into several more detailed points. The design for this system is a fairly complex task, but if taken a step at a time, it can be done painlessly.

Mr. Smiley wants the program to run on Windows 98 so that he can leverage his knowledge of the relatively standardized user interface style for Windows applications. After working with the list's general requirements for a while, you realize that several things will have to be done to get the project off the ground.

Document/View Architecture

A program design strategy that promotes platform portability by separating a program's data (the document) from the display of that data (the view).

An obvious first step is to conceptually separate the user interface (the GUI) from the data the GUI displays. This separation is typically known as a *document/view architecture*. The document portion of the program holds all the data and is platform independent. The view portion of the program displays the data residing in the document and uses graphics commands relevant to each GUI platform (and they're all very different).

Next, you'll want to identify the subsystems that make up the
complete system. You can then review the general requirements
and come up with a more detailed analysis of the design for each
program subsystem. You identify the following six main subsystems for Menu Maker:

- Recipe creation and editing
- Menu creation and editing
- Inventory
- Sales
- Reporting
- Printing/print preview

Identifying Classes Needed to Build the System

Assuming that the system requirements have been identified at
an acceptable level of detail, you can begin the process of identifying the objects you think the system will need to use as its
component parts.

It's very important to think about the relationships of objects,
how they interrelate, and how they interface and interact. Map
out a basic strategy for the system, sketching out object relationships like an architect sketches the objects in a blueprint.
Although it's often difficult to keep track of object relationships
in a complex system, if you create a list of the classes you think
you'll need, and determine the basic relationships between them,
you're off to a good start.

Try to think in terms of simple, individual objects and the properties and capabilities of those objects. It may take several iterations of design—often with pencil and paper, sketching out the
classes, class relationships, and possible class hierarchies—before
you begin to get a feel for how the system will work. Like a
sculptor shaping clay, you can mold the system design into the
shape you see it needs to take, often discovering hidden relationships you don't expect.

Sometimes a design path turns out to be a dead end, and you
have to turn back to take a different path. This is much easier to

Tip

The beauty of object-oriented
programming is that well-
designed classes are standalone
components that can be
plugged in wherever you need
them. Try to design your classes
to be as generic and reusable
as possible.

The Unified Modeling Language (UML)

The Unified Modeling Language (UML) is the culmination of over a decade of object-oriented notation strategies and CASE development. UML is an effort to combine the best parts of the most popular object-oriented notations.

do when you're working with abstract algorithms and object relationships on paper than when you've impatiently sat down and hacked out thousands of lines of code, unaware of the dead end waiting around the next turn. Reckless coding like this more often than not ends up in frustration and abandonment of code. Sometimes lots of code—which means lots of programming hours—and remember, time is money!

Instead of coding blindly at the outset, spend some time thinking about what each object needs to be able to do, and not about how it should do it. Leave the coding for later! System design is not programming—it's architecture; it's art. Whenever possible, encapsulate the data each class will need so that no other classes duplicate that functionality. Extract any commonality out into base classes and begin to develop small class hierarchies to form subsystems of the main system. You can do this planning on paper or with any of a variety of data modeling and CASE tools available for visually modeling a complex system and its component subsystems.

For the Menu Maker project, you decide to concentrate on the classes that make up the back end of the system, leaving the GUI portion separate. The visual programming tools you use for the project will allow you to create the front-end user interface (windows, dialog boxes, toolbars, and so on) that interface with the back-end classes. After some deliberation and planning, you generate the following list of classes that make up the back end of the system:

- Recipe creation and editing: `CRecipeItem`, `CRecipe`, `CRecipeEditor`
- Menu creation and editing: `CMenuItem`, `CMenu`, `CMenuEditor`
- Inventory: `CInventoryItem`, `CInventory`
- Sales: `CSalesItem`, `CSales`
- Reporting: `CReport`
- Printing/print preview: `CPrint`, `CPrintPreview`

Table 25.1 describes the basic purpose for each of these classes.

TABLE 25.1   Classes Identified for the Menu Maker Project

Class Name	Purpose
CRecipeItem	This class represents the individual ingredients used in a recipe. It must encapsulate the following items: name, description, category (meat, fruit, and so on), market price, and nutritional information (calories, fat, cholesterol content, and so on), quantity, measuring unit.
CRecipe	This class encapsulates a list of CRecipeItem objects, along with the following items: name, description, category (appetizers, seafood, sandwiches, desserts, and so on), market price, menu price, and nutritional information (calories, fat, cholesterol content, and so on). Each dish served by the restaurant is represented by a CRecipe object.
CRecipeEditor	This helper class manages the adding and editing of recipes.
CMenuItem	This class encapsulates the name of an individual dish that appears on the restaurant's menu, along its description and price.
CMenu	This class is a collection of all the items available on the restaurant's menu.
CMenuEditor	This helper class manages the adding and editing of the restaurant's menu and its items.
CInventoryItem	This class represents an individual food item to be stocked in the restaurant's kitchen and coolers (includes beverages, meats, vegetables, and so on).
CInventory	This class keeps track of how much food is in stock and when it's time to order more.
CSalesItem	This class represents the sale of an individual menu item, such as an appetizer, a salad, a steak, or a beer (preferably European).
CSales	This class encapsulates a list of CSalesItem objects, giving the combined sales for the restaurant.
CReport	This class accesses the other classes to get information about sales and inventory.
CPrint	This class implements the printing of report data.
CPrintPreview	This class implements a preview of what a printed report will look like.

As you can see, quite a few classes are required for the Menu Maker project. Table 25.1 provides a sketch of the classes we might need. With a few more iterations through the design phase, we may find that some of these classes can be absorbed into others, reducing the number of classes in the system. Or we may find that new classes become apparent as the design is shaped and then finalized. In this chapter, we'll consider just the classes listed in Table 25.1 as a prototype or a sketch and develop the concepts further. Figure 25.1 shows the basic subsystems defined by the classes we've identified.

FIGURE 25.1

The basic subsystems that make up the back-end classes in the restaurant system.

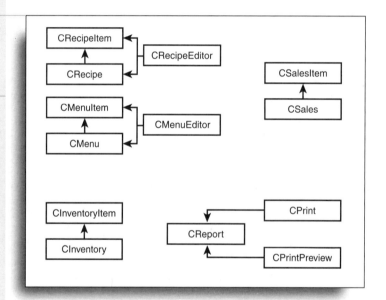

Designing Interfaces

An *interface* is a mechanism that enables interaction between two systems. In software design, interfaces are important because they permit different modules to interact, allowing you to build complex systems. Efficient, easy-to-use, and easy-to-maintain interfaces are important in quality software design.

An interface should be solidified to the point that the implementation of a class could be written in 20 different ways by 20 different programmers, and each version would work seamlessly with the interface (header). This is how the Standard C++

Library is designed. The interfaces (headers) for all library components are provided, and each compiler vendor must either create an implementation for each library component or license an implementation from some other vendor.

Using Modular Source Files

The use of software modules is essential to any serious programming project. By breaking down designs into logically related components, you can develop standalone modules and sets of interrelated modules that integrate well in any program.

Modules should contain a series of related services—preferably as class methods, but possibly as global routines. To reduce the amount of coupling between modules, you should minimize global data and fully think out and promote class interfaces as the technique for communication between modules.

Creating Interface (Header) Files

The interface to a module is the most important thing to the user of that module. The interface should be solidified early in the system design process, allowing for any type of functionality the user might require of the module. When the interface is complete, it should not change. This is especially true of object-oriented systems in which base class interfaces that change can trigger a chain reaction in any derived classes. A few simple changes to a base class interface can wreak havoc on the next build of a program.

The implementation of an interface isn't important to the end user—that is, it's not important exactly *how* the modularized code works, as long as it works. Solidify your interfaces with a specification of some sort, such as a class declaration. Place each class declaration into its own header file for maximum separation of interface and implementation, and for ease of code reuse in other projects.

Keeping your modules as close as possible to the ideal of a "black box" is the best path to take. Using protected and private class members that have clean interfaces and access routines will make your code much more robust than using public members or global functions. Figure 25.2 shows the basic relationships between the classes in the restaurant system.

FIGURE 25.2

The relationships between subsystems in the restaurant system.

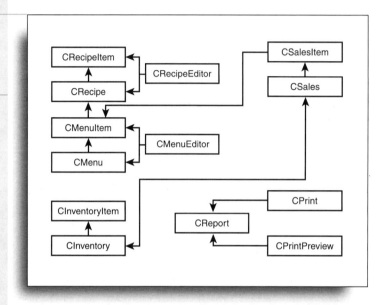

To begin, the interfaces for each of the identified classes will look very similar to each other. Consider the interface for the CRecipeItem class, shown in Listing 25.1.

LISTING 25.1

① Lines 7-8: Begin single-inclusion

LISTING 25.1   **The Preliminary Interface for the *CRecipeItem* Class**

```
1: //////////////////////////////////////////////////////
2: //  Module  : RecipeItem.h
3: //
4: //  Purpose : Interface for the CRecipeItem class
5: //////////////////////////////////////////////////////
6:
7: #ifndef __RECIPEITEM_H__
8: #define __RECIPEITEM_H__
9:
10: class CRecipeItem
11: {
```

①

```
12:     friend class CRecipe;
13:     friend class CRecipeEditor;
14:
15: public:
16:     CRecipeItem();
17:     virtual ~CRecipeItem();
18:
19:     // ...
20: };
21:
22: #endif //__RECIPEITEM_H__
```

LISTING 25.1 CONTINUED

2 Lines 12-13: CRecipe
and CRecipeEditor
are friend classes

3 Line 22: End single-inclusion

As you can see, this class interface file contains only a constructor and a destructor and declares the CRecipe and CRecipeEditor classes to be friend classes. The preliminary interfaces for the rest of the recipe subsystem, encompassed by the CRecipe and CRecipeEditor classes, are shown in Listings 25.2 and 25.3.

LISTING 25.2   **The Preliminary Interface for the *CRecipe* Class**

```
 1: ////////////////////////////////////////////////////
 2: //   Module  : Recipe.h
 3: //
 4: //   Purpose : Interface for the CRecipe class
 5: ////////////////////////////////////////////////////
 6:
 7: #ifndef __RECIPE_H__
 8: #define __RECIPE_H__
 9:
10: #include "RecipeItem.h"
11:
12: class CRecipe
13: {
14:     friend class CRecipeEditor;
15:
16: public:
17:     CRecipe();
18:     virtual ~CRecipe();
19:
20:     // ...
21: };
```

LISTING 25.2

1 Lines 7-8: Begin single-
inclusion

2 Line 14: CRecipeEditor
is a friend class

**Building Object-Oriented
Programs**

Coupling between related
groups of classes provides the
means to implement small subsystems that make up larger
subsystems within the complete
system that results in an object-
oriented program.

continues...

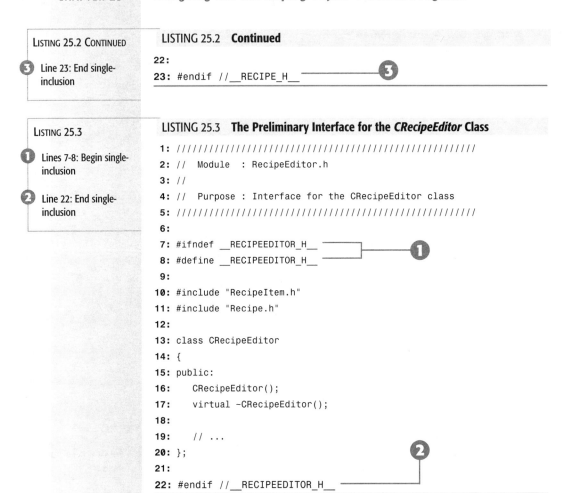

LISTING 25.2 CONTINUED

③ Line 23: End single-inclusion

LISTING 25.2 Continued

```
22:
23: #endif //__RECIPE_H__
```
③

LISTING 25.3

① Lines 7-8: Begin single-inclusion

② Line 22: End single-inclusion

LISTING 25.3 The Preliminary Interface for the *CRecipeEditor* Class

```
 1: ///////////////////////////////////////////////////////
 2: //  Module  : RecipeEditor.h
 3: //
 4: //  Purpose : Interface for the CRecipeEditor class
 5: ///////////////////////////////////////////////////////
 6:
 7: #ifndef __RECIPEEDITOR_H__
 8: #define __RECIPEEDITOR_H__
 9:
10: #include "RecipeItem.h"
11: #include "Recipe.h"
12:
13: class CRecipeEditor
14: {
15: public:
16:    CRecipeEditor();
17:    virtual ~CRecipeEditor();
18:
19:    // ...
20: };
21:
22: #endif //__RECIPEEDITOR_H__
```
① (lines 7-8)
② (line 22)

Creating Implementation Files

As you've seen many times in this book, an implementation file implements the functionality declared in its corresponding interface file. By putting your source code in the implementation file, you can compile it into object code and distribute just the header with the .obj file. This approach hides your implementation from the other programmers to whom you might distribute the object file. By including the header in a program source file, and linking with the corresponding object file, other programmers can take advantage of your code, while its internal implementation is kept hidden.

Corresponding to these header files are the source files that contain the implementations of any non-inline class methods declared in the headers. The preliminary implementation of the CRecipeItem class in Listing 25.4 contains only a constructor and destructor, just as the class interface currently specifies.

LISTING 25.4   **The Preliminary Implementation of the *CRecipeItem* Class**

```
 1: //////////////////////////////////////////////////////
 2: //   Module  : RecipeItem.cpp
 3: //
 4: //   Purpose : Implementation of class CRecipeItem
 5: //////////////////////////////////////////////////////
 6:
 7: #include "RecipeItem.h" ────────❶
 8:
 9: //////////////////////////////////////////////////////
10: // Constructor/Destructor
11:
12: CRecipeItem::CRecipeItem()
13: {
14:     // ...                        ❷
15: }
16:
17: CRecipeItem::~CRecipeItem()
18: {
19:     // ...                        ❸
20: }
```

LISTING 25.4

❶ Line 7: Include the interface for the class

❷ Lines 12-15: Skeletal implementation of the constructor

❸ Lines 17-20: Skeletal implementation of the destructor

The rest of the recipe subsystem is implemented in a similar manner. As the interface solidifies in the header, at least the stubs of class methods can be created in the corresponding source files. The constructor and destructor definitions in Listing 25.4 are such *stub functions*—functions that have a function body that contains no code. These stubs can later be fully

Stub Function

A stub function is a function that has a function body containing no source code—a function that's not yet implemented but that is present to keep the compiler and linker from complaining.

implemented, but for now the creation of the skeletal class system is the thrust of the coding. Figure 25.3 shows a temporary test project in the Microsoft Visual C++ Developer Studio after creating the preliminary header and source files for each class we've identified.

FIGURE 25.3

The restaurant classes in a temporary test project in the Microsoft Visual C++ Developer Studio.

Devising Class Methods

Method

A member function of a class.

After you've identified the list of classes you need for a project, you need to think about how those classes will interact and process their data. Each class will have certain public class methods that expose the class's functionality. Each class will likely also have protected and private methods that are used internally. On a class-by-class basis, add to the specification the probable methods each class will need. CASE tools really help out in this respect.

Interfaces in Action

Each class source file and header uses the interfaces of any other class that it relies on for data. By including the headers for other classes in the system, the classes become integrated and can use the services provided. For example, a recipe is made up of a number of items used to create a specific dish. The CRecipe class therefore needs to use the CRecipeItem class, as identified in Figure 25.2. This relationship is provided by including the CRecipeItem class declaration in the CRecipe class header.

The same concept applies to all the classes. Using the class relationships revealed in Figure 25.2, you can identify which classes need access to which other classes, and how the subsystems should fit together.

Accessibility Issues

It's convenient to allow certain classes with tighter coupling in a subsystem to get direct access to the members of other classes in the subsystem. To allow this access, you can declare a class as a friend of another class. Consider the CRecipeItem class, which declares both the CRecipe and CRecipeEditor classes as friends:

```
class CRecipeItem
{
    friend class CRecipe;
    friend class CRecipeEditor;

public:
    CRecipeItem();
    virtual ~CRecipeItem();

    // ...
};
```

Now the implementations of the CRecipe and CRecipeEditor classes can directly access the members of the CRecipeItem class. Other classes do not have access to any protected members that are added to the CRecipeItem class later in the development process.

Circular References

Make sure that your classes are designed in such a way that no two class headers, either directly or indirectly, rely on each other. This type of inter-dependency between two classes is called a *circular reference* and is the sign of a poorly designed system.

Testing and Integrating Modules

Each class and routine in a module must be thoroughly debugged and tested. By creating small driver programs to test classes or sets of classes forming program subsystems, you can be assured that a set of modules is appropriately integrated and debugged. The driver program should test every public class method and global function.

Avoiding Multiple Definitions

Header Files and File Inclusion

Make sure that you use single-inclusion preprocessor directives to avoid the problem of multiple definitions of classes in your object code files. By using these "inclusion guards," you can prevent linker errors related to this problem.

The use of single-inclusion directives (inclusion guards) to wrap the interface code in a header file is very important in preventing linker errors related to multiple definitions. This simple technique can save you a lot of headaches. Make it a habit—it can't hurt.

SEE ALSO

➤ For more information about single-inclusion directives, see page 299

Another thing to make sure of is that any function definition that's not part of a class declaration and that isn't inline should be in the source file, not the header. The same goes for variable declarations that are definitions. Put these definitions into the implementation source file and then use extern declarations for them in the header. For example, we can define these objects at file scope in a source file, like this:

```
// MySource.cpp
//

#include "MySource.h"

int SomeInt;
float SomeFloat;
CSomeClass sc;

// ...
```

To make these objects visible outside the module, you declare them in the corresponding header file as extern, telling the compiler, "You'll find these guys somewhere else during compilation, but not here," like this (note the single-inclusion directives):

```
// MySource.h
//

#ifndef __MYSOURCE_H__
#define __MYSOURCE_H__

class CSomeClass { };

extern int SomeInt;
extern float SomeFloat;
extern CSomeClass sc;

#endif //__MYSOURCE_H__
```

Testing Functionality

Once a module is coded, you must test it thoroughly. To do this, you should create a driver program to test the module's classes and functionality. Begin by running the module through your debugger and stepping through the code, verifying that it works properly.

Next, you should test the module with a variety of data, calling class members and global functions to verify that they work properly. While debugging, step through the code, verifying that each component of each class is functioning properly. It's much easier to fix bugs in freshly written code than in code written months or years earlier.

Integrating Modules

Once a module has been thoroughly debugged and tested, it's ready for integration into a program. The integration of multiple modules into a cohesive set of program files is sometimes a bit challenging. The easiest thing to do is to put file inclusions where they're needed, either in a header or a source file.

Driver Program

A simple program designed to test and debug a class (or a set of classes) or a module (or a set of modules).

If some data type or declaration is needed in a header, you should include, within the header, the additional header that provides the data type or declaration. If some data type or declaration is needed in a source file, include the header that provides the data type or declaration in the source file. For example, because the CRecipe class uses CRecipeItem objects, you must include RecipeItem.h in the CRecipe header (refer to Listing 25.2).

Reusing Code

By writing code that's generic, robust, and reusable, you can turn any programming project into an investment. If you think about function and class design with reusability in mind, it may take longer to produce the code the first time, but you won't have to reproduce it a second time.

Being able to plug classes and modules into a project can save countless hours of development time. You should also consider using function and class templates to make your code more generic and reusable. Code reuse is the single-most productive objective to which a programmer can strive.

Using Templates

Implement generic programming with templates

Create and use function and class templates

Understand how to use template parameters

Convert existing classes into class templates

Conceptualizing Templates

The introduction of experimental templates into C++ in the late 1980s was a major breakthrough for the language. After a decade of experimentation, modification, and fine-tuning, templates have become firmly rooted in the Standard C++ Library. Templates provide the basis of generic programming in C++ and make possible the Standard Template Library, one of the major features of the Standard C++ Library.

For years I wrote off templates as being just another programming trick that I could do without, but after I tried using them, there was no turning back. Templates provide an incredible amount of power for C++ programmers, allowing you to write generic code that will work with multiple data types. In abstract terms, templates are *parameterized types*. A template uses the parameter or parameters sent to it to define a new data type, called a *specialization* of the template, at compile time.

Parameterized Type

A template for a function or class that uses parameters to specify generic data type(s) used by or defining the function or class. The compiler generates a type-specific version of the template when it encounters an instantiation of a template object.

Specialization

The compiler-generated, type-specific version of a template.

Avoiding Redundant Code

Remember the multiplication functions from Chapter 8, "Overloading Functions"? These functions were cumbersome to use, and it was too difficult to remember which types you had defined them for. To refresh your memory, here are a few of the definitions for these functions:

```
float Mult2Floats(float num1, float num2)
    { return num1 * num2; }

int Mult2Ints(int num1, int num2)
    { return num1 * num2; }

float MultFloatLong(float num1, long num2)
    { return num1 * float(num2); }

double MultDoubleInt(double num1, int num2)
    { return num1 * double(num2); }
```

I then introduced a better solution, using function overloading to create several `Multiply()` functions that worked with different data types. Here are the corresponding overloaded definitions for these same functions:

```
float Multiply(float num1, float num2)
   { return num1 * num2; }

int Multiply(int num1, int num2)
   { return num1 * num2; }

float Multiply(float num1, long num2)
   { return num1 * float(num2); }

double Multiply(double num1, int num2)
   { return num1 * double(num2); }
```

The problem with these functions is that they're so annoyingly similar; the code is redundant. All these functions do the same basic thing—they multiply two objects passed in as parameters. If only there were some generic means of writing a single Multiply() function that would work with any data type. There is! Function templates enable you to create such generic functions.

Creating Function Templates

A function template uses the concept that all data types are classes, even the intrinsic C++ types like int and float. Internally, C++ does treat the intrinsic types as classes, so you can correctly speak of int variables and float variables as int objects and float objects. The parameters a template uses are specified within angle brackets (< >). To create a function template, you use the following general syntax:

```
template <class T>
ReturnType FunctionName(ParameterList) { ... }
```

The template keyword tells the compiler that a template is being defined, and the <class T> clause tells the compiler that some type T is the parameter type that will be used in the function. Type T can be any data type, such as an intrinsic type, or a user-defined structure or class—even another template. Here's an example showing how to create a generic Square() function that will work with any data type that supports the operator*():

```
template <class T>
T Square(T num) { return num * num; }
```

When you call this function in your source code, the compiler generates custom code to match the data type you've sent as an argument to the function template's T parameter—a generic type. Of course, if the data type doesn't support the * operator, the compiler will choke, generating an error instead of source code. The program in Listing 26.1 demonstrates the use of this template function.

LISTING 26.1

① Line 12: Declare the generic Square() function template

② Line 21: Call the Square() function with a float parameter

LISTING 26.1   A Program Demonstrating the Use of a Simple Global Function Template

```
1  ///////////////////////////////////////////////////////
2  //   Module   : FunctionTemplate1.cpp
3  //
4  //   Purpose : Demonstrates the use of simple global
5  //             function templates.
6  ///////////////////////////////////////////////////////
7
8  #include <iostream.h>
9
10 // A generic Square() prototype
11 //
12 template <class T> T Square(T num); ──────①
13
14 ///////////////////////////////////////////////////////
15 // main()
16
17 void main()
18 {
19    // float
20    //
21    cout << "The square of 5.5f is " << Square(5.5f) ──②
22       << endl;
23
24    // double
25    //
26    cout << "The square of 5.5 is " << Square(5.5)
27       << endl;
28
```

```
29    // int
30    //
31    cout << "The square of 10 is " << Square(10)
32        << endl;
33 }
34
35 //////////////////////////////////////////////////////////
36 // Square() — A template function
37
38 template <class T>
39 T Square(T num) { return num * num; }
```

LISTING 26.1 CONTINUED

3 Line 31: Call the Square()
function with an int parameter

4 Lines 38-39: The definition of
the Square() function
template

The output for this program shows that the compiler uses the
function template to correctly generate the correct source code
for each data type:

```
The square of 5.5f is 30.25
The square of 5.5 is 30.25
The square of 10 is 100
```

On line 12 you declare the function template for the generic
Square() function. On line 21, in main(), the Square() function is
called with a float parameter, so at compile time the compiler
generates an overloaded Square() function for floats. On line 31
the Square() function is called with an int parameter, so at compile time the compiler generates an overloaded Square() function
for integers. The definition for the function template is shown
on lines 38 and 39, taking a parameter of type T and returning a
value of type T.

It's true that a macro could accomplish the same thing as this
function template, for example:

```
#define Square(n) ((n)*(n))
```

However, this macro bypasses all C++ type checking, opening
the door to all kinds of side effects that can plague a program
with bugs. Templates provide complete type safety because the
compiler generates C++ code for the actual data types sent to the
template when an instance of the template class is instantiated.

Using Multiple Generic Class Types

Templates aren't limited to a single parameter—they can use more than one generic class type in their declaration and definition. For example, here's a "regular" Multiply() function—one of the overloaded functions you saw earlier:

```
float Multiply(float num1, int num2)
    { return num1 * (float)num2; }
```

Here's the same Multiply() function defined as a template that uses two generic class types instead of float and int explicitly:

```
template <class A, class B>
A Multiply(A num1, B num2)
    { return num1 * num2; }
```

This one template function can replace all the overloaded Multiply() functions you saw defined earlier—and any others you can think of that take two parameters and support the multiplication operator! The program in Listing 26.2 demonstrates the use of this multiclass template function.

LISTING 26.2

❶ Lines 12-13: Declare a function template taking two parameters

LISTING 26.2   A Program That Uses a Template Function with Multiple Generic Class Types as Parameters

```
 1 /////////////////////////////////////////////////////////
 2 //  Module  : FunctionTemplate2.cpp
 3 //
 4 //  Purpose : Demonstrates the use of a global function
 5 //            template taking multiple parameters.
 6 /////////////////////////////////////////////////////////
 7
 8 #include <iostream.h>
 9
10 // A generic Square() prototype
11 //
12 template <class A, class B>
13 A Multiply(A num1, B num2);
14
15 /////////////////////////////////////////////////////////
16 // main()
17
18 void main()
```

```
19 {
20    // float * int
21    //
22    cout << "5.5f * 4 == " << Multiply(5.5f, 4)  ──────②
23       << endl;
24
25    // double * long
26    //
27    cout << "10.2 * 6L == " << Multiply(10.2, 6L)  ──────③
28       << endl;
29
30    // int * int
31    //
32    cout << "10 * 10 == " << Multiply(10, 10)  ──────④
33       << endl;
34 }
35
36 ///////////////////////////////////////////////////////
37 // Multiply() -- A template function
38
39 template <class A, class B>
40 A Multiply(A num1, B num2)
41    { return num1 * num2; }
```

LISTING 26.2 CONTINUED

② Line 22: Call the Multiply() function template with float and int parameters

③ Line 27: Call the Multiply() function template with double and long parameters

④ Line 32: Call the Multiply() function template with two integer parameters

The output from this program shows that the specialized functions are correctly generated by the compiler from the function template:

```
5.5f * 4 == 22
10.2 * 6L == 61.2
10 * 10 == 100
```

The Multiply() function template declared on lines 12 and 13 takes two parameters, class A and class B. These two classes can each represent any data type that understands the operator * for multiplication. On line 22 you instantiate the Multiply() function template using the parameter types float and int, returning a float value. On line 27 you instantiate the Multiply() function template using the parameter types double and long, returning a double value. On line 32 you instantiate the Multiply() function template using the int type for both parameters, returning an int value.

The function template definition is given on lines 39 through 41, with the second operand (num2) typecast to type A before the multiplication. This assumes that the type used for num2 supports this type of cast operation.

Creating a Basic Class Template

Global template functions are powerful, but they're just the tip of the iceberg. The real power of templates becomes apparent when you use them to define classes themselves. Just as a function template can be used to generate a multitude of similar functions, a class template allows the compiler to generate a multitude of similar classes. Class templates are especially useful for container classes. The compiler uses the template definition to create actual data types as needed.

Designing a Template Skeleton

Note

Template classes can take several parameters, depending on the complexity and purpose of the class.

A simple class template will generally use the following skeletal format:

```
template <class T>
class BasicClass
{
protected:
    T myObj;
};
```

This skeletal template declares the protected myObj data member as being of data type T. This class can be easily extended to actually perform some functions using myObj.

Fleshing Out the Template

Now that you've defined the template skeleton, let's add a few class methods to flesh it out a bit. By adding Get() and Set() member functions you can provide indirect access to the protected myObj member. Here's the revised template, showing these methods in place in the class, along with a constructor to initialize myObj:

```
template <class T>
class BasicClass
{
public:
   BasicClass(const T& t) : myObj(t) { }

   T Get() const { return myObj; }
   void Set(const T& t) { myObj = t; }

protected:
   T myObj;
};
```

You can then instantiate a `BasicClass` object that is specialized to use a `float` parameter type like this:

```
BasicClass<float> f;
```

By providing a `typedef` for a specialized class template, you can make your code more readable and maintainable. For example, here's a type definition for the `BasicClass` template, specialized to use the `float` type:

```
typedef BasicClass<float> Float;
```

You can then use the specialized template `typedef`, like this:

```
Float f(5.5f);
cout << f.Get() << endl;

f.Set(12.3f);
cout << f.Get() << endl;
```

Creating a More Complex Class Template

In addition to generic parameterized class types, templates can also take specific types as parameters and can have default values as well. For example, here's a simple class template that takes a generic type and an intrinsic type as parameters:

```
template <class T, int size = 10>
class BasicArray
{
```

```
public:
    T& operator[](const int& index);

protected:
    T myArray[size]; // automatic initialization
};
```

By utilizing the template parameter size, the compiler can automatically set the size of the array at compile time. The program
in Listing 26.3 demonstrates the use of the BasicArray class
template.

LISTING 26.3

Line 15: Declare the
BasicArray class template
to use a default parameter
value

Line 22: The array uses
automatic storage class,
storing size elements

LISTING 26.3 **A Program That Uses a Class Template to Create Three Arrays of Different Types and Sizes**

```
1  /////////////////////////////////////////////////////
2  //  Module  : BasicArray.cpp
3  //
4  //  Purpose : Demonstrates a class template that wraps
5  //            an automatic array.
6  /////////////////////////////////////////////////////
7
8  #include <iostream.h>
9
10 class OutOfBounds { }; // for exception handling
11
12 /////////////////////////////////////////////////////
13 // Class template to wrap an array
14 //
15 template <class T, int size = 10> ———————①
16 class BasicArray
17 {
18 public:
19     T& operator[](const int& index);
20
21 protected:
22     T myArray[size]; // automatic initialization ————②
23 };
24
25 /////////////////////////////////////////////////////
26 // BasicArray<T>::operator[]() — Defining the
27 // operator outside the class template decaration
```

```
28
29 template <class T, int size>
30 T& BasicArray<T, size>::operator[](const int& index)
31 {
32     if ((index < 0) || (index >= size))
33         throw OutOfBounds();
34
35     return myArray[index];
36 }
37
38 //////////////////////////////////////////////////////
39 //  main()
40
41 void main()
42 {
43     try
44     {
45         // Create some arrays using the template
46         //
47         BasicArray<float> bc1; // uses default size value
48         BasicArray<int, 20> bc2;
49         BasicArray<char, 30> bc3;
50
51         // Use the arrays
52         //
53         bc1[5]  = 5.5f;
54         bc2[10] = 12;
55         bc3[15] = 'X';
56
57         cout << "bc1[5]  == " << bc1[5] << endl;
58         cout << "bc2[10] == " << bc2[10] << endl;
59         cout << "bc3[15] == " << bc3[15] << endl;
60     }
61     catch(OutOfBounds)
62         { cerr << "Array index out of bounds!\n"; }
63
64     catch(...)
65         { cerr << "Catching unknown exception!\n"; }
66 }
```

The output from this program demonstrates that the specialized arrays were correctly generated by the compiler, showing the values of the specified elements:

```
bc1[5]  == 5.5f;
bc2[10] == 12;
bc3[15] == X;
```

Line 10 defines the exception class OutOfBounds, which is used to catch an exception where an invalid array element is specified for an instantiated class template. The BasicArray class is declared from lines 15 through 23, with the template taking two parameters (line 15). The first parameter is a generic type T, but the second is an integer, providing a default array size of 10. The array class contains an operator[] declaration on line 19, and on line 22 the actual array data member is initialized to have as many elements as specified by the size template parameter.

The operator[] function is defined from lines 29 through 36, checking for an invalid element index on line 32. If the element index is invalid, an OutOfBounds exception is thrown on line 33. If the element index is in bounds, the actual array element is returned as a reference to type T on line 35.

A try block, beginning on line 43, enables exception handling for the main() function. On line 47 a specialized BasicArray object (bc1) of type float is instantiated, using the default element size (10) provided by the class template. Line 48 instantiates a BasicArray object of type int, reserving space for 20 elements by explicitly providing the second template parameter. Line 49 likewise instantiates a BasicArray object of type char, reserving space for 30 elements by explicitly providing the second template parameter.

Lines 53 through 55 assign appropriate data type values to arbitrary elements that fall within the array bounds, using the operator[] to get to the BasicArray class template's internal array. Lines 57 through 59 use the operator[] to retrieve the values from these same array elements, displaying them to the screen using cout.

If the array element indexes used on lines 53 through 59 were to somehow be out of bounds of a given array, the catch handler on

line 61 would trap the resulting OutOfBounds exception, and lines
64 and 65 provide a catch-all exception handler for those
unexpected conditions that sometimes crop up.

Converting Existing Classes into Class Templates

Existing classes are often good candidates for conversion to template classes. The conversion is usually fairly easy, changing
intrinsic and user-defined types to parameterized types as
needed. In fact, it's usually a good idea to create class templates
as regular, non-template classes first, so you can work out any
bugs inherent in the design. A fully debugged class can usually
become a class template with little modification.

Creating a Generic Linked List Class

In the following sections, you'll see how easy it is to convert an
existing class into a class template. I'll use the CIntList class
from Chapter 24, "Implementing Dynamic Storage in C++," as
the basis for a generic doubly linked list template class I'll call
CGenericList. You can use this generic container class to store
integers just like the original CIntList class, but you can also
use it to store other intrinsic data types, custom structures, and
classes.

The class data members and class methods will be nearly the
same as those in the original CIntList class, but as the basis for
the list the template will use the parameterized type T instead of
the intrinsic type int.

The foundation of the generic linked list class is a generic node
class, but before you can create a list of generic nodes, you need
to define exactly what a generic node is. This means that for the
generic list I'll also need to convert the CIntNode into the new
CGenericNode class.

Note

Sometimes a class requires a lot
of modification to become a
template class, and some
classes aren't suited to use as
templates at all. Experimentation
with templates to find out what
works and what doesn't is the
best way to learn about their
limitations.

Generic Node Class

A linked list node that can be of
any type specified by the template class parameters.

Implementing a Generic Node Class

In addition to the actual data stored in a node (in this case, the parameterized type T), each node in the list must contain a pointer to the previous node and a pointer to the next node, as well as the data itself. The data members for the CGenericNode class include a pointer to the next node (mypNext), a pointer to the previous node (mypPrev), and the generic data itself (myObj). I'll begin the node class conversion by converting the CIntNode class to CGenericNode. For comparison, here's the original CIntNode class declaration, so you have an idea of the changes that you need to make:

```
class CIntNode
{
public:
    CIntNode() : mypPrev(0), mypNext(0) { }
    int Value() const { return myInt; }
    void Value(const int& i) { myInt = i; }

    friend class CIntList;

protected:
    CIntNode *mypPrev;
    CIntNode *mypNext;
    int myInt;
};
```

Any function return types or parameters that are integers need to be replaced with the parameterized type T. Likewise, the protected data member myInt becomes myObj, of type T instead of type int. The first set of changes to the code can be accomplished by performing a global search and replace with your text editor, simply changing all occurrences of CIntNode to CGenericNode. Next, by adding the expression template<class T> to the beginning of the class declaration, you have a template class. The return and parameter types for the Value() methods need to change from int to T, giving the following class declaration for the CGenericNode class:

```
template <class T>
class CGenericNode
```

```
    {
    public:
        CGenericNode() : mypPrev(0), mypNext(0) { }
        T Value() const { return myObj; }
        void Value(const T& t) { myObj = t; }

        friend class CGenericList<T>;

    protected:
        CGenericNode *mypPrev;
        CGenericNode *mypNext;
        T myObj;
    };
```

See how easy this is? There's one more important addition to the code, though. To allow the CGenericList class direct access to the protected CGenericNode class members, you must declare this class as a friend of CGenericNode. Notice that the friend class declaration above uses angle brackets to specify T as the parameter type. Because of the way the compiler sees templates when compiling, a forward declaration of the CGenericList class is needed—*before* the compiler sees the CGenericNode class declaration—like this:

```
// Forward class template declaration
//
template <class T> class CGenericList;
```

This gives us the complete source for the CGenericNode header file, shown in Listing 26.4.

LISTING 26.4   **The Header for the *CGenericNode* Class**

```
 1 /////////////////////////////////////////////////////
 2 //  Module   : GenericNode.h
 3 //
 4 //  Purpose : Interface for the CGenericNode class
 5 /////////////////////////////////////////////////////
 6
 7 #ifndef __GENERICNODE_H__
 8 #define __GENERICNODE_H__
 9
10 // Forward class template declaration
```

continues...

LISTING 26.4

1 Line 12: This forward declaration allows the compiler to know about the CGenericList class template before encountering its declaration

2 Line 25: Declare the CGenericList class template of type T to be a friend

LISTING 26.4 **Continued**

```
11 //
12 template <class T> class CGenericList; ————————① 

13
14 ////////////////////////////////////////////////////////////
15 // Class CGenericNode
16
17 template <class T>
18 class CGenericNode
19 {
20 public:
21    CGenericNode() : mypPrev(0), mypNext(0) { }
22    T Value() const { return myObj; }
23    void Value(const T& t) { myObj = t; }
24
25    friend class CGenericList<T>; ————————————② 

26
27 protected:
28    CGenericNode *mypPrev;
29    CGenericNode *mypNext;
30    T myObj;
31 };
32
33 #endif //__GENERICNODE_H__
```

Problems with Separating the Class Interface and Implementation

The C++ standard designates the export keyword for use with templates to enable complete separation of interface and implementation, but most compilers (including the ones that I use) don't support the export keyword yet...the standard is still too new as of this writing. Many compilers use pragmas or command-line switches for the compiler or linker to make this happen, but the process isn't standardized across compilers—it's not even close!

You should be able to declare an interface for a template class in a header file, separate from the implementation, just like a

regular class. For example, here's a simple template class called
`CTemp`, which contains a single member function and no data
members:

```
// class template interface in temp.h
//
template <class T>
class CTemp
{
public:
   T Square(const T& t);
};
```

You *should* be able to define the implementation of the template
class member function in a separate .cpp file, like this:

```
#include "temp.h"

// class template implementation in temp.cpp
//
export template <class T>
T CTemp<T>::Square(const T& t)
   { return t * t; }
```

Unfortunately, most compilers don't support the `export` keyword
yet, so you either have to figure out their `pragmas` or command-
line switches, or end up with a multitude of linker errors. The
easy solution to this disturbing problem is to put both the interface *and* the implementation into the same header file. As a
result, I've stuffed both the interface and implementation for the
generic list into the header file to prevent linker errors.

Altering the List Class Interface and Implementation

I'll begin the generic list class conversion by converting the
`CIntList` class to `CGenericList`. Just as you did with the node
class, changing the class name in the code can be accomplished
by performing a global search and replace with your text editor,
simply replacing all occurrences of `CIntList` with `CGenericList`.
Next, by adding the expression `template<class T>` to the class
declaration, it becomes a class template. Adding the expression
`template<class T>` to the beginning of each member function
definition makes it a part of the new template class.

> **Note**
>
> The most common method of
> implementing class templates is
> to put both the interface and
> implementation into a header
> file that you can include in your
> programs.

> **Note**
>
> When templatizing a class, you
> can implement generic pro-
> gramming by changing all
> occurrences of a specific data
> type in the class to a para-
> meterized type supplied to the
> class template.

Any function return types or parameters that are of type int need to be replaced with the parameterized type T. Likewise, any appearance of CIntNode must be replaced with CGenericNode. For comparison, here's the original CIntList class declaration:

```
class CIntList
{
public:
    CIntList() : mypHead(0), mypTail(0), mypCur(0),
        mySize(0) { }
    virtual ~CIntList() { if (mypHead) Clear(); }

    // Public Member functions
    //
    bool AddHead(const int& i);
    bool AddTail(const int& i);
    void Clear();
    CIntNode* Current() { return mypCur; }
    CIntNode* Find(const int& i);
    CIntNode* Head() { return mypHead; }
    bool Insert(const int& i, CIntNode* pNode);
    CIntNode* Next();
    CIntNode* Prev();
    void Remove(CIntNode *pNode);
    void Reset() { mypCur = mypHead; }
    int Size() const { return mySize; }
    CIntNode* Tail() { return mypTail; }

protected:
    // Protected data members
    //
    CIntNode *mypHead;
    CIntNode *mypTail;
    CIntNode *mypCur;
    int mySize;
};
```

By altering the class declaration with the changes described previously, you end up with the following class declaration for the new CGenericList class:

```
template <class T>
```

```
class CGenericList
{
public:
    CGenericList() : mypHead(0), mypTail(0), mypCur(0),
        mySize(0) { }
    virtual ~CGenericList() { if (mypHead) Clear(); }

    // Public Member functions
    //
    bool AddHead(const T& t);
    bool AddTail(const T& t);
    void Clear();
    CGenericNode<T>* Current() { return mypCur; }
    CGenericNode<T>* Find(const T& t);
    CGenericNode<T>* Head() { return mypHead; }
    bool Insert(const T& t, CGenericNode<T> *pNode);
    CGenericNode<T>* Next();
    CGenericNode<T>* Prev();
    void Remove(CGenericNode<T> *pNode);
    void Reset() { mypCur = mypHead; }
    int Size() const { return mySize; }
    CGenericNode<T>* Tail() { return mypTail; }

protected:
    // Protected data members
    //
    CGenericNode<T> *mypHead;
    CGenericNode<T> *mypTail;
    CGenericNode<T> *mypCur;
    int mySize;
};
```

All that's left to do now is make some modifications to the class methods.

Adding a Node

The CGenericList::AddHead() function allocates a generic node, assigns a value to the node, and adds the node to the head of the list. The only parameter needed is a type T, giving you the following function definition header for the CGenericList::AddHead() function:

```
template <class T>
bool CGenericList<T>::AddHead(const T& t)
```

Each class member function that isn't defined within the class declaration must use the `template <class T>` clause to specify it as a template member function. Adding a node to the tail of the list is very similar, and the function `CGenericList::AddTail()` uses a similar function definition header:

```
template <class T>
bool CGenericList<T>::AddTail(const T& t)
```

These functions are nearly identical to those in Chapter 24, but allocating a generic node requires the use of angle brackets with type T to tell the compiler which actual type to create during compilation, like this:

```
CGenericNode<T> *pTemp = new CGenericNode<T>;
if (pTemp == 0)
{
    cerr << "New node memory allocation failed." << endl;
    return false;
}
```

Note

Compiler-generated template classes can increase the size of your executable files considerably, so be aware that this code-bloat can occur.

During compilation the compiler substitutes the actual data type that you specify in place of the generic type T. So, if you declare a variable of type `CGenericNode<float>`, the compiler generates the following code for this member function:

```
CGenericNode<float> *pTemp = new CGenericNode<float>;
if (pTemp == 0)
{
    cerr << "New node memory allocation failed." << endl;
    return false;
}
```

The only other difference between the new template `AddHead()` and `AddTail()` member functions and the original `CIntList` versions of these functions is in the setting of the node value. `myInt` changes to `myObj` and the value assigned is `t` (of type T), instead of `i` (of type `int`):

```
mypHead->myObj = t;
```

Traversing the List

To allow a program to traverse the list either forward or backward, the friendly member functions CGenericList::Next() and CGenericList::Prev() are provided. The CGenericList::Next() function points the mypCur pointer to the next node in the list to move its position one node forward along the list. The only changes from the original function are to add the T parameter to the type name, giving us this function definition:

```
template <class T>
CGenericNode<T> * CGenericList<T>::Next()
{
    if (mypCur)
        mypCur = mypCur->mypNext;

    return mypCur;
}
```

Similarly, the CGenericList::Prev() function can be defined like this, pointing the mypCur pointer to the previous node in the list to move its position one node backward along the list:

```
template <class T>
CGenericNode<T> * CGenericList<T>::Prev()
{
    if (mypCur)
        mypCur = mypCur->mypPrev;

    return mypCur;
}
```

Finding an Item

The changes to the Find() method are just as minor. Starting at the head of the list, you can define the CGenericList::Find() function like this:

```
template <class T>
CGenericNode<T> * CGenericList<T>::Find(const T& t)
{
    CGenericNode<T> *pTemp = mypHead;
```

```
    while (pTemp)
    {
        if (pTemp->myObj == t)
            return pTemp;
        pTemp = pTemp->mypNext;
    }
    return 0;
}
```

The use of type T in place of type int, and object t instead of object i, is really the only change. The while loop traverses the list, looking for a node that matches the item being sought. If the item is found, a pointer to that node is returned.

Inserting a Node

Inserting a node at a specific location requires two pieces of information: the generic value to insert and the address of the node where you want the insertion to occur. This yields the following function definition header:

```
template <class T>
bool CGenericList<T>::Insert(const T& t,
    CGenericNode<T> *pNode)
```

By using the CGenericList::Find() function to locate the insertion point, you have the address you need.

The first step is to allocate a new node:

```
CGenericNode<T> *pTemp = new CGenericNode<T>;
```

Next, you can set the value for the node:

```
pTemp->myObj = t;
```

The rest of the function is the same as the original.

Deleting All Nodes from the List

To delete all nodes from the list, you provide the CGenericList::Clear() function. This function uses a temporary node pointer:

```
CGenericNode<T> *pTemp;
```

This is used to store the value of the head's `mypNext` pointer. In a `while` loop, the address of the head's next node is assigned to `pTemp` and the head is then deleted. The temp node then becomes the new head, and the loop iterates until all the nodes are deleted, giving this transformed `CGenericList::Clear()` function:

```
template <class T>
void CGenericList<T>::Clear()
{
    CGenericNode<T> *pTemp;

    while (mypHead)
    {
        pTemp = mypHead->mypNext;
        delete mypHead;
        mypHead = pTemp;
    }
    mySize = 0;
}
```

Deleting a Node

Porting the `CGenericList::Remove()` function is just as easy as the others. The function takes a pointer to a `CGenericNode` object as a parameter, giving the following function definition header:

```
template <class T>
void CGenericList<T>::Remove(CGenericNode<T> *pNode)
```

Everything else stays the same. The entire interface and implementation source code for the `CGenericList` class is given in Listing 26.5, showing you the complete versions of its generic member functions.

LISTING 26.5   **The Complete Source Code for the Interface and Implementation of the *CGenericList* Class**

```
1  /////////////////////////////////////////////////////
2  //  Module  : GenericList.h
3  //
4  //  Purpose : Interface for the CGenericList class
5  /////////////////////////////////////////////////////
```

continues…

LISTING 26.5   Continued

```
6
7  #ifndef __GENERICLIST_H__
8  #define __GENERICLIST_H__
9
10 #include <iostream.h>
11 #include <assert.h>
12 #include "GenericNode.h"
13
14 //////////////////////////////////////////////////////////
15 // Class CGenericList
16
17 template <class T>
18 class CGenericList
19 {
20 public:
21     CGenericList() : mypHead(0), mypTail(0), mypCur(0),
22         mySize(0) { }
23     virtual ~CGenericList() { if (mypHead) Clear(); }
24
25     // Public Member functions
26     //
27     bool AddHead(const T& t);
28     bool AddTail(const T& t);
29     void Clear();
30     CGenericNode<T>* Current() { return mypCur; }
31     CGenericNode<T>* Find(const T& t);
32     CGenericNode<T>* Head() { return mypHead; }
33     bool Insert(const T& t, CGenericNode<T> *pNode);
34     CGenericNode<T>* Next();
35     CGenericNode<T>* Prev();
36     void Remove(CGenericNode<T> *pNode);
37     void Reset() { mypCur = mypHead; }
38     int Size() const { return mySize; }
39     CGenericNode<T>* Tail() { return mypTail; }
40
41 protected:
42     // Protected data members
43     //
44     CGenericNode<T> *mypHead;
45     CGenericNode<T> *mypTail;
46     CGenericNode<T> *mypCur;
```

```
47    int mySize;
48 };
49
50 //////////////////////////////////////////////////////////
51 // CGenericList::AddHead()
52
53 template <class T>
54 bool CGenericList<T>::AddHead(const T& t)
55 {
56    // Allocate new node
57    //
58    CGenericNode<T> *pTemp = new CGenericNode<T>;
59    if (pTemp == 0)
60    {
61       cerr << "New node memory allocation failed."
62          << endl;
63       return false;
64    }
65
66    // Add the node to the head of the list
67    //
68    if (mypHead)
69    {
70       pTemp->mypNext  = mypHead;
71       mypHead->mypPrev = pTemp;
72       mypHead = pTemp;   // Assign as new head
73    }
74    else  // New list, head & tail are the same
75    {
76       mypHead = pTemp;   // Assign as new head
77       mypTail = pTemp;   // Assign as new tail
78       mypCur  = pTemp;
79    }
80    mySize++;
81
82    // Set the new node's value
83    //
84    mypHead->myObj = t;
85
86    return true;
87 }
88
```

LISTING 26.5

1 Lines 53-87: Add a node to the head of the list

LISTING 26.5 CONTINUED

2 Lines 92-126: Add a node
   to the tail of the list

LISTING 26.5 **Continued**

```
89  /////////////////////////////////////////////////////
90  // CGenericList::AddTail()
91
92  template <class T>
93  bool CGenericList<T>::AddTail(const T& t)
94  {
95      // Allocate new node
96      //
97      CGenericNode<T> *pTemp = new CGenericNode<T>;
98      if (pTemp == 0)
99      {
100         cerr << "New node memory allocation failed."
101             << endl;
102         return false;
103     }
104
105     // Add the node to the tail of the list
106     //
107     if (mypTail)
108     {
109         mypTail->mypNext = pTemp;
110         pTemp->mypPrev   = mypTail;
111         mypTail = pTemp;   // Assign as new tail
112     }
113     else
114     {
115         mypHead = pTemp;   // Assign as new head
116         mypTail = pTemp;   // Assign as new tail
117         mypCur  = pTemp;
118     }
119     mySize++;
120
121     // Set the new node's value
122     //
123     mypTail->myObj = t;
124
125     return true;
126  }
127
```

```
128 //////////////////////////////////////////////////
129 // CGenericList::Clear()
130
131 template <class T>
132 void CGenericList<T>::Clear()
133 {
134     CGenericNode<T> *pTemp;
135
136     while (mypHead)
137     {
138         pTemp = mypHead->mypNext;
139         delete mypHead;
140         mypHead = pTemp;
141     }
142     mySize = 0;
143 }
144
145 //////////////////////////////////////////////////
146 // CGenericList::Find()
147
148 template <class T>
149 CGenericNode<T> * CGenericList<T>::Find(const T& t)
150 {
151     CGenericNode<T> *pTemp = mypHead;
152
153     while (pTemp)
154     {
155         if (pTemp->myObj == t)
156             return pTemp;
157         pTemp = pTemp->mypNext;
158     }
159     return 0;
160 }
161
162 //////////////////////////////////////////////////
163 // CGenericList::Insert()
164
```

LISTING 26.5 CONTINUED

3 Lines 131-143: Clear the list by deleting all nodes

4 Lines 146-160: Find an item in the list

continues…

LISTING 26.5 CONTINUED

⑤ Lines 165-190: Insert a
new node into the list at a
specific node

LISTING 26.5   **Continued**

```
165 template <class T>
166 bool CGenericList<T>::Insert(const T& t,
167     CGenericNode<T> *pNode)
168 {
169     assert(pNode != 0);
170
171     // Allocate a new node
172     //
173     CGenericNode<T> *pTemp = new CGenericNode<T>;
174     if (!pTemp)
175     {
176         cerr << "Error allocating new node!\n";
177         return false;
178     }
179     pTemp->myObj = t;        // set the value
180
181     // Shift pointers to link this node into the list
182     //
183     pNode->mypNext->mypPrev = pTemp;
184     pTemp->mypNext = pNode->mypNext;
185     pTemp->mypPrev = pNode;
186     pNode->mypNext = pTemp;
187
188     mySize++;
189     return true;
190 }
191
192 ////////////////////////////////////////////////////////
193 // CGenericList::Next()
194
195 template <class T>
196 CGenericNode<T> * CGenericList<T>::Next()
197 {
198     if (mypCur)
199         mypCur = mypCur->mypNext;
200
201     return mypCur;
202 }
203
204 ////////////////////////////////////////////////////////
205 // CGenericList::Prev()
206
207 template <class T>
208 CGenericNode<T> * CGenericList<T>::Prev()
```

⑤

```
209 {
210     if (mypCur)
211         mypCur = mypCur->mypPrev;
212
213     return mypCur;
214 }
215
216 ////////////////////////////////////////////////////////
217 // CGenericList::Remove()
218
219 template <class T>
220 void CGenericList<T>::Remove(CGenericNode<T> *pNode)
221 {
222     if (!pNode)
223         return;
224
225     if (mySize == 1)
226     {
227         this->Clear();
228         return;
229     }
230
231     if (pNode == mypHead)
232     {
233         mypHead = pNode->mypNext;
234         mypHead->mypPrev = 0;
235     }
236     else if (pNode == mypTail)
237     {
238         mypTail = pNode->mypPrev;
239         mypTail->mypNext = 0;
240     }
241     else
242     {
243         pNode->mypNext->mypPrev = pNode->mypPrev;
244         pNode->mypPrev->mypNext = pNode->mypNext;
245     }
246
247     delete pNode;
248     pNode = 0;
249     mySize—;
250 }
251
252 #endif // __GENERICLIST_H__
```

LISTING 26.5 CONTINUED

6 Lines 219-250: Remove a specific node from the list

The class constructor initializes all the class data members to zero on lines 21 and 22, and the destructor calls the `CGenericList::Clear()` function to delete the list when the object goes out of scope.

Lines 27 through 39 give the member function declarations for the class, and the protected data members are declared from lines 44 through 47. The `CGenericList::Current()` method on line 30 returns a pointer to the current node. The `CGenericList::Head()` method on line 32 returns a pointer to the first node in the list. The `CGenericList::Reset()` method on line 37 resets the current item pointer to point at the head of the list. The `CGenericList::Size()` method on line 38 returns the number of items in the list, and the `CGenericList::Tail()` method on line 39 returns a pointer to the tail of the list.

Although this may seem like a lot of code, it's completely generic and allows you to automatically create doubly linked lists for a multitude of data types.

Creating a Driver Program

In order to test the functionality of the `CGenericList` class, you'll create a driver program. You can now use the `CGenericList` class to create several types of lists. For example, using intrinsic C++ data types, you could create these four different lists:

```
CGenericList<int>    list1;   // integer list
CGenericList<float>  list2;   // float list
CGenericList<char>   list3;   // char list
CGenericList<double> list4;   // double list
```

The driver program in Listing 26.6 tests the generic list class using the following `Point2d` structure:

```
struct Point2d
{
   int x, y;
   bool operator==(const Point2d& pt)
      { return ((x == pt.x) && (y == pt.y)); }
};
```

LISTING 26.6   **A Driver Program to Test the *CGenericList* Class**

```
 1 /////////////////////////////////////////////////////
 2 //  Module  : Driver.cpp
 3 //
 4 //  Purpose : A driver program to test the CGenericList
 5 //            class.
 6 /////////////////////////////////////////////////////
 7
 8 #include <iostream.h>
 9 #include "GenericList.h"
10
11 struct Point2d
12 {
13     int x, y;
14     bool operator==(const Point2d& pt)
15         { return ((x == pt.x) && (y == pt.y)); }
16 };
17
18 // Function prototypes
19 //
20 void DisplayListNodes(CGenericList<Point2d>& list);
21
22 /////////////////////////////////////////////////////
23 // main()
24
25 void main()
26 {
27     try
28     {
29         CGenericList<Point2d> list;  // Create a list
30
31         Point2d pt1 = { 100, 100 };
32         list.AddHead(pt1);   // Add a node at the head
33         DisplayListNodes(list);
34
35         Point2d pt2 = { 200, 200 };
36         list.AddHead(pt2);   // Add a node at the head
37         DisplayListNodes(list);
38
39         Point2d pt3 = { 300, 300 };
40         list.AddTail(pt3);   // Add a node at the tail
41         DisplayListNodes(list);
```

LISTING 26.6

❶ Lines 11-16: Define a
Point2d class

❷ Lines 31-41: Create, populate,
and display a linked list of
Point3d objects, adding
nodes one at a time

continues…

LISTING 26.6 CONTINUED

3 Lines 45-52: Remove each existing node one at a time

4 Lines 76-82: Display the head of the list

LISTING 26.6   **Continued**

```
42
43        // Remove the nodes one at a time
44        //
45        list.Remove(list.Find(pt1));
46        DisplayListNodes(list);
47
48        list.Remove(list.Find(pt2));
49        DisplayListNodes(list);
50
51        list.Remove(list.Find(pt3));
52        DisplayListNodes(list);
53   }
54   catch(...)
55   {
56        cerr << "Catching unknown exception!\n";
57   }
58 }
59
60 /////////////////////////////////////////////////////////
61 // DisplayListNodes()
62
63 void DisplayListNodes(CGenericList<Point2d>& list)
64 {
65     list.Reset();
66
67     if (list.Size() == 0)
68     {
69         cout << "The list is empty...\n";
70         return;
71     }
72
73     cout << "\nList has " << list.Size() << " nodes:\n";
74     CGenericNode<Point2d> *pHead = list.Head();
75
76     if (pHead)
77     {
78         cout << "  list.Head()->Value().x == "
79             << pHead->Value().x << endl;
80         cout << "  list.Head()->Value().y == "
81             << pHead->Value().y << endl << endl;
82     }
```

3

4

```
83
84     CGenericNode<Point2d> *pNode;
85     for (int i = 1; i < list.Size() - 1 ; ++i)
86     {
87       pNode = list.Next();
88       if (pNode)
89       {
90         cout << "  list.Next()->Value().x == "
91            << pNode->Value().x << endl;
92         cout << "  list.Next()->Value().y == "
93            << pNode->Value().y << endl << endl;
94       }
95     }
96
97     if (list.Head() == list.Tail()) return;
98
99     CGenericNode<Point2d> *pTail = list.Tail();
100    if (pTail)
101    {
102      cout << "  list.Tail()->Value().x == "
103         << pTail->Value().x << endl;
104      cout << "  list.Tail()->Value().y == "
105         << pTail->Value().y << endl << endl;
106    }
107 }
```

LISTING 26.6 CONTINUED

5 Lines 84-95: Display non-head/non-tail nodes

6 Lines 99-106: Display the tail of the list

The output from this program demonstrates the generic linked list class in action:

```
List has 1 nodes:
  list.Head()->Value().x == 100
  list.Head()->Value().y == 100

List has 2 nodes:
  list.Head()->Value().x == 200
  list.Head()->Value().y == 200

  list.Tail()->Value().x == 100
  list.Tail()->Value().y == 100

List has 3 nodes:
  list.Head()->Value().x == 200
  list.Head()->Value().y == 200
```

```
list.Next()->Value().x == 100
list.Next()->Value().y == 100

list.Tail()->Value().x == 300
list.Tail()->Value().y == 300

List has 2 nodes:
list.Head()->Value().x == 200
list.Head()->Value().y == 200

list.Tail()->Value().x == 300
list.Tail()->Value().y == 300

List has 1 nodes:
list.Head()->Value().x == 300
list.Head()->Value().y == 300

The list is empty...
```

The driver program begins by defining the Point2d structure from lines 11 through 16. This is followed by the declaration of the DisplayListNodes() function on line 20, specifying Point2d as the parameter type. This function is defined from lines 64 through 108 and demonstrates traversing the list from head to tail, as well as using the other CGenericList methods.

Line 30 creates a list object to contain objects of type Point2d, and lines 32 and 33 create and add a point to the head of the list. Line 34 displays the contents of the list—currently a single node. Lines 36 through 38 perform the same task, first adding a different point to the list and then displaying the list, this time containing two nodes. Lines 39 through 41 add a point to the tail of the list and then display the list, this time containing three nodes.

Lines 45 through 52 remove each of the three nodes one at a time, displaying the list with each removal. The CGenericList::Remove() method is used to do this, using a nested call to CGenericList::Find() to find the node to delete. Lines 55 through 57 catch any unexpected exceptions that might occur.

Using Dynamic Casting and Runtime Type Identification

See how polymorphic objects can provide runtime type information

Use the new C++ casting operators

Learn to cast dynamically

See how C++ static casting is like C-style casting

Getting and Using Runtime Type Information

When working with class hierarchies, it's sometimes convenient or necessary to create a pointer of one type and convert it later to some other pointer type. You can always safely cast a derived object pointer to a base object pointer because the base class is part of the derived class. You can then use the derived object pointer to call functions from the base class. On the other hand, a base class can sometimes—but not always—be type cast as a pointer to a derived class.

The compiler can't always resolve these casts because they're sometimes ambiguous. To determine whether the cast is appropriate, C++ offers a facility called *Runtime Type Information* (RTTI). By attempting a special type cast to a certain object type, you can use RTTI to check an object at runtime to see whether it's an object of a specified type. If the object is of the expected type, a valid pointer results; otherwise, the cast returns zero (because the object isn't of the expected type).

Old-School Type Casting (C Style)

The C programming language doesn't support object-oriented programming; therefore, it doesn't support inheritance. A standard type cast provides a way to explicitly convert the data type of an object, in a specific situation, from one data type to another. The cast used by ANSI C follows this general syntax:

```
(DataType)Expression
```

In this syntax, `DataType` is the data type you want to convert `Expression` to.

After a type cast operation is performed on `Expression`, the compiler treats `Expression` as an object of type `DataType`. You can use casts to convert objects of any scalar type to or from any other scalar type. Here are a few examples:

```
int num1 = 10;
float num2 = (float)num1;        // cast int to float
```

```
void* pVoid   = new char[255];
char* pCast = (char*)pVoid;      // cast void* to char*
delete [] pCast;
```

New-School Type Casting (C++ Style)

In C++, you can certainly use ANSI C-style casts, but C++ provides several casting operators that C doesn't support. These operators and their purposes are listed in Table 27.1. You'll further examine each of these operators later in this chapter.

TABLE 27.1 Casting Operators Available in C++

Operator	Description
dynamic_cast	Returns a valid object pointer only if the object used as its operand is of an expected type.
static_cast	Can be used to explicitly perform any implicit type conversion, much like the ANSI C cast.
const_cast	Can be used to remove any const, volatile, or unaligned attributes from a class.
reinterpret_cast	Allows any pointer type to be converted into any other pointer type; also allows any integral type to be converted into any pointer type and vice versa.

Using C++ inheritance and polymorphism, if you derive a class from a base class that contains virtual functions, you can use a pointer to that base class to make calls to the inherited virtual functions in a derived object.

In a class hierarchy, derived objects can safely cast up the hierarchy tree to any inherited object type in the tree. Consider the simple class hierarchy shown in Figure 27.1. In this hierarchy, CShape is the base class for CSquare, which is the base class of CRectangle.

FIGURE 27.1

A simple hierarchy of shapes.

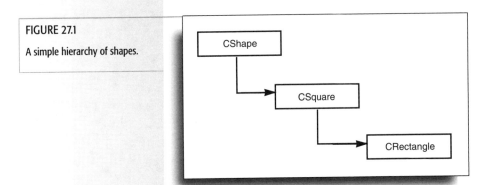

A CRectangle object would contain a CSquare subobject and a CShape subobject. This is the *complete object*. An inherited base class object becomes a *subobject* of the larger derived object. Figure 27.2 shows how a complete object of type CRectangle contains CSquare and CShape subobjects.

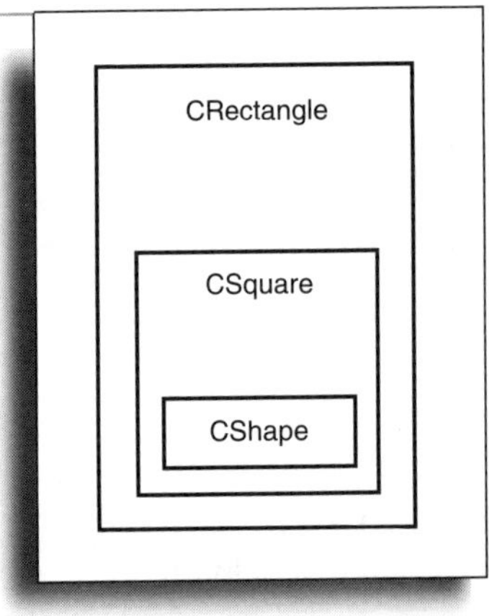

FIGURE 27.2

The inherited classes of the hierarchy create subobjects within complete objects.

Before we look at an example of where you might need to use RTTI, take a look at the header file in Listing 27.1. This header defines a simple class hierarchy of shapes.

LISTING 27.1   **A Header File Defining a Simple Hierarchy of Shapes**

```
1: //////////////////////////////////////////////////////////
2: //  Module  : Shapes.h
3: //
4: //  Purpose : A header defining a simple hierarchy
```

```
 5: //             of shape classes.
 6: ////////////////////////////////////////////////////
 7:
 8: #ifndef __SHAPES_H__
 9: #define __SHAPES_H__
10:
11: #include <iostream.h>
12:
13: ////////////////////////////////////////////////////
14: //   Class CShape
15:
16: class CShape
17: {
18: public:
19:    virtual void Draw()
20:       { cout << "Calling CShape::Draw()\n"; };
21: };
22:
23: ////////////////////////////////////////////////////
24: //   Class CSquare
25:
26: class CSquare : public CShape
27: {
28: public:
29:    CSquare() : myLength(0.0f) { }
30:    CSquare(const float length) : myLength(length) { }
31:
32:    virtual void Draw()
33:       { cout << "Calling CSquare::Draw()\n"; };
34:
35:    float Length() const { return myLength; }
36:    void Length(const float length)
37:       { myLength = length; }
38:
39:    virtual float Area()
40:       { return myLength * myLength; }
41:    virtual float Perimeter()
42:       { return myLength * 4.0f; }
43:
44: protected:
45:    float myLength;
46: };
```

continues…

LISTING 27.1

1 Lines 16–21: The CShape base class

2 Lines 32–33: The overloaded CSquare::Draw() method

LISTING 27.1 CONTINUED

3 Lines 58–59: The
overloaded
CRectangle::
Draw() method

LISTING 27.1   **Continued**

```
47:
48: /////////////////////////////////////////////////////////
49: //  Class CRectangle
50:
51: class CRectangle : public CSquare
52: {
53: public:
54:     CRectangle() : myWidth(0.0f) { }
55:     CRectangle(const float length, const float width)
56:         : myWidth(width) { myLength = length; }
57:
58:     void Draw()
59:         { cout << "Calling CRectangle::Draw()\n"; };
60:
61:     float Width() const { return myWidth; }
62:     void Width(const float width) { myWidth = width; }
63:
64:     float Area()
65:         { return myLength * myWidth; }
66:     float Perimeter()
67:         { return (myLength * 2.0f) + (myWidth * 2.0f); }
68:
69: protected:
70:     float myWidth;
71: };
72:
73: #endif //__SHAPES_H__
```

Now that we have some hierarchical classes to work with, take a look at the program in Listing 27.2. This program creates three objects, each of a different specific type, using a pointer to the base class to create each base and derived object.

LISTING 27.2   **A Program That Demonstrates Polymorphic Member Function Calls**

```
1: /////////////////////////////////////////////////////////
2: //  Module  : Shapes1.cpp
3: //
4: //  Purpose : Polymorphically calling virtual
5: //            member functions.
```

```
6:  //////////////////////////////////////////////////////
7:
8:  #include "shapes.h"
9:
10: //////////////////////////////////////////////////////
11: //  main()
12:
13: void main()
14: {
15:     // Create an array containing three different
16:     // object types
17:     //
18:     CShape *pArray[3] =
19:     {
20:         new CShape,
21:         new CSquare(5.0f),
22:         new CRectangle(10.0f, 5.0f)
23:     };
24:
25:     // Draw each object
26:     //
27:     for (int i = 0; i < 3; ++i)
28:         pArray[i]->Draw();
29:
30:     // Clean up
31:     //
32:      for (i = 0; i < 3; ++i)
33:         delete pArray[i];
34: }
```

LISTING 27.2

1. Line 18–23: Create an array of base class pointers

2. Lines 27–28: Draw objects using the pointers

3. Lines 32–33: Delete each object in the array

The output for this program is as follows:

```
Calling CShape::Draw()
Calling CSquare::Draw()
Calling CRectangle::Draw()
```

Line 8 includes shapes.h so that the classes from Listing 27.1 are available to main(). Line 18 declares an array of three pointers to CShape objects. Lines 19 through 23 initialize the elements of the array with objects. As you can see, each of the pointers is of the base class type CShape, but only the first object (pArray[0]) is really a CShape object; the other two are derived object types that inherit (and thus contain) a CShape object as a subobject.

On lines 27 and 28, a `for` loop iterates through the array elements, calling the `Draw()` method for each. Because the `Draw()` method is virtual in the base classes, the compiler resolves these function calls polymorphically and automatically. Remember that each element is of type `CShape*`; if this array were passed to a function, the actual data type information for an individual element would be unknown because each element looks like a base `CShape` object. (To find out what type of object the pointer *really* points to, you could use RTTI.) Lines 32 and 33 are used to individually delete the array elements created earlier by using `new` for each element in the array declaration.

C++ runtime type information makes it possible to see whether a pointer actually points to a complete object. If so, the pointer can be safely cast to point to another object in its hierarchy. C++ provides the `dynamic_cast` operator to perform these types of casts, along with a runtime check that makes the operation type safe.

Using the *dynamic_cast* Operator

L-Value

An expression that evaluates to a type other than **void** and that designates a variable, usually appearing on the left side of an assignment statement.

The `dynamic_cast` operator can return either a subobject or a complete object. The object returned depends on the type of object you're casting and the direction of the cast, either up or down the hierarchy. The syntax for a `dynamic_cast` operation is shown here:

```
dynamic_cast <DataType>(Expression)
```

Enable RTTI for Your Compiler

Some compilers require you to explicitly enable RTTI using command-line compiler switches. For example, Microsoft Visual C++ 5.0 requires the use of the /GR switch—without this switch the code generates errors.

The `dynamic_cast` operation converts *Expression* to an object of type *DataType*; *DataType* must be a pointer, a reference to a previously defined class type, or a void pointer (`void*`). If *Expression* is a pointer, *DataType* must be a pointer. If *DataType* is a reference, *Expression* must be an L-value. Here's an example of a `dynamic_cast` expression, converting a square to a rectangle:

```
CSquare *pSquare;
CRectangle* pRect = dynamic_cast<CSquare*>(pSquare);
```

Suppose that you have an array of `CShape` pointers similar to what you saw in Listing 27.2. Now suppose that program design criteria say, "Don't draw objects that are `CRectangle` objects." The program in Listing 27.3 shows the use of the `dynamic_cast` operator to draw only certain shapes in the hierarchy.

LISTING 27.3   **A Program That Demonstrates Dynamic Casting**

```cpp
1: //////////////////////////////////////////////////////////
2: // Module  : DynamicCast.cpp
3: //
4: // Purpose : Demonstrates the use of dynamic_cast
5: //////////////////////////////////////////////////////////
6:
7: #include <iostream.h>
8: #include "shapes.h"
9:
10: //////////////////////////////////////////////////////////
11: // main()
12:
13: void main()
14: {
15:    // Create an array containing three different
16:    // object types
17:    //
18:    CShape *pArray[3] = ─────────────────────────────────── ❶
19:    { ─┐
20:       new CShape,
21:       new CSquare(5.0f),                          ❷
22:       new CRectangle(10.0f, 5.0f)
23:    }; ─┘
24:
25:    // Draw each object except CRectangles
26:    //
27:    CRectangle* pRect;
28:    for (int i = 0; i < 3; ++i)
29:    {
30:       // Does pArray[i] point to a CRectangle? (upcast)
31:       //
32:       pRect = dynamic_cast<CRectangle*>(pArray[i]); ────── ❸
33:       if (!pRect)
34:          pArray[i]->Draw();
35:    }
36:
37:    // Clean up
38:    //
39:    for (i = 0; i < 3; ++i)
40:       delete pArray[i];
41: }
```

LISTING 27.3

❶ Line 18: Declare an array of three CShape objects

❷ Lines 19–23: Initialize the array elements

❸ Line 32: Use RTTI to see whether the object is a CRectangle object

The output from this program shows that CRectangle objects are, in fact, excluded from drawing, as expected:

```
Calling CShape::Draw()
Calling CSquare::Draw()
```

Lines 18 through 23 of this program define an array of objects identical to the array in Listing 27.2. On line 27, the CRectangle pointer pRect is declared. The dynamic_cast operation attempted on line 32 determines whether the current array element is actually a CRectangle object. If the pRect pointer is zero after the conversion operator, then the object is *not* a CRectangle object. Line 33 checks for a non-zero pointer before drawing the object on line 34. By identifying rectangles, either as subobjects or complete objects, the RTTI allows you to react accordingly for that object type.

Using the *const_cast* Operator

Using the const_cast operator, you can remove the const and volatile attributes from a class, if any exist. The operator uses the following syntax:

```
const_cast <DataType> (Expression)
```

Using the const_cast operator, you can convert a pointer type to an identical pointer type that has any const, volatile, and __unaligned attributes removed. The resulting pointer or reference refers to the original object. This type of conversion is usually performed to cast away the "const-ness" of an object. You must take care with these kinds of conversions—depending on the type of object referenced by the cast pointer, using the pointer might cause unexpected and undefined behavior.

For example, if you have const pointer to an object, the object is read-only. You can cast away the const-ness of the object using the const_cast operator, like this:

```
const int* pInt = new int(10);    // Create a new object

int* p = const_cast<int*>(pInt); // cast away const

*pInt = 20;    // Error, can't change const int*
*p   = 15;    // OK, p is non-const
```

This snippet first creates a new const integer object initialized to the value 10. Next, the const modifier is cast away using const_cast on pInt, returning the non-const int pointer p, which is the same memory address as pInt. Once the cast is performed, you can use p to modify the value stored in pInt. Again, it's the programmer's responsibility to avoid potential problems that can arise when casting.

Using the *reinterpret_cast* Operator

Using the reinterpret_cast operator, you can convert any pointer type into any other pointer type. You can also use this operator to convert any integral type to into any pointer type— and vice versa. Its syntax is like the other casting operators:

```
reinterpret_cast <DataType>(Expression)
```

Because the reinterpret_cast operator has few restrictions, this freedom can lead to unsafe type casts. You can use the operator to cast from some class to some unrelated class, or to unsafely cast pointers to unrelated types, such as from char* to double*. In fact, you can't safely use the result of a reinterpret_cast for anything except to cast an expression back to its original type. You should reserve the use of this operator for low-level casting, where you're sure of the safety of the cast.

Using the *static_cast* Operator

You can use the static_cast operator for things like converting a base class pointer to a derived class pointer. The static_cast conversion uses no runtime check, however, so it's up to the programmer to ensure that objects are cast to the correct data types. If unrelated object types are used in the conversion, access violations are bound to occur. The program in Listing 27.4 demonstrates the use of the static_cast operator.

Note

You can't use the reinterpret_cast operator to cast away the const, volatile, or unaligned attributes of a class—you must use the const_cast operator to do this.

Note

You can use the static_cast operator to explicitly convert an integral value to an enumeration type.

LISTING 27.4 **A Program That Demonstrates the Use of the *static_cast* Operator**

```
1: /////////////////////////////////////////////////////
2: //  Module  : StaticCast.cpp
3: //
```

continues...

LISTING 27.4

① Lines 21–22: Use
static_cast
to perform type casts

② Lines 33–35: Send three
object types into the
func( ) function

③ Lines 43–44: Compare
the use of
dynamic_cast
and static_cast

LISTING 27.4   **Continued**

```
 4: //  Purpose : Demonstrates the use of static_cast
 5: /////////////////////////////////////////////////////
 6:
 7: #include <iostream.h>
 8: #include "shapes.h"
 9:
10: // Function Prototypes
11: //
12: void func(CShape* pShape);
13:
14: /////////////////////////////////////////////////////
15: //  main()
16:
17: void main()
18: {
19:     double d = 55.5;
20:     char ch = 'X';
21:     int i    = static_cast<int>;           ━━━━━ ①
22:     float f  = static_cast<float>(ch);
23:
24:     cout << "d  == " << d  << endl;
25:     cout << "ch == " << ch << endl;
26:     cout << "i  == " << i  << endl;
27:     cout << "f  == " << f  << endl << endl;
28:
29:     CRectangle   rect;
30:     CSquare      square;
31:     CShape       shape;
32:
33:     func(&rect);       ━━━━━┐
34:     func(&square);          ├━━ ②
35:     func(&shape);      ━━━━━┘
36: }
37:
38: /////////////////////////////////////////////////////
39: //  func()
40:
41: void func(CShape* pShape)
42: {
43:     CSquare* pSquare1 = dynamic_cast<CSquare*>(pShape);   ━━┐
44:     CSquare* pSquare2 = static_cast<CSquare*>(pShape);    ━━┴━ ③
45:
```

```
46:     if (pSquare1) pSquare1->Draw();
47:     if (pSquare2) pSquare2->Draw();
48:     cout << endl;
49: }
```

The output from this program is as follows:

```
d  == 55.5
ch == X
i  == 55
f  == 88


Calling CRectangle::Draw()
Calling CRectangle::Draw()

Calling CSquare::Draw()
Calling CSquare::Draw()

Calling CShape::Draw()
```

This program begins by declaring the func() function on line 12. In main(), the static_cast operator is used to convert type double to type int and type char to type float. Lines 24 through 27 display the results of this casting.

Lines 29 through 31 declare three shape objects—a rectangle, a square, and a base class shape. These three objects are then sent one at a time into the func() function (lines 33 through 35). This function has a CShape pointer parameter and performs a couple of casts on the object it receives as an argument. The first cast occurs on line 43, using the dynamic_cast operator for type-safe conversion of the received object into a CSquare object. The second cast occurs on line 44, using the static_cast operator for a more general conversion that's at the discretion of the programmer.

As you can see from the program output, when rect and square are sent to func() (lines 33 and 34), all's well. The third call to func(), on line 35, has a different result. The dynamic_cast test fails because a CShape object isn't a CSquare object. The static_cast cast obliviously casts the pointer to a square anyway and draws the object. Polymorphism kicks in and calls the

`CShape::Draw()` method, which is not the intended result. What this boils down to is that if pShape really points to an object of type CSquare, pSquare1 and pSquare2 will be assigned identical values.

If pShape points to an object of type CShape instead of to the complete CSquare class, dynamic_cast will safely return zero. The static_cast operation relies on your assertion that pShape points to an object of type CSquare and simply returns a pointer to a CSquare object that doesn't really exist. This can cause big problems, so be careful.

PART

IV

Using the Standard
C++ Library

Introducing the
Standard C++ Library

An Overview of the Standard C++ Library

The Standard C++ Library is a treasure trove of programming gems guaranteed to be available on all C++ compilers that support the standard—and these days, that includes almost all commercial compilers. The standard library provides an incredible amount of functionality that's ready and waiting for you to plug in to your programs. The problem when first getting started using the Standard C++ Library is that it contains so much functionality it can be overwhelming.

In this chapter, we'll take a whirlwind tour of the standard library and its components, and we'll explore some of the reasons behind its design. A common question is, "What can the standard library do for me—is it worth the time to learn it?" Should you learn it? The answer is a definite *yes*. Your programs can use a large number of functions and objects defined in the Standard C++ Library. We'll look at some of the more useful components of the Standard C++ Library in the remaining chapters in this book.

Using the Standard Namespace

All Standard C++ Library entities are wrapped in the standard namespace: std. To use any library entity, you must therefore use this namespace to provide the proper scope. For example, the Standard C++ Library defines the familiar cout object in the standard header file <iostream>. To use the object, you can explicitly state its scope, like this:

SEE ALSO

➤ *For more information about namespaces in general, see page 384*

➤ *For more information about the standard namespace, see page 400*

```
std::cout << "Warning: Forward shields at 34 percent...\n";
```

In many cases, it's easier to use a using declaration to take care of the scope automatically:

```
#include <iostream>

using std::cout;
using std::endl;

void main()
{
    cout << "Warning: Starboard thrusters are offline..."
        << endl;
}
```

By issuing a general using directive for the entire namespace, all standard components can be used without explicit namespace scoping, as in this example:

```
#include <iostream>

using namespace std;   // using directive for std namespace

void main()
{
    cout << "Warning: Life support is offline..."
        << endl;
}
```

SEE ALSO

➤ *For more information about namespace access, see page 391*

Identifying Standard C++ Header Files

Every entity that makes up a part of the Standard C++ Library is declared or defined in one or more standard header files. A *hosted implementation* of standard C++ uses the entire set of standard C++ headers and fully implements the standard C++ language. A *freestanding implementation* of standard C++ uses only a subset of the standard C++ headers and only partially implements the standard C++ language.

Namespace

A C++ declaration area that adds a secondary name to an identifier, helping to insure that no duplicate global identifier names exist in a program.

Hosted Implementation

A hosted implementation of C++ is an implementation of standard C++ that uses the entire set of standard C++ headers and fully implements the standard C++ language.

Freestanding Implementation

A freestanding implementation of C++ is an implementation of standard C++ that uses only a subset of the standard C++ headers and only partially implements the standard C++ language.

A hosted implementation is comprised of 49 standard headers, of which 19 are Standard C Library headers in disguise. The standard C++ headers use no file extensions; those headers that are actually ANSI C library headers use their customary names prefixed with a letter c. For example, the ANSI C library header <string.h> is known in the Standard C++ Library as <cstring>. The Standard C++ Library also declares a standard string class, defined in the standard header <string>. Understanding the distinction between these similarly named files is the first step to understanding the library.

The 19 headers that redefine the ANSI C headers as part of the Standard C++ Library include, alphabetically: <cassert>, <cctype>, <cerrno>, <cfloat>, <ciso646>, <climits>, <clocale>, <cmath>, <complex>, <csetjmp>, <csignal>, <cstdarg>, <cstddef>, <cstdio>, <cstdlib>, <cstring>, <ctime>, <cwchar>, and <cwctype>.

The 30 remaining headers declare and define components unique to the Standard C++ Library. These 30 headers include, alphabetically: <algorithm>, <bitset>, <deque>, <exception>, <fstream>, <functional>, <iomanip>, <ios>, <iosfwd>, <iostream>, <istream>, <iterator>, <limits>, <list>, <locale>, <map>, <memory>, <numeric>, <ostream>, <queue>, <set>, <sstream>, <stack>, <stdexcept>, <streambuf>, <string>, <strstream>, <utility>, <valarray>, and <vector>.

Of these 30 standard C++ headers, the majority fall into two major categories: Standard Template Library (STL) headers and input/output streams headers.

Introducing the Standard Template Library

The Standard Template Library (STL) has revolutionized C++ programming. STL is the result of years of dedicated research into the possibilities of generic programming and is a major part of the Standard C++ Library. STL provides an incredible amount of generic programming power that can be immediately useful in your programs.

The Standard Template Library is mainly composed of generic container class templates and a set of many efficient template algorithms designed to work with, and manipulate, the containers. The classes declared and defined in STL use templates to their fullest capacity, enabling truly generic programming for C++ programmers.

SEE ALSO

➤ *For more information about STL, see page 692*

Using the Standard C Library

The Standard C Library is fully compatible with C++ and is part of the Standard C++ Library. Of course, there are a few distinctions between the two. First, the Standard C Library headers all end with a .h file extension. The Standard C++ Library equivalent puts a c in front of the header name and uses no file extension whatsoever. For example, the C header <stdio.h> becomes <cstdio> in C++, and the C function printf() from <stdio.h> becomes std::printf() in <cstdio>.

Again, you can promote a name into the current namespace with a using declaration, like this:

```
#include <cstdio>

using std::printf();

void main()
{
    printf("Calling Standard C++ printf()...");
}
```

Identifying the Components of the Standard C++ Library

A large number of functions and objects are defined in the Standard C++ Library. These functions and objects provide robust and efficient implementations for fundamental operations your programs might need, such as file input/output. The Standard C++ Library is composed of several categories of components:

- Diagnostics
- Input/output
- Language support
- Localization
- Numerics
- Strings
- General utilities
- Algorithms (STL)
- Containers (STL)
- Iterators (STL)

SEE ALSO

➤ *To learn more about iterators, see page 698*

Diagnostics

Three standard headers provide diagnostic services for your programs to aid in the debugging process and to provide the standard C++ exception handling classes used for reporting standard exceptions. Table 28.1 lists the standard headers used for diagnostics.

TABLE 28.1 **Headers Declaring or Defining Diagnostic Objects**

Header	Purpose
`<cassert>`	Includes the standard C header `<assert.h>` within the `std` namespace, providing standard C assertions.
`<cerrno>`	Includes the standard C header `<errno.h>` within the `std` namespace, providing C-style error handling.
`<stdexcept>`	Defines several classes used for reporting standard C++ exceptions.

The standard exception classes defined in `<stdexcept>` are as follows:

- `logic_error`   The base class for all exceptions thrown to report logic (programming) errors.

- `domain_error` The base class for all exceptions thrown to report a domain error.

- `invalid_argument` The base class for all exceptions thrown to report an invalid argument.

- `length_error` The base class for all exceptions thrown to report an attempt to generate an object that's too long to be specified.

- `out_of_range` The base class for all exceptions thrown to report an argument that's out of its valid range.

- `runtime_error` The base class for all exceptions thrown to report errors detectable only when the program executes.

- `range_error` The base class for all exceptions thrown to report an out-of-range error.

- `overflow_error` The base class for all exceptions thrown to report an arithmetic overflow.

- `underflow_error` The base class for all exceptions thrown to report an arithmetic underflow.

Input/Output

The input/output mechanism supplied by standard C++ is the *stream*, which is central to the standard `iostream` classes (sometimes referred to as the `iostream` library). The stream concept is central to the C++ way of handling input from and output to devices, including external files.

The `iostream` classes can be redirected to interact with devices as extended files. By redirecting a stream, you can communicate with and control the keyboard, screen, printer, and communication ports. In addition to the `iostream` library, C++ inherits several related facilities from standard C. Table 28.2 list the standard headers that provide input/output facilities for standard C++.

Stream

A linear, ordered sequence of bytes.

TABLE 28.2   **Headers Declaring or Defining Input and Output Streams**

Header	Purpose
<cstdio>	Includes the standard C header <stdio.h> within the std namespace, providing the printf() family of functions.
<cstdlib>	Includes the standard C header <stdlib.h> within the std namespace for character type functions, providing character type functions.
<cwchar>	Includes the standard C header <wchar.h> within the std namespace, providing the printf() family of functions for wide characters.
<fstream>	Defines several class templates that support iostream operations on sequences stored in external files.
<iomanip>	Defines several manipulators that each take a single argument. A *manipulator* performs actions on streams.
<ios>	Defines several types and functions essential to the operation of iostreams—iostream base classes.
<iosfwd>	Forward declarations to several class templates used throughout the iostreams library.
<iostream>	Declares objects that control reading from, and writing to, the standard streams.
<istream>	Defines the class template basic_istream, which handles extractions for the iostreams; and the class template basic_iostream, which handles insertions and extractions.
<ostream>	Defines class template basic_ostream, which handles extractions for the iostreams classes; also defines several related manipulators.
<sstream>	Defines several class templates supporting iostreams operations on strings.
<streambuf>	Defines class template basic_streambuf, which is essential to the operation of the iostreams classes.

SEE ALSO

➤ *For more information about file streams, see page 805*
➤ *For more information about iostreams, see page 800*

Language Support

A small portion of the Standard C++ Library is dedicated to providing features that facilitate language support. These support facilities include numeric limits, exception handling, argument lists, and so on. Table 28.3 lists the standard headers that facilitate language support.

Language Support

The base C++ language provides only the bare bones of what Standard C++ needs to be a comprehensive software development system. Additional headers and libraries provide the language support that C++ needs to give it the full power to compete with (and surpass) other programming languages.

TABLE 28.3 Headers Providing Additional Language Support

Header	Purpose
<cfloat>	Includes the standard C header <float.h> within the std namespace, providing C-style floating-point-limit macros.
<climits>	Includes the standard C header <limits.h> within the std namespace, providing C-style numeric scalar-limit macros.
<csetjmp>	Includes the standard C header <setjmp.h> within the std namespace, providing C-style stack unwinding.
<csignal>	Includes the standard C header <signal.h> within the std namespace, providing C-style signal handling.
<cstdarg>	Includes the standard C header <stdarg.h> within the std namespace, providing variable-length function argument lists.
<cstddef>	Includes the standard C header <stddef.h> within the std namespace, providing C library language support.
<cstdlib>	Includes the standard C header <stdlib.h> within the std namespace, providing program termination functionality.
<ctime>	Includes the standard C header <time.h> within the std namespace, providing access to the system clock.
<exception>	Defines several types and functions related to standard C++ exception handling.
<limits>	Defines the class template numeric_limits, whose specializations describe arithmetic properties of scalar data types.

Localization

Two standard headers define structures, functions, and classes designed to provide locale information, storing information about cultural differences between locales. Table 28.4 lists these standard headers.

TABLE 28.4   **Headers That Support Localization**

Header	Purpose
`<clocale>`	Includes the standard C header `<locale.h>` within the `std` namespace.
`<locale>`	Defines many class templates and function templates that encapsulate and manipulate locales, which represent cultural differences.

Numerics

Standard C++ provides extensive support for working with complex mathematical and numeric-related equations, allowing you to provide elegant solutions to complex problems. Table 28.5 lists the standard C++ headers providing numeric and mathematical support.

TABLE 28.5   **Headers That Support Numerics**

Header	Purpose
`<cmath>`	Includes the standard C header `<math.h>` within the `std` namespace, providing standard math functions.
`<complex>`	Provides a class template describing an object that stores both the real part and the imaginary part of a complex number.
`<cstdlib>`	Includes the standard C header `<stdlib.h>` within the `std` namespace, providing C-style random numbers.
`<numeric>`	Defines several function templates useful for computing numeric values, providing generalized numeric operations.
`<valarray>`	Defines the class template `valarray` along with many supporting template classes and functions, providing numeric vectors and operations.

Strings

Because we read and write every day, strings of characters are extremely important in our lives—it's how we communicate. Because this is so, strings are among the most generally useful types of objects, and standard C++ provides a vast amount of support for creating and working with strings. Table 28.6 lists the standard headers that provide support for strings.

TABLE 28.6 **Headers That Support Strings**

Header	Purpose
`<cctype>`	Includes the standard C header `<ctype.h>` within the `std` namespace, providing character classification.
`<cstdlib>`	Includes the standard C header `<stdlib.h>` within the `std` namespace, providing C-style string and character functions.
`<cstring>`	Includes the standard C header `<string.h>` within the `std` namespace, providing C-style string and character functions.
`<cwchar>`	Includes the standard C header `<wchar.h>` within the `std` namespace, providing C-style wide character support.
`<cwctype>`	Includes the standard C header `<wctype.h>` within the `std` namespace, providing C-style wide character string functions.
`<string>`	Defines the container template class `basic_string` and various supporting templates.

Utilities

A small portion of the Standard C++ Library is devoted to utilities that are useful in most programming situations. These utilities include date and time functions, *function object* templates, memory management features, as well as specialized utilities useful when working with STL. Table 28.7 lists the standard headers that provide utility support for Standard C++.

SEE ALSO

➤ *For more information about function objects, see page 694*

Function Object

A function object is an instance of a class that defines an overloaded function call operator: `operator()`.

Allocator

An allocator is an object that manages allocation and deallocation of storage for arrays of objects of generic type **T**.

TABLE 28.7 **Headers Declaring or Defining General Library Utilities**

Header	Purpose
`<ctime>`	Includes the standard C header `<time.h>` within the `std` namespace, providing C-style date and time functions.
`<functional>`	Defines several templates that help construct function objects.
`<memory>`	Defines a class, an operator, and several templates used to allocate and free objects—these templates are *allocators* for containers.
`<utility>`	Defines several general-use templates useful throughout the Standard Template Library, including operators and pairs.

SEE ALSO
➤ *For more information about allocators, see page 696*

Identifying STL Components

The interfaces for STL classes have been carefully designed, providing a common, uniform set of methods and identifiers that work with a wide variety of class types. There are six major components that make up STL:

- Container classes, including sequence containers (such as vectors and lists) and sorted associative containers (such as sets and maps).
- Generic algorithms, to manipulate the containers.
- Iterators, acting as pointers to container elements.
- Function objects, whose class specifications define an overloaded function call operator: `operator()`.
- Allocators, to control storage.
- *Adaptors*, to change the interfaces of containers, iterators, and function objects.

SEE ALSO
➤ *For more information about adaptors, see page 695*

Adaptor

An adaptor is a generic component that modifies the interface of another component.

Algorithms

The algorithms introduced as part of the Standard C++ Library provide generic template functions that work on most (if not all) containers, including containers of intrinsic C++ types. A few other useful algorithms, such as `bsearch()` and `qsort()`, can be found in the Standard C Library. Table 28.8 lists the standard headers that provide support for algorithms in standard C++.

TABLE 28.8   **Headers Declaring or Defining Standard Algorithms**

Header	Purpose
`<algorithm>`	Defines numerous general algorithms as template functions.
`<cstdlib>`	Includes the standard C header `<stdlib.h>` within the `std` namespace, providing the algorithms `bsearch()` and `qsort()`.

SEE ALSO
➤ *To learn more about the generic algorithms, see page 820*

Containers

Containers are a large part of the Standard Template Library, and provide generic containers of many types. Table 28.9 lists the standard headers that provide container support for standard C++.

SEE ALSO

➤ *For more information about containers and their uses, see page 714*

TABLE 28.9 **Headers Declaring or Defining Standard Containers**

Header	Purpose
`<deque>`	Describes an object controlling a varying-length sequence of elements of type T, permitting insertion and removal of an element at either end—a double-ended queue of T.
`<list>`	Defines the container class template `list` along with three supporting templates—a doubly linked list of T.
`<map>`	Defines the container class templates `map` and `multimap`, along with their supporting templates, providing an associative array of T.
`<queue>`	Defines the class templates `priority_queue` and `queue`, along with two supporting templates.
`<set>`	Defines the container class templates `set` and `multiset`, along with their supporting templates.
`<stack>`	Defines the template class `stack` and two supporting templates.
`<vector>`	Defines the container class template `vector`, along with three supporting templates, providing a one-dimensional array of T.

SEE ALSO

➤ *To learn more about generic containers, see page 714*

Iterators

As you know, iterators are pointer-like objects used to iterate through the elements in a container. An iterator can be used to manipulate, in various ways, an object in a container. Table 28.10 describes the sole header that provides iterators for the Standard C++ Library.

SEE ALSO

➤ *For more information about iterators, see page 698*

Iterator

Iterators are pointer-like objects used to iterate through the elements in a container.

TABLE 28.10   The Standard Header *<iterator>* Declares and Defines Iterator Templates

Header	Purpose
`<iterator>`	Defines a number of classes, class templates, and function templates used for the declaration and manipulation of iterators.

SEE ALSO

➤ *To learn more about iterators, see page 707*

Function Objects

Function objects are instances of classes that contain an overloaded function call operator: `operator()`. Function objects are used as replacements for function pointers and as arguments to generic algorithms. The generic algorithms can accept either function pointers or objects with `operator()` defined. The function object class templates are declared in the header `<functional>`. This header also provides two class templates you can use to derive your own function objects. There are several predefined function objects, which are divided into the following three categories:

- Arithmetic function objects: Function objects providing basic arithmetic operations such as plus and minus.
- Comparison function objects: Function objects providing comparison operations, such as equal-to or not-equal-to.
- Logical function objects: Function objects providing logic operations such as logical-or and logical-and.

Table 28.11 shows the arithmetic function objects provided by the Standard C++ Library.

TABLE 28.11   The Arithmetic Function Objects Provided by the Standard C++ Library

Function	Operation
`plus`	addition (x + y)
`minus`	subtraction (x - y)
`times`	multiplication (x * y)

Function	Operation
divides	division (x / y)
modulus	remainder (x % y)
negate	negation (-x)

Table 28.12 shows the comparison function objects provided by the Standard C++ Library.

TABLE 28.12   The Comparison Function Objects Provided by the Standard C++ Library

Function	Operation
equal_to	equality test (x == y)
not_equal_to	inequality test (x != y)
greater	greater comparison (x > y)
less	less-than comparison (x < y)
greater_equal	greater-than or equal comparison (x >= y)
less_equal	less-than or equal comparison (x <= y)

Table 28.13 shows the logical function objects provided by the Standard C++ Library.

TABLE 28.13   The Logical Function Objects Provided by the Standard C++ Library

Function	Operation
logical_and	logical AND (x && y)
logical_or	logical OR (x ¦¦ y)
logical_not	logical negation (!x)

Adaptors

Adaptors modify the interface of some other component. The standard library contains several types of adaptors, including these:

Traversal Order

Iterators traverse the items in a sequence, such as an array or a linked list, from first to last. This is the traversal order. Reverse traversal order iterates through sequence items from last to first.

- Reverse iterators, which adapt an iterator into a new iterator type that's exactly like the original, but with the traversal order reversed.

- Insert iterators, which adapt generic algorithms to allow insertion rather than their default behavior of overwriting.

- Various container adapters, which adapt container interfaces.

- Various function adapters, which adapt function interfaces.

Allocators

Each STL container class uses a special class called Allocator to store information about the memory model used by the program. The Allocator class stores information about pointers, references, sizes of objects, and other entities related to the memory model because different memory models have different requirements. Although new allocator classes can be derived for certain circumstances, in most cases, the default Allocator class is all you'll ever need.

Using Iterators and Containers

Learn about iterators and why they're useful

Explore iterator operations and classes

See the differences between sequence containers and associative containers

Examine the standard container classes

Understanding Iterators

Iterators and containers are closely related. Conceptually, an *iterator* is something that an algorithm can use to traverse the sequence of objects in a container; an iterator knows how to iterate through the contents of a container. Standard Template Library (STL) container classes such as vector, list, and map all use iterators to represent container elements. The generic algorithms provided by the standard library work with the generic containers, but not all algorithms work with all containers. A hierarchy of iterator types determines which algorithms will work with which containers.

The standard library uses iterators designed to provide a consistent set of interfaces across a variety of container types so that the same basic source code will work no matter what container class is used. To really get a handle on what an iterator is and does, think back to the CIntList class presented in Chapter 24, "Implementing Dynamic Storage in C++." This class had Next() and Prev() methods, as well as Head() and Tail() methods. The basic problem with the approach used in Chapter 24 is that these functions are bound too closely to the container to make the container useful for more than one thing at a time.

Suppose that you're writing a program that has to be able to look at and traverse the contents of a single container in three different ways, simultaneously. This isn't possible with the structure presented in Chapter 24, because you can only move Next() and Prev(), holding the current element pointer. By transplanting the access and traversal methods from the container to a separate iterator class, you can get as many iterators as you want, and you can do different things with each.

As an example of why iterators are useful with containers, let's create a new container class, called CContainer, and then create a driver program to test it. After testing the initial container class, we'll modify the container to use an iterator class. First, we need a simple container class—in this case, an array. The class declaration in Listing 29.1 takes care of that.

LISTING 29.1   The Header for the Simple Container Class *CContainer*

```
1: //////////////////////////////////////////////////
2: //   Module  : Container.h
3: //
4: //   Purpose : Interface for a simple container class
5: //////////////////////////////////////////////////
6:
7: #ifndef __CONTAINER_H__
8: #define __CONTAINER_H__
9:
10: class OutOfRange();   // Exception handler class
11:
12: //////////////////////////////////////////////////
13: // Class CContainer
14:
15: class CContainer
16: {
17: public:
18:    CContainer() { }
19:    CContainer(int size);
20:    ~CContainer() { delete [] myIntArray; }
21:
22:    void Add(int num);
23:    int GetCur() { return myIntArray[myIndex]; }
24:    int DisplayGetNext();
25:    bool IsEnd() { return (myIndex >= myEmpty); }
26:    void Reset() { myIndex = 0; }
27:
28: private:
29:    int  myEmpty;
30:    int  myIndex;
31:    int *myIntArray;
32:    int  mySize;
33: };
34:
35: #endif //__CONTAINER_H__
```

LISTING 29.1

❶ Lines 22-26: Public member functions

❷ Lines 29-32: Private data members

The CContainer class is basic at best, but it has enough functionality to illustrate a simple container. The class's four private
data members are declared on lines 29 through 32. Line 23

implements the CContainer::GetCur() method, which simply returns the value of the current array element, as determined by the value of the myIndex member. Line 25 implements the CContainer::IsEnd() method, which returns true if the value of the myIndex member is greater than or equal to the value of the myEmpty member (which holds the next available index). The CContainer::Reset() method in line 26 resets the current array index to zero. The class destructor automatically deletes the contained array when the object goes out of scope. The remaining member functions are implemented in the header's corresponding source file, which is shown in Listing 29.2.

LISTING 29.2

1 Line 16: Preallocate the array during construction

2 Lines 25-26: Add an item to the array

LISTING 29.2   **The Implementation of the *CContainer* Class**

```
1:  //////////////////////////////////////////////////////////
2:  //  Module  : Container.cpp
3:  //
4:  //  Purpose : Implementation of a simple container
5:  //////////////////////////////////////////////////////////
6:
7:  #include <cstring>
8:  #include "container.h"
9:
10: //////////////////////////////////////////////////////////
11: // Constructor
12:
13: CContainer::CContainer(int size) : mySize(size),
14:     myIndex(0), myEmpty(0)
15: {
16:     myIntArray = new int[mySize];        1
17:     memset(myIntArray, 0, sizeof(int)* mySize);
18: }
19:
20: //////////////////////////////////////////////////////////
21: // CContainer::Add()
22:
23: void CContainer::Add(int num)
24: {
25:     if (myEmpty < mySize)
26:         myIntArray[myEmpty++] = num;    2
27: }
```

```
28:
29: /////////////////////////////////////////////////////////
30: // CContainer::DisplayGetNext()
31:
32: int CContainer::DisplayGetNext()
33: {
34:     if (myIndex < myEmpty)
35:         return myIntArray[myIndex++];
36:     return myIntArray[myIndex];
37: }
```

The implementation of the CContainer class methods is trivial. The constructor runs from lines 13 through 18, allocating the container array to the specified size and initializing all elements to zero.

The CContainer::Add() method runs from lines 23 through 27, and it simply checks to see whether the specified index is less than the allocated array size and if so, adds the integer num to the array at the current index, which is then incremented to the next element.

The CContainer::DisplayGetNext() method runs from lines 32 through 37, and it does pretty much the same thing CContainer::Add() does, except that it returns the stored value instead of assigning it and then increments to the next array element.

The driver program in Listing 29.3 shows the use of a CContainer object in a program.

LISTING 29.3   A Driver Program to Test the *CContainer* Class

```
1: /////////////////////////////////////////////////////////
2: //  Module  : ContainerMain.cpp
3: //
4: //  Purpose : Demonstrates a simple container class.
5: /////////////////////////////////////////////////////////
6:
7: #include <iostream>
8: #include "container.h"
9:
```

continues…

LISTING 29.3 **Continued**

```
10: /////////////////////////////////////////////////////
11: // main()
12:
13: void main()
14: {
15:     CContainer bag(10);  ──── 1
16:
17:     for (int i = 0; i < 10; ++i)
18:         bag.Add(i);  ──── 2
19:
20:     bag.Reset();
21:     while (!bag.IsEnd())
22:         std::cout << bag.DisplayGetNext() << " ";  ──── 3
23: }
```

The output from this program is simply the following string of numbers:

```
0 1 2 3 4 5 6 7 8 9
```

The program begins by allocating the container array to 10 elements on line 15. Lines 17 and 18 assign values to the 10 elements using the CContainer::Add() function. The CContainer::Reset() function on line 20 resets the current array index to the first element in the sequence. The while loop on lines 21 and 22 iterates through the sequence of elements, displaying the current element value and incrementing to the next element with a single call to the CContainer::DisplayGetNext() function.

Creating an Iterator Class

To explain the concept of an iterator—which is extremely important in STL programming with the standard library—we'll create a simple iterator class (from scratch), called CIterator, that iterates over the objects in a container class. The CIterator class will drive the container class, relieving the container of the responsibilities of iterating through the sequence.

Because of the iterator, the container class requires less functionality than it had in the previous example, so the class interface for the revised container class is simpler, as you can see in Listing 29.4.

Note

The iterator and container classes demonstrated here are developed from scratch and don't use any functionality from the Standard Template Library.

LISTING 29.4   **The Header for the *CContainer2* Class**

```
1: ////////////////////////////////////////////////////
2: //   Module   : Container2.h
3: //
4: //   Purpose : Interface for a simple container class
5: ////////////////////////////////////////////////////
6:
7: #ifndef __CONTAINER2_H__
8: #define __CONTAINER2_H__
9:
10: ////////////////////////////////////////////////////
11: // Class CContainer2
12:
13: class CContainer2
14: {
15: public:
16:     CContainer2() { }
17:     CContainer2(int size) : mySize(size)
18:     {
19:         mypArray = new int[mySize];
20:         memset(mypArray, 0, sizeof(int)* mySize);
21:     }
22:     ~CContainer2() { delete [] mypArray; }
23:
24:     friend class CIterator; ———①
25:
26: private:
27:     int *mypArray;
28:     int mySize;
29: };
30:
31: #endif //__CONTAINER2_H__
```

LISTING 29.4

① Line 24: Declare an iterator class as a friend

The new version of the container class is CContainer2, and it performs the same initialization in the constructor as did its previous incarnation (lines 19 and 20). The destructor still deletes the array automatically (line 22). The rest of the functionality has been moved into the CIterator class, which is shown in Listing 29.5. As a result, there's no need for an implementation file for the CContainer2 class—the header contains the full implementation.

LISTING 29.5

1 Line 18: Take a reference to a container during construction

LISTING 29.5   **The Header for the *CIterator* Class**

```
 1: //////////////////////////////////////////////////////
 2: //  Module  : Iterator.h
 3: //
 4: //  Purpose : Interface for a simple iterator class.
 5: //////////////////////////////////////////////////////
 6:
 7: #ifndef __ITERATOR_H__
 8: #define __ITERATOR_H__
 9:
10: #include "container2.h"
11:
12: //////////////////////////////////////////////////////
13: // Class CIterator
14:
15: class CIterator
16: {
17: public:
18:     CIterator(CContainer2& c) : myContainer, ──── 1
19:         mypData(myContainer.mypArray) { }
20:
21:     void Reset() { mypData = myContainer.mypArray; }
22:     bool IsEnd()
23:     {
24:         return ((mypData - myContainer.mypArray) >=
25:             myContainer.mySize);
26:     }
27:
28:     void Add(int num) { *mypData = num; }
29:
30:     int GetNext()
31:     {
```

```
32:        if (!IsEnd())
33:            return *mypData++;
34:        else
35:            return *mypData;
36:    }
37:
38: private:
39:    CContainer2& myContainer;
40:    int *mypData;
41: };
42:
43: #endif  //__ITERATOR_H__
```

The iterator class is fully implemented in the iterator.h header file, with the constructor on lines 18 and 19 taking a reference to a container as a parameter. This container reference (myContainer) is used to drive the container object. The iterator uses pointer arithmetic to iterate through the container sequence, with the mypData member pointing to the current element. The CIterator::Reset() method in line 21 sets the current element pointer to the address of the container array—the first element in the sequence.

The CIterator::IsEnd() method in lines 22 through 26 uses pointer arithmetic to determine whether the current element is the last in the sequence. On line 28, the CIterator::Add() member function assigns a value to the current element. The CIterator::GetNext() method (lines 30 through 36) returns the value of the current element and increments the mypData pointer to the next element if the current element isn't the last in the sequence.

The driver program in Listing 29.6 shows the use of the iterator class to control the container class.

LISTING 29.6   A Driver Program to Test the *CIterator* Class

```
1: /////////////////////////////////////////////////////
2: //  Module  : IteratorMain.cpp
3: //
4: //  Purpose : Demonstrates a simple container class.
```

continues...

LISTING 29.6 **Continued**

```
 5: //////////////////////////////////////////////////////
 6:
 7: #include <iostream>
 8: #include "iterator.h"
 9:
10: //////////////////////////////////////////////////////
11: // main()
12:
13: void main()
14: {
15:     CContainer2 bag(10);
16:     CIterator  itor(bag);
17:
18:     int i = 0;
19:     while (!itor.IsEnd())
20:     {
21:         itor.Add(i++);
22:         itor.GetNext();
23:     }
24:
25:     itor.Reset();
26:     while (!itor.IsEnd())
27:     {
28:         std::cout << itor.GetNext() << " ";
29:     }
30: }
```

The output for this program is the same as that for the previous program:

```
0 1 2 3 4 5 6 7 8 9
```

The program begins by constructing a container object (bag) with a 10-element capacity (line 15). Next comes the construction of an iterator object (itor) on line 16, sending the container as an argument.

The while loop in lines 19 through 23 assigns values to the container elements by calling CIterator::Add() for each element, using CIterator::GetNext() to increment to the next element. Line 25 calls the CIterator::Reset() method to reset the current element pointer to the first element in the sequence. The while loop in lines 26 through 29 then iterates through the sequence, displaying the value of each element as long as `CIterator::IsEnd()` returns `false`.

Okay, enough iterator theory—now let's take a look at the iterators provided by the Standard C++ Library.

Types of Standard Iterators

All the standard library iterators are derived from a base iterator class that has this declaration in the standard header `<iterator>`:

```
template<class C, class T, class Dist = ptrdiff_t>
struct iterator
{
    typedef C iterator_category;
    typedef T value_type;
    typedef Dist distance_type;
};
```

The members `iterator_category`, `value_type`, and `distance_type` act as aliases for the template parameters `C`, `T`, and `Dist`. The standard header `<iterator>` also declares five basic iterator types as follows:

```
struct input_iterator_tag;
struct output_itcrator_Lag;
struct forward_iterator_tag;
struct bidirectional_iterator_tag;
struct random_access_iterator_tag;
```

These types correspond to the following five basic types of iterators, listed here in order of increasing power:

1. Output iterator
2. Input iterator
3. Forward iterator
4. Bidirectional iterator
5. Random-access iterator

The Standard Template Library uses iterators extensively to integrate algorithms and containers. Table 29.1 gives a summary for each of the iterator types, along with the name used in the standard header `<iterator>`.

TABLE 29.1   **The Five Standard Iterator Categories**

Iterator Type	Name	Description
Output iterator	OutIt	An output iterator is used to write values into a sequence.
Input iterator	InIt	An input iterator is used to read values from a sequence.
Forward iterator	FwdIt	A forward iterator can act as an output iterator (for writing) or an input iterator (for reading); it allows reading and writing and traversal in one direction.
Bidirectional iterator	BidIt	A bidirectional iterator can act as a forward iterator but allows traversal in reverse order as well.
Random-access iterator	RanIt	A random-access iterator can act as a bidirectional iterator but also allows pointer-like arithmetic operations.

Note

You can use an object pointer in place of a random-access iterator. If the object supports the proper read/write access to its sequence, it can act as any category of iterator.

Each classification of iterator has a different set of capabilities, encompassing all the capabilities of the previous classification. Figure 29.1 shows the hierarchy of capabilities of the standard iterator classifications.

FIGURE 29.1

The standard C++ iterator category hierarchy.

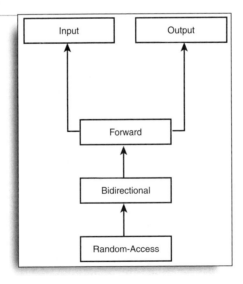

Exploring Iterator Operations

A fundamental concept in the STL is iterator arithmetic, which is made possible by operator template functions in the standard header <iterator>. The operators provided by the header include the following:

- operator==()
- operator!=()
- operator<()
- operator>()
- operator<=()
- operator>=()
- operator-()
- operator+()

In addition to these operators, several function templates are provided by <iterator>, as described in Table 29.2.

TABLE 29.2 **The Template Functions Provided for Iterators in the Standard Header *<iterator>***

Function	Description
back_inserter()	Returns a back_insert_iterator object, used when appending a new element to the end of the sequence.
front_inserter()	Returns a front_insert_iterator object, used when adding a new element to the beginning of the sequence.
inserter()	Returns an insert_iterator object, used when inserting a new element into the sequence.
advance()	Advances an iterator by incrementing it a specified number of times.
distance()	Returns the distance from one element to another in a sequence.

Iterator Classes

The standard library's iterator classes serve up the iterators used by all standard library containers and can serve as base classes for your own iterators for your own containers. Table 29.3 describes each of the iterator classes provided by standard C++.

TABLE 29.3 **The Standard C++ Iterator Classes**

Class	Purpose
iterator	Acts as the base class for all standard iterators.
back_insert_iterator	Describes an output iterator object that provides services for a container class having the member function push_back() to append new elements to the end of the sequence.
front_insert_iterator	Describes an output iterator object that provides services for a container class having the member function push_front() to append new elements to the beginning of the sequence.
insert_iterator	Describes an output iterator object that provides services for a container class having the member function insert() to insert new elements into the sequence.
istream_iterator	Describes an input iterator object that provides services for a stream object, extracting objects from an input stream.
istreambuf_iterator	Describes an input iterator object that provides services for a stream buffer object, extracting elements from an input stream buffer.
ostream_iterator	Describes an output iterator object that provides services for a stream object, inserting objects into an output stream.
ostreambuf_iterator	Describes an output iterator object that provides services for a stream buffer object, inserting objects into an output stream buffer.
reverse_bidirectional_ iterator	Describes an object that behaves like a bidirectional iterator that accesses, in reverse order, a sequence traversed in order by a bidirectional iterator.

Class	Purpose
reverse_iterator	Describes an object that behaves like a random-access iterator that accesses, in reverse order, a sequence traversed in order by a random-access iterator.

The hierarchy of standard iterators is simple and efficient, with all iterator classes derived from the base class iterator (see Figure 29.2). Note that this hierarchy is based on C++ inheritance and has nothing to do with the categorical hierarchy of iterator types shown in Figure 29.1.

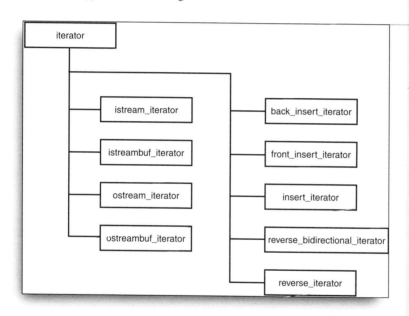

FIGURE 29.2

The standard C++ iterator class hierarchy by inheritance.

Using Input Iterators

An input iterator (InIt) can read a value from a sequence but is not necessarily able to write to it. Although an input iterator *may* be able to write a value to the sequence, it's not guaranteed to be able to do so. Input iterators must define a dereference operator*() for pointer-like access. The following example uses an iterator I and a value V:

```
V = *I;
```

Input iterators must also define the increment operator++(), used like this:

```
V = *I++;
```

Finally, input iterators must also define the inequality operator!=(), used like this:

```
if (I != V) return;
```

Using Output Iterators

The opposite of an input iterator is an output iterator (OutIt). An output iterator can write a value to a sequence but cannot necessarily read from it. Although an output iterator *may* be able to read a value from the sequence, it's not guaranteed to be able to do so. Output iterators must define a dereference operator*() for pointer-like access, as in the iterator I:

```
*I = 15;
```

Output iterators must also define the increment operator++(), as in this example:

```
*I++ = 15;
```

To generalize, an output iterator I can have a value V stored only indirectly on it, and then it must be incremented, like this:

```
*I++ = V;        // one-step increment
*I = V; ++I;     // two-step increment
```

For example, the general algorithm copy, from the standard header <algorithm>, uses both input and output iterators, as in this definition:

```
template<class InIt, class OutIt>
OutIt copy(InIt first, InIt last, OutIt x)
{
   while (first != last)
     *x++ = *first++;
   return x;
}
```

SEE ALSO

➤ *For more information about general algorithms, see page 820*

Because a regular C++ pointer has all the properties needed to be an input or output iterator, you can also use the copy algorithm with pointers as the iterators, like this:

```
// Create two arrays
//
int array1[10];
int array2[10];

// Fill the first array
//
for (int i = 0; i < 10; ++i)
   array1[i] = i;

// Copy the first array to the second array
//
copy(&array1[0], &array1[9], &array2[0]);
```

Using Forward Iterators

A forward iterator can both read values from and write values to a sequence, acting as both an input and an output iterator. A forward iterator (ForIt) can traverse the sequence in only one direction. You can make multiple copies of a forward iterator, and each copy can be dereferenced and incremented independently.

Using Bidirectional Iterators

A bidirectional iterator (BidIt) is just like a forward iterator, except that it can also traverse the sequence in reverse order (in two directions). This means that a bidirectional iterator must support the decrement operator −() in addition to the forward iterator capabilities.

A bidirectional iterator is the lowest iterator type you can use to iterate a doubly linked list. In fact, the generic container class list is a generic doubly linked list, and it uses bidirectional iterators to traverse the list both forward and backward.

Using Random-Access Iterators

Random-access iterators are the most powerful of all the iterator types; they can do everything the other four types can do. In addition, you can perform integer arithmetic on a random-access iterator (RanIt) in a manner similar to that used on a regular object pointer (such as addition and subtraction); you can also perform comparisons like the one in this sample function, where both a and b are random-access iterators:

```
template <class RanIt>
RanIt func(RanIt& a, RanIt& b) { return (a < b); }
```

Understanding Containers

The container classes provided by the standard library are generic containers that, thanks to C++ templates, serve as completely abstract data types. There are two families of container classes provided by the STL:

- *Sequence Containers*, including vectors, lists, and deques.
- *Associative Containers*, including sets, multisets, maps, and multimaps.

These containers constitute a family of classes that share a common interface design. Sequence containers are classes that contain a sequence of items that are located by index or iterative value, and have a linear search time proportional to the number of items in the sequence. Associative containers are classes that use keys to allow quick lookups of items in a sequence, resulting in far better performance than linear searches. The rest of this chapter examines these standard container classes, looking at their capabilities and uses.

Sequence Containers

Sequence containers store elements in a sequence. There are differences in performance between the three main sequence container types, as described in Table 29.4.

TABLE 29.4   **The Three Sequence Container Classes**

Class	Description
Vector	A sequence container that provides random access and fast insertions and deletions at the end of the sequence.
Deque	A sequence container that provides random access and fast insertions and deletions at both the beginning and the end of the sequence.
List	A sequence container that provides linear access and fast insertions and deletions anywhere in the sequence.

Each of the sequence container classes uses the following template parameters:

```
template <class T, class A = allocator<T> >
```

In this syntax, T is the data type to use and A is the storage allocator, which defaults to the standard allocator for type T.

Each standard container class defines several public types with creative use of type definitions to implement a standard interface. All the standard containers define the following types:

- value_type   The type of element stored in the container.
- reference   The type of element location (such as T&).
- iterator   The iterator type that refers to values of type reference.
- difference_type   A signed integral type representing the difference between two iterators.
- size_type   An unsigned integral type representing the non-negative value of the difference between two iterators.
- reverse_iterator   An iterator type that refers to values of type reference and defines the increment and decrement operators opposite their normal meaning, resulting in a reverse sequence traversal.

In addition to these types, the containers also define constant iterators for the reference, iterator, and reverse_iterator types. This results in these constant iterator types: const_reference, const_iterator, and const_reverse_iterator.

Vectors

A vector is a sequence container that provides random access and fast insertions and deletions at the end of the sequence. Vectors provide random-access iterators (the fastest, most powerful kind), which means that *all* the generic algorithms work on a vector (because random-access iterators can act as any other type of iterator). As an example of what the standard container class declarations look like, take a look at the declaration for the vector template class, shown in Listing 29.7.

LISTING 29.7

1 Line 4: Template parameters for the standard class vector

LISTING 29.7   **The Interface for the Standard Library Class Vector**

```
1: ///////////////////////////////////////////////////
2: // Class vector
3:
4: template<class T, class A = allocator<T> >  ──── 1
5: class vector
6: {
7: public:
8:    // Type definitions
9:    //
10:   typedef A allocator_type;
11:   typedef A::size_type size_type;
12:   typedef A::difference_type difference_type;
13:   typedef A::reference reference;
14:   typedef A::const_reference const_reference;
15:   typedef A::value_type value_type;
16:   typedef T0 iterator;
17:   typedef T1 const_iterator;
18:   typedef reverse_iterator<iterator, value_type,
19:       reference, A::pointer, difference_type>
20:       reverse_iterator;
21:   typedef reverse_iterator<const_iterator, value_type,
22:       const_reference, A::const_pointer,
23:       difference_type> const_reverse_iterator;
24:
25:   // Constructors
26:   //
```

```
27:     explicit vector(const A& al = A());
28:     explicit vector(size_type n, const T& v = T(),
29:         const A& al = A());
30:     vector(const vector& x);
31:     vector(const_iterator first, const_iterator last,
32:         const A& al = A());
33:
34:     // Methods
35:     //
36:     void reserve(size_type n);
37:     size_type capacity() const;
38:     iterator begin();
39:     const_iterator begin() const;
40:     iterator end();
41:     iterator end() const;
42:     reverse_iterator rbegin();
43:     const_reverse_iterator rbegin() const;
44:     reverse_iterator rend();
45:     const_reverse_iterator rend() const;
46:     void resize(size_type n, T x = T());
47:     size_type size() const;
48:     size_type max_size() const;
49:     bool empty() const;
50:     A get_allocator() const;
51:     reference at(size_type pos);
52:     const_reference at(size_type pos) const;
53:     reference operator[](size_type pos);
54:     const_reference operator[](size_type pos);
55:     reference front();
56:     const_reference front() const;
57:     reference back();
58:     const_reference back() const;
59:     void push_back(const T& x);
60:     void pop_back();
61:     void assign(const_iterator first,
62:         const_iterator last);
63:     void assign(size_type n, const T& x = T());
64:     iterator insert(iterator it, const T& x = T());
65:     void insert(iterator it, size_type n, const T& x);
66:     void insert(iterator it, const_iterator first,
67:         const_iterator last);
68:     iterator erase(iterator it);
```

LISTING 29.7 CONTINUED

2 Lines 27-32: Constructors for the vector class

continues…

LISTING 29.7 CONTINUED

3 Line 74: The allocator for the class as a protected data member

LISTING 29.7   **Continued**

```
69:     iterator erase(iterator first, iterator last);
70:     void clear();
71:     void swap(vector x);
72:
73: protected:
74:     A allocator;  ──── 3
75: };
```

The functions provided by the `vector` class are described in Table 29.5.

TABLE 29.5   **The Class Methods Provided by** *vector*

Method	Description
assign()	Replaces the entire sequence with another sequence.
at()	Returns a reference to the specified element position (index).
back()	Returns a reference to the last element of the sequence (must be nonempty).
begin()	Returns a random-access iterator pointing to the first element of the sequence. If the sequence is empty, the iterator points just beyond the end of the empty sequence.
capacity()	Returns the storage currently allocated to hold the sequence.
clear()	Calls `erase()` for each element in the sequence.
empty()	Returns `true` if the sequence is empty.
end()	Returns a random-access iterator pointing just beyond the end of the sequence.
erase()	Removes a specified element from the sequence.
front()	Returns a reference to the first element of the controlled sequence (must be nonempty).
get_allocator()	Returns a reference to the class allocator.
insert()	Inserts an element or a sequence of elements into the sequence.
max_size()	Returns the length of the longest sequence that the object can control.

Method	Description
operator[]()	Returns a reference to the specified element position (index).
pop_back()	Removes the last element of the controlled sequence (must be nonempty).
push_back()	Inserts an element at the end of the sequence.
rbegin()	Returns the beginning of the reverse sequence: a reverse iterator pointing just beyond the end of the sequence.
rend()	Returns the end of the reverse sequence: a reverse iterator pointing at the first element of the sequence (or just beyond the end of an empty sequence).
reserve()	Reserves storage to ensure enough capacity().
resize()	Reserves storage to ensure enough size().
size()	Returns the number of elements in the sequence.
swap()	Swaps the contents of two vectors.
vector()	Class constructor.

The program in Listing 29.8 shows how to create and use a vector.

LISTING 29.8   A Program Demonstrating the Use of Class *vector*

```
 1: /////////////////////////////////////////////////////
 2: //  Module  : vector.cpp
 3: //
 4: //  Purpose : Demonstrates the standard vector class.
 5: /////////////////////////////////////////////////////
 6:
 7: #include <iostream>
 8: #include <vector>
 9:
10: using std::cout;
11: using std::endl;
12:
13: /////////////////////////////////////////////////////
14: // main()
15:
```

LISTING 29.8

1 Lines 10-11: Promote declarations into the current namespace

continues…

LISTING 29.8   **Continued**

```
16: void main()
17: {
18:     // Create a 10-element vector
19:     //
20:     std::vector<int> v(10);  ──1
21:
22:     // Fill it
23:     //
24:     for (int i = 0; i < 10; ++i)
25:         v[i] = i;
26:
27:     cout << "Maximum size of vector: "
28:         << v.max_size() << endl;
29:
30:     cout << "Actual size of vector: "
31:         << v.size() << endl << endl;
32:
33:     // Traverse the vector
34:     //
35:     std::vector<int>::iterator itor = v.begin();
36:     while (itor != v.end())
37:     {
38:         cout << *itor++ << " ";  ──2
39:     }
40:     cout << endl;
41:
42:     // Traverse the vector in reverse order
43:     //
44:     std::vector<int>::reverse_iterator ritr = v.rbegin();
45:     while (ritr != v.rend())  ──3
46:     {
47:         cout << *ritr++ << " ";
48:     }
49:     cout << endl;
50: }
```

The output from this program is as follows:

```
Maximum size of vector: 1073741823
Actual size of vector: 10

0 1 2 3 4 5 6 7 8 9
9 8 7 6 5 4 3 2 1 0
```

Lines 10 and 11 of this program promote the standard cout and endl object into the current namespace, cleaning up the code somewhat. On line 20, a vector specialized to contain integers is constructed with 10 elements. The for loop running on lines 24 and 25 fills the vector directly, using the vector::operator[]() function to access the elements.

Line 28 uses the vector::max_size() method to display information about the vector's maximum capacity, and line 30 uses the vector::size() method to get the number of elements currently being contained.

An iterator specialized for vectors of integers is defined on line 35. This iterator is assigned a value using the vector::begin() method to return an iterator pointing to the first element in the vector. The while loop running from lines 36 through 39 uses the iterator to display the container's element values, incrementing the iterator with each loop iteration. Lines 44 through 48 perform a similar task, using a reverse iterator to traverse the sequence in reverse order.

Deques

A deque is a sequence container that provides random access and fast insertions and deletions at both the beginning and end of the sequence. This functionality makes a deque very much like a double-ended vector. The deque class doesn't provide the capacity() or reserve() functions found in vector (because they only exist in vector to increase performance when inserting at the beginning of the sequence). The deque class doesn't need these functions because it's designed to insert directly at the front of the sequence, as well as at the back.

Other deque member functions are the same as those in vector, with the addition of the push_front() method, which inserts an element at the beginning of the sequence. The program in Listing 29.9 is nearly the same as the one in Listing 29.8, except that it uses a deque instead of a vector.

LISTING 29.9

① Lines 10-11: Promote declarations into the current namespace

② Line 20: Create a deque object with zero elements

③ Line 38: Display deque elements with an iterator

LISTING 29.9   **A Program Demonstrating the Use of the Standard Library** *deque* **Class**

```cpp
 1: ///////////////////////////////////////////////////
 2: //   Module  : deque.cpp
 3: //
 4: //   Purpose : Demonstrates the standard deque class.
 5: ///////////////////////////////////////////////////
 6:
 7: #include <iostream>
 8: #include <deque>
 9:
10: using std::cout;
11: using std::endl;
12:
13: ///////////////////////////////////////////////////
14: // main()
15:
16: void main()
17: {
18:     // Create a 0-element deque
19:     //
20:     std::deque<int> d(0);
21:
22:     // Fill it
23:     //
24:     for (int i = 0; i < 10; ++i)
25:        ((i % 2) == 0) ? d.push_front(i): d.push_back(i);
26:
27:     cout << "Maximum size of deque: "
28:        << d.max_size() << endl;
29:
30:     cout << "Actual size of deque: "
31:        << d.size() << endl << endl;
32:
33:     // Traverse the deque
34:     //
35:     std::deque<int>::iterator itor = d.begin();
36:     while (itor != d.end())
37:     {
38:        cout << *itor++ << " ";
39:     }
40:     cout << endl;
```

```
41:
42:     // Traverse the deque in reverse order
43:     //
44:     std::deque<int>::reverse_iterator ritor = d.rbegin();
45:     while (ritor != d.rend())
46:     {
47:        cout << *ritor++ << " ";    ————4
48:     }
49:     cout << endl;
50: }
```

LISTING **29.9** CONTINUED

4 Line 47: Display deque elements with a reverse iterator

The output from this program is as follows:

```
Maximum size of deque: 1073741823
Actual size of deque: 10

8 6 4 2 0 1 3 5 7 9
9 7 5 3 1 0 2 4 6 8
```

As in the program in Listing 29.8, lines 10 and 11 of the program in Listing 29.9 promote the standard cout and endl object into the current namespace. On line 20, a deque specialized to contain integers is constructed with zero elements. The for loop running on lines 24 and 25 fills the deque directly, using the deque::push_front() and deque::push_back() functions in combination with a modulus expression to store even numbers at the front of the deque and odd numbers at the back.

Line 28 uses the deque::max_size() method to display information about the deque's maximum capacity; line 31 uses the deque::size() method to get the number of elements currently being contained.

An iterator specialized for deques of integers is defined on line 35. This iterator is assigned a value using the deque::begin() method to return an iterator pointing to the first element in the sequence. The while loop in lines 36 through 39 uses the iterator to display the container's element values, incrementing the iterator with each loop iteration. Lines 44 through 48 perform a similar task, using a reverse iterator to traverse the sequence in reverse order.

Lists

A `list` is a sequence container that provides linear access and fast insertions and deletions anywhere in the sequence. Although a `vector` is similar to a `deque`, a `list` is much different. The standard `list` container is a doubly linked list of elements (nodes). The `list` class declares methods that have interfaces like the other containers, but a completely different implementation. Table 29.6 describes the class methods for the standard `list` container.

TABLE 29.6   **The Class Methods Provided by** *list*

Method	Description
assign()	Replaces the entire sequence with another sequence.
back()	Returns a reference to the last element of the sequence (must be nonempty).
begin()	Returns a random-access iterator pointing to the first element of the sequence. If the sequence is empty, the iterator points just beyond the end of the empty sequence.
clear()	Calls `erase()` for each element in the sequence.
empty()	Returns `true` if the sequence is empty.
end()	Returns a random-access iterator pointing just beyond the end of the sequence.
erase()	Removes a specified element from the sequence.
front()	Returns a reference to the first element of the controlled sequence (must be nonempty).
get_allocator()	Returns a reference to the class allocator.
insert()	Inserts an element or a sequence of elements into the sequence.
list()	The class constructor.
max_size()	Returns the length of the longest sequence that the object can control.
merge()	Merges the elements of two lists into a single list.
pop_back()	Removes the last element of the controlled sequence (must be nonempty).

pop_front()	Removes the first element of the controlled sequence (must be nonempty).
push_back()	Inserts an element at the end of the sequence.
push_front()	Inserts an element at the beginning of the sequence.
rbegin()	Returns the beginning of the reverse sequence: a reverse iterator pointing just beyond the end of the sequence.
remove()	Removes from the sequence all elements equal to a specified value.
remove_if()	Removes from the sequence all elements equal to a specified value if a condition is true.
rend()	Returns the end of the reverse sequence: a reverse iterator pointing at the first element of the sequence (or just beyond the end of an empty sequence).
resize()	Reserves storage to ensure enough size().
reverse()	Reverses the order in which elements appear in the sequence.
size()	Returns the number of elements in the sequence.
sort()	Orders the elements in the sequence in some specified way.
splice()	Inserts a list sequence into the sequence.
swap()	Swaps the contents of two lists.
unique()	Removes duplicate elements from the sequence. Duplicate elements must be side by side in the sequence.

The program in Listing 29.10 demonstrates the use of the standard list class.

LISTING 29.10   A Program Demonstrating the Use of the Standard *list* Container Class

```
1: ///////////////////////////////////////////////////
2: //   Module  : list.cpp
3: //
4: //   Purpose : Demonstrates the standard list class.
5: ///////////////////////////////////////////////////
```

continues…

LISTING 29.10

① Line 13: Declare a type alias for a list of integers

② Lines 31-32: Add items to the list

LISTING 29.10   **Continued**

```
6:
7: #include <iostream>
8: #include <list>
9:
10: using std::cout;
11: using std::endl;
12:
13: typedef std::list<int>  IntList;  ————①
14:
15: void TraverseAndDisplay(IntList::iterator& itor,
16:                              const IntList& l);
17:
18: /////////////////////////////////////////////////////////
19: // main()
20:
21: void main()
22: {
23:     // Create a list
24:     //
25:     IntList lst;
26:
27:     // Fill it
28:     //
29:     for (int i = 0; i < 5; ++i)
30:     {
31:         lst.push_front(i);   ┐
32:         lst.push_back(i);    ┘ ②
33:     }
34:
35:     cout << "Maximum size of list: "
36:         << lst.max_size() << endl;
37:
38:     cout << "Actual size of list: "
39:         << lst.size() << endl << endl;
40:
41:     // Traverse the list
42:     //
43:     TraverseAndDisplay(lst.begin(), lst);
44:
45:     // Remove duplicate elements
46:     //
```

```
47:     cout << "\nRemoving duplicate elements...\n" ;
48:     lst.unique();
49:     cout << "Actual size of list: "
50:        << lst.size() << endl << endl;
51:     TraverseAndDisplay(lst.begin(), lst);
52:
53:     // Sort the remaining elements
54:     //
55:     cout << "\nSorting remaining elements...\n";
56:     lst.sort();
57:     TraverseAndDisplay(lst.begin(), lst);
58:
59:     // Remove duplicate elements
60:     //
61:     cout << "\nRemoving duplicate elements...\n\n";
62:     lst.unique();
63:     cout << "Actual size of list: "
64:        << lst.size() << endl << endl;
65:     TraverseAndDisplay(lst.begin(), lst);
66:
67:     // Traverse the list in reverse order
68:     //
69:     cout << "\nReverse element order...\n\n" ;
70:     IntList::reverse_iterator ritor = lst.rbegin();
71:     while (ritor != lst.rend())
72:     {
73:        cout << *ritor++ << " ";
74:     }
75:     cout << endl;
76: }
77:
78: /////////////////////////////////////////////////////
79: // TraverseAndDisplay()
80:
81: void TraverseAndDisplay(IntList::iterator& itor,
82:                          const IntList& l)
83: {
84:     while (itor != l.end())
85:     {
86:        cout << *itor++ << " ";
87:     }
88:     cout << endl;
89: }
```

LISTING 29.10 CONTINUED

3 Line 56: Sort the list

4 Line 62: Remove duplicate entries

5 Line 73: Traverse the list in reverse order using a reverse iterator

6 Line 86: Traverse the list using an iterator

The output from this program is as follows:

```
Maximum size of list: 1073741823
Actual size of list: 10


4 3 2 1 0 0 1 2 3 4


Removing duplicate elements...
Actual size of list: 9


4 3 2 1 0 1 2 3 4


Sorting remaining elements...
0 1 1 2 2 3 3 4 4


Removing duplicate elements...

Actual size of list: 5


0 1 2 3 4


Reverse element order...


4 3 2 1 0
```

This program begins by creating a list with the default constructor on line 25. The for loop in lines 29 through 33 uses the list::push_front() and list::push_back() methods to add duplicate values to the front and back of the list. Lines 36 and 38 get the maximum size and element count for the list, and line 43 calls the TraverseAndDisplay() function to traverse and display the list. Line 48 calls list::unique() to remove any duplicate elements appearing more than once in a row (the two zeros in the program output); the following statements display the list items again, showing that the duplicate zero has been removed.

On line 56, the list::sort() method is called to sort the list, which is then displayed again (this time, sorted). Now that there are numerous duplicate values side by side, the list::unique() method is called again on line 62, removing all duplicates, as you can see when the list is displayed yet again on line 65. Lines 70 through 74 make use of a reverse iterator to traverse the list backwards.

The `TraverseAndDisplay()` function in linc 81 takes a reference to an iterator (`itor`) and a `const` reference to a list (`l`), using the iterator to traverse the list in the `while` loop in lines 84 through 87, displaying the dereferenced iterator value using the `cout` object.

Associative Containers

Associative containers are designed to retrieve data as quickly as possible. They accomplish this by using keys associated with each element in the sequence—this item/key combination is very fast. In addition to the standard sequence container classes, the standard library provides the following sorted associative containers:

- *Sets*, which hold a sequence of unique objects called *keys*.
- *Multisets*, which hold a sequence of nonunique objects called *keys*.
- *Maps*, which hold a sequence of unique objects identified by value and key.
- *Multimaps*, which hold a sequence of nonunique objects identified by value and key.

Each of the associative container classes uses the following template parameters:

```
template<class Key, class Pred = less<Key>,
    class A = allocator<T> >
```

In this syntax, `Key` is the data type to use, `Pred` is a stored function object that specifies the type of comparison function to use, and `A` is the storage allocator (which defaults to the standard allocator for type `Key`).

The associative container classes use the same type definitions used by the sequence container classes: `value_type`, `Reference`, `Iterator`, `difference_type`, `size_type`, `reverse_iterator`, `const_reference`, `const_iterator`, and `const_reverse_iterator`. Additionally, the associative container classes define these types:

- `key_type` A type alias for template parameter type `Key`.
- `key_compare` A type alias for template parameter type `Pred`.
- `value_compare` A type alias for template parameter type `Pred`.

These associative container types correspond to the type definitions in the associative container class declarations. For example, this excerpt from the set template class declaration defines these types:

```
Template <class Key, class Pred = less<Key>,
    class A = allocator<T> >
class set
{
public:
    typedef Key key_type;
    typedef Pred key_compare;
    typedef Pred value_compare;
    //
    // ...
    //
};
```

Sets and Multisets

A *set* is an object that controls a varying-length sequence of elements, as specified by the template class set. Each element in a set serves a dual role, acting both as a sort key *and* a value. The set object orders its elements by calling the stored function object Pred, which is accessed by calling the key_comp() method. A set object always ensures that each key is unique.

A *multiset* is just like a set in that it controls a varying-length sequence of elements, but a multiset is specified by the template class multiset and, unlike a set object, a multiset object allows duplicate keys. The member functions for the standard template classes set and multiset are given in Table 29.7.

TABLE 29.7   **The Member Functions for the Standard Template Classes *set* and *multiset***

Method	Description
begin()	Returns a bidirectional iterator pointing to the first element of the sequence. If the sequence is empty, the iterator points just beyond the end of the empty sequence.
clear()	Calls erase() for each element in the sequence.

Method	Description
count()	Returns the number of elements within a specified range.
empty()	Returns true if the sequence is empty.
end()	Returns a bidirectional iterator pointing just beyond the end of the sequence.
equal_range()	Returns a pair of iterators representing the first and last elements in a range in which an item might be inserted in sorted order.
erase()	Removes a specified element from the sequence.
find()	Returns an iterator designating the first element in the controlled sequence whose sort key matches key.
get_allocator()	Returns a reference to the class allocator.
insert()	Inserts an element into the sequence in sorted order.
key_comp()	Returns the stored function object that determines the order of elements in the sequence.
lower_bound()	Returns an iterator representing the first element in the sequence in which an item might be inserted in sorted order.
max_size()	Returns the length of the longest sequence that the object can control.
multiset()	Constructor for class multiset.
rbegin()	Returns a reverse bidirectional iterator that points just beyond the end of the controlled sequence (the beginning of the reverse sequence).
reference()	Describes an object that can act as a reference to an element in the sequence.
rend()	Returns a reverse bidirectional iterator that points at the first element of the sequence (or just beyond the end of an empty sequence).
set()	Constructor for class set.
size()	Returns the length of the sequence.
swap()	Swaps the contents of two sets or multisets.
upper_bound()	Returns an iterator representing the last element in the sequence in which an item might be inserted in sorted order.
value_comp()	Returns a function object that determines the order of elements in the sequence.

Maps and Multimaps

A *map* is an object that controls a varying-length sequence of elements, as specified by the template class map. Each element in a map contains both a sort key and an associated value (hence the name *associative containers*). The map object orders its elements by calling the stored function object Pred, which is accessed by calling the key_comp() method. A map object always ensures that each key is unique.

A *multimap* is just like a map in that it controls a varying-length sequence of elements, but a multimap is specified by the template class multimap and, unlike a map object, a multimap object allows duplicate keys. The member functions for the standard template classes map and multimap are given in Table 29.8.

TABLE 29.8   The Member Functions for the Standard Template Classes *map* and *multimap*

Method	Description
begin()	Returns a bidirectional iterator pointing to the first element of the sequence. If the sequence is empty, the iterator points just beyond the end of the empty sequence.
clear()	Calls erase() for each element in the sequence.
count()	Returns the number of elements within a specified range.
empty()	Returns true if the sequence is empty.
end()	Returns a bidirectional iterator pointing just beyond the end of the sequence.
equal_range()	Returns a pair of iterators representing the first and last elements in a range in which an item might be inserted in sorted order.
erase()	Removes a specified element from the sequence.
find()	Returns an iterator designating the first element in the controlled sequence whose sort key matches key.
get_allocator()	Returns a reference to the class allocator.
insert()	Inserts an element into the sequence in sorted order.

Method	Description
`key_comp()`	Returns the stored function object that determines the order of elements in the sequence.
`lower_bound()`	Returns an iterator representing the first element in the sequence in which an item might be inserted in sorted order.
`map()`	Constructor for class `map`.
`max_size()`	Returns the length of the longest sequence that the object can control.
`multimap()`	Constructor for class `multimap`.
`rbegin()`	Returns a reverse bidirectional iterator that points just beyond the end of the controlled sequence (the beginning of the reverse sequence).
`reference()`	Describes an object that can act as a reference to an element in the sequence.
`rend()`	Returns a reverse bidirectional iterator that points at the first element of the sequence (or just beyond the end of an empty sequence).
`size()`	Returns the length of the sequence.
`swap()`	Swaps the contents of two maps or multimaps.
`upper_bound()`	Returns an iterator representing the last element in the sequence in which an item might be inserted in sorted order.
`value_comp()`	Returns a function object that determines the order of elements in the sequence.

The program in Listing 29.11 demonstrates the use of a map to store a series of names with corresponding nicknames as keys.

LISTING 29.11 A Program That Uses a *map* to Store Names

```
1: //////////////////////////////////////////////////////
2: //  Module  : map.cpp
3: //
4: //  Purpose : Demonstrates the standard map class.
5: //////////////////////////////////////////////////////
6:
7: #include <iostream>
```

continues…

LISTING 29.11

❶ Lines 22-29: This structure member returns the full name of a person

❷ Line 34: A type alias for a specialized map template

LISTING 29.11 **Continued**

```cpp
 8: #include <string>
 9: #include <map>
10:
11: using namespace std;
12:
13: // A simple user-defined data type
14: //
15: struct Person
16: {
17:     string FirstName;
18:     string LastName;
19:
20:     // Helper function
21:     //
22:     Person& SetName(const string& first,
23:         const string& last)
24:     {
25:         FirstName = first;
26:         LastName  = last;
27:
28:         return *this;
29:     }
30: };
31:
32: // A map type for the Person data type
33: //
34: typedef map<string, Person> MAP_STRING2PERSON;
35:
36: /////////////////////////////////////////////////////////
37: //   main()
38:
39: void main()
40: {
41:     MAP_STRING2PERSON m;
42:     MAP_STRING2PERSON::iterator itor;
43:
44:     cout << "Maximum size of map : "
45:         << m.max_size() << endl;
46:
47:     cout << "Actual size of map  : "
48:         << m.size() << endl << endl;
```

❶ (lines 22-29)

❷ (line 34)

```
49:    cout << "Filling map with new entries..." << endl;
50:
51:    // Fill the map with nicknames, mapped to people.
52:    // These names would ordinarily be read from a file
53:    //
54:    Person person;
55:
56:    m["Rob"]  = person.SetName("Robert", "McGregor");
57:    m["Brad"] = person.SetName("Bradley", "Sasala");
58:    m["Tom"]  = person.SetName("Thomas", "Newton");
59:    m["Ron"]  = person.SetName("Ronald", "Masters");
60:    m["Dave"] = person.SetName("David", "Barnhart");
61:    m["Rudy"] = person.SetName("Sue", "Balla");
62:
63:    cout << "The map has " << m.size() << " entries.\n";
64:
65:    // Ask the user for a nickname
66:    //
67:    string nickname;
68:    string realname;
69:
70:    itor = m.end();
71:    while(itor == m.end())
72:    {
73:       cout << "\nEnter a nickname: ";
74:       cin >> nickname;
75:
76:       // Print full name corresponding to nickname
77:       //
78:       if((itor = m.find(nickname)) != m.end())
79:       {
80:          nickname = (*itor).first;
81:          person   = (*itor).second;
82:
83:          realname = person.FirstName + " " +
84:             person.LastName;
85:
86:          cout << "The nickname " << nickname
87:             << " belongs to "
88:             << realname << endl;
89:       }
90:       else
```

LISTING 29.11 CONTINUED

3 Lines 56-61: Add items to the map

4 Line 78: Search for a name in the map

continues...

LISTING 29.11 CONTINUED

6 Lines 98-105: Iterate through all map items

LISTING 29.11 **Continued**

```
91:          cout << "Nickname not found, try again...\n";
92:    }
93:
94:    // Display all mapped names
95:    //
96:    cout << "\nOur lucky contestants:";
97:    itor = m.begin();
98:    while (itor != m.end())
99:    {
100:       nickname = (*itor).first;
101:       person   = (*itor).second;
102:       cout << endl << nickname << " is really "
103:          << person.FirstName + " " + person.LastName;
104:       itor++;
105:    }
106:
107:    // Clear the map - could use the clear() method
108:    //
109:    cout << "\n\nEmptying the map...\n";
110:    m.erase(m.begin(), m.end());
111:    cout << "The map has " << m.size() << " entries.\n";
112: }
```

A test run of the program resulted in the following output:

```
Maximum size of map : 134217727
Actual size of map  : 0

Filling map with new entries...
The map has 6 entries.

Enter a nickname: red
Nickname not found, try again...

Enter a nickname: Ron
The nickname Ron belongs to Ronald Masters

Our lucky contestants, sorted:
Brad is really Bradley Sasala
Dave is really David Barnhart
Rob is really Robert McGregor
```

```
Ron is really Ronald Masters
Rudy is really Sue Balla
Tom is really Thomas Newton

Emptying the map...
The map has 0 entries.
```

This program begins by defining the Person structure (lines 15 through 30), which stores a first name and a last name. The member function Person::SetName() returns a reference to an initialized Person object—this is useful for adding Person objects to the map. On line 34, the type definition MAP_STRING2PERSON is declared as an alias to a map that stores Person objects associated with string keys.

The main() function begins on line 39 by declaring a MAP_STRING2PERSON map object and an iterator for that specialized map type. Line 45 calls the map::max_size() method to display the maximum number of items the map can hold. Line 48 calls the map::size() method to display the actual number of items the map contains.

On line 54, a Person object (person) is defined. This object is used for temporary storage of Person data when adding entries to the map. Lines 56 through 61 use the Person::SetName() method, which returns a reference to an initialized Person object. In each case, the resulting reference, in conjunction with the map::operator[](), is assigned to a map entry using a nickname string as the key.

On line 63, the map size is checked again; this time, the check reveals that six items are now contained in the map. On line 70, the map iterator (itor) is assigned the value returned by map::end(). This iterator value is checked in the while statement on line 71 to see whether the end of the map has been reached. The user is asked for a nickname on line 74, and the user's input is stored in the standard string object nickname. On line 78, the map::find() method is called to attempt to locate the nickname key in the map.

If the map::find() call is successful, the resulting iterator points to the item being sought; otherwise, the iterator is assigned the value returned by map::end(). If map::find() is successful, the iterator is dereferenced and the nickname string and person object are retrieved from the map using the iterator::first and iterator::second members on lines 80 and 81. On lines 83 and 84, the person's complete name is concatenated into the string object realname, and the nickname and realname strings are displayed on lines 86 through 88.

If the map::find() call is not successful, line 91 tells the user that the nickname was not found, and the while loop iterates until a valid nickname is entered. On line 97, itor is assigned the value returned by map::begin(), which returns an iterator pointing to the first element in the map. Using the same iterator dereferencing technique you saw on lines 80 and 81, all names in the map are displayed (lines 98 through 105). The names appear in sorted order because the map sorts the names as they are inserted into the map. The final action of the program is to clear all elements from the map, using the map::erase() method with the iterators returned by map::first() and map::last() as arguments.

Using Strings

Learn about the standard C++ string data type

Investigate the *basic_string* class template

Examine the standard string operators

Explore the standard string member functions

Learn to use standard strings with C-style string functions

Characters and Standard Strings

Strings of characters are the basis of written communication, and they are the basis of programming, too—we need them to write source code in an editor, to construct electronic documents, to generate reports, and so on. You've seen strings used in this book since Chapter 1: The ANSI C solution to strings is a null-terminated array of characters; although the Standard C++ Library provides full support for these primitive strings, they're a bit clumsy to work with.

String classes have traditionally been some of the most often defined classes that programmers create for themselves in their endeavors to make strings less clumsy—more like a built-in C++ type. For years, programmers have come up with many diverse, clever, and unique designs and implementations of string classes. The Standard C++ Library provides a comprehensive string class fashioned after STL containers, using STL templates: the *standard string*. Finally, after years of workarounds, string standardization finally looms on the horizon. The main problem with the standard string class is that it's huge—it has so much functionality that it's hard to get a handle on just what the standard string class can do.

Creating Character Strings

The facilities of the Standard Template Library make possible the generic template class basic_string, which serves as the basis of the standard string. The string class is a specialization of the basic_string class that uses the intrinsic data type char, and is defined in the standard header <string> as shown here:

```
typedef basic_string<char> string;
```

Likewise, the wide string class wstring is a specialization of the basic_string class that uses the wide character data type wchar_t, and is defined in the standard header <string> as shown here:

```
typedef basic_string<wchar_t> wstring;
```

SEE ALSO

➤ *For more information about wide characters, see page 741*

Identifying International Concerns

The main reason the basic_string class was designed as a template is so that it can provide strings of not only characters but of other objects as well—typically, strings of wide characters. The problem is that some languages require more storage to hold their character sets. That's why there are two types of character sets: single byte and multibyte.

Single-Byte Character Sets

Most character sets used in computers are of the single-byte variety. This simply means that each character is identified by a value one byte wide. These character sets are 8-bit (single-byte) sets that can hold a maximum of 256 characters. Single-byte character sets are used in Western languages like English, German, and Spanish.

Multibyte Character Sets

Many non-Western languages such as Asian languages use large numbers of characters that can't all fit into the same 256-character single-byte schemes used for many Western languages. Internationalization of software led to the development of multibyte character sets that can hold many more characters and that can fully accommodate the extensive characters used by these non-Western languages.

The requirements of these complex written languages led to the development of the double-byte character set (DBCS) that's used by Asian languages and of the global character encoding standard called Unicode. Unicode can depict all characters and symbols commonly used throughout the world, including technical symbols. A Unicode character is a full 16 bits wide, allowing up to 65,536 characters—a far cry from the original 256!

Creating Other Types of Strings

The <string> templates (those template classes and specializations declared in the standard header <string>) were designed with characters in mind. Other types of strings are possible, but

> **Note**
>
> If you are working on projects that will be used internationally with non-English languages, using the standard wstring class specialization is the better option than the standard string specialization.

only if the data type used to specialize the <string> templates meets all the requirements as far as character properties are concerned. These character properties, or traits, define everything the templates need to know about a string element. This information is stored in the aptly named char_traits structure.

The string class is designed to work with types other than characters, which means that some foreign language with a large set of written symbols could be easily represented by a specialization of the char_traits class. One foreign language containing a vast array of arcane symbols comes immediately to mind—Klingon. Those quirky Klingon symbols can be represented as string elements in a basic_string specialization, something like this:

```
// Structure defining the Klingon character type
//
struct kchar_t
{
  // Klingon character info
  // ...
};
typedef basic_string<kchar_t> KString;
```

Defining Character Traits

If an object is to be used as an element of a string sequence, it must be capable of taking on an integer representation. To define a character type, the standard library provides a template structure called char_traits; this structure defines the properties of a character type. Listing 30.1 shows the generic char_traits structure.

LISTING 30.1   **The Class Template Defining Character Traits**

```
1: // Generic char_traits template
2: //
3: struct char_traits<E>
4: {
5:   typedef E char_type;
6:   typedef T1 int_type;
7:   typedef T2 pos_type;
8:   typedef T3 off_type;
```

```
 9: typedef T4 state_type;
10:
11: static void assign(E& x, const E& y);
12: static E *assign(E *x, size_t n, const E& y);
13: static bool eq(const E& x, const E& y);
14: static bool lt(const E& x, const E& y);
15: static int compare(const E *x, const E *y, size_t n);
16: static size_t length(const E *x);
17: static E *copy(E *x, const E *y, size_t n);
18: static E *move(E *x, const E *y, size_t n);
19: static const E *find(const E *x, size_t n, const E& y);
20: static E to_char_type(const int_type& ch);
21: static int_type to_int_type(const E& c);
22: static bool eq_int_type(const int_type& ch1,
23:   const int_type& ch2);
24: static int_type eof();
25: static int_type not_eof(const int_type& ch);
26: };
```

Of course, the generic char_traits template must be specialized to provide useful character properties. The standard string class specializes the char_traits template for a string of characters (char) and a string of wide characters (wchar_t). So that it can take advantage of library functions that manipulate objects of type char, the specialization takes on the following form:

```
class char_traits<char>;
```

Likewise, to allow manipulation of objects of type wchar_t, the specialization takes on the following form:

```
class char_traits<wchar_t>;
```

Investigating the *basic_string* Class

The basic_string class is a container similar to a vector, but its methods are tailored to work with strings. Examining a class's specification is a great way to learn what the class can do. Because the basic_string template in <string> contains the interface for the string class, it's presented in small subsections throughout this chapter.

Note

The standard string template **basic_string** uses the **char_traits** specializations to define character set properties of the string.

Everything in the `basic_string` class is declared using public access except the allocator, which is protected. Many methods are declared as `const`, which offers some additional protection (later in this chapter we'll look at the class members in more detail, by classification and purpose). For now, you should just be aware of these major classifications of class members:

- String operators
- String iterators
- String construction
- String functions

Using String Operators

The `basic_string` class template provides three operators, listed in Table 30.1. These operators are supplemented by the binary operator templates defined in the standard header <string>.

TABLE 30.1   **The Member Operators Provided by the *basic_string* Class Template**

Operator	Description
`operator+=`	Appends the operand sequence to the end of the string sequence.
`operator=`	Replaces the existing string sequence with the operand sequence.
`operator[]`	Returns a reference to the element of the sequence at specified position.

Here's an example using all three `basic_string` class member operators:

```cpp
#include <iostream>
#include <string>

void main()
{
  std::string str = "This is a";      // operator=
  str += " Test String\n";            // operator+=
  std::cout << "The string is: " << str;
```

```
      std::cout << "The fourth char of str is: '"
        << str[3] << "'" << std::endl;   // operator[]
    }
```

This code results in the following output:

```
The string is: This is a Test String
The fourth char of str is: 's'
```

In addition to these three unary member operators, the standard header <string> also provides nine binary operator functions as overloaded templates that handle a variety of operands. These operator templates are listed in Table 30.2.

TABLE 30.2   Binary Operator Function Templates Defined in *<string>*

Operator	Description
operator+	Concatenates two objects of template class `basic_string`.
operator!=	Compares two objects of template class `basic_string` for inequality.
operator==	Compares two objects of template class `basic_string` for equality.
operator<	Compares two objects of template class `basic_string` to see whether the left operand is lexicographically less than the right operand.
operator<<	Inserts an object of template class `basic_string` into a specified stream.
operator<=	Compares two objects of template class `basic_string` to see whether the left operand is lexicographically less than or equal to the right operand.
operator>	Compares two objects of template class `basic_string` to see whether the left operand is lexicographically greater than the right operand.
operator>=	Compares two objects of template class `basic_string` to see whether the left operand is lexicographically greater than or equal to the right operand.
operator>>	Extracts an object of template class `basic_string` from a specified stream, replacing the existing sequence, if any.

String Iterators

Like all standard container classes, the `string` class provides iterators for traversing the sequence of container objects. These iterators are obtained through the use of several familiar member functions, described in Table 30.3.

TABLE 30.3   **The *basic_string* Iterator Functions**

Function	Description
`begin()`	Returns a random-access iterator pointing to the first element of the sequence. If the sequence is empty, the iterator points just beyond the end of the empty sequence.
`end()`	Returns a random-access iterator pointing just beyond the end of the sequence.
`rbegin()`	Returns the beginning of the reverse sequence: a reverse iterator pointing just beyond the end of the sequence.
`rend()`	Returns the end of the reverse sequence: a reverse iterator pointing at the first element of the sequence (or just beyond the end of an empty sequence).

String Construction

The declaration for class `basic_string` contains many overloaded template functions; seven of these template functions are the following overloaded constructors:

```
template <class E, class T = char_traits<E>,
  class A = allocator<T> >
class basic_string
{
public:

  //...

  // Constructors
  //
  explicit basic_string(const A& al = A());
  basic_string(const basic_string& rhs);
  basic_string(const basic_string& rhs, size_type pos,
```

```
     size_type n, const A& al = A());
  basic_string(const E *s, size_type n,
    const A& al = A());
  basic_string(const E *s, const A& al = A());
  basic_string(size_type n, E c, const A& al = A());
  basic_string(const_iterator first,
    const_iterator last, const A& al = A());


  //...
};
```

You can initialize strings using C-style null-terminated strings, string literals, and other strings. Integers are incompatible, so a single character, which is an integral type, is invalid for constructing a string object. Some examples of using the string constructors are given in Listing 30.2.

LISTING 30.2   **A Program Demonstrating Various String Constructors**

```
 1: ////////////////////////////////////////////////////
 2: // Module : construct.cpp
 3: //
 4: // Purpose : Demonstrates string class constructors.
 5: ////////////////////////////////////////////////////
 6:
 7: #include <iostream>
 8: #include <string>
 9:
10: ////////////////////////////////////////////////////
11: // main()
12:
13: void main()
14: {
15:   std::string str1;
16:   std::string str2("Hal? Open the door, Hal!");
17:   std::string str3(str2);
18:   std::string str4(str3 + "!");
19:   std::string str5(54, '/');
20:   std::string str6(str3, 0, 4);
```

LISTING 30.2

① Lines 15-20: Use various string constructors

continues…

LISTING 30.2 CONTINUED

2 Lines 22-27: Display the
  resulting strings

LISTING 30.2   **Continued**

```
21:
22:   std::cout << "str1: " << str1 << std::endl;
23:   std::cout << "str2: " << str2 << std::endl;
24:   std::cout << "str3: " << str3 << std::endl;
25:   std::cout << "str4: " << str4 << std::endl;
26:   std::cout << "str5: " << str5 << std::endl;
27:   std::cout << "str6: " << str6 << std::endl;
28: }
```

The output from this program dumps the contents of the strings after construction, as follows:

```
str1:
str2: Hal? Open the door, Hal!
str3: Hal? Open the door, Hal!
str4: Hal? Open the door, Hal!!
str5: //////////////////////////////////////////////////////
str6: Hal?
```

This program uses a different constructor for each string. The first constructor in line 15 is the default constructor, resulting in an empty string. The constructor on line 16 is initialized with a string literal. The constructor on line 17 is initialized with a string. The constructor on line 18 uses the concatenation operator in the construction expression. The constructor on line 19 creates 54 copies of the slash character ('/'), and the constructor on line 20 grabs four characters from str3, starting at sequence element zero.

Using String Functions

The declaration for class basic_char contains many overloaded member template functions, and these can be categorized by purpose into these types:

- Assignment methods
- Appending and inserting methods
- Informational methods
- Standard C-style string conversion methods

- String comparison methods
- String search and replace methods
- Substring manipulation methods

Let's take a closer look at these diverse and highly useful member functions.

Assignment Methods

The `basic_string` class provides three overloaded assignment operators and five overloaded assignment methods, as seen in this section of the `basic_string` class:

```
template <class E, class T = char_traits<E>,
  class A = allocator<T> >
class basic_string
{
public:

  //...

  // Assignment operators and methods
  //
  basic_string& operator=(const basic_string& rhs);
  basic_string& operator=(const E *s);
  basic_string& operator=(E c);

  basic_string& assign(const basic_string& str);
  basic_string& assign(const basic_string& str,
    size_type pos, size_type n);
  basic_string& assign(const E *s, size_type n);
  basic_string& assign(const E *s);
  basic_string& assign(size_type n, E c);
  basic_string& assign(const_iterator first,
    const_iterator last);

  // ...
};
```

The `basic_string::assign()` method is demonstrated in the program in Listing 30.3.

LISTING 30.3

🕐 Lines 21-24: Use the
assign() function

LISTING 30.3   **A Program That Demonstrates the String *assign()* Functions**

```
 1: ////////////////////////////////////////////////////////
 2: // Module : assign.cpp
 3: //
 4: // Purpose : Demonstrates the string class assign()
 5: //          function,
 6: ////////////////////////////////////////////////////////
 7:
 8: #include <iostream>
 9: #include <string>
10:
11: ////////////////////////////////////////////////////////
12: // main()
13:
14: void main()
15: {
16:   std::string str1;
17:   std::string str2;
18:   std::string str3;
19:   std::string str4;
20:
21:   str1.assign("Testing...");
22:   str2.assign("Hal? Open the door, Hal!");
23:   str3.assign(str2);
24:   str4.assign(str3 + "!");
25:
26:   std::cout << "str1: " << str1 << std::endl;
27:   std::cout << "str2: " << str2 << std::endl;
28:   std::cout << "str3: " << str3 << std::endl;
29:   std::cout << "str4: " << str4 << std::endl;
30: }
```

This program produces output similar to that from the previous
example. The code in Listings 30.2 and 30.3 are nearly identical,
but Listing 30.3 uses the basic_string::assign() method instead
of the basic_string::operator=() and class constructors used by
Listing 30.2, as you can see here:

```
str1: Testing...
str2: Hal? Open the door, Hal!
str3: Hal? Open the door, Hal!
str4: Hal? Open the door, Hal!!
```

Appending and Inserting Methods

Appending a string to an existing string is a common operation. The `basic_string` class provides the `basic_string::operator+=()` function to allow you to append a string with an operator, like this:

```
string str1 = "Who is";
string str2 = " John Galt?";
str1 += str2;
```

This code produces the string `Who is John Galt?`

The `basic_string` class also provides several overloaded `append()` and `insert()` functions, as seen in this section of the class declaration:

```
template <class E, class T = char_traits<E>,
  class A = allocator<T> >
class basic_string
{
public:

  //...

  // Append functions
  //
  basic_string& append(const basic_string& str);
  basic_string& append(const basic_string& str,
    size_type pos, size_type n);
  basic_string& append(const E *s, size_type n);
  basic_string& append(const E *s);
  basic_string& append(size_type n, E c);
  basic_string& append(const_iterator first,
    const_iterator last);

  // Insert functions
  //
  basic_string& insert(size_type p0,
    const basic_string& str);
  basic_string& insert(size_type p0,
    const basic_string& str, size_type pos,
    size_type n);
```

```
basic_string& insert(size_type p0,
  const E *s, size_type n);
basic_string& insert(size_type p0, const E *s);
basic_string& insert(size_type p0, size_type n,
  E c);
iterator insert(iterator it, E c);
void insert(iterator it, size_type n, E c);
void insert(iterator it, const_iterator first,
  const_iterator last);

// ...
};
```

The program in Listing 30.4 shows the append() and insert() functions in action.

LISTING 30.4   A Program Showing the Use of the String *append()* and *insert()* Functions

```
 1: /////////////////////////////////////////////////////////
 2: // Module : append_insert.cpp
 3: //
 4: // Purpose : Demonstrates the string class append()
 5: //      and insert() members.
 6: /////////////////////////////////////////////////////////
 7:
 8: #include <iostream>
 9: #include <string>
10:
11: using std::cout;
12: using std::endl;
13: using std::string;
14:
15: /////////////////////////////////////////////////////////
16: // main()
17:
18: void main()
19: {
20:  // Create some string objects
21:  //
```

```
22:   string s1 = "Have a";
23:   string s2 = " ";
24:   string s3 = "nice day";
25:   string s4 = "A mind is a thing to waste!";
26:   string s5 = "terrible ";
27:
28:   s1.append(s2); // s1 == "Have a "
29:   cout << "s1 == " << s1 << endl;
30:
31:   s1.append(s3); // s1 == "Have a nice day"
32:   cout << "s1 == " << s1 << endl;
33:
34:   // Append 1 element from s4 starting at position 26
35:   //
36:   s1.append(s4, 26, 1); // s1 == "Have a nice day!"
37:   cout << "s1 == " << s1 << endl;
38:
39:   // Append a regular char array
40:   //
41:   char *array = " Please...";
42:   s1.append(array);
43:   cout << "s1 == " << s1 << endl;
44:
45:   // Insert
46:   //
47:   cout << "s4 == " << s4 << endl;
48:   s4.insert(12, s5);
49:   cout << "s4 == " << s4 << endl;
50:
51:   s4.insert(s4.end(), 5, '!');
52:   cout << "s4 == " << s4 << endl;
53: }
```

1

2

LISTING 30.4

1 Lines 22-26: Create some strings to manipulate

2 Line 36: Append a single character from one string to another

This program produces the following output:

```
s1 == Have a
s1 == Have a nice day
s1 == Have a nice day!
s1 == Have a nice day! Please...
s4 == A mind is a thing to waste!
s4 == A mind is a terrible thing to waste!
s4 == A mind is a terrible thing to waste!!!!!!
```

This program begins by creating five strings and assigning each a literal string value (lines 22 through 26). These statements are followed by the first append operation on line 28, where the `string::append()` function is called to append string s2 to string s1. Line 31 calls the function again, appending string s3 to string s1. Line 36 calls a different version of `string::append()` to extract a substring from another string object and append that substring to itself. In this case, the string s1 is extracting from string s4 one character, at position 26 (the exclamation point). On line 43, a regular character array is appended.

On line 48, string s4 inserts string s5 into its sequence at position 12 (just before t in thing). Line 52 finishes up the program, inserting five exclamation points at the end of string s4.

Informational Methods

The `basic_string` informational methods deal with memory issues related to container size and capacity—they provide information about a string. These methods appear in the `basic_string` class declaration like this:

```
template <class E, class T = char_traits<E>,
  class A = allocator<T> >
class basic_string
{
public:

  //...

  // Informational methods
  //
  size_type capacity() const;
  bool empty() const;
  size_type length() const;
  size_type max_size() const;
  size_type size() const;
  void reserve(size_type n = 0);
  void resize(size_type n, E c = E());

  A get_allocator() const;
```

```
  // ...
};
```

These methods are described in Table 30.4.

TABLE 30.4 **The Informational Methods Provided by the Standard**
basic_string **Class**

Function	Description
capacity()	Returns the amount of storage currently allocated to hold the sequence.
empty()	Returns true if the sequence is empty.
length()	Returns the length of the sequence (just as size() does).
max_size()	Returns the length of the longest sequence that the object can contain.
size()	Returns the length of the sequence.
reserve()	Reserves storage for the string.
resize()	Resizes the string to contain more elements.
get_allocator()	Returns the allocator for the string.

Standard C-Style String Conversion Methods

The basic_string conversion methods designed to work with C-style strings appear in the basic_string class declaration like this:

```
template <class E, class T = char_traits<E>,
  class A = allocator<T> >
class basic_string
{
public:

  //...

  // String conversion methods
  //
  size_type copy(E *s, size_type n,
   size_type pos = 0) const;
  const E *c_str() const;
  const E *data() const;
```

Note

The string conversion functions allow you to use C-style strings with common ANSI C library functions.

```
    // ...
};
```

These class member functions are described in Table 30.5.

TABLE 30.5   **The String Conversion Methods Provided by the Standard**
basic_string **Class**

Function	Description
copy()	Copies a specified number of elements from the sequence, starting at a specified position.
c_str()	Returns a pointer to a read-only, C-style, null-terminated string.
data()	Returns a pointer to the first element of the sequence.

The string conversion functions convert standard strings to C-style strings. The use of these functions is shown in the following code snippets. Using the string::c_str() method is painless, giving a temporary const pointer to the underlying character array, like this:

```
// Using the string::c_str() member
//
string s1 = "std::string makes it easy!";
const char *ps1 = s1.c_str();   // must be const
cout << ps1 << endl;
```

Using the string::data() method is just as easy, giving a temporary const pointer to the first array element, like this:

```
// Same thing using the string::data() member
//
string s2 = "std::string makes it easy!";
const char *ps2 = s2.data();
cout << ps2 << endl;
```

Using the string::copy() method gives you the power to copy a string to a modifiable character array, like this:

```
// Modifiable, using the string::copy() member
//
string s3 = "std::string makes it easy!";
char *ps3 = new char[s3.length()+1];
```

```
s3.copy(ps3, s3.length());
ps3[s3.length()] = '\0';  // add null terminator!!
cout << ps3 << endl;
delete [] ps3;
```

In this last case, you must add the null-terminator, or the cout object will likely overrun the string bounds, causing an error.

String Comparison Methods

The overloaded basic_string::compare() methods perform various types of string comparisons. These methods appear in the basic_string class declaration like this:

```
template <class E, class T = char_traits<E>,
  class A = allocator<T> >
class basic_string
{
public:

  //...

  // String comparison methods
  //
  int compare(const basic_string& str) const;
  int compare(size_type p0, size_type n0,
   const basic_string& str);
  int compare(size_type p0, size_type n0,
   const basic_string& str, size_type pos, size_type n);
  int compare(const E *s) const;
  int compare(size_type p0, size_type n0,
   const E *s) const;
  int compare(size_type p0, size_type n0,
   const E *s, size_type pos) const;

  // ...
};
```

The basic_string::compare() methods all return an integer value. If the return value is less than zero, the string being compared is lexicographically less than the string object performing the comparison. If the return value is zero, the strings are equal. If the return value is greater than zero, the string being

Note

String comparisons are often used to find or match data in a data file. For example, a data file might be scanned until the name *John Smith* is found, and then some action would be taken with the data following that point.

Lexicographical Comparisons

A lexicographical comparison alphabetically compares the characters of two strings, just like words are organized in a dictionary. Using the dictionary metaphor, if word A comes before word B in the dictionary, word A is said to be lexicographically less than word B. Using the same terminology, word B is said to be lexicographically greater than word A. For example, the word *apple* is lexicographically less than the word *zebra*.

compared is lexicographically greater than the string object performing the comparison. As an example, take a look at the program in Listing 30.5.

LISTING 30.5

① Lines 20-22: Create some strings

② Line 26: Use the compare() function

LISTING 30.5   **A Program That Demonstrates the Standard String** *compare()* **Method**

```cpp
1: ///////////////////////////////////////////////////
2: // Module : compare.cpp
3: //
4: // Purpose : Demonstrates the string class compare()
5: //        member.
6: ///////////////////////////////////////////////////
7:
8: #include <iostream>
9: #include <string>
10:
11: using std::cout;
12: using std::endl;
13: using std::string;
14:
15: ///////////////////////////////////////////////////
16: // main()
17:
18: void main()
19: {
20:   string str1 = "Rob";
21:   string str2 = "Carleen";
22:   string str3 = "Tara";
23:
24:   cout << "The string " << str1
25:     << " compares the string " << str2 << " giving: "
26:     << str1.compare(str2) << endl;
27:
28:   cout << "The string " << str2
29:     << " compares the string " << str3 << " giving: "
30:     << str2.compare(str3) << endl;
31:
32:   cout << "The string " << str3
33:     << " compares the string " << str1 << " giving: "
34:     << str3.compare(str1) << endl;
35: }
```

The output from this program shows how the comparison works:

```
The string Rob compares the string Carleen giving: 1
The string Carleen compares the string Tara giving: -1
The string Tara compares the string Rob giving: 1
```

String Find and Replace Methods

The basic_string class provides lots of overloaded functions for finding strings and substrings. These overloaded methods perform various types of string searching; they appear in the basic_string class declaration like this:

```
template <class E, class T = char_traits<E>,
  class A = allocator<T> >
class basic_string
{
public:

  //...

  // String finding methods
  //
  size_type find(const basic_string& str,
   size_type pos = 0) const;
  size_type find(const E *s, size_type pos,
   size_type n) const;
  size_type find(const E *s, size_type pos = 0) const;
  size_type find(E c, size_type pos = 0) const;

  size_type rfind(const basic_string& str,
   size_type pos = npos) const;
  size_type rfind(const E *s, size_type pos,
   size_type n = npos) const;
  size_type rfind(const E *s,
   size_type pos = npos) const;
  size_type rfind(E c, size_type pos = npos) const;
```

```
                size_type find_first_of(const basic_string& str,
                size_type pos = 0) const;
                size_type find_first_of(const E *s, size_type pos,
                size_type n) const;
                size_type find_first_of(const E *s,
                 size_type pos = 0) const;
                size_type find_first_of(E c,
                 size_type pos = 0) const;

                size_type find_last_of(const basic_string& str,
                 size_type pos = npos) const;
                size_type find_last_of(const E *s, size_type pos,
                 size_type n = npos) con/t;
                size_type find_last_of(const E *s,
                 size_type pos = npos) const;
                size_type find_last_of(E c,
                 size_type pos = npos) const;

                size_type find_first_not_of(const basic_string& str,
                 size_type pos = 0) const;
                size_type find_first_not_of(const E *s,
                 size_type pos, size_type n) const;
                size_type find_first_not_of(const E *s,
                 size_type pos = 0) const;
                size_type find_first_not_of(E c,
                 size_type pos = 0) const;

                size_type find_last_not_of(const basic_string& str,
                 size_type pos = npos) const;
                size_type find_last_not_of(const E *s,
                 size_type pos, size_type n) const;
                size_type find_last_not_of(const E *s,
                 size_type pos = npos) const;
                size_type find_last_not_of(E c,
                 size_type pos = npos) const;

                // ...
            };
```

These functions are described in Table 30.6.

TABLE 30.6 **The String-Finding Functions of Class** *basic_string*

Function	Description
find()	Returns the position of the first occurrence of the specified string in the sequence, beginning on or after a specified position.
rfind()	Returns the position of the last occurrence of the specified string in the sequence, beginning on or after a specified position.
find_first_of()	Returns the position of the first occurrence of the specified string in the sequence, beginning on or after a specified position.
find_last_of()	Returns the position of the last occurrence of the specified string in the sequence, beginning on or after a specified position.
find_first_not_of()	Returns the first position in the sequence that doesn't match the specified string, beginning on or after a specified position.
find_last_not_of()	Returns the last position in the sequence that doesn't match the specified string, beginning on or after a specified position.

In addition to just finding strings, standard strings can replace strings, too—the basic_string class provides several overloaded functions that replace strings and substrings. These overloaded methods perform various types of string replacement; they appear in the basic_string class declaration like this:

```
template <class E, class T = char_traits<E>,
  class A = allocator<T> >
class basic_string
{
public:

  //...

  // String finding methods
  //
  basic_string& replace(size_type p0, size_type n0,
   const basic_string& str);
  basic_string& replace(size_type p0, size_type n0,
```

```
              const basic_string& str, size_type pos,
              size_type n);
          basic_string& replace(size_type p0, size_type n0,
              const E *s, size_type n);
          basic_string& replace(size_type p0, size_type n0,
              const E *s);
          basic_string& replace(size_type p0, size_type n0,
              size_type n, E c);
          basic_string& replace(iterator first0,
              iterator last0, const basic_string& str);
          basic_string& replace(iterator first0,
              iterator last0, const E *s, size_type n);
          basic_string& replace(iterator first0,
              iterator last0, const E *s);
          basic_string& replace(iterator first0,
              iterator last0, size_type n, E c);
          basic_string& replace(iterator first0,
              iterator last0, const_iterator first,
              const_iterator last);

      //...
      };
```

The program in Listing 30.6 shows the use of the find and replace functions.

LISTING 30.6   **A Program Demonstrating the String *find* and *replace* Functions**

```
 1: //////////////////////////////////////////////////////////
 2: // Module : find_replace.cpp
 3: //
 4: // Purpose : Demonstrates the string class find and
 5: //           replace members.
 6: //////////////////////////////////////////////////////////
 7:
 8: #include <iostream>
 9: #include <string>
10:
11: using std::cout;
12: using std::endl;
13: using std::string;
14:
```

```
15: ///////////////////////////////////////////////////////
16: // main()
17:
18: void main()
19: {
20: //     0    1    2
21: //     012345678901234567890
22:    string s = "Testing... Testing...";
23:    cout << "s == \"" << s << "\"\n\n";
24:    cout << "Looking for \"ing\"\n\n";
25:    int pos[7];
26:
27:    pos[0] = s.find("ing");
28:    pos[1] = s.rfind("ing");
29:    pos[2] = s.find_first_of("ing");
30:    pos[3] = s.find_last_of("ing");
31:    pos[4] = s.find_first_not_of("ing");
32:    pos[5] = s.find_last_not_of("ing");
33:    pos[6] = s.find("Shaken not stirred"); // -1
34:
35:    for (int i = 0; i < 7; ++i)
36:      cout << "pos[" << i << "] == " << pos[i] << endl;
37:
38:    // Replace some stuff...
39:    //
40:    cout << "\nReplacing 'e' with 'a'\n";
41:    s.replace(1, 1, "a");
42:    s.replace(s.rfind("e"), 1, "a");
43:    cout << "s == \"" << s << "\"\n";
44:
45:    cout << "\nReplacing \"ing...\" with 'e'\n";
46:    s.replace(s.find("ing..."), 6, "e");
47:    s.replace(s.rfind("a"), 1, "e");
48:    cout << "s == \"" << s << "\"\n";
49: }
```

LISTING 30.6 CONTINUED

1 Line 22: Create a test string

2 Lines 25-33: Find substring positions

3 Lines 46-47: Replace substrings

The output for this program is as follows:

```
s == "Testing... Testing..."

Looking for "ing"
```

```
pos[0] == 4
pos[1] == 15
pos[2] == 4
pos[3] == 17
pos[4] == 0
pos[5] == 20
pos[6] == -1

Replacing 'e' with 'a'
s == "Tasting... Tasting..."

Replacing "ing..." with 'e'
s == "Taste Testing..."
```

This program begins by creating the test string s on line 22; then it declares an array of seven integers (pos[]) on line 25. These seven elements hold the positions of substrings found using the various find functions from lines 27 through 33. The most interesting case here is pos[6], which ends up with a value of -1 (because the string Shaken not stirred is not found within the string Testing... Testing...). Lines 35 and 36 iterate through the pos array, displaying the position values returned by the find functions. Study the output and the code for a while, and you will see the light.

Line 41 actually uses the string::replace() method to replace a substring that starts at position 1 and is one element long, with the substring e. Line 42 uses the string::rfind() method to find the last occurrence of a, and string::replace() replaces it with a. This turns Testing...Testing... into Tasting...Tasting.... The replace statements on lines 46 and 47 are similar, replacing the first ing with e, and replacing the last a with e. This turns Tasting...Tasting... into Taste Testing....

In addition to the find and replace functions, the subscript operator[] function you saw earlier in this chapter gives you access to individual elements in the sequence. Using this operator, you can work with a standard string as if it were a regular character array. For example, you can output a string's contents with one single character per line like this:

```
string s = "Spa";

for (int i = 0; i < s.length() + 1; ++i)
  cout << s[i] << endl;
```

This code results in the following output onscreen:

```
s
p
a
```

It's easy to swap characters with the subscript operator, too, for example:

```
string s = "Spa";

s[2] = 'y';
cout << s << endl;
```

This code yields the string Spy instead of the original Spa.

Substring Manipulation Methods

The standard string supports substring manipulation with the basic_string::substr() method, which reads part of a string. The method appears in the basic_string class declaration like this:

```
template <class E, class T = char_traits<E>,
  class A = allocator<T> >
class basic_string
{
public:

  //...

  // Substring method
  //
  basic_string substr(size_type pos = 0,
   size_type n = npos) const;

  //...
};
```

You use the `basic_string::substr()` method by specifying the starting position and number of elements to read from the string, like this:

```
string s1 = "Testing... Testing...";
string s2;

for (int i = 0; i < s1.length() + 1; ++i)
{
  s2 = s1.substr(0, i);
  cout << "" << s2 << endl;
}
```

The value returned is the substring you requested, assigned to string s2. When the `for` loop in this snippet iterates, it grabs one more character each time, as `i` increments, producing this lovely patterned output:

```
T
Te
Tes
Test
Testi
Testin
Testing
Testing.
Testing..
Testing...
Testing...
Testing... T
Testing... Te
Testing... Tes
Testing... Test
Testing... Testi
Testing... Testin
Testing... Testing
Testing... Testing.
Testing... Testing..
Testing... Testing...
```

Well, that wraps up our discussion of strings.... In the next chapter, we'll take a look at the number-crunching power of standard C++.

Working with Numerics

Identifying Numeric Headers

The Standard C++ Library provides loads of functionality for numeric processing, a common programming task. Table 31.1 describes each of the standard headers that support numeric operations for standard C++.

TABLE 31.1   Standard Headers That Support Numeric Operations

Header	Purpose
<cmath>	Includes the standard C header <math.h> within the std namespace, providing standard math functions.
<cstdlib>	Includes the standard C header <stdlib.h> within the std namespace, providing random number generation.
<complex>	Provides a class template describing an object that stores both the real part and the imaginary part of a complex number.
<valarray>	Defines the class template valarray along with many supporting template classes and functions, providing numeric vectors and operations.
<limits>	Defines the class template numeric_limits. Specializations of this template class describe arithmetic properties of the scalar data types.
<numeric>	Defines algorithmic function templates useful for computing special numeric values based on sequences.

Using Standard Math Functions

To use the math functions inherited from ANSI C, just include the standard header <cmath> in your programs. Instantly, you get access to a wide variety of very useful standard math functions. These functions are described in Table 31.2.

TABLE 31.2   Some Commonly Used Math Functions Declared in the Standard Header <cmath>

Function	Description
abs()	Returns the absolute value of its argument.
acos()	Returns the arccosine of its argument.

Function	Description
asin()	Returns the arcsine of its argument.
atan()	Returns the arctangent of its argument.
atan2()	Returns the arctangent of the quotient of its two arguments.
atof()	Converts a string argument to a double.
atoi()	Converts a string argument to an integer.
atol()	Converts a string argument to a long.
ceil()	Returns the smallest integer (the numeric ceiling) greater than or equal to its argument.
cos()	Returns the cosine of its argument.
cosh()	Returns the hyperbolic cosine of its argument.
exp()	Returns the exponential value of its argument.
fabs()	Returns the absolute value of its floating-point argument.
floor()	Returns the greatest integer (the numeric floor) less than or equal to its argument.
fmod()	Returns the floating-point remainder of its argument.
labs()	Returns the absolute value of its long integer argument.
log()	Returns the natural logarithm of its argument.
log10()	Returns the base 10 logarithm of its argument.
modf()	Splits a floating-point value into fractional and integer parts.
pow()	Raises a number to a specified power.
sin()	Returns the sine of its argument.
sinh()	Returns the hyperbolic sine of its argument.
sqrt()	Returns the square root of its argument.
tan()	Returns the tangent of its argument.
tanh()	Returns the hyperbolic tangent of a number.

These functions are straightforward and easy to use. For example, to calculate the cosine of a number, just do this:

```
double Val = 45.29;
double CosVal = cosine(val);
```

To compute the value of 10 to the third power, use the pow() function, like this:

```
double retVal = pow(10.0, 3.0);
```

Generating Random Numbers

The standard library header <cstdlib> provides a standard way to generate random numbers, using the standard library functions described in Table 31.3.

TABLE 31.3   **The Random Number Functions Found in the Standard Header** *<cstdlib>*

Function	Description
srand()	Seeds the random number generator.
rand()	Generates a pseudo-random number.

The problem with the rand() function is that the numbers returned aren't **really** random—they're only *pseudo-random*. The numbers generated depend on the seed value specified with srand(). If you use the same seed value each time, the same "random" numbers will be generated. To provide truly random numbers, a common method is to seed the random number generator using the system clock on your computer, virtually ensuring that duplicate seeds won't be used in separate runs of the program. The standard library function time() returns the system time. Using the return value of time() as the seed value for srand() works like this:

```
srand((unsigned)time(0));
```

To get a random number within a certain range, you can define a function to return such a random number. Listing 31.1 presents a simple class called CRand. This class generates random numbers within a specified minimum and maximum range.

LISTING 31.1   **The Header for a Random Number Generating Class**

```
 1: ////////////////////////////////////////////////////
 2: //   Module : rmrandom.h
 3: //
 4: //   Purpose : Interface and implementation of a
 5: //             random number generating class.
 6: ////////////////////////////////////////////////////
 7:
 8: #ifndef __RMRANDOM_H__
 9: #define __RMRANDOM_H__
10:
11: #include <cstdlib>  // for srand(), rand()
12: #include <ctime>    // for time()
13:
14: ////////////////////////////////////////////////////
15: // CRand class
16:
17: class CRand
18: {
19: public:
20:
21:    // Seed the random number generator
22:    // during construction
23:
24:    CRand() { srand((unsigned)time(0)); }
25:    CRand(unsigned seed) { srand(seed); }
26:
27:    // Get a random number
28:    //
29:    int GetRandom(int min, int max)
30:    {
31:       if (max < 0) max = 0;
32:       if ((min == max) && (min == 0))
33:          return 0;
34:       return rand() % (max + 1 - min) + min;
35:    }
36: };
37:
38: #endif  // __RMRANDOM_H__
```

LISTING 31.1

1 Lines 23-24: Seed the random number generator during construction

2 Lines 29-35: Generate a random number within a given range

This class wraps a call to rand() in the CRand::GetRandom() function. Because the constructor seeds the random number generator with the current time value, all you have to do is declare a CRand object and call its GetRandom() function, specifying a range as parameters. To test the CRand class, a simple driver program is in order. This driver program is provided in Listing 31.2.

LISTING 31.2

1 Line 16: Create a CRand object

2 Line 20: Call CRand::
GetRandom() to generate a
number between 0 and 100,
inclusive

LISTING 31.2   **A Driver Program to Test the *CRand* Class**

```
1: //////////////////////////////////////////////////////
2: //   Module  : random.cpp
3: //
4: //   Purpose : Demonstrates the random number class
5: //             CRMRand.
6: //////////////////////////////////////////////////////
7:
8: #include <iostream>
9: #include "rmrandom.h"
10:
11: //////////////////////////////////////////////////////
12: //   main()
13:
14: void main()
15: {
16:     CRand rand;  ———— ①
17:
18:     for (int i = 0; i < 10; ++i)
19:         std::cout << "Random number " << i + 1 << ": "
20:             << rand.GetRandom(0, 100) << std::endl;  ———— ②
21: }
```

The random numbers output by this program during a test run of the program were as follows:

```
Random number 1: 95
Random number 2: 12
Random number 3: 82
Random number 4: 44
Random number 5: 60
Random number 6: 60
Random number 7: 8
Random number 8: 67
Random number 9: 35
Random number 10: 14
```

Working with Complex Numbers

Complex numbers have a real part and an imaginary part. A discussion of complex number theory is beyond the scope of this book, but the Standard C++ Library provides the standard header <complex> to define a template class for complex numbers. In addition to the generic complex class, the header also defines three specializations of the complex class:

- complex<double>

- complex<float>

- complex<long double>

Table 31.4 describes the template functions available in the standard header <complex>.

TABLE 31.4   The Template Functions Available for Use with Complex Numbers in the Standard Header *<complex>*

Function	Description
abs()	Returns the absolute value of its argument.
arg()	Returns the phase angle of its argument.
conjg()	Returns the conjugate of its argument.
cos()	Returns the imaginary cosine of its argument.
cosh()	Returns the hyperbolic cosine of its argument.
exp()	Returns the exponential value of its argument.
imag()	Returns the imaginary part of a complex number.
log()	Returns the natural logarithm of its argument.
log10()	Returns the base 10 logarithm of its argument.
norm()	Returns the squared magnitude of its argument.
operator!=()	Returns true if both the real and imaginary parts of two complex number operands are not equal.
operator*()	Returns the complex product of two operands.
operator+()	Returns the complex sum of two operands.
operator-()	Returns the complex difference of two operands.
operator/()	Returns the complex quotient of two operands.

continues…

TABLE 31.4   **Continued**

Function	Description
operator<<()	Inserts, into a specified output stream, the complex value of a specified complex object.
operator==()	Returns true if both the real and imaginary parts of two complex number operands are equal.
operator>>()	Attempts to extract, from a specified input stream, the complex value of a specified complex object.
polar()	Returns the complex value of a specified magnitude and phase angle.
pow()	Raises a specified complex number to a specified power.
real()	Returns the real part of a complex number.
sin()	Returns the imaginary sine of its argument.
sinh()	Returns the hyperbolic sine of its argument.
sqrt()	Returns the square root of its argument.

Introducing *valarrays*

The Standard C++ Library provides a container class designed to contain numeric values; this template class is called valarray, declared in the Standard C++ Library header <valarray>. As does a vector, this template class describes an object that controls a varying-length sequence of elements of type T, stored as an array of type T. The class provides several operators useful for mathematical operations on complex numbers, as well as some template functions. All these operators and functions are described in Table 31.5.

TABLE 31.5   **The Operators and Functions Defined by the Standard *valarray* Template Class**

Function or Operator	Description
cshift()	Shifts elements circularly left a specified number of places.
fill()	Fills every element with the same specified value.

Function or Operator	Description
free()	Erases the array, leaving it with zero elements.
max()	Returns a value corresponding to the largest array element value.
min()	Returns a value corresponding to the smallest array element value.
operator T *()	Returns a pointer to the first element of the array, which must have at least one element.
operator!()	Returns a copy of the array, in which each element E is set to !E.
operator%=()	Performs a modulus operation between all internal elements and the valarray passed as a reference parameter.
operator&=()	Performs a bitwise AND operation between all elements of itself and the valarray passed as a reference parameter.
operator>>=()	Performs a right-shift operation between all elements of itself and the valarray passed as a reference parameter.
operator<<=()	Performs a left-shift operation between all elements of itself and the valarray passed as a reference parameter.
operator*=()	Performs a multiplication operation between all elements of itself and the valarray passed as a reference parameter.
operator+=()	Performs an addition operation between all elements of itself and the valarray passed as a reference parameter.
operator-()	Negates each element in the valarray.
operator-=()	Performs a subtraction operation between all elements of itself and the valarray passed as a reference parameter.
operator/=()	Performs a division operation between all elements of itself and the valarray passed as a reference parameter.
operator=()	Replaces a sequence with another sequence.
operator[]()	Permits direct access to valarray elements.
operator^=()	Performs a bitwise XOR operation between all elements of itself and the valarray passed as a reference parameter.

continues…

TABLE 31.5   **Continued**

Function or Operator	Description
operator¦=()	Performs a bitwise OR operation between all elements of itself and the valarray passed as a reference parameter.
operator~()	Performs a bitwise NOT operation between all elements of itself and the valarray passed as a reference parameter.
resize()	Changes the size of the container.
shift()	Performs a bit-shift operation on the elements of the array.
size()	Returns the number of elements in the array.
sum()	Returns the sum of all the elements in the array.

Exploring Numeric Algorithms

Generic Numeric Algorithms

An algorithm is a formalized process or set of rules used for calculations. All standard C++ algorithms, including those found in the standard header <numeric>, are templates that operate on container sequences in some way.

Four *generic numeric algorithms* are declared in the standard header <numeric>, which is designed to be fast and efficient. These four algorithms are described in Table 31.6.

TABLE 31.6   **The Template Functions That Implement the Standard Generic Numeric Algorithms Found in *<numeric>***

Algorithm	Description
accumulate()	Accumulates a value from a sequence of numbers.
inner_product()	Accumulates a value from two sequences of numbers.
partial_sum()	Calculates the end result of a set of incremental changes by adding adjacent element values.
adjacent_difference()	Calculates the end result of a set of incremental changes by subtracting adjacent element values.

These generic numeric algorithm functions deal with numeric-intensive operations and are declared in the standard header <numeric>, as shown in Listing 31.3.

LISTING 31.3 **The Generic Numeric Algorithms Found in the Standard Header**
<numeric>

```
 1: //////////////////////////////////////////////////
 2: // Numeric algorithm declarations
 3:
 4: // accumulate algorithm
 5: //
 6: template <class InIt, class T>
 7:     T accumulate(InIt first, InIt last, T val);
 8: template <class InIt, class T, class Pred>
 9:     T accumulate(InIt first, InIt last, T val, Pred pr);
10:
11: // inner_product algorithm
12: //
13: template <class InIt1, class InIt2, class T>
14:     T inner_product(InIt1 first1, InIt1 last1,
15:         Init2 first2, T val);
16: template <class InIt1, class InIt2, class T,
17:     class Pred1, class Pred2>
18:     T inner_product(InIt1 first1, InIt1 last1,
19:         Init2 first2, T val, Pred1 pr1, Pred2 pr2);
20:
21: // partial_sum algorithm
22: //
23: template <class InIt, class OutIt>
24:     OutIt partial_sum(InIt first, InIt last,
25:         OutIt result);
26: template <class InIt, class OutIt, class Pred>
27:     OutIt partial_sum(InIt first, InIt last,
28:         OutIt result, Pred pr);
29:
30: // adjacent_difference algorithm
31: //
32: template <class InIt, class OutIt>
33:     OutIt adjacent_difference(InIt first, InIt last,
34:         OutIt result);
35: template <class InIt, class OutIt, class Pred>
36:     OutIt adjacent_difference(InIt first, InIt last,
37:             OutIt result, Pred pr);
```

Let's take a closer look at each of these algorithms to see how
you can use them.

778

The *accumulate* Algorithm

The accumulate algorithm accumulates a value from a sequence of numbers. Two template functions are declared in the standard header <numeric> to implement this algorithm:

```
template <class InIt, class T>
    T accumulate(InIt first, InIt last, T val);


template <class InIt, class T, class Pred>
    T accumulate(InIt first, InIt last, T val, Pred pr);
```

In these functions the parameter first denotes the first number in the range, and the parameter last denotes the last number in the range. The parameter val is used to initialize an internal accumulator variable, used to do the accumulation. The first version of the function uses the operator+ by default, and the second version uses a predicate specifying some other binary operation to use for the accumulation.

These overloaded template functions iterate from first to last, repeatedly adding the value of *first++ to val until first equals last, returning the accumulated value initialized by val. For example, given the set of integers {1, 2, 3, 4, 5}, the accumulation would be as follows:

```
1 + 2 + 3 + 4 + 5 = 15
```

The sample program in Listing 31.4 demonstrates the use of accumulate().

LISTING 31.4   A Program That Demonstrates the *accumulate* Algorithm

```
 1: ////////////////////////////////////////////////////////
 2: //   Module  : accumulate.cpp
 3: //
 4: //   Purpose : Demonstrates the accumulate algorithm
 5: ////////////////////////////////////////////////////////
 6:
 7: #include <iostream>
 8: #include <vector>
 9: #include <numeric>
10:
11: using namespace std;
```

```
12:
13: typedef vector<int> IntVector; ———①
14:
15: /////////////////////////////////////////////////////////
16: //  main()
17:
18: void main()
19: {
20:     // Create a vector of integers
21:     //
22:     IntVector iv;
23:
24:     // Fill it with values
25:     //
26:     for (int i = 1; i < 11; ++i)
27:         iv.push_back(i); ———②
28:
29:     // Accumulate
30:     //
31:     cout << " 0 + 1 + 2 + 3 + ... + 9 + 10 == "
32:         << accumulate(iv.begin(), iv.end(), 0) << endl; ┐
33:                                                          ├ ③
34:     cout << "10 + 1 + 2 + 3 + ... + 9 + 10 == "          │
35:         << accumulate(iv.begin(), iv.end(), 10) << endl; ┘
36: }
```

LISTING 31.4

① Line 13: A type alias for vector<int>

② Line 27: Add values to the vector

③ Lines 32-35: Accumulate values using accumulate()

The output from this program is as follows:

```
 0 + 1 + 2 + 3 + ... + 9 + 10 == 55
10 + 1 + 2 + 3 + ... + 9 + 10 == 65
```

This program begins by defining the type alias IntVector for the vector specialization vector<int> on line 13. This definition is followed by the creation of an IntVector object iv on line 22. The for loop on lines 26 and 27 adds items to the vector using the vector::push_back() method.

The accumulate() function is called on line 32, accumulating a value composed of all elements in the vector, as specified by the iterator values iv.begin() and iv.end(). The third argument is the additional amount to accumulate—in this case, a zero. The accumulate() function is called again on line 35, this time with the third argument having a value of 10 as the additional amount to accumulate. In both cases, the cout object displays the resulting accumulation value.

The *inner_product* Algorithm

The inner_product algorithm accumulates a value from two sequences of numbers. The algorithm is implemented in the inner_product() function declared in the standard header <numeric>, using the following function templates:

```
template <class InIt1, class InIt2, class T>
    T inner_product(InIt1 first1, InIt1 last1,
        Init2 first2, T val);
```

```
template <class InIt1, class InIt2, class T,
    class Pred1, class Pred2>
    T inner_product(InIt1 first1, InIt1 last1,
        Init2 first2, T val, Pred1 pr1, Pred2 pr2);
```

In these functions the parameter first1 denotes the first number in the range of the first sequence, and the parameter last1 denotes the last number in the sequence range. The parameter first2 denotes the first number in the range of the second sequence, and its range is assumed to be the same as that of the first sequence. The parameter val is used to initialize an internal accumulator variable, used to do the accumulation. The first version of the function performs binary addition and multiplication operations by default, and the second version uses two predicates specifying some other binary operations to use for the inner product calculation.

Given two sequences of numbers, the inner_product algorithm calculates the sum of products of elements in corresponding positions in the two sequences. For example, given the two sets of numbers {1, 2, 3} and {4, 5, 6} and an initial value of 10, the inner product is calculated like this (using the default addition and multiplication operations):

```
10 + (1 * 4) + (2 * 5) + (3 * 6) = 42
```

The program in Listing 31.5 demonstrates how to perform this very operation with C++ code.

LISTING 31.5   **A Program That Demonstrates the *inner_0product()* Function**

```
 1: //////////////////////////////////////////////////////
 2: //  Module  : inner_product.cpp
 3: //
 4: //  Purpose : Demonstrates the inner_product algorithm
 5: //////////////////////////////////////////////////////
 6:
 7: #include <iostream>
 8: #include <vector>
 9: #include <numeric>
10:
11: using namespace std;
12:
13: typedef vector<int> IntVector; ————①
14:
15: //////////////////////////////////////////////////////
16: //  main()
17:
18: void main()
19: {
20:     // Create two vectors of integers
21:     //
22:     IntVector iv1, iv2;
23:
24:     // Fill them with values
25:     //
26:     for (int i = 1; i < 4; ++i)
27:     {
28:         iv1.push_back(i); ——————
29:         iv2.push_back(i + 3); ——— ②
30:     }
31:
32:     // Calculate the inner product
33:     //
34:     int result = inner_product(iv1.begin(), iv1.end(),——
35:         iv2.begin(), 10); ————————————————— ③
36:
37:     cout << "Given the following two sets of numbers:\n"
38:         << "   1, 2, 3   and   4, 5, 6\n\n";
39:     cout << "The inner product, plus 10, is:\n"
40:         "10 + (1 * 4) + (2 * 5) + (3 * 6) = " << result
41:         << endl;
42: }
```

LISTING 31.5

① Line 13: A type alias for vector<int>

② Lines 28-29: Add items to the vectors

③ Lines 34-35: Compute the inner product values using inner_product()

The output from this program reveals the inner product of the two sets of numbers:

```
Given the following two sets of numbers:
   {1, 2, 3} and {4, 5, 6}

The inner product, plus 10, is:
10 + (1 * 4) + (2 * 5) + (3 * 6) = 42
```

This program begins by defining the type alias `IntVector` for the vector specialization `vector<int>` on line 13. This definition is followed by the creation of two `IntVector` objects (`iv1` and `iv2`) on line 22. The `for` loop running from lines 26 through 30 adds items to the vectors using the `vector::push_back()` method. The second vector's items are offset by 3 to give us the proper data set.

The `inner_product()` function is called on lines 34 and 35, computing the inner product for each pair of elements in the vectors, as specified by the iterator values `iv1.begin()` and `iv1.end()`. The third argument is the iterator pointing to the start of the second vector (`v2.begin()`). Note that the function assumes that the arrays are the same size, so it doesn't need a `v2.end()` iterator. The value of the inner product is stored in the variable `result`, which is displayed using `cout` on line 40.

The *partial_sum* Algorithm

The `partial_sum` algorithm calculates partial sums, or the end result of a set of incremental changes attained by adding adjacent element values. The algorithm is implemented in the `partial_sum()` function declared in the standard header `<numeric>`, using the following function templates:

```
template <class InIt, class OutIt>
    OutIt partial_sum(InIt first, InIt last,
        OutIt result);

template <class InIt, class OutIt, class Pred>
    OutIt partial_sum(InIt first, InIt last,
        OutIt result, Pred pr);
```

The first version of the function performs a binary addition operation by default, and the second version uses a predicate specifying some other binary operation to use for the accumulation. As an example of a partial sum, given the set of numbers {1, 2, 3, 4}, you would calculate the partial sum like this:

{1, 1+2, 1+2+3, 1+2+3+4}

The result of this operation is the sequence {1, 3, 6, 10}. The resulting set of numbers represents the partial sum. This algorithm is useful for calculating changes between numbers, such as an array of fluctuating stock prices. Here's another example, using the set of numbers {1, 3, 5, 7}. Given this set of numbers you would calculate the partial sum like this:

{1, 1+3, 1+3+5, 1+3+5+7}

The result of this operation is the sequence {1, 4, 9, 16}. The program in Listing 31.6 demonstrates the use of this algorithm.

The *adjacent_difference* Algorithm

The adjacent_difference algorithm is the opposite of the partial_sum algorithm. It's implemented in the adjacent_difference() function declared in the standard header <numeric>, using the following overloaded function templates:

```
template <class InIt, class OutIt>
    OutIt adjacent_difference(InIt first, InIt last,
        OutIt result);

template <class InIt, class OutIt, class Pred>
    OutIt adjacent_difference(InIt first, InIt last,
        OutIt result, Pred pr);
```

The adjacent_difference() function defined in the standard header <numeric> provides a generic numeric algorithm for calculating adjacent differences, or the end result of a set of incremental changes attained by subtracting adjacent element values (note that this makes adjacent_difference() the inverse operation of partial_sum()).

As an example, let's use the result set of numbers from the partial_sum example given in the preceding section: {1, 3, 6, 10}. You would calculate the adjacent difference like this:

{1, 3-1, 6-3, 10-6}

The result is the sequence {1, 2, 3, 4}. Note that this operation "undoes" the partial_sum operation. Listing 31.6 demonstrates the use of the partial_sum() and adjacent_difference() functions.

LISTING 31.6   A Program That Demonstrates the Use of the *partial_sum()* and *adjacent_difference()* Functions

```
 1: //////////////////////////////////////////////////////
 2: //  Module  : partial_adjacent.cpp
 3: //
 4: //  Purpose : Demonstrates the partial_sum and
 5: //            adjacent_difference algorithms.
 6: //////////////////////////////////////////////////////
 7:
 8: #include <iostream>
 9: #include <vector>
10: #include <numeric>
11:
12: using namespace std;
13:
14: typedef vector<int> IntVector;
15:
16: void DisplayVectorElements(IntVector& iv);
17:
18: //////////////////////////////////////////////////////
19: //  main()
20:
21: void main()
22: {
23:     // Create three vectors of integers
24:     //
```

```
25:     IntVector iv1, iv2(4), iv3(4);
26:
27:     // Fill the first vector with four values
28:     //
29:     for (int i = 1; i < 5; ++i)
30:         iv1.push_back(i);
31:
32:     // Display the vector elements
33:     //
34:     DisplayVectorElements(iv1);
35:
36:     // Find the partial sum and display
37:     //
38:     partial_sum(iv1.begin(), iv1.end(), iv2.begin());
39:     DisplayVectorElements(iv2);
40:
41:     // Find the adjacent difference and display
42:     //
43:     adjacent_difference(iv2.begin(), iv2.end(),
44:         iv3.begin());
45:     DisplayVectorElements(iv3);
46: }
47:
48: /////////////////////////////////////////////////////
49: //  DisplayVectorElements()
50:
51: void DisplayVectorElements(IntVector& iv)
52: {
53:     IntVector::iterator itor = iv.begin();
54:
55:     cout << "\nVector elements are as follows:\n";
56:     while (itor != iv.end())
57:         cout << *itor++ << " ";
58:     cout << endl;
59: }
```

LISTING 31.6

1 Line 25: Create three IntVector objects

2 Lines 29-30: Fill the first vector with values

3 Line 38: Find the partial sum

4 Line 43: Find the adjacent difference

5 Lines 56-57: Display the elements of an IntVector

The output from this program demonstrates how the `partial_sum()` and `adjacent_difference()` functions produce inverse results:

```
Vector elements are as follows:
1 2 3 4


Vector elements are as follows:
1 3 6 10


Vector elements are as follows:
1 2 3 4
```

This program, like the last two, begins by defining the `IntVector` type on line 14. Three `IntVector` objects are created on line 23, the first (`iv1`) with no elements preallocated, the second (`iv2`) and third (`iv3`) with four elements each. The `for` loop on lines 29 and 30 adds values to the vector, and line 34 calls the `DisplayVectorElements()` function to dump to the screen all elements from vector `iv1`.

The `partial_sum()` function is called on line 38, computing the partial sum for each pair of elements in vector `iv1`, as specified by the iterator values `iv1.begin()` and `iv1.end()`. The third argument is the iterator pointing to the start of the second vector (`v2.begin()`), the target location for the resulting partial sum data set. Line 39 calls the `DisplayVectorElements()` function again, this time dumping to the screen all elements from vector `iv2`.

The `adjacent_difference()` function is called on lines 43 and 44, computing the adjacent difference for each pair of elements in vector `iv2`, as specified by the iterator values `iv2.begin()` and `iv2.end()`. The third argument is the iterator pointing to the start of the third vector (`v3.begin()`), the target location for the resulting adjacent difference data set. Line 45 calls the `DisplayVectorElements()` function one last time, this time dumping to the screen all elements from vector `iv3`.

The `DisplayVectorElements()` function runs from lines 51 through 59 and uses the `vector<int>::iterator` type on line 53 to get an iterator (`itor`) that points at the start of the array. Using this iterator in a `while` loop sends each element value to the screen on lines 56 and 57.

Working with Files and Streams

Working with Streams

Like its predecessor C, C++ doesn't directly support input/output (I/O) operations as part of the base language as it does for object-oriented programming features such as inheritance and polymorphism, or generic programming such as templates. C++ directly supports these other features by keywords and architecture inherent to the language. As it was in C, I/O in C++ has been left up to programmers to define for themselves, using the base language features to implement it.

After more than a decade of tradition and evolution, stream objects have become part of the Standard C++ Library as template classes. Originally defined in the traditional iostreams library for I/O of characters to and from devices and external files, the role of streams has been templatized, as has most of the traditional C++ library.

A *stream object* acts as both source and destination for bytes, whether the bytes go to the screen, to a file, or somewhere else. There are several types of stream classes, and each stream class is characterized by its type and by its customized insertion and extraction operators. The collective group of classes that make up the input and output facilities of standard C++ are called the *standard iostreams library*.

Stream Object

An instance of a stream class, which manipulates a linear, ordered sequence of bytes in some way.

Identifying Stream Types

You've seen the cout and cin objects used throughout this book. These objects represent the simplest use of iostreams. By using the cin stream object, you can extract values from the standard input device. This is made possible by the declarations and implementation of the base input stream class basic_istream. By using the cout stream object, you can insert values into the standard output device. This is made possible by the declarations and implementation of the base output stream class basic_ostream.

These input and output operations are called *insertions* and *extractions* in stream terminology, and they are performed by extractors and insertors. For example, the familiar cout object is an insertor, and the cin object is an extractor. The base class `basic_ios` handles format control for both extractors and insertors, controlling the appearance of the byte stream. The format information defined in `basic_ios` is manipulated by objects called *manipulators*. A manipulator alters the bytes in a stream in some way, such as formatting all characters as upper-case, or converting a decimal number to hexadecimal format.

The iostreams library used in traditional C++ for the past decade has been recently replaced with the standard iostreams template classes in the Standard C++ Library. The headers making up the standard iostreams library are, alphabetically, `<fstream>`, `<iomanip>`, `<ios>`, `<iosfwd>`, `<iostream>`, `<istream>`, `<ostream>`, `<sstream>`, `<streambuf>`, and `<strstream>`. These headers are introduced in Table 32.1.

TABLE 32.1 The Headers Comprising the Standard iostreams Library

Header	Purpose
`<fstream>`	Defines several template classes that support iostreams operations on sequences stored in external files.
`<iomanip>`	Defines several manipulators that take a single argument.
`<ios>`	Defines several types and functions basic to the operation of iostreams, including many format manipulators.
`<iosfwd>`	Forward declarations for the iostreams classes.
`<iostream>`	Declares global stream objects (such as `cin` and `cout`) that control reading from and writing to the standard streams.
`<istream>`	Defines the template class `basic_istream` along with several extractors.
`<ostream>`	Defines the template class `basic_ostream` along with several insertors and manipulators.
`<sstream>`	Defines several template classes that support iostreams operations on sequences stored in character arrays—easily converted to and from objects of template class `basic_string`.
`<streambuf>`	Defines the template class `basic_streambuf`.
`<strstream>`	Defines several classes that support iostreams operations on sequences stored in C-style character arrays.

Note

The iostreams headers support conversions between straight text and encoded or formatted text, and input and output to external files.

The standard iostreams library contains many classes, but several of these classes are of interest only to advanced users. This chapter examines only the classes that are more commonly used, including the base classes that provide essential functionality for standard stream operations.

With the exception of the root base class `ios_base`, the base classes are provided as template classes. In practice, these templates revert back to the traditional C++ way of doing things because the standard library provides template class specializations for type `char`. Figure 32.1 shows the hierarchy of the most commonly used iostreams classes. The next few sections of this chapter take a look at the services provided by these base classes.

FIGURE 32.1

Commonly used base classes and their corresponding character specialization classes.

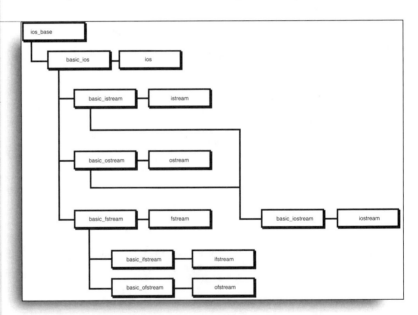

As you can see from Figure 32.1, the `basic_*` classes have character specializations that drop the `basic_` prefix from the class name. For example, `basic_ios` is specialized for characters as `ios`, and `basic_fstream` is specialized for characters as `fstream`.

Introducing the *ios_base* Class

The `ios_base` class is the root base class for the standard iostreams library. This class provides the storage and member functions common to derived input and output stream classes that aren't dependent on template parameters.

The `ios_base` class provides two arrays: one of type `long`, and one of type `void*`—both of which are extensible. The `io_base` class also provides several data types that act as flags for the class and its descendants. These data types include the following:

- Format flags, in the type alias `fmtflags`, used to provide format information for the stream.

- I/O state information, in the type alias `iostate`, used to keep track of the current state of I/O operations, such as stream corruption.

- Open mode, in the type alias `openmode`, used to specify what type of read/write access a stream has.

- Seek direction, in the type alias `seekdir`, used to specify where in the stream data should be sought.

- Event information, in the type alias `event`, used to store a callback event used as an argument to a function registered with the `ios_base::register_callback()` function.

Table 32.2 describes the member function of the `ios_base` class.

TABLE 32.2   **The Methods Provided by the *basic_ios* Class**

Member	Description
`flags()`	Sets or retrieves format flag information about a stream.
`getloc()`	Returns the internal locale object, which encapsulates locale information useful for internationalization.
`imbue()`	Stores a locale object, returning the previously stored value.
`ios_base()`	The class constructor.
`iword()`	Returns a reference to a specified element of the extensible array having elements of type `long`.
`operator=()`	Copies any stored formatting information and copies any extensible arrays to a new stream object.

continues...

Callbacks

A callback is a function pointer that is registered with and called by the operating system or some library. Callbacks allow you to define custom functions to handle various important situations.

TABLE 32.2 **Continued**

Member	Description
precision()	Returns the stored display precision, specifying the number of decimal places.
pword()	Returns a reference to a specified element of the extensible array having elements of type void*.
register_callback()	Stores a function pointer and an index that are used for stream callback events.
setf()	Sets new format flag information into the stream, returning any previously stored format flags.
unsetf()	Clears all format flag bits.
width()	Sets or retrieves the field width of a stream.
xalloc()	Returns a stored static value that you can use as a unique index argument when calling the member functions iword() or pword().

Format Flags

Stream formatting information is stored in values known as *format flags*. These flags are defined in the class ios_base, and are described in Table 32.3.

TABLE 32.3 **The iostreams Format Flags Enumerated Values**

Flag	Description
boolalpha	Flags a stream to insert or extract Boolean objects as names such as true and false instead of as numeric values (such as 1 and 0).
dec	Flags a stream to insert or extract integer values in floating-point format (with decimals).
fixed	Flags a stream to insert floating-point values in fixed-point format, without using exponents.
hex	Flags a stream to insert or extract integer values in hexadecimal format.
internal	Flags a stream to pad to a field width as needed by inserting internal fill characters.
left	Flags a stream to left-justify characters by padding with fill characters on the right.

oct	Flags a stream to insert or extract integer values in octal format.
right	Flags a stream to right-justify characters by padding with fill characters on the left.
scientific	Flags a stream to insert floating-point values in scientific format, using exponents.
showbase	Flags a stream to insert a prefix that reveals the base of a generated integer field (for example, hex 9 becomes 0x9).
showpoint	Flags a stream to force a decimal point in a floating-point field, even when there is no fractional part present.
showpos	Flags a stream to insert a plus sign in a nonnegative-generated numeric field.
skipws	Flags a stream to skip leading whitespace before certain extractions.
unitbuf	Flags a stream to flush output after each insertion.
uppercase	Flags a stream to insert uppercase equivalents of lowercase letters in certain insertions.

I/O State Flags

In addition to the member functions listed in Table 32.2, the `ios_base` class provides an enumerated type used to store stream state information. The `ios_base::iostate` data member stores this information, which can have the following distinct flag values:

Flag Value	Description
badbit	Used to record stream buffer corruption.
eofbit	Used to register that the end of a file was reached while extracting from a stream.
failbit	Used to record a failure when extracting a valid field from a stream.
goodbit	Indicates that no bits are set and that the stream is in good shape.

Open Mode Flags

The `ios_base` class also provides an enumerated type used to store the opening mode for several iostreams objects.

The `ios_base::openmode` data member stores this information, which can have the following distinct flag values:

Flag Value	Description
app	Seeks to the end of a stream before each insertion.
ate	Seeks to the end of a stream when the stream object is created.
binary	Reads a file as a binary stream, rather than as a text stream.
in	Permits extraction from a stream.
out	Permits insertion into a stream.
trunc	Truncates an existing file when the stream object is created.

Seek Direction Flags

Seeking data in a stream alters the current read or write position of a sequence (such as an array, stream, or file). The `ios_base::seekdir` data member uses the seek direction flags to store the seek mode, which is used as an argument to the member functions of several iostreams classes. The seek direction can have any of the following distinct flag values:

Flag Value	Description
beg	Seeks relative to the beginning of a sequence.
cur	Seeks relative to the current position within a sequence.
end	Seeks relative to the end of a sequence.

Event Flags

Streams can respond to certain events through the use of a callback function. The `ios_base::event` data member uses the event flags to store a callback event type. This type is used as an argument to a function registered with the member function `ios_base::register_callback()`, and can have any of the following distinct flag values:

Flag Value	Description
copyfmt_event	Identifies a callback that occurs near the end of a call to the member function copyfmt().
erase_event	Identifies a callback that occurs at the beginning of a call to the member function copyfmt(), or at the beginning of a call to the destructor for *this.
imbue_event	Identifies a callback that occurs at the end of a call to the member function imbue(), just before the function returns.

Introducing the *basic_ios* Class

The template class basic_ios is the base class for the classes basic_istream, basic_ostream, and basic_fstream. Table 32.4 describes the members of the basic_ios class.

TABLE 32.4   **The Members of the *basic_ios* Class**

Member	Description
bad()	Returns true if the badbit I/O state flag is set.
basic_ios()	Class constructor.
clear()	Clears a stream's I/O state flags.
copyfmt()	Copies stream format and other information, and fires off the erase_event and copyfmt_event callback events.
eof()	Returns true if the eofbit I/O state flag is set.
exceptions()	Clears or sets the stream's exception mask, which is an object of type ios_base::iostate.
fail()	Returns true if the failbit I/O state flag is set.
fill()	Sets or retrieves the fill character used by a stream.
good()	Returns true if the goodbit I/O state flag is set.
imbue()	Sets or retrieves locale information about a steam.
init()	Initializes a stream with default data member values.
narrow()	Creates a char value from a char_type value.

continues...

TABLE 32.4 **Continued**

Member	Description
operator!()	Returns fail().
operator void*()	Returns a null pointer if the failbit I/O state flag is set.
rdbuf()	Returns the stream buffer pointer.
rdstate()	Returns the stream's state information.
setstate()	Sets the stream's state information.
tie()	Sets up or breaks a connection between an istream and an ostream object.
widen()	Creates a char_type value from a char value.

The class ios is a synonym for template class basic_ios, specialized for elements of type char. The class has the following declaration in the standard header <ios>:

```
typedef basic_ios <char, char_traits<char> > ios;
```

In addition to the basic_ios class specification, the standard header <ios> provides a variety of manipulator functions that can manipulate the stream's format flags. These manipulators are described in Table 32.5, and they appear in <ios> like this:

```
// <ios> Manipulators
//
ios_base& boolalpha(ios_base& str);
ios_base& noboolalpha(ios_base& str);
ios_base& showbase(ios_base& str);
ios_base& noshowbase(ios_base& str);
ios_base& showpoint(ios_base& str);
ios_base& noshowpoint(ios_base& str);
ios_base& showpos(ios_base& str);
ios_base& noshowpos(ios_base& str);
ios_base& skipws(ios_base& str);
ios_base& noskipws(ios_base& str);
ios_base& unitbuf(ios_base& str);
ios_base& nounitbuf(ios_base& str);
ios_base& uppercase(ios_base& str);
ios_base& nouppercase(ios_base& str);
ios_base& internal(ios_base& str);
```

```
ios_base& left(ios_base& str);
ios_base& right(ios_base& str);
ios_base& dec(ios_base& str);
ios_base& hex(ios_base& str);
ios_base& oct(ios_base& str);
ios_base& fixed(ios_base& str);
ios_base& scientific(ios_base& str);
```

TABLE 32.5 **The Manipulators Defined in the Standard Header <*ios*>**

Flag	Description
boolalpha()	Symbolic representation of true and false.
noboolalpha()	Undoes boolalpha().
showbase()	Shows the base of a number, prefixing octal and hex numbers with 0 and 0x, respectively.
noshowbase()	Undoes showbase().
showpoint()	Displays a decimal point in a floating-point number having no fractional part.
noshowpoint()	Undoes showpoint().
showpos()	Inserts a plus sign in a nonnegative numeric field.
noshowpos()	Undoes showpos().
skipws()	Skips whitespace.
noskipws()	Doesn't skip whitespace.
unitbuf()	Flushes output after each insertion.
nounitbuf()	Doesn't flush output after each insertion.
uppercase()	Inserts uppercase equivalents of lowercase letters in certain insertions.
nouppercase()	Doesn't insert uppercase equivalents of lowercase letters in certain insertions.
internal()	Pads to a field width as needed by inserting internal fill characters.
left()	Left-justifies characters by padding with fill characters on the right.
right()	Right-justifies characters by padding with fill characters on the left.

continues…

TABLE 32.5   **Continued**

Flag	Description
dec()	Inserts or extracts integer values in floating-point format (with decimals).
hex()	Inserts or extracts integer values in hexadecimal format.
oct()	Inserts or extracts integer values in octal format.
fixed()	Inserts floating-point values in fixed-point format, without using exponents.
scientific()	Inserts floating-point values in scientific format, using exponents.

Introducing the *basic_istream* Class

The template class basic_istream describes an object that controls extraction of elements and encoded objects from a stream buffer. Table 32.6 describes the members of the basic_istream class.

TABLE 32.6   **The Members of the *basic_istream* Class**

Member	Description
basic_istream()	Class constructor.
gcount()	Returns the number of elements extracted by the last unformatted input function.
get()	Extracts data from an input stream.
getline()	Extracts data from an input stream until a specified delimiter is found, the specified limit is reached, or the end of the file is reached.
ignore()	Extracts and discards a specified number of elements.
ipfx()	An input prefix function called internally by input functions before extracting data from the stream.
isfx()	An input suffix function called internally by input functions after extracting data from the stream.
operator>>()	This overloaded extraction operator extracts data from an input stream.

Member	Description
peek()	Returns the next element without extracting it from the stream.
putback()	Puts an element back into the input stream.
read()	Extracts bytes from the stream until a specified limit is reached or until the end of the file is reached.
readsome()	Extracts up to a specified number of elements and stores them in an array.
seekg()	Changes the position pointer for the stream, (usually a file stream).
sync()	Synchronizes the stream's internal buffer with the external source of elements.
tellg()	Gets the value for the stream's get pointer.
unget()	Puts the most recently read element back into the stream.

The class istream is a synonym for template class basic_istream, which is specialized for elements of type char. The class has the following declaration in the standard header <istream>:

```
typedef basic_istream<char, char_traits<char> > istream;
```

Introducing the *basic_ostream* Class

The template class basic_ostream describes an object that controls insertion of elements and encoded objects into a stream buffer. Table 32.7 describes the members of the basic_ostream class.

TABLE 32.7 **The Members of the *basic_ostream* Class**

Member	Description
basic_ostream()	Class constructor.
flush()	Flushes the buffer associated with a stream.
operator<<()	Overloaded insertion operator used to write elements to a stream.
opfx()	An output prefix function called internally by input functions before inserting data into a stream.

continues…

TABLE 32.7   Continued

Member	Description
osfx()	An output suffix function called internally by input functions after inserting data into a stream.
put()	Inserts a single element into the output stream.
seekp()	Changes the position value for the stream (usually a file stream).
tellp()	Gets the position value for the stream.
write()	Inserts a specified number of bytes from a buffer into the stream.

The class ostream is a synonym for template class basic_ostream, which is specialized for elements of type char. The class has the following declaration in the standard header <ostream>:

```
typedef basic_ostream <char, char_traits<char> > ostream;
```

Introducing the *basic_iostream* Class

The template class basic_iostream is a product of multiple inheritance, containing both a basic_istream object and a basic_ostream object. As such, basic_iostream contains all the members of both classes and can act as an input stream and an output stream.

The class iostream is a synonym for template class basic_iostream, specialized for elements of type char. The class has the following declaration in the standard header <istream>:

```
typedef basic_iostream<char, char_traits<char> > iostream;
```

Introducing the *basic_fstream* Class

The template class basic_fstream is the base class for the template classes basic_ifstream and basic_ofstream. Table 32.8 describes the members of the basic_fstream class.

TABLE 32.8   **The Members of the *basic_fstream* Class**

Member	Description
close()	Closes a file stream.
is_open()	Determines whether a file stream is open.
open()	Opens a file stream.

The class fstream is a synonym for template class basic_fstream, which is specialized for elements of type char. The class has the following declaration in the standard header <fstream>:

```
typedef basic_fstream<char, char_traits<char> > fstream;
```

Using Stream Manipulators

Stream manipulators are used to manipulate stream object data in various ways. A manipulator typically does something to the stream data itself, as opposed to inserting or extracting stream data. An exception to this is the std::endl manipulator, which inserts a newline character or character sequence into an output stream. Manipulators are typically used to format the data in the stream.

Creating Formatted Stream Data

Formatting stream data is a common task, and the use of various manipulators is necessary to coerce data into the desired format. Consider a simple example that uses the cout object. By using manipulators on cout, we can force data into whatever format is appropriate for a given situation. Listing 32.1 demonstrates several ways of manipulating the stream format for cout.

LISTING 32.1   **A Program That Demonstrates Formatting Output Stream Data Using *cout***

```
1: //////////////////////////////////////////////////////
2: //  Module  : format.cpp
3: //
4: //  Purpose : Demonstrates formatting stream data
```

continues...

LISTING 32.1 **Continued**

```
 5: //                using manipulators.
 6: /////////////////////////////////////////////////////
 7:
 8: #include <iostream>
 9: #include <iomanip>
10:
11: using std::cout;
12: using std::endl;
13: using std::ios;
14:
15: void Display(float a[], int count, int width);
16:
17: /////////////////////////////////////////////////////
18: // main()
19:
20: void main()
21: {
22:     float af[2] = { 1.0f, 123.287f };
23:
24:     cout << "Default format for true & false:\n";
25:     cout << true << ", " << false << endl;
26:
27:     cout << "\nSetting ios::boolalpha:\n";
28:     cout.setf(ios::boolalpha); ────❶
29:     cout << true << ", " << false << endl;
30:
31:     cout << "\nDefault numeric format:\n";
32:     Display(af, 2, 10);
33:
34:     cout << "\nSetting ios::showpoint:\n";
35:     cout.setf(ios::showpoint); ────❷
36:     Display(af, 2, 10);
37:
38:     cout << "\nSetting ios::showpos:\n";
39:     cout.setf(ios::showpos);
40:     Display(af, 2, 10);
41:     cout.unsetf(ios::showpos);
42:
43:     cout << "\nSetting fixed precision at "
44:         << "two decimal places:\n";
45:     cout.setf(ios::fixed); ────❸
```

```
46:      cout << std::setprecision(2) << 10.5498 << endl;
47:
48:      cout << "\nSetting ios::scientific:\n";
49:      cout.setf(ios::scientific);
50:      Display(af, 2, 10);
51:      cout.unsetf(ios::scientific);
52:
53:      cout << "\nSetting ios::hex for decimal 34:\n";
54:      cout.setf(ios::hex, ios::basefield);
55:      cout.setf(ios::showbase);
56:      cout << 34 << endl;
57: }
58:
59: /////////////////////////////////////////////////////////
60: // Display()
61:
62: void Display(float a[], int count, int width)
63: {
64:    for (int i = 0; i < count; ++i)
65:    {
66:       cout.width(width);
67:       cout << a[i] << endl;
68:    }
69: }
```

LISTING 32.1 CONTINUED

④ Lines 54-55: Specify hexadecimal formatting

This program uses manipulators to produce the following output:

```
Default format for true & false:
1, 0

Setting ios::boolalpha:
true, false

Default numeric format:
        1
    123.287

Setting ios::showpoint:
    1.00000
    123.287
```

```
Setting ios::showpos:
  +1.00000
  +123.287

Setting fixed precision at two decimal places:
10.55

Setting ios::scientific:
      1.0
  1.2e+002

Setting ios::hex for decimal 34:
0x22
```

This program simply uses manipulators to display stream data in various ways. The program begins by including both the <iostream> and <iomanip> standard headers (lines 8 and 9). On line 15, a prototype for the Display() function is provided. This function takes three parameters: an array of floats and two integers. Display() is defined from lines 62 through 69 and uses the ios::width() member function to set the stream width to whatever amount is specified by the Display() function's width parameter. Each array item is then output to the console, one item per line.

The main() function begins on line 20 and immediately defines the float array af[] on line 22 (this is the array we'll send to the Display() function). The two floats in af[] come into play later. Line 25 sends the default values for true and false (1 and 0) to the screen. Line 28 sets the ios::boolalpha manipulator flag, so that when line 29 (which is exactly the same as line 25) sends true and false to the screen, they appear as the strings true and false.

Line 31 calls the Display() function to display the contents of the af[] array, using 10 for the width parameter. The float values appear onscreen in their default format, dropping the decimal point from 1.0f because there's no fractional part. Calling the ios::setf() function with the ios::showpoint flag as a parameter, followed by the same Display() call on line 36, results in the first array element appearing as 1.00000.

A similar call to `ios::setf()` on line 39 sets the `ios::showpos` flag, which causes the positive array numbers to display a plus sign when output on line 40. A call to the corresponding `ios::unsetf()` on line 41 unsets the `ios::showpos` flag.

Setting the `ios::fixed` flag on line 45, followed by the `std::setprecision()` call on line 46, causes the call on line 50 to display the number `10.5498` with two decimal places, rounding off to `10.55`. The call to set the `ios::scientific` flag on line 49 causes the `Display()` call on line 50 to display the array numbers using scientific exponentiation.

The final formatting trick is to display the decimal number `34` as the hex number `0x22` by setting the `ios::hex` and `ios::basefield` flags on line 54, followed by setting the `ios::showbase` flag to prefix the hex `22` with an `0x` to denote hexadecimal.

Using File Streams

So far, we've dealt only with streams that read from and write to the standard output (console streams). In addition to these streams, file streams are very important for programs that have to work with and store external data. The standard file stream objects provide native support for file operations using standard streams. Because the file streams are inherited from the standard console streams, they include all the functionality of the base stream objects.

Writing and Reading Text Files

A common task for a program is to open a text file and read in some data, which is then processed in some way. Using the `fstream` object, you can easily write and read text files in your C++ programs. You can also create your own libraries of functions and derived objects to make the task even easier. The program in Listing 32.2 writes a text file to disk and then reads the text back in and displays it using the `cout` object.

LISTING 32.2 **A Program That Writes Some Text to a File and Then Reads It Back and Displays It Onscreen**

```cpp
 1: //////////////////////////////////////////////////////
 2: //   Module  : text.cpp
 3: //
 4: //   Purpose : Demonstrates creating and reading a
 5: //             basic text file.
 6: //////////////////////////////////////////////////////
 7:
 8: #include <iostream>
 9: #include <fstream>               1
10: #include <string>
11:
12: //////////////////////////////////////////////////////
13: // main()
14:
15: void main()
16: {
17: // input and output file objects
18: //
19:     std::fstream fin, fout;       2
20:
21:     // Open a new file for output
22:     //
23:     fout.open("c:/test.txt", std::ios::out);
24:     if (!fout.is_open()) return;
25:
26:     // Write some text to the file, then close it
27:     //
28:     for (int i = 0; i < 10; ++i)               ┐
29:       fout << "This is line #" << i + 1 << std::endl;  ┘  3
30:     fout.close();
31:
32:     // Open the new file for input
33:     //
34:     fin.open("c:/test.txt", std::ios::in);
35:     if (!fin.is_open()) return;
36:
37:     // Read and display all text from the file
38:     //
39:     std::string str;
40:     while (!fin.eof())
41:     {
42:       std::getline(fin, str, '\n');       4
```

```
43:        std::cout << str << std::endl;
44:     }
45:     fin.close();
46: }
```

The output from this program is written into the text file
test.txt and is then read back out of the file and displayed
onscreen, yielding the following program output:

```
This is line #1
This is line #2
This is line #3
This is line #4
This is line #5
This is line #6
This is line #7
This is line #8
This is line #9
This is line #10
```

This program includes the standard header <fstream> on line 9
to provide the iostreams objects created on line 19. Line 23
attempts to create a new file called test.txt, open for output,
and line 24 checks to see whether the file was really opened for
writing. If the call to fout.is_open() returns false, the program
returns from main() and terminates. If the file is open for output,
the for loop on lines 28 and 29 writes ten lines of text to the file,
which is then closed on line 30.

Line 34 attempts to open the newly created file for input, and
line 35 checks to see whether the file was opened successfully. As
before, if the call to fin.is_open() returns false, the program
returns from main() and terminates.

Line 39 creates a string object (str) that's used with the
std::getline() function on line 42 to grab a line of text from the
file—the newline character is specified as the delimiter for each
line. This all occurs within the while loop that runs from lines
40 through 44; the loop control condition is a call to fin.eof(),
which returns true when the end of the file is reached.

Working with Multiple Files

Working with multiple files is just as easy as working with a single file—you simply create several file stream objects. You can

use file streams to perform many useful activities (such as generating the HTML code for World Wide Web pages on the fly, based on some template file and list of criteria).

The program in Listing 32.3 merges names and text from two separate files into a third file—like a basic mail-merge program. The list, in this case, is a list of names in a straight ASCII text file (list.txt), which contains the following entries:

```
Mr. Louis Goldin
Mr. Rob Boydston
Ms. Amy Whitson
Mr. Jose Bermudez
Mr. Tim Fullerton
Mr. Paul Mosely
```

These entries are merged, one by one, with a text file that uses bracketed items (tags) to indicate where the merged information is to be placed. The names in the preceding list are divided into the following tags: <HONORIFIC>, <FIRST>, and <LAST>. The text in the template file (template.txt) contains these tags, interspersed with other text that could be used to form the basis of an annoying mass email message campaign for the fictitious company Spammers, Inc. The template.txt file contents are shown in Figure 32.2.

FIGURE 32.2

The contents of the template.txt file contains merge tags.

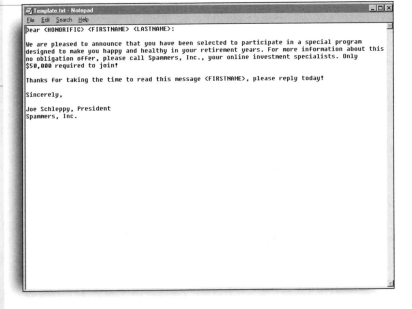

LISTING 32.3   **A Program That Merges Names and Text from Two Separate Files into a Third File**

```
 1: //////////////////////////////////////////////////////
 2: //   Module   : file_merge.cpp
 3: //
 4: //   Purpose : Merges two text files into a third
 5: //////////////////////////////////////////////////////
 6:
 7: #include <iostream>
 8: #include <fstream>
 9: #include <string>
10:
11: using std::cout;
12: using std::endl;
13: using std::string;
14:
15: const int MAX = 10000;
16:
17: struct Person
18: {
19:     string honorific;
20:     string first;
21:     string last;
22: };
23:
24: //////////////////////////////////////////////////////
25: //   main()
26:
27: void main()
28: {
29:     std::ifstream fin1, fin2;
30:     std::ofstream fout;
31:
32:     char *infile1 = "list.txt";
33:     char *infile2 = "template.txt";
34:     char *outfile = "merge.txt";
35:
36:     char ach[MAX];
37:     string str1, str2;
38:
39:     fin1.open(infile1, std::ios::in);
40:     if (!fin1.is_open())
```

LISTING 32.3

❶ Lines 17-22: Declare the Person structure

continues…

LISTING 32.3 **Continued**

```
41:        return;
42:
43:     fin2.open(infile2, std::ios::in);
44:     if (!fin2.is_open())
45:     {
46:        fin1.close();
47:        return;
48:     }
49:     memset(ach, 0, MAX);
50:     fin2.read(ach, MAX);
51:     fin2.close();
52:
53:     str1 = ach;
54:
55:     fout.open(outfile, std::ios::app); // append
56:     if (!fout.is_open())
57:     {
58:        fin1.close();
59:        return;
60:     }
61:
62:     // Read all names from the list file
63:     //
64:     Person person;
65:     while (!fin1.eof())
66:     {
67:        fin1 >> person.honorific;
68:        fin1 >> person.first;
69:        fin1 >> person.last;
70:
71:        if (person.honorific.length() > 0)
72:        {
73:           str2 = str1; // working copy of text.txt
74:
75:           while (1)
76:           {
77:              int pos = 0;
78:              pos = str2.find("<FIRSTNAME>", pos + 1);
79:              if (pos == -1) break;
80:              str2.replace(pos, 11, person.first);
81:
```

```
82:              pos = 0;
83:              pos = str2.find("<LASTNAME>", pos + 1);
84:              if (pos == -1) break;
85:              str2.replace(pos, 10, person.last);
86:
87:              pos = 0;
88:              pos = str2.find("<HONORIFIC>", pos + 1);
89:              if (pos == -1) break;
90:              str2.replace(pos, 11, person.honorific);
91:          }
92:          fout << str2 << endl;
93:      }
94:  }
95:  fin1.close();
96:  fout.close();
97: }
```

The output from this program is written into the text file
merge.txt; as you can see in Figure 32.3, the merge from
list.txt and template.txt to merge.txt is successful.

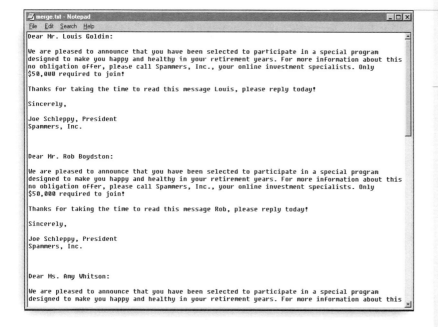

FIGURE 32.3

A portion of the output file
merge.txt as it appears in the
Windows Notepad applet.

This program begins by declaring a constant value MAX on line 15. This constant is used to specify the maximum number of characters read from a file in one gulp. Lines 17 through 22 define the Person structure, which holds three strings: honorific, first, and last. These three strings are read from the list file list.txt.

Lines 29 and 30 declare three stream objects: fin1, fin2, and fout. The names of the files to work with are specified on lines 32, 33, and 34 as infile1, infile2, and outfile, respectively. On line 36, the character buffer ach[] is declared to hold MAX characters. Line 37 declares two strings: str1 and str2. These strings are used to hold file data stored in the temporary buffer ach[].

Line 39 attempts to open infile1 for input, and line 40 verifies that the file is indeed open. Likewise, line 43 attempts to open infile2 for input, and line 44 verifies that it has been opened. If this test fails, infile1 is closed and the program terminates. On line 49, the character buffer ach[] is initialized to contain all zeros using the ANSI C memset() function. Line 50 reads up to MAX characters from infile2 into the buffer ach[]. If the end of the file is reached (which is the idea here), the reading stops. The file is closed on line 51, and ach[] now contains the contents of the file template.txt in memory. As the final step in this first process, str1 is assigned the contents of ach[], so that str1 now contains the contents of the file template.txt in memory.

Line 55 attempts to open outfile for appending using the ios::app flag, and line 56 verifies that the file is open. Line 64 declares a variable of type Person (person) and then we enter a while loop starting on line 65. The conditional test for this loop is the return value from the method fin1.eof(), such that when the end of infile1 is reached, the loop terminates.

The interior of the while loop begins by reading three strings from infile1 using the fin1 extraction operator>> on lines 67, 68, and 69. These file reads fill the person structure. Line 71 verifies that the person.honorific field actually contains some characters, and if so, makes a working copy of str1 (the contents of template.txt), storing it in str2. This approach keeps the original template.txt text intact in str1 while allowing us to modify str2 to suit our needs.

On line 71, we enter an endless `while` loop. Using the integer variable `pos`, we find any occurrences of the string `<FIRSTNAME>` on line 78 by calling the `string::find()` method. The location of the string within `str2` is returned back into `pos`, which contains the value `-1` if the string isn't found. If this is the case, we break out of the endless loop on line 79. On line 80, we replace the text `<FIRSTNAME>`, which is 11 characters long, with the contents of `person.first` by calling the `string::replace()` method. This same process is repeated again from lines 82 through 85, and from lines 87 through 90, replacing `<LASTNAME>` with `person.last`, and `<HONOROFIC>` with `person.honorific`.

Line 92 writes the modified text to the `outfile` `merge.txt`, and the process loops again for each name found in `list.txt`. The final steps are to close the files on lines 95 and 96.

Writing and Reading a Binary File

Because many programs use binary files to store their data externally for future use, you should know how to write and read binary files as well as writing and reading text files. Reading and writing binary files is somewhat faster than reading and writing text files, and binary files generally take less storage space.

The program in Listing 32.4 demonstrates writing various types of data, including a user-defined structure, to a binary file.

LISTING 32.4 **A Program That Creates a Binary File and Then Reads and Displays Its Contents**

```
 1: ////////////////////////////////////////////////////////
 2: //  Module  : binary.cpp
 3: //
 4: //  Purpose : Demonstrates creating and reading a
 5: //             binary file.
 6: ////////////////////////////////////////////////////////
 7:
 8: #include <iostream>
 9: #include <fstream>
10: #include <string>
11: #include <cstring>
12:
```

continues…

LISTING 32.4 CONTINUED

① Lines 17-37: A test structure used to test binary file writing and reading

LISTING 32.4   **Continued**

```
13: using namespace std;
14:
15: // A test structure
16: //
17: struct myStruct
18: {
19:     int    x, y;
20:     float  z;
21:     string str;
22:     char   ch[10];
23:     myStruct() { }
24:     myStruct(int rx, int ry, float rz,
25:         string& rstr, char* pch)
26:     {
27:         try
28:         {
29:             x = rx;
30:             y = ry;
31:             z = rz;
32:             str = rstr;
33:             strcpy(ch, pch);
34:         }
35:         catch(...) { throw; }
36:     }
37: };
38:
39: // Helper function prototype
40: //
41: void DisplayMyStruct(string& str, const myStruct& ms);
42:
43: ////////////////////////////////////////////////////////
44: // main()
45:
46: void main()
47: {
48:     fstream fin, fout; // input and output file objects
49:
50:     // Open a new file for output
51:     //
52:     fout.open("test.bin", fstream::out);
53:     if (!fout.is_open()) return;
```

①

```
54:
55:    // Create some data and fill the structures
56:    //
57:    char c1 = 'R';
58:    char c2 = 'M';
59:
60:    string str1 = "This is test #1";
61:    string str2 = "This is test #2";
62:    string str3 = "This is test #3";
63:
64:    myStruct ms1(1, 2, 3.5f, str1, "1111111111");
65:    myStruct ms2(1, 2, 3.5f, str2, "2222222222");
66:
67:    // Write the data to the file, then close it
68:    //
69:    fout.write(&c1, 1);
70:    fout.write(&c2, 1);
71:
72:    fout.write(reinterpret_cast<const char*>(&ms1),
73:       sizeof(myStruct));
74:    fout.write(reinterpret_cast<const char*>(&ms2),
75:       sizeof(myStruct));
76:    fout.close();
77:
78:    // Open the new file for input
79:    //
80:    fin.open("c:/test.bin", ios_base::in);
81:    if (!fin.is_open()) return;
82:
83:    // Read and display all data from the file
84:    //
85:    char c3, c4;
86:    fin.read(&c3, 1);
87:    fin.read(&c4, 1);
88:
89:    myStruct ms3, ms4;
90:    fin.read(reinterpret_cast<char*>(&ms3),
91:       sizeof(myStruct));
92:    fin.read(reinterpret_cast<char*>(&ms4),
93:       sizeof(myStruct));
94:    fin.close();
95:
```

LISTING 32.4 CONTINUED

2 Lines 72-75: Write binary data to a file

3 Lines 90-93: Read binary data back out of the file

continues…

LISTING 32.4   Continued

```
 96:    cout << "c3 == " << c3 << endl;
 97:    cout << "c4 == " << c4 << endl << endl;
 98:
 99:    DisplayMyStruct(string("ms3"), ms3);
100:    DisplayMyStruct(string("ms4"), ms4);
101:
102:    system("pause");
103: }
104:
105: /////////////////////////////////////////////////////
106: // DisplayMyStruct()
107:
108: void DisplayMyStruct(string& str, const myStruct& ms)
109: {
110:    cout << str << ".x   == " << ms.x   << endl;
111:    cout << str << ".y   == " << ms.y   << endl;
112:    cout << str << ".z   == " << ms.z   << endl;
113:    cout << str << ".str == " << ms.str << endl;
114:    cout << str << ".ch  == " << ms.ch  << endl << endl;
115: }
```

This program produces the following output, which is read from
a binary file and displayed to the screen:

```
c3 == R
c4 == M

ms3.x   == 1
ms3.y   == 2
ms3.z   == 3.5
ms3.str == This is test #1
ms3.ch  == 1111111111

ms4.x   == 1
ms4.y   == 2
ms4.z   == 3.5
ms4.str == This is test #2
ms4.ch  == 2222222222
```

This program uses a structure called myStruct to test binary
file writes and reads. This simple structure is defined from
lines 17 through 37 and provides a constructor for easy initialization of the members. On line 41, the prototype for the

`DisplayMyStruct()` function is declared. This function runs from lines 108 through 115 and simply displays each member of the structure to the screen using `cout`.

The `main()` function begins by declaring two stream objects on line 48: `fin` and `fout`. These objects are used for input and output, respectively. Line 52 attempts to open a binary file (`test.bin`) for output. If this attempt is successful, the character variables `c1` and `c2` are declared and initialized with my initials (`R` and `M`) on lines 57 and 58. Similarly, the three string objects `str1`, `str2`, and `str3` are declared and initialized on lines 60 through 62. Finally, the two `myStruct` objects `ms1` and `ms2` are declared and initialized (using `str1` and `str2`) on lines 64 and 65.

These objects are then written to the binary file. Lines 69 and 70 write the values of `ch1` and `ch2` to the file using the `ostream::write()` method, writing one character each. Lines 72 and 73 write the `ms1` object to the file, specifying the number of bytes written by using the `sizeof()` operator. Because the `ostream::write()` method works with constant character pointers, the `reinterpret_cast` operator is used to convert `ms1` to a `const char*`, the proper format. Lines 74 and 75 do the same for the `ms2` object, and the file is closed.

On line 80, the file is opened for input; on line 85, two new `char` variables (`ch3` and `ch4`) are declared. Lines 86 and 87 read the values of `ch3` and `ch4` from the file using the `ostream::read()` method, reading one character each. Line 89 declares two new `myStruct` objects (`ms3` and `ms4`). Lines 90 and 91 read the `ms3` object from the file, specifying the number of bytes to read by using the `sizeof()` operator. The `reinterpret_cast` operator is again used to convert the `char` pointer back into the proper format—a `myStruct` object. Lines 92 and 93 do the same for the `ms4` object, and the file is closed on line 94.

Lines 96 and 97 send the values of `c3` and `c4` to the screen to verify that the read worked properly, and two calls to `DisplayMyStruct()` on lines 99 and 100 do the same for the `ms3` and `ms4` objects.

The `DisplayMyStruct()` function running from lines 108 through 115 simply displays all the data in the structure provided as a parameter.

Examining Algorithms

Understand the concept of generic algorithms

See the difference between in-place and copy algorithms

Learn about the modifying and nonmodifying sequence
algorithms

Discover the sorted sequence algorithms

Explore the heap operation, comparison, and
permutation algorithms

Generic Algorithms

The Standard C++ Library provides a wide assortment of generic algorithms designed to be efficient and yet work with a wide variety of data types. These generic algorithms use iterators to perform their magic. In this chapter, you'll see how these algorithms can cut your programming time by providing plug-in solutions. These algorithms can be divided into the following seven general categories, based on their semantics and usage:

- **Nonmodifying sequence algorithms.** These algorithms operate on a container without changing its contents.
- **Modifying sequence algorithms.** These algorithms operate on a container and modify its contents.
- **Sorted sequence algorithms.** These algorithms include sorting and merging, binary searches, and operations on sorted container sequences.
- **Heap operation algorithms.** These algorithms make it easy to sort a sequence when needed.
- **Comparison algorithms.** These algorithms allow element selection based on comparisons.
- **Permutation algorithms.** These algorithms provide ways of permutating a sequence.
- **Generalized numeric algorithms.** You explored these kinds of algorithms back in Chapter 31, "Working with Numerics."

Within each category of algorithm are subcategories that define the way an algorithm works. These subcategories provide variations of an algorithm that include the following:

- **In-place algorithms.** These algorithms place the result of the algorithm into the same container on which it operates.
- **Copying algorithms.** These algorithms place the result of the algorithm into a copy of the original container on which it operates, or sometimes into a different (nonoverlapping) area of the same container on which it operates.

- **Function parameter algorithms.** These algorithms accept a function object as a parameter. The function object is typically a standard library predicate, defined in the standard header <functional>.

Some of the standard algorithms implement both in-place and copy versions, making them even more useful in more situations. Most of the generic algorithms are defined in the standard header <algorithm>; these algorithms are the subject of study in this chapter. The remaining four generic algorithms are defined in the standard header <numeric>, and were covered in Chapter 31.

The generic algorithms make extensive use of iterators as template parameters, which denote the *least* powerful category of iterator permitted as an actual argument type. Iterators with more power in the iterator hierarchy can, of course, replace lower-powered iterators at any time. The iterators, in order of power, are as follows:

- OutIt: Indicates an output iterator

- InIt: Indicates an input iterator

- FwdIt: Indicates a forward iterator

- BidIt: Indicates a bidirectional iterator

- RanIt: Indicates a random-access iterator

SEE ALSO

➤ *For more information about iterators in general, see page 698*

➤ *For more information about the standard iterator hierarchy, see page 709*

Exploring the Nonmodifying Sequence Algorithms

The Standard C++ Library provides generic nonmodifying algorithms that search for specific container elements, count container elements meeting certain criteria, and check container elements for equality—all activities that don't modify the container itself. Table 33.1 briefly describes each of the nonmodifying sequence algorithms. These algorithms are, for the most part, unrelated, aside from the fact that they don't modify container contents.

Note

Like the numeric algorithms presented in Chapter 31, the algorithms in the standard header <algorithm> are implemented by overloaded template functions that operate on containers. For each algorithm, each overloaded template function uses the name of the algorithm as the function name and implements slightly different functionality.

TABLE 33.1 **The Nonmodifying Sequence Algorithms Defined in the Standard Header *<algorithm>*, Listed Alphabetically**

Algorithm	Description
adjacent_find	Searches a sequence for adjacent pairs of equal elements.
count	Counts the number of times a value appears in a sequence.
count_if	Counts the number of times a value appears in a sequence for which the given predicate is `true`.
equal	Compares two ranges of elements. Returns `true` only if corresponding pairs of elements in both ranges are equal.
find	Searches a container for the first occurrence of an element.
find_end	Finds the last occurrence of a specified sequence as a sub-sequence.
find_first_of	Finds a value from one sequence in another sequence.
find_if	Searches a container for the first occurrence of an element for which the given predicate is `true`.
for_each	Applies a function object to each element in a sequence.
mismatch	Compares two ranges of elements. Returns a pair of iterators that are the first corresponding positions at which unequal elements occur in a pair of sequences.
search	Finds the first occurrence of a specified sequence as a sub-sequence.
search_n	Finds the *n*th occurrence of an element in a sequence.

With one exception (`for_each`), we can further categorize the nonmodifying algorithms by operation, giving the following subcategories:

- Counting algorithms
- Find algorithms
- Search algorithms
- Sequence comparison algorithms

The following sections look at each of the nonmodifying algorithms.

Counting Algorithms

The counting algorithms provide generic counting of elements meeting specified values. The counting algorithms are count and count_if. The declarations for these algorithms as found in the standard header <generic> are given in the next sections.

The *count* Algorithm

The count algorithm counts the number of times a value appears in a sequence. This algorithm is implemented in the count() function declared in the standard header <algorithm> using the following function template:

```
template <class InIt, class T>
   size_t count(InIt first, InIt last, const T& val);
```

The *count_if* Algorithm

The count_if algorithm counts the number of times a value appears in a sequence for which the given predicate is true. This algorithm is implemented in the count_if() function declared in the standard header <algorithm> using the following function template:

```
template <class InIt, class Prcd, class Dist>
   size_t count_if(InIt first, InIt last, Pred pr,
   Dist& n);
```

Find Algorithms

There are several find algorithms, each targeting a certain method of finding elements in a sequence. The find algorithms are adjacent_find, find, find_first_of, and find_if. The declarations for these algorithms as found in the standard header <generic> are given in the following sections.

The *adjacent_find* Algorithm

The adjacent_find algorithm searches a sequence for adjacent pairs of equal elements. This algorithm is implemented in the adjacent_find() function declared in the standard header <algorithm> using the following function templates:

```
template <class FwdIt>
   FwdIt adjacent_find(FwdIt first, FwdIt last);

template <class FwdIt, class Pred>
   FwdIt adjacent_find(FwdIt first, FwdIt last, Pred pr);
```

The *find* Algorithm

The find algorithm searches a container for the first occurrence of an element. This algorithm is implemented in the find() function declared in the standard header <algorithm> using the following function template:

```
template <class InIt, class T>
   InIt find(InIt first, InIt last, const T& val);
```

The *find_first_of* Algorithm

The find_first_of algorithm finds a value from one sequence in another sequence. This algorithm is implemented in the find_first_of() function declared in the standard header <algorithm> using the following function templates:

```
template <class FwdIt1, class FwdIt2>
   FwdIt1 find_first_of(FwdIt1 first1, FwdIt1 last1,
      FwdIt2 first2, FwdIt2 last2);

template <class FwdIt1, class FwdIt2, class Pred>
   FwdIt1 find_first_of(FwdIt1 first1, FwdIt1 last1,
      FwdIt2 first2, FwdIt2 last2, Pred pr);
```

The *find_if* Algorithm

The find_if algorithm searches a container for the first occurrence of an element for which the given predicate is true. This algorithm is implemented in the find_if() function declared in the standard header <algorithm> using the following function template:

```
template <class InIt, class Pred>
   InIt find_if(InIt first, InIt last, Pred pr);
```

The *for_each* Algorithm

The for_each algorithm applies a function to each element in a sequence. This algorithm is implemented in the for_each() function declared in the standard header <algorithm> using the following function template:

```
template <class InIt, class Fun>
   Fun for_each(InIt first, InIt last, Fun f);
```

Note

The for_each algorithm is especially useful for performing some operation on each item in a sequence. An example might be printing the value of sequence item–without the need of a loop to iterate through the sequence.

Search Algorithms

The standard library includes three search algorithms: find_end, search, and search_n. The declarations for these algorithms as found in the standard header <generic> are given in the following sections.

The *find_end* Algorithm

The find_end algorithm finds the last occurrence of a specified sequence as a subsequence. This algorithm is implemented in the find_end() function declared in the standard header <algorithm> using the following function templates:

```
template <class FwdIt1, class FwdIt2>
   FwdIt1 find_end(FwdIt1 first1, FwdIt1 last1,
      FwdIt2 first2, FwdIt2 last2);

template <class FwdIt1, class FwdIt2, class Pred>
   FwdIt1 find_end(FwdIt1 first1, FwdIt1 last1,
      FwdIt2 first2, FwdIt2 last2, Pred pr);
```

The *search* Algorithm

The search algorithm finds the first occurrence of a specified sequence as a subsequence. This algorithm is implemented in the search() function declared in the standard header <algorithm> using the following function templates:

```
template <class FwdIt1, class FwdIt2>
   FwdIt1 search(FwdIt1 first1, FwdIt1 last1,
      FwdIt2 first2, FwdIt2 last2);

template <class FwdIt1, class FwdIt2, class Pred>
   FwdIt1 search(FwdIt1 first1, FwdIt1 last1,
      FwdIt2 first2, FwdIt2 last2, Pred pr);
```

The *search_n* Algorithm

The search_n algorithm finds the *n*th occurrence of an element in a sequence. This algorithm is implemented in the search_n() function declared in the standard header <algorithm> using the following function templates:

```
template <class FwdIt, class Dist, class T>
   FwdIt search_n(FwdIt first, FwdIt last,
      Dist n, const T& val);

template <class FwdIt, class Dist, class T, class Pred>
   FwdIt search_n(FwdIt first, FwdIt last,
      Dist n, const T& val, Pred pr);
```

Sequence Comparison Algorithms

The two sequence comparison algorithms compare sequence elements: equal and mismatch. The declarations for these algorithms as found in the standard header <generic> are given in the following sections.

The *equal* Algorithm

The equal algorithm compares two ranges of elements. It returns true only if all corresponding pairs of elements in both ranges are equal. This algorithm is implemented in the equal() function declared in the standard header <algorithm> using the following function templates:

```
template <class InIt1, class InIt2>
   bool equal(InIt1 first, InIt1 last, InIt2 x);
```

```
template <class InIt1, class InIt2, class Pred>
    bool equal(InIt1 first, InIt1 last, InIt2 x,
    Pred pr);
```

The *mismatch* Algorithm

The `mismatch` algorithm compares two ranges of elements. The algorithm returns a pair of iterators that are the first corresponding positions where unequal elements occur in a pair of sequences. This algorithm is implemented in the `mismatch()` function declared in the standard header `<algorithm>` using the following function templates:

```
template <class InIt1, class InIt2>
    pair<InIt1, InIt2> mismatch(InIt1 first, InIt1 last,
    InIt2 x);
```

```
template <class InIt1, class InIt2, class Pred>
    pair<InIt1, InIt2> mismatch(InIt1 first, InIt1 last,
        InIt2 x, Pred pr);
```

Exploring the Modifying Sequence Algorithms

The Standard C++ Library provides generic modifying algorithms that copy, replace, remove, rotate, and transform specific container elements—all activities that modify the container's contents. Table 33.2 briefly describes each of the modifying sequence algorithms. These algorithms are, for the most part, unrelated, aside from the fact that they modify container contents.

TABLE 33.2   The Modifying Sequence Algorithms Defined in the Standard Header *<algorithm>*, Listed Alphabetically

Algorithm	Description
copy	Copies elements from one sequence to another.
copy_backward	Copies elements from one sequence to another sequence, starting with the last element.

continues…

TABLE 33.2   Continued

Algorithm	Description
fill	Replaces each element in a sequence with a given value.
fill_n	Replaces the first *n* elements in a sequence with a given value.
generate	Replaces each element in a sequence with the value returned by an operation.
generate_n	Replaces the first *n* elements in a sequence with the value returned by an operation.
iter_swap	Swaps two elements using iterators.
random_shuffle	Reorders elements into a uniformly pseudo-random order.
remove	Removes elements equal to a specified value.
remove_copy	Copies a sequence, removing elements equal to a specified value in the new sequence.
remove_copy_if	Copies a sequence, removing elements equal to a specified value in the new sequence if a predicate returns true.
remove_if	Removes elements equal to a specified value if a predicate returns true.
replace	Replaces with another value each element in a sequence that matches some specified value.
replace_copy	Copies a sequence to another sequence, replacing with another value each element in the sequence that matches some specified value.
replace_copy_if	Copies a sequence to another sequence, replacing with another value each element in the sequence that matches some specified value only if a predicate returns true.
replace_if	Replaces with another value each element in a sequence that matches some specified value only if a predicate returns true.
reverse	Reverses the order of the elements in a sequence.
reverse_copy	Copies one sequence into another, reversing the order of the elements in the new sequence.
rotate	Performs a circular shift of all elements in a sequence.
rotate_copy	Copies one sequence into another, performing a circular shift of all elements in the new sequence.

Algorithm	Description
swap	Exchanges two sequence elements.
swap_ranges	Exchanges elements of one sequence with those of another sequence using a specified range.
transform	Performs a specified operation on every element in a sequence.
unique	Removes duplicate elements of a sequence if they are adjacent.
unique_copy	Copies a sequence, removing duplicate elements from the new sequence if they are adjacent.

With one exception (transform), we can further categorize the modifying algorithms by operation, giving the following subcategories:

- Copy algorithms
- Replace algorithms
- Remove algorithms
- Fill and generate algorithms
- Reverse and rotate algorithms
- Swap algorithms

The following sections look at the algorithms in each of these subcategories of the modifying algorithms.

Copy Algorithms

The copy algorithms copy elements from one sequence to another; each algorithm performs a different function based on different criteria. The copy algorithms include copy and copy_backward. Their declarations, as found in the standard header <generic>, are given in the following sections.

The *copy* Algorithm

The copy algorithm copies elements from one sequence to another. This algorithm is implemented in the copy() function declared in the standard header <algorithm> using the following function template:

Note

The copy algorithms are useful for making working copies of sequences that you don't want to modify directly.

```
template <class InIt, class OutIt>
    OutIt copy(InIt first, InIt last, OutIt x);
```

The *copy_backward* Algorithm

The copy_backward algorithm copies elements from one sequence to another starting with the last element. This algorithm is implemented in the copy_backward() function declared in the standard header <algorithm> using the following function template:

```
template <class BidIt1, class BidIt2>
    BidIt2 copy_backward(BidIt1 first, BidIt1 last,
    BidIt2 x);
```

Fill and Generate Algorithms

The fill and generate algorithms are used to systematically assign values to sequence elements. These algorithms include fill, fill_n, generate, and generate_n. The declarations for these algorithms as found in the standard header <generic> are given in the following sections.

The *fill* Algorithm

The fill algorithm replaces each element in a sequence with a given value. This algorithm is implemented in the fill() function declared in the standard header <algorithm> using the following function template:

```
template <class FwdIt, class T>
    void fill(FwdIt first, FwdIt last, const T& x);
```

The *fill_n* Algorithm

The fill_n algorithm replaces the first *n* elements in a sequence with a given value. This algorithm is implemented in the fill_n() function declared in the standard header <algorithm> using the following function template:

```
template <class OutIt, class Size, class T>
    void fill_n(OutIt first, Size n, const T& x);
```

The *generate* Algorithm

The generate algorithm replaces each element in a sequence with the value returned by an operation. This algorithm is implemented in the generate() function declared in the standard header <algorithm> using the following function template:

```
template <class FwdIt, class Gen>
   void generate(FwdIt first, FwdIt last, Gen g);
```

The *generate_n* Algorithm

The generate_n algorithm replaces the first *n* elements in a sequence with the value returned by an operation. This algorithm is implemented in the generate_n() function declared in the standard header <algorithm> using the following function template:

```
template <class OutIt, class Pred, class Gen>
   void generate_n(OutIt first, Dist n, Gen g);
```

Replace Algorithms

The replace algorithms are used to replace values in existing sequence elements. These algorithms include replace, replace_copy, replace_copy_if, and replace_if. The declarations for these algorithms as found in the standard header <generic> are given in the following sections.

The *replace* Algorithm

The replace algorithm replaces with another value each element in a sequence that matches some specified value. This algorithm is implemented in the replace() function declared in the standard header <algorithm> using the following function template:

```
template <class FwdIt, class T>
   void replace(FwdIt first, FwdIt last,
      const T& vold, const T& vnew);
```

The *replace_copy* Algorithm

The replace_copy algorithm copies a sequence to another sequence, replacing with another value each element in the sequence that matches some specified value. The copied sequence contains the replaced values. This algorithm is implemented in the replace_copy() function declared in the standard header <algorithm> using the following function template:

```
template <class InIt, class OutIt, class T>
  OutIt replace_copy(InIt first, InIt last, OutIt x,
      const T& vold, const T& vnew);
```

The *replace_copy_if* Algorithm

The replace_copy_if algorithm copies a sequence to another sequence, replacing with another value each element in the sequence that matches some specified value only if a predicate returns true. The copied sequence contains the replaced values. This algorithm is implemented in the replace_copy_if() function declared in the standard header <algorithm> using the following function template:

```
template <class InIt, class OutIt, class Pred, class T>
  OutIt replace_copy_if(InIt first, InIt last, OutIt x,
      Pred pr, const T& val);
```

The *replace_if* Algorithm

The replace_if algorithm replaces with another value each element in a sequence that matches some specified value only if a predicate returns true. This algorithm is implemented in the replace_if() function declared in the standard header <algorithm> using the following function template:

```
template <class FwdIt, class Pred, class T>
  void replace_if(FwdIt first, FwdIt last,
      Pred pr, const T& val);
```

Remove Algorithms

The remove algorithms are used to remove existing elements from a sequence. These algorithms include remove, remove_copy, remove_copy_if, and remove_if. The declarations for these algorithms as found in the standard header <generic> are given in the following sections.

The *remove* Algorithm

The remove algorithm removes elements equal to a specified value. This algorithm is implemented in the remove() function declared in the standard header <algorithm> using the following function template:

```
template <class FwdIt, class T>
   FwdIt remove(FwdIt first, FwdIt last, const T& val);
```

The *remove_copy* Algorithm

The remove_copy algorithm copies a sequence, removing elements equal to a specified value from the new sequence. This algorithm is implemented in the remove_copy() function declared in the standard header <algorithm> using the following function template:

```
template <class InIt, class OutIt, class T>
   OutIt remove_copy(InIt first, InIt last, OutIt x,
      const T& val);
```

The *remove_copy_if* Algorithm

The remove_copy_if algorithm copies a sequence, removing elements equal to a specified value in the new sequence if a predicate returns true. This algorithm is implemented in the remove_copy_if() function declared in the standard header <algorithm> using the following function template:

```
template <class InIt, class OutIt, class Pred>
   OutIt remove_copy_if(InIt first, InIt last,
      OutIt x, Pred pr);
```

The *remove_if* Algorithm

The remove_if algorithm removes elements equal to a specified value if a predicate returns true. This algorithm is implemented in the remove_if() function declared in the standard header <algorithm> using the following function template:

```
template <class FwdIt, class Pred>
   FwdIt remove_if(FwdIt first, FwdIt last, Pred pr);
```

Reverse and Rotate Algorithms

The reverse and rotate algorithms are used to reorder the sequence of elements in a container. These algorithms include random_shuffle, reverse, reverse_copy, rotate, and rotate_copy. The declarations for these algorithms as found in the standard header <generic> are given in the following sections.

The *random_shuffle* Algorithm

The random_shuffle algorithm reorders elements into a uniformly pseudo-random order. This algorithm is implemented in the random_shuffle() function declared in the standard header <algorithm> using the following function templates:

```
template <class RanIt>
    void random_shuffle(RanIt first, RanIt last);
```

```
template <class RanIt, class Fun>
    void random_shuffle(RanIt first, RanIt last, Fun& f);
```

The *reverse* Algorithm

The reverse algorithm reverses the order of the elements in a sequence. This algorithm is implemented in the reverse() function declared in the standard header <algorithm> using the following function template:

```
template <class BidIt>
    void reverse(BidIt first, BidIt last);
```

The *reverse_copy* Algorithm

The reverse_copy algorithm copies one sequence into another, reversing the order of the elements in the new sequence. This algorithm is implemented in the reverse_copy() function declared in the standard header <algorithm> using the following function template:

```
template <class BidIt, class OutIt>
    OutIt reverse_copy(BidIt first, BidIt last, OutIt x);
```

The *rotate* Algorithm

The rotate algorithm performs a circular shift of all elements in a sequence. This algorithm is implemented in the rotate()

Note

The reverse_copy algorithm leaves the sequence unchanged, putting the reverse copy into a separate sequence. This differs from the copy_backward algorithm, which directly modifies a single sequence.

function declared in the standard header <algorithm> using the following function template:

```
template <class FwdIt>
    void rotate(FwdIt first, FwdIt middle, FwdIt last);
```

The *rotate_copy* Algorithm

The rotate_copy algorithm copies one sequence into another, performing a circular shift of all elements in the new sequence. This algorithm is implemented in the rotate_copy() function declared in the standard header <algorithm> using the following function template:

```
template <class FwdIt, class OutIt>
    OutIt rotate_copy(FwdIt first, FwdIt middle,
        FwdIt last, OutIt x);
```

Swap Algorithms

The swap algorithms move elements from one location to another in a container. These algorithms include iter_swap, swap, and swap_ranges. The declarations for these algorithms as found in the standard header <generic> are given in the following sections.

The *iter_swap* Algorithm

The iter_swap algorithm swaps two elements pointed to by iterators. This algorithm is implemented in the iter_swap() function declared in the standard header <algorithm> using the following function template:

```
template <class FwdIt1, class FwdIt2>
    void iter_swap(FwdIt1 x, FwdIt2 y);
```

The *swap* Algorithm

The swap algorithm exchanges two sequence elements (these elements can be in the same sequence or in different sequences). This algorithm is implemented in the swap() function declared in the standard header <algorithm> using the following function template:

```
template <class T>
    void swap(T& x, T& y);
```

The *swap_ranges* Algorithm

The swap_ranges algorithm exchanges elements of one sequence with those of another sequence within a specified range. This algorithm is implemented in the swap_ranges() function declared in the standard header <algorithm> using the following function template:

```
template <class FwdIt1, class FwdIt2>
    FwdIt2 swap_ranges(FwdIt1 first, FwdIt1 last, FwdIt2 x);
```

The *transform* Algorithm

The transform algorithm performs a specified operation on every element in a sequence. This algorithm is implemented in the transform() function declared in the standard header <algorithm> using the following function templates:

```
template <class InIt, class OutIt, class Unop>
    OutIt transform(InIt first, InIt last, OutIt x,
        Unop uop);

template <class InIt1, class InIt2, class OutIt, class Binop>
    OutIt transform(InIt1 first1, InIt1 last1, InIt2 first2,
        OutIt x, Binop bop);
```

The first version performs a specified unary operation, and the second version performs a specified binary operation.

Unique Algorithms

The unique algorithms remove duplicate adjacent elements within a sequence. These algorithms include unique and unique_copy. The declarations for these algorithms as found in the standard header <generic> are given in the following sections.

The *unique* Algorithm

The unique algorithm removes duplicate elements within a sequence if they are adjacent. This algorithm is implemented in the unique() function declared in the standard header <algorithm> using the following function templates:

```
template <class FwdIt>
   FwdIt unique(FwdIt first, FwdIt last);

template <class FwdIt, class Pred>
   FwdIt unique(FwdIt first, FwdIt last, Pred pr);
```

The *unique_copy* Algorithm

The unique_copy algorithm copies a sequence, removing duplicate elements from the new sequence if they are adjacent. This algorithm is implemented in the unique_copy() function declared in the standard header <algorithm> using the following function templates:

```
template <class InIt, class OutIt>
   OutIt unique_copy(InIt first, InIt last, OutIt x);

template <class InIt, class OutIt, class Pred>
   OutIt unique_copy(InIt first, InIt last, OutIt x,
      Pred pr);
```

Exploring the Sorted Sequence Algorithms

The Standard C++ Library provides several generic algorithms related to sorted sequences and sort operations. Table 33.3 briefly describes each of the sorting and searching algorithms.

**TABLE 33.3   The Sorted Sequence Algorithms Defined in the Standard Header
<algorithm>, Listed Alphabetically**

Algorithm	Description
binary_search	Finds a value in a sorted sequence using repeated bisection.
equal_range	Searches a sorted sequence for a subsequence having a specified value.
inplace_merge	Merges two consecutive sorted sequences.
lower_bound	Finds the first occurrence of a value in a sorted sequence.

continues...

TABLE 33.3 Continued

Algorithm	Description
includes	Returns true if a specified subsequence is present in a sequence.
merge	Merges two sorted sequences.
nth_element	Places a sequence element into the position it would occupy if the sequence were sorted.
partial_sort	Sorts the first part of a sequence.
partial_sort_copy	Makes a copy of a sequence, sorting the first part of the new sequence.
partition	Places elements matching a predicate first in the sort order.
set_difference	Compares two sequences, creating a sorted third sequence that contains elements found in the first sequence but not in not the second.
set_intersection	Compares two sequences, creating a sorted third sequence that contains elements found in both of the first two sequences.
set_symmetric_difference	Compares two sequences, creating a sorted third sequence that contains all elements found in the first but not the second, and all elements found in the second but not the first.
set_union	Creates a new sequence that contains elements found in two sequences, eliminating duplicates.
sort	Sorts a sequence.
stable_partition	Sorts a sequence, placing elements that match a predicate first while maintaining relative order.
stable_sort	Sorts a sequence, maintaining relative order of equal elements.
upper_bound	Finds the last occurrence of a value in a sorted sequence.

Relative Order and Stability

The stable_partition and stable_sort algorithms are called stable because they maintain the relative position of equivalent elements. This is useful when sorting elements containing multiple fields (for example, sorting elements first by Zip code, then by last name).

We can further categorize the sorted sequence algorithms by operation, giving the following subcategories:

- Binary search algorithms
- Merge algorithms

- Partition algorithms
- Set operation algorithms
- Sorting algorithms

The following sections look at each of the sorted sequence algorithms.

Binary Search Algorithms

The binary search algorithms make searching sorted sequences orders of magnitude faster than linear searches on unsorted sequences. These algorithms include `binary_search`, `equal_range`, `lower_bound`, and `upper_bound`. The declarations for these algorithms as found in the standard header `<generic>` are given in the following sections.

The *binary_search* Algorithm

The `binary_search` algorithm finds a value in a sorted sequence using *repeated bisection*. This algorithm is implemented in the `binary_search()` function declared in the standard header `<algorithm>` using the following function templates:

```
template <class FwdIt, class T>
    bool binary_search(FwdIt first, FwdIt last, const T& val);

template <class FwdIt, class T, class Pred>
    bool binary_search(FwdIt first, FwdIt last, const T& val,
        Pred pr);
```

The *equal_range* Algorithm

The `equal_range` algorithm searches a sorted sequence for a subsequence having a specified value. This algorithm is implemented in the `equal_range()` function declared in the standard header `<algorithm>` using the following function templates:

```
template <class FwdIt, class T>
    pair<FwdIt, FwdIt> equal_range(FwdIt first, FwdIt last,
        const T& val);
```

Repeated Bisection and Binary Searching

The `binary_search` algorithm uses a technique called repeated bisection to efficiently search a sequence. Repeated bisection entails dividing a sorted sequence range in half (dividing it into two sections—that's why the search is called *binary*), then deciding which half to search next. This division of ranges is repeated until the element being sought is found, or until all elements have been exhausted without finding the desired element.

```
template <class FwdIt, class T, class Pred>
   pair<FwdIt, FwdIt> equal_range(FwdIt first, FwdIt last,
      const T& val, Pred pr);
```

The *lower_bound* Algorithm

The `lower_bound` algorithm finds the first occurrence of a value in a sorted sequence. This algorithm is implemented in the `lower_bound()` function declared in the standard header `<algorithm>` using the following function templates:

```
template <class FwdIt, class T>
   FwdIt lower_bound(FwdIt first, FwdIt last,
      const T& val);
```

```
template <class FwdIt, class T, class Pred>
   FwdIt lower_bound(FwdIt first, FwdIt last,
      const T& val, Pred pr);
```

The *upper_bound* Algorithm

The `upper_bound` algorithm finds the last occurrence of a value in a sorted sequence. This algorithm is implemented in the `upper_bound()` function declared in the standard header `<algorithm>` using the following function templates:

```
template <class FwdIt, class T>
   FwdIt lower_bound(FwdIt first, FwdIt last,
      const T& val);
```

```
template <class FwdIt, class T, class Pred>
   FwdIt lower_bound(FwdIt first, FwdIt last,
      const T& val, Pred pr);
```

Merge Algorithms

The merge algorithms combine sequences in various ways. These algorithms include `inplace_merge` and `merge`. The declarations for these algorithms as found in the standard header `<generic>` are given in the following sections.

The *inplace_merge* Algorithm

The `inplace_merge` algorithm merges two consecutive sorted sequences. This algorithm is implemented in the `inplace_merge()` function declared in the standard header `<algorithm>` using the following function templates:

```
template <class BidIt>
   void inplace_merge(BidIt first, BidIt middle,
      BidIt last);

template <class BidIt, class Pred>
   void inplace_merge(BidIt first, BidIt middle,
      BidIt last, Pred pr);
```

The *merge* Algorithm

The `merge` algorithm merges two sorted sequences. This algorithm is implemented in the `merge()` function declared in the standard header `<algorithm>` using the following function templates:

```
template <class InIt1, class InIt2, class OutIt>
   OutIt merge(InIt1 first1, InIt1 last1,
      InIt2 first2, InIt2 last2, OutIt x);

template <class InIt1, class InIt2, class OutIt, class Pred>
   OutIt merge(InIt1 first1, InIt1 last1,
      InIt2 first2, InIt2 last2, OutIt x, Pred pr);
```

Partition Algorithms

The partition algorithms place every element that satisfies a predicate requirement before every element that doesn't satisfy that requirement, rearranging a sequence as needed. For example, the predicate might specify partitioning all elements in a sequence that are greater than 100 from those not greater than 100.

The partition algorithms include `partition` and `stable_partition`. The declarations for these algorithms as found in the standard header `<generic>` are given in the following sections.

The *partition* Algorithm

The partition algorithm places first in the sort order those elements matching a predicate. This algorithm is implemented in the partition() function declared in the standard header <algorithm> using the following function template:

```
template <class BidIt, class Pred>
   BidIt partition(BidIt first, BidIt last, Pred pr);
```

The *stable_partition* Algorithm

The stable_partition algorithm sorts a sequence, placing elements that match a predicate first while maintaining relative order. This algorithm is implemented in the stable_partition() function declared in the standard header <algorithm> using the following function template:

```
template <class FwdIt, class Pred>
   FwdIt stable_partition(FwdIt first, FwdIt last,
      Pred pr);
```

Set Operation Algorithms

The algorithms that operate on sets work only with sorted sequences because typical set operations such as intersect and difference are terribly slow on unsorted sequences. The set algorithms include includes, set_difference, set_intersection, set_symmetric_difference, and set_union. The declarations for these algorithms as found in the standard header <generic> are given in the following sections.

The *includes* Algorithm

The includes algorithm returns true if a specified subsequence is present in a sequence. This algorithm is implemented in the includes() function declared in the standard header <algorithm> using the following function templates:

```
template <class InIt1, class InIt2>
   bool includes(InIt1 first1, InIt1 last1,
      InIt2 first2, InIt2 last2);
```

```
template <class InIt1, class InIt2, class Pred>
   bool includes(InIt1 first1, InIt1 last1,
      InIt2 first2, InIt2 last2, Pred pr);
```

The *set_difference* Algorithm

The set_difference algorithm compares two sequences, creating a sorted third sequence that contains elements found in the first sequence but not found in the second. This algorithm is implemented in the set_difference() function declared in the standard header <algorithm> using the following function templates:

```
template <class InIt1, class InIt2, class OutIt>
   OutIt set_difference(InIt1 first1, InIt1 last1,
      InIt2 first2, InIt2 last2, OutIt x);

template <class InIt1, class InIt2, class OutIt, class Pred>
   OutIt set_difference(InIt1 first1, InIt1 last1,
      InIt2 first2, InIt2 last2, OutIt x, Pred pr);
```

The *set_intersection* Algorithm

The set_intersection algorithm compares two sequences, creating a sorted third sequence that contains elements found in both of the first two sequences. This algorithm is implemented in the set_intersection() function declared in the standard header <algorithm> using the following function templates:

```
template <class InIt1, class InIt2, class OutIt>
   OutIt set_intersection(InIt1 first1, InIt1 last1,
      InIt2 first2, InIt2 last2, OutIt x);

template <class InIt1, class InIt2, class OutIt, class Pred>
   OutIt set_intersection(InIt1 first1, InIt1 last1,
      InIt2 first2, InIt2 last2, OutIt x, Pred pr);
```

The *set_symmetric_difference* Algorithm

The set_symmetric_difference algorithm compares two sequences, creating a sorted third sequence that contains all elements found in the first sequence but not found in the second, and all elements found in the second sequence but not found in the first. This algorithm is implemented in the set_symmetric_ difference() function declared in the standard header <algorithm> using the following function templates:

```
template <class InIt1, class InIt2, class OutIt>
    OutIt set_symmetric_difference(InIt1 first1, InIt1 last1,
        InIt2 first2, InIt2 last2, OutIt x);

template <class InIt1, class InIt2, class OutIt, class Pred>
    OutIt set_symmetric_difference(InIt1 first1, InIt1 last1,
        InIt2 first2, InIt2 last2, OutIt x, Pred pr);
```

The *set_union* Algorithm

The set_union algorithm creates a new sequence that contains elements found in two sequences, eliminating duplicates. This algorithm is implemented in the set_union() function declared in the standard header <algorithm> using the following function templates:

```
template <class InIt1, class InIt2, class OutIt>
    OutIt set_union(InIt1 first1, InIt1 last1,
        InIt2 first2, InIt2 last2, OutIt x);

template <class InIt1, class InIt2, class OutIt, class Pred>
    OutIt set_union(InIt1 first1, InIt1 last1,
        InIt2 first2, InIt2 last2, OutIt x, Pred pr);
```

Sorting Algorithms

The algorithms that actually sort sequences include nth_element, partial_sort, partial_sort_copy, sort, and stable_sort. The declarations for these algorithms as found in the standard header <generic> are given in the following sections.

The *nth_element* Algorithm

The nth_element algorithm places a sequence element into the position it would occupy if the sequence were sorted. This algorithm is implemented in the nth_element() function declared in the standard header <algorithm> using the following function templates:

```
template <class RanIt>
    void nth_element(RanIt first, RanIt nth, RanIt last);
```

```
template <class RanIt, class Pred>
   void nth_element(RanIt first, RanIt nth, RanIt last,
      Pred pr);
```

The *partial_sort* Algorithm

The partial_sort algorithm sorts the first part of a sequence (from first to middle, as given in the declarations below). This algorithm is implemented in the partial_sort() function declared in the standard header <algorithm> using the following function templates:

```
template <class RanIt>
   void partial_sort(RanIt first, RanIt middle, RanIt last);


template <class RanIt, class Pred>
   void partial_sort(RanIt first, RanIt middle,
      RanIt last, Pred pr);
```

Note

The **partial_sort** parameter **middle** can actually point anywhere within the range from first to last. In fact, using the same iterator for both **middle** and **last** will sort the entire range.

The *partial_sort_copy* Algorithm

The partial_sort_copy algorithm makes a copy of a sequence and sorts the first part of the new sequence. This algorithm is implemented in the partial_sort_copy() function declared in the standard header <algorithm> using the following function templates:

```
template <class InIt, class RanIt>
   RanIt partial_sort_copy(InIt first1, InIt last1,
      RanIt first2, RanIt last2);


template <class InIt, class RanIt, class Pred>
   RanIt partial_sort_copy(InIt first1, InIt last1,
      RanIt first2, RanIt last2, Pred pr);
```

The *sort* Algorithm

The sort algorithm sorts a sequence. This algorithm is implemented in the sort() function declared in the standard header <algorithm> using the following function templates:

```
template <class RanIt>
   void sort(RanIt first, RanIt last);


template <class RanIt, class Pred>
   void sort(RanIt first, RanIt last, Pred pr);
```

The *stable_sort* Algorithm

The stable_sort algorithm sorts a sequence, placing elements that match a predicate first while maintaining relative order. This algorithm is implemented in the stable_sort() function declared in the standard header <algorithm> using the following function templates:

```
template <class BidIt>
    void stable_sort(BidIt first, BidIt last);

template <class BidIt, class Pred>
    void stable_sort(BidIt first, BidIt last, Pred pr);
```

Exploring the Heap Operation Algorithms

The Standard C++ Library provides generic heap operation algorithms to work with heaps. Table 33.4 briefly describes each of the heap operation algorithms.

Heap

A particular representation of a random access data structure.

TABLE 33.4   **The Heap Operation Algorithms Defined in the Standard Header *<algorithm>*, Listed Alphabetically**

Algorithm	Description
make_heap	Creates a sequence to be used as a heap.
pop_heap	Removes an element from a heap.
push_heap	Adds an element to a heap.
sort_heap	Sorts a heap.

The declarations for these algorithms as found in the standard header <generic> are given in the following sections.

The *make_heap* Algorithm

The make_heap algorithm creates a sequence to be used as a heap. This algorithm is implemented in the make_heap() function declared in the standard header <algorithm> using the following function templates:

```
template <class RanIt>
   void make_heap(RanIt first, RanIt last);


template <class RanIt, class Pred>
   void make_heap(RanIt first, RanIt last, Pred pr);
```

The *pop_heap* Algorithm

The pop_heap algorithm removes the first element from a heap. This algorithm is implemented in the pop_heap() function declared in the standard header <algorithm> using the following function templates:

```
template <class RanIt>
   void pop_heap(RanIt first, RanIt last);


template <class RanIt, class Pred>
   void pop_heap(RanIt first, RanIt last, Pred pr);
```

The *push_heap* Algorithm

The push_heap algorithm adds an element to the beginning of a heap. This algorithm is implemented in the push_heap() function declared in the standard header <algorithm> using the following function templates:

```
template <class RanIt>
   void push_heap(RanIt first, RanIt last);


template <class RanIt, class Pred>
   void push_heap(RanIt first, RanIt last, Pred pr);
```

The *sort_heap* Algorithm

The sort_heap algorithm sorts a heap. This algorithm is implemented in the sort_heap() function declared in the standard header <algorithm> using the following function templates:

```
template <class RanIt>
   void sort_heap(RanIt first, RanIt last);


template <class RanIt, class Pred>
   void sort_heap(RanIt first, RanIt last, Pred pr);
```

Exploring the Comparison Algorithms

The Standard C++ Library provides generic algorithms to compare sequences and elements. Table 33.5 briefly describes each of the comparison algorithms.

TABLE 33.5   The Comparison Algorithms Defined in the Standard Header *\<algorithm\>*, Listed Alphabetically

Algorithm	Description
lexicographical_compare	Performs a lexicographical comparison of two sequences to determine which is first.
max	Returns the larger of two arguments.
max_element	Returns an iterator to the largest value in a sequence.
min	Returns the smaller of two arguments.
min_element	Returns an iterator to the smallest value in a sequence.

The declarations for these algorithms as found in the standard header \<generic\> are given in the following sections.

The *lexicographical_compare* Algorithm

The lexicographical_compare algorithm performs a lexicographical comparison of two sequences to determine which sequence is first. This algorithm is implemented in the lexicographical_compare() function declared in the standard header \<algorithm\> using the following function templates:

```
template <class InIt1, class InIt2>
   bool lexicographical_compare(InIt1 first1, InIt1 last1,
      InIt2 first2, InIt2 last2);

template <class InIt1, class InIt2, class Pred>
   bool lexicographical_compare(InIt1 first1, InIt1 last1,
      InIt2 first2, InIt2 last2, Pred pr);
```

The *max* Algorithm

The max algorithm returns the larger of two arguments. This algorithm is implemented in the max() function declared in the standard header <algorithm> using the following function templates:

```
template <class T>
   const T& max(const T& x, const T& y);
template <class T, class Pred>
   const T& max(const T& x, const T& y, Pred pr);
```

The *max_element* Algorithm

The max_element algorithm returns an iterator to the largest value in a sequence. This algorithm is implemented in the max_element() function declared in the standard header <algorithm> using the following function templates:

```
template <class FwdIt>
   FwdIt max_element(FwdIt first, FwdIt last);

template <class FwdIt, class Pred>
   FwdIt max_element(FwdIt first, FwdIt last, Pred pr);
```

The *min* Algorithm

The min algorithm returns the smaller of two arguments. This algorithm is implemented in the min() function declared in the standard header <algorithm> using the following function templates:

```
template <class T>
   const T& min(const T& x, const T& y);

template <class T, class Pred>
   const T& min(const T& x, const T& y, Pred pr);
```

The *min_element* Algorithm

The min_element algorithm returns an iterator to the smallest value in a sequence. This algorithm is implemented in the min_element() function declared in the standard header <algorithm> using the following function templates:

```
template <class FwdIt>
    FwdIt min_element(FwdIt first, FwdIt last);

template <class FwdIt, class Pred>
    FwdIt min_element(FwdIt first, FwdIt last, Pred pr);
```

Permutation

One of several possible arrangements of elements in a sequence.

Exploring the Permutation Algorithms

The Standard C++ Library provides two generic algorithms to perform permutations on sequences. Table 33.6 briefly describes both of these algorithms.

TABLE 33.6   **The Permutation Algorithms Defined in the Standard Header** **<*algorithm*>, Listed Alphabetically**

Algorithm	Description
next_permutation	Permutes a sequence into the next lexicographical ordering of permutations.
prev_permutation	Permutes a sequence into the previous lexicographical ordering of permutations.

The declarations for these algorithms as found in the standard header <generic> are given in the following sections.

The *next_permutation* Algorithm

The next_permutation algorithm permutes a sequence into the next lexicographical ordering of permutations. This algorithm is implemented in the next_permutation() function declared in the standard header <algorithm> using the following function templates:

```
template <class BidIt>
    bool next_permutation(BidIt first, BidIt last);

template <class BidIt, class Pred>
    bool next_permutation(BidIt first, BidIt last, Pred pr);
```

The *prev_permutation* Algorithm

The prev_permutation algorithm permutes a sequence into the previous lexicographical ordering of permutations. This algorithm is implemented in the prev_permutation() function declared in the standard header <algorithm> using the following function templates:

```
template <class BidIt>
    bool prev_permutation(BidIt first, BidIt last);

template <class BidIt, class Pred>
    bool prev_permutation(BidIt first, BidIt last, Pred pr);
```

Index

Symbols

& (ampersand)
  address-of operator, 65
  AND operator, 68, 427-431
  reference operator, 266

&& (Logical AND), 68

&=( ) operator, valarrays, 775

* (asterisk)
  dereference operators, 251
  indirection operator, 65, 247
  Multiplication, 67
  pointer-to-member operator, 509

*( ) function, numerics, 773

*=( ) operator, valarrays, 775

\ (backslash character), preprocessors, 297

{ (braces), 17

^ (exclusive OR) operator, 68
  bits, 427, 433-437

^=( ) operator, valarrays, 775

. (dot operator)
  pointers, 253
  structures, 217
  unions, 237

= (equal sign), 63
  assignment operator, 80

=( ) operator
  ios base class, 792
  valarrays, 775

== (equal to), 68, 80
  binary string class, 745

==( ) function, numerics, 774

! (logical NOT operator), 66

!( ) operator
  basic ios class, 796
  valarrays, 775

!= operator
  binary string class, 745
  inequality operator, 68, 80

!=( ) function, numerics, 773

< (less than operator), 68, 80
  binary string class, 745

<< (insertion operator), 25
  cout, 26

<< (left-shift operator), 67
  binary string class, 745
  bits, 428, 440-441

<<( ) function, numerics, 774

<<( ) operator, basic ostream class, 799

<<=( ) operator
  valarrays, 775

<= (less-than-or-equal-to operator), 68, 80
  binary string class, 745

- (minus sign)
  decrement operator, pointers, 263
  subtraction, 67

-( ) function, numerics, 773

-( ) operator, valarrays, 775

-- (decrement operator), 65-66

-=( ) operator
  valarrays, 775

| (inclusive OR) operator, 68
  bits, 427, 431-433

|=( ) operator, valarrays, 776

|| (Logical OR), 68

% (Modulus), 67

%=( ) operator, valarrays, 775

+ (plus sign)
  binary string class, 745
  plus operator, 63, 65, 67

+( ) function, numerics, 773

++ (increment operator), 65-66

+=( ) operator, valarrays, 775

(pound symbol)
  make files, 454
  preprocessors, 296
  stringizing operator, 314-315

(token pasting operator), 315-316

. (member-selection operator), 64

... (ellipsis), 185

/ (slash), division operator, 67

/( ) function
  numerics, 773

/* (comments), 21

/=( ) operator
  valarrays, 775

Boolean, 78-82
conditional, 91
operands, 62-63
operators, 62-63
binary, 67-68
conditional, 69
pointer-to-member, 68-69
unary, 65-67
postfix, 64-65
primary, 64
type casting, 69-70

extensions
binary object code, 12
interface files, 11

extern keyword, 48

extern specifier, 58

external linkage, 507
preprocessors, 296

extraction operator, 25, 30

extractions, streams, 788

F

fabs( ) function, 769

Fahrenheit/Celsius conversions
do statements, 117-119
for statements, 107-110
while statements, 113-115

fail( ) member function, basic ios class, 795

failbit iostate flag, 793

fields
bits, 422
declaring, 423
memory controls, 424-427
unnamed, 423
input files, payroll example, 230

FILE macro, 319

file streams, 805
binary, reading/writing, 813-817
multiple, 807-810, 812-813
text, reading/writing, 805-807

files
binary object code, 12
executable, building, 12
header
assertions, 365-368, 370-371
debugging macros, 454-458
dynamic arrays, 579-580
linked lists, 600-602
Standard C++ Library. See Standard C++ Library
headers, iterators, 703-705
implementation (source files), 11
software modules, 624-626
include, 11
interface (header files), 11, 54
make, 12, 453-454
source, 54
compiling, 11-12
linking, 12-13
testing, 13-14

fill algorithms, 827, 830

fill( ) member function
basic ios class, 795
valarrays, 774

filling structures, 217

filtering, AND (&) operator, 429

find algorithms, 823-824

Find( ) member function
associative containers
map/multimap, 732
set/multiset, 731
basic string class, 759-765
dynamic arrays, 572, 576
generic linked lists, 651-652
linked lists, 591, 596-597

find_end algorithm, 825

find_first of( ) member functions, basic string class, 761

find_first_not_of( ) member functions, basic string class, 761

find_first_of algorithm, 824

find_if algorithm, 824

find_last_not_of( ) member functions, basic string class, 761

find_last_of( ) member functions, basic string class, 761

fixed flag, 792

fixed( ) manipulator, basic ios class, 798

flags
ios_base class, 792-793
event, 794-795
format, 793
iostate, 793
openmode, 793-794
seekdir, 794

flags( ) member function, ios base class, 791

float keyword, 24

float values, unions, 238

floating-point numbers, 42-43
constants, 51

floor( ) function, 769

flush( ) member function, basic_ostream class, 799

fmod( ) function, 769

for each algorithm, 825

for keyword, 24

for Loop to Generate Temperature Conversions (Listing 5.2), 108, 110

for statement, 73
initializing arrays, 140

format flags, ios_base class, 792-793

formatting, stream data, 801-805

H

listings